Basic Contributions to Psychology
Readings

Second Edition

Basic Contributions to Psychology
Readings

Second Edition

edited by
Robert L. Wrenn
The University of Arizona

Brooks/Cole Publishing Company
Belmont, California
A Division of Wadsworth Publishing Company, Inc.

L. C. Cat. Card No.: 79–102375
Printed in the United States of America

1 2 3 4 5 6 7 8 9 10–73 72 71 70

Preface to the Second Edition

This book of readings was initially constructed from a pool of research references commonly found in introductory psychology texts. The interested reader may want to check my methods for obtaining the pool of references found in the Preface to the First Edition (following this preface). The study on which the first edition was based has been recently redone. The specific references found in common in all five introductory psychology texts sampled and in four out of the five texts sampled are included at the end of each preface. The publication date for the sample of texts for the first edition averaged 1961, whereas texts sampled for the second edition were published, on the average, in 1968. The first and second editions of this book were based in large part, although not exclusively, on these reference lists. The purpose for this approach to the development of readings is to offer a more empirical basis for selecting readings for a first course in psychology.

In all fairness, it should be pointed out that there are certain shortcomings to this approach. Not everyone would agree that "treasures from the past" are in fact treasures. Perhaps psychology readers and texts should avoid perpetuating what might be considered faulty methods and consequently dubious conclusions of some pioneering ventures in our field. However, these errors are not always easily recognized, since their assessment depends—at least in part—on where psychology is going, which, of course, has not yet been adequately established. There is also the question of whether the writers of the five texts from which these readings are taken based their texts on other than subjective considerations and whether they wrote their books independent of one another's judgments. Finally, since I chose from among the lists of references taken from the beginning texts, rather than include them all, my own subjective appraisal of what should be accepted and deleted from this list constitutes a major source of subjectivity. Notwithstanding the above possible sources of error in judgment, I rest my case on what I feel to be a more tightly prescribed set of rules in formulating readings than I have witnessed in other available readers. This means that this book of readings will coordinate quite well with most introductory psychology texts. Whether introductory psychology texts, in turn, coordinate well with the total field of psychology or with today's world, however defined, is a separate issue that cannot be resolved here.

The criteria used to make final selections from the reference lists would only be apparent to another editor. Some references are simply unavailable for reprint because the copyright holder is unwilling to release the material. (While on the subject of copyright, some reprint permission contracts require that all footnotes be retained, but others do not. An attempt has been made to delete footnotes where possible, which will undoubtedly be appreciated by most students.) Lengthy monographs and books cannot be reproduced in their entirety, which forces the editor to abandon them completely or to reprint an essential element. Some references would require as much footnoting space to explain to the beginning student what is meant as would the reference itself. Some references overlap in content and thus force the editor to choose among them, since including them all would be redundant. In short, the basis for retaining, deleting, and adding references has been guided by those reference changes found in introductory psychology texts since the first edition of this book. It should be made quite clear, however,

179591

that the reference lists served only as a guide and that practical considerations as well as my personal preferences also guided the decisions of what selections would actually be included.

A glossary of terms and a subject-author index have been added to this edition. As was true of the first edition, a manual of test items is also available under separate cover. Requests for biographical data have been sent to each author, and these returns have been incorporated within the biographical sketch that precedes each selection. Questions before each selection to guide the reader and suggested readings at the end of each chapter are again included.

I would again like personally to acknowledge my appreciation to the authors and particularly to the American Psychological Association for their assistance in obtaining copyright permissions. Credits to author and publisher are found on the first page of each article. My secretary, Mrs. Karen Ferlanto, and her assistant, Miss Barbara Ball, did all the detail work of typing this edition into shape for the publisher. Debra Moser, a psychology student, conducted the tabulation of changes in references cited in the elementary texts. Finally, I extend my appreciation to Bonnie Fitzwater and Terry Hendrix of Brooks/Cole Publishing Company for cajoling, pampering, prodding, accepting, urging, and loving me into a state of productivity so that this book might be suitably revised.

Robert L. Wrenn

Works Cited by All Five Authors of Elementary Texts (*N*=13)

Bruce, R. W. Conditions of transfer of training. *J. exp. Psychol.,* 1933, 16, 343–361.

Ebbinghaus, H. *Memory,* 1885, 1913.

Festinger, L. *A theory of cognitive dissonance,* 1957.

Gibson, E. J. & Walk, R. D. The "visual cliff." *Sci. Amer.,* 1960, 202 (4), 64–71.

Jenkins, J. G. & Dallenbach, K. M. Oblivescence during sleep and waking. *Amer. J. Psychol.,* 1924, 35, 605–612.

Jones, H. E. & Conrad, H. S. The growth and decline of intelligence. *Genet. Psychol. Monog.* 1933, 13, 223–298.

Kinsey, A. C., et al. *Sexual behavior in the human male,* 1948.

McClelland, D. C., et al. *The achievement motive,* 1953.

Newman, H. H., et al. *Twins: A study of heredity and environment,* 1937.

Pavlov, I. P. *Conditioned reflexes,* 1927.

Schachter, S. & Singer, J. E. Cognitive, social, and physiological determinants of emotional state. *Psychol. Rev.,* 1962, 69, 379–399.

Wechsler, D. *Wechsler Adult Intelligence Scale,* 1955.

Wolpe, J. *Psychotherapy by reciprocal inhibition,* 1958.

Works Cited by 4 out of 5 Authors of Elementary Texts (*N*=45)

Ax, A. F. The physiological differentiation between fear and anger in humans. *Psychosom. Med.,* 1953, 15, 433–442.

Barker, R., et al. Frustration and regression, an experiment with young children. *Univer. Iowa Stud. Child Welf.,* 1941, 18, No. 386.

Bekesy, G. V. *Experiments in hearing,* 1960.

Bexton, W. H., et al. Effects of decreased variation in the sensory environment. *Canad. J. Psychol.,* 1954, 8, 70–76.

Boring, E. G. *A history of experimental psychology,* 1929, 1950.

Broadbent, D. E. *Perception and communication,* 1958.

Cannon, W. B. Hunger and thirst. In C. Murchison (Ed.), *A handbook of general experimental psychology,* 1934.

Dollard, J. & Miller, N. E. *Personality and psychotherapy,* 1950.

Duncker, K. On problem solving. *Psychol. Monog.,* 1945, 58, No. 270.

Eccles, J. *The physiology of the synapses,* 1964.

Erickson, S. C. Variability of attack in massed and distributed practice. *J. exp. Psychol.,* 1942, 31, 339–345.

Festinger, L. & Carlsmith, J. M. Cognitive consequences of forced compliance. *J. abnorm. soc. Psychol.,* 1959, 58, 203–210.

Gates, A. I. Recitation as a factor in memorizing. *Arch. Psychol.,* 1917, 6, No. 40.

Gibson, E. J. & Walk, R. D. The effect of prolonged exposure to visually presented patterns on learning to discriminate them. *J. comp. physiol. Psychol.,* 1956, 49, 239–242.

Harlow, H. F. The formation of learning sets. *Psychol. Rev.,* 1949, 56, 51–65.

Harrell, T. W. & Harrell, M. S. Army General Classification Test scores for civilian occupations. *Educ. Psychol. Meas.,* 1945, 5, 229–239.

Hebb, D. O. *Organization of behavior,* 1949.

Hernández-Peón, R., et al. Modification of electric activity in the cochlear nucleus during "attention" in unanesthetized cats. *Science,* 1956, 123, 331–332.

Hollingshead, A. B. & Redlich, F. C. *Social class and mental illness: A community study,* 1958.

Hull, C. L. *Principles of behavior,* 1943.

Hunter, W. The delayed reaction in animals and children. *Behav. Monog.,* 1913, 2, No. 6.

Krech, D., et al. *Individual in society,* 1962.

Lewin, K., et al. Patterns of aggressive behavior in experimentally created "social climates." *J. soc. Psychol.,* 1939, 10, 271–299.

Lindsley, D. B. Emotion. In S. S. Stevens (Ed.), *Handbook of experimental psychology,* 1951, 473–516.

Masserman, J. *Principles of dynamic psychiatry,* 1946, 1961.

Mead, M. *Sex and temperament in three primitive societies,* 1935.

Miller, N. E. Fear as an acquired drive. *J. exp. Psychol.,* 1948, 38, 89–101.

Murray, H. A. *Explorations in personality,* 1938.

McNemar, Q. *The revision of the Stanford-Binet Scale,* 1942.

Olds, J. & Milner, P. Positive reinforcement produced by electrical stimulation of septal area and other regions of rat brain. *J. comp. physiol. Psychol.,* 1954, 47, 419–427.

Riggs, L. A., et al. The disappearance of steadily fixated visual test objects. *J. opt. soc. Amer.,* 1953, 43, 495–501.

Riesen, A. H. Arrested vision. *Sci. Amer.,* 1950, 183, 16–19.

Rogers, C. *Client-centered therapy,* 1951.

Senden, M. V. *Raum—und Gestaltauffassung bei operierten Blindgeborenen vor und nach operation,* 1932.

Sheldon, W. H. & Stevens, S. S. *The varieties of temperament,* 1942.

Skodak, M. & Skeels, H. M. A final follow-up of one hundred adopted children. *J. genet. Psychol.,* 1949, 75, 3–19.

Stratton, G. M. Vision without inversion of the retinal image. *Psychol. Rev.,* 1897, 4, 341–360, 463–481.

Thurstone, L. L. & Thurstone, T. G. Factorial studies of intelligence. *Psychomet. Monog.,* 1941, No. 2.

Tsang, Y. C. Hunger motivation in gastrectomized rats. *J. comp. Psychol.,* 1938, 26, 1–17.

Underwood, B. J. Interference and forgetting. *Psychol. Rev.,* 1957, 64, 49–60.

Underwood, B. J. Ten years of massed practice on distributed practice. *Psychol. Rev.,* 1961, 68, 229–247.

Wallas, G. *The art of thought,* 1926.

Wechsler, D. *Wechsler Intelligence Scale for children,* 1949.

White, R. Motivation reconsidered: The concept of competence. *Psychol. Rev.,* 1959, 66, 297–333.

Woodworth, R. S. & Schlosberg, H. *Experimental psychology,* 1954.

Preface to the First Edition

Any book title that begins "Basic Contributions" or "Classic Studies" suggests that the author is daring or, perhaps, foolhardy. Consensus on what research or theory has had the greatest influence on a field of study depends upon who is doing the judging and upon what is being judged. This book of readings consists mainly of studies found in a sample of five introductory psychology texts. The selections are highly visible and cited often. Although this procedure has added objectivity to the choice of selections, the essential problem over what is basic or classic in the field of psychology is not completely resolved. Of the 3,587 references cited in the sample of introductory texts, only twenty were cited in all texts. When the criterion was revised to include references cited by four out of five texts, the list was increased to ninety-three. From this list of ninety-three references the majority of the readings for this book were taken. The means by which introductory texts were sampled to identify familiar studies and the list of references drawn upon for this book are discussed in the author's article entitled "Literature in Psychology Viewed from the Elementary Text," *The Psychological Record*, 14 (1964), 291–300. An abridged reprint of this article is included at the end of the preface.

Except for the first and last chapters of the book, chapter format generally follows that of the typical beginning text in psychology. The selections, however, are not necessarily of recent origin. This was thought to be a good matching of effort: the contemporary emphasis of most elementary psychology texts with the more prototypic studies found in this book of readings.

Some of the readings originally considered for this book were either too technical or too jargon-laden to be of value to the beginning student. Where this occurred, a substitute selection was found. The substitute selection either retains the essential meaning of the original work, or it is an article on a similar topic by the same author. The selections include articles written by fourteen past, or present, presidents of the American Psychological Association. Effort was made to include selections that are of human interest and at the same time adhere to adequate research design and methodology.

It is imperative to acknowledge the many authors who wrote the selections included in this book. Credits to author and publisher are found on the entry page of each article. My wife, Marcy, contributed to the book by handling many jobs that were rightfully mine. My thanks go also to many of my colleagues, whose advice and consultation I sought. The University of Arizona Library staff was most helpful, even courteous, in spite of my numerous requests. The lion's share of clerical and detail work was accomplished by Ana K. Knezevich, receptionist-secretary for the University of Arizona Counseling Bureau. Finally, my appreciation goes to Charles T. Hendrix, Psychology Editor for Brooks/Cole Publishing Company. He not only coordinated the whole affair adeptly but proved to be a most congenial associate.

Literature in Psychology Viewed from the Elementary Text

The importance of the first course in psychology, what it should include and how it should be taught, has been of concern to such writers as Birney and McKeachie (1942), Harper (1952) and Pressey (1949). Its importance stems from the fact that it is the only course in psychology many students will ever take. It may be the only course many graduate students will ever teach. Since the first course is generally conducted as a survey of the field, the text as well as the teacher's influence will shape the beginning undergraduate student's perception of the field. Harassed graduate students preparing for major exams will often thumb through the beginning text for well-known studies and for ideas on organizing their thoughts. Some psychologists (Albee, 1963; Daniel, 1962; Wolfle, 1947) have conducted content analyses of elementary texts as an indication of changing trends of emphasis in the field over the years.

The elementary text is influential in these several ways and perhaps for other reasons as well. The present analysis attempts to answer questions such as these: What articles, research studies and books would you likely find *common* reference to in a survey of several leading texts? From which journals are most studies taken? Can cues as to the present status of the field be taken from these data? Are the "classics" in our field adequately represented? A partial answer to these somewhat sweeping questions can be gained by a simple tally of works referenced in representative elementary texts.

Sample

Five texts were selected as a sample of total population. These texts were well known and are generally thought to be among the leading contenders in the field: Hilgard, E. R., *Introduction to Psychology, 1962;* Morgan, C. T., *Introduction to Psychology, 1961;* Munn, N. L., *Psychology: The Fundamentals of Human Adjustment, 1961;* Ruch, F. L., *Psychology and Life, 1958;* Sanford, F. H., *Psychology: A Scientific Study of Man, 1962.* (At least one of the above texts has been revised since the present study was completed.) Certainly other texts from the long list of those available might have been included. The diversity and proliferation of elementary texts are such that an adequate sample and analysis of them would seem virtually impossible. It was felt, however, that the above texts would be sufficiently representative of texts used in the first course to warrant their use. This is not a compelling rationale, but it is a workable one.

Method

All references specifically cited in each of the five texts were tabulated alphabetically by lead author. Any complete reference to a book, a part of a book, a journal article, a dissertation, a thesis or an unpublished study was included. Films, proper names cited without literature reference, pictures and graphs not fully referenced were *not* included in the tabulation. The use of complete reference as the criterion for inclusion is one not only of convenience. In some cases it would have been nearly impossible to determine the exact source of the text author's reference unless it was given as a complete reference. There are also a number of reference errors in any text which lists several hundred references. The extent to which a reference is discussed in the text is, of course, not indicated simply by the fact that the work is cited at the end of a chapter, in a footnote, or at the end

of the book. Yet to discern the degree of use for the 3,587 references tallied is a more formidable task than intended by this study.

Results

The results of this tabulation have been broken down into three general categories. First, an analysis is made of the extent to which text authors agree on the references they cite. Secondly, the journals most frequently used and from which research studies were more likely to be taken were enumerated. Finally, attention is given to the percentage of references taken from a given decade in recent psychological history.

Author Agreement

In viewing the degree of agreement among text authors on what references to include, considerable independence of selection seems the rule.[1] Parenthetically it might be stated that the variability in references chosen seems to reflect a difficulty more generally encountered in defining the field. Wurtz (1961), for example, in compiling a list of important psychological books sent in by 80 respondents found that almost 47 percent of the 180 authors listed were mentioned by only one respondent. Table 1 depicts a similar trend in the

TABLE 1. DEGREE OF CORRESPONDENCE AMONG FIVE TEXTS WITH RESPECT TO REFERENCE CITATIONS. (a)

No. texts in agreement	No. references cited	% all references
5	20*	.5
4	73*	2.0
3	164	4.6
2	425	11.8
one text only	2905	80.8
Total	3587	99.7

(a) Texts are: Hilgard, E. R., *Introduction to Psychology,* 1962; Morgan, C. T., *Introduction to Psychology,* 1961; Munn, N. L., *Psychology: The Fundamentals of Human Adjustment,* 1961; Ruch, F. L., *Psychology and Life,* 1958; Sanford, F. H., *Psychology: A Scientific Study of Man,* 1962.

* A list of these 93 references can be found in the original article or can be obtained by writing directly to the author. The list is too long to be published here. These references served as the basis for the selections chosen for this book of readings.

[1] Two of the textbook authors were asked what determined the particular set of references they chose for inclusion in their text. One author emphasized that the references cited gave his basis of defense (evidence) for the way in which he handled a given topic in the field. The second author also emphasized the idea that his selection of references was for the purpose of "making a point." The question of what constitutes an appropriate reference would seem to be a matter of individual judgment.

TABLE 2. FREQUENCY OF TOP TEN WORKS FROM THREE SEPARATE
STUDIES AND EXTENT THEY ARE INCLUDED IN THE ELEMENTARY TEXT

Agreement of Elementary Texts	Ruja	Sundberg	Wurtz	Total
all	1	0	3	4*
4	2	4	3	9**
3	3	2	2	7
2	2	1	1	4
1	0	2	1	3
None	2	1	0	3
Total:	10	10	10	30

* Included Allport's *Personality*, James' *Principles*, Pavlov's *Conditioned Reflexes* and Ebbinghaus' *Memory*.
** Included Hull's *Principles*, Hilgard's *Theories*, Boring's *History*, Morgan & Stellar's *Physiol.*, Woodworth & Schlosberg's *Experimental* and Skinner's *Behavior of Organisms*.

amount of agreement of specific references used.

By somewhat different design and approach Ruja (1956), Sundberg (1960) and Wurtz (1961) have attempted to determine the degree of consensus among psychologists on important works in the field. Ruja combed through three well-known journals and found the ten publications most frequently cited during the period 1949–1952. In a survey during 1958–1959 Sundberg obtained a list of ten books recommended as important books by over half of the psychology departments in his sample. Wurtz surveyed the opinions of 80 psychologists and ranked the works

TABLE 3. FREQUENCY OF JOURNALS
QUOTED BY ALL AUTHORS

Rank	No. Times Cited	Name of Journal
1	197	J. exp. Psychol.
2	138	J. comp. physiol. Psychol.
3	120	J. abnorm. soc. Psychol.
4	91	Psychol. Rev.
5	90	J. genet. Psychol.
6	75	Amer. J. Psychol.
7	68	Psychol. Bull.
8.5	60	Amer. Psychologist
8.5	60	Psychol. Monog.
10	59	J. Psychol.
11	55	J. appl. Psychol.
12	48	Science
13	47	Sci. Amer.
14	44	J. consult. Psychol.
15	38	J. gen. Psychol.
16	37	J. soc. Psychol.
17	34	J. educ. Psychol.
18	31	Genet. Psychol. Monog.
19	26	Archives Psychol.

listed by ten or more respondents. A direct comparison of these three lists of ten each is not possible. Two of the lists contain only books while the third includes journal articles. Sundberg's list is almost exclusively made up of commonly used graduate level texts while Wurtz's list reflects "classics" of the field. (At that, only three of the 30 works—Hull's *Principles,* Boring's *History* and Hilgard's *Theories of Learning*—are mentioned on two of the three lists.) Cutting across these operational differences, and drawing from a larger representation of the field, 20 of these 30 works are mentioned in common by three or more of the elementary texts utilized in this study. (See Table 2.)

Journal Frequency

If the elementary text can be thought of as a general mirror of literature in the field, then the journals supplying the bulk of research literature to these texts warrant analysis. In the five texts sampled, a total of 295 separate journals were cited. There is a little more commonality here— 148 of these journals, or 50 per cent, were mentioned only once by one author. Table 3 lists the 19 top-ranking journals most often cited in the five texts. By inspection it was judged that, with minor exceptions, each text holds very close to the frequency ranking shown in Table 3.

The interests of psychologists as indicated by A.P.A. divisional membership do not seem proportionately reflected in the journals drawn upon for the elementary text. This seeming discrepancy in emphasis is not surprising to psychologists. The beginning student, on the other hand, may find many of his expectations of the field upended by the research content he encounters in the first course. As Daniel (1962) has pointed out, the image many non-psychology college faculties hold of psychology as a social science is not particularly supported in the beginning text by the emphasis on psychology as biological science. This image gives some support for identifying psychology as a behavioral science rather than fighting for the image of *either* natural or social science. To use an analogy, it might just be that psychology is still in the Oedipal stage of development—fearing castration by its "scientific" father while hanging onto the skirts of its "philosophy" mother. Perhaps a behavioral emphasis would deter a fixation at this stage of development.

1. The lack of commonality in references cited among elementary text authors reflects the diverse nature of the field and a difficulty in defining it.

2. A basic core of psychological literature can be identified by a survey of elementary text references. Some degree of stability can be inferred by comparing works from various surveys that have been conducted on different operational bases.

3. The interests of psychologists as indicated

TABLE 4. FREQUENCY AND PERCENTAGE OF REFERENCES CITED BY THE
FIVE AUTHORS OF ELEMENTARY TEXTS BROKEN DOWN BY
PUBLICATION DECADE

	Journal Articles		Books	
	f	$\%$	f	$\%$
Prior to 1900	10	.5	14	.9
1900–1909	9	.5	20	1.2
1910–1919	26	1.3	25	1.5
1920–1929	103	5.3	85	5.1
1930–1939	323	16.7	201	12.1
1940–1949	455	23.5	356	21.6
1950–1959	951	49.1	847	51.4
1960 +	60	3.1	100	6.1
	1937	100.0	1648	99.9

Date of Publication

Finally, when references from the beginning text are tallied by date of publication, there is some justification for the historically oriented psychologist to wish that more of the older "classical" studies had been included.

Over half of all references cited have been published since 1950, while only two to four percent of all references are dated prior to 1920. The emphasis of present day texts is on the present. As might be expected, however, the 20 references cited in common by all texts support the "tried and true" hypothesis. Only two of the twenty references from that list have been published since 1950 with over two-thirds of them dating prior to World War II.

Conclusions

A frequency comparison of references cited in elementary texts is only one of several approaches possible in assessing the current status of literature in the field. This method, however, offers a quick survey of literature content from materials that are readily accessible to most psychologists. In common with other surveys of this type it is a means of identifying important literature for the neophyte teacher of the first course. As a general index to the literature it may be a point of departure for formulating suggested readings for graduate students. If systematically followed up every five years or so it would supplement what we personally feel to be changing trends of emphasis in psychology. The application of this method to contemporary elementary texts yields the following general conclusions:

by A.P.A. divisional membership do not seem proportionately reflected in the journals most heavily drawn upon for the elementary texts.

4. Finally, studies or references cited in common by most elementary text authors have been in the literature for roughly 30 years. This "recognition lag" contrasts sharply in time with the publication date of the bulk of references.

References

Albee, G. W. American psychology in the sixties. *Amer. Psychologist,* 1963, 18, 90–95.

Birney, R., and McKeachie, W. The teaching of psychology: a survey of research since 1942. *Psychol. Bull.,* 1955, 52, 51–68.

Daniel, R. S. What is general about general psychology? Presidential address, Division 2, APA, September, 1962.

Harper, R. S. The first course in psychology. *Amer. Psychologist,* 1952, 7, 722–727.

Pressey, S. L. The place and functions of psychology in undergraduate programs. *Amer. Psychologist,* 1949, 4, 148–150.

Ruja, H. Productive psychologists. *Amer. Psychologist,* 1956, 11, 148–149.

Sundberg, N. D. Basic readings in psychology. *Amer. Psychologist,* 1960, 15, 343–345.

Wolfle, D. The sensible organization of courses in psychology. *Amer. Psychologist,* 1947, 2, 437–445.

Wurtz, K. R. A survey of important psychological books. *Amer. Psychologist,* 1961, 16, 192–194.

Works Cited by All Five Authors of Elementary Texts (N=20)

Allport, G. W. *Personality,* 1937.

Bridges, K. M. B. Emotional development in early infancy. *Child Develop.,* 1932, 3, 324–341.

Coleman, J. C. *Abnormal psychology and modern life,* 1950, 1956.

Ebbinghaus, H. *Memory,* 1885, 1913.

Gates, A. I. Recitation as a factor in memorizing. *Arch. Psychol.,* 1917, 6, No. 40.

Ghiselli, E. E. & Brown, C. W. *Personnel and industrial psychology,* 1955.

Harrell, T. W. & Harrell, M. S. Army General Classification Test scores for civilian occupations. *Educ. Psychol. Meas.,* 1945, 5, 229–239.

Jacobson, E. The electrophysiology of mental activities. *Amer. J. Psychol.,* 1932, 44, 677–694.

James, W. *Principles of psychology,* 1890.

Jenkins, J. G. & Dallenbach, K. M. Oblivescence during sleep and waking. *Amer. J. Psychol.,* 1924, 35, 605–612.

Kinsey, A. C., et al. *Sexual behavior in the human male,* 1948.

Köhler, W. *The mentality of apes,* 1925.

Lewin, K. *A dynamic theory of personality,* 1935.

Luchins, A. A. Mechanization in problem solving: The effect of Einstellung. *Psychol. Monog.,* 1942, 54, No. 248.

Murray, H. A. *Explorations in personality,* 1938.

Newman, H. H., et al. *Twins: A study of heredity and environment,* 1937.

Pavlov, I. P. *Conditioned reflexes,* 1927.

Wallas, G. *The art of thought,* 1926.

Wechsler, D. *Wechsler Intelligence Scale for children,* 1949.

Wolfe, J. B. Effectiveness of token rewards for chimpanzees. *Comp. Psychol. Monog.,* 1936, 12, No. 60.

Works Cited by 4 Out of 5 Authors of Elementary Texts (N=73)

Allport, G. W. & Odbert, H. S. Trait names: A psycholexical study. *Psychol. Monog.,* 1936, No. 211.

Allport, G. W., et al. *A study of values,* 1951, 1960.

Barker, R., et al. Frustration and regression, an experiment with young children. *Univer. Iowa Stud. Child Welf.,* 1941, 18, No. 386.

Bartlett, F. C. *Remembering,* 1932, 1950.

Bexton, W. H., et al. Effects of decreased variation in the sensory environment. *Canad. J. Psychol.,* 1954, 8, 70–76.

Boring, E. G. *A history of experimental psychology,* 1929, 1950.

Bruner, J. S., et al. *A study of thinking,* 1956.

Cannon, W. B. Hunger and thirst. In C. Murchison (Ed.), *A handbook of general experimental psychology,* 1934.

Carmichael, L. (Ed.), *Manual of child psychology,* 1954.

Carmichael, L. The development of behavior in vertebrates experimentally removed from the influence of external stimulation. *Psychol. Rev.,* 1926, 33, 51–58.

Cook, T. W. Massed and distributed practice in puzzle solving. *Psychol. Rev.,* 1934, 41, 330–355.

Cronbach, L. J. *Essentials of psychological testing,* 1949, 1960.

Davis, C. M. Self-selection of diet by newly weaned infants. *Amer. J. dis. Child.,* 1928, 36, 651–679.

Deese, J. *The psychology of learning,* 1958.

Dollard, J. & Miller, N. E. *Personality and psychotherapy,* 1950.

Erickson, S. C. Variability of attack in massed and distributed practice. *J. exp. Psychol.,* 1942, 31, 339–345.

Estes, W. K. An experimental study of punishment. *Psychol. Monog.,* 1944, 57, No. 263.

Ford, C. S. & Beach, F. A. *Patterns of sexual behavior,* 1951.

Gardner, E. *Fundamentals of neurology,* 1958.

Guetzkow, H. & Bowman, P. H. *Men and hunger,* 1946.

Harlow, H. F. The formation of learning sets. *Psychol. Rev.,* 1949, 56, 51–65.

Hebb, D. O. *Organization of behavior,* 1949.

Hilgard, E. R. *Theories of learning,* 1956.

Hull, C. L. *Principles of behavior,* 1943.

Hull, C. L. Quantitative aspects of the evolution of concepts. *Psychol. Monog.,* 1920, 28, No. 123.

Hurlock, E. B. *Developmental psychology,* 1953, 1959.

Johnson, D. M. *The psychology of thought and judgment,* 1955.

Jones, H. E. & Conrad, H. S. The growth and decline of intelligence. *Genet. Psychol. Monog.,* 1933, 13, 223–298.

Kellogg, W. N. & Kellogg, L. A. *The ape and the child,* 1933.

Keys, A. B., et al. *The biology of human starvation,* 1950.

Klineberg, O. *Social psychology,* 1954.

Kretschmer, E. *Physique and character,* 1925.

Lee, E. S. Negro intelligence and selective migration. *Amer. Soc. Rev.,* 1951, 16, 227–233.

Leonard, W. E. *The locomotive god,* 1927.

Lewin, K., et al. Patterns of aggressive behavior in experimentally created "social climates." *J. soc. Psychol.,* 1939, 10, 271–299.

Lindsley, D. B. Emotion. In S. S. Stevens (Ed.), *Handbook of experimental psychology,* 1951. Pp. 473–516.

McClelland, D. C. *Personality,* 1951.

McClelland, D. C., et al. *The achievement motive,* 1953.

McGeoch, J. A. & Irion, A. L. *Psychology of human learning,* 1952.

McNemar, Q. *The revision of the Stanford-Binet Scale,* 1942.

Mead, M. *Sex and temperament in three primitive societies,* 1935.

Morgan, C. T. & Stellar, E. *Physiological psychology,* 1950.

Moruzzi, G. & Magoun, H. W. Brain stem reticular formation and activation of the E.E.G. *E.E.G. Clin. Neurophysiol.,* 1949, 1, 455–473.

Mowrer, O. H. *Learning theory and personality dynamics,* 1950.

Murphy, G. *Historical introduction to modern psychology,* 1949.

Noyes, A. P. *Modern clinical psychiatry,* 1948.

Olds, J. Physiological mechanisms of reward. In M. Jones (Ed.), *Nebraska symposium on motivation,* Vol. III. 1955. Pp. 73–139.

Olds, J. & Milner, P. Positive reinforcement produced by electrical stimulation of septal area and other regions of rat brain. *J. comp. physiol. Psychol.,* 1954, 47, 419–427.

Osgood, C. E. The nature and measurement of meaning. *Psychol. Bull.,* 1952, 49, 197–327.

Patrick, C. Creative thought in artists. *J. Psychol.,* 1937, 4, 35–73.

Penfield, W. & Rasmussen, T. *The cerebral cortex of man,* 1950.

Poincaré, H. Mathematical creation. In *Foundations of science,* 1913.

Rogers, C. R. *Client-centered therapy,* 1951.

Rotter, J. B. *Social learning and clinical psychology,* 1954.

Schjelderup-Ebbe, T. Social behavior of birds. In C. Murchison (Ed.), *Handbook of social psychology,* 1935.

Shaffer, L. F. Fear and courage in aerial combat. *J. consult. Psychol.,* 1947, 11, 137–143.

Shaffer, L. F. & Shoben, E. J., Jr. *The psychology of adjustment,* 1956.

Sheldon, W. H. & Stevens, S. S. *The varieties of temperament,* 1942.

Sheldon, W. H., et al. *The varieties of human physique,* 1940.

Skinner, B. F. Teaching machines. *Science,* 1958, 128, 969–977.

Skinner, B. F. *The behavior of organisms,* 1938.

Sleight, R. B. The effect of instrument dial shape on legibility. *J. appl. Psychol.,* 1948, 32, 170–188.

Stevens, S. S. & Davis, H. *Hearing,* 1938.

Terman, L. M. & Merrill, M. A. *Measuring intelligence,* 1937.

Thigpen, C. H. & Cleckley, H. M. *The three faces of Eve,* 1957.

Tinbergen, N. *The study of instinct,* 1951.

Tsang, Y. C. Hunger motivation in gastrectomized rats. *J. comp. Psychol.,* 1938, 26, 1–17.

Tyler, L. E. *The psychology of human differences,* 1956.

Vinacke, W. E. *The psychology of thinking,* 1952.

Wechsler, D. *Measurement and appraisal of adult intelligence,* 1958.

Wever, E. G. *Theory and hearing,* 1949.

White, R. W. *The abnormal personality,* 1956.

Woodworth, R. S. & Schlosberg, H. *Experimental psychology,* 1954.

Contents

11 The Psychologist and the World Community   *326*

Glossary   *355*

Index   *361*

***Basic Contributions
to Psychology***
Readings

Second Edition

1   *The Beginnings and Process of a Science*

Where does scientific psychology fit into the history of life evolution? An analogy may illustrate how recent a development it is. If the 2 billion years of life on earth were collapsed into one calendar year, single-cell forms of life would emerge on January 1, invertebrate animals would appear on about July 1, and large reptiles would roam the earth during August and September. These reptiles would disappear on October 1. Early that same month mammals would appear. Finally, primitive man would walk onto the scene on December 31. But not until seconds before midnight would man begin to live in organized groups. Thus any scientific progress made by man would occur during the last second of the year. And, since psychology in this country did not emerge as a separate discipline until the early 1900s, it would enter at the last stroke of the clock.

A major reason for psychology's arrival at the last moment may be found in man's reluctance, throughout history, to use a scientific approach in solving his personal and social problems. Bringing psychology from the armchair to the laboratory was not an easy task. This reluctance, or resistance, to apply the methods of science to human behavior stems partly from man's unreasoning fear of the unknown and from his belief in the value of magic or chance. In fact, before applying the methodology of science to himself, man had to accept its usefulness in less personally oriented fields of observation.

The Rise of Modern Science, Edwin G. Boring. In the first selection, Boring identifies the main influences that have led man to a discovery of scientific principles. Of particular interest is the influence of *Zeitgeist* on scientific progress. *Zeitgeist* is the total cultural background within which a scientific discovery becomes known. Boring traces this phenomenon from the beginning of Greek civilization through the Renaissance. Also discussed are the five events, or "causes," that forcefully changed society's attitude toward new scientific ideas. Boring is a psychologist-historian who is respected by students of psychology as well as history for his thorough treatment of the history of experimental psychology.

Science and Values, Henri Poincaré. Poincaré, a French mathematician, discusses how a scientist's personal values relate to the quality of his observations. He asks the question "How does one coordinate scientific and moral truth?" Although he raises doubts about the absolute nature of truth, he points out that events and phenomena do proceed in an orderly manner. This fact, perhaps, is what inspires the scientist to continue his efforts.

Planning an Experiment, Donald G. Marquis. Although the subject of this reading is planning a program of research in psychology, Marquis' remarks are quite applicable to the individual experimental situation and to the beginning student in psychology as well as the seasoned research psychologist. He gives a description of the basic steps of the scientific method. "Program design," he says, "is scientific method in its full and complete form." The methodological steps he describes apply directly to the types of behavioral studies the beginning student is likely to undertake.

Psychology and Biology: Some Relationships, John P. Scott. Scott, a biologist, compares the growth of biology with the growth of psychology. Biology is closely related to psychology in its special concern for the functioning of living organisms. Life functions and behavior interact with each other in ways not yet completely understood. The two sciences mutually assist each other in solving their separate problems. Scott describes ways of furthering and augmenting the close relationship between the two sciences.

Humanistic Psychology: A New Break-Through, J. F. T. Bugental. The future of psychology as a scientific process is the focus of this selection. Bugental challenges the validity of eight specific assumptions that psychologists have traditionally accepted. This essay is controversial, and it illustrates, better than the other four selections, that psychology is an evolving science. It is placed last in this chapter as a reminder to the student that no science can remain static and expect to survive.

The Rise of Modern Science

Edwin G. Boring

Edwin G. Boring (1886–1968), Professor Emeritus, Harvard University, received his Ph.D. from Cornell University in 1914. An early president of the American Psychological Association (1928), Boring began his career as an electrical engineer. Fired from Clark University in 1922 because of his interest in freedom of speech, Boring stated, "Later Clark, with a new liberal president, gave me an honorary degree" (Sc.D., 1956). Among his many achievements was the editorship of Contemporary Psychology *from 1957 to 1961. Boring was responsible for making the concept of the* Zeitgeist *current in psychology.*

1. *When did science begin?*

2. *What conditions seem to provoke insights of scientific value?*

3. *What major events brought about a change in attitude toward the new science?*

The progress of science is the work of creative minds. Every creative mind that contributes to scientific advance works, however, within two limitations. It is limited, first, by ignorance, for one discovery waits upon that other which opens the way to it. Discovery and its acceptance are, however, limited also by the habits of thought that pertain to the culture of any region and period, that is to say, by the *Zeitgeist:* an idea too strange or preposterous to be thought in one period of western civilization may be readily accepted as true only a century or two later. Slow change is the rule—at least for the basic ideas. On the other hand, the more superficial fashions as to what is important, what is worth doing and talking about, change much more rapidly, depending partly on

their antagonists. A psychologist's history of psychology is, therefore, at least in aspiration, a dynamic or social psychology, trying to see not only what men did and, what they did not do, but also why they did it or why, at the time, they could not do it.

This matter becomes clearer when we realize that there are two theories of history, the *personalistic* and the *naturalistic*. The personalistic theory, which is also the theory of common sense, says that astronomy forged ahead because Copernicus had the insight to see and the courage to say that the heliocentric view of the solar system is more plausible than a geocentric. The naturalistic theory, on the other hand, holds that it was almost inevitable that the heliocentric view should be realized in the Age of Enlightenment, that it should then, as men's attitudes toward themselves shifted, come to seem plausible, and that Copernicus was, therefore, only the agent or perhaps the symptom of inexorable cultural change. Did Wundt found the new experimental psychology somewhere around 1860 or did the times compel the changes to which Wundt merely gave expression? Certainly Copernicus' and Wundt's discovery and partly on the social interaction of the wise men most concerned with the particular matter in hand—the cross-stimulation of leaders and their followers, of protagonists and opinions on these matters would not help us, for no one ever knows surely about his own motives or the sources of his insights, and the man of genius in his most brilliant flash of creative insight would not claim that his originality was uncaused—not in our modern culture would he claim it. As a matter of fact this dilemma is not real but a Kantian antinomy. Copernicus' and Wundt's thinkings are themselves both natural phenomena, and the course of history is no more nor less inexorable when it is interpreted as including the minute neural events which are the flashes of insight of those geniuses whose names mark the mileposts of science. Actually the naturalistic theory includes the personalistic. You get the personalistic view when you ignore the antecedents of the great man, and you get the naturalistic view back again when you ask what made the great man great. On either view there are Great Men, with nervous systems whose operations provide the opportunities for especially rapid scientific progress.

A truer dilemma arises when we ask about the rate of scientific progress. Does science run along on a plateau and then suddenly shoot ahead because of an important discovery, or does it move steadily, inevitably, onward, always by small increments? Is its course discrete and step-wise or is it gradual and continuous? Mature opinion favors many small steps as the general rule. Nearly all great discoveries have had their anticipations which the historian digs up afterward. Disproved theories hang on indefinitely, often for a century or more, until displaced by some positive substitute. Again and again it seems as if the crucial insight either does not come until the *Zeitgeist* has prepared for its reception, or, if it comes too soon for the *Zeitgeist,* then it does not register and is lost until it is unearthed later when the culture is ready to accept it.

Undoubtedly the smooth course of history on analysis would prove to be ultimately quantal, consisting of little bursts of progress, as this bit of discovery or that thrust of insight registers. It is when you consider larger units—the entire contribution of one man, the progress of a decade or a century—that you get the perception of large steps. Yet there have been moments when progress was rapid. An instance is Newton's conceiving of the principle of uni-

versal gravitation, a conception that certainly was formed quickly in 1666, although Voltaire's story that the idea came to Newton in an instant when he noticed the earth and an apple falling toward each other may exaggerate the suddenness of this basic insight. Be this as it may, the description of progress has necessarily to be made in terms of its differentials, those increments of change which are important enough and big enough to show whither knowledge is going.

The Emergence of Science

How did science begin? There is an argument that science has no beginning in human history but is as old as perception, that it begins in the evolutionary scale with the capacity to generalize in perceiving an object. In observation both science and perception look to underlying generalities, seeing in the observed object the uniformities of nature.

Take what psychologists call *object constancy*. The retinal image of a seen object gets smaller as the object recedes although both the physical object itself and the perception of it remain constant in size. The uniformity of nature here is the rule that objects do not change size when they move or when their observers move. That is a scientific physical generalization. The human organism is, however, so constructed that its perception, in general, follows the same general rule: the organism sees the same object as the same size regardless of the distance between it and the object. So the scientific generality is 'understood' by the organism in the sense that its perception includes this generalization. The generalizing organism can be man, an ape, a chick or even a lower animal form, since some degree of objective generalization is present in all perception. Perhaps this analogy is too fanciful, since it makes the first scientist an organism no higher in the animal scale than a chicken or perhaps even a protozoan; nevertheless the similarity serves to warn us that we shall not find in human history an exact moment when science began.

Science in the modern sense of a social institution in which many men cooperate and one generation carries on the work of the preceding requires the existence of a written language, of books and eventually of libraries, all of which make communication free and allow the younger generation to consult the wisdom of the ancients long since dead. Egyptian priests could pass on the lore of the heavens to their successors, but dependence on oral communication alone is fatal to extensive progress, since memory traces change, deteriorate and presently are lost in death. Scientific progress needs written language and books.

When one takes the very longest view of the emergence of science, then indeed there are apparent huge steps—periods of rapid development and sudden change. The first 'mutation' came with the emergence of Greek civilization, the 'Greek miracle,' as it is often called, and the second came with the Renaissance and its shift of interest away from theological dogma to a concern with nature and eventually with the experimental method.

As contrasted with the systematized knowledge of the previous ages in Egypt, Mesopotamia and the Aegean, the Greek civilization of the third, fourth and fifth centuries B.C seems indeed a miracle. These are the centuries of Plato (*ca.* 427–347 B.C.), Aristotle (384–322 B.C.) and Archimedes (*ca.* 287–212 B.C.). Aristotle, the greatest mind that ever lived, as some think, catalogued knowledge and increased it by his own wise pronouncements. Archimedes, as mathematician and physicist, actually anticipated the modern modes of scientific thinking in his way of dealing with general principles of nature. The total picture of this civilization, preserved to us and promoted by the use of an easily written language and the existence of books, shows a penetrating interest in knowledge and truth and an esthetic maturity in architecture and the arts that astonishes historians, astonishes them because, while they can describe the events, they cannot say why they occurred.

On the other hand, we must not forget that Greek civilization was meager as compared with our own. The Greeks were just as intelligent as we—there is no evidence that two millennia of evolution have improved man in the dimension in respect of which he excels the great apes. The educated Greek could live a full rich life—the richer because he was free to sample all knowledge and the cultivated arts and free of the modern pressure to adjust himself to more factual knowledge than he could possibly understand. He lived largely in the here and now. He had no history to learn and understand. Even Thucydides wrote history mostly within the span of his own memory. The ancient Greek had no important foreign languages to acquire, nor great foreign literatures to absorb and not much literature of his own. He felt no need to study other cultures. The Greek of the golden age lived in the best culture that had ever existed and that for him was surely enough. He did not need to travel to be educated, for there was no better place to go. Distances, moreover, seemed great. The gods could live on Olympus in northern Greece with no fear of inquisitive mortals' prying into their abode. There were no watches, no clocks. Discourse in Plato's Academy did not start at seven minutes past the hour. The economic system, which included slave labor, made it possible for the élite to give themselves fully to the advancement of a civilization to which the modern westerner owes an immeasurable debt. It was not, however, a civilization adapted to the emergence of experimental science. It favored intuition, insight and the intellectual processes, but not the extraction of secrets from nature by mechanical contrivance and experimental technique. That was not to come until almost two thousand years later.

In the Dark Ages (*ca.* 500–1200) and the Middle Ages (*ca.* 1200–1500), although science was advanced in the Byzantine culture of the east, the cultural life of western Europe was dominated by theological interest. When a man's thoughts passed beyond the immediate concern of his here and now, they were centered on the prospects of his soul and its chances of avoiding hell-fire. Thinking men were eager enough to know the truth, but the values of the times were such that they thought that the truth would be revealed to them in accordance with the divine will, and they looked for dogmas to guide them. Having accepted seven as a sacred number, it did not seem to them that God would place more than seven bodies in the immediate celestial universe—the Earth, the sun, the moon, Venus, Mars, Jupiter and Saturn—and Galileo's discovery of four moons for Jupiter appeared to them as sacrilegious. We are inclined to condemn the Middle Ages for their lack of science, their acceptance of unprovable dogma, their failure to advance what we call civilization; yet men of intelligence equal to that of today's Nobel Prize winners held these dogmatically determined attitudes toward truth as vehemently as any scientist defends his modern version of reality. Both medievalism and modernism depend on many *a priori* values, and our interest in the medieval in this book lies only in the fact that it furnished the kind of thinking from which modern science had to emerge. This emergence changed basic values; it did not, of course, eliminate them.

Actually modern science did not make its appearance until the Renaissance and the accompanying revival of learning.

The New Learning

What started the Renaissance off? We may be at a loss to explain the origin of the miracle of Greek civilization, but we can indeed say something of the dynamics of the revival of learning, of which one phase was the substitution of interest in evidentially established fact for theologically sanctioned dogma. It is usual to mention five events as 'causes' of the changed attitudes which made the new learning possible.

(1) The first of these is the invention of gunpowder and its use in warfare (15th century). That change helped to outmode the feudal system, to lay the basis for the democratization of society by weakening the bonds of personal fealty. The strengthening of national units at the expense of feudal estates broadened intellectual horizons and made learning easier.

(2) The invention of the printing press in 1440 suddenly made possible the mass production of books, multiplying many fold the effect that the invention of a written language had already had on civilization.

(3) The fall of Constantinople to the Turks in 1453 marked the end of the Byzantine Empire and the dissipation of its culture toward the west. The revival in Italy of interest in Greek civilization was furthered by the escape thither from Constantinople of Greek scholars.

(4) The discovery of America in 1492 was a phase of a period of geographical exploration and a search for convenient trade routes from western Europe to the far east. This event was due to no private whim of Columbus' but to the fact that the Middle Ages were passing and that concern with business and trade was beginning to surpass interest in the soul and theological dogma. Exploration was motived by the desire for wealth, and presently in the sixteenth century wealth was found, not only in trade with the Indies, but also in the silver and gold of Mexico and Peru. Besides the precious metals and the profits from trade, there was land—free land for the colonist who had the strength to take it and cultivate it. It is probable that no single factor has influenced more the character of the last four centuries in western Europe and America than the existence of 'free' land, even though it had first to be won from savages and then won again from nature to be called free.

Some historians have held that the democratic, practical spirit of America was due to its shifting westward frontier, beyond which there was always free land for every man with the wit and strength to become lord of his own acres. That may indeed be true, but there is also a much larger sense in which the free land of both the far west and the far east gave a special character to the four centuries which constitute modernity. In the Middle Ages power was derived from God—directly in the Church, or indirectly through the divine rights of kings, or, once established, by inheritance, as in the case of nobles. The powerful—kings, nobles, feudal lords and the Church—held the land, which thus became the symbol of power. In the new age the colonist could acquire land by hard work and the merchant could buy land. Gradually economic forces shifted the grounds for social status from hereditary or divine right to the possession of wealth in land or goods. This process of democratization played an enormously important rôle in the rise of science, because it both undermined the prestige of the givers of dogma and prepared the way for the promotion of science as soon as the commercial usefulness of science was demonstrated—and that was very soon.

(5) The fifth item of which so much has been made as a determiner of the new age of thought is the Copernican theory, published in 1543, the year of Copernicus' death. The geocentric theory of the celestial universe was also an anthropocentric theory: the universe was seen to revolve about man on the earth.

The heliocentric theory made more sense scientifically, but it demoted man to an unimportant peripheral position on one of many planets. There are even those today who ascribe the present prevalence of psychoneurosis partly to man's loss of a sense of prestige and importance under the Copernican theory. Not only did the Copernican revolution rob man of his geocentric position in the universe, it also robbed him of his definite celestial site for heaven and depreciated the importance of his own soul as it multiplied the possibilities of many other souls on other planets.

As we have already noted, it is difficult in these matters of historical causation to tell cause from effect, reason from symptom. Many of the relationships are circular. The discovery of free lands, the gold and silver of the Incas and the riches of the Indies, helped to establish the spirit of the new age, but the spirit of the new age helped in turn to further exploration. The Copernican theory was both the effect of new modes of thinking and the cause of their promotion. Copernicus needed the changing interests of men of intellect to encourage him to press the simpler but heterodox view of the celestial bodies; yet he recognized that the Church would be against him and he hesitated, putting his theory forward as a speculation and not publishing it before his death. So the effect of change was to make more change easier, but progress was slow. We might, for instance, add the Reformation to our list of causes. Luther nailed his ninety-five theses to the church door in 1517, but his act was the result of growing general dissatisfaction with the Church as well as the cause of more dissatisfaction. Some historians list the emergence of science as a reason for the new age. It too was both an effect and a cause of the changing times. It was part of the new learning.

Science and Values

Henri Poincaré

Henri Poincaré (1854–1912), a French mathematician, received his doctorate from the University of Paris in 1879. Considered by many the greatest mathematician of his time, he was a scholar of many subjects: mathematics, physics, astronomy, and philosophy. Psychologists have been particularly interested in his personal description of the creative function of mathematical discovery and invention.

1. Why is scientific truth neither moral nor immoral?

2. How does scientific truth differ from moral truth?

3. Can reality be determined independently of the mind that conceives it?

The search for truth should be the goal of our activities; it is the sole end worthy of them.

Doubtless we should first bend our efforts to assuage human suffering, but why? Not to suffer is a negative ideal more surely attained by the annihilation of the world. If we wish more and more to free man from material cares, it is that he may be able to employ the liberty obtained in the study and contemplation of truth.

But sometimes truth frightens us. And in

From Henri Poincaré, *The Foundations of Science,* trans. G. B. Halsted (Lancaster, Pa.: The Science Press, 1913), pp. 205–209.

fact we know that it is sometimes deceptive, that it is a phantom never showing itself for a moment except to ceaselessly flee, that it must be pursued further and ever further without ever being attained. Yet to work one must stop, as some Greek, Aristotle or another, has said. We also know how cruel the truth often is, and we wonder whether illusion is not more consoling, yea, even more bracing, for illusion it is which gives confidence. When it shall have vanished, will hope remain and shall we have the courage to achieve? Thus would not the horse harnessed to his treadmill refuse to go, were his eyes not bandaged? And then to seek truth it is necessary to be independent, wholly independent. If, on the contrary, we wish to act, to be strong, we should be united. This is why many of us fear truth; we consider it a cause of weakness. Yet truth should not be feared, for it alone is beautiful.

When I speak here of truth, assuredly I refer first to scientific truth; but I also mean moral truth, of which what we call justice is only one aspect. It may seem that I am misusing words, that I combine thus under the same name two things having nothing in common; that scientific truth, which is demonstrated, can in no way be likened to moral truth, which is felt. And yet I can not separate them, and whosoever loves the one can not help loving the other. To find the one, as well as to find the other, it is necessary to free the soul completely from prejudice and from passion; it is necessary to attain absolute sincerity. These two sorts of truth when discovered give the same joy; each when perceived beams with the same splendor, so that we must see it or close our eyes. Lastly, both attract us and flee from us; they are never fixed: when we think to have reached them, we find that we have still to advance, and he who pursues them is condemned never to know repose. It must be added that those who fear the one will also fear the other; for they are the ones who in everything are concerned above all with consequences. In a word, I liken the two truths, because the same reasons make us love them and because the same reasons make us fear them.

If we ought not to fear moral truth, still less should we dread scientific truth. In the first place it can not conflict with ethics. Ethics and science have their own domains, which touch but do not interpenetrate. The one shows us to what goal we should aspire, the other, given the goal, teaches us how to attain it. So they can never conflict since they can never meet. There can no more be immoral science than there can be scientific morals.

But if science is feared, it is above all because it can not give us happiness. Of course it can not. We may even ask whether the beast does not suffer less than man. But can we regret that earthly paradise where man brute-like was really immortal in knowing not that he must die? When we have tasted the apple, no suffering can make us forget its savor. We always come back to it. Could it be otherwise? As well ask if one who has seen and is blind will not long for the light. Man, then, can not be happy through science, but to-day he can much less be happy without it.

But if truth be the sole aim worth pursuing, may we hope to attain it? It may well be doubted. Readers of my little book 'Science and Hypothesis' already know what I think about the question. The truth we are permitted to glimpse is not altogether what most men call by that name. Does this mean that our most legitimate, most imperative aspiration is at the same time the most vain? Or can we, despite all, approach truth on some side? This it is which must be investigated.

In the first place, what instrument have we at our disposal for this conquest? Is not human intelligence, more specifically the intelligence of the scientist, susceptible of infinite variation? Volumes could be written without exhausting this subject; I, in a few brief pages, have only touched it lightly. That the geometer's mind is not like the physicist's or the naturalist's, all the world would agree; but mathematicians themselves do not resemble each other; some recognize only implacable logic, others appeal to intuition and see in it the only source of discovery. And this would be a reason for distrust. To minds so unlike can the mathematical theorems themselves appear in the same light? Truth which is not the same for all, is it truth? But looking at things more closely, we see how these very different workers collaborate in a common task which could not be achieved without their cooperation. And that already reassures us.

Next must be examined the frames in which

nature seems enclosed and which are called time and space. In 'Science and Hypothesis' I have already shown how relative their value is; it is not nature which imposes them upon us, it is we who impose them upon nature because we find them convenient. But I have spoken of scarcely more than space, and particularly quantitative space, so to say, that is of the mathematical relations whose aggregate constitutes geometry. I should have shown that it is the same with time as with space and still the same with 'qualitative space'; in particular, I should have investigated why we attribute three dimensions to space. I may be pardoned then for taking up again these important questions.

Is mathematical analysis, then, whose principal object is the study of these empty frames, only a vain play of the mind? It can give to the physicist only a convenient language; is this not a mediocre service, which, strictly speaking, could be done without; and even is it not to be feared that this artificial language may be a veil interposed between reality and the eye of the physicist? Far from it; without this language most of the intimate analogies of things would have remained forever unknown to us; and we should forever have been ignorant of the internal harmony of the world, which is, we shall see, the only true objective reality.

The best expression of this harmony is law. Law is one of the most recent conquests of the human mind; there still are people who live in the presence of a perpetual miracle and are not astonished at it. On the contrary, we it is who should be astonished at nature's regularity. Men demand of their gods to prove their existence by miracles; but the eternal marvel is that there are not miracles without cease. The world is divine because it is a harmony. If it were ruled by caprice, what could prove to us it was not ruled by chance?

This conquest of law we owe to astronomy, and just this makes the grandeur of the science rather than the material grandeur of the objects it considers. It was altogether natural, then, that celestial mechanics should be the first model of mathematical physics; but since then this science has developed; it is still developing, even rapidly developing. And it is already necessary to modify in certain points the scheme from which I drew two chapters of 'Science and Hypothesis.'

The progress of science has seemed to imperil the best established principles, those even which were regarded as fundamental. Yet nothing shows they will not be saved; and if this comes about only imperfectly, they will still subsist even though they are modified. The advance of science is not comparable to the changes of a city, where old edifices are pitilessly torn down to give place to new, but to the continuous evolution of zoologic types which develop ceaselessly and end by becoming unrecognizable to the common sight, but where an expert eye finds always traces of the prior work of the centuries past. One must not think then that the old-fashioned theories have been sterile and vain.

Were we to stop there, we should find in these pages some reasons for confidence in the value of science, but many more for distrusting it; an impression of doubt would remain; it is needful now to set things to rights.

Some people have exaggerated the rôle of convention in science; they have even gone so far as to say that law, that scientific fact itself, was created by the scientist. This is going much too far in the direction of nominalism. No, scientific laws are not artificial creations; we have no reason to regard them as accidental, though it be impossible to prove they are not.

Does the harmony the human intelligence thinks it discovers in nature exist outside of this intelligence? No, beyond doubt a reality completely independent of the mind which conceives it, sees or feels it, is an impossibility. A world as exterior as that, even if it existed, would for us be forever inaccessible. But what we call objective reality is, in the last analysis, what is common to many thinking beings, and could be common to all; this common part, we shall see, can only be the harmony expressed by mathematical laws. It is this harmony then which is the sole objective reality, the only truth we can attain; and when I add that the universal harmony of the world is the source of all beauty, it will be understood what price we should attach to the slow and difficult progress which . . . enables us to know it better.

Planning an Experiment

Donald G. Marquis

Donald G. Marquis, Professor at the Sloan School of Management, Massachusetts Institute of Technology, received his Ph.D. from Yale University in 1932. A past president of the American Psychological Association, he now directs a multidisciplinary program studying the organization and management of large-scale research. Committed to the value of inquiry, Marquis has for many years helped develop students of psychology into researchers.

1. *In formulating a problem, why should one weed out value assumptions from the factual propositions?*

2. *On what grounds should a theory be based?*

3. *Must the six proposed steps always proceed in the order given by the author?*

I do not believe that it takes a genius to design a research program, nor is it necessary to wait for that rare flash of scientific insight. An example from another field of science may indicate more clearly what I mean. In meteorology there is no theory comparable to that in physics or chemistry. It is conceivable that hundreds of students of weather could carry out in their individual laboratories and field stations a multitude of little unrelated studies. One of them would clock the sunrise in Central standard time; another would report the movement of the moon in Eastern daylight saving time; one of them would record wind velocity on a 7-point descriptive scale; another would devise a windmill gadget and report velocities in reliable but arbitrary units of revolutions per minute.

Abridged from Donald G. Marquis, "Research Planning at the Frontiers of Science," *American Psychologist*, 3 (1948), 432–435. Copyright 1948 by the American Psychological Association and reproduced by permission.

One would study temperature in Albuquerque, another rainfall in Cheyenne. In spite of all the diligence and individual ingenuity of this earnest band of researchers it would be a slow and wasteful process to accumulate useful meteorological knowledge. But because the problem is sufficiently important, the meteorologists have gotten together and agreed to collect commensurate data by standardized methods in all parts of the world. With these data available there has been steady growth in theory and in the accuracy of prediction. This is an extreme example. In most frontier fields it may not be possible to undertake so comprehensive a program but rather to have many programs proceeding simultaneously, each large enough to provide an adequate test of the conceptual theory involved but permitting several alternative approaches to the same general problem.

What, then, is the essential feature of program design? It is the attempt to plan a comprehensive, integrated series of studies in relation to a particular set of concepts focused on a central problem. It is the attempt to broaden and lengthen the scope of a research sufficiently so that we can tell whether it is really getting anywhere. It is scientific method in its full and complete form. I shall list six steps in program design. The temporal sequence of the steps is not fixed although there is a natural order.

1. The first step may be called *problem*

formulation. In the selection of a problem there appears to be no restriction on the kind of topic which can be attacked scientifically. "The religious attitudes of middle-west farmers" is as acceptable a problem as the limits of their visual sensitivity. There are, however, two important limitations governing the formulation of a problem for scientific study. The first is that a value proposition cannot be verified by any present scientific methods. It is necessary therefore to separate the value assumptions from the factual propositions which can be investigated. Most of the problems arising from the practical situations of living come to us with a mixture of value and factual questions. We cannot, for example, test the proposition that spaced practice is better than massed practice. Analyzing this problem into its components, we formulate the proposition that spaced practice results in more rapid learning than massed practice, and we do not examine the question of whether rapid learning is desirable or not. Such analysis of a problem poses few difficulties in physical and biological science but is a frequent source of confusion in dealing with topics like labor relations, race prejudice, and therapy.

A second limitation on the scientific method of inquiry is that the phenomenon under study must exist in replication. There is no known method by which a single unique event can be the subject of research. If we are interested in what appears to be a unique situation, such as the explanation of the suicide of a particular individual or the form of organization of the world state, it is necessary to reformulate the problem in terms of those aspects of the situation which can be identified in several instances. This is a serious limitation on the scope of scientific investigation and one which is not completely accepted by all persons who become interested in the significant and real problems of practical life.

2. The second step is *review of knowledge*—of what has been learned or said by others about the topic. The library is the usual source of this material but personal informants are often utilized, for example, in anthropological field work. Although this step is clearly recognized by everyone, the difficulties of achieving it are becoming serious as a result of the tremendous growth in the literature of every field. Abstract journals, bibliographies, summaries and reviews are important aids in this respect and should be extended into frontier fields more adequately than at present. If research is organized into programs it becomes feasible for each to undertake a comprehensive review of current knowledge, and the Office of Naval Research has recognized this need in arranging contracts which include specific provision for literature summaries.

3. The third step is *preliminary observation* of the events under study. This may be quite unstructured observation which enriches the second-hand library knowledge and suggests new leads for investigation. It may also be more controlled observation in the nature of trying out methods of measurement, formulating codes for classification of data, identifying sub-samples of the population and pretesting promising hypotheses. In its most developed form it may be methodological research—a comparison of two or more ways of describing, measuring or scoring the phenomena. A variety and diversity of observational methods is desirable at this point in order to explore most fruitfully the best possible ways of formulating and categorizing the data.

4. The fourth step is *theory construction*—the formulation of specific and rigorous hypotheses for subsequent test. Now the investigator draws upon everything that he has learned from his review of previous work and from preliminary observation. While theory construction can sometimes be achieved in the comfort of the armchair, I do not want to imply that it is easy or routine. It is indeed the crucial test of the creative scientist.

I think we are beginning to realize more clearly that a theory, to be useful, must be built around concepts which have specific and unequivocal relation to empirical observation and measurement. Only in this way can theory be verified. Most of what we have called theory in the new fields of psychology has not been of this type. Our theories have a long life span of controversy because of the difficulties of testing them. Their concepts are not such as can be identified or measured. They were invented on the basis of a priori considerations rather than being abstracted from empirical study and as a result, they do not lend themselves to unequivocal test. It is certainly typical, and perhaps inevitable, that the first theories in a new field, since they aim at broad understanding, are speculative and untestable. Man's desire for explanation does not permit a vacuum in his comprehension of the world. Hence the crystal spheres theory in astronomy; the earth, air, fire and water theory in physical science; the demonological theory of mental disease; the social contract theory of the state; and the instinct theory of human behavior. In the history of science it has usually been necessary to abandon such theories completely rather than to try to modify them to a form which permits testing. We can perhaps accelerate the long-range development of scientific knowledge in frontier fields by emphasis upon the construction of theory out of empirical or operationally-defined concepts. Such theories will necessarily be limited in scope. It is inevitable that the most useful theories will, for some time to come, be small conceptual systems dealing with a restricted range of phenomena.

5. The fifth step is *verification*—the testing of the hypotheses or of deductions from them. If our concepts have been properly chosen and if methods of measurement have been devised, we find adequate guides for verification in our present knowledge of statistical methods. This step in program design is the one which has received the most extensive attention and while it is crucial for science, it is not the primary topic of my discussion. Perhaps the most frequent present limitation in the verification stage is found in the selection of a population for study. Too often in the formulation of a problem we fail to think through the definition of the universe to which our theory is applicable and we are apt to overlook the necessity to select a representative sample of that universe for verification purposes. Considerations of convenience, habit and inadequate funds usually determine that the research will be carried out on any available group of college sophomores, nursery school children, or military personnel. Such studies may be very fruitful and have a definite place in the preliminary observation step. Usually, however, they cannot be made a

coordinate part of a total integrated body of knowledge.

The processes of verification may take quite different forms, of which the controlled experiment is only one example. Correlation studies, comparative studies, genetic studies, surveys, intensive case studies, and field studies each have a definite place if they are relevant tests of the theory which has been formulated.

The results of the verification process do not all turn out as the theory predicted. This is not entirely unfortunate, since it provides the clue for reformulation of the theory and hence advance in knowledge. The scientist then proceeds with further tests of his revised theory and in this manner theory construction goes along with experiment and observation in a continuous reciprocal alternation.

6. The sixth and last step in program design is *application* of the verified theory. In pure research, of course, application is not involved since the results are used only to modify the theory. But pure research is rare in frontier fields and application must usually be made directly from the research results rather than indirectly through the theory. Application involves three processes itself: first is a value decision on the desired objective, second is the diagnosis of the specific situation, and third is the selection of the relevant verified knowledge and its application. Consider, for example, the clinical psychologist dealing with a client requesting vocational counseling. A decision must first be made whether a job is to be chosen on the basis of salary, status, interests or some combination of factors. Scientific theory does not determine what job the individual should take; it can only point out the probability of certain consequences of a vocational choice. The decision must be made by the counselor or, better, by the client, in reference to his value system. The diagnosis requires pertinent information about the individual and about the possible jobs. It is then possible to apply knowledge such as "the greater the congruence of a person's abilities with the requirements of an occupation, the greater are the chances of that individual's success and satisfaction in that occupation."

Psychology and Biology:
Some Relationships

John P. Scott

John P. Scott, Regents' Professor of Psychology and Director, Center for Research on Social Behavior, Bowling Green State University, received his Ph.D. from the University of Chicago in 1935. Known for his conception of the critical-period unit in development, he is the author of four books: Animal Behavior (*1958*), Aggression (*1958*), *with J. L. Fuller,* Genetics and the Social Behavior of the Dog (*1965*), *and* Early Experience and the Organization of Behavior (*1968*).

1. What is meant by the phrase "The old religious and philosophical dualism of mind and body still handicaps psychological thought"?

2. What events or techniques have been mutually beneficial to biology and psychology?

3. How do biology and psychology differ in their systems of terminology?

Any student who enters the field of science is struck immediately by a sort of hierarchy which extends from the older to the more recently developed sciences. Whether he compares this hierarchy to the caste system in India or the "peck order" which is developed by barnyard chickens depends upon his taste, but, generally speaking, mathematicians tend to be the high priests, physicists and chemists are of a lower but still acceptable rank, whereas social scientists rank as untouchables. Each of the higher-ranking scientists tends to assume that the methods of his science are superior to those in the lower orders and that he automatically knows all about the inferior sciences by virtue

of his own experience. The low-ranking scientist, on the other hand, tends to listen to these opinions with an attitude of respect and submission.

Such social reactions of scientists would form an interesting study for a social psychologist interested in group relations, but even without such a study it is obvious that these common attitudes and assumptions are by no means correct. The sciences which have developed more lately have profited by the mistakes of their predecessors and frequently have been able to go ahead to new refinements of thought and technique. In early physics there was a tendency to set up theories on the basis of crude mechanical models such as the comparison of electricity with a current of water, and this tradition persists even to the present day in physical explanations of the action of the human brain. The new analogies are more refined than the old ones, but even the electronic calculator has the deficiencies of all such models.

It is equally obvious, to anyone who has attempted to cross over between two fields of science, that learning in the more basic field does not guarantee competence or even acquaintanceship with developments in the newer field. Speaking as one who was originally trained as a biologist, I find that psychology has greatly profited from earlier scientific developments, and as a result is in many ways technically superior. At the same time, this late development has also resulted in certain losses.

Historical Origins of Biology and Psychology

Most sciences were originally started by amateurs, and biology was no exception. It was not until the time of Linnaeus that biology became a serious study, which at this time consisted chiefly of describing and cataloguing the various kinds of plants and animals. As the subject became accepted into colleges and universities it was not originally considered science at all, and in the catalogues of the last century courses were described in natural philosophy which included chemistry and physics, and natural history which included biology. The early biologist did not have to be a scientist and this greatly helped his freedom of ideas and development. Biologists were chiefly interested in the historical problem of evolution and, as such, devoted nearly half a century to collecting the facts of anatomy, embryology, and geographical distributions. The period may be called one of comparison, and in comparative anatomy this technique reached its height. About 1900, with the rediscovery of Mendelism, the emphasis in biology changed toward experimentation rather than description and comparison, and this trend has been maintained ever since.

Psychology, on the other hand, began as pure philosophy and even when I studied the subject as an undergraduate some 25 years ago the department was labeled philosophy and psychology. There are still a great many hangovers from this period, the principal one of which is a tendency to cling to a priori reasoning. The old religious and philosophical dualism of mind and body still handicaps psychological thought, and in the investigation of any human problem psychologists are prone to start with similar ancient conceptions. Psychology never enjoyed a great period of description and comparison; in fact, psychology was not seriously studied until the turn of the century when experimentalism was already in vogue in the sister science of biology. There was a brief flowering of comparative psychology before the first World War but the job was never completed and, as Beach has pointed out, psychologists devoted themselves thereafter to the experimental study of learning, sometimes without having the basic facts on which to found their theories. Recently, the pressure of clinical problems has forced many psychologists to the realization that observation and description are necessary precursors to experimentation.

It will be seen that biology and psychology have had a strongly interrelated historical development. From an analytical point of view it is proper that this should be so. In one respect psychology may be considered a special branch of biology, being closely related to the all-inclusive science of ecology, or the study of the organism and its environment. In still another sense, psychology is more inclusive than biology because science itself may be considered a human behavioral attribute and the study of all science properly becomes a subdivision of psychology.

Mutual Contributions of Biology and Psychology

One of the most obvious ways in which biology and psychology have mutually benefited has been through the development of statistical methods which have been sometimes described as biometry. Work along these lines largely began with Galton's interest in the inheritance of human abilities and physical characteristics, and a great development of methods followed under the leadership of Karl Pearson. This, in turn, led to further advances, at first applied to experimental biology and later applied to psychology. Certain special problems of correlation attracted the attention of psychologists such as Thurstone and led to the development of even more advanced statistical methods which are now being applied in biology as well as psychology.

A great many basic theories and ideas came from the field of biology. One of the most important of these was the idea of the organism as a whole, which is, of course, the basis of the study of behavior, and this has gradually replaced the old dualism of mind and body. The physiological studies of Pavlov on conditioned reflexes are still the foundation of most theories of learning. Cannon's idea of homeostasis, particularly as related to hunger and fear, greatly stimulated the study of emotions and motivation by psychologists.

Psychological findings are so important to human welfare that there is always a temptation for the research worker to generalize from any discovery and propound a simple universal theory of behavior, and it is probably this tendency that accounts for the formation of many of the different schools of psychology. At the same time both biologists and psychologists have developed the theory of multiple factor causation which removes the necessity of ascribing behavior to any one universal factor and indicates that all schools of psychology probably have their places in the scheme of science and that there is no necessary conflict between them.

Both psychologists and biologists have their blind spots and this sometimes leads to apparent contradictions and controversies. Because of the importance of heredity in the theory of evolution, biologists stress hereditary factors, and when a behavioral phenomenon is studied will tend to ascribe it entirely to heredity without ever considering the possibility of learning. Similarly psychologists have been preoccupied with the idea of learning because of its practical importance in education and most of them are likely to assume that any behavioral phenomenon must be learned and will admit the possible action of hereditary factors only as a last resort. This tendency is still apparent and demonstrates the need for greater communication between the two sciences.

One great historical difference in the development of the two sciences is seen in the reactions of biologists and psychologists to the problem of terminology. Biology got its start at the time when classical education was still in vogue, and a regular system of terminology from Greek and Latin roots was developed. From the point of view of semantics this scheme has great advantages. A new phenomenon can be given a new name and an exact definition which makes it possible to think clearly concerning it. Derived from Greek or Latin roots, the term is usually hard to pronounce and does not get into popular usage with the resulting tendency toward loss of meaning. By contrast, psychology reached its great development when classical education was declining and psychologists have tended to use common terms and attempt to redefine them with the result that psychological terminology often has many resemblances to schoolboy slang in that the words used are known to everyone, but the meaning is comprehended only by the initiated. Such a term as "conditioning" is confusing to the beginner because he already knows other meanings of the term and its use adds nothing to the understanding of the scientist. In many cases, however, the more precise terminology developed in the biological sciences is being taken over where it applies to psychological phenomena, particularly in physiological psychology.

A final field in which biology and psychology are making mutual contributions is in the technique of observation. Animal behaviorists with biological training are doing the basic collecting of observational facts on animal species which is a prerequisite to understanding details of behavior which can be subjected to experimentation. Up until recently no one had made a basic behavioral study of the Norway rat which psychologists had studied intensively in the laboratory for over 30 years. One of the facts which emerged from these studies by Calhoun and others is that rats are highly social animals and as such are affected by the behavior of the experimenters as well as each other. Once the rat is understood as a rat it is possible to make intelligent comparisons of rat and human behavior for, while rats and humans may have some things in common, certain other items of behavior may have a quite different significance to the rat.

For example, a great deal has been made out of certain experiments on the tendency of laboratory rats to transfer food from one point to another, and these ideas have been associated with the ideas of hoarding, miserliness, retention, and the like. Rat populations studied under natural and seminatural conditions are found to exist in organized social groups which reject strangers and which are themselves organized into dominance hierarchies. If there is but one source of food in the territory of a group, it is usually controlled by the dominant animals, which, however, carry the food away to various outlying points. Such stores may be visited by the less dominant rats when unable to reach the central supply. If they do reach it, they may simply scatter it at a distance. Is this hoarding, or is it food storing or possibly even food sharing? Since the food is always concealed in burrows or shelters, it is perhaps most likely that the behavior trait has adaptive value in that the food is placed in positions where it can be eaten—by others as well as the carrier—in comparative safety from predators.

I found a similar lack of information a few years ago when I began the study of social development in animals. Only a few thorough studies had ever been done on small numbers of animals and most of those before 1900. After thorough observational studies of puppies, mice, and sheep it turned out that the course of development in any species is different from that in any other and tends to be related to the particular social organization of the species. Experiments on the effect of early experience can only be done intelligently with a knowledge of normal behavioral events. A few days difference in timing may make a great difference in the ultimate result. Some species begin to learn immediately after birth; others show no permanent learning for several weeks. The course of sensory and motor development is extremely variable. All of this descriptive material throws new light on human development and suggests new possibilities and lines of research.

While psychologists are seldom observers, psychology has contributed greatly to the technique of observation. The use of duplicate observers and the statistical techniques of reliability have been developed by psychologists and are of great help to biologically trained students of animal behavior. Furthermore, the psychological studies of perception have been and will be of great value in giving students better training in observation. One technique which may be suggested is the use of moving pictures in which behavioral situations can be exactly repeated and discrimination more easily taught than in most real-life situations.

I would conclude that psychology students should, as part of their training, have more emphasis placed on the technique of objective observation. The techniques of experimental psychological testing have worked out very well in classroom situations and in providing information concerning classroom learning. This has rightly been one of the chief preoccupations of psychologists and should not be neglected. However, many of the important unsolved problems of human behavior lie in the field of social relationships and personality interaction where a paper and pencil test cannot possibly duplicate real-life situations. As the clinical psychologists have found, observation is the only answer, and observation should go further than an oral interview which is likely to reflect the subject's reaction to the particular personality of the interviewer. To the student interested in clinical work, sound training in the technique of observation should be invaluable.

Such training can also be used to directly stimulate thought and promote the interest of students. As a preliminary exercise one may be sent out into a strange social situation and given instructions to record as accurately as possible what people around him are doing. Usually he will experience an intense awareness of what is going on, which can be related later in the classroom to such principles as the effect of change and accommodation on stimulation. Great individual differences in accuracy will appear, and the student can be trained to discriminate between what he sees and what he interprets. It is probably best to avoid structuring the situation, except that no more than two students should ever attempt to make an observation at the same time, and, if so, should attempt to observe entirely independently, so that later studies of observer reliability can be made.

The experience may eventually be stimulating for research, for while experiments are designed to test new ideas, new ideas rarely come from them. Many of the important psychological ideas come directly from clinical observation, and the most original discoveries come from the observation of a curious fact and the inevitable question, Why should this happen? As observation is improved there should be a corresponding improvement in the quality and depth of psychological research.

Humanistic Psychology:
A New Break-Through

J. F. T. Bugental

James Bugental, presently on leave from Psychological Service Associates, Los Angeles, and serving as Research Consultant to the Educational Policy Research Center at the Stanford Research Institute, in Menlo Park, California, received his Ph.D. from Ohio State University in 1948. Principally interested in individual and group psychotherapy, he is the author of more than 50 articles, reviews, and books on the subject. Fostering an existential-analytic approach to psychotherapy, Bugental is concerned that practitioners of psychology emphasize the "positive and creative aspects of human experience" rather than become preoccupied with the pathological aspect.

1. *Do the eight points of attack seem reasonable to you? If not, why not?*

2. *Why is the author so set against a part-function approach?*

3. *Can a process approach to the study of man be conducted scientifically?*

I want to present the thesis that a major break-through is occurring at the present time in psychology. Like man's other major changes—the introduction of the steam engine, the decline of feudalism, the beginnings of the laboratory method in psychology—its presence and potentialities are difficult to recognize for those of us who are so deep in daily concerns. Yet, I am convinced that the parallels I cite are not vainglorious. I think we are on the verge of a new era in man's concern about man which may—if allowed to run its course—produce as profound changes in the human condition as those we have seen the physical sciences bring about in the last century. The essence of this change is, I believe, the eroding away of some of the familiar parameters of psychological

science and the concurrent emergence of a new appreciation for the fundamental inviolability of the human experience.

Psychology, as any social institution, is a constantly evolving set of assumptions, information, and speculations. As with any institution, it has its periods of stability and of rapid change. Sometimes the change may be clearly dated from a particular event, as with the rise of behaviorism after Watson's epochal book appeared. Sometimes the forces producing the change are more scattered, as in the rise of the mental testing wave. In either instance, hindsight reveals numerous stirrings before the change process became clearly apparent. This is certainly so at the present. Writings by many social scientists have prepared the way for what is now emerging (viz., James, Allport, Cantril, May, Maslow, Fromm, Rogers, and many others). What has brought this development to the fore now may be argued, but certainly some of the influences will include: the large number of psychologists now involved in the practice of psychotherapy, the failure of many promising approaches to produce a truly embracing and adequate theory of human personality from our existing orientations, the press of public interest in, and need for, psychological science and service. One may speculate also that just as when a single organism encounters a threat to its life maintenance, it evokes counter forces (e.g., antibodies), so this development may be part of an evolutionary response to the biology-threatening forces of nuclear destruction.

Psychological Parameters Undergoing Change

Let us examine eight parameters which have been traditionally accepted as given in psychology but which, I think, are being questioned increasingly as a result of the wave of change which is now occurring.

These eight parameters are:

1. The model of man as a composite of part functions
2. The model of a science taken over from physics
3. The model of a practitioner taken over from medicine
4. The pattern of a compartmentalized, subdivided graduate school faculty and curriculum as the appropriate agency for preparing students for psychological careers
5. The criterion of statistical frequency as a demonstration of truth or reality
6. The illusion that research precedes practice
7. The myth of the "clinical team"
8. The fallacy that diagnosis is basic to treatment

What I want to do now is to examine each of these models with a view to recognizing what changes may be occurring in them.

1. The Model of Man as a Composite of Part Functions. What has been said above already indicates my view that this fundamental conception of the nature of man is in the process of basic alteration. So long as we sought mental elements, in whatever form and given whatever sophistication of naming, we operated on the basis that the total human being could be sufficiently understood if only we had an inclusive catalogue of his parts. This is at root inevitably a structuralistic conception. Today we are more and more recognizing that we need a process conception of the human being. So basic do I feel this difference to be that I would propose that in the coming years we will increasingly recognize that the study of the part functions of human behavior is indeed

a different science than is the study of the whole human being. We are familiar with making this sort of division between psychology and physiology. It seems to me that part functions of what we have traditionally thought of as psychology—that is, such segments as habits, test scores, single percepts, learned items—differ more from the functioning of the total person than does the reflex arc from memory for nonsense syllables.

I propose that the defining concept of man basic to the new humanistic movement in psychology is that *man is the process that supersedes the sum of his part functions.*

2. The Model of a Science Taken Over from Physics. So long as we accepted the model of man as a composite of his part functions then it was appropriate for us to seek for the ultimate units of behavior. Such attempts followed the two main lines of the search for mental elements under Titchner or for the simple stimulus-response bond under the behaviorists, or on the other side the seeking for basic instincts or primary cathexes under the orthodox psychoanalytic banner. Physics has demonstrated tremendous versatility in increasing our knowledge of the physical world by analytic methods. But physics has built its record because of the fundamental interchangeability of the units which it studied. A true psychology of human beings is a psychology of noninterchangeable units. The past 50 years have seen a tremendous accumulation of data about people treated as interchangeable units. And yet it is clearly the case that only where we are concerned with masses of persons do these data yield useful results. This may seem a harsh judgment, but I think it is an accurate one. If psychology is the study of the whole human being, and this I believe is its primary mission, then results which are only true of people in groups are not truly psychological but more sociological. Just as psychology is emerging as distinct from the study of part functions, so it is distinguishing itself from the study of group phenomena.

Before leaving these comments on a model of a science taken over from physics, it would be worthwhile noting that physics itself has found that it must move beyond logical positivism and the mechanistic causality which long were its guideposts. Attention to process and to the experimenter's interconnection with the experiment are beginning to be recognized as essential to the further development of pure physics. How much more pertinent are they to psychology!

3. The Model of a Practitioner Taken Over from Medicine. The medical model for the practitioner has a long history which dates back, of course, to the shaman, the medicine man, and the occult priest. Psychological practitioners have taken it for granted that they must function in a similar fashion. This is increasingly being found to be a false assumption. Indeed many practitioners of psychotherapy find that such a pattern is all too readily accepted by patients and used as a resistance to taking responsibility in their own lives. A new concept of the practitioner is emerging to which it is difficult yet to give an adequate name. Lowell Kelly has suggested the term "consultants in living" which has much to commend it, though it does seem somewhat pretentious. Certainly the point is that we cannot follow a pattern of esoterically diagnosing our patients' difficulties and writing prescriptions in Latin and an illegible scrawl, which the patient dutifully carries to the pharmacist for compounding and then takes with complete ignorance of the preparation or its intended effects. We are recognizing more and more that essential to the psychotherapeutic course is the patient's own responsible involvement in the change process.

4. The Pattern of a Compartmentalized, Subdivided Graduate School Faculty and Curriculum as the Appropriate Agency for Preparing Students for Psychological Careers. Something of the ferment within psychology has been represented in the typical graduate school faculty. Especially in our larger schools, there has been a pattern of subdivision of the department into various specialties. Sometimes these reach rather extreme numbers of subpsychologies. The result has been a fragmented approach to our field which has created much confusion and threat for graduate students. I wish I could report that I see as many signs of healthful change in this area as in some of the others upon which I report; nevertheless, there are stirrings which indicate a recognition that our pattern of many specialties—clinical, counseling, industrial, child—is proving more self-defeating than

implementing. My own feeling is that we must move toward recognizing three basic subdivisions of psychology: that concerned with part functions, that concerned with group functions, and that concerned with the total person as the unit. Quite probably for each of these there will need to be a research and teaching phase and a practitioner phase. All three are increasingly being employed in the solution of practical problems, and the number of practitioners in all three is sure to grow tremendously in the coming years. Much of the resentment of our experimental brothers toward the practitioners is apt gradually to fade away as more and more of the experimentalists themselves are drawn into consulting functions. Tryon has written his prediction that the academic ivory tower is a thing of the past and that the experimentalists soon will be deeply involved in practitioner roles. This will certainly have a profound effect on our graduate school educational philosophies.

5. The Criterion of Statistical Frequency as a Demonstration of Truth. In the abstract, the criterion of statistical frequency seems to be an excellent one. Certainly those things that happen regularly and uniformly seem to be self-evident samples of the nature of reality. However, in actual practice this is not borne out. Despite increasing elaboration of statistical methodologies, despite greater and greater refinement of laboratory procedure, the product of years of conscientious effort has not been such as to warrant confidence that we will eventually arrive at a genuine understanding of human behavior by this route. And this is not surprising when we look back to the model on which these efforts are founded. The effort to find the basic subperson unit of behavior has been vain. The total person is the basic unit. Only as we find ways to understand the behaving person can we understand his behavior. It is manifestly impossible with present techniques to control all factors involved in any behavioral sequence in which the human normally engages. Nor is this simply a matter of developing more and more tests and using larger and larger computers. Our definition of the human being as the process that supersedes the sum of its factors indicates that there is still a nonmeasurable aspect. There is still the person himself. It is not a matter of more time being needed; it is a matter of recognizing that we are following an unprofitable course.

Another way of conceptualizing the problem may throw light on it: This is to recognize that our traditional scientific approach as represented in so many journal articles, dissertations, and master's theses, has been founded on a finite universe conception. That is to say, implicitly it is postulated that the universe is a closed system in which there is a fixed quantum of potential knowledge. Today science generally—whether physical, biological, or social—is coming to recognize that knowledge is infinite even as the universe is infinite. Once we could study any isolated correlation between two psychological variables with the hope that eventually that correlation would link up with other such isolated studies and some embracing systematization would emerge inductively. We must recognize today that this is not so. Within a universe of infinite variability we can go on infinitely collecting isolated items of data, of correlations and variation, and no link-up will necessarily emerge. Investigators who have repeated experiments conducted by other investigators have not uniformly been able to replicate their findings, because of the infinite variety of variables, because of the infiniteness of potential knowledge.

6. The Illusion that Research Precedes Practice. We have long had the popular myth that the scientist develops knowledge and the engineer applies it. For this we could substitute that the researcher develops knowledge and the practitioner applies it. This has not been so in psychology, and it has never been so in physics and engineering either. More than one authority in the physical sciences has recognized that physics has received more contributions from engineering than it has given to engineering. Similarly, in clinical psychology, we have made more contributions to the body of psychological knowledge from the practitioner's end than have been received by the practitioner from the research investigators. One need hardly elaborate this point beyond citing the work of Freud as an overriding example. Perhaps one additional highly important instance is the reintro-

duction of humanism into psychology. This reintroduction—which is the revitalizing, indeed the saving event of this period in the history of psychology—is in large part due to the contribution of clinical practice. More particularly it is in great part due to the experience of psychologists who have been engaged in the practice of psychotherapy. The names of the leaders in the field who are in the forefront of this development are the names of people who have had intensive immersion in the work of psychotherapy: Carl Rogers, Abraham Maslow, Rollo May, Erich Fromm, and so on.

Again we can point to the influence of the model of the finite universe in which knowledge can be accumulated at random and eventually integrated and made available for the practitioner. Since we have disavowed this model, since we recognize that it is not veridical with the universe, then we must recognize that we need the practitioners' contributions to highlight those areas of greatest significance socially. We need the practitioners' testing of findings for pertinence and applicability; we need the practitioners' contribution of proposing questions for research inquiry.

7. The Myth of the Clinical Team. Let me make clear at the outset that I do know that in some settings the clinical team has proven a very useful and productive concept, but I am equally convinced that in most settings it is not, that in many instances it has been a disguise for the domination of the team by one or another of the professionals. Similarly, many times it has resulted in the subordination of the potential contributions of the two professionals not in the dominant role. But most importantly, the clinical team is founded again on the segmentalist view of human beings. The three-headed monster of the clinical team is not able, by its very nature, to meet the patient in genuine interpersonal encounter. The clinical team may be an excellent device to gather information about people, chiefly information which treats people as representatives of various classes or groupings of society. It may be a useful administrative tool to make case assignments or dispositions, but it is not a therapeutically useful tool. I am convinced that psychotherapy, which is truly depth psychotherapy, requires an authentic encounter between two human beings and that the divided responsibility, and relationships which the clinical team presupposes militate against such an authentic encounter.

One may also note that the clinical team is of questionable social viability. Today when the number of persons needing treatment so far exceeds the number of practitioners to meet this demand, the multiplication of persons working with any one patient is of dubious utility. Some work now being done on the use of lay persons capable of genuine interpersonal relationships suggests that there may be better ways of meeting this problem. Work such as that of Margaret Rioch at the National Institute of Mental Health, in training mature women to serve as counselors without requiring them to go through the usual professional curriculum, illustrates this possibility. True, these people need supervision and help, but they have demonstrated that they can make a genuine contribution. Again, some studies reported informally by Fillmore Sanford are pertinent. He told of sending a research team into a community and asking at random of the citizens, "To whom would you talk if you had an important personal problem?" In this manner they were able to triangulate and locate a small group of mature human people who, in a native and unschooled way, could give meaningful help to their fellows. If these people then are given help from professional sources and not contaminated in what they can do, they can meet human need also. Finally, some work may be mentioned in which we are investigating the possibility of using paired people involved in a sensitivity training experience to intensify the "product" of that experience. Our results are most encouraging, though most preliminary, at this time.

8. The Fallacy that Diagnosis is Basic to Treatment. We have traditionally thought that we could only help the person when we had accumulated a great deal of information about that person. At one time we made elaborate diagnostic studies of each applicant for psychotherapy. Today we know that the accumulation of diagnostic information for most people contributes little to the actual therapeutic work, when that therapeutic work is of an outpatient, interview type. Diagnostic information is inevitably part-function information, while psychotherapy that is most effective is whole-person, relationship centered. Diagnostic information is knowledge *about* the patient, the most effective psychotherapy requires knowledge *of* the patient. This difference is more than a play on words. Knowledge about a patient treats that patient as an object, or a thing to be studied and manipulated. Knowledge of the patient recognizes the patient's essential humanity and individuality. It involves a knowing and relating, a being with, as opposed to a manipulating. Diagnostic information is useful when the need is to treat people as objects, as representatives of classes, rather than as individuals. For administrative functions, it often is essential. For research purposes it may be crucial, but for the psychotherapeutic purpose itself, diagnosis is not important once the grosser disturbances have been ruled out.

Conclusion

I have tried to give one view of a tremendously exciting development in our field of psychology. If I see it correctly, we are leaving the stage of preoccupation with part functions and getting back to what psychology seemed to most of us to mean when we first entered the field. We are returning to what psychology still seems to mean to the average, intelligent layman, that is, the functioning and experience of a whole human being.

Psychology has been going through an adolescence. This is an analogy we have often made. As an adolescent, psychology has little valued what its parents could give, while it has modeled itself on the glamorous outsider, physics. Now I hope that psychology has matured and at last is coming into its adulthood. As with most adolescents reaching maturity, it begins to look back at the old folks with some appreciation. (Was it Mark Twain who said that at 14 he didn't realize someone could be as stupid as his father and still live, while at 21 he was amazed at how much the old man had learned in 7 years?) Perhaps this can be so with psychology, and psychology can turn again to its parents, the humanities and philosophy, and from these take new strength to meet the challenges of our day.

Two great human traditions are converging,

and from their convergence we may expect a tremendous outpouring of new awareness about ourselves in our world. One such tradition is that of science; the other is the humanities. It is as though we are suddenly made heirs to a tremendous storehouse of data which has been but little utilized scientifically before, or—to use a different analogy—as though a whole new hemisphere of our globe had been discovered by some new Columbus. Certainly much exploration and development must be done, but at last we are reaching its shores.

Suggested Readings

Boring, E. G. *A History of Experimental Psychology.* New York: Appleton-Century-Crofts, 1950.

Dennis, W. *Readings in the History of Psychology.* New York: Appleton-Century-Crofts, 1948.

Feigl, H., and M. S. Scriven, eds. *Minnesota Studies in the Philosophy of Science,* Minneapolis: University of Minnesota Press, 1956.

Garrett, H. E. *Great Experiments in Psychology.* New York: The Century Co., 1930.

James, W. *Principles of Psychology.* New York: Holt, 1890.

Murphy, G. *Historical Introduction to Modern Psychology.* New York: Harcourt, Brace & Co., 1949.

Ogburn, W. F., and D. Thomas. "Are Inventions Inevitable?" *Political Science Quarterly,* 37 (1922), 83–98.

Whitehead, A. N. *Science and the Modern World.* New York: Macmillan, 1925.

2　　　*The Developing Individual*

Scientists representing various disciplines have attempted to describe the process of human growth and development. The American psychologist, in his attempts, has traditionally concerned himself more with the influence of environmental "causes" on the development of the individual than with the influence of heredity. However, he has been aware of the question "How much of human behavior is caused by heredity and how much is caused by environmental influences?" In his attempts to answer this question, he has encountered difficulty in controlling one influence while testing the other. As a result, the psychologist has come to the conclusion that fulfillment of an inheritance depends on the environment within which it unfolds. The interdependent factors of heredity and environment, it has now been observed, work together toward a maturity of behavior. Moreover, they work together before birth as well as after birth.

The selections chosen for this chapter deal with attempts to resolve the heredity-environment issue. Also included are studies that describe other basic methods of approach used by the psychologist to define the process of growth and development.

The Interdependence of Heredity and Environment, Leonard Carmichael. Examples of how the "nature-nurture," or heredity-environment, controversy has been approached may be found in the first two selections. Carmichael demonstrates the importance of physical maturation to swimming movements in salamanders. He uses the technique of minimizing any possible learning of the swimming movements through practice.

The Ape and the Child, W. N. Kellogg and L. A. Kellogg. This husband-and-wife team demonstrates another approach to the study of development. They describe an experiment in which an ape and a human child are reared together. Throughout the study they controlled only the environment of the ape and child so they could observe and catalog the differences in the separate heredities. The "ape and child" study was undertaken to examine which of several theories best accounts for the bizarre behavior of "wild" children.

The Development of Emotions, Katherine M. B. Bridges. This selection describes a study of emotional development. It demonstrates the value of beginning a scientific inquiry with an accurate description. It describes, through recorded observations of children made from birth to two years of age, how the generalized emotional state of excitement at birth becomes increasingly differentiated and more specific as a child ages.

Frustration and Regression, Roger Barker, Tamara Dembo, and Kurt Lewin. This selection provides supporting evidence for the hypothesis that a child will seek earlier modes of emotional adjustment when he encounters frustrating circumstances. The authors compare the behavior of children before and after frustration has been induced. Their findings disclose, among other things, that the course of normal development is not always a smooth, progressive affair. Obstacles to the achievement of a goal may be met by behavior that has been learned previously and is thus less mature than it could be.

The Development of Visual Perception in Man and Chimpanzee, Austin H. Riesen. The last two selections again emphasize the value of animal research as a means of testing questions that would be impossible to test with human subjects. The short selection by Riesen demonstrates the developmental problems resulting from a visually deprived environment and the adaptability of the organism to stimulus intervention.

Affection in the Monkey, Harry F. Harlow. Harlow focuses on the development of sexual-affectionate patterns of behavior. The psychologist, because he must work within the codes and mores of a given society, has always had difficulty in gaining scientific knowledge about the primary conditions that foster or inhibit mature affectionate relationships in the adult human organism. Harlow's study, which describes the development of affection in the rhesus monkey, may add to our understanding of how the human organism learns to establish close affectionate relationships.

The Interdependence of Heredity and Environment

Leonard Carmichael

Leonard Carmichael is Vice-President for Research and Exploration, National Geographic Society, Washington, D.C. A past president of the American Psychological Association, he received his doctorate from Harvard University in 1924. With Dr. H. H. Jasper he took the first electroencephalograms in the United States. The scientific study of the early development of behavior of animals is Carmichael's special field of study.

1. *Why were subhuman vertebrates chosen to be subjects in this study?*

2. *What is being controlled for by the use of a control group?*

3. *Do the results demonstrate that swimming movements are dependent upon the maturation of innate factors? What do the results indicate?*

The behavior of an adult vertebrate differs radically from the behavior of a young individual of the same species. What are the factors which bring about this differential transformation? Is this modification of activity the result of environmentally conditioned learning or of the maturing of certain innate behavior patterns or 'instincts'? The experiments recorded in this paper were undertaken in an effort to throw some additional empirical light upon certain phases of this question.

From Leonard Carmichael, "The Development of Behavior in Vertebrates Experimentally Removed from the Influence of External Stimulation," *Psychological Review*, 33 (1926), 51–58. Reprinted by permission of the author and the American Psychological Association.

Part I. Experimental

The specific problem of the present investigation was the determination of the nature and the speed of the process by which developing vertebrates first acquire the ability to carry out muscular movements. The work was done upon the embryos of the frog (*Rana sylvatica*) and the salamander (*Amblystoma punctatum*). A relatively short time is required for the development of these embryos from fertilized eggs into larvæ with well-coordinated swimming movements. The fundamental procedure of the investigation consisted in the comparison of the movements of larvæ which were allowed to develop 'normally' with the movements of larvæ which were reared under such experimental conditions that they showed no gross bodily movements until released by the experimenter.

The embryos used in these experiments developed from eggs found in masses in small pools in the neighborhood of Princeton, New Jersey. In all cases the eggs were in very early stages of cell division when they were brought into the laboratory. The technique of the experiments, save where noted to the contrary, was the same for both the *rana* and *amblystoma* embryos.

In the laboratory the protecting jelly was

removed from the individual eggs. This some-what tedious process was accomplished by holding a few of the jelly-surrounded eggs upon a piece of very damp paper toweling by means of a wide-mouthed pipette. Then, by the use of needles, the individual eggs were teased out of the jelly. The bare eggs were kept at all times in covered glass dishes filled with tap water. The embryos were allowed to grow in these dishes until the head and tail 'buds' could be observed. Body movements do not appear in these organisms until a stage much later than this early head and tail bud period; indeed at this stage the peripheral nervous system has not developed.[1]

The embryos in this early head and tail bud stage were, in all of the experiments, divided into two similar groups. One of these sets, the *control group,* was placed in a development dish filled with tap water. The other set, the *experimental group,* was placed in a develop-ment dish filled with a solution of chloretone (chlorbutanol). Previous work had shown that living organisms placed in a solution con-taining certain concentrations of this drug con-tinue to grow, but they never exhibit any body movements in response to external stimulation while they are under the influence of the anæsthetic.[2] The present experiments con-firmed this observation. Some little difficulty was experienced in determining the optimal concentration of the drug in which to raise the experimental groups. If the solution was too weak the embryos would show some slight movement in response to strong stimula-tion while still supposedly under the influence of the anæsthetic. When movement of this sort occurred the entire experimental group had to be discarded. On the other hand, if the solu-tion was too strong the embryos developed morphological abnormalities. Typical of such

[1] *Cf.* C. J. Herrick and G. E. Coghill, "The Devel-opment of Reflex Mechanisms in Amblystoma," *J. comp. Neur.,* 25 (1915), 67, 82.

[2] *Cf.* H. Randolph, "Chloretone (Acetonchloro-form): An Anæsthetic and Mascerating Agent for Lower Animals," *Zool. Anz.,* 23 (1900), 436–439. Also *cf.* R. G. Harrison, "An Experimental Study of the Relation of the Nervous System to the Developing Musculature in the Embryo of the Frog," *Amer. J. Anat.,* 3 (1904), 197–220. The writer is indebted to Professor S. R. Detwiler for suggesting the use of this method in the problem reported here.

defects was a great bloating of the body which either resulted in death or seriously interfered with later observations on movement. The best concentrations of chloretone for the proper development of the *rana* and *amblystoma* em-bryos were found to be somewhat different. Good results were obtained with the frog em-bryos raised in a solution containing, by weight, 3 parts of chloretone in 10,000 parts of water. For *amblystoma* the best results were obtained in a solution containing 4 parts of chloretone in 10,000 parts of water. Acceptable results how-ever were secured in solutions differing slightly from those noted above.

In all cases the experimental and control groups were kept in covered glass dishes on the same table. No especial effort was made to regulate the temperature or the light of the room in which the investigation was carried on. Both the experimental and control groups were thus at all times subject to the same conditions. Morphologically the development of the control and the experimental embryos was, in the best examples, quite similar. In all cases the larvæ in the tap water grew more rapidly in size than did those in the chloretone solution.

At a certain point, as previously noted by Drs. Herrick and Coghill, the developing em-bryos of the control group began to respond to the stimulation of slight touches of a slender rod. Very soon after such responses had been first elicited, both in the frog and salamander embryos, a coördination of responses was effected which culminated in rapid swimming movements. Similar stimulation elicited no movement in the experimental embryos at this stage or at any other period, so long as the animals lived and were kept in an anæsthetic solution of proper concentration. From day to day these drugged larvæ showed a gradual mor-phological development; otherwise they were absolutely 'inert.'

In the organisms raised under these experi-mental conditions, therefore, bodily movement in response to external stimulation was absent during growth. Long before muscular response commenced in the normal embryo these experi-mental larvæ were placed in the chloretone solution, and until released by the investigator they gave no evidence whatsoever of behavior.

The method of liberating each embryo from the influence of the drug consisted in lifting it with a pipette from the chloretone solution and placing it in a large dish of tap water. The time after the organism was placed in the unmedicated water until it elicited the first movement in response to the stimulation of a slender rod was taken by the use of a stop watch. The tables given below indicate this time to the nearest minute for the frog and salamander embryos.

The conclusion of the present preliminary experiments is, therefore, that in a period of time which averages less than twelve minutes, embryos raised under conditions of absolute artificial inactivity are able to respond to external stimulation. In varying lengths of time

Part II. Theoretical

May the results of this experiment be interpreted as giving additional support to the theory that the maturing of innate factors alone accounts for the development of the neuromuscular mechanism upon which behavior depends? Certainly the results of the experiments recorded above seem to show that the reflex system of these organisms is able to function in a manner which is biologically useful to the animal in a very short time after the first signs of behavior are noted. But is this rapidity of

TABLES SHOWING THE TIME AFTER REMOVING EMBRYO FROM ANÆSTHETIC
BEFORE FIRST RESPONSE TO STIMULATION WAS OBSERVED

TABLE I—AMBLYSTOMA

Embryo number	1	2	3	4	5	6	7	8	9	10
Time in minutes	14	25	9	7	6	8	8	7	24	13

Embryo number	11	12	13	14	15	16	17	18
Time in minutes	9	9	12	11	5	5	28	8

TABLE II—RANA

Embryo number	1	2	3	4	5	6	7
Time in minutes	10	14	11	7	9	15	15

after this first movement, but in all cases in less than thirty minutes, the previously drugged embryos showed coördinated swimming movements. In fact a number of the eighteen *amblystoma* embryos swam so well in less than one half hour after they had shown the first sign of movement, that they could with difficulty, if at all, be distinguished from the members of the control group who had been free swimmers for five days.[3]

[3] Due to many imperfections of technique in the rearing of the earlier series, the 25 cases tabulated are the only ones, out of the many hundreds originally studied, in which the conditions of experimentation were sufficiently controlled to assure scientific accuracy. The writer hopes to make further studies in this problem in subsequent seasons when the material is again available. The results recorded here upon *amblystoma* as well as upon *rana* confirm in most respects certain observations previously made by Professor Harrison (*loc. cit.*) upon the frog.

development a sign that these swimming movements were already determined in the fertilized egg? May we class this behavior with those functions of which Professor Woodworth has written, ". . . the only question, regarding such traits, is whether the environment is going to be such as to enable this young individual to live and mature and unfold what is latent within it"?[4] It does not seem to the present writer that this 'maturation hypothesis'[5] is necessarily substantiated by the facts discovered in the experiments reported above. Much recent work upon the development of the neuromuscular

[4] R. S. Woodworth, "Psychology: A Study of Mental Life," 1921, p. 91.
    Cf. also A. I. Gates, "Psychology for Students of Education," 1924, pp. 110*ff*.
[5] *Cf.* F. H. Allport, "Social Psychology," 1924, p. 44.

system, as I have shown elsewhere,[6] points to the fact that the growth of this system can only be understood in terms of continuous living function. The intricate development of such interrelated structures as receptors, nerve trunks, central apparatus and motor end-organs appears to be determined by functional stimulation within the organism itself. The excitation and response of the elements of the neuromuscular system is itself a part of the growth process. It may thus be said that during growth these systems are continuously functioning, and yet before a certain stage has been reached they are not able to serve their typical *purpose* in the organism. This of course does not mean that development is a non-functional and a mysteriously teleological event determined alone by certain elements of the original germ.[7] Indeed, as Dr. Child has well said, "The older conception of ontogeny as a process of construction of a machine which, after construction is completed, begins to function seems less and less satisfactory as our knowledge advances. Living protoplasm is functioning at all times and development is a process of functional construction, that is, beginning with a given structure and function, the continuance of function modifies the structural substratum, and this in turn modifies further function and so on."[8]

It should be remembered, too, that in the experiments recorded above, the swimming reaction was not perfect at the first trial. From the initial twitch to the fully coördinated swimming movements, a continuum of increasingly complex responses could be noted in each organism as it developed through the short period indicated above. It is at present impossible to state to what extent this apparent gradual perfection of behavior was due to a process analogous to very rapid learning, and how much of it was due to the gradual removal of the 'masking' influence of the drug. The observations, however, show no sudden arrival of fitness.

For the reasons given above there is no obligation on the part of the student to assume that behavior in the experimental cases was the result *merely* of the maturation of certain innate factors.

Is it possible, on the other hand, to account for the results of these experiments without any reference to heredity? Dr. Kuo, for example, would dismiss the entire concept of heredity from a behavioristic psychology.[9] May this program be applied to the experimental findings recorded above? It seems to the writer that the facts observed cannot be explained without any reference to heredity. The rapidity and uniformity of the development of the swimming reaction in the experimental larvæ and the unmistakable differences in behavior between the frog and the salamander embryos, even when raised under apparently identical conditions, seems to suggest the basic importance of certain non-environmental influences in the development of responses.

Indeed, it is difficult to see how the facts recorded here, as well as the results of many similar experiments, can be explained save on the assumption that heredity and environment are *interdependently* involved in the perfection of behavior. Is development anything other than a process by which, what is in the last analysis, an hereditary 'given' is transformed by an environmental 'present'?[10]

If this view be true it will appear that any attempted separation of the parts played by heredity and environment in the drama of development can be in logical terms only. Moreover, the sterile products of such verbal analysis

---

[6] L. Carmichael, "Heredity and Environment: Are They Antithetical?" *J. abn. soc. Psychol.,* 20 (1925), 245–261.

[7] In passing it should be noted that there is a real difference in meaning between *function* in the sense of activity and *function* in the sense of biological use. Almost always in development the first sort of function is propædeutic to the second. This distinction is not sufficiently emphasized in Sir Charles Sherrington's paper "On Some Aspects of Animal Mechanism" (*Science,* 56, 1922, pp. 345–355). In this article he considers nerve regeneration, which is a process similar in many respects to nerve development, and asserts that: 'What is constructed is functionally useless until the whole is complete.' In a similar manner, this distinction might modify the argument of Professor Ogden, based in part upon this paper of Sherrington, that intelligent behavior is analogous to nerve regeneration because it too is based upon a 'functionless procedure.' ("Crossing the Rubicon between Mechanism and Life," *J. Phil.,* 22 (1925), 281–293).

[8] C. M. Child, "The Origin and Development of the Nervous System," 1921, pp. 114*f.*

[9] Z. Y. Kuo, "A Psychology without Heredity," *Psychol. Rev.,* 31 (1924), 427–448.

[10] As I have suggested before (L. Carmichael, *loc. cit.,* p. 260), this *interdependence* view of the development of behavior has much in common with the "convergence theory" of Professor W. Stern. *Cf.* his "Psychology of Early Childhood," 1924, p. 51.

are of more than dubious value to science; they may even do much positive harm in education or industry if applications are based upon them.

In summary, it may be said that the preliminary experiments recorded here successfully demonstrate that in a typical vertebrate form the development of the structures upon which behavior depends may apparently occur during a period when there is no observable response to environmental stimulation. The structures so developed however are not able at their initial appearance to serve the purpose which they ultimately perform in the adult organism.

Theoretically, it is held that these facts do not demonstrate that behavior is alone dependent upon the maturation of certain hypothetical innate factors. Likewise the results do not show that all behavior may be explained alone in terms of environmental conditioning. It seems probable indeed that the development of behavior in this typical case, if not in all cases, can only be conceived as resulting from the *interdependent* action of both heredity and environment in determining the functional development of the individual.

The Ape and the Child

W. N. Kellogg and L. A. Kellogg

W. N. Kellogg, Professor Emeritus, Florida State University, received his Ph.D. from Columbia University in 1929. Primarily interested in the investigation of animal behavior (porpoises and sea lions), Kellogg has also concerned himself with the sensory processes of the blind. Although elected to office in various psychological associations, Kellogg feels that he functions more in the role of research biologist than he does as psychologist.

1. *What features of the "home-setting environment" are most difficult for the experimenters to keep alike?*

2. *Why were the experimenters sensitive to such anthropomorphic expressions as "the ape was afraid"?*

3. *If the experimenters were to conduct the study a second time, what would they do differently?*

Let us suppose that by some queer accident a human infant, the child of civilized parents, were abandoned in the woods or jungle where it had as companions only wild animals. Suppose, further, that by some miraculous combination of circumstances it did not die, but survived babyhood and early childhood, and grew up in these surroundings. What would be the nature of the resulting individual who had matured under such unusual conditions, without clothing, without human language, and without association with others of its kind? That this is not so fanciful a conception as to lie altogether outside the realm of possibility is attested by the fact that about a dozen instances of "wild" foundlings of this sort are known to history. To be sure the reports about them are in many cases so garbled and distorted that the true facts are hard to sift out. In some, how-

Abridged from W. N. Kellogg and L. A. Kellogg, *The Ape and the Child* (New York: Hafner Publishing Co., 1967; originally printed by McGraw-Hill in 1933), pp. 3–7, 11–13, 16–17, 131, 311–316, 323–327. Reprinted by permission of the publisher.

ever, the accuracy of the accounts is well established.

One of the earliest of these children to attract scientific notice was "the wild boy of Aveyron" who was found roaming a French forest by a group of sportsmen in the year 1799. He had apparently been living on roots, berries, and such other provender as might be found in the woods. When discovered he was naked, scarred, and unkempt, and sought to resist capture by hurriedly climbing into a tree. Although he appeared to be fully 11 or 12 years old, he was quite unable to talk and was without knowledge of the most rudimentary habits of personal cleanliness. He was taken to Paris and subjected to a long period of methodical and painstaking education by a young French doctor named Itard. Despite the fact that considerable progress was made toward fitting him for the complexities of civilized life, the training on the whole was regarded as unsuccessful.

The customary way of explaining the fact that a human being of this sort does not respond well to the efforts of those who would civilize and educate it, is to say that it is feeble-minded, that it is mentally deficient, or that it is congenitally lacking in the ability to learn and adapt to its new surroundings. Even had such children lived under civilized conditions, they would still have failed to duplicate the accomplishments of normal individuals. The opportunities enjoyed by the average child would have left them little better in their ability to react than they were when they were found. This reasoning carries with it the assumption that because these children were not up to the average for their ages when their reeducation was discontinued, there must have been something wrong with them before they were placed in the jungle or prison surroundings. That they were unable to adapt completely to civilizing influences is taken as proof of an original deficiency. In fact, going one step further, it is often argued that the "wild" children were probably abandoned in the first place because they displayed idiotic or imbecilic tendencies at a very young age. Their unusual environment in this sense is a sort of result rather than the cause of their condition. The cause is ultimately a matter of hereditary deficiency—a basic lack in the genes of the parent cells.

But there is a second way of accounting for the behavior of the "wild" children, according to the theory of external or environmental influences. It would be quite possible according to the latter view to take the child of criminal delinquents, provided he was normal at birth, and by giving him the proper training, to make him a great religious or moral leader. Conversely it would be possible to take the child of gifted and upright parents and by placing him in a suitable environment, to produce a criminal of the lowest order. Heredity, in this view, assumes a secondary role and education or training becomes the important item.

Instead of supposing that the "wild" children were inherently feeble-minded, as is usually done, the proponent of the environmental doctrine would hold that originally such children were probably normal. He would point, no doubt, to the fact that a child who is deficient in any respect whatever would have a smaller chance of survival in a jungle enviroment than one with normal abilities. On the strength of this supposition, it might be maintained that the "wild" children had made natural and adequate adjustments to their environment. They could even be said to have developed responses which were peculiarly suited to their immediate needs. Those placed with animals may actually have learned, in a literal sense of the word, to be wild themselves, in the same way that a Caucasian child reared among Chinese grows into the Chinese customs and language, or a baby that has been kidnaped by gypsies knows in later years only the gypsy manner of living.

Without doubt, one of the most significant tests which could be applied to a problem of this nature would be to put to rigid experimental proof the stories of the "wild" children themselves. To accomplish this end it would be necessary to place a normal human infant in uncivilized surroundings and to observe and record its development *as it grew up* in this environment. Such an experiment should throw important light upon the precise influence of outside stimulation in the development of the young baby. Yet obviously, in spite of all the scientific zeal which could be brought to bear upon an undertaking of this kind, it would be both legally dangerous and morally outrageous to carry out.

Although it would be impossible, therefore,

to duplicate the conditions under which these foundlings are reported to have been discovered, it would be both possible and practical, it occurred to us, to reverse these conditions. Instead of placing a child in a typical animal environment, why not place an animal in a typical human environment? Why not give one of the higher primates exactly the environmental advantages which a young child enjoys and then study the development of the resulting organism? This plan is in fact similar to that suggested by Professor Lightner Witmer, who wrote in 1909:

I venture to predict that within a few years chimpanzees will be taken early in life and subjected for purposes of scientific investigation to a course of procedure more closely resembling that which is accorded the human child.

If such an experiment were to produce valid results, it would admit of no halfway measures. To carry it out in any comprehensive manner one would have to obtain an infant anthropoid ape, as young as possible, and rear it in every respect as a child is reared—even to the most minute detail. According to our plan, the animal subject was to be fed upon a bottle, clothed, bathed, fondled, and given careful human treatment in every phase of its daily existence. It would be placed in a perambulator and wheeled. It would be induced at the proper time to walk upright as the human child is assisted in this process. It would learn to eat with a spoon as soon as it was able to eat at all by itself. Throughout its upbringing its mistakes would be gently and persistently corrected as are the mistakes of a child. It would be made a thoroughly humanized member of the family of the experimenters, who would serve respectively in the capacities of adopted "father" and "mother." Many of the highly developed customs of our society might thus become integral parts of its behavior equipment in much the same manner that they are built into the human baby. As far as its immediate surroundings were concerned, the animal would never be given the opportunity to learn any other ways of acting except the human ways.

One important consideration upon which we would insist was that the *psychological* as well as the *physical* features of the environment be entirely of a human character. That is, the reactions of all those who came in contact with the subject, and the resulting stimulation which these reactions afforded the subject, should be without exception just such as a normal child might receive. Instances of anthropoid apes which have lived in human households are of course by no means unknown. But in all the cases of which we have any knowledge the "human" treatment accorded the animals was definitely limited by the attitude of the owner and by the degree of his willingness to be put to boundless labor. It is not unreasonable to suppose, if an organism of this kind is kept in a cage for a part of each day or night, if it is led about by means of a collar and a chain, or if it is fed from a plate upon the floor, that these things must surely develop responses which are different from those of a human. A child itself, if similarly treated, would most certainly acquire some genuinely *un*childlike reactions. Again, if the organism is talked to and called like a dog or a cat, if it is consistently petted or scratched behind the ears as these animals are often treated, or if in other ways it is given *pet stimuli* instead of *child stimuli,* the resulting behavior may be expected to show the effects of such stimulation.

Having outlined the project, we may now pass to a brief statement of its consummation. On June 26, 1931, a young female chimpanzee in the colony of the Anthropoid Experiment Station of Yale University at Orange Park, Florida, was forcibly separated from her mother, in whose cage she had previously been living. This little animal, named Gua, had been born in captivity in the Abreu Colony in Cuba on November 15, 1930. She was turned over to the writers following the separation and was soon thereafter taken to their home, where her humanizing was begun. Her age at that time was 7½ months, or almost exactly 2½ months less than that of the writers' only child, Donald, who had been born August 31, 1930. From the point of view of experimental technique, the close correspondence between the ages of the boy and the ape proved indeed to be a fortunate coincidence.

These two individuals lived together as companions, playmates, and members of the same household until March 28, 1932. Their surroundings and treatment were as nearly alike as it was possible to make them. At that time, 9 months after the initiation of the research, Gua had attained the age of 16½ months, while Donald was 19 months old. The experiment was then discontinued and the ape was returned by a gradual habituating process to the more restricted life of the Experiment Station. During the nine months a continuous series of tests, comparisons, observations, and experiments were made upon the two subjects. These covered nearly every phase of their structure and behavior for which we had or could construct measuring facilities. Many of the tests unfortunately were of a crude and inaccurate nature; others were more precise.

Conclusions

I. Differences Favorable to the Child

We turn first to some important differences between the two individuals and consider the performances in which Gua remains upon another level from the boy. A difference "favorable" to Donald is not necessarily one in which he shows any special aptitude, nor is it one in which Gua is necessarily deficient or inferior. Only as the ape does not duplicate the performance of a human being is the resulting difference considered under this category. The items listed here represent therefore the principal ways in which the chimpanzee deviates in one way or another from human norms or standards.

Within this larger class of differences we may then make a secondary grouping according to our predetermined plan, into (1) those responses which would probably have developed as they did even though Gua had been kept in a thoroughly non-human environment, (2) those which seem to us to be more directly dependent upon the specific nature of the civilized surroundings, and (3) those which are doubtful. But even though we make such a division to the best of our ability, it is too much to expect that all who read this passage will agree with the writers in the placing of every item. An endeavor such as this leaves room for individual opinion. Still, the results of our efforts should not conflict by too wide a margin with the judgment of others who might undertake the same task.

1. *Non-environmental Differences.* The first clearcut differences in behavior to be noted as we skim over the early findings consist of Gua's higher blood pressure and her lower pulse rate. In this grouping also should come her greater consumption of water, which is due no doubt to her probably possessing fewer sweat glands than the child. That Gua's mouth is more mobile as an organ of prehension is likewise independent of the civilized environment. It is the same with her more consistent avoidance of bright lights, her (apparently) keener hearing, and her many distinctive emotional reactions. Similarly we should place her greater propensity to bite and chew, her inability to pick up small objects with the fingers, and her deficiency in articulation in this category. Her further deficiencies in exploration and manipulation, her attention to stimuli for only a relatively short time, and her inferiority in imitation seem also to us to belong under this heading.

These characteristics we think are independent of the specific humanizing features of the environment in which Gua lived. Certainly this need not mean that the influence of some sort of environment cannot be proven in every one of them. But it does mean that they would probably have developed much as they are in almost any environment which permits healthy and regular growth. They are qualities which for the most part are traceable to bony development, the chemistry of the muscles, the character of the nerve centers including the brain, and the shape and form into which the parts of the organism naturally arrange themselves unless fundamentally altered by violent, irregular, or abnormal outside factors. They are ways of behaving which to our way of thinking would not be strongly affected by training or education.

2. *Environmental Differences.* There are other differences in behavior between the subjects; but there are none *involving the ape's deviation from human standards* in which the particular influence of the civilized surroundings can be shown to play an indispensable part. We therefore find ourselves unable to list any reactions under this heading.

3. *Unclassified Items.* Can it be said that the reason Gua possessed a greater tendency than the child to avoid strange humans was because she in some way had learned from her

associates to behave in this way? Although there are grounds for considering this characteristic an environmental one, it is possible, we must admit, to build up a case for the opposing view. This is consequently a difference between the subjects which comes in the doubtful grouping. Their particular food preferences and aversions may similarly be traceable to the human surroundings, yet here also we are less sure of such a statement. In the matters of the greater psychological dependency of the ape and her stronger attachment to one person, there is even greater uncertainty.

The important point in this connection: The majority of the differences in behavior thus far listed show the chimpanzee to be unaffected in any special or dominant way by the particular civilized aspects of her surroundings.

II. *Likenesses between the Two*

When we take up the aspects in which Gua was like Donald, we find a shift in emphasis, for in this category a large proportion of the reactions of the chimpanzee seem to be explainable as a result of humanizing influences. Within this second major grouping there may again be some question about many of the responses classified, concerning both their influence by the civilized environment and also the degree of their similarity from one subject to the other. It is to be pointed out in this connection that the reactions given are not necessarily *exclusively* human, but they are nevertheless respects in which Gua resembled the child.

1. *Non-environmental Likenesses.* Of the similar features of behavior which seem to be relatively independent of the human situation, the reflexes of the two are important. So also are their common drowsy reactions of nodding and of rubbing the eyes. Probably the perception of motion, as in motion pictures, should be placed here, as well as the susceptibility of both subjects to the illusion of reversed sound localization. Their like responsiveness to tickling is no doubt chiefly a matter of similar sense organs and nerve connections, while the sleeping postures of the ape probably resembled those of the child because of the shape and proportions of her body. Perhaps, in addition, we should classify Gua's tendency to forget and her man-like laughter under this heading, although there is a serious question about the latter.

2. *Environmental Likenesses.* The upright walking of the subjects, which in many respects was similar, would probably have failed to develop as it did without the humanizing influences. We should therefore consider it an environmental likeness. Here also may be put many of the common play reactions of the two, such as playing with shoes, playing with human faces, playing ball and tag, and playing with the telephone and typewriter. Their like reactions to sizable bodies of water we should classify in this category along with the conditioning to vocal commands and to other specific stimuli, since all these were of necessity controlled or elicited by particular outside influences. Similarly many other definite tasks in which the ape came close to the child's performance, such as pointing to the nose, work with the form board, and scribbling.

3. *Unclassified Items.* Concerning playing in the sand, the affectionate behavior of one subject for the other, and the avoiding reactions of each to animals, the classification is less clear. Of course these responses could hardly have appeared as they did except for immediate environmental influences. And yet, the particular human phases of the environment can hardly be considered indispensable; for it is conceivable that similar behavior might well have developed in quite different surroundings. The hand preferences of both individuals, which shifted as a result of outside stimulation, might similarly have changed much as they did under vastly different environmental conditions.

III. *Differences Favorable to the Ape*

There remains a third major class of characteristics in which Gua was neither like Donald nor peculiarly like an animal. These are respects in which the chimpanzee was different from the child, yet in which she went beyond him and so behaved like a human older and more mature than he. Her progress in this regard may be ascribed largely to her more rapid rate of development.

1. *Non-environmental Differences.* Among the human-like advances of the ape which were probably not outgrowths of the civilized environment belong her superior muscular coordi-

nation and more rapid rate of involuntary movement. Her demonstrations of greater strength, accuracy in auditory localization, the compensatory movements during rotation, and her superiority in remembering may also be considered independent of any necessary human effects.

2. *Environmental Difference.* In this, the most important group, is shown the capacity of the chimpanzee to acquire responses peculiar to the civilized surroundings which are more complex or more proficient than those of the child himself. Since the performance of Donald was about average for his age, the respects in which the ape surpassed him are respects in which she was generally more advanced than the average human approximately as old as herself. They cast no necessary reflection upon the child, but are rather points of special credit for the ape. She may thus be said to have become "more humanized" than the human subject in the acquisition of behavior of which the child was still incapable.

Here should be placed Gua's skipping. Here also we should put her greater cooperation and obedience, which is a feature of the behavior of well-trained older children. And here belongs her tendency to kiss for forgiveness and her skillful opening of doors. Her more frequent sly behavior suggests the mischievousness of a lively boy, while her superior anticipation of the bladder and bowel reactions may be cited as a more obvious mark of progress. Finally, under this heading should be placed her striking ability to eat with a spoon and drink from a glass, which compare favorably to the corresponding abilities of children considerably older than the ape. These items in our opinion are traceable to the influence of special factors in the human environment which were favorable to their acquisition.

Perhaps at this point, while we are in an appropriately critical attitude, we should turn for a moment upon our own work and consider some significant deficiencies in this investigation itself. For since we have now completed our survey of the abilities of the subjects, we can readily see ways in which the research could have been improved. Without doubt the most important factor in this regard involves the ages of the subjects at the start of the

project. In fact, if such a task were to be undertaken a second time, there are two inflexible requirements we would demand. First, the ape should be obtained, in accordance with the original plans, at the age of a month or younger. This would eliminate the unknown influence of an earlier wild or captive environment and would permit more comprehensive conclusions upon the genesis of various types of behavior.

Second, the ape should be reared not in a family with one child, but in a family of several children, the youngest of which is at the start at least a year older than the animal subject. There are advantages both to the anthropoid and to the humans which should accrue from these conditions. The ape would have as continual associates children who were its equal or superior in maturation and agility. Its companions would thus be constantly able to serve as leaders in the development of new behavior. The children, on the other hand, should be correspondingly less inclined to follow or imitate the animal.

Third, in a repetition of the same research it would also be desirable to continue over a longer period of time, although this can hardly be classed as an inflexible requirement. There is always the tendency to say, "Yes, of course. But even though the ape was superior in some respects she would not have remained so if the comparison had covered a long enough interval." Such an outcome without question presents a possibility of great importance. It is also quite possible, nevertheless, that the matter of time would prove less significant than at first it may appear. For example, had the experiment continued for twice as long and the results remained much as they are, the same objection could be raised. Had it lasted three or four times as long with similar findings, one could always say the same thing. Indeed, if we are entirely open-minded on the subject, we can hardly overlook the logical possibility that the ape might continue to demonstrate a superiority in many outstanding ways. Such a contingency from an unprejudiced viewpoint should be placed on a parity with the possibility that the child would eventually triumph in those respects in which he was found to be less proficient than the ape. It is rather, therefore, to determine in which way the further development would lead, whether for "better" or for "worse," that it would be advisable to keep on for a longer interval.

The Developing Individual   35

We note, finally, by way of criticism, that there is a strong tendency in an investigation of this type to commit the error of anthropomorphism, that is, to ascribe to the animal and to the young child adult- and manlike attributes which they do not actually possess. Of course no one can ever tell except by the somewhat doubtful methods of inference or analogy whether animals or even human infants are capable at all of such complex mental experiences as of *feeling* or *thinking*. And yet, if one sees them behave in peculiar or unusual ways, he may be sorely tempted to interpret that behavior as it appears to him. In such cases one runs the risk of giving the objective actions a mental quality based upon his own experience. Hence, if a tiny baby, immediately after spilling some milk, begins to cry, the incautious onlooker may say, "He is angry or disappointed." In all strictness, however, the elements of "anger" or "disappointment" are added by the observer. All that is objectively known is that (1) the milk is spilled and (2) the baby cries. It is possible, to be sure, that the observer is correct in his appraisal, but, unless the baby in some way can tell him, the correctness of his inference must forever remain unknown.

This inclination to see in all other organisms the same feelings, emotions, thoughts, and impulses which man himself experiences has met with such severe treatment at the hands of many contemporary scientists that some have tended, so it seems, to lean in the opposite direction. As a result, elaborate precautions are often taken in scientific discussion to avoid the use of words which by the remotest suggestion possess an introspective or anthropomorphic savor.

But note that in the present research we set out at the start to discover just how manlike an animal could be. We deliberately attempted, in other words, to make the non-human subject *as anthropomorphic as possible.* All the conditions of the study were directed towards this very end. How, then, can we recount manlike activity without ascribing to the subject the manlike qualities which this activity implies? The question of anthropomorphism in this particular instance seems to present an unusual difficulty. Probably the most obvious answer to this question is to confine oneself rigidly to the discussion of behavior, and this in the main is what we have endeavored to do. We have therefore tried to avoid such expressions as, "The ape was afraid," and have usually substituted instead, "She acted *as if* she was afraid," or "She *seemed* to be afraid." Yet to a large extent even statements of this sort, which cover broad general phases of behavior, are colored by the impressions of the onlooker. We have taken the view that such impressions, if carefully evaluated, were better recorded than left out, since their omission often fails to give the picture completeness. The description cannot be composed entirely of details. There must perforce be some generalities. If included, on the contrary, they may do violence to the actual events.

It is impossible to escape such arguments. The reader of a written report must accept his facts as somewhat tarnished or affected by the hands through which they have already passed. He is committed to form his own conclusions through the intermediate eyes of the observers. The personal element can seldom if ever be eradicated from observations of this sort. But to the extent that the observer, like a field glass or a telescope, presents a distorted or foggy view, he may be accused of misrepresentation.

We sincerely hope to avoid any such accusation. It has been our wish to give an accurate and non-partisan account of the development of the subjects without on the one hand sensationally glorifying the capacities of the chimpanzee or on the other hand attacking or belittling them. We have tried to remain on the sidelines as careful but unbiased observers. If we have failed, we are genuinely sorry. If, in addition, we have in any way offended the sensitive or critical reader, we beg his indulgence for the unknown influence of personal attitudes, which it seems no one can ever quite escape.

The Development of Emotions

Katherine M. B. Bridges

Katherine M. Banham Bridges is Associate Professor Emeritus of Psychology at Duke University. After receiving her Ph.D. in psychology from the University of Montreal in 1934, she began her career with an interest in the mental health problems of children. Bridges' work with juvenile delinquents led her to be concerned with questions relating to the development of the emotions. The following selection is a good sample of her thinking on this subject.

1. *Do you suspect that there is some correlation between measured intelligence and emotional development? Is it positive or negative? On what basis would you defend your answer?*

2. *When does a child begin to develop affection for another child? Can you think of environments or situations that would alter this development? Did the author acknowledge this fact or account for its control in her study?*

The emotional behavior of 62 infants in the Montreal Foundling and Baby Hospital was carefully observed and recorded daily over a period of three or four months. The circumstances attendant upon these reactions were noted, and the whole data was studied from the point of view of development from age to age. A summary of the findings will be presented in the following paragraphs. They will be seen to lend support to the writer's theory of the genesis of the emotions and to add further illuminating detail.

The babies under observation were in separate wards more or less according to age. In different rooms were infants under one month, one to three months, three to six months, six to nine months, nine to twelve months, and twelve to

From K. M. B. Bridges, "Emotional Development in Early Infancy," *Child Development*, 3 (1932), 324–341. Reprinted by permission of the author and the Society for Research in Child Development, Inc.

fifteen months. An older group of children between fifteen and twenty-four months of age played together in the nursery.

Table 1 shows the number of children at the different ages whose behavior was observed for this study.

Development in the emotional behavior of the young child comprises 3 main classes of

TABLE 1

AGE (MONTHS)	NUMBER OF CHILDREN
Under 1	3
1–3	16
3–6	23
6–9	18
9–12	11
12–15	20
15–18	8
18–21	5
21–24	6
Over 24	2

change. From birth onward there is a gradual evolution of the emotions taking place. The earliest emotional reactions are very general and poorly organized responses to one or two general types of situation. As weeks and months go by the responses take on more definite form in relation to more specific situations. It seems that in the course of genesis of the emotions there occurs a process of differentiation. Coincident with the partial isolation of certain responses is a combining of the simpler reactions within the unit responses and the formation of bonds of association between these emotional syndromes and detailed aspects of the provoking situations. In this manner slowly appear the well known emotions of anger, disgust, joy, love, and so forth. They are not present at birth in their mature form.

In addition to the progressive evolution of the emotions, there is, going on at the same time, a gradual change in the mode of response of each specific emotion. Muscles are developing, new skills are being learned. So that the anger, for instance, expressed by the eighteen-month-old differs in detail of form from the anger manifested by the ten-month-old baby. Fresh bonds of association are being made between emotional behavior and the always slightly varying attendant circumstances. Different situations come to have emotional significance for the growing child and subsequently provoke emotional responses. Thus a gradual substitution takes place of the situations which prompt the emotions. In the language of the behaviorists, emotional responses become conditioned to fresh stimuli.

Excitement, the Original Emotion

After observing the behavior of babies *under one month* of age, the writer felt more than ever convinced that the infant does not start life with 3 fully matured pattern reactions, such as have been mentioned by behaviorists and named fear, rage and love. Unfortunately the writer was not able to observe the infants within a few hours of birth, but this fact in no way invalidates observations made on children two or three weeks old. Moreover, if the above named emotional responses are really the 3 great primary emotions from which all our adult emotions are derived, surely they may still be observed a month or more after birth. And, even if the process of conditioning begins before or immediately upon birth, one may expect the original emotion-producing stimuli to elicit their natural responses at least for two or three weeks after birth.

It was observed in the hospital that, on presentation of certain strong stimuli the infants became agitated, their arm and hand muscles tensed, their breath quickened, and their legs made jerky kicking movements. Their eyes opened, the upper lid arched, and they gazed into the distance. The stimuli producing such agitation or excitement were: bright sun directly in the infant's eyes, sudden picking up and putting down on the bed, pulling the child's arm through his dress sleeve, holding the arms tight to the sides, rapping the baby's knuckles, pressing the bottle nipple into the child's mouth, and the noisy clatter of a small tin basin thrown on to a metal table whence it fell to the radiator and the floor.

The loud sound startled only four of the one- and two-month-old babies, while six others lay practically undisturbed. None of the infants cried after hearing the noise. The same experiment was tried upon children of successive ages up to fifteen months. Under two or three months the reaction was one of sudden but rather mild general excitement as described above. Children of three or four months and older gave more of a jump and looked definitely in the direction of the sound. Afterwards they remained still with eyes and mouth open, and stared towards the source of the commotion. One baby of eight months stiffened and turned away on the second trial. The corners of his mouth turned down, his eyes moistened and he looked to the adult for sympathy and comfort. Another child of eleven months sat wide-eyed and still, the corners of his mouth drooping as if he were ready to burst into tears. The older children merely stood, or sat, alert and attentive without further sign of distress.

Lowering the babies suddenly into their cribs, and in some cases lifting them quickly, also startled and excited them. Sometimes they would cry following upon such a surprise. Rocking a quiet child would cause him to open his eyes attentively. But gently rocking a crying infant would often, though not always, cause him to reduce his activity, stop crying, and eventually become tranquil. Gentle handling, slow patting, wrapping in warm blankets, and nursing easily soothed an agitated or crying infant, making him relax and yawn and become sleepy.

Light pinching of the arm left the three- or four-week-old baby unmoved. Deeper pressure caused him to kick slightly, breathe faster and move his arms. A sharp flick on the hand produced similar agitation, but a second rap resulted in a sudden check to breathing followed by a prolonged cry and other signs of distress. The first exciting experience had been found disagreeable and the second rap produced unmistakable distress.

Time after time on waking suddenly from sleep the infants were observed to wave their arms jerkily, kick, open and close their eyes, flush slightly, and breathe quickly and irregularly. Some grunted, some cried spasmodically for a moment or two, while others cried loudly for several minutes. The combined stimulation of light, of sounds, of damp or restricting bed clothes, and the change from sleeping to waking breathing-rate seemed to produce a temporary agitation and often distress. Waking apparently requires emotional adjustment.

The hungry child before feeding would often show restless activity, waving, squirming, mouthing and crying at intervals. The infant who had been lying in one position for a long time and the tired child before falling asleep would also show emotional agitation. Their breath would come jerkily, uttering staccato cries of "cu-cu-cu-ah," and they would thrust out their arms and legs in irregular movements. At the moment the nipple was put into the hungry baby's mouth he again breathed quickly, occasionally cried, waved the free arm, and kicked in excited agitation.

The emotional reactions of the tiny infant are certainly not highly differentiated. The most common response to highly stimulating situations seems to be one of general agitation or excitement. It is a question which word most aptly describes the behavior. The former perhaps conveys more the idea of general disturbance, although the two words are often used synonymously. This vague emotional response to a large variety of circumstances must surely be one of the original emotions, if not the only one.

A kind of general excitement over new and startling or other highly stimulating circumstances may be seen at any age. The behavior manifestations vary from time to time, but the main characteristics of accelerated response, alertness, slight tension or restlessness remain as constant attributes. In the babies, excitement is frequently manifested in kicking movements. The month-old infants kick jerkily with both feet at random. In another month or so,

the kicking becomes more regular, the legs being thrust out alternately. By five or six months the babies express their emotions in combined leg thrusts, kicking with one foot, and in swinging the legs from the hips. At fourteen months when the children can stand they will hold on to a support and "mark time" with their feet or stamp. Stamping, jumping and running express excited agitation at a still later age.

Two- and three-month-old babies may be seen to suck their thumbs or fingers rapidly in moments of stress. At seven months and over, children bite, pull and suck their garments, as well as their fingers. This behavior seems to produce a gradual subsidence of the emotion. Body-rocking accompanied in many instances by rhythmic vocalizations is another expression of mixed emotion. Hungry, annoyed, excited or restless children will sit and rock for minutes on end. The five-month-old baby lies prone and pushes with his knees, or sways when lying dorsally. Seven-month-old infants support themselves on their arms and rock back and forth murmuring "m̄m-ŭm, m̄m-ŭm." After nine months they sit up and rock to and fro, or they kneel and bounce up and down holding on to the crib bars. Sometimes they sit and bump their backs against the side of the crib. This kind of behavior was observed in the nursery up to eighteen months of age.

Rhythmical movements were observed not only to be the outcome of emotional excitement or tension, but they were seen to have a soothing and pacifying effect. These must be attempts at adjustment on the part of the organism to reduce tension and restore emotional equilibrium or tranquility. In the light of these observations, it can be easily understood how long walks, games, field sports, singing, dancing, and sea-voyages are found to be so universally health-giving and positively curative for "nervous wrecks."

Distress and Its Derivatives

It is a moot question whether "distress" is an original emotion or whether it is a very early differentiated reaction to disagreeably painful and unsatisfying experiences. It may be that it is a part of the general emotional response of excitement which copes more satisfactorily with obnoxious stimuli. Tense muscles resist or remove pressure; activity warms a chilled body and reduces tension; and cries, at first reflex due to the rush of air in and out of the lungs, bring comfort and aid. These responses become differentiated from excitement, associated together and conditioned to the disagreeable stimuli as a result of experience. If such differentiation actually takes place, it must begin immediately after birth. For the two emotions of excitement and distress are already distinguishable in a three-weeks-old infant.

On the other hand, it is possible that there is a native emotional response to pain, particularly muscle pain. The sympathetic branch of the autonomic nervous system is predominantly active and the overt behavior is definitely that of distress. Other stimuli, such as loud sounds and sudden falling merely produce startled excitement. Blanton observed that the infant's cry of colic had a specially shrill character accompanied by rigidity of the abdominal walls. She also noted that infants during the first days of life cried from "(1) hunger; (2) in response to noxious stimuli (including rough handling, circumcision, lancing and care of boils, sores, etc.); and (3) possibly fatigue or lack of exercise." The writer has observed the same phenomena in three-weeks-old babies. But, hunger, rough handling, and fatigue were also noticed on many occasions to produce a restless excitement rather than specific distress.

It is not easy, in the case of the very young infant, to distinguish distress from general agitation. Perhaps the most characteristic marks of the former are greater muscle tension, interference with movement and with breathing, closing of the eyes, and loud rather high-pitched crying. In children of two months and over, the eyes become moist and tears may flow. The crying of the infant *under a month* or even six weeks often seems to be part of the general activity in excitement. Breath comes more or less regularly, the cry emerging on both intake and expiration of air. There are no tears, and the skin does not flush. Movement is free though rather jerky; and the mouth is held open in an elliptic, round, or square shape.

The cry of distress, recognizable in the *month-old* baby, is irregular. There are short intakes of breath and long cries on expiration. The eyes are "screwed up" tight, the face flushed, the fists often clenched, the arms tense, and the legs still or kicking spasmodically. The mouth is open and square in shape or, more usually kidney-shaped with the corners pulled down. The pitch of the cry is high and somewhat discordant, and sounds something like "ah, cu-ah, cu-ah, cu-æh."

Cries of distress were heard from month-old babies in the hospital on the following occasions: on waking suddenly from sleep, struggling to breathe through nostrils blocked with mucous, when the ears were discharging, when lying awake before feeding time, after staying long in the same position, lying on a wet diaper, when the child's buttocks were chafed, and when the fingers were rapped. The three main causes of distress at this age, therefore, seemed to be discomfort, pain, and hunger.

Crying from discomfort and on awakening usually developed slowly, and sounded like "cu-cu-cu-cah-ah—." The cry of pain came suddenly, often after a holding of the breath. The sound was a loud shrill prolonged "ă-ă-ă," and lowered in pitch slightly from the first emission. The cries of hunger were rather like those of discomfort. The former came perhaps more in intermittent waves; the intervening moments being taken up with mouthing or sucking movements. Occasionally the hungry child would utter a sharp loud cry, as if in pain, and then whine or moan for a time.

Two-month-old babies cry less of the total waking time; but slighter discomforting stimuli seem to cause distress more frequently than in the case of the younger infants. They are more disturbed by a wet diaper, by flatulence, and by tight clothing which restricts movement and makes breathing difficult. Their movements are freer and they tend to move their heads from side to side when they are distressed. While one-month-old babies kick irregularly with jerky movements, the two-month-old kicks his legs alternately and more regularly. He waves his arms up and down when agitated or distressed, as well as in spontaneous play. The sound or sight of an approaching person will not quiet his distress; but being picked up will do so, or being fed if he is hungry.

By *three months* of age a child will cry and show other signs of distress when placed in an unusual position or moved to a strange place; as, for instance, when lain temporarily at the foot of another child's bed. He will wave his arms laterally as well as up and down, and will kick more vigorously. The hospital baby has learned to associate feeding time with the presence of an adult; for, when he is hungry he shows some excitement at the close approach of a person. He stares at the person's face, waves, kicks, breathes faster, and opens his mouth. If no food is forthcoming, he becomes more tense and jerky in his movements and begins to cry. He is distressed at the delay in normal proceedings.

Should the adult remain tantalizingly near for some minutes without either picking up the child or feeding him, his cry increases in intensity, his eyes become moist with tears, he holds his breath longer, and utters prolonged flat "ă-ă-ă" sound reminiscent of an older child's "paddy" or temper cry. The infant's motor responses were all set for being picked up and fed, and then he was thwarted and disappointed. His excitement changed into bitter distress with a semblance of angry vexation.

The slight change in vowel sound of the cry, the long holding of breath combined with more than usually vigorous leg thrusts and arm movements, seemed to suggest that the emotion of anger is beginning to evolve from general distress at about this age. Although for the most part the distress shown at discomfort differs almost imperceptibly from distress in response to disappointment, occasionally the latter includes, to a marked degree, those behavior elements peculiar to the emotion of anger. The situations which evoke these demonstrations of temper in the tiny infant are a stop or check in the progressive satisfaction of a physical need. In the above instance the child's appetite was aroused but not satisfied. Lack of even the first sign of a need being satisfied merely produces vague distress.

A *four-month-old* baby shows distress at the same general sort of situation that troubles the younger child. He is, however, less frequently disturbed by bodily discomfort. He moves about sufficiently to relieve tired muscles and local pressures, and to eliminate gas from his stomach. He cries vigorously at delay in the feeding process and may show decided temper on such occasions. His arms then stiffen and tremble; he screws up his eyes, flushes, holds breath and utters prolonged and irregular cries

on expiration of breath; he kicks violently, pushes with his feet and looks at any adult, presumably to see the effect. He is getting very fond of attention at this age, and will show distress and often anger when a person leaves the room or ceases to pay attention and play with him.

At *five months,* the baby's interest in small objects, such as rattles, stuffed animals and, of course, his milk bottle, causes him to be distressed when these objects are removed. He may express his displeasure as formerly by crying, squirming, waving and kicking, but he may also be heard merely to call out in a protesting tone of voice, "ah aye," without the half-closing of the eyes and the accompanying tensions of crying.

By this age the child may show slight revulsion for certain foods, coughing, spluttering, frowning and crying while he is being fed. Chopped vegetables and soup too thick in consistency were specially disliked by some babies in the hospital. Cereals, milk, and sweetish foods were almost always taken readily. It was noted that babies under three months often refused to drink sterile water. They just let it run out of their mouths without swallowing. There was no emotion involved in this reaction. Similarly, three- and four-month-old babies sometimes rejected their thin vegetable soup, but were not very disturbed about it. A genuine emotional revulsion did not appear till five months or later. Perhaps this is the beginning of the emotion of disgust. Revulsion at nauseating sights and smells, the adult form of disgust, apparently does not develop until two or more years of age.

Several of the babies in the hospital *between six and eighteen months* were observed to splutter and choke, and refuse to swallow spinach more than other vegetables. The mouthfuls that were rejected were usually, though not always, those containing large or stringy pieces of spinach. When the latter was chopped fine it was swallowed a little more easily; but only when it was mixed with other vegetables was it eaten without any protest. There must be factors other than consistency and size of morsel to account for this objection to spinach.

It seemed to the writer that some cans of spinach tasted more bitter than others and were less palatable on that account. In order to find how the children would react to a bitter taste, two teaspoonful each of unsweetened grapefruit juice were given to nine children in the nursery. Four of them pursed or curled their lips, 1 turned his head away, and 1 frowned. The others sat still and solemn, and kept tasting their lips attentively for some time. There were certainly individually different reactions to this bitter-sour, astringent taste. Several of the children definitely disliked it and none of them seemed to like it. It is possible then that there is a bitter taste to spinach which may in part account for children's aversion to it. Another factor, that of the dark green colour of spinach may influence older children's and adults' feeling reaction towards it. One two-year-old in the hospital on turning away and refusing to eat the vegetable was seen to point to it and say "dirty."

The *six-month-old* baby's attention is usually arrested by the presence of a stranger. His movements are inhibited and he watches the newcomer intently. He is not pleased and one could hardly say he is afraid. But he seems diffident and uncertain what to do, or utterly unable to move for a few moments. At seven months he reacts in the same way to the approach of a stranger, though the general inhibition of movement is greater and lasts longer. After a few moments or several seconds of tension he may begin to cry slowly, or burst suddenly into tears. The whole body is usually rigid and inactive. The eyes, previously wide open, close tight and the head bends. Should the stranger touch the child he will probably turn or draw away. Here is the emotion of fear already differentiated. Frightened distress results when the child through inhibition, ignorance, or inability finds himself unable to respond at all adequately to the situation.

At *seven months* of age an infant calls out protestingly when a familiar person ceases to attend to him, instead of crying distressfully like a four-month-old. He still cries and kicks angrily if some object in which he was deeply engrossed is taken from him. He does so also after being highly excited by a playful adult when the latter goes away or stops playing with him. He now makes prolonged attempts to get at objects out of reach. If he fails to attain his objective he may give up and cry in helpless distress, or he may just grunt in protestation.

A *nine-month-old* child will struggle longer and make more varied attempts to reach the object of his desire. Should he fail to do so after putting forth considerable effort he may become tense and red in the face with anger. He will kick and scream and look for assistance, while tears flow copiously. The cry at this age is becoming exceedingly loud, and tears flow more readily than at the earlier ages. Prolonged crying at four or five months is accompanied by slight lacrimal secretion, but after six months of age tears often flow down the child's cheeks as he cries, especially after an adult's attention has been attracted.

Strangers are still quite terrifying to the nine-month-old baby. His movements are more completely arrested by the unfamiliar presence than those of the six-month-old. He will remain immovable for several minutes unless the newcomer approaches very close to him. In that case he will lie face down or bend his head and probably begin to cry. At ten months of age he may even be so frightened as to flop down suddenly on the bed and scream loudly. Then follows prolonged and tearful crying.

When children of *ten months* and over are hungry, uncomfortable, tired, or fretful and unwell, they will set up a whine or cry as the result of suggestion when another child cries. They do not, however, ordinarily imitate crying when they are occupied and happy. Under these circumstances they may call or babble in a pitch similar to that of the other child's cry. Small objects which can be manipulated interest them so intensely that they can be distracted from a distressing trouble fairly easily at this age. These objects need not necessarily be new so long as they are freshly presented.

Year-old babies often cry suddenly when they feel themselves falling, or when they lose their grip while climbing. If they miss the assistance of a helping hand they will also sit down and cry loudly. Sometimes their emotion is anger at the thwarting or failure of their endeavors. They scream, flush, and tremble in rage. At other times they sit motionless in fright and look for aid or comforting sympathy. When strangers approach the *twelve-* or *thirteen-month-old* baby he may hold his hand behind his ear in a withdrawing motion and stare apprehensively. He may actually hide his eyes behind his hands or look away so as not to see the awe-inspiring or annoying intruder.

At *fourteen months* or thereabouts we may see the real temper tantrum. At least, that is the age when it became noticeable in the hospital. If a child is not given his food or a coveted toy exactly when he wants it he may respond by throwing himself suddenly on the bed or floor. He then screams, holds his breath, trembles, turns red, kicks or thrusts his feet out together. Tears flow and he will wave away anything that is not the desired object. These outbursts may occur frequently for a few weeks, or only spasmodically for another year or eighteen months. The children under observation seemed to have their "off-days" when they were fretful and easily distressed or roused to anger. Such days were usually when they were incubating or recovering from colds, when the hospital routine was disturbed, or after the children had been excited by parents' visits.

Distressful crying becomes less common as the months go by. Extreme hunger and weariness after a long day or great activity may be accompanied by whining and intermittent outbursts of tears. Anger is expressed more in protesting shouts, pushing and kicking, but less in tearful screaming. So long as adults are present, however, the interference and rough handling of another child may bring forth cries and tears. A *fifteen-month-old* may show his annoyance by hitting a child who has taken his toy or who is holding on to the thing he most wants. He may even bite him or pull his hair without a preliminary scream or shout.

The attention of familiar and interested adults is much sought by children of *fifteen to eighteen months*. If such attention is given to another child there may be signs of deep distress. The neglected one may stiffen, stand motionless, bend his head and burst into tears. Here is perhaps the beginning of jealousy, distress at the loss of, or failure to receive, expected attention and affection. Some children will show aggressive annoyance when another receives the attention they covet. They do this usually by hitting the envied child.

A *twenty-one-month-old* child will show less mistrust of strangers than will a younger infant. He may, however, run away and watch the newcomer for a time at a safe distance. After eighteen months he shows anger at adult interference by obstinate refusal to comply with their requests. He may shake his head and refuse either to be fed or to feed himself. At two he will play with his food, throwing it about instead of eating it, as a spite against some offending or scolding adult. Distress is shown chiefly at pain and acute discomfort, though the child will cry miserably at much less discomfort if a sympathetic adult is close at hand.

The children in the nursery group, *between fifteen and twenty-four months,* were more or less unconcerned when being undressed for the annual physical examination. This part of the procedure was familiar and not unpleasant. Several of the children cried and stiffened somewhat when placed on the table in the examining room. One or two continued to show distress throughout the examination. Others smiled cheerily at the attendant nurse or the doctor, until they felt sudden and unexpected local pressure. All of the children cried at some time during the procedure. The most distressing events were when a flashlight was thrown into the eyes, and when the throat and ears were examined with the aid of the usual tongue-depressor and otoscope. The children had to be held firmly and their movements curbed during these operations.

It was patent to the observer that the children were undergoing rather different emotions according to their fast-developing individual idiosyncracies. Some were mainly startled and afraid, their movements were paralyzed. Some seemed to be just generally distressed at the unusual proceeding and the discomfort; while others were chiefly annoyed at the interference with their freedom. Several children showed signs of all three emotions. These individual differences probably have their foundation in variants in the physical constitutions of the children, both hereditary and acquired. They are certainly very much determined by the particular experiences the infants have gone through since their birth. A continuous study of behavior week by week reveals the actual differentiation and consolidation of individual traits of temperament.

Two or three of the nursery children over fourteen months developed fears for specific objects or persons. Toy animals that squeaked frightened one or two, causing them to draw away, stare wide-eyed and perhaps cry. This squeak could hardly be called a "loud low sound" such as Watson describes as one of the original fear-producing stimuli. The sound is, however, rather unusual and comes at first as a surprise to the babies. One child was afraid of a particular aggressive little boy. No doubt he had gone up and hit her unexpectedly some time when the nurses were not watching. One youngster showed fear of a dark grey dog with a rough fur, rather different from the soft teddy-bears and other stuffed animals in the nursery.

Parents often remark how their children may suddenly show fear of some surprisingly trivial and inoffensive object. The answer to this may be found in certain partial associations with disturbing events of the past. It may also be found in the particular mental set of the child's mind and body when he came in contact with the object. He may have become suddenly aware of its presence and perceived it as an unwelcome intruder upon an entirely different line of thought or action. Still another phenomenon may account for the peculiar fears and objections of children. Timid behavior may be actually learned and preserved as a social asset, one of the numerous means of drawing attention.

The nursery child who cried and crawled away after touching the rough-haired, stuffed animal was flattered with the attention of all the adults in the room. A nurse brought the dog up to the child, smiling and saying "nice doggie." He looked up at her face, saw her kindly smile, then bent his head and began to whimper again. Another nurse laughed appreciatively as he put his hand to his eye, and tried to coax him with a toy cat. He turned away quickly, cried out again, then looked up to see the effect on the adults. He was having a delightful time out of his apparent fear.

Delight and Its Derivatives

Delight is much later in becoming differentiated from general excitement than distress. The baby under a month old is either excited or quiescent. Gentle stroking, swaying and patting soothe him and make him sleepy. When satisfied after a meal he is no longer excited nor even distressed by hunger. And yet he is not positively delighted. He is just unemotionally content, and either tranquil or busy mouthing and staring at distant objects. When he is *over two weeks old* he will sometimes give a faint

reflex smile upon light tapping at the corners of his mouth. This is hardly an emotional response.

One- and two-month-old babies cry and kick from hunger before they are fed, rather than show delight on presentation of the much desired food. They become calm, however, immediately when given their milk, but not at the mere approach of the adult who brings it. At two months infants will give fleeting smiles upon being nursed, patted, wrapped warmly, spoken to, tickled, or gently rocked. Perhaps this is the beginning of the emotion of delight.

By *three months* of age the emotion of delight is becoming more clearly differentiated from agitated excitement on the one hand and non-emotional quiescence or passivity on the other. The child kicks, opens his mouth, breathes faster, and tries to raise his head upon sight of his bottle. He gives little crooning sounds when being fed, nursed or rocked. He smiles when an adult comes near and talks to him; and he will even stop crying momentarily at the sound of a person's voice. He may also show delight in distant moving objects. One baby in the hospital, for instance, lay and watched the moving leaves of the creeper on the window for a minute or two at a time. Her eyes were wide and her mouth rounded and open. At times she would breathe fast, or inspire deeply, and utter murmurings of "uh-uh-uh." Her arms would wave up and down and her legs kick alternately.

The chief characteristics of delight are: free as against restrained movement; open eyes and expansion of the face in a smile as contrasted with the puckering of the forehead and closing of the eyes in distress; body movements or muscle tension of incipient approach rather than withdrawal; audible inspirations and quickened breathing; soft, lower pitched vocalizations than those of distress or excitement; more or less rhythmic arm and leg movements; prolonged attention to the object of interest; and cessation of crying. Although behavior varies in detail from child to child at successive ages, delight is always recognizable from certain general types of response. Free and rhythmic movements, welcoming and approaching gestures, smiles and vocalizations of middle pitch are most common features.

A *four-month-old* baby laughs aloud when some person smiles and frolics with him. He smiles in response to another's smile and even when anyone approaches his crib, whether they be strangers or not. He spreads out his arms, lifts his chin, and tries to raise his body in approach to the attentive person. He takes active delight in his bath, kicking and splashing the water. Food, though sometimes welcomed eagerly, is often neglected for the more interesting attendant who talks and smiles at him.

At *five months* a child vocalizes his delight in sounds of "uh-uh-ung" in addition to waving, laughing, kicking and wriggling around. He shows special interest in small objects that he can handle and explore. Musical or noisy rattles are popular at this age. When hungry he kicks, breathes fast, and calls out eagerly at the first sign of the person who brings his food. His smiles are more transient, however, and his movements less vigorous on approach of a stranger.

By *six months* of age a child will reach towards a familiar person but will lie still and observe a stranger dubiously. He crows and coos frequently, taking pleasure in his own movements and sounds. In the hospital the babies of this age would watch each other through the bars of their cribs, sometimes laughing and kicking in response to the sight of the other's movements. They would swing their legs rhythmically when lying on their backs, or sway sideways when lying prone.

A *seventh-month-old* baby is becoming increasingly interested in small objects and in the act of reaching and grasping those close at hand. He will even struggle to attain things somewhat out of his reach. When his efforts meet with success he often smiles, takes a deep breath and expresses his satisfaction in a sort of grunt. After a moment or two spent in examination and manipulation of the object, he goes exploring again with fresh vigor. Possibly this is the beginning of the emotion of elation, exhilarating pleasure in personal accomplishments. Resting periods, after the delightful satisfaction of feeding or explorative activity, are often taken up with a rhythmical rocking back and forth, the child supporting himself on his hands and knees.

At *eight months* of age the child seems to take more delight than ever in self-initiated purposeful activity. He babbles and splutters and laughs to himself. Especially does he seem delighted with the noise he makes by banging spoons or other playthings on the table. Throwing things out of his crib is another favorite pastime. He waves, pats, and coos, drawing in long breaths, when familiar adults swing him or talk to him. He will watch the person who nurses him attentively, exploring her, patting gently, and often smiling. Here are perhaps the earliest demonstrations of affection. The child will also pat and smile at his own mirror image. But his behavior is rather more aggressive and inquisitive than really affectionate.

A *nine-month-old* baby is very popular with adults. He laughs frequently, bounces up and down and tries to mimic their playful actions. He pats others babies exploratively but does not show particular affection for them. Strange adults may frighten him at first. But, after studying them for some time in the distance, he will smile responsively and join in play with them. By *ten months* of age the child is taking more interest in other babies. He will mimic their calls and even their laughter. The hospital babies of this age would pat and bang and laugh in imitation of each other.

An *eleven-month-old* baby takes great delight in laughter, not only his own but that of another. He will laugh in order to make another child laugh, then jump and vocalize and laugh again in response. At twelve months of age he will repeat any little action that causes laughter. He is becoming increasingly affectionate. He puts his arms around the familiar adult's neck, and strokes and pats her face. Sometimes he will actually bring his lips close to her face in an incipient kissing movement. He looks eagerly for attention; and may stand holding a support and changing weight from one foot to the other in rhythmic motion, as a solace when neglected.

Between *twelve and fifteen months* a child usually learns to walk with a little help. This performance, though often accompanied by panting and tense effort, causes great delight and even elation when a few steps have been accomplished. The child calls out, smiles and waves ecstatically (i.e. rapidly or jerkily). Without further encouragement from adults, he will then set out again with renewed fervor. When attentive adults are too enthusiastic in their appreciation, the little one may become positively tense with excitement. His efforts may consequently meet with less success, and then he cries in vexatious disappointment.

There is already a noticeable difference between the responsiveness of different *fifteen-month-old* children to demonstrated affection. Some children come readily to be nursed and petted, others require a little coaxing. One or two will kiss back when kissed, while others merely cling closely to the adult caressing them. At this age the children begin to show definite affection for each other. They take hands, sit close to one another, put their arms about one another's neck or shoulders, pat and smile at each other. Eighteen-month-olds will also jabber nonsense amicably together. Again, with regard to playmates as well as adults some children are more affectionate than others.

These variations in affection no doubt have a number of causal factors. They depend upon the child's physical constitution and his condition of health at the moment. Sick children may be very clinging and affectionate with adults, or, in some instances, refractory and irritable. They may be both by turns. Whether a child is affectionate or not also depends upon the nature of his dominant interest at the moment. Affection for a grown person depends upon the child's attitude towards adults in general; and that again is largely a matter of the amount of fondling or scolding the child has received. Affection for other children is considerably determined by the agreeable or exasperating nature of chance contacts.

Between *fifteen and twenty-one months* the children find increasing enjoyment in walking and running about. They chase each other laughingly and enjoy snatching one another's toys. They come back again and again to adults to be lifted high or swung round. The nursery slide is very popular at this age. One or two of the hospital children pulled away and watched apprehensively in the distance after the first slide. A little encouragement from the nurses and the eager shouts of the other children soon overcame their fear, and they joined the sliding group again.

Gramophone music was listened to intently by almost all the nursery children. Some of them responded by swaying or nodding motions

to time. The children at this age were beginning to find individual interests in things and to express their enjoyment each in their own peculiar way. Absorbed preoccupation, tight clasping, biting, and varied manipulation of the attractive object were common expressions of interest. Some children would knock one object against another in play, some would collect things, and others would find pleasure in throwing and scattering toys about. These variations in appreciative interest in things and activities may be the precursors of the more mature emotion of joy.

Most of the eighteen-month-olds in the hospital were anxious to attract attention. They called out or came running to greet an adult. They would smile and hold out their arms to a familiar nurse in expectation of being lifted. A stranger they would watch solemnly for a while. Then they would approach slowly, touch and explore her clothes, or hit and watch for the effect. The children seemed to recognize their nurses at this age, whether the latter appeared in uniform or not. Babies of seven to twelve months, however, would sometimes turn away in fear or hostility when the nurses approached them wearing outdoor clothes.

Slight preferences for certain nurses were noticed as early as six months, but definitely affectionate attachments were observed chiefly between the ages of twelve and twenty-four months. One or two youngsters of eighteen months showed preferences for certain playmates. A twin boy and girl seemed especially fond of each other. The children would be more responsive and playful with those they liked, more delighted at their approach and very anxious to keep them close. Some children were friendly with almost everybody including strange visitors. Others showed more specific and decided likes and dislikes. When a terrifying stranger was present, some times a child would show more than usual affection for his familiar nurse, but at other times he would be restrained and aloof from everybody. Similarly when a beloved parent was nursing a child on visiting day he might be hostile to anyone else; but more often he would smile agreeably at everybody including awe-inspiring strangers.

A specific "like" does not necessarily enhance a specific "dislike" by force of contrast, though this does sometimes happen. If the disliked object threatens the satisfaction or enjoyment of the object preferred then the dislike becomes stronger. Similarly a preferred object may be enjoyed with greater intensity in the presence of, or following upon, something disliked. It is a comforting relief from distress. This effect of contrast is perhaps what Freud terms "ambivalence." There are situations, however, where it has no noticeable effect. For instance, as cited above, a child made happy by one person may like everybody for the moment, regardless of previous attitudes towards them. A troubled child may be annoyed with everybody, even his favorite playmates. Strong emotions may thus have a decided "halo" effect.

Although children between *eighteen months and two years* of age tease and hit each other frequently, they show more affection for one another than younger infants. They not only pat and stroke fondly, but they will kiss and hug each other on occasion. The older children in the nursery group were seen to direct the younger ones' activities and point out their errors by gesture and exclamation. There was no evidence, however, of the parental affection and almost self-sacrificing care shown by four-year-olds for their much younger playmates.

Noisy activities delighted the eighteen- to twenty-four-month old youngsters. They took pleasure in tearing and pulling things to pieces and in lifting large but portable objects, such as their own chairs. They jabbered happily to each other at table. One child would repeatedly make strange noises to arouse the attention and laughter of another. With adults they would practice newly learned words and would seek to share their enjoyments. When the children received new toys in the hospital they would cling to them and guard them jealously from the other children. But they would hold them out for the nurses to share in their appreciation. Here is a mark of trusting friendship for their kindly guardians such as the children had not yet developed for one another. They would always rather share the other child's plaything than give up or share their own.

Affection, thus, begins as delight in being fondled and comforted by an elder. It becomes differentiated from general delight and manifested in tender caressing responses at about eight months of age. This earliest affection is essentially reciprocal in nature. Spontaneous affection for adults may be seen, however, by eleven or twelve months of age. Both reciprocal and spontaneous affection for other children make their appearance around fifteen months, but they are not as strong as affection for adults.

Specific affection for the grown-ups who give special attention may be manifested as early as demonstrative affection itself, i.e. eight or nine months. These preferences persist as long as the care and attention continue. Attachments between two children were not observed in the hospital till after fifteen months of age. They were usually very temporary, lasting only for a few hours or days. The behavior of a child-friend is so much more erratic and less dependable than that of an adult. Friendships between eighteen- to twenty-four-month-old children would sometimes last, however, for several weeks. There seemed to be no preference in these attachments either for the same or the opposite sex. Little girls would become friends together, or little boys, or a boy and girl would show mutual affection for one another.

Summary and Conclusion

The emotional behavior of young infants as observed in the Montreal Foundling and Baby Hospital seemed to lend support to the writer's theory of the genesis of the emotions. Emotional development was found to take place in three ways. The different emotions gradually evolved from the vague and undifferentiated emotion of excitement. The form of behavior response in each specific emotion changed slowly with developing skills and habits. Different particular situations would arouse emotional response at succeeding age-levels, although these situations would always be of the same general type for the same emotions.

The one-month-old baby showed excitement in accelerated movement and breathing, upon any excessive stimulation. He exhibited distress by crying, reddening of the face and tense jerky movements at painful and other disagreeable stimulations. But he was more or less passive and quiescent when agreeably stimulated.

By three months of age the child was seen to exhibit delight in smiles, deep inspirations and somewhat rhythmic movements when his bodily needs were being satisfied. Between three and four months angry screaming and vigorous leg-thrusts, in response to delay in anticipated feeding, were observed. A few weeks later anger was aroused when an adult's playful attention was withdrawn.

Distress and delight came to be expressed more in specific vocalizations with increasing age. General body movements gave place to precise responses to details of a situation. A four-month-old baby would laugh aloud with delight and cry tearfully when distressed. A child of five months was seen to cough and reject foods of a certain taste and consistency in incipient disgust. He would reach towards objects that caused him delight. By six months of age he showed definite fear when a stranger approached. He remained motionless and rigid, his eyes wide and staring. It is possible that "non-institutional" children might show fear in response to other unusual or unexpected events a little earlier than this. There was little variation in the daily routine of the children under observation, and fear was a rare occurrence.

By seven months of age the child showed positive elation, and renewed his activity as a result of success in his own endeavours. At eight months he began to show reciprocal affec-

tion for adults, and by twelve months spontaneous affection. Delight was manifested in much laughter, bouncing up and down, and banging with the hand.

Between nine and twelve months of age the hospital babies would hide their heads, like ostriches, upon the approach of a relatively unfamiliar person. They would scream and become flushed with anger when their efforts or desires were thwarted; and they would cry out in fear and sit motionless after perceiving themselves falling.

It was observed that a child learns to kiss soon after twelve months of age, and by fifteen months he expresses his affection for other children. Anger over disappointment becomes more dramatic in its manifestation. The true temper-tantrum makes its appearance roughly about fourteen months of age. By eighteen months anger at adults is expressed in obstinate behavior; and annoyance at interfering children is manifested in hitting, pulling and squealing.

Eighteen-month-olds would constantly seek the attention of adults, and take great delight in running about and making noises. One or two children of this age showed depressed, and others angry, jealousy when another child received the coveted attention. A few specific

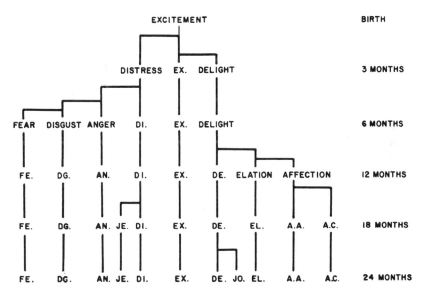

FIGURE 1. *Showing the Approximate Ages of Differentiation of the Various Emotions During the First Two Years of Life.*
Key: *A.A. = Affection for adults, A.C. = Affection for children, An. = Anger, De. = Delight, Dg. = Disgust, Di. = Distress, El. = Elation, Ex. = Excitement, Fe. = Fear, Je. = Jealousy, Jo. = Joy.*

fears were noticed; and several children developed particular affectionate attachments.

Thus it seems that in the course of development, emotional behavior becomes more and more specific, both as regards arousing stimuli and form of response. Distress, though more readily aroused, comes to find adequate expression in a variety of actions, and delight becomes sensitive appreciation and joy in numerous pursuits. The emotions, evolve slowly, and the exact age of differentiation is difficult to determine.

A diagram showing the approximate ages of the appearance of the different emotions, as observed in the Montreal Foundling Hospital, is given in Figure 1. Study of a number of children in private homes might suggest a somewhat different age arrangement.

Emotional behavior and development are very much determined by particular events and experiences and the routine of living. It is, therefore, to be expected that "institution babies" will show some deviations in their reactions from those of children at home. The former will probably exhibit fear of a larger number of things than other children, due to their very limited experience. On the other hand, they may show greater tolerance of interference, as a result of much practice in self-control in the nursery. They may also be more affectionate with other children, in consequence of the many happy play-hours spent together.

The daily round of feeding, washing, dressing and sleeping, however, has so many factors in common for all babies, that the observations made on the emotional development of a few hospital children, and the suggested inferences presented above, may have at least some general significance for infants brought up under other circumstances.

Frustration and Regression

Roger Barker, Tamara Dembo, and Kurt Lewin

Roger Barker, Professor of Psychology at the University of Kansas and Director of the Midwest Psychological Field Station, received his Ph.D. from Stanford University in 1934. Barker studied under two eminent psychologists, Kurt Lewin and Lewis Terman. Among other notable awards, he received the A.P.A. Distinguished Scientific Contribution Award in 1964. Barker has actively pursued "the development of methods and concepts for studying interrelations between the environment of behavior and behavior outside the contrived situations of the experimental laboratory" (ecological psychology). Tamara Dembo, Professor of Psychology at Clark University, received her Ph.D. from the University of Berlin in 1930. Kurt Lewin (1890–1947) studied psychology in Germany and is further described at the beginning of his article in Chapter 10.

1. *Explain what value or purpose is served when a frustrated child regresses.*

2. *Should a control have been made for such variables as social-class status? How would such a control affect the validity of the findings?*

Experimental Procedures

General Arrangements

Technically it has been the aim of this investigation to compare the behavior of children in a nonfrustrating or free play situation with their

Abridged from R. Barker, T. Dembo, and K. Lewin, "Frustration and Regression: An Experiment with Young Children," *University of Iowa Studies in Child Welfare,* 18 (1941), 47–57, 205–208. Reprinted by permission of author and publisher.

behavior in a frustrating situation. We have been especially concerned with productivity, or creativity of behavior.

Every child was observed on two occasions: first, in a free play situation during which the subject was placed in a standardized playroom and allowed to play without restriction, and second, in a frustrating situation during which the subject was placed in the same room with the same toys as on the first occasion, but to which a number of much more attractive, but inaccessible, toys had been added. The latter arrangement was provided by replacing one of the walls of the original room with a wire net partition through which the subject could easily see the fine toys, but through which locomotion was impossible.

The Subjects

The subjects in the experiment were children taken from three age groups of the preschool laboratories of the Iowa Child Welfare Research Station during the academic year 1935–1936. The number of children from each group is as follows: ten children from first group (2 to 3 years), twelve children from second group (3 to 4 years), and eight children from third group (4 to 5 years). The chronological ages and IQ's ranged from 28 to 61 months, and 100 to 157, respectively. The Kuhlmann-Binet was used with the ten youngest subjects; the Stanford-Binet with the older subjects.

Establishing a Free Atmosphere for the Child

In a free play situation every effort was made to establish optimal conditions for constructive play. For this reason insecurity on the part of the child was very undesirable and attempts were made to eliminate it.

To help give the children a feeling of security in order that they might behave freely and spontaneously, and also to allow the experimenter to become acquainted with them, several precautions were taken:

1. Before starting experimentation, the experimenter took part in the activities of the preschool for ten days.

2. A child was used as a subject only if his initial attitude toward the experimenter and toward coming to the experimental room was positive.

Each child was asked to take part in the

experiment in the following way: "Do you want to come and play with me?" (This is a general procedure used by experimenters and testers in the preschool laboratories.)

Although the children in the school are accustomed to being tested and to participating in experiments with different people, willingness to participate varies from child to child and from situation to situation. Some children, upon hearing the experimenter invite another child to "come and play," spontaneously ask to go too; others go only after being requested, but comply willingly and without hesitation; still others are reluctant to go. These latter children were not used as subjects.

3. The children were familiar with the building in which the experiments were conducted, having to stop in it every day for routine medical inspection, and going to it frequently for tests and examinations.

4. Upon going to the experiment the child had to put on his wraps, and was helped by the experimenter. The experimenter tried to keep the child in a good mood, and to make the situation an open and free one while putting on and taking off the child's wraps and walking across the street with him. At the same time, these situations gave an opportunity to observe the child and his attitude toward the experimenter.

5. In all cases, where the above mentioned precautions did not seem sufficient to develop free and spontaneous behavior, we introduced a special preliminary play period. In this preliminary period the child was taken to the experimental room for fifteen or twenty minutes of play with blocks and balls during which the experimenter tried gradually to gain his confidence by playing with him. This precaution was required at the beginning of the school year, since at that time many children were newcomers to the preschool, and the general situation was strange to them. Later, when the children felt more secure and free, both in the school and with the experimenters, it was not thought necessary to use a preliminary play period.

The Free Play Situation

The arrangement of the experimental room in the free play situation is shown in Figures 1 and 2. It was 14 by 8½ feet, had two doors, and

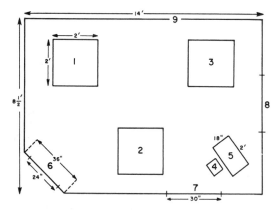

FIGURE 1. *Diagram of the Free Play Situation.*

1. Square of paper on which the following toys are placed: a child's chair, teddy bear, doll, cup, small truck and trailer, saucer, teapot, ironing board and iron, and telephone receiver. 2. Square of paper on which the following toys are placed: box of crayons, two pieces of writing paper. 3. Square of paper on which the following toys are placed: motor boat, sail boat, duck, frog, fishing pole. 4. Experimenter's chair. 5. Experimenter's table. 6. Observation screen. 7. Entrance door. 8. Window. 9. Opaque partition (now functioning as a wall).

a window. The wall (See 9, Figure 1) consisted of two wooden frames, 12 by 3 feet, covered with wire mesh netting. These frames could be moved up and down in a vertical slot along the walls adjacent to them like window frames. In the free play experiment, the frames were in such a position that one of them rested on the floor, while the other extending from the top of this lower one, nearly reached the ceiling. On the back of each frame, that is, behind the wire mesh netting, an opaque canvas covering was stretched. The canvas was the same color as the room, making the partition appear to be the fourth wall.

One door (See 7, Figure 1) was used as the entrance door; the other (See 6), into which a one-way observation screen was built, was locked. Behind this one-way vision screen one of the experimenters was seated to act as an observer. The second experimenter, who conducted the experiment, sat in a child's chair (See 4) at a small table (See 5) near the window (See 8).

On the floor of the room were three squares of paper each 24 by 24 inches. A set of standardized play materials was placed on

FIGURE 2. *The Setup in the Free Play Situation.*

each. On the square designated as 1 (Figure 1), were a child's chair on which a small teddy bear and a doll were seated, a cup, a small truck and trailer, a saucer, a teapot without a lid, an ironing board and an iron (but nothing to iron), and a telephone receiver which squeaked when shaken. On square 2 were placed a box of crayons and two pieces of writing paper, 8½ by 11 inches.[1] On square 3 there was a small wooden motor boat, a sail boat, a celluloid duck, a frog, and a fishing pole and line on the end of which was a magnet.

After entering the experimental room with the child, the experimenter approached square 1, and picking up each toy said, "Look, here are some things to play with. Here is a teddy bear and a doll. Here is an iron to iron with, etc." In proceeding this way, the experimenter named and demonstrated every toy on all three squares. Then he said, "You can play with everything. You can do whatever you like with the toys, and I'll sit down here and do my lesson." The experimenter then sat on the chair at the table.[2]

The child was left to play alone for a thirty-minute period. During this time the experimenter, as if occupied with his own work, sat at

[1] In the early experiments a peg-board, beads, a rolling wagon, and plasticene were also placed here.
[2] This procedure was modified slightly in later experiments in order to make the child more curious about the toys. When the child was brought into the room, the toys were not yet distributed on the squares. A basket with the play materials stood in the corner and the experimenter took the basket and in the presence of the child distributed the toys on the squares. The experimenter named the single objects as he put them down.

his table in the corner and took notes. If the child made a social approach, the experimenter responded, but attempts were made to keep this at a minimum without, however, becoming abrupt or curt. The experimenter entered the play situation of the child as little as possible, at the same time behaving naturally. The objective was to minimize the social factors in the situation and to provide an atmosphere of security and freedom for the child.

After a half hour, the experimenter made the first "leaving suggestion" to the child. He said, "I'm about through. Will you be ready to go pretty soon?" If the child said "No" or did not answer, the experimenter waited for about a minute and then said, "Shall we go to the

preschool now?" If this suggestion was not accepted, the experimenter made a third leaving suggestion after a minute or two. If the child did not want to leave at the third suggestion, the experimenter started to leave the room, saying, "I have to go now." In every case this was sufficient to make the child want to leave the experimental room.

The Frustration Situation

Three parts of the frustration experiment can be distinguished in the temporal order of their occurrence: (a) the prefrustration, (b) the frustration, and (c) the postfrustration periods.

Prefrustration Period. The arrangement of the room in the prefrustration period is shown in Figures 3 and 4. The partition dividing the room was lifted so the room was twice the size it had been in the free play situation.

The squares, 1, 2, and 3, were in their usual places, but all toys except those on square 2 had been removed and incorporated in the much more elaborate and attractive new set of toys in the new part of the room.

In the added part of the room was a big doll house (3 by 3 feet), brightly painted and decorated. The child could enter the house through a doorway. Inside there was a bed upon which the doll was lying, and a chair in which the teddy bear sat. The ironing board with the iron on it stood against one wall and the telephone, this time on its base with a dial and bell, was in the corner. There was a stove with cooking

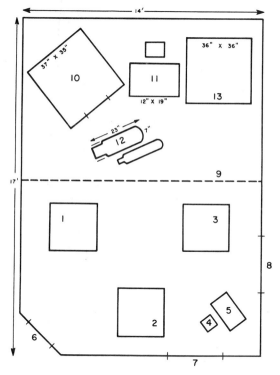

FIGURE 3. *Diagram of the Prefrustration Period of the Frustration Experiment.*
1. Square of paper (without toys). 2. Square of paper on which are placed crayons and paper. 3. Square of paper (without toys). 4, 5, 6, 7, 8, as explained in caption of Figure 1. 9. Lifted partition. 10. Toy house containing the following toys: doll, chair, teddy bear, bed, ironing board, iron, telephone, stove with cooking utensils, cupboard, electric lights, curtain, and carpet. 11. Tea table with tea set. In front of it a child's chair. 12. Large truck and trailer. Nearby a small truck and trailer. 13. A lake with real water containing: island with light house, wharf, ferry boat, small boats, fishes, ducks, and frogs.

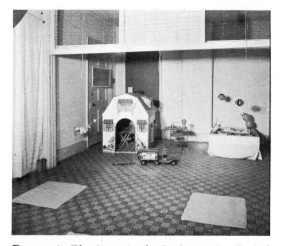

FIGURE 4. *The Setup in the Prefrustration Period of the Frustration Experiment.*

utensils, and a cupboard. The house had electric lights, curtains, and a carpet.

Outside the house was a laundry line on which the doll's clothes hung. A rubber bunny sat near the entrance to the house. A large delivery truck (23 inches long) stood near the house, and behind it was the small truck and trailer used in the preceding experiment. Nearby was a child's table prepared for a luncheon party. On the table were cups, saucers, dishes, spoons, forks, knives, a small empty teapot, and a large teapot with water in it.

In the other corner of the new part of the room was a toy lake (3 by 3 feet) filled with real water. It contained an island with a lighthouse, a wharf, a ferry boat, small boats, fishes, ducks, and frogs. The lake had sand beaches.

In all cases the children showed evidences of

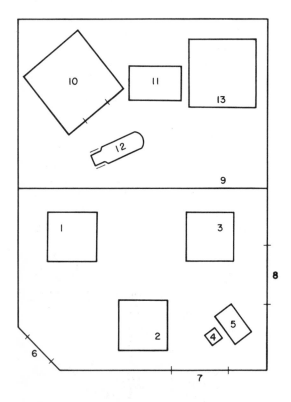

FIGURE 5. *Diagram of the Frustration Period of the Frustration Experiment.*

1, 2, 3. Squares of paper on which the same toys are placed as in the Free Play Situation (see Figure 1). 4, 5, 6, 7, 8, same as Figure 1. 9. Transparent partition through which the house, with toys (10), tea table with tea set (11), big truck and trailer (12), lake with lake toys (13), are visible.

great interest in the new toys, and at once started to investigate them. Each child was left entirely free to explore and play as he wished. During this time, the experimenter "did his lessons."

If, after several minutes, the child had played with only a limited number of objects, the experimenter approached and demonstrated the other toys, e.g., he dailed the telephone, or showed the child how to get the water from the spout of the teapot. In general, the experimenter called to the child's attention every toy he had overlooked. Following this the experimenter returned to his place, and waited until the child had become thoroughly involved in play; this varied from five to fifteen minutes.

The transition from prefrustration to frustration was made the following way: The experimenter collected in a basket all the play materials which had been used in the free play experiment and distributed them, as before, on the squares. He then approached the child and said, "And now let's play at the other end," pointing to the "old" part of the room. The child went or was led to the other end of the room and the experimenter lowered the wire partition and fastened it by means of a large padlock. The part of the room containing the new toys was now physically inaccessible but visible through the wire mesh netting.

Frustration Period. The arrangement of the room in this part of the experiment is shown in Figures 5 and 6. With the lowering of the partition, the frustration period began. This part of the experiment was conducted exactly as the free play experiment. The experimenter

FIGURE 6. *The Setup in the Frustration Period of the Frustration Experiment.*

wrote at his table, leaving the child completely free to play or not, as he desired. Here again the child's questions were answered, but the experimenter remained aloof from the situation in as natural a manner as possible.

Thirty minutes after the lowering of the partition, the experimenter made the first leaving suggestion. Contrary to the behavior in the free play experiment, the child was usually willing to leave at the first suggestion.

After the experimenter had made sure that the child wanted to leave, the partition was lifted. Usually the child was pleasantly surprised and, forgetting his desire to leave, joyfully hurried over to the fine toys. If the child did not return spontaneously, the experimenter suggested his doing so, and a second suggestion was never necessary.

Postfrustration Period. The lifting of the partition at the end of the frustration period was not done with an experimental purpose, but to satisfy the desire of the child to play with the toys and to obviate any undesirable after effects. The child was allowed to play with the house, lake, etc., until he was ready to leave.

Summary: Experimental Results

Thirty children between two and five years of age were observed individually while playing with a standardized set of toys in a free play situation and in a frustration situation for half an hour on different days. A record of all behavior was made and the effect of frustration on the constructiveness of play was determined.

Constructiveness of Play in Free Play Situation

1. A seven-point constructiveness scale was developed on the basis of which each play unit of each child in both the free play and the frustration situation was rated.

2. The constructiveness of play with the same toy varies greatly from child to child.

3. The mean constructiveness of primary play in the free play situation is correlated $+.81$[3] with both mental and chronological age.

4. The constructiveness of play is positively related to length of play unit.

5. The constructiveness of play is lower for secondary play (play which occurs simulta-

[3] See the Glossary for an explanation of correlation (Ed.).

neously with another nonplay action) than for primary play (play which receives the full attention of the child).

6. The qualitative analysis indicates that constructiveness of play measured by the scale is related to degree of differentiation, degree of hierarchical organization, originality, and adequacy of play behavior.

The Strength of Frustration in the Frustration Situation and Mood

1. The amount of time spent in attempts to overcome the barrier to the inaccessible toys by physical or social means (amount of barrier behavior) varies greatly from child to child.

2. The amount of time spent in trying to leave the experimental room by physical or social means (escape behavior) is positively related to the amount of barrier behavior.

3. The proportion of the total time occupied with barrier and escape behavior in a situation such as the frustration situation can be used as a measurement of the average strength (potency) of the background of frustration during the experimental period.

4. The potency of a background of frustration can be measured for a given natural "psychological episode" by determining the proportion of the total time occupied with barrier and escape behavior in that episode.

5. In the frustration situation freedom of expression as indicated by play monologue, and friendly conversation with experimenter, decreases; and masking social behavior increases.

6. The frequency of happy actions decreases and of unhappy actions increases in frustration. This change is positively related to strength of frustration.

7. The frequency of restlessness and of aggressive actions is positively related to the strength of frustration.

Regression in Frustration

1. A background of frustration decreases the average constructiveness of play with accessible toys. On the average, the constructiveness regresses by an amount equivalent to 17.3 months mental age. For the younger subjects, 28 to 41 months of age, this average regression is 9.6 months; for the older subjects,

42 to 61 months of age, the average regression is 21.5 months.

2. The maximum constructiveness of play decreases in frustration; although not as much as the average constructiveness of play.

3. The amount of secondary play increases in the frustration situation.

4. The average length of play units decreases in the frustration situation with the strong frustration group.

5. The lowering of the constructiveness of play in frustration is partly due to the increase in the amount of secondary play and to the decrease in the average length of play unit. However, the decrease in constructiveness holds, also, for primary play of the same length of play unit in the free play situation and frustration situation.

6. The amount of regression in constructiveness of play is a function of the strength of frustration. This is shown by the difference in the effect on children showing strong or weak frustration in the experimental setting, and by a comparison of behavior of the same children under different strengths of frustration.

7. In the strong frustration group the regression was equivalent to 24 months, and in the weak group to 4 months mental age.

8. The greater regression in strong frustration holds also for primary play and for play units of the same length.

9. The amount of regression in the constructiveness of primary play of equivalent length of unit in the free play situation and the frustration situation is positively related to the relative strength (potency) of the background of frustration.

10. A background of weak frustration in some cases seems to increase the constructiveness of play.

11. If the play unit with the accessible toys takes on the meaning of a substitute for the inaccessible toys, the mood of the person will under certain conditions be happy and the constructiveness level of play will not indicate regression.

12. Constructiveness of play is not related to the preference for particular toys. The regression in the constructiveness of play is not due to the selection in frustration of toys with a naturally low constructiveness level.

13. The amount of negative emotionality increases with the strength of frustration.

14. The qualitative analysis indicates that the lowering of constructiveness of play is similar in nature to the change in behavior occurring under conditions of high emotionality where restless movements, stereotyped repetition of sentences, and stuttering are frequent. Both changes involve a reduction in degree of differentiation and level of hierarchical organization within a unit of activity, and a certain lack of realism.

The Development of Visual Perception in Man and Chimpanzee

Austin H. Riesen

Austin Riesen received his doctorate from Yale in 1939. During World War II he was involved in aviation psychology. Shortly thereafter he became affiliated with the Yerkes Laboratories of Primate Biology, in Orange Park, Florida. In 1963 Riesen became Chairman of the Psychology Department at the University of California at Riverside. His chief interests are developmental and comparative perception and sensory deprivation. Riesen is presently making films of primate behavior at the San Diego Zoo.

1. Why were chimpanzees rather than human infants chosen as research subjects?

2. What implications might be drawn from this study as points of discussion for or against special education classes for physically or socially handicapped children?

The study of innate visual organization in man is not open to direct observation during early infancy, since a young baby is too helpless to respond differentially to visual excitation. A first attack on this problem has been made by investigating the visual responsiveness of persons born blind and later made able to see by cataract removal. To evaluate the apparent contradictions between these clinical reports and experimental findings with lower mammals and birds, chimpanzees were reared in darkness until sufficiently mature for the testing of visual responsiveness. The results, which corroborate and extend data reported for man by Senden (3), may require changes in current theories of learning and perception.

Two chimpanzees were reared in darkness to the age of 16 months.* The animals were then brought periodically into the light for a regularly repeated series of observations. By the time of the first observations the animals had developed postural and locomotor skills roughly comparable to normally reared chimpanzees of the same age or approximating in a general way those of a two-year-old human child. At this time the total light experience, received in half a dozen brief (45-second) episodes daily, as required by the routine care of the animals, was approximately 40 hours. At 21 months of age the female was brought permanently into normal indoor illumination. At the present writing the animals are 26 months of age.

The first tests of visual reactions with both subjects demonstrated the presence of good pupillary responses to changes in light intensity, pronounced startle reactions to sudden increases of illumination, and a turning of the eyes and head toward sources of light. In the darkroom there was pursuit of a moving light with both eye and head movements. The eyes, however, did not fixate steadily on a light. Dur-

Austin H. Riesen, "The Development of Visual Perception in Man and Chimpanzee," *Science*, Aug. 1, 1947, 106 (2744), 107–108. Reprinted by permission.

* The early rearing in the darkroom was arranged by H. G. Birch, whose part in this experiment is gratefully acknowledged.

ing all tests, episodes of a resilient "spontaneous" nystagmus occurred, the quick phase usually toward, and the slow phase away from, the light source. With the subject sitting stationary at the center of a rotating drum marked in alternating black and white stripes, tests for optokinetic responses were made. Characteristic pursuit eye movements with quick jerks in the opposite direction were obtained.

Aside from the reflexes just described, and the pursuit of a moving light, the two animals were, in effect, blind. The acquisition of visually mediated responses proceeded very gradually, with no evidence of any sudden increased responsiveness such as might be expected if, for example, the failure to respond was at first due to a general lack of attention to visual stimulation. No fixation of any object, still or moving, could be elicited in any of the early tests. For a long time there was no eye blink when an object was brought rapidly toward the eyes. An object brought slowly toward the face produced no response until contact was made, when the animal reacted with a quick jerk in the typical startle pattern. With the female this was observed for the last time on the 30th day after she was moved into the daylight room. Her first blink to a threatened blow in the face occurred on the 5th day, but occurred consistently only after 48 days, at which time she had been in the light for a total of 570 hours, was 22½ months old, and had for a month received some pushing around daily in short play periods with a younger but visually sophisticated chimpanzee.

Many repetitions of experience with objects presented visually were necessary before any recognition of such objects appeared in either subject. The feeding bottle, for example, was thoroughly familiar tactually and kinesthetically. If the bottle or nipple touched the hand, arm, or face, either animal promptly seized the nipple in its mouth. First signs of *visual* recognition occurred in the female when she protruded her lips toward the bottle on the 33rd meal, or the 11th day, following her shift into the daylight room. The first reaching for the bottle with the hand (done before 12 months of age by normally reared animals) appeared on the 48th meal, or 16th day in the light. With the male, whose visual experience was limited to mealtime, many more feedings were required

before these responses appeared. The first reaching responses of both animals were grossly inaccurate.

A training procedure employing electric shock showed that the learning of avoidance responses was also an extremely slow and gradual process.

These results can best be interpreted in conjunction with the data of Senden. Lacunae in each set of findings, clinical and experimental, are in many respects filled by the other.

In the first place, there is no question that the chimpanzee subjects were well motivated. Sufficient hunger to produce whimpering, and shock severe enough to bring vocal protests, did not alter the fact of failure to "see." The similar slowness of learning of the human patients therefore cannot be accounted for merely by a defect of motivation. The emotional disturbances would seem to have been the result of slow learning, just as Senden concluded, rather than its cause; that is to say, the patient lost some of his enthusiasm when he found how difficult it was to make effective use of the new and at first interesting sensations.

Secondly, the verbal assistance given the human patients make it clear that the difficulty is not simply a failure to attend to visual sensations. With attention successfully directed to a newly-introduced stimulation, as attested to by the patient's partial success in describing it, learning to identify remained a tediously slow process, with the notable exception of color naming. Since color names were learned easily, it cannot be said that "visual attention" was absent.

The prompt visual learning so characteristic of the normal adult primate is thus not an innate capacity, independent of visual experience, but requires a long apprenticeship in the use of the eyes. At lower phylogenetic levels the period of apprenticeship is much shorter. The chick makes effective use of vision immediately upon hatching and shows further improvement of efficiency with the practice afforded by a dozen pecks (*1*). Rats reared in darkness, when first exposed to light, show no clear utilization of vision but learn to jump in response to visual cues within 15 minutes and after an hour or two may be indistinguishable from the normally reared animal (*2*). The chimpanzees of the present study received 50 hours of exposure before the first visually mediated learning was evident; and man, to judge by some of Senden's cases, may require an even longer exposure.

The comparative data conform to the generally recognized principle that organisms whose potential adaptations to the environment are most complex, *i.e.* those that show the greatest intelligence at maturity, also require the longest period of development. This has generally been regarded as a period of maturation. The clinical and experimental data discussed here, however, show that this long period is also essential for the organization of perceptual processes through learning.

References

1. Cruze, W. W. *J. comp. Psychol.,* 1935, 19, 371–409.
2. Hebb, D. O. *J. genet. Psychol.,* 1937, 51, 101–126; *J. comp. Psychol.,* 1937, 24, 277–299; Lashley, K. S., and Russell, J. T. *J. genet. Psychol.,* 1934, 45,136–144.
3. Senden, M. v. *Raum- und Gestaltauffassung bei operierten Blindgeborenen vor und nach der Operation.* Leipzig: Barth, 1932.

Affection in the Monkey

Harry F. Harlow

Harry Harlow is Research Professor at the University of Wisconsin and Director of the Primate Laboratory and the Wisconsin Regional Primate Center. He received his Ph.D. from Stanford University in 1930. A past president of the American Psychological Association, Harlow was also a consultant on the Army's Scientific Advisory Panel. Editor of the Journal of Comparative and Physiological Psychology *from 1951 to 1963, Harlow is a recipient of the Distinguished Psychologist Award and the National Medal of Science.*

1. What conclusion is drawn from the observation that male and female monkeys show differences in sex behavior at two months of age?

2. What conditions in this study led to the development of "neurotic" adult monkeys?

3. What criterion was used to establish the "normalcy" of an adult monkey?

The inspiration for this address came from observational data obtained from seven guinea pigs—two males and three females in a colony and two females brought in temporarily.

Abridged from Harry F. Harlow, "The Heterosexual Affectional System in Monkeys," *American Psychologist,* 17 (1962), 1–9. Copyright 1962 by the American Psychological Association and reproduced by permission.

Observations were provided by my ten-year-old daughter Pamela. These observations were made with love and endearment, and the behavior observed was endearment and love. Furthermore, these observations were made at a level of objectivity difficult for an adult to attain in this field.

Male and female guinea pigs are very fond of each other. They stare blissfully into the limpid pink or ruby or midnight-blue pools of each other's eyes. They nuzzle and they cuddle and the end production is not characterized by rush or rape. After all, one does not have to hurry if there is no hurry to be had. This, Pamela has witnessed several times. A caged, virgin adult female was brought by a friend for mating. Twirp, Pamela's large, black, gentle male, was put into the cage with the new female. He purred, nuzzled her, brushed up against her, smelled and licked her, and gradually conquered the frightened animal. A half-hour later they were snuggled up next to each other, peaceful and content, and they lived in bliss for several weeks until another friend brought in her female and Twirp repeated his patient, gentle approach. Twirp has convinced me that some male guinea pigs, at least, are endowed with an innate sense of decency, and I am happy to say that this is the way most male monkeys behave. I presume that there are some men who have as deep a depth of dignity as guinea pigs.

The guest stands, unfortunately, ended peaceful coexistence in the colony. For many months the five adult guinea pigs had lived amiably in one large cage, with Twirp in command and the second male playing second fiddle. While Twirp was host to the visiting females, White Patch commanded the permanent harem. When Twirp was reintroduced to the colony cage, it took but ten seconds to discover that he would not be tolerated. White Patch bared his teeth and lunged at Twirp, and to save the males, a new cage was acquired.

This led to various divisions of the females and led Pamela to discover particular male guinea pigs like particular female guinea pigs, and they squeal piteously when separated, even when the female is so bulging with babies that she can offer the male nothing in terms of drive reduction. Particular female guinea pigs like particular male guinea pigs. Tastes seem fairly stable, for even after weeks of peaceful residence with the unfavored male, the female will still attempt to get to her favorite male, and after weeks of quiet residence with unfavored females, the male will still try to get to his favorite female.

The females, like the males, defend their rights. In the happy one-cage days two females were separated from the group to care for their litters. White Thrush, in an advanced stage of pregnancy, lived alone with the males. When Chirp was returned to the colony cage after three weeks of maternal chores, both males approached enthusiastically, making friendly gestures. But Hell hath no fury like a female guinea pig spurned, and White Thrush would not tolerate infidelity. She hissed at Chirp, and lunged, and as Chirp fled from the cage, White Thrush pursued, teeth bared. The males also pursued, clucking and purring in anticipation.

The males won, and White Thrush sulked the rest of the day. Guinea pigs apparently have a well-developed heterosexual affectional system.

Sex behavior in the guinea pig has been intensively investigated, and there are exhaustive studies on what has been called the sex drive, but I know of no previous mention of or allusion to the guinea pig's heterosexual affectional system. No doubt this stems from the paradigm which has been established for research in this area.

In a typical experiment a male guinea pig and a female guinea pig in estrus are taken from their individual cages, dropped into a barren chamber, and observed for 15 minutes. In such a situation there is a high probability that something is going to happen and that it will happen rapidly and repeatedly. The thing that happens will be reliable and valid, and all that one needs to do to score it is to count. It is my suggestion that from this time onward it be known as the "flesh count." Sometimes I wonder how men and women would behave if they were dropped naked into a barren chamber with full realization that they had only fifteen minutes to take advantage of the opportunities offered them. No doubt there would be individual differences, but we would obtain little information on the human heterosexual affectional system from such an experiment.

Sex is not an adventitious act. It is not here today and gone tomorrow. It starts with the cradle, and as a part of the human tragedy it wanes before the grave. We have traced and are tracing the development of the heterosexual affectional system in monkeys.

We believe that the heterosexual affectional system in the rhesus monkey, like all the other affectional systems, goes through a series of developmental stages—an infantile heterosexual stage, a preadolescent stage, and an adolescent and mature heterosexual stage. Although these stages are in considerable part overlapping and cannot be sharply differentiated in time, we would think of the infantile stage as lasting throughout the first year and being characterized by inadequate and often inappropriate sexual play and posturing. The preadolescent stage, beginning in the second year and ending in the third year in the female and the fourth year in the male, is characterized by adequate and appropriate sexual play and posturing, but incompleteness. The adolescent and adult stage is characterized by behaviors which are similar in form but give rise to productive outcomes which are also reproductive.

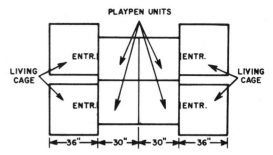

FIGURE 2. *Playpen test situation.*

We have traced the development of the infantile heterosexual stage during the first year of life in two test situations using observational techniques. One is our playroom, illustrated in Figure 1, which consists of a room 8 feet high with 36 feet of floor space. In this room are a platform, ladder, revolving wheel, and flying rings to encourage the infants' adaptation to a three-dimensional world, and there is an assortment of puzzles and toys for quieter activities. Two groups of four infants each, half of each group male and half female, have been observed in the playroom daily over many months. The second apparatus is shown in Figure 2. This is the playpen situation, and it consists of four large living cages and adjoining pens. Each living cage houses a mother and infant, and a three-inch by five-inch opening in the wall between cage and playpen units enables the infants to leave the home cage at any time but restrains the mothers. The playpen units are separated by wire-mesh panels which are removed one or two hours a day to allow the infants to interact in pairs during the first 180 days and both in pairs and in groups of four during the next half-year of life. Again, we are

referring to data gathered from two playpen setups, each housing four infants and their real or surrogate mothers. Insofar as the infantile heterosexual stage is concerned, it makes little or no difference from which situation we take our data.

The outstanding finding in both the playroom and playpen is that male and female infants show differences in sex behavior from the second month of life onward. The males show earlier and more frequent sex behavior than do females, and there are differences in the patterns displayed by the sexes. The males almost never assume the female sex-posture patterns, even in the earliest months. The females, on the other hand, sometimes display the male pattern of sex posturing, but this is infrequent after ten months of age. Predominantly, females show the female pattern and exceptional instances are to other females, not males. Frequency of sex behavior for both males and females increases progressively with age. There is no latency period—except when the monkeys are very tired.

The early infantile sexual behaviors are fragmentary, transient, and involve little more than passivity by the female and disoriented grasping and thrusting by the male. Thus, the male may thrust at the companion's head in a completely disoriented manner or laterally across the midline of the body. However, it is our opinion that these behaviors are more polymorphous than perverse.

Thus, as soon as the sexual responses can be observed and measured, male and female sexual behaviors differ in form. Furthermore, there are many other behaviors which differ between males and females as soon as they can be observed and measured. Figure 3 shows the

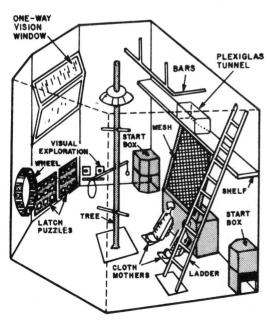

FIGURE 1. *Playroom test situation.*

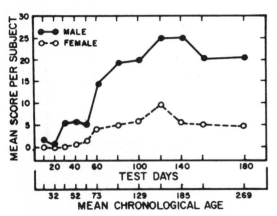

FIGURE 3. *Frequency of threat responses by males and females in the playroom.*

development of threat responses by males and females in the playroom, and these differences are not only statistically significant,[1] but they also have face validity. Analysis of this behavior shows that males threaten other males and females but that females are innately blessed with better manners; in particular, little girl monkeys do not threaten little boy monkeys.

The withdrawal pattern—retreat when confronted by another monkey—is graphed for the playroom in Figure 4, and the significance is obvious. Females evince a much higher incidence of passive responses, which are characterized by immobility with buttocks oriented toward the male and head averted, and a similar pattern, rigidity, in which the body is stiffened and fixed.

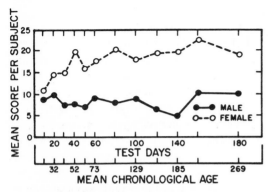

FIGURE 4. *Frequency of withdrawal responses by males and females in the playroom.*

[1] A statistically significant response difference is one that, on application of statistical tests, appears to be related to the experimental effects and did not occur by chance (Ed.).

Infant male and female monkeys show clear-cut differences in behavior of far greater social significance than neonatal and infantile sex responses. Grooming patterns, which are basic to macaque socialization, show late maturation, but as is seen in Figure 5, when they appear, they sharply differentiate the two sexes. Caressing is both a property and prerogative of the females. Basic to normal macaque socialization is the infant-infant or peer-peer affectional system, and this arises out of and is dependent upon the play patterns which we have described elsewhere and only mention here. As is shown in the solid lines of Figure 6, play behavior in the playroom is typically initiated by males, seldom by females. However, let us not belittle the female, for they also serve who only stand and wait. Contact play is far more frequent among the males than the females and is almost invariably initiated by the males. Playpen data graphed in Figure 7 show that real rough-and-tumble play is strictly for the boys.

I am convinced that these data have almost total generality to man. Several months ago I was present at a school picnic attended by 25 second-graders and their parents. While the parents sat and the girls stood around or skipped about hand in hand, 13 boys tackled and wrestled, chased and retreated. No little girl chased any little boy, but some little boys chased some little girls. Human beings have been here for two million years, and they'll probably be here two million more.

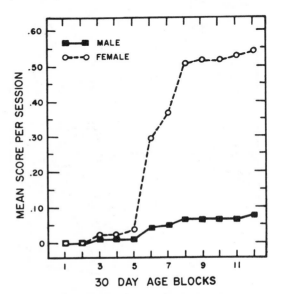

FIGURE 5. *Frequency of grooming responses made by males and females in the playroom.*

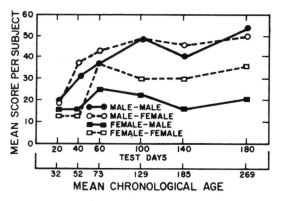

FIGURE 6. *Frequency of play-initiations by males and females to monkeys of the same (male-male, female-female) and other sex (male-female, female-male). Observations are from the play-room.*

These secondary sex-behavior differences probably exist throughout the primate order, and, moreover, they are innately determined biological differences regardless of any cultural overlap. Because of their nature they tend automatically to produce sexual segregation during middle and later childhood, but fortunately this separation is neither complete nor permanent. Behavioral differences may very well make it easy through cultural means to impose a sexual latency period in the human being from childhood to puberty. We emphasize the fact that the latency period is not a biological stage in which primary sex behavior

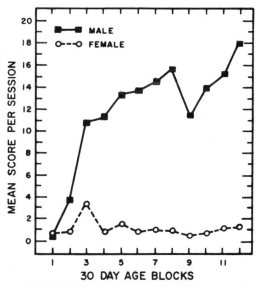

FIGURE 7. *Frequency of occurrence of "rough-and-tumble" play for two males and two females in the playroom through the first year of life.*

is suppressed, but a cultural stage built upon secondary behavioral differences.

We believe that our data offer convincing evidence that sex behaviors differ in large part because of genetic factors. However, we claim no originality for the discovery of intersex behavioral differences. In 1759 Laurence Sterne in his book *Tristram Shandy* described male and female differences at the most critical period in Tristram Shandy's development; indeed, it would not be possible to conceive of a more critical period.

"Pray, my dear, quoth my mother, *have you not forgot to wind up the clock?——— Good G——!* cried my father, making an exclamation, but taking care to moderate his voice at the same time———*did ever woman, since the creation of the world, interrupt a man with such a silly question?"*[2]

Men and women have differed in the past and they will differ in the future.

It is possible that the listener has been dismayed by the frequent reference to sex and the relatively infrequent reference to affection. Out of these infantile behavior patterns, both sexual and nonsexual, develop the affectional bonds and the social ordering that appear to be important or even essential to the full development of the heterosexual affectional system of macaques. Traumatic affectional errors, both transient and prolonged, may have devastating effects upon subsequent social and sexual behaviors.

For some years we have been attempting to establish experimental neuroses in infant monkeys by having them live on unfriendly and inconsistent mother surrogates. One preparation was a rejecting mother that on schedule or demand separated her baby when a wire frame embedded in her spun-nylon covering was displaced violently upward and backward. The baby was disturbed, but as soon as the frame was returned to its resting position, the baby returned to cling to its surrogate mother as tightly as ever. Next we developed an air-blast mother with a series of nozzles down the entire center of her body which released compressed

[2] Laurence Sterne, *The Life and Opinions of Tristram Shandy, Gentleman.* J. A. Work, ed. (New York: The Odyssey Press, 1940) p. 5.

air under high pressure—an extremely noxious stimulus to monkeys. The blasted baby never even left the mother, but in its moments of agony and duress, clung more and more tightly to the unworthy mother. Where else can a baby get protection? Apparently our infant had never read Neal Miller's theory that avoidance gradients are precipitous and approach gradients gradual and tenuous, for love conquered all.

We next devised a shaking mother, which on schedule or demand shook her infant with unconscionable violence until its teeth chattered. The infant endured its tribulations by clinging more and more tightly. At the present time we believe we may be on the threshold of success through Jay Mowbray's creation of the porcupine mother, which extrudes brass spikes all over its ventral surface. Preliminary studies on two infants suggest that they are emotionally disturbed. Whether or not we eventually succeed, the fact remains that babies are reluctant to develop experimental neuroses, and at one time we even wondered if this were possible.

During the time that we were producing these evil mothers, we observed the monkeys which we had separated from their mothers at birth and raised under various mothered and nonmothered conditions. The first 47 baby monkeys were raised during the first year of life in wire cages so arranged that the infants could see and hear and call to other infants but not contact them. Now they are five to seven years old and sexually mature. As month after month and year after year have passed, these monkeys have appeared to be less and less normal. We have seen them sitting in their cages strangely mute, staring fixedly into space, relatively indifferent to people and other monkeys. Some clutch their heads in both hands and rock back and forth—the autistic behavior pattern that we have seen in babies raised on wire surrogates. Others, when approached or even left alone, go into violent frenzies of rage, grasping and tearing at their legs with such fury that they sometimes require medical care.

Eventually we realized that we had a laboratory full of neurotic monkeys. We had failed to produce neurotic monkeys by thoughtful planning and creative research, but we had succeeded in producing neurotic monkeys through misadventure. To err is human.

Because of housing pressures some of these monkeys and many of our surrogate-raised monkeys lived in pairs for several years while growing to sexual maturity, but we have seldom seen normal sex behavior, and we certainly have not had the validating criterion of newborn baby monkeys. Instead, these monkeys treat each other like brother and sister, proving that two can live in complete propinquity with perfect propriety as long as no one cares.

Their reason for being, as we saw it, was to produce babies for our researches, and so at this point we deliberately initiated a breeding program which was frighteningly unsuccessful. When the older, wire-cage-raised males were paired with the females at the peak of estrus, the introduction led only to fighting, so violent and vicious that separation was essential to survival. In no case was there any indication of normal sex behavior. Frequently the females were the aggressors; even the normal praying mantis waits until the sex act is completed.

Pairing such cloth-surrogate-raised monkeys as were sexually mature gave little better end results. Violent aggression was not the rule, and there was attempted sex behavior, but it was unreproductive since both the male and female behaviors were of the infantile type we have already described.

At this point we took the 17 oldest of our cage-raised animals, females showing consistent estrous cycles and males obviously mature, and engaged in an intensive re-education program, pairing the females with our most experienced, patient, and gentle males, and the males with our most eager, amiable, and successful breeding females. When the laboratory-bred females were smaller than the sophisticated males, the girls would back away and sit down facing the males, looking appealingly at these would-be consorts. Their hearts were in the right place, but nothing else was. When the females were larger than the males, we can only hope that they misunderstood the males' intentions, for after a brief period of courtship, they would attack and maul the ill-fated male. Females show no respect for a male they can dominate.

The training program for the males was equally unsatisfactory. They approached the females with a blind enthusiasm, but it was a misdirected enthusiasm. Frequently the males would grasp the females by the side of the body and thrust laterally, leaving them working at cross purposes with reality. Even the most persistent attempts by these females to set the boys straight came to naught. Finally, these females either stared at the males with complete contempt or attacked them in utter frustration. It became obvious that they, like their human counterpart, prefer maturer men. We realized then that we had established, not a program of breeding, but a program of brooding.

We had in fact been warned. Our first seven laboratory-born babies were raised in individual cages while being trained on a learning test battery. William Mason planned to test their social behaviors subsequently, and great care had been taken to keep the babies socially isolated and to prevent any physical contacts. Neonatal baby monkeys require 24-hour-a-day care, and infant monkeys need ministrations beyond a 40-hour week. We had assigned the evening care to Kathy, a maternal bit of fluff who had worked for several years as a monkey tester while studying to become an elementary school teacher.

Checking on his wards one night near 10 P.M., Mason found Kathy sitting on the floor surrounded by seven baby monkeys, all eight of the primates playing happily together. Before the horrified scientist could express his outrage, Kathy had risen to her full height of five feet two. Already anticipating the carping criticisms which he was formulating, she shook her finger in his face and spoke with conviction: "Dr. Mason, I'm an education student and I know that it is improper and immoral to blight the social development of little children. I am right and you are wrong!"

Although we were angry with Kathy, we did think there was a certain humor in the situation and we did not worry about our monkeys. We simply transferred Kathy to an office job. Alas, she could not have been more right and we could not have been more wrong! We have already described the social-sexual life of these 7 monkeys and the next 40 to come.

Two years later we had more than theoretical reasons to be disturbed because Mason tested a group of these isolation-raised monkeys, then between 2.5 and 3.5 years of age, and found evidence of severe social abnormalities, which might be described as a sociopathic syndrome.

He matched the laboratory-raised monkeys on the basis of weight and dentition patterns with monkeys that had been born and raised in the wild for the first 12 to 18 months, then captured and subjected to various kinds of housing and caging treatments for the next year or two. In the test situations the laboratory-raised monkeys, as compared with feral monkeys, showed infantile sexual behavior, absence of grooming, exaggerated aggression, and absence of affectional interaction as measured by cooperation.

We are now quite certain that this sociopathic syndrome does not stem from the fact that the baby monkeys were raised in the laboratory but from *how* they were raised in the laboratory. Our infants raised in the laboratory by real monkey mothers and permitted opportunity for the development of normal infant-infant affection demonstrate normal male and female sexual behavior when they enter the second year of life. Furthermore, our playroom and playpen studies show that infant monkeys raised on cloth mothers but given the opportunity to form normal infant-infant affectional patterns, also develop normal sexual responses.

In a desperate attempt to assist a group of 18 three- to four-year-old cloth-surrogate-raised monkeys, half of them males and half females, we engaged in a group-psychotherapy program, placing these animals for two months on the monkey island in the Madison Zoo, as shown in Figure 8. Their summer vacation on the enchanted island was not without avail, and social grooming responses rapidly developed and were frequent in occurrence. After a few days of misunderstanding, patterns of social ordering developed, and a number of males and females developed friendship patterns. Unfortunately, sexual behavior was infrequent, and the behavior that was observed was completely inadequate—at least from our point of view. In desperation we finally introduced our most experienced, most patient, and most kindly breeding male, Smiley, and he rapidly established himself as king of the island and prepared to take full advantage of the wealth of opportunity which surrounded him. Fortunately, the traumatic experiences he encountered with unreceptive females have left no

FIGURE 8. *Group of cloth-surrogate-raised monkeys on the monkey island in the Madison Zoo.*

FIGURE 9. *Typical behavior of unmothered mother toward her infant. Mother is looking upward while crushing her baby against the cage floor.*

apparent permanent emotional scars, and now that he has been returned to our laboratory breeding colony, he is again making an important contribution to our research program. If normal sexual behavior occurred, no member of our observational team ever saw it, and had a female become pregnant, we would have believed in parthenogenesis.

But let us return to the monkeys that we left on the island and the older ones that we left in their cages. A year has passed, and the frustrations that both we and our monkeys experienced are in some small part nothing but a memory. We constructed larger and more comfortable breeding cages, and we designed a very large experimental breeding room 8 feet by 8 feet by 8 feet in size with appropriate platforms and a six-foot tree. Apparently we designed successful seraglios for I can report that not all love's labors have been lost. It does appear that the males are completely expendable unless they can be used in a program of artificial insemination. Certainly we can find no evidence that there is a destiny that shapes their ends unless some Skinnerite can help us with the shaping process. We have, however, had better success with some of the females, particularly the females raised on cloth surrogates.

Even so, one of the wire-cage-raised females is a mother and another is pregnant. Three cloth-surrogate females are mothers and four or five are expectant. We give all the credit to three breeding males. One, Smiley, does not take "no" for an answer. Smiley has a way with females. Patient, gentle, and persuasive, he has overcome more than one planned program of passive resistance. One female did not become pregnant until the fifth successive month of training. Month after month she has changed, and now she is mad about the boy. Male No. 342 behaves very much like Smiley. Even when females threaten him, he does not harm them. Given time, he has been able to overcome more than one reluctant dragon, and he is a master of the power of positive suggestion.

Breeding male No. 496 has helped us greatly, particularly with the younger, cloth-surrogate-raised females. His approach differs from that of Smiley and No. 342. His technique transcends seduction, and in contract bridge terms it may be described as an approach-forcing system.

Combining our human and male-monkey talents, we are winning the good fight and inparting to naive and even resistant female monkeys the priceless gift of motherhood. Possibly it is a Pyrrhic victory. As every scientist knows, the solution of one scientific problem inevitably leads to another, and this is our fate (Figure 9). Month after month female monkeys that

never knew a real mother, themselves become mothers—helpless, hopeless, heartless mothers devoid, or almost devoid, of any maternal feeling.

Suggested Readings

Carmichael, L., ed. *Manual of Child Psychology*. New York: Wiley, 1954.

Davis, C. M. "Self-Selection of Diet by Newly Weaned Infants," *Amer. J. dis. child,* 36 (1928), 651–679.

Dennis, W., and Dennis, M. G. "The Effect of Cradling Practices upon the Onset of Walking in Hopi Children," *J. genet. Psychol.,* 56 (1940), 77–86.

Gesell, A., and Thompson, H. "Twins T and C from Infancy to Adolescence," *Genet. Psychol. Monog.,* 24 (1941), 3–122.

Harris, D. B., ed. *The Concept of Development*. Minneapolis: University of Minnesota Press, 1957.

Hess, E. H. "Imprinting," *Science,* 130 (1959), 133–141.

Hunt, J. McV. "The Effects of Infant Feeding Frustration upon Adult Hoarding Behavior," *J. abnorm. soc. Psychol.,* 36 (1941), 338–360.

Hurlock, E. B. *Developmental Psychology*. New York: McGraw-Hill, 1959.

Munn, N. L. *The Evolution and Growth of Human Behavior*. Boston: Houghton Mifflin Co., 1955.

Newman, H. H., F. N. Freeman, and K. H. Holzinger. *Twins: A Study of Heredity and Environment*. Chicago: University of Chicago Press, 1937.

Riesen, A. H. "The Development of Visual Perception in Man and Chimpanzee," *Science* 106 (1949), 107–108.

Sears, R. R. "Relation of Early Socialization Experiences to Aggression in Middle Childhood,"*J. abnorm. soc. Psychol.,* 63 (1961), 466–492.

Sears, R. R., E. E. Maccoby, and H. Levin. *Patterns of Child Rearing*. Evanston, Illinois: Row, Peterson, 1957.

Sperry, R. W. "The Growth of Nerve Circuits," *Scient. Amer.,* November 1959.

Tinbergen, N. *The Study of Instinct*. London: Oxford University Press, 1951.

3   *Measuring Individual Differences*

It is quite obvious that people come in different sizes, shapes, and colors. It is obvious to us because we can see physical differences between people and we have learned that we can usually count on what we see. If we were asked to compare the physical differences between two people, we could easily do so by using measurements of height, weight, and color of skin. *Behavioral differences,* however, are not so clearly recognizable. What are some of these differences? How stable are they once we recognize them? The selections in this chapter will help to answer these questions.

The Prediction Problem, Paul Horst. Individual differences are traditionally classified according to intellectual and personality traits. Such traits include perception, achievement, aptitude, interest, and attitude. Of course, these terms mean nothing unless we know what observations and operations stand behind them. The general guidelines for an understanding of these operations are presented in this selection. Horst discusses the problem of *prediction,* which is generally thought of as the most significant area of behavioral measurement.

Toward a Broadened Construct of Intelligence, David Wechsler. The remaining selections are placed in an order that progresses from a discussion of the theoretical aspects of individual behavior through a discussion of specific behavior traits. Thus the second selection, by Wechsler, contains a capsule view of the history of mental measurement. He takes the point of view that "general intelligence is the function of the personality as a whole and is determined by emotion and conative factors." This consideration is currently important, since intelligence tests are under close scrutiny and their usefulness with minority-group members is being hotly debated in many quarters. Wechsler is best known for his pioneering work in the area of intelligence measurement. The Wechsler Intelligence Scales for Children and Adults are the most widely used individual tests of intelligence.

What Is a Trait of Personality?, Gordon W. Allport. This article is included here under the assumption that personality plays an important role in determining a person's intellectual life. The author defines personality by the use of eight evaluative criteria.

Gifted Men: Scientists and Nonscientists, Lewis M. Terman. Terman compares various factors that distinguish gifted scientists from gifted nonscientists. This special study intensively followed gifted individuals over a 30-year period. It is perhaps the best-conducted study of its kind and is based on the largest body of data ever gathered on individuals of superior intelligence. Terman authored the Stanford-Binet Test, the first individual intelligence test to be extensively used in this country.

The Prediction Problem

Paul Horst

Paul Horst, Professor Emeritus of Psychology, University of Washington, received his Ph.D. from the University of Chicago in 1931. With a long-term concern for problems of prediction and selection, Horst retains a special interest in the prediction of personal adjustment.

1. If you are taking an introductory course in psychology, what criterion would you use to predict your success in the course? What personal and situational factors would you want to isolate prior to your prediction?

In all realms of human activity, individuals differ in performance. The aim of prediction studies is to estimate, in advance of participation, the level of an individual's performance in a given activity. To this end prediction research seeks to ascertain the personality traits, skills, and capacities which are associated with differences in level of performance and the situational factors in the environment which influence performance. In this chapter are discussed the types of factors associated with differences in performance, and the kinds of situational factors which must be taken into consideration.

Factors Associated with Individual Differences in an Activity

Given the fact of individual differences in performance of an activity, the problem becomes that of determining what factors associated with this variation are needed in making predictions. These factors are of two kinds,

Abridged from Paul Horst, "The Prediction of Personal Adjustment," *Social Science Research Council Bulletin,* No. 48 (1941), pp. 12–19.

personal and situational. The former comprises all those traits or characteristics that pertain to the person, whether physiological or psychological in nature. The situational factors may be any of the many influences on a person's activity which are external to and relatively independent of him, e.g., supervision in the vocational field, or type of high school attended in the school situation. Personal and situational factors are constantly interacting and are interrelated in their influence on a person's level of performance in an activity. As a matter of fact, the situational factors must always be understood in the way they are defined by the individual himself. While for purposes of discussion the two types of factors will be considered separately, their intimate interrelations should always be kept in mind.

Situational Factors Associated with Variation in an Activity

Situational or extrapersonal factors frequently account for some of the variation in an activity and must therefore be considered in the prediction of individual behavior. Examples of the importance of situational factors for prediction can be multiplied, but a few will suffice. Many studies of sales personnel have demonstrated the influence of situational factors, such as the effect of supervision or field organization on volume of sales.[1] External factors are important, too, in other vocations. In the factory, for example, supervision, lighting conditions, age of machines, etc., all affect workers' productivity. In the transportation field, the kind of route a motorman operates influences the number of accidents he has as well as does his degree of carefulness.[2]

The importance of situational factors in parole has been indicated by many studies. From a study of success of prisoners released on parole or conditional release, Sanders concludes that ". . . the success rate . . . varies widely according to the type of parole advisor."[3] Parole supervision is only one of a large number of situational factors which affect success or failure on parole. Among factors which may influence the success of the parolee are the neighborhood to which he returns when released from prison, his marital situation, whether or not he has a job.

Success in marital adjustment is related not only to the personality and cultural background (here called personal factors) of the married person, but also to certain of the conditions of life after marriage. Burgess and Cottrell found that amount of unemployment after marriage was significantly related to success. Another situational factor of importance was the size of the community in which the couple lived, which was found to be inversely related to marital success.[4]

In the educational field, it has been recognized that to make adequate predictions, situational variables such as housing conditions in college or amount of outside employment must be considered as well as intelligence, personality, interest, and other personal factors. It may be, too, that the higher achievement of students in some classes as compared with others is partly a function of differences in the ability of teachers. In a study by E. E. Oberholzer

". . . about 41% of the differences between classes was accounted for in terms of the rated differences between the teachers in their ability to carry out their work."[5]

Content of high school curriculum may also be regarded as a situational factor in predicting school success. An intensive study of the influence of this factor on achievement in college is the eight-year investigation begun in 1932 by the Progressive Education Association. The purpose of this research has been to determine whether graduates of good progressive schools which emphasize the needs and interests of the pupils and ignore specific college-entrance requirements could do as well in college as students coming from the traditional type of secondary schools. The subjects of the research have been 1500 students who were products of three years of training in progressive schools and a control group of 1500 matching the experimental group in I.Q., age, race, sex, type of family, economic background and size of community but attending high schools with curricula oriented to college-entrance requirements. Elaborate follow-up studies have been made of these two groups whose members have now been in college from one to four years.[6]

What are called situational factors vary all the way from the rather obvious kinds of factors cited above to very subtle settings in which personality development takes place. For example, a student who comes from a home with strict authoritarian parents and has learned to react to that situation by a protective attitude of apathy may show marked difference in attitude and performance in his work under two teachers, one of whom is dictatorial and one of whom is quite nonauthoritarian in method.

Manipulable and Nonmanipulable Situational Factors

Situational factors may be usefully classified into two categories: those which are manipu-

---

[1] See, e.g., H. G. Kenagy and C. S. Yoakum, *The Selection and Training of Salesmen.* New York: McGraw-Hill Book Co., 1925, pp. 1–8.

[2] Morris S. Viteles, "Standards of Accomplishment: Criteria of Vocational Selection," *Journal of Personnel Research,* 4 (1926), 484.

[3] Barkev S. Sanders, "Testing Parole Prediction," *Proceedings of the Sixty-Fifth Annual Congress, American Prison Association,* Atlanta, Ga., 1935, p. 230.

[4] E. W. Burgess and Leonard S. Cottrell, Jr., *Predicting Success or Failure in Marriage,* New York: Prentice-Hall, Inc., 1939, pp. 250, 264.

[5] From an unpublished report by the Committee on Evaluation of Newer Practices in Education, G. Derwood Baker, Chairman.

[6] For a nontechnical discussion of the experiment, see Dorothy Dunbar Bromley, "Education for College or for Life," *Harper's Magazine,* 182 (March 1941), 407–416.

lable, and those which are relatively nonmanipulable. This distinction is rather important, for it is the manipulable factors in the situation which make social control possible.

Nonmanipulable situational factors are significant in prediction research provided they account for some of the variation in the success of individuals in the group whose activity is being studied. In the case of army pilots, for example, individuals may vary in the number of planes they shoot down because more enemy planes are operating in one pilot's territory than in another. This might be considered a nonmanipulable factor because the number of enemy planes in any given territory can not as a rule be varied by the system within which the army pilot is operating, namely, the country for which he is fighting. (It can, of course, be varied by another system, namely, the country against which he is fighting.) In marriage, the amount of satisfaction or happiness attainable by a wife may be limited by the particular culture in which she is living. Factors of this sort must be taken into account in analyzing the variation with respect to the activity of a group of individuals. They may be thought of as defining the range of success in the activity. In general, there is relatively little that can be done within the system in which the individuals are operating to modify or change factors such as these.

Situational factors subject to manipulation are of particular interest because of the opportunity they offer for controlling, within limits, the amount of individual variation in the activity. Such control may be exercised to increase the probabilities of success in given cases. In parole, for example, it has been repeatedly emphasized by investigators that a man's success is a function of many factors which are independent of him, and that those which lend themselves to control should be manipulated in such a way as to help insure a successful parole. Despite this emphasis, it has been frequently noted that too little use is made of such manipulable factors. Parolees are often returned to disorganized families and unwholesome community environments despite the fact that success on parole is less likely under such conditions. If these situation factors were im-

proved, the chances for success would be greatly increased.[7]

Two types of manipulation may be distinguished: (1) manipulation having the same effect on all persons and (2) manipulation having a differential effect on different persons. As an example of the first, a hypothetical situation may be cited in which a soap salesman is moved from a hard water to a soft water territory where presumably less soap is consumed. Such manipulation of a situational factor would have the same effect on all salesmen, namely, to reduce the maximum potential volume of their sales from what it previously had been. The second type of manipulation is illustrated by the case of a change of supervisor and its effect on sales of soap salesmen. A new supervisor may serve as a means of increasing the sales volume of one salesman, but of decreasing it in the case of another salesman who operates less successfully than under his former supervisor. The first type of manipulation has a relatively constant effect for all persons, whereas the effect of the latter may vary considerably for different persons. It is, perhaps, the latter type of manipulation which is more significant for social efficiency.

In the intensive analysis of manipulable situations and the person's relation to them, the case study can make an important contribution.

The case study is particularly helpful when an attempt is made to analyze a prediction situation from the standpoint of changing the person about whom the prediction is made. A reward-punishment analysis of the concrete situation might often show that manipulation of rewards could be arranged to develop in him the skills desired or tested for. Such an analysis is not at present likely to be particularly fruitful if only the conventional statistical test items are relied upon, because, with a multitude of variables, it is difficult to isolate the influence statistically of any single variable. Ultimately, if the number of items or variables can be reduced to a few meaningful clusters, the effectiveness of quantitative devices not only for prediction but also for changing the person about whom the prediction is made can be greatly enhanced.

---

[7] See *Attorney General's Survey of Release Procedures*, Vol. IV, *Parole*. Washington, D.C.: Department of Justice, 1939, pp. 305–306.

The problem of prediction is to ascertain the personal and situational elements which are associated with successful performance of an activity, so that these may be used to estimate the degree of success of a given individual prior to his engaging in the activity. In research, the prediction process proceeds somewhat as follows: (a) given an activity in which individuals are known to vary in their performance, a measure of success or failure in the activity is established; (b) given this criterion, the personal and situational factors associated with individual differences in the performance of the activity must be isolated, and these must be of such a nature that they (or some index of them) are present and can be analyzed prior to engagement in the activity; (c) given such pre-activity factors which are associated with success or failure in the activity to a known extent, it is then possible to make predictions.

Toward a Broadened Construct of Intelligence

David Wechsler

David Wechsler was for many years Chief Psychologist at Bellevue Hospital. Although now retired, he continues as Clinical Professor at the New York University College of Medicine. In 1967 he was Visiting Professor of Psychology at the Hebrew University in Jerusalem. In college Wechsler "majored in philosophy; did best work in biology, was most fascinated by entomology, but eventually was inspired by R. S. Woodworth and Carl Spearman to find a niche in psychology." He received his Ph.D. from Columbia University in 1925. Wechsler is best known for his authorship of Intelligence Scales. Less well known is the fact that he invented the psychogalavanograph, forerunner of what we now know as the lie detector (polygraph).

1. How many situations can you think of in which an "IQ" is used to determine an individual's placement or status?

2. What statistical technique has been most closely associated with the study of intelligence? Why was it chosen?

3. How did Dr. Wechsler arrive at the conclusion that achievement is determined by more than intellectual factors? Can you follow his reasoning?

It is always a good omen for science when different men in different places make independent discoveries or arrive at similar conclusions. In the last two decades psychologists in their efforts to define the nature of general intelligence seem to have arrived at the threshold of such a situation. In this paper I wish to present to you what appears to me to be the germ of the impending re-orientation: it is this, that general intelligence cannot be equated with intellectual ability however broadly defined, but must be regarded as a manifestation of the personality as a whole.

Abridged from David Wechsler, "Cognitive, Conative, and Non-intellective Intelligence," *American Psychologist*, 5 (1950), 78–83. Copyright 1950 by the American Psychological Association and reproduced by permission.

From an historical point of view, the first one to argue against the identification of general intelligence with intellectual ability was Henri Bergson. Already in his *"Donées Immediate de la Conscience"* and more emphatically in his *"Evolution Creatrice,"* he pointed out the insufficiencies of the human intellect or, what was for him the same, normative logic, in dealing effectively with man's total environment.

I shall not here restate Bergson's arguments nor his attempted solution of endowing the human mind with a new faculty, creative intuition, and its generating force, the "elan vital." I wish only to call your attention to the fact that in our attempts at measuring intelligence we have persisted in treating intelligence as if it consisted exclusively of intellectual elements or factors. What, in fact, are these intellectual elements which we have continued to use and to posit in appraising intelligence? They are abstract reasoning, verbal, spatial, numerical, and a few other specified factors, all of which in some particularized manner deal with man's cognitive ability. Shades of Bergson, are we confirming his claim that human intelligence, as the psychologist conceives it, can only deal with geometric and logical symbols?

Now, the remarkable thing is that while this is what we are saying in our tests of intelligence, most of us don't believe it. What is more important, it isn't true! Our contemporary definitions of intelligence assert as much: intelligence according to these is not only the ability to learn, to abstract, to profit from experience, but also to adjust and to achieve. Everyone with clinical experience knows that the latter involve other capacities besides eductive, verbal, numerical, spatial, and the other intellective factors that have been demonstrated. Yes, but what are they? The answer is: they are *not* intellective. They are capacities and traits dependent upon temperament and personality which are not restricted to logical and abstract perception; they are, in my opinion, factors of personality itself. It is this point of view, independently sensed or suggested, at times only tangentially, by a number of investigators including Goldstein, Alexander, Wechsler, and more recently by Halstead and Eysenck, which I presented six years ago for the first time under the term *"Non-intellective Factors of Intelligence."* I wish now to present to you more fully the evidence in its support and to justify what appears to be not only the need for a reorientation in our concept of general intelligence, but of a new psychometric that will, in fact, measure what is purported in our definition of intelligence.

Let me begin by restating the issue in terms of the actual psychometric problem. The crux of this problem, as we have already noted, is the discrepancy between what the clinical psychologist does and what he says he does in clinical practice. If we examine any of the current psychological tests of intelligence, we shall find them to consist of sample tasks measuring, by definition, a variety of mental abilities. One would imagine that any summary of the results obtained with such tests would be essentially a report of the degree to which an individual possesses these abilities and the manner in which they vary. However, it will be found that once a summative score is obtained from them, whether in terms of MA, IQ, or whatnot, the clinical psychologist proceeds to enlarge his summary to include not only specific psychologic interpretations but broad social and biological implications as well.

An IQ is thus used, not only to determine comparative mental endowment, capacity to learn, presence of special abilities and disabilities, and evaluation of degree of mental deficiency, but also as a basis for school placement, for vocational guidance, for psychiatric diagnosis, and for the prediction of adjustment potentials in a variety of situations from infancy to old age, including such areas as child adoption, juvenile delinquency, fitness for military service, college success, and old age counseling.

Assuming that intelligence tests may be used in all these situations, and within limits I believe they may, the question arises how this is possible under the concept that general intelligence is a matter of a single basic or even a combination of a number of intellectual abilities. It is this question which I shall try to answer this evening. But I must first call your attention to the fact you are all aware of, that this is not the usual criticism of intelligence tests. The historic and continued objection to intelligence tests is not that they measure too much, but that they do not measure enough, or at least, not well enough.

You are all acquainted with the arguments against intelligence tests, and I shall not repeat them; the damaging criticism pertains, not as is generally emphasized, to the question of reliability, but to one of basic validity. Even such studies as those of Wellman, Goldfarb and others, showing changes in IQ produced by a variety of social and environmental factors, though relevant, are not crucial. The crucial instances are those where individuals obtain identical IQs (say an IQ of 65) but, on overall appraisal, must nevertheless be rated differently, say, one as a defective and the other as not defective. Such instances are not necessarily common, but neither are they rare exceptions. Here is a situation which needs explaining and cannot be by-passed.

The first to attack this problem was E. L. Thorndike. His answer, as always characteristic of his approach, was straightforward and to the point. Our tests measure intelligence to be sure, he said, but there is not just one unique, but several different kinds of intelligence, namely, abstract, social and practical. The first is manifested by the individual's ability to work with symbols, the second by his ability to deal with people, and the third by his ability to manipulate objects. Thorndike, himself, seems to have been primarily interested in the first kind of intelligence and, having made the above trichotomy, and along with it the distinction between tests which measure breadth, as against those which measure altitude, left the working out of these concepts to others. But relatively little has been done to verify or refute the hypothesis.

In the 1920's Moss published a test of social intelligence which consisted essentially of items involving memory and recognition of names and faces, and a series of multiple-choice questions involving social situations, in which the correct answer seemed to have been based on the notion that "the customer is always right." Although Moss's test for a time had some vogue among business firms, clinical psychologists, as far as I have been able to discover, seldom if ever make use of it.

The other important effort at producing a test of social intelligence is Doll's Vineland Social Maturity Scale. This Scale, as you know, consists of a series of questions listing a variety of social acquisitions, that is, of approved and useful acts and achievements, which

a child may be expected to have learned from infancy to adolescence. The Scale is hardly a test in the ordinary sense of the term, since it involves no test performance or response by the subject, and can be completed, as it usually is, by other persons. But it does correlate fairly well with other tests of intelligence and has been shown by Doll and others to correlate positively and significantly with a number of practical criteria of social adjustment.

Clinical psychologists appear to have accepted performance tests, almost from the start, as a measure of practical intelligence. Only they seem to have regarded practical intelligence, as measured by these tests, as a kind of special aptitude rather than as a kind of intelligence. For many years the situation in clinical practice was something like this: a child would be given routinely a Binet test. Then, if his Binet MA did not seem to do justice to him, he would be given a Pintner-Paterson or similar performance battery as a supplementary test. But the child's score on the performance test, except in instances of language handicaps, would seldom be integrated with, or serve to alter, his Binet intelligence rating. Instead, it would usually be used as evidence of a compensatory useful special ability. Thus, if a child attained an IQ of 85 on the Binet, and one of 110 on the Pintner-Paterson, the reporting psychologist would ordinarily give the rating as "dull normal" intelligence with good practical or manipulative ability. It was not until the publication of the Bellevue Scales that any consistent attempt was made to integrate performance and verbal tests into a single measure of intelligence. The Bellevue tests have had increasingly wider use, but I regret to report that their popularity seems to derive, not from the fact that they make possible a single global rating, but because they enable the examiner to obtain separate verbal and performance IQ's with one test.

The Aristotelian hierarchical white-collar concept of intelligence dies hard. This, in spite of the fact that performance tests often can and do contain a larger amount of *g* (see below) than do the verbal tests. Thus, in his differential study of *"Abstract and Concrete Intelligence,"* W. P. Alexander, after correcting for communality, specific factors, and chance errors of measurement, found the theoretical g loadings for verbal and practical ability to be .60 and .81, respectively. Alexander concludes that "a perfect performance battery would be a better measure of g than a perfect verbal battery."

This and other findings by Alexander bring me to what constitutes the most compelling evidence for the reorientation in our concept of intelligence mentioned at the onset of this paper. I refer to the findings contributed by factor analysis. Here two important names appear on the horizon: Carl Spearman and L. L. Thurstone. I believe that the answers which they have given to the problem of the nature of general intelligence are incorrect. But I am sure that without the inspiration and without the tools which they furnished us, the solution of the problem would be altogether impossible.

Such a statement before a gathering of clinical psychologists may be unorthodox, because to many, factor analysis is almost anathema. But I can assure you, on the authority of expert consultants, that the mathematics of factor analysis is quite elementary, and on the basis of my own experience with it, extremely practical; and, with due apologies to Freud, even "sexy." For with what, in effect, does factor analysis concern itself, but with the bedfellowship of psychometric tests. For, mind you, it embraces matrices, correlational to be sure, and then tells you what test stays close to what other tests when axes are rotated. Now that, I submit, is what clinical psychologists want to know: what test, what factor, or, if you will, what function or what trait goes with what other factor, or function, or trait. And when the findings are examined some very interesting and unsuspected relationships come to light. For example, some tests of intelligence, like some human beings, are extremely promiscuous. Thus, vocabulary, the paragon of verbal tests, correlates very frequently, and to a considerable measure, with Block Designs, the perfect example of a performance test. But to return to a more serious vein, the importance of factor analysis is, of course, that it enables us to discover what our tests measure and the extent to which they measure the things they purport.

What are the elements which factor analysis has shown our intelligence tests to measure?

The first is abstract reasoning. This is Spearman's g or eduction. Spearman argued that g was the only independent factor, and while he hesitated to identify g with general intelligence, his actual applications are tantamount to it. In equating g with general intelligence Spearman was in error, not because the tetrad equation is incorrect but because, in point of fact, it is not satisfied as he claimed. Spearman's answer to this finding was that we cannot expect the tetrad equation to be satisfied by all the tests of general intelligence but only by "good" tests of intelligence, like analogies and mathematical reasoning which require eduction. But of course, if you select your tests, you can choose them so highly saturated with a single factor that the residuals vanish. This is all that the tetrad equation says, and it was the perceptive insight of Thurstone which recognized the tetrad equation for what it was, namely, a mathematically special case of a more general solution of the factorial problem. What was needed was a statistical analysis which would permit the emergence of other factors when present. By the use of his expanded technique, it has now been shown that intelligence tests, such as they are, contain not one but several independent factors. Some five or six have been definitely identified; they are, to repeat, induction, verbal, spatial, numerical, and one or two other factors. Notice, however, that these factors, like Spearman's eduction, are all cognitive.

At this point it is important to bear in mind what a factor stands for in factor analysis. Basically, it is an identifiable independent variable which accounts for a certain portion of the total test variance in a correlational matrix. The amount of variance it accounts for in any given test is called the test's factor loading. In a perfectly factorialized correlation matrix, the sum of the factorial loadings of the extracted factors should be 100 per cent, that is, account for the total test variance.

Now, it is a remarkable finding that when matrices of intelligence tests are factored, the amount of variance accounted for is seldom more than 60 per cent of the total, and, what is perhaps of equal significance, the greater the number of different tests included, the smaller, generally, the total per cent of variance accounted for; and this is seemingly independent of the number of factors extracted. In the case of our present intelligence test batteries, factors beyond the first 3 or 4 usually contribute so little to the already accounted-for variance that it is generally not profitable to extract them. It is the observation of this important finding that in the factorialization of batteries of intelligence tests, there always remained a considerable per cent of unaccounted-for variance, which began to arouse my interest some years ago. It seemed to hold the key to our problem.

If after successive attempts at factoring out all the components of intelligence, there always remained a large residue of these unknown elements, the obvious inference to be made was that our intelligence tests measured other things than those accounted for by the extracted factors. The second inference was that those other factors were numerous and occurred in relatively small amounts, because it was impossible to extract single additional factors which would account for any considerable portion of the residual variance. I assumed that the principal reason for this was that the test batteries usually factored did not include tests which contained sufficient amounts of these other factors to enable some of the remaining tests to cluster about them. Provisionally I called these residual components the nonintellective factors of intelligence. But in terms of more recent findings, I believe they can be more justly designated as the personality components of general intelligence, which in fact they are.

The evidence for this conclusion comes from a number of sources. As early as 1913, Webb, in factoring a battery of tests, along with a number of ratings which attempted to appraise traits of character, was able to extract a factor "W." "W" in a broad sense seemed to relate to a moral and conative propensity, which he called conscientiousness or purposeful consistency. A few years later, in Spearman's own laboratory, Lankes and Wynn Jones demonstrated the existence of another non-intellective factor, "p," or perseveration, which characterized their subjects tendency to resist changes in set, and which Spearman related to his law of inertia. In 1921, W. M. Brown discussed character traits as factors in intelligence tests, and in 1933, R. B. Cattell reported correlations between tests of temperament and ratings in intelligence. But perhaps the most crucial findings are those of W. P. Alexander who, in an extensive factor analysis of a large series of verbal

and performance tests, supplemented by tests of achievement and academic marks, showed that in addition to the now familiar *g,* V (verbal ability), and P (practical ability), a considerable portion of variance had to be ascribed to two other extracted factors, namely, X and Z. X was a factor which determined the individual's interests and "concerns," in Alexander's words, "temperament rather than ability"; while Z was "an aspect of temperament related to achievement," in the case of Alexander's subjects, to school achievement.

The factor loadings of X and Z varied greatly from test to test, but even some of Spearman's ostensibly pure tests of *g* contained some Z and nearly all the performance tests showed considerable X or Z loadings. As might be expected, these factors played an even greater role in academic or technical achievement. For success in science, for example, the X factor loading was .74,[1] as against only .36 for *g,* and for English .48 as against .43 for the *g* loading. From these findings one might even infer that lack of intellectual ability, beyond a certain point, accounts for relatively little of school failures. Indeed Dorothea McCarthy recently offered the "hypothesis," and I quote, "that emotional insecurity . . . is the basic cause of most educational disabilities and learning failures, which are not due to mental defect."

What are we to make of these two findings? First, that factors other than intellectual contribute to achievement in areas where, as in the case of learning, intellectual factors have until recently been considered uniquely determinate, and, second, that these other factors have to do with functions and abilities hitherto considered traits of personality. Among those partially identified so far are factors relating primarily to the conative functions like drive, persistence, will, and perseveration, or in some instances, to aspects of temperament that pertain to interests and achievement. This, to be sure, is just the beginning, but one of the reasons that not much more has been done is that psychologists have continued to assume that personality has little to do with intelligence. To Thurstone as well

[1] This is a correlation between a measure of success in science and the *x* factor. It is a positive correlation (+), and the plus sign is taken for granted. See the Glossary for an explanation of correlation (Ed.).

as to Spearman, general intelligence seems to be first and foremost a cognitive function, by Spearman to be accounted for by a single pervasive factor, by Thurstone by a number of factors.

It is curious that the clinical psychologist, so little impressed by or, at least, so little conversant with factor analysis, has almost from the start dealt with intelligence test findings as if the personality components in intelligence were already an established fact. For what does psychological diagnosis on the basis of intelligence test findings consist of but inferring adjustive capacities of the subject as a personna? It appears that the clinician, like the character in Molière's *"Malade Imaginaire,"* has been speaking prose all his life without knowing it.

One might add that diagnosing personality and personality disorder, at the level it is being done, is not very difficult. Practically every good individual test of intelligence lends itself to such application to a greater or lesser degree, the Bellevue Scales and the new Children's Test of Intelligence perhaps a little more readily. This does not mean that they are tests of personality, but they do suggest that our intelligence tests contain elements which are essentially factors of the personality as a whole rather than of specific cognitive abilities. When the neurotic does poorly on the Digit Span Test, it is not because of defective memory, but generally because of a basic anxiety mobilized by the test, as by any other situation, in which he is seemingly on trial. Conversely, when a mental defective does relatively well on the Maze Test, it is generally not because he has better planning ability, but because he is less impulsive. Similarly, a large variety of traits and personality factors may be inferred from test performance—for example, energy level from a subject's performance on the Digit Symbol, asocial tendencies from general comprehension, masculinity-femininity from the picture completion test. These are only a few of the traits and diagnostic constellations with which every clinician who has done psychological diagnosis is familiar.

The point here is not that personality traits can be discovered in psychometric performance, or, what needs no special argument, that personality and abnormal conditions influence intelligence test findings, but that personality traits *enter into* the effectiveness of intelligent behavior, and, hence, into any global concept of intelligence itself. It is one thing if a child does poorly on an intelligence test because he is disinterested or upset and quite another if he is congenitively impulsive or emotionally unstable.

One would naturally suppose that if intelligence is a function of the personality as a whole, one should find significant positive or negative correlations with measures of personality itself. Such, indeed, are the findings, but the results are extremely hard to evaluate. This is in part due to the fact that the studies in this area have been done primarily with the intent of discovering the extent to which intelligence accounts for variance in personality. In an article which appeared in 1940, Irving Lorge reviews the studies published to that date on the general relationship between measures of intelligence and various measures or estimates of personality. The personality tests included most of the current and older inventories (Woodworth, Laird, Thurstone, Bernreuter, Allport, et al), as well as the association experiment and the personality measures of Hartshorn, May, and Maller. Some 200 correlation coefficients were analyzed. The range of coefficients[2] was from +.70 to −.49 with a median of +.04. Disregarding the signs, half of the ratios were between .00 and .15, and one quarter of them .30 and above. Lorge's general feeling about the findings is that the range is so "extraordinary that anybody can make any statement." Nevertheless, his conclusion is "that some correlation between intelligence and personality exists."

All this is rather meager fare, but the findings are perhaps as satisfactory as could be expected. Apart from the known unreliability of paper-and-pencil inventories, there is the more disturbing fact of their uncertain validity and relevance. At times they do not measure the traits claimed for them, at others they measure only small segments of the personality, although in different ways; and at still other times, traits which are purely nominal. The latter, for example, was shown by Flanagan to be the case with the Bernreuter Inventory di-

[2] See the Glossary for an explanation of correlation coefficients (Ed.).

chotomies. In the original publication the test was scored for six different traits, which by factorialization were then reduced to two.

Flanagan's study is a good example of how factor analysis aids us in getting at basic components. Mere evidence of concomitant variation is not enough; in fact, it is often misleading. For example, defective hearing may have a measurable effect on both learning arithmetic and size of vocabulary, but, obviously, has no basic relation to either arithmetical reasoning or verbal ability. A variable to be basic and scientifically significant must be independent. In the case of man's cognitive functions, these independent variables, in so far as they are relevant to general intelligence, have been pretty well identified. It may be possible to add one or two to Thurstone's list, but not many more. Those of personality are yet to be discovered. We have some knowledge of what the factors to be measured are likely to be, some on the basis of researches like those of Webb, Alexander, Guilford, Cattell, and Eysenck, others on the basis of general observation and clinical experience. The latter have thus far gone unrecognized, not only because we have no tests for them but because clinicians, like their more academic colleagues, still think of intelligence as consisting primarily of cognitive abilities. Any bit of behavior that seems concerned with or related to instinct, impulse, or temperament is ipso facto considered as having no direct relation to general intelligence.

Such, for example, is curiosity. This was one of the traits which Terman in his studies of genius found most frequently among his gifted children. But he did not have, nor do we as yet have, any test of curiosity. No attempt has been made to extract curiosity as a factor of intelligence. We all know how important curiosity is for biologic adaptation as well as scientific achievement. It is, to quote McDougall, "at the basis of many of man's most splendid achievements, for rooted in it are his speculative and scientific tendencies," and ". . . in men in whom curiosity is innately strong, it may become the main source of intel-

lectual energy and effort." But what is curiosity? "It is the impulse to approach and examine more closely the object which attracts it," that is an instinct, and according to McDougall, one of the basic instincts.

One need not be afraid or ashamed to acknowledge impulse, instinct and temperament as basic factors in general intelligence. It is indeed because I believe they are that I have brought before you the arguments and evidence presented. My main point has been that general intelligence cannot be equated with intellectual ability, but must be regarded as a manifestation of the personality as a whole. I have tried to show that factors other than intellectual enter into our concept of general intelligence, and that in everyday practice, we make use of them knowingly or not.

What is needed is that these factors be rigorously appraised. Factor analysis has been emphasized because, at present, it is the only method which enables us to demonstrate and discover independent variables. We already have some clues as to what the non-intellective but relevant factors of intelligence may be. What we now need are tests which not only identify but measure them. This in effect demands broadening our concept of general intelligence and calls for a revised psychometric to measure these added variables as sub-tests of all general intelligence scales.

To say that general intelligence can be social and practical, as well as abstract, was just a beginning. We had to know what basic components of the mind were responsible for making an individual effective in one rather than in another area.

To realize that general intelligence is the function of the personality as a whole and is determined by emotion and conative factors is also just a beginning. We now need to know what non-intellective factors are relevant and to what degree. This is the task which lies immediately before us.

What Is a Trait of Personality?

Gordon W. Allport

Gordon Allport (1897–1967) was Professor of Psychology at Harvard University, from which he received his Ph.D. in 1922. A past president of the American Psychological Association, Allport was the author of many articles and books in psychology. He was especially interested in the psychology of prejudice and was well known for the Study of Values test he devised with the assistance of colleagues Vernon and Lindzey.

1. Allport feels that reflexes and habits are not basic units in the study of human behavior. What school of psychology is he criticizing when he makes this statement? What school does he seem to fall within?

2. How does Allport handle the criticism that the doctrine of traits is disproved when a person is judged with a trait of neatness in dress but is found to keep a sloppy and disordered desk?

At the heart of all investigation of personality lies the puzzling problem of the nature of the unit or element which is the carrier of the distinctive behavior of a man. *Reflexes* and *habits* are too specific in reference, and connote constancy rather than consistency in behavior; *attitudes* are ill-defined, and as employed by various writers refer to determining tendencies that range in inclusiveness from the *Aufgabe* to the *Weltanschauung; dispositions* and *tendencies* are even less definitive. But *traits,* although appropriated by all manner of writers for all manner of purposes, may still be salvaged, I think, and limited in their reference to a certain definite conception of a generalized

From Gordon W. Allport, "What Is a Trait of Personality?" *Journal of Abnormal and Social Psychology,* 25, No. 4 (1931), 368–372.

response-unit in which resides the distinctive quality of behavior that reflects personality. Foes as well as friends of the doctrine of traits will gain from a more consistent use of the term.

The doctrine itself has never been explicitly stated. It is my purpose with the aid of eight criteria to define *trait,* and to state the logic and some of the evidence for the admission of this concept to good standing in psychology.

1. *A trait has more than nominal existence.* A trait may be said to have the same kind of existence that a habit of a complex order has. Habits of a complex, or higher, order have long been accepted as household facts in psychology. There is no reason to believe that the mechanism which produces such habits (integration, *Gestaltung,* or whatever it may be) stops short of producing the more generalized habits which are here called traits of personality.

2. *A trait is more generalized than a habit.* Within a personality there are, of course, many independent habits; but there is also so much integration, organization, and coherence among habits that we have no choice but to recognize great systems of interdependent habits. If the habit of brushing one's teeth can be shown, statistically or genetically, to be unrelated to the habit of dominating a tradesman, there can be no question of a common trait involving both

these habits; but if the habit of dominating a tradesman can be shown, statistically or genetically, to be related to the habit of bluffing one's way past guards, there is the presumption that a common trait of personality exists which includes these two habits. Traits may conceivably embrace anywhere from two habits to a legion of habits. In this way, there may be said to be major, widely extensified traits, and minor, less generalized traits in a given personality.

3. *A trait is dynamic, or at least determinative.* It is not the stimulus that is the crucial determinant in behavior that expresses personality; it is the trait itself that is decisive. Once formed a trait seems to have the capacity of directing responses to stimuli into characteristic channels. This emphasis upon the dynamic nature of traits, ascribing to them a capacity for guiding the specific response, is variously recognized by many writers. The principle is nothing more than that which has been subscribed to in various connections by Woodworth, Prince, Sherrington, Coghill, Kurt Lewin, Troland, Lloyd Morgan, Thurstone, Bentley, Stern, and others. From this general point of view traits might be called "derived drives" or "derived motives." Whatever they are called they may be regarded as playing a motivating role in each act, thus endowing the separate adjustments of the individual to specific stimuli with that *adverbial* quality that is the very essence of personality.

Some psychologists may balk at the doctrine of the absorption of driving power into the integrated mechanism of traits. If so, it is equally possible, without violence to the other criteria of this paper, to accept the view that a trait is a generalized neural set which is activated ecphorically or redintegratively. But it seems to me that this second doctrine is only slightly less dynamic than the first. The difference is simply one between trait considered as a drive aroused through the operation of a specific stimulus, and trait conceived as powerfully directive when an effective stimulus arouses the organism to action.

4. *The existence of a trait may be established empirically or statistically.* In order to know that a person has a *habit* it is necessary to have evidence of repeated reactions of a constant type. Similarly in order to know that an individual has a trait it is necessary to have evidence of repeated reactions which, though

not necessarily constant in type, seem none the less to be consistently a function of the same underlying determinant. If this evidence is gathered casually by mere observation of the subject or through the reading of a case-history or biography, it may be called empirical evidence.

More exactly, of course, the existence of a trait may be established with the aid of statistical techniques that determine the degree of coherence among the separate responses. Although this employment of statistical aid is highly desirable, it is not necessary to wait for such evidence before speaking of traits, any more than it would be necessary to refrain from speaking of the habit of biting fingernails until the exact frequency of the occurrence is known. Statistical methods are at present better suited to intellective than to conative functions, and it is with the latter that we are chiefly concerned in our studies of personality.

5. *Traits are only relatively independent of each other.* The investigator desires, of course, to discover what the fundamental traits of personality are, that is to say, what broad trends in behavior do exist independently of one another. Actually with the test methods and correlational procedures in use, completely independent variation is seldom found. In one study expansion correlated with extroversion to the extent of $+.39$,[1] ascendance with conservatism, $+.22$, and humor with insight, $+.83$, and so on. This overlap may be due to several factors, the most obvious being the tendency of the organism to react in an integrated fashion, so that when concrete acts are observed or tested they reflect not only the trait under examination, but also simultaneously other traits; several traits may thus converge into a final common path. It seems safe, therefore, to predict that traits can never be completely isolated for study, since they never show more than a relative independence of one another.

In the instance just cited, it is doubtful whether humor and insight (provided their close relationship is verified in subsequent studies) represent distinct traits. In the future perhaps it may be possible to agree upon a certain magnitude of correlation below which it will be acceptable to speak of *separate* traits,

[1] See the Glossary for an explanation of correlation coefficients (Ed.).

and above which *one* trait only will be recognized. If one trait only is indicated it will presumably represent a broadly generalized disposition. For example, if humor and insight cannot be established as independent traits, it will be necessary to recognize a more inclusive trait, and name it perhaps "sense of proportion."

6. *A trait of personality, psychologically considered, is not the same as moral quality.* A trait of personality may or may not coincide with some well-defined, conventional, social concept. Extroversion, ascendance, social participation, and insight are free from preconceived moral significance, largely because each is a word newly coined or adapted to fit a psychological discovery. It would be ideal if we could in this way find our traits first and then name them. But honesty, loyalty, neatness, and tact, though encrusted with social significance, *may* likewise represent true traits of personality. The danger is that in devising scales for their measurement we may be bound by the conventional meanings, and thus be led away from the precise integration as it exists in a given individual. Where possible it would be well for us to find our traits first, and then seek devaluated terms with which to characterize our discoveries.

7. *Acts, and even habits, that are inconsistent with a trait are not proof of the nonexistence of the trait.* The objection most often considered fatal to the doctrine of traits has been illustrated as follows: "An individual may be habitually neat with respect to his person, and characteristically slovenly in his handwriting or the care of his desk."

In the first place this observation fails to state that there are cases frequently met where a constant level of neatness is maintained in all of a person's acts, giving unmistakable empirical evidence that the trait of neatness is, in some people at least, thoroughly and permanently integrated. All people must not be expected to show the same degree of integration in respect to a given trait. *What is a major trait in one personality may be a minor trait, or even nonexistent in another personality.*

In the second place, we must concede that there may be opposed integrations, *i.e.,* contradictory traits, in a single personality. The same individual may have a trait *both* of neatness *and* of carelessness, of ascendance *and* submission, although frequently of unequal strength.

In the third place there are in every personality instances of acts that are unrelated to existent traits, the product of the stimulus and of the attitude of the moment. Even the characteristically neat person may become careless in his haste to catch a train.

But to say that not all of a person's acts reflect some higher integration, is not to say that no such higher integrations exist.

8. *A trait may be viewed either in the light of the personality which contains it, or in the light of its distribution in the population at large.* Each trait has both its unique and its universal aspect. In its unique aspect, the trait takes its significance entirely from the role it plays in the personality as a whole. In its universal aspect, the trait is arbitrarily isolated for study, and a comparison is made between individuals in respect to it. From this second point of view traits merely extend the familiar field of the psychology of individual differences.

There may be relatively few traits, a few hundred perhaps, that are universal enough to be scaled in the population at large; whereas there may be in a single personality a thousand traits distinguishable to a discerning observer. For this reason, after a scientific schedule of universal traits is compiled, there will still be the field of *artistic* endeavor for psychologists in apprehending correctly the subtle and unique traits peculiar to one personality alone, and in discovering the *pattern* which obtains *between* these traits in the same personality.

Gifted Men: Scientists and Nonscientists

Lewis M. Terman

Lewis Terman (1877–1956) received his Ph.D. from Clark University in 1905. In 1916 he developed the Stanford Revision of the Binet-Simon Intelligence Scale. During World War I he was one of several psychologists actively engaged in developing selection procedures for army recruits. He was president of the American Psychological Association in 1923. In 1925 Terman published the first volume of his now famous Genetic Studies of Genius. *He is best known for his pioneer work in intelligence measurement and his longitudinal study of the gifted.*

1. Before reading this selection, try to predict what environmental factors would differentiate gifted scientists from gifted nonscientists. Check your predictions as you read.

2. The intellectual ability of this group of gifted men increased from age 29 to 41. How might you account for this?

I. Sources of Data Used

The subjects in this study were the approximately 800 male members of a gifted group who were selected in childhood on the basis of an intelligence test and whose careers have been followed for 30 years. As children all had made intelligence scores that rated them in the top 1 per cent for their respective ages. Four field studies of the group have been made: (a) at the time most of them were selected in 1921–22; (b) in 1927–28; (c) in 1939–40; and (d) in 1950–51. On each of these occa-

Abridged from L. M. Terman, "Scientists and Nonscientists in a Group of 800 Gifted Men," *Psychological Monographs,* 68, No. 7 (1954), 1–4, 35–41. Copyright 1954 by the American Psychological Association and reproduced by permission.

sions field assistants administered a variety of tests in addition to tests of intelligence, and collected extensive case history information from the subjects and from their parents and teachers. Apart from the field studies the group has been followed up from time to time by sending a General Information Blank to be filled out by each subject and a Home Information Blank to be filled out by a parent or other relative. By these means almost continuous contact has been maintained with all but a few of the subjects, including slightly more than 800 males and 600 females. Of the entire group (both sexes) only some 30 subjects have been lost track of. The 800 males here reported upon do not include any who were deceased before 1940.

As this group is the only one of its kind that has been studied so intensively over so long a period of time (and at a total cost of a quarter of a million dollars), it seemed desirable to sift all the data collected to 1951 in order to find what items of information might differentiate between those who became scientists and those who did not, and between various subgroups of the scientists. This search has been limited to males because only a small number of the gifted women became scientists.

II. Classification of Subjects

In the autumn of 1951 the educational and vocational records of all the male subjects were examined as a basis for classifying them into groups for comparative study. Dr. F. E. Terman, Dean of the School of Engineering at Stanford University, gave helpful advice on the classification of doubtful cases. The groups then decided upon were as follows:

1. Men with a considerable record of basic research in a field of physical science or engineering ($N = 51$).
2. Engineers who had done research that was primarily applied rather than basic ($N = 27$).
3. Engineers whose work had involved no appreciable amount of research of any kind ($N = 77$).
4. Men with a record of research in a biological science or in medicine ($N = 26$).
5. A medical group engaged chiefly in the practice of medicine with only incidental research or none ($N = 35$).
6. A group whose undergraduate majors were in a physical or biological science but whose later careers involved little or no research in any field ($N = 68$).
7. Men who as undergraduates had majored in one of the social sciences but whose later careers involved no research of importance ($N = 200$).[1]
8. Men whose undergraduate majors were in the various fields of the humanities ($N = 127$).
9. Men who had not attended college or had attended less than three years ($N = 177$). Because of limited schooling this group was not regarded as comparable with the other groups and for this reason was omitted from the statistical evaluation of group differences.

After the case history data to 1940 had been coded and punched for IBM treatment, the cards were sorted for the first eight groups listed above and group comparisons were made by the chi-square technique on some 250 items of information. By the time this had been done, an examination of the results suggested the desirability of revising the original classification of the subjects despite the amount of recomputation this would involve. The changes made and the reasons therefore were as follows:

---

[1] There was also a group of 19 men who had engaged extensively in social science research, but this group has been omitted from the study because of its small size and heterogeneous make-up.

1. The two groups of engineers (numbered 2 and 3 in the above list) were combined into a single group. There were two reasons why this seemed desirable: (*a*) on most of the items of information the statistical results for the two groups agreed so closely as to indicate that they belonged together; and (*b*) combining them would make a sizable group of 104 subjects.
2. The second change was to combine the medical practitioners with the group that had done research in medicine or biology (groups 5 and 4 above). The reasons for this change are the same as for combining the two groups of engineers; that is, few items of information differentiated between the researchers and the medical practitioners, and combining them provided an N of 61.
3. The third change involved taking 51 lawyers who had majored in a social science out of the social science group (number 7 above) and combining these with 32 lawyers who had majored in the humanities (number 8 above), thus forming a separate group of 83 lawyers without regard to their undergraduate major. The desirability of putting lawyers in a group of their own is indicated by the fact that a good many items of information clearly differentiate them from the social science group on the one hand and from the humanities group on the other.

With these changes the groups to be compared are reduced from eight to seven. The make-up of the groups as they now stand will be described in the paragraphs that follow.

1. *Physical Science Research* ($N = 51$). This group, designated PSR, is composed of men who were doing or had done basic research in any field of physical science. It includes 18 engineers, 17 chemists, 9 physicists, 3 geologists, 2 astronomers, and 1 each in mathematics and oceanography. Thirty-two of the group had taken the degree of Ph.D. or Sc.D. Other graduate degrees included E.E. or C.E., 5; M.A. or M.S., 6. Eight of the group held only a bachelor's degree, though some of these had done considerable graduate work.

2. *Engineers* ($N = 104$). The E group as now constituted includes 27 men who are doing or have done applied research and 77 who are practicing engineers with no research record. Fields of engineering most frequently represented are mechanical, 25; civil, 24; chemical, 19; electrical, 14; architectural, 7; aeronautical, 5; six other fields, 10. However, several of these practicing engineers could be almost equally well classified in either of two fields. Of the total E group, 21 have one or more graduate degrees, 60 have a bachelor's degree only (though of these 6 have had one or more years of graduate work), and 23 have no degree. On

the whole, group E rates far below the PSR group in scientific training and achievement.

3. *Medical-Biological* ($N = 61$). The M-B group includes 26 who have done medical or biological research and 35 doctors of medicine who are engaged chiefly in medical practice. Fields of research represented by the research group include anatomy, biochemistry, fisheries, general biology, criminology, microbiology, Oriental diseases, pharmacology, physiology, psychiatry, public health, and surgery. The 35 practitioners include (according to their own designations) 12 general practitioners, 9 surgeons, 3 internists, 2 ophthalmologists, 2 psychiatrists, 2 radiologists, an anaesthetist, a gynecologist, a pediatrician, a laboratory director, and a medical director of a state-wide medical group-insurance service. Degrees held by the total M-B group of 61 are as follows: M.D., 48; Ph.D., 11; M.A. plus three years, 1; A.B. plus three years, 1. Of those who hold the M.D., one has also the D.P.H., one the M.P.H., and one the Sc.D. About half of the members of the M-B group have taught either in medical schools or in other university departments. Seven are, or have been, heads of departments.

4. *Physical or Biological Science, Nonresearch* ($N = 68$). This group, designated PBS, is composed of men who as undergraduates majored in a physical or biological science but who later in many cases turned to other fields of work. Their undergraduate majors classify as follows: chemistry, 15; engineering, 14; mathematics, 10; physics, 6; forestry, 5; and 1 to 3 each in astronomy, botany, dentistry, entomology, pharmacy, premedicine, and zoology. All are college graduates except 8 who had three or more years of college but took no degree. About half of the group had one to three years of graduate work. Four graduated from Annapolis and 2 from West Point. Eleven of the group are teachers of science (5 in high schools, 4 in junior colleges, and 2 in colleges). Some 30 of the others are or have been engaged in work more or less related to their science major; among these are a few who have at one time or another been employed as engineers or chemists and several who have become sales managers, superintendents, or manufacturers. However, some of the PBS group have entered vocations that make little or no use of their science training; among these are 2 ranchers, a realtor, a jeweler,

a professor of Greek who had majored in engineering, a professor of education who had majored in physics, a premedical graduate who is a lithographer, an engineer who is an investment banker, an advertising executive, and 3 chemistry majors of whom one became an accountant, one a personnel expert, and one the proprietor of an automobile agency. Another, who took a master's degree in engineering, is one of America's best-known writers of science fiction. This is one case in which the science training paid off despite a radical shift from the original goal. There is reason to believe that several members of the PBS group should never have chosen a science major.

5. *Social Scientists* ($N = 149$). The SS group is composed of men who majored in one of the social sciences but have not, to any appreciable extent, engaged in research. The most frequent undergraduate majors were economics and political science, with smaller numbers in business, history, psychology, and anthropology. Fifteen of the SS group left college without taking a degree. A majority of those who graduated had one to three years of graduate work. The greatest number of graduate degrees were in business administration, with smaller numbers in economics, history, political science, psychology, education, and journalism. The group includes some 110 whose postcollege careers have been confined chiefly to business. The business fields most frequently represented are accounting, banking and investments, management (including office managers, superintendents, presidents, vice-presidents, and owners), sales and sales management, ranching, statistics, and government specialists in economics. Among those who entered other fields than business are 8 who teach in high schools or colleges, 5 journalists, 3 prominent members of the U.S. Department of State, and 3 outstanding radio writers or producers. The 20 others not engaged in business are distributed in a dozen miscellaneous occupations.

6. *Lawyers* ($N = 83$). A large majority of the L group are engaged in general practice, though several have specialized in such fields as corporation law, motion picture law, petroleum law, taxation, etc. Three of the lawyers are now judges and another is a director and vice-

president of a leading aircraft industry. Several members of the group have taught for a time in law schools. One has served several years as a state legislator and is now state controller. Three are employed by the federal government and three by the Army or Navy. Although most of the L group rate high in professional success, 4 or 5 are not engaged in any kind of legal work.

7. *The Humanities Group* (*N* = 95). The H group is composed of men who as undergraduates majored in a field of the humanities. The majors most frequent were English, 30; philosophy, 15; languages, 14; art, 11; and music, 7. The remaining 18 majors were scattered among five different fields, including architecture, education, prelaw, journalism, and theology. Twenty of the group left college after completing the junior year. Of the 75 who graduated, 12 continued to the Ph.D. (or Th.D.), 20 to the M.A., and 5 took other professional degrees. Fourteen others completed from one to three years of graduate work without taking a graduate degree. By recent occupation the group classifies as follows: 28 educators (15 college teachers, 9 high school teachers, and 4 administrators), 23 in higher business occupations (5 public relation specialists, 4 executives in business or industry, 4 advertising executives, 3 investment and security brokers or analysts, 3 controllers or accounting executives, 2 tax analysts, 1 sales manager, and 1 insurance analyst), 7 authors or journalists, 6 clergymen, 5 in sales or clerical work, 3 motion picture or radio writers or directors, 3 librarians, 3 small business owners, 3 in skilled trades, 2 in protective service occupations, 2 artists, an Army officer, an actor, an architect, a landscape architect, and a farmer. Three are not employed because of ill health and 2 are recently deceased.

The noncollege group (hereinafter designated as NC) is composed of 177 men who did not attend college or attended less than three years. Slightly more than a third of the group (69) discontinued their schooling with high school or had less than a year of additional business or technical training; 67 had one year of college and/or additional specialized professional or technical training, and 41 had 2 years

of college. Some of the latter group also had further training along special lines. By recent vocation they classify as follows: in business occupations, 50 (including 15 who are executives in business or industry; 12 in banking, finance, or insurance; 11 in accounting, auditing, statistics, cost analysis, etc.; 8 in technical sales work, sales engineering, or sales management; and 4 in advertising or public relations). Thirty are in skilled trades or retail business and 16 in clerical or sales work. Ten are in the entertainment field (3 writers and producers for radio and television, 2 motion picture directors, and 5 musicians), 6 are officers in police or fire departments, 4 are farmers, 4 are authors or journalists, and 4 are Army or Navy officers. The remainder are distributed among a variety of occupations with only 1 or 2 in each. Among these are a clergyman, an engineer, and a school teacher, as well as a bartender and a truck driver. Two are not employed for health reasons, and 11 are deceased, of whom 3 were war casualties.

Although the NC group was not included in the chi-square evaluation of group differences, the status of this group on most of the variables will be given for the information of readers who may be interested in comparing it with the other groups.

III. Summary

It remains to bring together the outstanding difference trends among our compared groups, especially differences between the science groups (PSR, E, and M-B) on the one hand and the nonscience groups (SS, L, and H) on the other.

For purpose of summary the differences fall roughly into five categories relating respectively to (a) family background, (b) abilities evidenced, (c) vocational interest scores, (d) social adjustment, and (e) occupational success and life satisfactions. For the more important variables under each of these categories the groups ranking very high and those ranking very low (in percentage frequencies) will be indicated. As a rule only the differences that are statistically significant will be cited.

Family Background

Eight variables in this category that yielded significant differences will be noted. For convenience in referring to them they are here listed and numbered.

1. Both parents were native-born;
2. The father's education included college graduation or more;
3. The father as of 1928 was in the professional class;
4. The father's areas of interests included two or more;
5. The mother's areas of interests included two or more;
6. The father has held (as of 1922) one or more positions of honor or trust;
7. The father has held (as of 1922) a religious position of honor or trust;
8. The subject (as of 1940) had two or more sibs, living or dead.

Group PSR is highest of all the groups on variables 1, 2, and 3, and is lowest on 8. Group E is lowest on variables 2 and 5, and high on none. Group M-B is highest on variable 6, is tied for highest on variable 8, and is close to highest on 2; it is the lowest of all the groups, however, on variable 4. Group PBS is highest on 4, lowest on 6 and 7, and second lowest on 3. Group SS is highest on 5, close to highest on 4, and lowest on 3. Group L is highest on 8 and close to highest on 2 and 4. Group H is highest on 7 and tied for highest on 4.

On the whole, it appears that the groups with the most favorable background are M-B and PSR, that those with the least favorable background are E and PBS, and that groups SS, L, and H hold an intermediate position.

Abilities Evidenced

Three special abilities described by the parent as superior in 1922 yielded highly reliable group differences. Highest on "mechanical ability" was group E with a frequency roughly twice that of SS, L, or H. Nearly tied for high on "nature study and science" were groups PSR and M-B, with frequencies nearly twice that of SS. On "dramatic ability" the situation was reversed, with groups H and L highest and groups PSR and E lowest.

On the number of parents who named some field of science as a suitable occupation for the child, groups PSR, E, and PBS were almost tied for top place with frequencies several times that of SS, L, or H. On teachers who suggested a science as a suitable occupation PSR was high-

est and M-B next highest, with lowest positions again occupied by SS, L, and H. On the child's preference for a science as an occupation, groups PSR, E, and M-B all had frequencies two or more times as high as SS, L, or H. On the child's specific choice of engineering as the preferred occupation, group E had a frequency over four times that of SS, L, or H.

Two ability tests have yielded significant differences. On a test of information in language and literature given in 1922, high scores were about three times as frequent in groups M-B and L as in group PSR. On the Concept Mastery test given in 1940 four groups (PSR, M-B, L, and H) were almost tied for top place, and groups PBS and SS were tied for low place.

The top groups on scholastic record, both in high school and college, were PSR and M-B; lowest in high school was SS and lowest in college were PBS and SS. On graduation from college before age 22, groups PSR, M-B, and L were tied for high place and groups E and PBS for low place.

Two fields on which subjects rated their interests in 1940 were science and mechanics. On interest in science the highest groups were PSR, E, and M-B, and the lowest SS and L. On interest in mechanics the high groups were E and PSR and the lowest SS, L, and H.

The above lines of evidence are well nigh unanimous in showing that early ability or interest in science is far more common among children who later become physical scientists, engineers, or biologists than among those who enter nonscientific fields. This has long been recognized but has not yet received the attention it deserves in educational and vocational guidance.

Vocational Interest Scores

The Strong blanks were scored for six kinds of scientists: chemist, engineer, psychologist, physician, architect, and math-science teacher. On every one of these occupations the PSR group was either highest or second highest in frequency of superior scores, group E was highest or second highest on three, and group M-B was highest or second highest on two. At the opposite extreme group SS ranked lowest or second lowest on all six, and group L was lowest or second lowest on five. The only one of the nonscience groups that rated high on any of these six occupations was group H, which scored second highest for architect.

Consider next the eight occupations of lawyer, author-journalist, artist, musician, minister, YMCA secretary, social-science teacher, and school superintendent. Here the situation was reversed, with the science groups ranking usually among the lowest. Group E was at the bottom in seven of the eight, and PSR near the bottom in two and high in none. Group M-B ranked second highest for two of these occupations (artist and minister) but neither very high nor very low in the others. At the other extreme, the highest or second highest rank was held by group H on six of these occupations, by group L on four, and by SS on two.

Then follow the data for eight business occupations, and on nearly all of these the three science groups ranked at or near the bottom. Exceptions were two high ranks for group E on purchasing agent and production manager. Group SS ranked highest on six of the eight business occupations and second highest on another; group L was highest on one and second highest on three. Group H, which most often ranked highest in the professional occupations discussed in the preceding paragraph, was among the lowest of all the groups on four business occupations and high on none.

Finally, on masculinity of interests the science groups ranked high and the nonscience groups low. On proportion scoring A in their own occupation, groups PSR and E were highest, and PBS lowest. On proportion who scored B+ or A on seven or more occupations, groups PSR and M-B were tied for top place and groups E and PBS were lowest.

In general the results of the vocational interest tests are clearly in line with the evidence offered in the preceding section of this summary.

Social Adjustment

There were some 18 variables that yielded significant group differences on matters related directly or indirectly to social adjustment. On a majority of these the nonscience groups made a better showing than the science groups. Most consistently high were groups L and SS; most consistently low were groups PSR and E. Data obtained in 1922 on four variables in this category put group L at the top on every one; these include sociality as rated by interest in plays and games, average of composite parent-teacher ratings on five social traits, and similar parent-teacher ratings on four moral and four volitional traits. The lowest or second lowest rank on all of these four variables is held by group E, and on two of them by PSR. Only one science group ranked as high as second from the top on any of the four; this was group M-B as rated by parents and teachers on social traits.

Data on social adjustment obtained in 1940 showed a similar picture. Participation in high school activities was greatest in groups L and H, and lowest in groups E and PSR. The self-rating on interest in politics showed group L highest and group E lowest. The self-rating on interest in social life showed groups SS and M-B almost equally high and group E again lowest. Also throwing light on social traits are the vocational interest scores on such "uplift" occupations as those of minister, YMCA secretary, social-science teacher, school superintendent, and life insurance salesman. On all but one of these occupations both the highest and next to highest ranks were held by groups SS, L, and H. The exception was group M-B which ranked second highest on score for minister. Group E was lowest or second lowest on all five of these occupations, and group PSR was lowest or second lowest on two of them.

The biographical blank filled out by subjects in 1951 furnished data for ten variables that yielded significant group differences on matters related to social adjustment. These include eight ratings on the following: interest in social success at ages 12–20, interest in outdoor sports at ages 12–20, social adjustment in childhood and youth, extent to which *S* felt "different" from other children, admiration for mother in childhood and youth, extent of affection and understanding between son and his father, extent to which *S* has suffered from inferiority feelings, and degree to which *S* has tended to conform to authority or convention (as contrasted with tendency to rebel). Two other variables were based on the proportion of *S*s who mentioned certain factors as having contributed to life accomplishment, the two factors that yielded significant group differences being "good social adjustment" and "good personality."

Here again the science groups tend to rate much lower than the nonscience groups. Group PSR was lowest of all the groups on six of the ten variables and second lowest on another. Group E was lowest or close to lowest on three and group M-B on four. The only high rank of a science group on any of these ten variables was that of group E, which was second on freedom from inferiority feelings. At the other extreme, group SS was highest for social adjustment on five of the ten variables and second highest on another. Group H was highest or second highest on four and group L on one. In the nonscience groups SS, L, and H, there was only a single variable on which one of these groups rated at the bottom for social adjustment; that was on feeling "different" from other children, most often reported by group H.

Occupational Success and Life Satisfactions

There are eight variables worth noting in this category that yielded significant group differences. These concern the proportion of subjects who—

1. reported that occupation was definitely chosen, not drifted into;
2. began first consideration of their life work before age 16;
3. chose the occupation that was first seriously considered;
4. reported an earned income of $10,000 or more in 1949;
5. checked their "work itself" as an aspect of life giving greatest satisfaction;
6. checked their "income" as an aspect of life giving greatest satisfaction;
7. reported that life offers satisfactory outlets for their mental capabilities;
8. double-checked "adequate education" as a factor in life success.

Highest place or close to highest went to group PSR on variables 2, 3, 5, 7, and 8; to group E on 2 and 3; and to group M-B on all except number 3. In the nonscience group L was highest or second highest on 1, 4, and 7. Group SS was lowest on 1, 2, 3, and 5; group H was lowest on 4 and 6, and second lowest on 2; group PBS was lowest on 4, 7, and 8.

The above summary of group differences has been confined to the seven groups utilized in the chi-square evaluations. On most of the variables data have also been presented for the NC group of 177 men who were excluded from the chi-square computations because of limited schooling. What are some of the characteristics of this group? Our percentage graph will enable the reader to compare it with each of the other seven groups on nearly all the variables discussed in the text. It is sufficient here to point out the individual variables which show a percentage frequency for the NC group radically divergent from the percentage frequency for the other seven groups combined. In the graph the latter frequency is given in the column headed "Total." Table 1 shows the more significant percentage differences between the "Total" column and the "NC" column.

The facts presented in Table 1 show that, compared to the other groups combined, the NC men (as a group) were from less cultured homes, achieved less in school, as adults test lower in intelligence, and are less successful vocationally. For two reasons, however, interpetation of the differences is by no means easy. In the first place, on a large majority of the hundred or so variables for which data have been presented, the NC group does not differ much, if at all, from the other groups combined. In the second place, it is impossible to say what is cause and what is effect. Are the NC men less successful vocationally chiefly because they had less education, or can the limited success in both school and vocation be accounted for largely by a general lack of ambition or drive? The latter has been a factor in many cases, and it is our opinion that educational background of the family has also played a part.

IV. Comments and Conclusions

As we have stated in an earlier section of this report, the value of our search for variables that would differentiate between scientists and nonscientists, and between different kinds of scientists, has been limited by the considerable heterogeneity of several of the individual groups. A more fundamental limitation is the fact that our study of gifted subjects undertaken in 1921 was not specifically designed to throw light on the problem with which we are here concerned. Its purpose was broader and much more general, namely: (a) to select children rating in the top 1 per cent for their respective ages in "general" intelligence; (b) to discover how a population thus selected compares with unselected children of corresponding age in family background and in such traits as physique, health, school achievement, interests, social adjustment, character, and personality; and (c) to follow the subjects for as many years as possible in order to check adult achievement against the promise of childhood and youth. The population selected with these ends in view numbered more than 1,500 subjects of both sexes and (with a few exceptions) ranged in age from 5 to 17 years.

A study and follow-up of gifted subjects for the express purpose of discovering the earlier and later correlates of achievement in science would need to differ in a number of respects from the 30-year study we have made. For one thing, it would be more economical to have, instead of a single group of subjects representing the generality of children with high IQ's, two gifted groups closely matched for superior IQ but otherwise as *unlike* as possible with respect to scientific promise. The selection of the two contrasting groups would need to be based largely on batteries of tests and ratings of special abilities and interests believed to be symptomatic of scientific talent. Group A should be composed entirely of subjects rating very high on a majority of the tests and ratings, group B of subjects rating very low on them. Preferably the age range of subjects when selected should be relatively narrow, perhaps from 8 to 12 years, and a single sex should be used to reduce the number of variables. The follow-up of two such groups would call for types of tests, interviews, questionnaires, and other procedures specially tailored to throw light on the degree of presence or absence of traits or behavior likely to be associated with scientific performances at later stages of development. A research of this kind undertaken now would have the great advantage of being able to use many techniques that did not exist 30 years ago or that existed then only in rudimentary form. Two groups, each of 300 subjects selected in the manner we have suggested and followed for a generation by the best techniques now available, would contribute far more to the prediction of scientific achievement

TABLE 1. COMPARISON OF NONCOLLEGE GROUPS WITH THE TOTAL OF OTHER GROUPS

ITEM	TOTAL	NC
	%	%
Father of S graduated from college	41	16
Father of S in professional class	35	16
Information quotient of S in language and literature 160 or higher, 1922	41	26
Recommended units at high school graduation 15 or more	88	63
Average college grade A or B (for those attending one year or more)	65	39
Concept Mastery score of S 110 or higher in 1940	43	19
Concept Mastery score of wife 110 or higher in 1940	38	20
S a member of two or more clubs or organizations, 1950	71	43
In childhood and youth more than moderate affection and understanding between father and son, report of S, 1951	38	24
Felt "different" from others in childhood and youth, report of S, 1951	57	45
Earned income of $10,000 or more for 1949	31	17
Occupation definitely chosen, not drifted into, report of S, 1940	65	39
First serious choice of life work was fulfilled, report of S, 1951	72	34
Checked "your work itself" as a source of life satisfaction, 1951	78	67
Had all the schooling he wanted at the time he left school, 1951 report	86	50
"Adequate education" double-checked as a source of life satisfaction, 1951 report	23	4

than would a much larger miscellaneous group selected only for high IQ and followed up by the kinds of shot-gun methods we have used.

Nevertheless, the present study of scientific achievement in our group of 800 men, despite its many inadequacies, has yielded valuable clues to many characteristic differences between scientists and nonscientists, and also to differences between groups of scientists. Especially significant for the purpose of counseling and guidance are the differences observable in childhood behavior, interests, and preoccupations that are found many years later to discriminate between scientists and nonscientists. The results we have obtained by Strong's vocational interest test argue strongly for the value of this test in vocational guidance, especially if later research confirms Strong's data on the relative permanence of an individual's interest patterns after the age of high school graduation. The group differences we have found on this test, given at the average age of 30 years, are all the more significant in view of the fact that very few of our men had been exposed to vocational counseling either in high school or college.

It is disappointing, however, that so many of the variables provided by the blank on Supplementary Biographical Data failed to yield significant group differences. It had been hoped that the ratings on parents and on parent-child relationships, together with other questions in the blank calling for information on factors influencing life achievement, might throw much-needed light on motivational factors. A few of these items proved to be discriminating but not enough of them to document what we believe to be the decisive role motivation has played in shaping the lives of these men. A new approach to this problem should be made when the next follow-up of the group is undertaken.

In closing we wish to call attention to a fact not primarily related to the purpose of this study; namely, the frequency of superior achievement in this group of 800 men, selected in childhood solely on the basis of high IQ, in comparison with what could have been expected of a group of 800 boys of corresponding age picked at random in the school population. The number who became research scientists, engineers, physicians, lawyers, or college teachers, or who were highly successful in business and other fields, is in each case many times the number a random group would have provided. But for the fact that a majority of our group reached college age shortly before or shortly after the beginning of the great depression, which prevented many from getting as much schooling as they would have obtained in normal times, the general level of achievement would have been even higher than it was.

Another fact that is of interest, though not germane to the purpose of the present study, is that the intellectual ability of the group, as measured by the Concept Mastery test, increased in the twelve-year period between 1939–40 and 1951–52. Form A of the test was given when the average age of the subjects was about 29 years, and Form B when the average was about 41. After the two forms of the test were equated for difficulty by administering them both to new populations (half in the AB and half in the BA order), Bayley and Oden analyzed the score changes of 772 gifted subjects who had taken both the earlier and the later test and found that the great majority of changes were in the upward direction. The average gain was statistically significant for both sexes, and for the older as well as for the younger subjects.

Suggested Readings

Allport, G. W. "Traits Revisited," *Amer. Psychol.*, 21 (1966), 1, 1–10.

Cronbach, L. J. *Essentials of Psychological Testing*. New York: Harper, 1960.

Guilford, J. P. *Personality*. New York: McGraw-Hill, 1959.

Harrell, T. W., and M. S. Harrell. "Army General Classification Test Scores for Civilian Occupations," *Educ. Psychol. Meas.*, 5 (1945), 229–239.

Jones, H. E., and H. S. Conrad. "The Growth and Decline of Intelligence," *Genet. Psychol. Monog.,* 13 (1933), 223–298.

Kallmann, F. J. *Heredity in Health and Mental Disorder,* New York: Norton, 1953.

Lee, E. S. "Negro Intelligence and Selective Migration," *Amer. soc. Rev.,* 16 (1951), 227–233.

OSS Assessment Staff. *Assessment of Men.* New York: Rinehart, 1948.

Terman, L. M., and M. A. Merrill. *Measuring Intelligence.* Boston: Houghton Mifflin, 1937.

Tyler, L. E. *The Psychology of Human Differences.* New York: Appleton-Century-Crofts, 1965.

Wechsler, D. *Measurement and Appraisal of Adult Intelligence.* Baltimore: Williams & Wilkins, 1958.

4   *Motivation*

Motivation is an abstraction and can be inferred only from observed behavior. The man who climbs to the top of the social ladder and the poor man who steals a loaf of bread to satisfy his hunger are both motivated individuals. Motivation is generally thought to be a force that maintains and guides a behavior until the initiating drive or quest has been satisfied. However, the strength of a motive and its duration may vary considerably among people.

Some theorists assume that many everyday behaviors can be understood if we trace a person's history and determine the degree to which his basic needs were initially satisfied. A more testable assumption is that physiological needs must be satisfied before higher-level needs can be realized. A hungry man is not motivated to love mankind. An explanation of the various theories and interpretations of motivation is best left to an introductory text. The readings in this chapter, however, substantially contribute to a better understanding of some of the theories, assumptions, and variations of motivation.

Hunger as a Source of Motivation, Harold Guetzkow and Paul H. Bowman. This selection focuses on the effects of food deprivation on behavior. An appreciation of the strength and persistence of the hunger drive can be gained by observing the behavioral changes that are induced by starvation. Guetzkow and Bowman describe an experiment, conducted at the University of Minnesota during World War II, in which 32 conscientious objectors were deprived of normal food intake.

Sex as a Source of Motivation, A. C. Kinsey, W. B. Pomeroy, and C. E. Martin. The second selection is taken from the Kinsey Report. Although Kinsey's research has been severely criticized for its poor sample design and uncontrolled interview conditions, the trends he identifies are probably realistic. This selection gives a good description of how the human male expends his sexual energy. The implications of the study, from the point of view of motivation, are perhaps obvious enough.

Pleasure Centers in the Brain, James Olds. Olds demonstrates the exciting possibility that certain areas of the brain are centers of motivation. The research subjects are rats that gratify themselves by the self-stimulation of their brains with electricity. This experiment demonstrates that a given stimulus—in this case electricity—is neither always noxious nor always pleasurable; it can be either. This selection further suggests that the real wonders of nature are within the organism itself.

The Achievement Motive, David C. McClelland. The three articles to follow are concerned with higher-order concepts of what motivates behavior. McClelland writes on the topic of achievement motives, which are considered so important in our striving American culture. The need to achieve is measured by means of fantasy stories elicited from subjects after they have viewed projective-test pictures. McClelland believes that similar procedures can, theoretically, be applied to the measurement of any other motive.

The Motivating Properties of Dissonance, Leon Festinger. A great deal of research has been conducted to test the hypotheses that Festinger proposes in this introduction to his theory of cognitive dissonance. In his own words, Festinger states, "I am proposing that dissonance, that is, the existence of nonfitting relations among cognitions, is a motivating factor in its own right." For this reason Festinger's work on cognitive dissonance has been included in this chapter, rather than in Chapters 7 and 8, which deal with the thinking process.

The Autonomy of Motives, Gordon W. Allport. The final selection is a discussion of the nature of motives. Proponents of the principle of functional autonomy argue that certain behaviors are maintained long after the initiating stimulus that produced them has been removed. Although this selection presents the evidence and rationale for the functional-autonomy principle, a question still persists: Do old habits become self-motivating, as Allport proposes, or do new motives take the place of the original ones?

Hunger as a Source of Motivation

Harold Guetzkow and Paul H. Bowman

Harold Guetzkow is Professor of Psychology and Political Science at Northwestern University. He received his Ph.D. from the University of Michigan in 1948 and is presently working on the computer simulation of international processes and problems. Paul Bowman graduated in clinical psychology from the University of Chicago and is presently Executive Director of a preventive community and school mental health program in Quincy, Illinois.

1. Do you think a starving person can be motivated to behave in some desired way without being fed? Please explain.

2. Are there behaviors or areas of life not affected in some way by the hunger state?

Changes in Motivation

In normal living there is an ebb and flow among the drives and impulses, first one dominating, then another. In starvation this pleasant balancing process is upset, and the hunger drive gradually dominates more and more of the person's activities and thoughts. Concomitant with this is a lessening of other drives, such as the diminution of sexual urges.

Hunger differs radically from the delightful nuances of appetite. Seldom do normal people clearly separate the two; never have they experienced the depth and omnipresence of dull, gnawing hunger pains. This kind of hunger is induced by the body consuming itself, such as leg and arm tissues wasting away.

When food is supplied, the individual is often caught between his desire to gulp it down rav-

Abridged from H. Guetzkow and P. H. Bowman, *Men and Hunger: A Psychological Manual for Relief Workers* (Elgin, Illinois: The Brethren Press, 1946), pp. 23–43. Reprinted by permission of the publisher.

enously and to consume the prized possession slowly, covetously, so that the flavor and odor of each morsel are fully appreciated. Some of our thirty-two grown men licked their plates to avoid waste. Toward the end of the semistarvation a number of the men would dawdle for two hours over a meal they had previously consumed in twenty minutes. No matter how the food was eaten, usually each man would leave the dining hall with his hunger undiminished. Many of the men toyed with their food, making weird and seemingly distasteful concoctions. Cold macaroni sandwiches were prepared by some men to tide them over the long midday stretch which extended from early morning until the evening meal. But the thought that there was a sandwich in one's pocket was excruciating, and often a man would break his best resolutions and jealously eat it, basking in the exquisite aroma which clung to the cold macaroni. Throughout the six months of starvation this group of American men, accustomed to the variety of food that America provides, appreciated and enjoyed a monotonous menu of potatoes, turnips, rutabagas, dark bread, and macaroni. Hunger! Hunger! Hunger! They wondered whether this horrible nightmare would ever end.

Contrariwise, their sexual urge gradually decreased, and it was the rare individual who continued courtship at the end of the starvation. Budding romances collapsed, and some men wondered how they could have been so interested in *that* girl. One fellow's girl friend visited him from a distant city during the low days of starvation, and she found his ostensible affection disappointingly shallow. His reservoir of affectional responses was drying up.

It is difficult to delineate other types of basic motivations. The tendency for spontaneous activity which is universal in healthy adults was notably lacking. The men were tired and weak. The urge to get up and do something simply was not there; energy came niggardly. A man could not take two steps at a time going upstairs. He wondered if it were not foolish to make that side-excursion, because he did not have enough energy to do the things he wanted to do. Dancing was not fun—he would rather go to a movie. The men seldom fatigued in a healthy way; they felt old, stuporous.

Behavioral Consequences of the Physical Changes

The profound physical changes which were induced by the prolonged semistarvation had very noticeable effects upon behavior. An outstanding physical change was the 30% reduction in strength. Fellows who were used to sharing in all kinds of physical tasks were unable to do them any more. This was very discouraging. A person knew undeniably that he was losing ground: he was becoming debilitated. His bony, drawn face was ugly; he saw that in the mirror. When he chanced upon a prestarvation photograph of himself, he would look at it, and then feel surprised that he had changed so much. His gawking ribs and bulging collar bone were uncomfortable. He could not sit on wooden furniture, for his "cushions" were gone and the bony buttocks offered slight comfort. The pallor which masked his face could not be removed, even when he tried to tan himself in the sun. He was a sight unfit to be seen. At times he was ashamed of himself, in baggy clothes that never fit. He had to be careful in moving fast; if he arose too rapidly, he would sometimes "blackout" and faint. When he tried to go up stairs he needed to pause in the middle of them. Sometimes he failed to lift his leg high enough, and would fall flat on his face. Other times a sidewalk crack would trip him. Often he could not change his direction of movement fast enough, if he walked with an unstarved individual. He would weave while walking, and bump his companion; this was annoying. He did not like persons to touch his skin or caress him in any way. He wondered if the rapid loss of his hair was natural or had been accelerated by the starvation. He became cold quickly, for his body temperature had dropped about one degree. He seemed never to have enough blankets on the bed at night. His poor circulation meant that limbs would go to "sleep." Swollen legs made walking uncomfortable and running almost impossible. In the long run, it was better to stay near a radiator, whiling away the time in a soft rocker.

Changes in Emotionality

In the preceding discussion of basic motivational changes, the general lack of drive toward spontaneous activity was highlighted. The most important emotional change coincides with this motivational apathy; namely, that there was a dulling of the emotional response of the individual with concomitant depression. Humor was gone. The men did not sing or whistle of their own accord. Music did not bring its former warmth. The dejection was exhibited in the lack of conversation at mealtimes. The men had not talked themselves out, but lacked the spark that fires curiosity. They were not interested in the ideas or activities of others, except as they were related to food-getting activities. Gloominess permeated many of their relationships. Smiles were not frequent, and the saddened faces grew longer each week as hunger gave way to more hunger. They saw the negative side of things now more than ever before. If there was a job to be done, the hurdles seemed so high and abundant—"Is it worth it?"—and discouragement and lack of confidence often followed in the wake of encounters with the real world. One man discovered during rehabilitation a change which had gone unnoticed in semistarvation; he had not blushed or become really frightened during starvation.

Superficially, the increased irritability of the semistarving men contradicts the generalization that they were apathetic and introversive. The two characteristics, nevertheless, existed side by side. Occasionally the men were irritable; most often they tended to be dull and bored. Over-powering frustration existed in the very fabric of their personalities because of the constant food deprivation. This frustration seemed to dictate their behavior in other areas. Petty defeats became very important and were the source of much irritation. Standing in line at the diet kitchen before being served was the source of explosive conduct. Indecisiveness on the part of the servers would give rise to ire, and to the suspicion that perhaps the cooks did not know what their ration should really be. The men "blew up" at each other on occasion. Mannerisms which formerly went unnoticed now became sources of friction. One man talked too loudly, another with too much affec-tation. Some persons spent too much time eating, or perhaps indulged in the disgusting habit of telling visitors how poorly they felt. During the worst times certain men refused to sit with each other at the dining room tables. They even felt impelled to leave the table if their "annoyers" happened to sit at the one at which they were eating. One man firmly or-dered another to "get the h— out of here."

Their expressions of irritation were directed not only to those of their own number; the technical and administrative personnel who conducted the experiment drew their share of fire. One man commented in a letter to a friend, "I'm so hungry I could eat anything, but I'd start on the fat staff first." The men were annoyed at seeing the staff eat their lunches, and were still more annoyed when the staff tried to conceal the fact that they were eating— "There he sat, fat, hiding his lunch, while the aroma from his orange still permeated the air." One fellow conducted a nursery school young-ster to and from school each day, until her childish antics grew so irritating that he re-signed the job with the realization that his patience was meager and his self-control very limited.

This lack of control of irritability was one expression of a general lack of evenness or steadiness in mood. Although most often the men were silent and sad, on occasion they would become elated or feel "high." These periods of elation would last a few hours, or more often a few days. Some men would explain how good they felt, that maybe there was some quickening going on inside them from the starvation and

that finally they had adjusted to the reduced ration. But this feeling never persisted, and their discouragement upon having been let down accentuated the next low period. One of the men who was eliminated from the experi-ment because of his inability to maintain the dietary restrictions underwent a severe alterna-tion between despondency and unfounded feel-ings of well-being. One night when he lost control over himself, he stopped at seventeen drugstores on a hike from the edge of town back to the laboratory, having an uproariously good time at each soda fountain. He kidded with the fountain girls, thought the lights more beautiful than ever, felt that the world was a very happy place. The world was with him. This degenerated into a period of extreme pes-simism and remorse; he felt that he had nothing to live for, that he had failed miserably to keep his commitment of staying on reduced rations.

Weather and Moods

Such cyclic tendencies were markedly influenced by the weather; warm, sunny days brightened the spirits immeasurably, while cold, damp, cloudy days lowered the men further in their abyss of dejection.

Although these men had no more social reasons for insecurity during starvation than during the previous three months of standard-ization, a number of them experienced anxiety and insecurity reactions. For instance, one man wanted to have a little money in the bank; just having it there made him feel more at ease. In another individual this anxiety expressed itself in a restlessness, a feeling that he wanted to go somewhere, but he did not know where.

In general, the emotional changes which took place may be thought of as a combination of shallowness of emotion—the depression com-ponent—and lack of control, with the resultant escape into emotional outbursts and anxiety.

Changes in Sociability

One of the more profound changes which took place was the decreased sociability of the men. There were important exceptions to this, but even the men who managed to continue their social contacts often felt animosity toward strangers, merely because they were strangers. The men built up a tremendous in-group feeling that tended to exclude both their nonstarving friends and the administrative and technical staff. They were apart from others—those who had been well fed. They were especially alienated by the individual who supposed he knew what it was like to be hungry because he had gone without food for a couple of days. It was hard to sit near one's comrade who had extra food. They became provoked at the laboratory staff for giving "too much" food to some, and thought it criminal to restrict the rations of others, even though they clearly understood the experimental plan demanded such adjustments in rations.

Conversation with outsiders as well as among themselves degenerated in quality and lost its sparkle: they were a tired, dead group of men. They could not keep up the pace of conversations; questions often came too rapidly. Sometimes men were invited to parties; but they were not tactful, and they could not think of things to say; they really "didn't give a d— if they were bores," and would often find chairs by the fireplace in which to slouch away the rest of the evening. Often they realized they were not gentlemen in the gallant way they formerly had been, and they did not care. What difference did it make if they were unshaven and sloppily dressed? They would prefer to go to movies alone, while formerly a "show" was not real entertainment unless a companion could share in the fun. Humor often eases the tensions which arise in normal social situations, but these starving men lacked humor—they could not pull quips; they could not make light of things. Even in movies, slapstick comedy bored. They never had "belly-laughs." In a store when shopping, they were easily pushed around by the crowd. Their usual reaction was resignation.

Besides this more superficial type of inability to be sociable and co-operative, which widely pervaded the group as a whole, a few of the men were unable to remain voluntarily on the restricted diet throughout its entirety. Some of the violations were of a minor nature and did not jeopardize the experimental conclusions; in those few cases where major deviations occurred the subject was excluded from the experiment, or the data obtained was discarded. This deterioration of their ethical control was all the more remarkable because these men had shown themselves to be sincere and upright throughout the two or more years of work they had performed in civilian public service units before coming to the laboratory. The laboratory had run vitamin experiments with other conscientious objectors and had not once found evidence of any violation of dietary regimens. The semistarvation pressure of hunger was, however, too much—their very beings revolted against the restriction. One of the individuals not only bought food, but also stole some from "locked" storerooms. Another individual sublimated his food cravings by stealing china cups from coffee shops. Although fasting is said at times to quicken one spiritually, none of the men reported significant progress in their religious lives. Most of them felt that the semistarvation had coarsened rather than refined them, and they marveled at how thin their moral and social veneers seemed to be.

Changes in Intellective Capacity

The psychological measurements which were made of intellective ability demonstrated that there were no changes in this area. However, the deterioration described above had side-reactions in the intellective area. The intensive preoccupation with food made it difficult for the men to concentrate upon the tasks they had intellectually decided they would work on. If a man tried to study, he soon found himself daydreaming about food. He would think about foods he had eaten in the past; he would muse about opportunities he had missed to eat a certain food when he was at this or that place. Often he would daydream by the hour about the next meal, which was not very far away: "Today we'll have menu No. 1. Gee, that's the smallest menu, it seems. How shall I fix the potatoes? If I use my spoon to eat them I'll be able to add more water. Should I make different varieties of beverages tonight? Haven't had my toast yet today. Maybe I should save some for a midnight snack with my buddy. What kind of a sandwich could I make? Maybe I'd better write these ideas down, so I don't forget them. If I eat a little faster the food would stay warm longer—and I like it warm. But then it's gone so quickly. . . ."

So ceaselessly he mused for an hour or two,

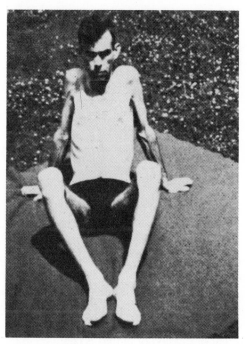

One starving engineer made a study of frozen-food lockers. Others became intensely interested in the physiology of nutrition.

Because of this all-pervasiveness of food thoughts, the men did not often have original ideas. It was hard for them to carry out their original plans and intentions. Some of the men used the device of turning to more physical and rote types of activities, such as wood-working and map-making. But even in these they had difficulty in persisting from day to day. The hunger drive often sidetracked them into other substitute activities, such as window-shopping and book-hunting. Often they would come home with "bargains"—clothes, toasters, books. One young fellow avidly collected National Geographics. After nine weeks of rehabilitation he was looking for ways of getting rid of them, as he knew he would always have access to them in libraries whenever he really needed them. Some substitute activities were more directly related to the food deprivation. Some took up smoking to "kill their hunger," but it did not. Others drank excessive amounts of water, to give them a "full" feeling. Until the laboratory prohibited the use of chewing gum, a few men indulged in "chain-chewing," consuming twenty to thirty packages a day, until their mouths ached and became sore.

Decisions came much harder. When one was out walking, he could not make up his mind which corner to take. The little matters in living in which decisions are inconsequential to the normal individual became major matters of deliberation with all of the torment that overtakes a person unable to choose between alternatives. It was often a relief for a semistarved man to walk with a healthy person, because then the starved one did not have to make up his mind about where to go. Our starving subjects appreciated someone who knew what he wanted to do. This lack of volition was reflected in their indecisiveness about word choice—it was often difficult to find the right word to use. Getting started on anything was very hard, but the task was much easier to do, once the individual got in motion, than he had imagined when he was contemplating it. Even reaching a decision was no guarantee of being at ease on a matter. One man worked three hours on the problem of how to eat his evening

until some external distraction would be strong enough to pull thoughts away from food.

About half of the group collected cookbooks and recipes. Toward the end of rehabilitation, one of the men told us how he now was throwing away his recipes. He had made out many that were senseless repetitions of others. Instead of having a single one for all flavors of custard pie, he had collected recipes for orange custard, for butterscotch custard, for lemon custard, for chocolate custard, and so forth.

meal and wrote his decisions down, only to find himself having to redecide the entire matter when he actually sat down to eat the meal.

There was a gradual blunting of perception and a dulling of consciousness which was not noticed by many of the men during the gradual starvation. Upon rehabilitation feeding, however, this unnoticed vagueness became apparent. Life then became sharper—things looked clearer; one could see more. Reading became more of a pleasure, and the meaning of the passages became clearer. During starvation the men found themselves often confused by trying to undertake, or even think about, too many things at a single time. They wrote many reminder-notes to themselves. They would have to check their experimental testing time-schedule more often, "just in case I might forget."

Sex as a Source of Motivation

A. C. Kinsey, W. B. Pomeroy, and C. E. Martin

Alfred Kinsey (1894–1956) was Professor of Zoology at Indiana University. With a Ph.D. from Harvard University in 1920, Dr. Kinsey achieved initial recognition for his evolutionary studies of gall wasps. His human sex research, for which he became internationally famous, began in 1938. W. B. Pomeroy is a clinical psychologist in private practice in New York City, but for 20 years he was with the Institute for Sex Research at Indiana University. Pomeroy received his Ph.D. from Columbia University in 1952. At present his research interest is in the study of transvestism. C. E. Martin was a graduate student at Johns Hopkins University at the time of this study and held a Bachelor of Arts degree from Indiana University.

1. Do the frequencies and modes of sexual outlet in this selection correspond with what is accepted by your church, school, or peer group? Why the disparity?

2. How do the authors feel about the use of the terms "normal" and "abnormal" when applied to the realm of sexual activity?

The six chief sources of orgasm for the human male are masturbation, nocturnal emissions, heterosexual petting, heterosexual intercourse, homosexual relations, and intercourse with animals of other species. The sum of the orgasms derived from these several sources constitutes the individual's total sexual outlet.

Abridged from A. C. Kinsey, W. B. Pomeroy, and C. E. Martin, *Sexual Behavior in the Human Male* (Philadelphia: W. B. Saunders Co., 1948), pp. 193–203. Reprinted by permission of the publisher and Dr. Paul H. Gebhard, Executive Director, Institute for Sex Research, Inc., Indiana University, Bloomington, Indiana.

Since practically all of the sexual contacts of the mature male involve emotional changes, all of which represent expenditures of energy, all adult contacts might be considered means of outlet, even though they do not lead to orgasm. These emotional situations are, however, of such variable intensity that they are difficult to assess and compare; and, for the sake of achieving some precision in analysis, the present discussion of outlets is confined to those instances of sexual activity which culminate in orgasm.

Frequency of Total Outlet

There are some individuals who derive 100 per cent of their outlet from a single kind of sexual activity. Most persons regularly depend upon two or more sources of outlet; and there are some who may include all six of them in some short period of time. The mean number of outlets utilized by our more than 5000 males is between 2 and 3 (means of 2.5 or 2.2)

(Table 1). This number varies considerably with different age groups and with different social levels.

There are, both theoretically and in actuality, endless possibilities in combining these several sources of outlet and in the extent to which each of them contributes to the total picture (Figure 1). The record of a single sort of sexual activity, even though it be the one most frequently employed by a particular group of males, does not adequately portray the whole sexual life of that group. Published figures on

outlet from that source. The fact that such a person may have had hundreds of heterosexual contacts will, in most cases, be completely ignored. Even psychologic studies have sometimes included, as "homosexual," persons who were not known to have had more than a single overt experience. In assaying the significance of any particular activity in an individual history, or any particular type of sexual behavior in a population as a whole, it is necessary to

TABLE 1. NUMBER OF SOURCES OF OUTLET IN ANY
5-YEAR PERIOD

No. of sources	SAMPLE POPULATION			U.S. POPULATION		
	Cases	Percent of population	Cumulated percent	Cases per 10,000	Percent of population	Cumulated percent
0	263	2.2	100.0	199	1.99	100.00
1	2,169	18.4	97.8	2,579	25.79	98.01
2	3,834	32.4	79.4	3,314	33.14	72.22
3	3,478	29.5	47.0	2,742	27.42	39.08
4	1,690	14.3	17.5	974	9.74	11.66
5	342	2.9	3.2	179	1.79	1.92
6	33	0.3	0.3	13	0.13	0.13
Total	11,809			10,000		
Mean[1]	2.45 ± 0.01			2.22		
Median	2.91			2.67		

Computed for the whole population involved in the present study, and computed for a theoretic adult male population with the age distribution found in the U.S. Census for 1940.

the frequency of marital intercourse, for instance, cannot be taken to be the equivalent of data on the frequency of total outlet for the married male; for marital intercourse may provide as little as 62 per cent of the orgasms of certain groups of married males. Similarly, studies of masturbation among college and younger students are not the equivalents of studies of total sexual outlet for such a group. Again, many persons who are rated "homosexual" by their fellows in a school community, a prison population, or society at large, may be deriving only a small portion of their total

[1] See the Glossary for a definition of the measures of central tendency: mean, median, mode (Ed.).

consider the extent to which that activity contributes to the total picture. Since all previously published rates on human sexual activity have been figures for particular outlets, such as masturbation or marital intercourse, the figures given in the present study on total outlet are higher than previous data would have led one to expect.

The average (mean) frequency of total sexual outlet for our sample of 3905 white males ranging between adolescence and 30 years of age is nearly 3.0 per week. It is precisely 2.88 for the total population of that age, or 2.94 for the sexually active males in that population (Table 2, Figure 2). For the total population, including all persons between adolescence and 85 years of age, the mean is 2.74 (Figure 3).

These average figures, however, are not entirely adequate, for they are based upon the particular groups of males who have contributed so far to this study. Subsequent analyses will show that there are differences in mean frequencies of sexual activity, dependent upon such factors as age, marital status, educational, religious, and rural-urban backgrounds, and on still other biologic and social factors. In order to be intelligible, any discussion of sexual outlet should be confined to a particular group of persons whose biologic condition, civil status, and social origins are homogeneous. Most of the present volume is concerned with the presentation of data for such homogeneous groups. If there is any advantage in having a generalized figure for the population of the country as a whole, that figure is best calculated by determining the frequencies for a variety of these homogeneous groups, determining the relative size of each of these groups in the national census, and then, through a process of weighting of means, reconstructing the picture for a synthetic whole.

For this synthesized population, which more nearly represents the constitution of the nation as a whole, we arrive at a figure of 3.27 per week for the total sexual outlet of the average white American male under thirty years of age (Table 2). For all white males up to age 85, the corrected mean is 2.34 per week. The latter figure is lower because of the inactivity of the older males.

Individual Variation

While approximately 3.3 is the mean frequency of total outlet for younger males, no mean nor median, nor any other sort of average, can be significant unless one keeps in mind the range of the individual variation and the distribution of these variants in the population as a whole. This is particularly true in regard to human sexual behavior, because differences in behavior, even in a small group, are much greater than the variation in physical or physiologic characters (Table 2, Figures 2 and 3). There are a few males who have gone for long periods of years without ejaculating: there is one male who, although apparently sound physically, had ejaculated only once in thirty years. There are others who have maintained average frequencies of 10, 20, or more per week for long periods of time: one male (a scholarly and skilled lawyer) has averaged over 30 per week for thirty years. This is a difference of several thousand times.

In considering structural characters of plants and animals, such as total height in the human, or length of wings, legs or other parts in other animals, a maximum that was two or three times the size of the minimum would command considerable attention. One of us has published data on individual variation in populations of insects. The populations represented individuals of single species, from single localities. There were many characters which varied. Extreme wing lengths, for instance, varied between 10 and 180 micrometer units. This difference of 18 times probably represents as extreme a linear variation as is known in any population of adults of any species of plant or animal. But differences between the extreme frequencies of sexual outlet in the human (Figures 2–3) range far beyond these morphologic differences. Calculation will show that the difference between one ejaculation in thirty years and mean frequencies of, say, 30 ejaculations per week throughout the whole of thirty years, is a matter of 45,000 times. This is the order of the variation which may occur between two individuals who live in the same town and who are neighbors, meeting in the same place of business, and coming together in common social activities. These sexually extreme individuals may be of equal significance, or insignificance, in the societal organization. They may be considered as very similar sorts of persons by their close friends who do not know their sexual histories. It has been notable throughout our field collections that a sample of as few as a hundred histories is likely to show a considerable portion of this full range of variation.

These differences in frequency of sexual activity are of great social importance. The publicly pretended code of morals, our social organization, our marriage customs, our sex laws, and our educational and religious systems are based upon an assumption that individuals are

TABLE 2. INDIVIDUAL VARIATION IN FREQUENCY OF TOTAL SEXUAL OUTLET

	INDIVIDUAL VARIATION IN TOTAL SEXUAL OUTLET					
	YOUNGER AGES: ADOLESCENT TO 30			ALL AGES: ADOLESCENT TO 85		
Frequencies per week	Cases	Sample population percent	U.S. population percent	Cases	Sample population percent	U.S. population percent
0.0	232	2.0	1.7	291	2.1	1.3
—	192	1.7	1.2	260	1.8	1.3
0.5	1136	9.9	8.3	1491	10.6	12.1
1.0	1397	12.2	11.3	1852	13.2	14.8
1.5	1235	10.8	11.2	1579	11.2	11.4
2.0	1240	10.8	10.4	1606	11.4	13.3
2.5	1066	9.3	9.6	1299	9.2	9.6
3.0	979	8.5	7.6	1194	8.5	7.7
3.5	910	7.9	8.1	1049	7.4	6.2
4.0	622	5.4	5.2	717	5.1	4.3
4.5	455	4.0	4.1	529	3.8	3.1
5.0	411	3.6	3.5	446	3.2	2.3
5.5	267	2.3	2.2	298	2.1	1.7
6.0	249	2.2	2.5	279	2.0	2.3
6.5	158	1.4	1.5	169	1.2	1.0
7.0	189	1.6	1.9	208	1.5	1.2
7.5	122	1.1	1.2	127	0.9	0.7
8.0	99	0.9	1.4	105	0.7	0.7
8.5	65	0.6	0.7	69	0.5	0.4
9.0	33	0.3	0.2	44	0.3	0.2
9.5	40	0.3	0.3	46	0.3	0.3
10.0	68	0.6	0.8	71	0.5	0.6
11.0	61	0.5	0.9	67	0.5	0.5
12.0	43	0.4	0.5	49	0.3	0.3
13.0	30	0.3	0.6	39	0.3	0.4
14.0	31	0.3	0.5	36	0.3	0.4
15.0	25	0.2	0.4	33	0.2	0.3
16.0	19	0.2	0.3	23	0.2	0.5
17.0	18	0.2	0.4	20	0.1	0.2
18.0	10	0.1	0.1	12	0.1	0.1
19.0	10	0.1	0.2	12	0.1	0.1
20.0	9	0.1	0.2	11	0.1	0.2
21.0	5	—	0.2	6	0.1	0.1
22.0	8	0.1	0.1	10	0.1	0.1
23.0	6	—	0.1	6	—	—
24.0	2	—	—	2	—	—
25.0	6	—	0.1	6	—	0.1
26.0	4	—	0.2	5	—	0.1
27.0	3	—	0.1	3	—	—
28.0	0	0	—	0	0	—
29.+	12	0.1	0.2	14	0.1	0.1
Total	11467	100.0	100.0	14083	100.0	100.0
Mean	2.88 ± 0.027		3.27	2.74 ± 0.024		2.34
Median	2.14			1.99		

Raw data, based on the available sample, are corrected for a population of the same age, marital status, and educational level as that shown for the total population in the U.S. Census of 1940.

and capacities. Persons interested in sex education look for a program which will satisfy children—meaning all the children—at some particular educational level, overlooking the fact that one individual may be adapted to a particular, perhaps relatively inactive, sort of sexual adjustment, while the next would find it practically impossible to confine himself to such a low level of activity. In institutional management, there has been almost complete unawareness of these possible differences between inmates. The problems of sexual adjustment

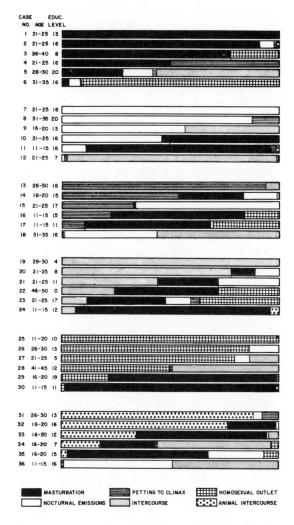

FIGURE 1. *Diverse examples of combinations of six sources of outlet. Each bar shows a combination of outlets used by one individual.*

much alike sexually, and that it is an equally simple matter for all of them to confine their behavior to the single pattern which the mores dictate. Even in such an obviously sexual situation as marriage, there is little consideration, under our present custom, of the possibility that the two persons who have mated may be far apart in their sexual inclinations, backgrounds, for persons committed to penal, mental, or other institutions, the problems of sexual adjustment for men and women in the army, the navy, or other armed forces, are a thousand different problems for any thousand of the persons involved.

While the curve shows three-quarters (77.7%) of the males with a range of variation that lies between 1.0 and 6.5 per week, there is still nearly a quarter (22.3%) of the males who fall into extreme ranges (total population, U.S. Correction). There are, for instance, 7.6 per cent of all the males whose outlets may average 7 or more per week for periods of at least five years in some part of their lives. Daily and more than daily arousal and sexual activity to the point of complete orgasm must occur among some of the friends and acquaintances which any person has. When the data on the female are subsequently published, they will show that there is even a wider range of variation there, although a larger number of the females are in the lower portion of the curve.

The possibility of any individual engaging in sexual activity at a rate that is remarkably different from one's own, is one of the most difficult things for even professionally trained persons to understand. Meetings of educators who are discussing sex instruction and policies to be followed in the administration of educational institutions, may bring out extreme differences of opinion which range from recommendations for the teaching of complete abstinence to recommendations for frank acceptance of almost any type of sexual activity. No other subject will start such open dissension in a group, and it is difficult for an observer to comprehend how objective reasoning can lead to such different conclusions among intelligent men and women. If, however, one has the histories of the educators involved, it may be found that there are persons in the group who are not ejaculating more than once or twice a year, while there may be others in the same group who are experiencing orgasm as often as ten or twenty times per week, and regularly. There is, inevitably, some correlation between these rates and the positions which these persons take in a public debate. On both sides of the argument, the extreme individuals may be totally unaware of the possibility of others in the group having histories that are so remote from their own. In the same fashion, we have listened to discussions of juvenile delinquency, of law enforcement, and of recommendations for legislative action on the sex laws, knowing that the policies that ultimately come out of such meetings would reflect the attitudes and sexual experience of the most vocal members of the group, rather than an intelligently thought-out program established on objectively accumulated data.

Even the scientific discussions of sex show little understanding of the range of variation in human behavior. More often the conclusions are limited by the personal experience of the author. Psychologic and psychiatric literature is loaded with terms which evaluate frequencies of sexual outlet. But such designations as infantile, frigid, sexually under-developed, under-active, excessively active, over-developed, over-sexed, hypersexual, or sexually over-active, and the attempts to recognize such states as nymphomania and satyriasis as discrete entities, can, in any objective analysis, refer to nothing more than a position on a curve which is continuous. Normal and abnormal, one sometimes suspects, are terms which a particular author employs with reference to his own position on that curve.

The most significant thing about this curve (Figures 2–3) is its continuity. It is not symmetrical, with a particular portion of the population set off as "normal," "modal," "typical," or discretely different. No individual has a sexual frequency which differs in anything but a slight degree from the frequencies of those placed next on the curve. Such a continuous and widely spread series raises a question as to whether the terms "normal" and "abnormal" belong in a scientific vocabulary. At the best, abnormal may designate certain individuals whose rates of activity are less frequent, or whose sources of sexual outlet are not as usual in the population as a whole; but in that case, it is preferable to refer to such persons as rare, rather than abnormal. Moreover, many items in human sexual behavior which are labelled abnormal, or perversions, in textbooks, prove, upon statistical examination, to occur in as many as 30 or 60 or 75 per cent of certain populations. It is difficult to maintain that such types of behavior are abnormal because they are rare.

The term "abnormal" is applied in medical pathology to conditions which interfere with the physical well-being of a living body. In a social sense, the term might apply to sexual activities which cause social maladjustment. Such an application, however, involves subjective determinations of what is good personal living, or good social adjustment; and these things are not

incidence of tuberculosis in the population as a whole; and the incidence of disturbance over sexual activities, among the persons who come to a clinic, is no measure of the frequency of similar disturbances outside of clinics. The impression that such "sexual irregularities" as "excessive" masturbation, pre-marital intercourse, responsibility for a pre-marital pregnancy, extra-marital intercourse, mouth-genital

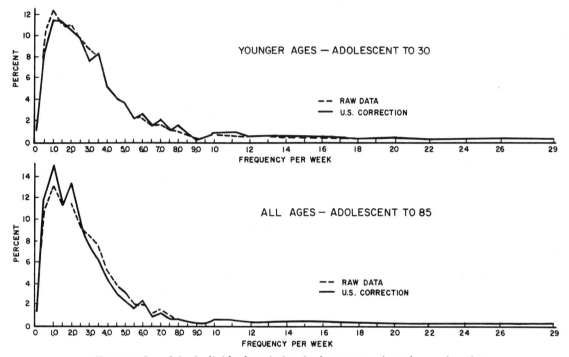

FIGURES 2 and 3. *Individual variation in frequency of total sexual outlet.*

as readily determined as physiologic well-being in an organic body. It is not possible to insist that any departure from the sexual mores, or any participation in socially taboo activities, always, or even usually, involves a neurosis or psychosis, for the case histories abundantly demonstrate that most individuals who engage in taboo activities make satisfactory social adjustments. There are, in actuality, few adult males who are particularly disturbed over their sexual histories. Psychiatrists, clinical psychologists, and others who deal with cases of maladjustment, sometimes come to feel that most people find difficulty in adjusting their sexual lives; but a clinic is no place to secure incidence figures. The incidence of tuberculosis in a tuberculosis sanitarium is no measure of the

contacts, homosexual activity, or animal intercourse, always produce psychoses and abnormal personalities is based upon the fact that the persons who do go to professional sources for advice are upset by these things.

It is unwarranted to believe that particular types of sexual behavior are always expressions of psychoses or neuroses. In actuality, they are more often expressions of what is biologically basic in mammalian and anthropoid behavior, and of a deliberate disregard for social convention. Many of the socially and intellectually most significant persons in our histories, successful scientists, educators, physicians, clergymen, businessmen, and persons of high position in governmental affairs, have socially taboo items in their sexual histories, and among them they have accepted nearly the whole range of so-called sexual abnormalities. Among the socially most successful and personally best adjusted persons who have contributed to the present study, there are some whose rates of outlet are as high as those in any case labelled nymphomania or satyriasis in the literature, or recognized as such in the clinic.

Clinical subjects who have such unusual items in their histories often do present psychopathologies—that is why they have gone to the clinics. But the presence of particular behavior, or the existence of a high rate, is not the abnormality which needs explanation. The real clinical problem is the discovery and treatment of the personality defects, the mental difficulties, the compulsions, and the schizophrenic conflicts which lead particular individuals to crack up whenever they depart from averages or socially accepted custom, while millions of other persons embrace the very same behavior, and may have as high rates of activity, without personal or social disturbance. It has been too simple a solution to discover the sexual items in a patient's history, to consider them symptoms of a neurosis, and to diagnose the disturbance as the outcome of the departure from the established mores. It is much more difficult to discover the bases of the unstable personalities that are upset by such sexual departures, and to treat the basic defects rather than to patch up the particular issues over which the disturbances occur. Clinicians would have more incentive for using such an approach if they were better acquainted with the normal frequencies of the so-called abnormal types of activity, and if, at least as far as sex is concerned, they could acquire a wider acquaintance with the sexual histories of well-adjusted individuals.

Most of the complications which are observable in sexual histories are the result of society's reactions when it obtains knowledge of an individual's behavior, or the individual's fear of how society would react if he were discovered. In various societies, under various circumstances, and even at various social levels of the population living in a particular town, the sex mores are fundamentally different. The way in which each group reacts to a particular sort of history determines the "normality" or "abnormality" of the individual's behavior—in that particular group. Whatever the moral interpretation, there is no scientific reason for considering particular types of sexual activity as intrinsically, in their biologic origins, normal or abnormal. Yet scientific classifications have been nearly identical with theologic classifications and with the moral pronouncements of the English common law of the fifteenth century. This, in turn, as far as sex is concerned, was based on the medieval ecclesiastic law which was only a minor variant of the tenets of ancient Greek and Roman cults, and of the Talmudic law. Present-day legal determinations of sexual acts which are acceptable, or "natural," and those which are "contrary to nature" are not based on data obtained from biologists, nor from nature herself. On the contrary, the ancient codes have been accepted by laymen, jurists, and scientists alike as the ultimate sources of moral evaluations, of present-day legal procedure, and of the list of subjects that may go into a textbook of abnormal psychology. In no other field of science have scientists been satisfied to accept the biologic notions of ancient jurists and theologians, or the analyses made by the mystics of two or three thousand years ago. Either the ancient philosophers were remarkably well-trained psychologists, or modern psychologists have contributed little in defining abnormal sexual behavior.

The reactions of our social organization to these various types of behavior are the things that need study and classification. The mores, whether they concern food, clothing, sex, or religious rituals, originate neither in accumulated experience nor in scientific examinations of objectively gathered data. The sociologist and anthropologist find the origins of such customs in ignorance and superstition, and in the attempt of each group to set itself apart from its neighbors. Psychologists have been too much concerned with the individuals who depart from the group custom. It would be more important to know why so many individuals conform as they do to such ancient custom, and what psychology is involved in the preservation of these customs by a society whose individual members would, in most cases, not attempt to defend all of the specific items in that custom. Too often the study of behavior has been little more than a rationalization of the mores masquerading under the guise of objective science.

While this problem will be met again in other places, the present discussion of frequencies of total sexual outlet provides a good opportunity for understanding the futility of classifying individuals as normal or abnormal, or well-adjusted or poorly adjusted, when in reality they may be nothing more than frequent or rare, or conformists or non-conformists with the socially pretended custom.

Pleasure Centers in the Brain

James Olds

James Olds is Professor of Behavioral Biology, California Institute of Technology, having received his Ph.D. from Harvard University in 1952. Such diverse groups as the American Association for the Advancement of Science, the American Psychiatric Association, and the Society of Experimental Psychologists have awarded him prizes and medals for his work on the behavioral consequences of brain stimulation.

1. Historically, why have brain functions been so difficult to investigate?

2. By what criteria did the author determine that electrical stimulation to the brain is "pleasurable"?

3. Do the findings of this study generalize to the functioning of the human brain?

The brain has been mapped in various ways by modern physiologists. They have located the sensory and motor systems and the seats of many kinds of behavior—centers where messages of sight, sound, touch and action are received and interpreted. Where, then, dwell the "higher feelings," such as love, fear, pain and pleasure? Up to three years ago the notion that the emotions had specific seats in the brain might have been dismissed as naive—akin perhaps to medieval anatomy or phrenology. But recent research has brought a surprising turn of affairs. The brain does seem to have definite loci of pleasure and pain, and we shall review

Abridged from J. Olds, "Pleasure Centers in the Brain," *Scientific American,* 195 (1956), 105–116. Reprinted with permission. Copyright © 1956 by Scientific American, Inc. All rights reserved.

here the experiments which have led to this conclusion.

The classical mapping exploration of the brain ranged mainly over its broad, fissured roof—the cortex—and there localized the sensory and motor systems and other areas which seemed to control most overt behavior. Other areas of the brain remained mostly unexplored, and comparatively little was known about their functions. Particularly mysterious was the series of structures lying along the mid-line of the brain from the roof down to the spinal cord, structures which include the hypothalamus and parts of the thalamus [*see diagram*]. It was believed that general functions of the brain might reside in these structures. But they were difficult to investigate, for two reasons. First, the structures were hard to get at. Most of them lie deep in the brain and could not be reached without damaging the brain, whereas the cortex could be explored by electrical stimulators and recording instruments touching the surface. Secondly, there was a lack of psychological tools for measuring the more general responses of an animal. It is easy to test an animal's reaction to stimulation of a motor center in the brain, for it takes the simple form of flexing a muscle, but how is one to measure an animal's feeling of pleasure?

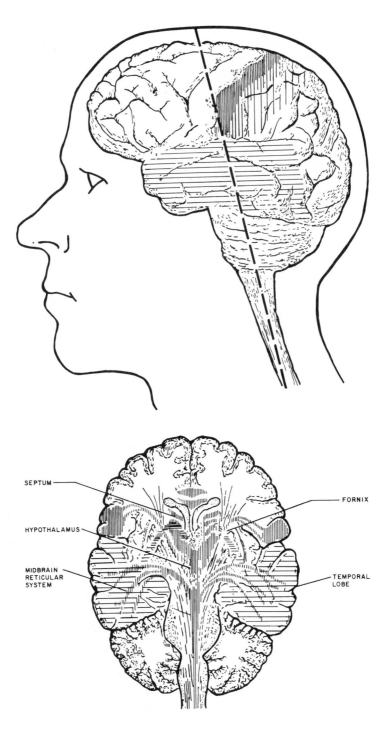

SEPTUM

HYPOTHALAMUS

MIDBRAIN
RETICULAR
SYSTEM

FORNIX

TEMPORAL
LOBE

Locations of function in the human brain are mapped in these two diagrams. The white areas in both diagrams comprise the motor system; the black crosshatched areas, the sensory system. Crosshatched are the "nonspecific" regions now found to be involved in motivation of behavior. The diagram at bottom shows the brain from behind, dissected along the heavy dashed line at top. The labels here identify the centers which correspond to those investigated in the rat. The fornix and parts of the temporal lobes, plus associated structures not labeled, together constitute the rhinencephalon or "smell-brain."

The first difficulty was overcome by the development of an instrument for probing the brain. Basically the instrument is a very fine needle electrode which can be inserted to any point of the brain without damage. In the early experiments the brain of an animal could be probed only with some of its skull removed and while it was under anesthesia. But W. R. Hess in Zurich developed a method of studying the brain for longer periods and under more normal circumstances. The electrodes were inserted through the skull, fixed in position and left there; after the skin healed over the wound, the animal could be studied in its ordinary activities.

Using the earlier technique, H. W. Magoun and his collaborators at Northwestern University explored the region known as the "reticular system" in the lower part of the mid-brain. They showed that this system controls the sleep and wakefulness of animals. Stimulation of the system produced an "alert" electrical pattern, even from an anesthetized animal, and injury to nerve cells there produced more or less continuous sleep.

Hess, with his new technique, examined the hypothalamus and the region around the septum (the dividing membrane at the mid-line), which lie forward of the reticular system. He found that these parts of the brain play an important part in an animal's automatic protective behavior. In the rear section of the hypothalamus is a system which controls emergency responses that prepare the animal for fight or flight. Another system in the front part of the hypothalamus and in the septal area apparently controls rest, recovery, digestion and elimination. In short, these studies seemed to localize the animal's brain responses in situations provoking fear, rage, escape or certain needs.

There remained an important part of the mid-line region of the brain which had not been explored and whose functions were still almost completely unknown. This area, comprising the upper portion of the middle system, seemed to be connected with smell, and to this day it is called the rhinencephalon, or "smell-brain." But the area appeared to receive messages from many organs of the body, and there were various other reasons to believe it was not concerned exclusively or even primarily with smell. As early as 1937 James W. Papez of Cornell University suggested that the rhinencephalon might control emotional experience and behavior. He based this speculation partly on the observation that rabies, which produces profound emotional upset, seems to attack parts of the rhinencephalon.

Such observations, then, constituted our knowledge of the areas of the brain until recently. Certain areas had been found to be involved in various kinds of emotional behavior, but the evidence was only of a general nature. The prevailing view still held that the basic motivations—pain, pleasure and so on—probably involved excitation or activity of the whole brain.

Investigation of these matters in more detail became possible only after psychologists had developed methods for detecting and measuring positive emotional behavior—pleasure and the satisfaction of specific "wants." It was B. F. Skinner, the Harvard University experimental psychologist, who produced the needed refinement. He worked out a technique for measuring the rewarding effect of a stimulus (or the degree of satisfaction) in terms of the frequency with which an animal would perform an act which led to the reward. For example, the animal was placed in a bare box containing a lever it could manipulate. If it received no reward when it pressed the lever, the animal might perform this act perhaps 5 to 10 times an hour. But if it was rewarded with a pellet of food every time it worked the lever, then its rate of performing the act would rise to 100 or more times per hour. This increase in response frequency from five or 10 to 100 per hour provided a measure of the rewarding effect of the food. Other stimuli produce different response rates, and in each case the rise in rate seems to be a quite accurate measure of the reward value of the given stimulus.

With the help of Hess's technique for probing the brain and Skinner's for measuring motivation, we have been engaged in a series of experiments which began three years ago under the guidance of the psychologist D. O. Hebb at McGill University. At the beginning we planned to explore particularly the mid-brain reticular system—the sleep-control area that had been investigated by Magoun.

Just before we began our own work, H. R.

Delgado, W. W. Roberts and N. E. Miller at Yale University had undertaken a similar study. They had located an area in the lower part of the mid-line system where stimulation caused the animal to avoid the behavior that provoked the electrical stimulus. We wished to investigate positive as well as negative effects—that is, to learn whether stimulation of some areas might be sought rather than avoided by the animal.

We were not at first concerned to hit very specific points in the brain, and in fact in our early tests the electrodes did not always go to the particular areas in the mid-line system at which they were aimed. Our lack of aim turned out to be a fortunate happening for us. In one animal the electrode missed its target and landed not in the mid-brain reticular system but in a nerve pathway from the rhinencephalon. This led to an unexpected discovery.

In the test experiment we were using, the animal was placed in a large box with corners labeled A, B, C and D. Whenever the animal went to corner A, its brain was given a mild electric shock by the experimenter. When the test was performed on the animal with the electrode in the rhinencephalic nerve, it kept returning to corner A. After several such returns on the first day, it finally went to a different place and fell asleep. The next day, however, it seemed even more interested in corner A.

At this point we assumed that the stimulus must provoke curiosity; we did not yet think of it as a reward. Further experimentation on the same animal soon indicated, to our surprise, that its response to the stimulus was more than curiosity. On the second day, after the animal had acquired the habit of returning to corner A to be stimulated, we began trying to draw it away to corner B, giving it an electric shock whenever it took a step in that direction. Within a matter of five minutes the animal was in corner B. After this, the animal could be directed to almost any spot in the box at the will of the experimenter. Every step in the right direction was paid with a small shock; on arrival at the appointed place the animal received a longer series of shocks.

Next the animal was put on a T-shaped platform and stimulated if it turned right at the crossing of the T but not if it turned left. It soon learned to turn right every time. At this point we reversed the procedure, and the animal had to turn left in order to get a shock. With some guidance from the experimenter it eventually switched from the right to the left. We followed up with a test of the animal's response when it was hungry. Food was withheld for 24 hours. Then the animal was placed in a T, both arms of which were baited with mash. The animal would receive the electric stimulus at a point halfway down the right arm. It learned to go there, and it always stopped at this point, never going on to the food at all!

After confirming this powerful effect of stimulation of brain areas by experiments with a series of animals, we set out to map the places in the brain where such an effect could be obtained. We wanted to measure the strength of the effect in each place. Here Skinner's technique provided the means. By putting the animal in the "do-it-yourself" situation (*i.e.,* pressing a lever to stimulate its own brain) we could translate the animal's strength of "desire"

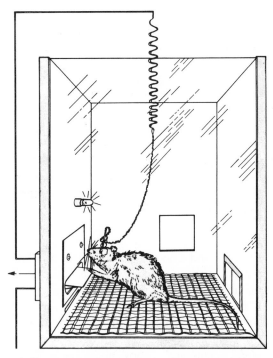

Self-stimulation circuit is diagrammed here. When the rat presses on treadle it triggers an electric stimulus to its brain and simultaneously records action via wire at left.

into response frequency, which can be seen and measured.

The first animal in the Skinner box ended all doubts in our minds that electric stimulation applied to some parts of the brain could indeed provide reward for behavior. The test displayed the phenomenon in bold relief where anyone who wanted to look could see it. Left to itself in the apparatus, the animal (after about two to five minutes of learning) stimulated its own brain regularly about once every five seconds, taking a stimulus of a second or so every time. After 30 minutes the experimenter turned off the current, so that the animal's pressing of the lever no longer stimulated the brain. Under these conditions the animal pressed it about seven times and then went to sleep. We found that the test was repeatable as often as we cared to apply it. When the current was turned on and the animal was given one shock as an *hors d'oeuvre,* it would begin stimulating its brain again. When the electricity was turned off, it would try a few times and then go to sleep.

The current used to stimulate was ordinary house current reduced by a small transformer and then regulated between one and five volts by means of a potentiometer (a radio volume control). As the resistance in the brain was approximately 12,000 ohms, the current ranged from about .000083 to .000420 of an ampere. The shock lasted up to about a second, and the animal had to release the lever and press again to get more.

We now started to localize and quantify the rewarding effect in the brain by planting electrodes in all parts of the brain in large numbers of rats. Each rat had a pair of electrodes consisting of insulated silver wires a hundredth of an inch in diameter. The two stimulating tips were only about one 500th of an inch apart. During a test the animal was placed in a Skinner box designed to produce a chance response rate of about 10 to 25 bar-presses per hour. Each animal was given about six hours of testing with the electric current turned on and one hour with the current off. All responses were recorded automatically, and the animal was given a score on the basis of the amount of time it spent stimulating its brain.

When electrodes were implanted in the classical sensory and motor systems, response rates stayed at the chance level of 10 to 25 an hour.

Rat seeks stimulus as it places its paw on the treadle. Some of the animals have been seen to stimulate themselves for 24 hours without rest and as often as 5,000 times an hour.

In most parts of the mid-line system, the response rates rose to levels of from 200 to 5,000 an hour, definitely indicative of a rewarding effect of the electric stimulus. But in some of the lower parts of the mid-line system there was an opposite effect: the animal would press the lever once and never go back. This indicated a punishing effect in those areas. They appeared to be the same areas where Delgado, Roberts and Miller at Yale also had discovered the avoidance effect—and where Hess and others had found responses of rage and escape.

The animals seemed to experience the strongest reward, or pleasure, from stimulation of areas of the hypothalamus and certain midbrain nuclei—regions which Hess and others had found to be centers for control of digestive, sexual, excretory and similar processes. Animals with electrodes in these areas would stimulate themselves from 500 to 5,000 times per hour. In the rhinencephalon the effects were milder, producing self-stimulation at rates around 200 times per hour.

Electric stimulation in some of these regions actually appeared to be far more rewarding to the animals than an ordinary satisfier such as

Rat feels stimulus as it presses on treadle. Pulse lasts less than a second; the current is less than .0005 ampere. The animal must release lever and press again to renew the stimulus.

food. For example, hungry rats ran faster to reach an electric stimulator than they did to reach food. Indeed, a hungry animal often ignored available food in favor of the pleasure of stimulating itself electrically. Some rats with electrodes in these places stimulated their brains more than 2,000 times per hour for 24 consecutive hours!

Why is the electric stimulation so rewarding? We are currently exploring this question, working on the hypothesis that brain stimulation in these regions must excite some of the nerve cells that would be excited by satisfaction of the basic drives—hunger, sex, thirst and so forth. We have looked to see whether some parts of the "reward system" of the brain are special-ized; that is, there may be one part for the hunger drive, another for the sex drive, etc.

In experiments on hunger, we have found that an animal's appetite for electric stimulation in some brain regions increases as hunger increases: the animal will respond much faster when hungry than when full. We are performing similar tests in other places in the brain with variations of thirst and sex hormones. We have already found that there are areas where the rewarding effects of a brain stimulus can be abolished by castration and restored by injections of testosterone.

Our present tentative conclusion is that emotional and motivational mechanisms can indeed be localized in the brain; that certain portions of the brain are sensitive to each of the basic drives. Strong electrical stimulation of these areas seems to be even more satisfying than the usual rewards of food, etc. This finding contradicts the long-held theory that strong excitation in the brain means punishment. In some areas of the brain it means reward.

The main question for future research is to determine how the excited "reward" cells act upon the specific sensory-motor systems to intensify the rewarded behavior.

At the moment we are using the self-stimulating technique to learn whether drugs will selectively affect the various motivational centers of the brain. We hope, for example, that we may eventually find one drug that will raise or lower thresholds in the hunger system, another for the sex-drive system, and so forth. Such drugs would allow control of psychological disorders caused by surfeits or deficits in motivational conditions.

Enough of the brain-stimulating work has been repeated on monkeys by J. V. Brady and J. C. Lilly (who work in different laboratories in Washington, D.C.) to indicate that our general conclusions can very likely be generalized eventually to human beings—with modifications, of course.

The Achievement Motive

David C. McClelland

David McClelland, Professor of Psychology, Harvard University, received his Ph.D. from Yale University in 1941. He is the author of numerous books and articles relating to personality. His particular interest is the achievement motive. McClelland is consultant and adviser to many educational and governmental committees.

1. Can you accept the three assumptions upon which this study is based?

2. Are n Achievement scores obtained by two independent judgments reliable? How does this compare with test-retest correlations?

3. How do n Achievement scores compare with the actual solution of achievement-oriented problems?

Contemporary psychological theory stresses the importance of motivation, but provides no satisfactory method for measuring it, at least at the human level. The present research was begun with the idea of remedying this defect. Psychology needs a measure of human motivation and we set out to find one. This report represents a brief description of some of the main findings obtained by our entire research group which has included the following people: David Angell, John W. Atkinson, Robert C. Birney, Russell A. Clark, Gerald A. Friedman, Jules Holzberg, Alvin M. Liberman, Edgar L. Lowell, John Perkins, Thornton B. Roby, Benjamin Simon, Joseph Veroff, and Josef Zatzkis.

Abridged from D. C. McClelland, "Measuring Motivation in Phantasy: The Achievement Motive," in H. Guetzkow, ed., *Groups, Leadership and Men* (Pittsburgh: Carnegie Press, 1951), pp. 191–205. Reprinted by permission of the publisher.

In retrospect, at least, our search appears to have been guided by three hypotheses. First, the method of measurement for maximum theoretical usefulness should be at least partially independent of the methods of measurement used to define the other two main variables in contemporary psychological theory, namely, perception and learning. The field of sensation and perception received a great boost when the psychophysical methods were invented or systematized and put into wide use over a century ago. Theoretical development in this field continues to draw heavily for its vitality on the application of these methods. Similarly, learning theory received a great boost around the beginning of the twentieth century when methods for studying problem-solving behavior (*e.g.,* conditioning, serial rote learning, maze learning, and the like) were developed. It seemed logical that motivation in turn would get its greatest lift as a theoretical variable if some methods for measuring it could be developed that were not identical with those that were already in use to measure perception and learning.

The second hypothesis which guided our search was that motives might be best measured in phantasy. There were two bases for this assumption. In the first place, phantasy fulfills our first requirement: it differs quite radically from problem-solving behavior on the one hand and veridical perception on the other. In the second place, clinical psychologists from Freud to Murray have found phantasy of immense practical value in developing the dynamic or motivational theory of personality. In fact, one could argue that the whole psychoanalytic school of thinking is built, operationally speaking, on an analysis of imaginative behavior, whether it be the free association of adults on a psychoanalytic couch or the imaginative play of children.

Our third hypothesis was that motives could be experimentally aroused by manipulating external conditions. Here we were guided by the immensely successful assumption of animal psychologists that motives are states of the organism which can be aroused normally by deprivation. While we felt that the animal model has so far not proven particularly useful in its direct application to measuring motivation at the human level, nevertheless it has proven so theoretically fruitful in the construction of elementary behavior theory that it should not be wholly ignored.

Quite simply then, our problem became one of attempting to arouse human motives experimentally and to measure the effects on phantasy. As a preliminary check we decided to test one of our basic hypotheses, namely, that phantasy would be sensitive to changes in conditions which everyone would agree were motivating. So Atkinson and McClelland conducted and reported an experiment in which they demonstrated that human subjects deprived of food for one, four, and sixteen hours wrote brief imaginative stories which changed in a number of important ways as hunger increased. From the shifts in the content of the stories they were able to develop a composite score which gave a rough idea of how long the subjects had been without food. This preliminary evidence together with earlier work done by Sanford seemed to clear the track for work on what became the main objective of the study, namely, the measurement of the strength of the achievement motive in phantasy.

Procedure

How could the achievement motive be experimentally aroused in human subjects? This was our first problem. Fortunately, there are several standard laboratory procedures for producing achievement orientation which are usually lumped together under the heading of "ego-involvement." They have in common the attempt to orient the subjects around success in some task which is or should be of great importance to them. In our case, we decided to define certain tasks as achievement-related for the subjects and to control their experiences of success or failure on these tasks. In this way we hoped to be able to control the intensity of the achievement motive aroused in various groups of subjects and to measure the effects of the different intensities on subsequent imaginative behavior. Specifically, we worked finally with six different "arousal conditions": (1) a *relaxed* condition in which the tasks the subjects performed were introduced casually as part of the blind exploration of some graduate students into a new problem, (2) a *neutral* condition in which the tasks were seriously introduced as ones on which the department of psychology wanted some norms, (3) an *ego-involved* condition in which the tasks were described as measures of intelligence and leadership capacity, (4) a *success* condition in which the subjects were allowed to succeed on the ego-involved tasks, (5) a *failure* condition in which the subjects were caused to fail on the ego-involved tasks, and (6) a *success-failure* condition in which the subjects first succeeded and then failed on the ego-involved tasks. In this way we attempted to explore the effect of the entire range of achievement-related experiences on imaginative behavior, although in the end our primary attention focused on the difference between the relaxed and ego-involved orientations rather than on the specific effects of success and failure.

How were we to measure the effects of these various arousal conditions on phantasy? Since our design calls for the scoring of a large number of records from sizable groups of subjects, we necessarily had to eliminate the type of elaborate phantasy production normally used by clinical psychologists. Instead we decided in favor of getting small, relatively standardized samples of imaginative behavior from each subject. In time our routine procedure involved asking a group of subjects to write brief five-minute stories in response to each of four pictures exposed for twenty seconds on a screen in front of the group. The stories were written around the following four questions spaced on an answer sheet:

What is happening?
What has led up to this situation?
What is being thought?
What will happen?

The instructions given were the standard ones for the Thematic Apperception Test. Their general tone is to urge the subject to be as creative as possible and not to think in terms of right and wrong answers. There were four slides in all, two of which came from the Murray Thematic Apperception Test and two of which were made up especially for this test. They suggested respectively a work situation (two men working at a machine), a study situation (a boy seated at a desk with a book in front of him), a father-son situation (TAT 7BM), and a young boy possibly dreaming of the future (TAT 8BM). Considerable work has been done by Atkinson with slides suggestive of other situations, but most of the work reported is based on these four which represent an attempt to sample the range of achievement-related activities.

The stories obtained by this method average about ninety words in length. How are they to be scored? Again we had to eliminate complex scoring systems and in the end hit upon the scheme of analyzing the stories in terms of the action sequence suggested by the questions on the answer sheet. That is, a plot or story usually has a beginning (or instigation), a middle (containing instrumental acts and obstacles), and an end (containing goal responses). Thus the categories we finally chose to score were aspects of the instigation action or problem-solving sequence commonly used as a model in contemporary learning theory. They included the following (arranged in accordance with the time order in which they normally appear in a story): statements of need or wish, instrumental activities, blocks or obstacles either internal or external in nature, anticipations of the outcome, positive or negative effect accompanying success or failure in reaching a goal, and the like. This scoring system is general enough to fit an action sequence centered around any motive and was also used in scoring for hunger in the Atkinson and McClelland study previously mentioned. The critical problem is that of finding a scoring definition for deciding whether statements are related to the motive in question—in the present instance, the achievement motive. What constitutes achievement imagery? This pre-

sented many serious and complicated problems but in the end we were able to formulate a definition which stated that any imagery (*e.g.,* statement in the story) which suggests *competition with a standard* is achievement related. In its simplest terms this means that someone in the story is *trying to do better* in relation to some achievement goal such as doing a better job or getting ahead in the world.

Results

Methodological

Scoring the stories for various achievement-related categories as finally defined is highly reliable. After training, two judges working together agreed on 91 per cent of the categories on two successive scorings of the same records. The agreement on individual n Achievement (need for Achievement) scores derived from summation of these categories is even higher. The correlation is .95[1] between n Achievement scores obtained on two different occasions by two judges working together. One judge, after experience with the system for three days, has obtained a correlation of .92 between his scores and those obtained by another judge more experienced with the system. Furthermore, after practice the system can be applied rapidly; it takes from three to five minutes on the average to score the four stories obtained for a given individual.

Many significant differences in the scoring categories were produced by the various methods of arousing the achievement motive. In general, there were large and significant increases in the number of subjects and number of stories showing achievement-related imagery as the experiences the subjects had just had became more achievement-oriented. For the sake of simplicity, we will disregard specific differences in the effects of success and failure and turn our attention only to the derivation of an over-all index of the strength of an individual's achievement motive, an index which we refer to as his n Achievement score, following Murray's convention. First, we noted all those characteristics such as stated need for achievement, anticipation of success and failure, *etc.,* which increased significantly from a

[1] See the Glossary for an explanation of correlation (Ed.).

lower to a higher state of achievement arousal; then we argued that the number of those characteristics in the stories written by a subject under normal or non-ego-involved conditions would indicate the normal strength of his concern for achievement. That is, we could look for the characteristics in a person's stories which we had found to be sensitive to experimental changes in achievement orientation, sum them up, and derive an over-all n Achievement score for that individual.

One of our first concerns was to see whether or not a measure derived in this way was applicable to groups of persons other than the male college students who had been the subjects in the various arousal conditions. To test the generality of the n Achievement measure, Veroff compared the stories written by high school students, both boys and girls, after neutral and ego-involving experiences. He found that the high school boys, representing a much larger segment of the population than our college men, also showed a significant over-all increase in mean n Achievement score from the neutral to the ego-involving condition. This strongly suggests that the characteristics scored are not peculiar to the highly selected portion of the population represented in college. In the second place, Veroff found no significant change in n Achievement score for girls following ego-involvement. There are many interesting explanations for this finding, but the conclusion it leads to here is that the method cannot be applied to women without some additional assumptions. Finally, we went outside our culture altogether and compared the stories written by Navaho high-school-age males under neutral and ego-involving conditions, and found once again that even in this different culture, our scoring system was applicable and showed a significant increase in mean n Achievement score from a condition of low achievement arousal to one of higher achievement arousal.

Our next concern was with the reliability of a person's n Achievement score. In other words, what are the chances that he will get the same or a similar score on two different occasions? Our reliabilities are on the whole low. A test-retest correlation for two three-picture measures taken a week apart was only .22 (not significant[2] with N[3] $= 40$). However, the two measures agreed significantly (72.5 per cent) in placing subjects above or below the mean on the two occasions, and the split-half reliability for a six- or eight-picture test runs over .70 (corrected for halving the test). On the whole, in the present state of development, the n Achievement measure appears adequate for classifying individuals into high and low achievement groups, or at the most into high, middle, and low achievement groups, but not for finer discriminations or for individual testing purposes. It is always possible, of course, that with a projective instrument of this sort high test-retest reliabilities cannot be obtained because the subject is "spoiled" by having taken such a test once previously. This may mean that the measure is more valid in the sense of being related to other types of behavior than it is reliable in the sense of being related to itself as obtained on a second occasion.

Relation of n Achievement Score to Other Kinds of Behavior

While our method of deriving the n Achievement score from differences in achievement arousal conditions gives the measure a kind of validity, the skeptical observer would still want to know more. In particular, is our presumed measure of motive strength related to other kinds of behavior in ways that on a theoretical or common-sense basis we would expect motivation to be related? For this reason, much of our energy has gone into exploring the relation of the n Achievement score to other variables. Chief among these are performance and learning. On theoretical, experimental, and common-sense grounds one would expect that more highly motivated subjects would, at least under certain circumstances, perform more quickly, and, under certain others, learn more efficiently than poorly motivated subjects. Thus, if our n Achievement score is an index of the strength of the achievement motive in individuals, we should be able to demonstrate that people with high n Achievement scores show evidence of better learning and performance. Of the several studies designed to test this hypothesis, the one by Lowell is perhaps the most definitive. He first administered a three-picture form of the TAT n Achievement Test to a group of male college students and then asked

[2,3] See the Glossary for an explanation (Ed.).

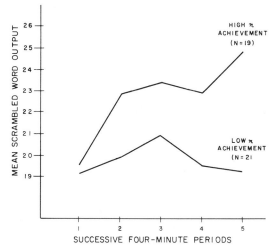

FIGURE 1. *Mean output of Scrambled Words for subjects above and below the mean in n Achievement score in successive four-minute periods.*

them to work on a twenty-minute Scrambled Words test which required them to rearrange a nonsense series of letters (for example, WTSE) until they had constructed a meaningful word (*e.g.,* WEST). The test was arranged in such a way that the subjects worked for two minutes on each of ten different pages of Scrambled Words, which were randomized from subject to subject to equate for difficulties. One week later Lowell administered to the same group of subjects another set of three TAT pictures and asked them to work on solving some simple addition problems for ten minutes. The n Achievement score for an individual was obtained in the usual manner by summing the significant characteristics in the stories obtained from all six pictures on the two different occasions. Figures 1 summarizes how groups of subjects with high and low n Achievement scores performed in different periods of the Scrambled Words task. The rather regular increases in performance from the first to the fifth four-minute period for the high n Achievement subjects strongly suggest a learning curve, while variations in output for the low n Achievement subjects display no consistent trend. The high need group shows a mean gain in output from the first to the last period of 5.32 words, whereas the low need group shows a gain of only .43 words, a difference in gain of 4.89 words which is well beyond the 1 per cent level (t = 3.76)[4]. In short, our expectations

are confirmed: there is definite and statistically significant evidence for superior learning in the high as compared with the low n Achievement group.

Figure 2 shows the results for the addition task. Here it is clear that the high n Achievement subjects solved more problems at every point in the test so that their over-all output is significantly greater than for the low n Achievement subjects (t = 2.40, P[5] < .05).

The difference in the findings reported in Figures 1 and 2 is important. Presumably the reason why the more highly motivated subjects showed learning in connection with the Scrambled Word task is because this task is sufficiently complex for the subject to find new and better ways of performing at it as they practice it. The Additions task, on the other hand, is so simple that presumably subjects are about at their maximum level of efficiency when they begin; no new methods of adding are likely to be discovered in the course of a ten-minute task. Thus we can argue that where learning is possible in a complex task, the highly motivated subjects will show it; where it is not possible or at least not likely in a very simple task, high n Achievement produces faster performance but not learning. Both of these findings support the hypothesis that the n Achievement score is measuring motivational strength.

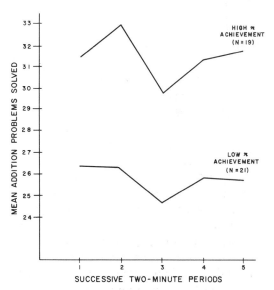

FIGURE 2. *Mean output of addition problems solved by subjects above and below the mean n Achievement score in successive two-minute periods.*

[4,5] See the Glossary for an explanation of *t* tests and probability (Ed.).

Motivation should also have some demonstrable connection with perception and memory. Out of several experiments done in this field, two are particularly striking and confirm each other. The first is the one reported by McClelland and Liberman on the effect of n Achievement on the recognition of need-related words. Having previously obtained n Achievement scores on their subjects, they measured how quickly a subject could recognize achievement related, security-related, and neutral words when they were exposed repeatedly at increasing illuminations for only .01 second. They found that subjects with high n Achievement scores were able to recognize positive achievement words like *success* and *strive* faster than subjects with low n Achievement scores. When they obtained a somewhat more stable measure of n Achievement by combining the score obtained from imagination with one based on a performance task to produce an over-all index of n Achievement rank, they were able to make a finer analysis of the data. That is, they found that subjects in the lowest third of the distribution of n Achievement ranks showed no particular trend with respect to recognizing either positive achievement words or negative achievement words like *unable* and *failure*. The subjects in the middle third of the distribution, however, showed a *slower* recognition time for the negative achievement words than did either the low or high thirds, and the high n Achievement third showed a much *faster* recognition of the positive achievement words than did either the middle or low thirds. In short, it looked as if, as n Achievement increased in intensity, it tended to orient subjects first around avoiding failure (decreased sensitivity to failure words) and then around attaining success (increased sensitivity to success words). Some further evidence that the middle n Achievement subjects were security-minded lay in the fact that they were also quicker at recognizing security-related words like *friend* or *comfort*. McClelland and Liberman concluded that "the group of subjects with moderate n Achievement are security-minded and chiefly concerned with avoiding failure, or with achieving a minimal level of aspiration, whereas the group of subjects with high n Achievement are concerned more directly with achieving success or attaining a maximum level of aspiration."

These findings were confirmed in a study reported by Atkinson on the memory for completed and incompleted tasks. In addition to having subjects who could be classified low, moderate, or high with respect to n Achievement on the basis of their stories, he had three types of test situations: (a) a relaxed orientation in which the experimenter was introduced quite informally as a "graduate student who wants to try out some tasks"; (b) a task orientation in which the experimenter simply directed the students' attention to how the tasks were to be performed without any effort to create an experimental atmosphere; and (c) an ego orientation in which the experimenter described the tasks as being measures of intellectual ability, leadership, *etc.,* and urged the students to do their best. Atkinson found in line with work previously reported that the number of *completed* tasks recalled, irrespective of motivation, increased from relaxed to task to ego orientation. But when a breakdown was made according to n Achievement score, he found strikingly opposite trends for the subjects in the high and middle thirds of the n Achievement distribution with respect to the incompleted tasks. For the subjects with high n Achievement there was a regular *increase* in the number of incompleted tasks recalled, whereas for the subjects with moderate n Achievement there was a regular *decrease* in the number of incompleted tasks recalled. For the subjects with lowest n Achievement there was no trend in the number of incompleted tasks recalled. In short, the data look very much like those obtained with perception. The subjects with moderate n Achievement are defensive; they appear to regard their inability to complete a task as a failure as they become more ego-oriented, and consequently attempt to avoid remembering it. Subjects with high n Achievement, however, apparently tend to regard their incompleted tasks as *challenges* which they remember better as the situation becomes more ego-oriented, presumably in order to complete them. Both of these studies strongly suggest that there are at least two kinds of achievement motivation, one of which appears to be oriented around avoiding failure and the other around the more positive goal of attaining success. It cannot be stated, of course, which type of motivation is more efficient, since either an excessive concern with success or with avoiding failure may be maladaptive, depending on the requirements of the situation.

Having demonstrated the relation of our measure to important behavior variables, we come to the more traditional validity checks. Is the n Achievement score related in any significant way to how much achievement "drive" a person is judged to have either by himself or by a clinician after careful study? Apparently not. There is no significant relationship between imaginative n Achievement score and either a psychiatrist's judgment of n Achievement or a person's own judgment of his n Achievement intensity. This is not as disturbing as it might at first seem to be. If ratings of motivational strength were adequate measures of motivation (*e.g.,* were significantly related to performance, level of aspiration, *etc.*), there would be no need to develop any such elaborate system as this for measuring motivation. The fact of the matter is that such judgments must necessarily be complexly determined. When a psychiatrist, for example, attempts to estimate the strength of an individual's achievement motive he must take into account a great many factors—the person's actual performance, his goals in life at least as they are consciously realized, his relation to his father, *etc.* The final rating, whether it be the psychiatrist's or the person's own, represents a synthesis or integration of these many factors and is not therefore, at least in the theoretical sense, "pure." That is, it does not represent any one aspect of personality but is a judgment involving many. It was just to avoid such complexly determined measures of motivation that the present research was undertaken.

We have found that n Achievement score is significantly related to the kinds of linguistic categories that a person uses in attempting to express himself, at least in an achievement-related situation, and so forth. Rather than dwell on any of these findings, let us turn to our attempts to explore the origins of n Achievement, assuming for the moment that our measure of it is valid.

The first study in this area was a cross-cultural one performed by Friedman. Quite surprisingly, he found that he could apply the n Achievement scoring system developed on male American college students to folk tales collected from eight different American Indian cultures. By selecting twelve such tales from each of the cultures and using the standard scoring system, he found he could obtain an over-all achievement index for each of the cultures which represented the amount of achievement-related imagery in the stories in his sample. He then correlated this index with ratings which had been made independently of data in the Yale cross-cultural files for a study by Whiting and Child on various child-rearing practices in the eight cultures. On theoretical grounds we predicted that n Achievement scores would be highly related to the amount of stress in the culture which was placed on independence training. Friedman found a relationship that was significant well beyond the 1 per cent level even with only eight cases, indicating that severity of independence training in childhood is highly correlated with the amount of achievement imagery in the folk tales current in a culture. This supports the hypothesis that achievement motivation develops out of parents' concern that children "stand on their own feet" rather early in life and learn to do things for themselves.

A more direct confirmation of this hypothesis was obtained by correlating n Achievement scores of male American college students with their own ratings of their parents' behavior toward them on several different dimensions, namely, Democratic-autocratic, Acceptance-rejection, Indulgence, and Casualness. The correlation for the Acceptance-rejection dimension was significant, being .49 for the father, .33 for the mother, and .48 for both parents combined. In other words, the higher the n Achievement score the more the student tended to rate both parents, but particularly the father, rejectant. Again this suggests that the son was either forced to stand on his own feet by his parents or *thought* he was forced to stand on his own feet (and therefore "rejected"). The sons were also asked to rate their parents on several different personality characteristics including the following: friendly, helpful, domineering, selfish, successful, clever, self-confident. Table 1 shows the results when the personality characteristics were grouped according to similarity.

Apparently, again, the sons who rated their parents as unfriendly, unhelpful, and unsuccessful tended to have higher n Achievement scores. In reverse, the sons who found their parents (especially their fathers) to be helpful, nurturent, friendly, and successful tended to have low n Achievement scores. Again this makes theoretical sense. Apparently n Achievement develops out of an insistence on independence, or doing things for oneself which is interpreted by sons later on during college as rejection and unfriendliness. Contrariwise, boys who are greatly helped by clever fathers and mothers never get a chance to want to achieve by themselves. There are other bits of evidence in our data on this general point, but they all support the same conclusion: n Achievement score is significantly related to severity of independence training in childhood.

The general outcome of our research to date may be summarized briefly as follows:

(1) It has demonstrated the great potentiality of an n Achievement score based on phantasy as a measure of the achievement motivation of individuals irrespective of their cultural background.

(2) By providing an independent measure of motivation, it has opened up great new areas for further research, such as the relation between achievement motivation and school grades.

(3) It has demonstrated that the method of deriving a measure of motivational strength from experimentally produced changes in phantasy is a practical one which could theoretically be applied to the measurement of any motive.

(4) It has led us to question seriously prevailing theories of motivation and to attempt a revision of those theories.

TABLE 1. CORRELATIONS BETWEEN N ACHIEVEMENT SCORE AND
PERSONALITY TRAITS ATTRIBUTED TO PARENTS (N = 30)

	FATHER	MOTHER	COMBINED
1. Friendly–Helpful	−.56	−.39	−.57
2. Domineering–Selfish	.10	.14	.14
3. Successful–Clever–Self-confident	−.37	−.41	−.44

Correlations of .36 and .46 are significant at the 5% and 1% levels respectively.

The Motivating Properties of Dissonance

Leon Festinger

Leon Festinger received his doctorate from the University of Iowa in 1942. He has been interested for many years in the area of social psychology, especially in the conditions that alter attitude, opinion, and belief systems. Festinger became a member of the Psychology Department at Stanford University in 1955 and is presently on the faculty at New York University.

1. *Is this discussion dissonant or consonant with your own beliefs about what motivates people?*

2. *Does your answer to the above question make you act or think as Festinger says you would be expected to?*

I. An Introduction to the Theory of Dissonance

It has frequently been implied, and sometimes even pointed out, that the individual strives toward consistency within himself. His opinions and attitudes, for example, tend to exist in clusters that are internally consistent. Certainly one may find exceptions. A person may think Negroes are just as good as whites but would not want any living in his neighborhood; or someone may think little children should be quiet and unobtrusive and yet may be quite proud when his child aggressively captures the attention of his adult guests. When such inconsistencies are found to exist, they may be quite dramatic, but they capture our interest primarily because they stand out in sharp contrast against a background of consist-

ency. It is still overwhelmingly true that related opinions or attitudes are consistent with one another. Study after study reports such consistency among one person's political attitudes, social attitudes, and many others.

There is the same kind of consistency between what a person knows or believes and what he does. A person who believes a college education is a good thing will very likely encourage his children to go to college; a child who knows he will be severely punished for some misdemeanor will not commit it or at least will try not to be caught doing it. This is not surprising, of course; it is so much the rule that we take it for granted. Again what captures our attention are the exceptions to otherwise consistent behavior. A person may know that smoking is bad for him and yet continue to smoke; many persons commit crimes even though they know the high probability of being caught and the punishment that awaits them.

Granting that consistency is the usual thing, perhaps overwhelmingly so, what about these exceptions which come to mind so readily? Only rarely, if ever, are they accepted psychologically *as inconsistencies* by the person involved. Usually more or less successful attempts are made to rationalize them. Thus, the person who continues to smoke, knowing that it is bad for his health, may also feel (*a*) he enjoys smoking so much it is worth it; (*b*) the chances of his health suffering are not as serious as some would make out; (*c*) he can't always avoid every possible dangerous contingency and still live; and (*d*) perhaps even if he stopped smoking he would put on weight which is equally bad for his health. So, continuing to smoke is, after all, consistent with his ideas about smoking.

But persons are not always successful in explaining away or in rationalizing inconsistencies to themselves. For one reason or another, attempts to achieve consistency may fail. The inconsistency then simply continues to exist. Under such circumstances—that is, in the presence of an inconsistency—there is psychological discomfort.

The basic hypotheses can now be stated. First, I will replace the word "inconsistency" with a term which has less of a logical connotation, namely, *dissonance*. I will likewise replace the word "consistency" with a more neutral term, namely, *consonance*. A more formal definition of these terms will be given shortly; for the moment, let us try to get along with the implicit meaning they have acquired as a result of the preceding discussion.

The basic hypotheses I wish to state are as follows:

1. The existence of dissonance, being psychologically uncomfortable, will motivate the person to try to reduce the dissonance and achieve consonance.

2. When dissonance is present, in addition to trying to reduce it, the person will actively avoid situations and information which would likely increase the dissonance.

Before proceeding to develop this theory of dissonance and the pressures to reduce it, it would be well to clarify the nature of dissonance, what kind of a concept it is, and where the theory concerning it will lead. The two hypotheses stated above provide a good starting point for this clarification. While they refer here specifically to dissonance, they are in fact very general hypotheses. In place of "dissonance" one can substitute other notions similar in nature, such as "hunger," "frustration," or "disequilibrium," and the hypotheses would still make perfectly good sense.

In short, I am proposing that dissonance, that is, the existence of nonfitting relations among cognitions, is a motivating factor in its

own right. By the term *cognition,* I mean any knowledge, opinion, or belief about the environment, about oneself, or about one's behavior. Cognitive dissonance can be seen as an antecedent condition which leads to activity oriented toward dissonance reduction just as hunger leads to activity oriented toward hunger reduction. It is a very different motivation from what psychologists are used to dealing with but, as we shall see, nonetheless powerful.

The Occurrence and Persistence of Dissonance

Why and how does dissonance ever arise? How does it happen that persons sometimes find themselves doing things that do not fit with what they know, or having opinions that do not fit with other opinions they hold? An answer to this question may be found in discussing two of the more common situations in which dissonance may occur.

1. New events may happen or new information may become known to a person, creating at least a momentary dissonance with existing knowledge, opinion, or cognition concerning behavior. Since a person does not have complete and perfect control over the information that reaches him and over events that can happen in his environment, such dissonances may easily arise. Thus, for example, a person may plan to go on a picnic with complete confidence that the weather will be warm and sunny. Nevertheless, just before he is due to start, it may begin to rain. The knowledge that it is now raining is dissonant with his confidence in a sunny day and with his planning to go to a picnic. Or, as another example, a person who is quite certain in his knowledge that automatic transmissions on automobiles are inefficient may accidentally come across an article praising automatic transmissions. Again, at least a momentary dissonance is created.

2. Even in the absence of new, unforeseen events or information, the existence of dissonance is undoubtedly an everyday condition. Very few things are all black or all white; very few situations are clear-cut enough so that opinions or behaviors are not to some extent a mixture of contradictions. Thus, a midwestern farmer who is a Republican may be opposed to his party's position on farm price supports; a person buying a new car may prefer the economy of one model but the design of another; a person deciding on how to invest his money

may know that the outcome of his investment depends upon economic conditions beyond his control. Where an opinion must be formed or a decision taken, some dissonance is almost unavoidably created between the cognition of the action taken and those opinions or knowledges which tend to point to a different action.

There is, then, a fairly wide variety of situations in which dissonance is nearly unavoidable. But it remains for us to examine the circumstances under which dissonance, once arisen, persists. That is, under what conditions is dissonance not simply a momentary affair? If the hypotheses stated above are correct, then as soon as dissonance occurs there will be pressures to reduce it. To answer this question it is necessary first to have a brief look at the possible ways in which dissonance may be reduced.

Let us now examine how dissonance may be reduced, using as an illustration the example of the habitual cigarette smoker who has learned that smoking is bad for his health. He may have acquired this information from a newspaper or magazine, from friends, or even from some physician. This knowledge is certainly dissonant with cognition that he continues to smoke. If the hypothesis that there will be pressures to reduce this dissonance is correct, what would the person involved be expected to do?

1. He might simply change his cognition about his behavior by changing his actions; that is, he might stop smoking. If he no longer smokes, then his cognition of what he does will be consonant with the knowledge that smoking is bad for his health.

2. He might change his "knowledge" about the effects of smoking. This sounds like a peculiar way to put it, but it expresses well what must happen. He might simply end up believing that smoking does not have any deleterious effects, or he might acquire so much "knowledge" pointing to the good effects it has that the harmful aspects become negligible. If he can manage to change his knowledge in either of these ways, he will have reduced, or even eliminated, the dissonance between what he does and what he knows.

But in the above illustration it seems clear that the person may encounter difficulties in trying to change either his behavior or his knowledge. And this, of course, is precisely the reason that dissonance, once created, may persist. There is no guarantee that the person will

be able to reduce or remove the dissonance. The hypothetical smoker may find that the process of giving up smoking is too painful for him to endure. He might try to find facts and opinions of others to support the view that smoking is not harmful, but these attempts might fail. He might then remain in the situation where he continues to smoke and continues to know that smoking is harmful. If this turns out to be the case, however, his efforts to reduce the dissonance will not cease.

Indeed, there are some areas of cognition where the existence of major dissonance is customary. This may occur when two or more established beliefs or values, all relevant to the area of cognition in question, are inconsistent. That is, no opinion can be held, and no behavior engaged in, that will not be dissonant with at least one of these established beliefs. Myrdal, in the appendix to his classic book, states this quite well in connection with attitudes and behavior toward Negroes. In discussing the simultaneous existence of opinions and values concerning human beings in general, Negroes in general, specific groups of Negroes, and so on, Myrdal states:

A need will be felt by the person or group, whose inconsistencies in valuations are publicly exposed, to find a means of reconciling the inconsistencies. . . . The feeling of need for logical consistency within the hierarchy of moral valuations . . . is, in its modern intensity, a rather new phenomenon. With less mobility, less intellectual communication, and less public discussion, there was in previous generations less exposure of one another's valuation conflicts.

While I find myself in disagreement with Myrdal in the importance he places on the public exposure of the dissonance, I feel it is a good statement of some of the reasons why strong dissonance exists in this area.

The notions introduced thus far are not entirely new; many similar ones have been suggested. It may be of value to mention two whose formulation is closest to my own. Heider, in an as yet unpublished manuscript, discusses the relationships among people and among sentiments. He states:

Summarizing this preliminary discussion of balanced, or harmonious, states, we can say that they are states characterized by two or more relations which fit together. If no balanced state exists, then forces toward the [balanced] state will arise. Either there will be a tendency to change the sentiments involved, or the unit relations will be changed through action or cognitive reorganization. If a change is not possible, the state of imbalance will produce tension, and the balanced states will be preferred over the states of imbalance.

If one replaces the word "balanced" with "consonant" and "imbalance" with "dissonance," this statement by Heider can be seen to indicate the same process with which our discussion up to now has dealt.

Osgood and Tannenbaum recently published a paper in which they also formulated and documented a similar idea with respect to changes in opinions and attitudes. In discussing the "principle of congruity," as they call it, they state: "Changes in evaluation are always in the direction of increased congruity with the existing frame of reference." The particular kind of "incongruity" or cognitive dissonance with which they deal in their study is produced by the knowledge that a person or other source of information which a subject regards positively (or negatively) supports an opinion which the subject regards negatively (or positively). They proceed to show that under such circumstances there is a marked tendency to change either the evaluation of the opinion involved or the evaluation of the source in a direction which would reduce the dissonance. Thus, if the source were positively evaluated and the opinion negatively evaluated, the person might end up reacting less positively to the source or more positively to the issue. It is also clear from their data that the particular outcome depends on whether the evaluation of the source or of the issue is initially more firmly rooted in the person's cognition. If his attitude toward the source is highly "polarized," then the opinion is more likely to change, and vice versa. Indeed, by careful initial measurement of the attitudes toward the sources and toward the opinions before the dissonance is introduced, and by careful measurement of how resistant each of these is to change, the authors are able to predict quite nicely the direction, and in some instances the amount, of change in evaluation.

The important point to remember is that there is pressure to produce consonant relations among cognitions and to avoid and reduce dissonance. Many other writers have recognized this, although few have stated it as concretely and as succinctly as the authors we have mentioned. The task which we are attempting is to formulate the theory of dissonance in a precise yet generally applicable form, to draw out its implications to a variety of contexts, and to present data relevant to the theory.

Resistance to Reduction of Dissonance

If dissonance is to be reduced or eliminated by changing one or more cognitive elements, it is necessary to consider how resistant these cognitive elements are to change. Whether or not any of them change, and if so, which ones, will certainly be determined in part by the magnitude of resistance to change which they possess. It is, of course, clear that if the various cognitive elements involved had no resistance to change whatsoever, there would never be any lasting dissonances. Momentary dissonance might occur, but if the cognitive elements involved had no resistance to change, the dissonance would immediately be eliminated. Let us, then, look at the major sources of resistance to change of a cognitive element.

Just as the reduction of dissonance presented somewhat different problems depending upon whether the element to be changed was a behavioral or an environmental one, so the major sources of resistance to change are different for these two classes of cognitive elements.

Resistance to Change of Behavioral Cognitive Elements. The first and foremost source of resistance to change for *any* cognitive element is the responsiveness of such elements to reality. If one sees that the grass is green, it is very difficult to think it is not so. If a person is walking down the street, it is difficult for his cognition not to contain an element corresponding to this. Given this strong and sometimes overwhelming responsiveness to reality, the problem of changing a behavioral cognitive element becomes the problem of changing the behavior which is being mapped by the element. Consequently, the resistance to change of the cognitive element is identical with the resistance to change of the behavior reflected by that element, assuming that the person maintains contact with reality.

Certainly much behavior has little or no resistance to change. We continually modify many of our actions and feelings in accordance with changes in the situation. If a street which we ordinarily use when we drive to work is being repaired, there is usually little difficulty in altering our behavior and using a different route. What, then, are the circumstances that make it difficult for the person to change his actions?

1. The change may be painful or involve loss. A person may, for example, have spent a lot of money to purchase a house. If for any reason he now wants to change, that is, live in a different house or different neighborhood, he must endure the discomforts of moving and the possible financial loss involved in selling the house. A person who might desire to give up smoking must endure the discomfort and pain of the cessation in order to accomplish the change. Clearly, in such circumstances there will be a certain resistance to change. The magnitude of this resistance to change will be determined by the extent of pain or loss which must be endured.

2. The present behavior may be otherwise satisfying. A person might continue to have lunch at a certain restaurant even though they served poor food if, for example, his friends always ate there. Or a person who is very domineering and harsh toward his children might not easily be able to give up the satisfactions of being able to boss someone, even if on various grounds he desired to change. In such instances, of course, the resistance to change would be a function of the satisfaction obtained from the present behavior.

3. Making the change may simply not be possible. It would be a mistake to imagine that a person could consummate any change in his behavior if he wanted to badly enough. It may not be possible to change for a variety of reasons. Some behavior, especially emotional reactions, may not be under the voluntary control of the person. For example, a person might have a strong reaction of fear which he can do nothing about. Also, it might not be possible to consummate a change simply because the new behavior may not be in the behavior repertory of the person. A father might not be able to change the way he behaves toward his children

simply because he doesn't know any other way to behave. A third circumstance which could make it impossible to change is the irrevocable nature of certain actions. If, for example, a person has sold his house and then decides he wants it back, there is nothing that can be done if the new owner refuses to sell it. The action has been taken and is not reversible. But under circumstances where the behavior simply cannot change at all, it is not correct to say that the resistance to change of the corresponding cognitive element is infinite. The resistance to change which the cognitive element possesses can, of course, not be greater than the pressure to respond to reality.

Resistance to Change of Environmental Cognitive Elements. Here again, as with behavioral cognitive elements, the major source of resistance to change lies in the responsiveness of these elements to reality. The result of this, as far as behavioral elements go, is to tie the resistance to change of the cognitive element to the resistance to change of the reality, namely, the behavior itself. The situation is somewhat different with regard to environmental elements. When there is a clear and unequivocal reality corresponding to some cognitive element, the possibilities of change are almost nil. If one desired, for example, to change one's cognition about the location of some building which one saw every day, this would indeed be difficult to accomplish.

In many instances, however, the reality corresponding to the cognitive element is by no means so clear and unambiguous. When the reality is basically a social one, that is, when it is established by agreement with other people, the resistance to change would be determined by the difficulty of finding persons to support the new cognition.

There is another source of resistance to change of both behavioral and environmental cognitive elements. We have postponed discussion of it until now, however, because it is a more important source of resistance to change for environmental elements than for others. This source of resistance to change lies in the fact that an element is in relationship with a number of other elements. To the extent that the element is consonant with a large number of other elements and to the extent that changing it would replace these consonances by dissonances, the element will be resistant to change.

The above discussion is not meant to be an exhaustive analysis of resistance to change or a listing of conceptually different sources. Rather, it is a discussion which attempts to make distinctions that will help operationally rather than conceptually. In considering any dissonance and the resistance to change of the elements involved, the important factor in the attempt to eliminate the dissonance by changing an element is the total amount of resistance to change; the source of the resistance is immaterial.

Limits of the Magnitude of Dissonance

The maximum dissonance that can possibly exist between any two elements is equal to the total resistance to change of the less resistant element. The magnitude of dissonance cannot exceed this amount because, at this point of maximum possible dissonance, the less resistant element would change, thus eliminating the dissonance.

This does not mean that the magnitude of dissonance will frequently even approach this maximum possible value. When there exists a strong dissonance that is less than the resistance to change of any of the elements involved, this dissonance can perhaps still be reduced for the total cognitive system by adding new cognitive elements. In this way, even in the presence of very strong resistances to change, the total dissonance in the system could be kept at rather low levels.

Let us consider an example of a person who spends what for him is a very large sum of money for a new car of an expensive type. Let us also imagine that after purchasing it he finds that some things go wrong with it and that repairs are very expensive. It is also more expensive to operate than other cars, and what is more, he finds that his friends think the car is ugly. If the dissonance becomes great enough, that is, equal to the resistance to change of the less resistant element, which in this situation would probably be the behavioral element, he might sell the car and suffer whatever inconvenience and financial loss is involved. Thus

the dissonance could not exceed the resistance the person has to changing his behavior, that is, selling the car.

Now let us consider the situation where the dissonance for the person who bought a new car was appreciable but less than the maximum possible dissonance, that is, less than the resistance to change of the less resistant cognitive element. None of the existing cognitive elements would then be changed, but he could keep the total dissonance low by adding more and more cognitions that are consonant with his ownership of the car. He begins to feel that power and riding qualities are more important than economy and looks. He begins to drive faster than he used to and becomes quite convinced that it is important for a car to be able to travel at high speed. With these cognitions and others, he might succeed in rendering the dissonance negligible.

It is also possible, however, that his attempts to add new consonant cognitive elements would prove unsuccessful and that his financial situation is such that he could not sell the car. It would still be possible to reduce the dissonance by what also amounts to adding a new cognitive element, but of a different kind. He can admit to himself, and to others, that he was wrong to purchase the car and that if he had it to do over again, he would buy a different kind. This process of divorcing himself psychologically from the action can and does materially reduce the dissonance. Sometimes, however, the resistances against this are quite strong. The maximum dissonance which could exist would, in such circumstances, be determined by the resistance to admitting that he had been wrong or foolish.

Avoidance of Dissonance

The discussion thus far has focused on the tendencies to reduce or eliminate dissonance and the problems involved in achieving such reduction. Under certain circumstances there are also strong and important tendencies to avoid increases of dissonance or to avoid the occurrence of dissonance altogether. Let us now turn our attention to a consideration of these circumstances and the manifestations of the avoidance tendencies which we might expect to observe.

The avoidance of an increase in dissonance

comes about, of course, as a result of the existence of dissonance. This avoidance is especially important where, in the process of attempting to reduce dissonance, support is sought for a new cognitive element to replace an existing one or where new cognitive elements are to be added. In both these circumstances, the seeking of support and the seeking of new information must be done in a highly selective manner. A person would initiate discussion with someone he thought would agree with the new cognitive element but would avoid discussion with someone who might agree with the element that he was trying to change. A person would expose himself to sources of information which he expected would add new elements which would increase consonance but would certainly avoid sources which would increase dissonance.

If there is little or no dissonance existing, we would not expect the same kind of selectivity in exposure to sources of support or sources of information. In fact, where no dissonance exists there should be a relative absence of motivation to seek support or new information at all. This will be true in general, but there are important exceptions. Past experience may lead a person to fear, and hence to avoid, the initial occurrence of dissonance. Where this is true, one might expect circumspect behavior with regard to new information even when little or no dissonance is present to start with.

The operation of a fear of dissonance may also lead to a reluctance to commit oneself behaviorally. There is a large class of actions that, once taken, are difficult to change. Hence, it is possible for dissonances to arise and to mount in intensity. A fear of dissonance would lead to a reluctance to take action—a reluctance to commit oneself. Where decision and action cannot be indefinitely delayed, the taking of action may be accompanied by a cognitive negation of the action. Thus, for example, a person who buys a new car and is very afraid of dissonance may, immediately following the purchase, announce his conviction that he did the wrong thing. Such strong fear of dissonance is probably relatively rare, but it does occur. Personality differences with respect to fear of dissonance and the effectiveness with which one is able to reduce dissonance are undoubtedly important in determining whether or not such avoidance of dissonance is likely to happen. The operational problem would be to independently identify situations and persons where this kind of a priori self-protective behavior occurs.

Summary

The core of the theory of dissonance which we have stated is rather simple. It holds that:

1. There may exist dissonant or "nonfitting" relations among cognitive elements.

2. The existence of dissonance gives rise to pressures to reduce the dissonance and to avoid increases in dissonance.

3. Manifestations of the operation of these pressures include behavior changes, changes of cognition, and circumspect exposure to new information and new opinions.

Although the core of the theory is simple, it has rather wide implications and applications to a variety of situations which on the surface look very different.

The Autonomy of Motives

Gordon W. Allport

Gordon Allport (1897–1967) was Professor of Psychology at Harvard University, where he received his Ph.D. in 1922. A past president of the American Psychological Association, Allport was the author of many articles and books on psychology. He was especially interested in the psychology of prejudice and was well known for the Study of Values test that he devised with the assistance of colleagues Vernon and Lindzey.

1. *Can you think of other psychological principles that might better explain the examples described in this article?*

2. *What are the author's feelings regarding the importance of a historical approach toward understanding behavior?*

To understand the dynamics of the normal mature personality a new and somewhat radical principle of growth must be introduced to supplement the more traditional genetic concepts thus far considered. For convenience of discussion this new principle may be christened the *functional autonomy of motives.*

Now, any type of psychology that treats *motives,* thereby endeavoring to answer the question as to *why* men behave as they do, is called a *dynamic psychology.* By its very nature it cannot be merely a descriptive psychology, content to depict the *what* and the *how* of human behavior. The boldness of dynamic psychology in striking for causes stands in marked contrast to the timid, "more scientific" view that seeks nothing else than the establishment of a mathematical function for the relation between some artificially simple stimulus and some equally artificial and simple response. If the psychology of personality is to be more than a matter of coefficients of correlation it *must* be a dynamic psychology, and seek first and foremost a sound and adequate theory of the nature of human dispositions.

Evidence for Functional Autonomy

Let us begin in a common sense way. An ex-sailor has a craving for the sea, a musician longs to return to his instrument after an enforced absence, a city-dweller yearns for his native hills, and a miser continues to amass his useless horde. Now, the sailor may have first acquired his love for the sea as an incident in his struggle to earn a living. The sea was merely a conditioned stimulus associated with satisfaction of his "nutritional craving." But now the ex-sailor is perhaps a wealthy banker; the original motive is destroyed; and yet the hunger for the sea persists unabated, even increases in intensity as it becomes more remote from the "nutritional segment." The musician may first have been stung by a rebuke or by a slur on his inferior performances into mastering his instrument, but now he is safely beyond power of these taunts; there is no need to continue, yet he loves his instrument more than anything else in the world. Once indeed the city dweller may have associated the hills around his mountain home with nutritional and erotogenic satisfactions, but these satisfactions he finds in his city home, *not* in the mountains; whence then comes all his hill-hunger? The miser perhaps learned his habits of thrift in dire necessity, or perhaps his thrift was a symptom of sexual perversion (as Freud would claim), and yet the miserliness persists, and even becomes stronger with the years, even after the necessity or the roots of the neurosis have been relieved.

Abridged from Gordon W. Allport, *Personality, A Psychological Interpretation* (New York: Holt, Rinehart and Winston, Inc., 1937), pp. 191–192, 196–197, 205–207. Reprinted with permission of the publishers.

Workmanship is a good example of functional autonomy. A good workman feels compelled to do clean-cut jobs even though his security, or the praise of others, no longer depends upon high standards. In fact, in a day of jerry-building his workman-like standards may be to his economic disadvantage. Even so he cannot do a slipshod job. Workmanship is not an instinct, but so firm is the hold it may acquire on a man that it is little wonder Veblen mistook it for one. A businessman, long since secure economically, works himself into ill-health, and sometimes even back into poverty, for the sake of carrying on his plans. What was once an instrumental technique becomes a master-motive.

Neither necessity nor reason can make one contented permanently on a lonely island or on an isolated country farm after one is adapted to active, energetic city life. The acquired habits seem sufficient to urge one to a frenzied existence, even though reason and health demand the simpler life.

The pursuit of literature, the development of good taste in clothes, the use of cosmetics, the acquiring of an automobile, strolls in the public park, or a winter in Miami, may first serve, let us say, the interests of sex. But every one of these instrumental activities may become an interest in itself, held for a lifetime, long after the erotic motive has been laid away in lavender. People often find that they have lost allegiance to their original aims because of their deliberate preference for the many ways of achieving them.

The maternal sentiment offers an excellent final illustration. Many young mothers bear their children unwillingly, dismayed at the thought of the drudgery of the future. At first they may be indifferent to, or even hate, their offspring; the "parental instinct" seems wholly lacking. The only motives that hold such a mother to child-tending may be fear of what her critical neighbors will say, fear of the law, a habit of doing any job well, or perhaps a dim hope that the child will provide security for her in her old age. However gross these motives, they are sufficient to hold her to her work, until through the practice of devotion her burden becomes a joy. As her love for the child develops, her earlier practical motives are forgotten. In later years not one of these original motives may operate. The child may be in-

competent, criminal, a disgrace to her, and far from serving as a staff for her declining years, he may continue to drain her resources and vitality. The neighbors may criticize her for indulging the child, the law may exonerate her from allegiance; she certainly feels no pride in such a child; yet she sticks to him. The tenacity of the maternal sentiment under such adversity is proverbial.[1]

Only such a principle as that under discussion can provide a flexible enough account of the plurality of motives and their countless expressions in human life. Its specific advantages stand out in the following summary:

1. It clears the way for a completely dynamic psychology of *traits, attitudes, interests,* and *sentiments,* which can now be regarded as the ultimate and true dispositions of the mature personality.

2. It avoids the absurdity of regarding the energy of life now, in the *present,* as somehow consisting of early archaic forms (instincts, prepotent reflexes, or the never-changing Id). Learning brings new systems of interests into existence just as it does new abilities and skills. At each stage of development these interests are always contemporary; whatever drives, drives *now.*

3. It dethrones the stimulus. A motive is no longer regarded as a mechanical reflex or as a matter of redintegration, depending entirely upon the capricious operation of a conditioned stimulus. In a very real sense dispositions select the stimuli to which they respond, even though *some* stimulus is required for their arousal.

4. It readily admits the validity of all other established principles of growth. Functional autonomy *utilizes* the products of differentiation, integration, maturation, exercise, imitation, suggestion, conditioning, trauma, and all

---

[1] Most mothers, to be sure, give their babies a somewhat warmer welcome from the start, but, even so, there is little evidence that the maternal instinct is a ready-made, full-fledged and invariable possession of all women. Even those who have early learned to be fond of babies find that with practice and experience the interest becomes constantly stronger, demanding no other satisfaction for itself than its own autonomous functioning. Some women become *so* absorbed in being good mothers that they neglect being the good wives they were earlier.

other processes of development; and allows, as they do not, considered by themselves, for their *structuration* into significant motivational patterns.

5. It places in proper perspective the problems of the origin of conduct by removing the fetish of the genetic method. Not that the historical view of behavior is unimportant for a complete understanding of personality, but so far as *motives* are concerned the cross-sectional dynamic analysis is more significant. Motives being always contemporary should be studied in their present structure. Failure to do so is probably the chief reason why psychoanalysis meets so many defeats, as do all other therapeutic schemes relying too exclusively upon uncovering the motives of early childhood.

6. It accounts for the force of delusions, shell shock, phobias, and all manner of compulsive and maladaptive behavior. One would expect such unrealistic modes of adjustment to be given up as soon as they are shown to be poor ways of confronting the environment. Insight and the law of effect should both remove them. But too often they have acquired a strangle hold in their own right.

7. At last we can account adequately for socialized and civilized behavior. The principle supplies the correction necessary to the faulty logic of *bellum omnium contra omnes.* Starting life as a completely selfish being, the child would indeed remain entirely wolfish and piggish throughout his days unless genuine transformations of motives took place. Motives being completely alterable, the dogma of Egoism turns out to be a callow and superficial philosophy of behavior, or else a useless redundancy.

8. It explains likewise why a person often *becomes* what at first he merely *pretends* to be—the smiling professional hostess who grows fond of her once irksome role and is unhappy when deprived of it; the man who for so long has counterfeited the appearance of self-confidence and optimism that he is always driven to assume it; the prisoner who comes to love his shackles. Such *personae,* as Jung observes, are often transformed into the real self. The mask becomes the *anima.*

9. The drive behind genius is explained. Gifted people demand the exercise of their talents, even when no other reward lies ahead. In lesser degree the various hobbies, the artistic, or the intellectual interests of any person show the same significant autonomy.

10. In brief, the principle of functional autonomy is a declaration of independence for the psychology of personality. Though in itself a general law, at the same time it helps to account, not for the abstract motivation of an impersonal and purely hypothetical mind-in-general as do other dynamic principles, but for the concrete, viable motives of any one mind-in-particular.

Suggested Readings

Cannon, W. B. "Hunger and Thirst," in C. Murchison, ed., *A Handbook of General Experimental Psychology.* Worcester, Mass.: Clark Univ. Press, 1934.

Ford, C. S., and F. A. Beach. *Patterns of Sexual Behavior.* New York: Harper, 1951.

French, E. G. "Effects of the Interaction of Motivation and Feedback on Performance," in J. W. Atkinson, ed., *Motives in Fantasy, Action, and Society.* New York: Van Nostrand, 1958.

Frenkel-Brunswick, E. "Motivation and Behavior," *Genet. Psychol. Monog.* 26 (1942), 121–265.

Harlow, H. F., M. K. Harlow, and D. R. Meyer. "Learning Motivated by a Manipulation Drive," *J. exp. Psychol.,* 40 (1950), 228–234.

Kinsey, A. C., W. B. Pomeroy, and C. E. Martin. *Sexual Behavior in the Human Male.* Philadelphia: Saunders, 1948.

Lindsley, D. B. "Emotion," in S. S. Stevens, ed., *Handbook of Experimental Psychology.* New York: Wiley, 1951.

Lindzey, G., ed., *Assessment of Human Motives.* New York: Rinehart, 1958.

Maslow, A. H. *Motivation and Personality*. New York: Harper, 1954.

Morgan, C. T., and J. D. Morgan. "Studies in Hunger: II," *J. genet. Psychol.,* 57 (1940), 153–163.

Moruzzi, G., and H. W. Magoun. "Brain Stem Reticular Formation and Activation of the E.E.G.," *E.E.G. clin. Neurophysiol.* 1 (1949), 455–473.

Olds, J. "Physiological Mechanisms of Reward," in M. Jones, ed., *Nebraska Symposium on Motivation*. Lincoln: Univ. of Nebraska Press, Vol. III, 1955, pp. 73–139.

Tsang, Y. C. "Hunger Motivation in Gastrectomized Rats," *J. comp. Psychol.,* 26 (1938), 1–17.

5   *The Nature of Learning*

Learning, like motivation, is an unwieldy term. It is unwieldy because it refers to almost any situation in which a change in performance occurs. Specifically, learning refers to those changes in behavior that result directly from experience. Learning is also the name of the process whereby such change is carried out. It does not refer to behavior changes that result from events occurring outside the control of the participant—such events as bodily injury, surgery, fatigue, disease, or sensory adaptation. Nevertheless there is an infinite variety of situations in which performance change does occur. Moreover, a number of reasonably well-established principles underlie the confusing array of learned behavior. These principles of learning are the result of the kind of thinking—although not inclusively so—to be found in the selections in this chapter.

Problems and Issues in the Study of Learning, Ernest R. Hilgard. The first two selections are concerned with some of the theoretical aspects of learning. Questions to be kept in mind while reading about the learning process are stated in this first selection, by Hilgard. These questions are important because issues in learning change from time to time according to whose theory has been chosen for revision. This selection, in addition, contains condensed statements of the problems and issues peculiar to learning research. It should serve as a guide for thought and imagination through the other selections in the chapter.

Framework for an Objective Theory of Behavior, Clark L. Hull. Hull provides a foundation on which to build a theory of learning. This particular selection refers to many of the philosophical issues of science: the determination of a unit of measurement, the role of intervening variables, objectivity versus subjectivity of approach, and so on. Hull is quite honest about his tendency to "regard, from time to time, the behaving organism as a completely self-maintaining robot." He is of particular interest because he epitomizes the logical, objective, and scientific attitude in psychology.

Classical Conditioning, Ivan P. Pavlov. The phrase "Pavlov's salivating dogs" competes with "Freud's Oedipal complex" for popular usage. Yet very few people have read Pavlov's narration of his pioneer work on the conditioned response. This is the type of study that has become known as classical conditioning. It displays a precision and reliability of work seldom seen in the field of learning. This precision is especially difficult, of course, when human subjects are used. Because classical conditioning is experimenter controlled, the subject's response is dependent on reinforcement—reward or punishment. This is in contrast to instrumental, or operant, conditioning, which is environmentally controlled and in which reinforcement is dependent on the subject's making the correct response.

Operant Conditioning, Burrhus F. Skinner. The two basic types of conditioning can be understood by contrasting the approach of Pavlov with that of Skinner. Skinner is a controversial figure in psychology. His work on automated learning, his antitheoretical approach to the study of learning, and his utopian novel, *Walden Two,* are a few of the subjects with which his name is associated.

Learning to Fear, Harold E. Jones and Mary C. Jones. The two preceding selections use the study of animal behavior to establish controlled experimental conditions. Harold and Mary Jones focus on the interrelation of animal and human. This selection is an empirical description of some practical procedures used to discover how children come to know fear. College students, it may be noted, have a greater fear of certain animals than do 8-year-olds. This fact strongly suggests that the attitudes one holds toward man and mankind are established early in life and are acquired from other people.

Problems and Issues in the Study of Learning

Ernest R. Hilgard

Ernest Hilgard, Professor Emeritus of Psychology and Education at Stanford University, received his Ph.D. from Yale University in 1930. Author of many articles and books and past president of the American Psychological Association, Hilgard began his career as a chemical engineer. His interest in psychology came "by way of running a student employment office at the University of Illinois." With D. G. Marquis in 1940, Hilgard introduced the terms "classical" and "instrumental" conditioning, now widely used concepts in learning.

1. *The term "learning" covers a variety of acquired skills. It has been said that the term is so broad it is meaningless. Do you think we should abandon the term? If not, in what way is it a useful concept?*

2. *Do you know of any way to test a person's capacity for learning? Does the measure you have in mind indicate capacity for all types of learning?*

The preferences of the theorist often lead him to concentrate upon one kind of learning situation to the neglect of the others. His theory is then appropriate to this situation, but becomes somewhat strained in relation to other problems of learning. A comprehensive learning theory ought to answer the questions which an intelligent non-psychologist might ask about the sorts of learning which are met in everyday life. A few such questions will be listed here.

1. *What are the limits of learning?* Here is raised the question of the capacity to learn, of individual differences among learners of the same species and of unlike species. There are questions not only of persistent differences in capacity, but of change in capacity with age. Who can learn what? Are the limits set at birth? Do people get more or less alike with practice? These are the sorts of questions which it is natural to raise.

2. *What is the role of practice in learning?* The old adage that practice makes perfect has considerable racial wisdom behind it. Surely one learns to roller skate or to play the piano only by engaging in the activity. But what do we know about practice in detail? Does improvement depend directly on the amount of repetition? If not, what are its conditions? What are the most favorable circumstances of practice? Can repetitive drill be harmful as well as helpful to the learner?

3. *How important are drives and incentives, rewards and punishments?* Everybody knows in a general way that learning can be controlled by rewards and punishments, and that it is easier to learn something which is interesting than something which is dull. But are the consequences of rewards and punishments equal and opposite? Is there a difference between intrinsic and extrinsic motives in their effect upon learn-

From *Theories of Learning*, 2nd edition, pp. 6–13, by Ernest R. Hilgard. Copyright © 1948, 1956, 1966, Appleton-Century-Crofts, Inc. Reprinted by permission of Appleton-Century-Crofts.

4. *What is the place of understanding and insight?* Some things are learned more readily if we know what we are about. We are better off as travelers if we can understand a timetable or a road map. We are helpless with differential equations unless we understand the symbols and the rules for their manipulation. But we can form vowels satisfactorily without knowing how we place our tongues, and we can read without being aware of our eye movements. Some things we appear to acquire blindly and automatically; some things we struggle hard to understand and can finally master only as we understand them. Is learning in one case different from what it is in the other?

5. *Does learning one thing help you learn something else?* This is the problem of formal discipline, as it used to be called, or of transfer of training, to use a more familiar contemporary designation. Some transfer of training must occur or there would be no use in developing a foundation for later learning. Nobody denies that it is easier to build a vocabulary in a language after you have a start in it, or that higher mathematics profits from mastery of basic concepts. The question is really one of how much transfer takes place, under what conditions, and what its nature is.

6. *What happens when we remember and when we forget?* The ordinary facts of memory are mysterious enough, but in addition to familiar remembering and forgetting, our memories may play peculiar tricks on us. Some things we wish to remember are forgotten; some things we would be willing to forget continue to plague us. In cases of amnesia there are often gaps in memory, with earlier and later events remembered. Then there are the distortions of memory, in which we remember what did not happen, as is so strikingly demonstrated in testimony experiments. What is taking place? What control have we over processes involved?

These six questions will serve as useful ones to ask of each of the major theories. They suffice to illustrate the kinds of questions which give rise to theories of learning. Now we wish to turn to certain issues that have arisen in the formulation of actual theories.

Learning theories fall into two major families: *stimulus-response* theories and *cognitive* theories, but not all theories belong to these two families. The stimulus-response theories include such diverse members as the theories of Thorndike, Guthrie, Skinner, and Hull. The cognitive theories include at least those of Tolman, the classical gestalt psychologists, and Lewin. Not completely and clearly classifiable in these terms are the theories of functionalism, psychodynamics, and the probabilistic theories of the model builders. The lines of cleavage between the two families of theories are not the only cleavages within learning theories; there are other specific issues upon which theories within one family may differ.

General Issues Producing a Cleavage Between Stimulus-Response and Cognitive Theories

The cleavages between the theorists of opposing camps are difficult to understand because many of the distinctions which at first seem to contrast sharply later are found to be blurred. All reputable theorists accept a common logic of experimentation, so that disagreements over experimentally obtained facts are readily arbitrated. In the end, all the theorists accept a common body of demonstrated relationships, at the factual or descriptive level; any theorist who denied an established fact, a reproducible experimental finding, would lose status among his scientific colleagues, and his theories would no longer command respect. The first rule that we must be prepared to accept, as we judge the relative merits of different theories is this: *All the theorists accept all of the facts.* Some experimental findings are doubted when they are first announced and the status of findings *as fact* may for a long time be doubted; but once the status as fact is established, all accept the fact as true. Hence the differences between two theorists are primarily differences in interpretation. Both theories may fit the facts reasonably well, but the proponent of each theory believes his view to be the more fruitful. We shall be better prepared later on to discuss the ways in which theories get validated or modified after we are acquainted with them in more detail. For the present, we must be prepared to accept the historical truth that opposing theories have great survival value, and that an appeal to the facts as a way of choosing between theories is a very complex process, not nearly as decisive in practice as we might expect it to be.

We may begin by examining three kinds of preferences on which stimulus-response theorists tend to differ from cognitive theorists.

1. "Peripheral" versus "Central" Intermediaries

Ever since Watson promulgated the theory that thinking was merely the carrying out of subvocal speech movements, stimulus-response theorists have preferred to find response or movement intermediaries to serve as integrators of behavior sequences. Such movement-produced intermediaries can be classified as "peripheral" mechanisms, as contrasted with "central" (ideational) intermediaries. The stimulus-response theorist tends to believe that some sort of chained muscular responses, linked perhaps by fractional anticipatory goal responses, serve to keep a rat running to a distant food box. The cognitive theorist, on the other hand, more freely infers central brain processes, such as memories or expectations, as integrators of goal-seeking behavior. The differences in preference survive in this case because both kinds of theorists depend upon *inferences* from observed behavior, and the inferences are not directly verified in either case. It is potentially easier to verify tongue movements in thinking than it is to discover a revived memory trace in the brain, but in fact such verification is not offered with the precision necessary to compel belief in the theory. Under the circumstances, the choice between the peripheral and the central explanation is not forced, and favoring one or the other position depends upon more general systematic preferences.

2. Acquisition of Habits versus Acquisition of Cognitive Structures

The stimulus-response theorist and the cognitive theorist come up with different answers to the question, What is learned? The answer of the former is "habits"; the answer of the latter is "cognitive structures." The first answer appeals to common sense: we all know that we develop smooth-running skills by practicing

them; what we learn is *responses*. But the second answer also appeals to common sense: if we locate a candy store from one starting point, we can find it from another because we "know where it is"; what we learn is *facts*. A smooth-running skill illustrates a learned habit; knowing alternate routes illustrates cognitive structure. If all habits were highly mechanical and stereotyped, variable nonhabitual behavior would force us to admit cognitive structures as part, at least, of what is learned. But the stimulus-response psychologist is satisfied that he can deduce from the laws of habit formation the behavior that the cognitive theorist believes supports his interpretation. Hence we cannot choose between the theories by coming up with "decisive" illustrations of what we learn, for both groups of theorists will offer explanations of all our examples. The competing theories would not have survived thus far had they been unable to offer such explanations.

3. Trial and Error versus Insight in Problem-Solving

When confronted with a novel problem, how does the learner reach solution? The stimulus-response psychologist finds the learner assembling his habits from the past appropriate to the new problem, responding either according to the elements that the new problem has in common with familiar ones, or according to aspects of the new situation which are similar to situations met before. If these do not lead to solution, the learner resorts to trial and error, bringing out of his behavior repertory one response after another until the problem is solved. The cognitive psychologist agrees with much of this description of what the learner does, but he adds interpretations not offered by the stimulus-response psychologist. He points out, for example, that granting all the requisite experience with the parts of a problem, there is no guarantee that the learner will be able to bring these past experiences to bear upon the solution. He may be able to solve the problem if it is presented in one form and not solve it if it is presented in another form, even though both forms require the same past experiences for their solution. According to the cognitive theorist, the preferred method of presentation permits a perceptual structuring leading to "insight," that is, to the understanding of the essential relationships involved. The stimulus-response psychologist tends, by preference, to look to the past history of the learner for the sources of solution, while the cognitive psychologist, by preference, looks to the contemporary structuring of the problem. His preference for the past does not require the stimulus-response psychologist to ignore the present structuring of the problem, nor does his preference for the present require the cognitive psychologist to ignore the past. One must not assume because there is a difference in preference that either theorist is blind to the totality of the learning situation. The facts of the insight experiment are accepted by both theorists, as are the facts of skill learning. We may remind ourselves again that no single experiment will demolish either the interpretation according to trial and error or the interpretation according to insight.

These three issues—peripheral versus central intermediaries, accquisition of habits versus acquisition of cognitive structures, and trial and error versus insight in problem-solving—give something of the flavor of the differences between these two major families of theories.

Specific Issues Not Confined to the Major Families

Some issues lie outside the conflict between the stimulus-response and the cognitive theories. Thus two stimulus-response psychologists may differ as to the role of reinforcement in learning, and two cognitive theorists may differ as to the necessity for a physiological explanation of learning. Three of these issues will suffice to alert us to the many problems that learning theorists face.

1. Contiguity versus Reinforcement

The oldest law of association is that ideas experienced together tend to become associated. This has come down in one form or another to the present day as the principle of association by contiguity, although it is now more fashionable to describe the association as between stimuli and responses rather than as between ideas. Several of our contemporary theorists accept the principle of contiguous association, notably Guthrie (a stimulus-response psychologist) and Tolman (a cognitive psychologist). Other theorists insist that learning does not take place through contiguity alone, unless there is some sort of reinforcement, some equivalent of reward or punishment.

2. One or More Kinds of Learning?

The contiguity-reinforcement dilemma may be resolved by accepting both, thus defining two varieties of learning. This solution has appealed to theorists such as Thorndike and Skinner and Mowrer. But these two varieties are not the only possibilities. Perhaps by using the common name "learning" to cover the acquisition of motor skills, the memorization of a poem, the solving of a geometrical puzzle, and the understanding of a period in history, we are deceiving ourselves by looking for common laws explanatory of processes that have little in common.

Hence the theorist has to choose between a single-factor theory and a multi-factor one. Tolman at one time pointed to the possibility of seven kinds of learning.

3. Intervening Variables versus Hypothetical Constructs

We have already considered a contrast between two types of intermediary, the peripheral and the central types. But as theories become more refined, additional problems arise over the way in which inferred intermediaries should be specified. One kind of intermediary found in theories is a mathematical constant that reappears in various contexts, such as the acceleration of a free-falling body (g) that appears in equations describing the movement of a pendulum, the path of a projectile, or the way in which balls roll down inclined planes. Such an integrating intervening variable need have no properties other than those expressed in its units of measurement, that is, it need have no independent existence, apart from the functional relationships it has in its systematic context. This kind of integrating intermediary, without surplus meanings, is called an *intervening variable*. By contrast, some kinds of intermediaries are concrete, tangible, palpable, with properties of their own. Suppose, for example, we describe the behavior that results when a cat is confronted with a barking dog. The cat arches its back, hisses, its hair stands on end, and numerous changes take place within its digestive and circulatory system. Many of the internal changes can be *explained* by the use of a demonstrable intermediary, adrenin, the hormone of the adrenal glands. Suppose that before adrenin was isolated a theorist had inferred that some substance in the blood stream was causing the internal changes. This would have been a *hypothetical construct* at this stage, an inferred intermediary with palpable qualities. The discovery of adrenin would have then confirmed the hypothesis that such a substance in the blood stream was, in fact, causing many of the changes. Adrenin, as a substance, has other properties than those inferred from bodily changes in emotion. In this it differs from a mere intervening variable, which has no further properties beyond its systematic ones.

Those who hold with intervening variables in their learning theories are free to choose such variables as they wish, provided they serve their systematic purposes of producing a more coherent and parsimonious theory than can be produced without them. Those who prefer hypothetical constructs must seek either demonstrable movements or secretions (if they are peripheralists), or some physiological brain processes (if they are centralists). Again, the issue over intervening variables or hypothetical constructs is not confined to one or the other of the major theoretical families.

One extreme position is that we can do away with intermediaries entirely (Skinner). Thus, on this issue as on the others, we have nearly all possible views represented.

This brief introduction to three contrasts between stimulus-response theories and cognitive theories, and three issues that are not confined to the two major families, should make it clear that what seem to be diametrically opposed points of view may turn out to be based on differences in preference, each being possible of persuasive statement, and to a point justifiable. The opposed cases are each made by intelligent men of good will.

Framework for an Objective Theory of Behavior

Clark L. Hull

Clark Hull (1884–1952) received his Ph.D. from the University of Wisconsin in 1918. Most of his academic career was spent at Yale University, where he worked on a variety of problems, ranging from hypnosis to aptitude testing. Hull is best known for his logically rigorous system or handling facts of learning. His unique approach to psychology can be found in his Mathematico-Deductive Theory of Rote Learning: A Study in Scientific Methodology *(1940) or in his more easily read* Principles of Behavior *(1943).*

1. *Does Hull advocate a molar or molecular study of behavior? Why?*

2. *What advantage is there in conceiving of "the behaving organism as a completely self-maintaining robot, constructed of materials as unlike ourselves as may be"?*

From *Principles of Behavior*, pp. 16–28, by Clark L. Hull. Copyright 1943, D. Appleton-Century Company, Inc. Reprinted by permission of Appleton-Century-Crofts.

The Basic Fact of Environmental-Organismic Interaction

At the outset of the independent life of an organism there begins a dynamic relationship between the organism and its environment. For the most part, both environment and organism are active; the environment acts on the organism, and the organism acts on the environment. Naturally the terminal phase of any given environmental-organismic interaction depends upon the activity of each; rarely or never can the activity of either be predicted from knowing the behavior characteristics of one alone. The possibility of predicting the outcome of such interaction depends upon the fact that both environment and organism are part of nature, and as such the activity of each takes place according to known rules, i.e., natural laws.

The environment of an organism may conveniently be divided into two portions—the internal and the external. The external environment may usefully be subdivided into the inanimate environment and the animate or organismic environment.

The laws of the internal environment are, for the most part, those of the physiology of the particular organism. The laws of the inanimate environment are those of the physical world and constitute the critical portions of the physical sciences; they are relatively simple and reasonably well known.

The laws of the organismic environment are those of the behavior of other organisms, especially organisms of the same species as the one under consideration; they make up the primary principles of the behavior, or "social," sciences and are comparatively complex. Perhaps because of this complexity they are not as yet very well understood. Since in a true or symmetrical social situation only organisms of the same species are involved, the basic laws of the activities of the environment must be the same as those of the organism under consideration. It thus comes about that *the objective of the present work is the elaboration of the basic molar[1] behavioral laws underlying the "social" sciences.*

Organismic Need, Activity, and Survival

Since the publication by Charles Darwin of the *Origin of Species* it has been necessary to think of organisms against a background of organic evolution and to consider both organis-

[1] By this expression is meant the uniformities discoverable among the grossly observable phenomena of behavior as contrasted with the laws of the behavior of the ultimate "molecules" upon which this behavior depends, such as the constituent cells of nerve, muscle, gland, and so forth. The term *molar* thus means coarse or macroscopic as contrasted with molecular, or microscopic.

mic structure and function in terms of *survival*. Survival, of course, applies equally to the individual organism and to the species. Physiological studies have shown that survival requires special circumstances in considerable variety; these include optimal conditions of air, water, food, temperature, intactness of bodily tissue, and so forth; for species survival among the higher vertebrates there is required at least the occasional presence and specialized reciprocal behavior of a mate.

On the other hand, when any of the commodities or conditions necessary for individual or species survival are lacking, or when they deviate materially from the optimum, a state of *primary need* is said to exist. In a large proportion of such situations the need will be reduced or eliminated only through the action on the environment of a particular sequence of movements made by the organism. For example, the environment will, as a rule, yield a commodity (such as food) which will mediate the abolition of a state of need (such as hunger) only when the movement sequence corresponds rather exactly to the momentary state of the environment; i.e., when the movement sequence is closely synchronized with the several phases of the environmental reactions. If it is to be successful, the behavior of a hungry cat in pursuit of a mouse must vary from instant to instant, depending upon the movements of the mouse. Similarly if the mouse is to escape the cat, its movements must vary from instant to instant, depending upon the movements of the cat.

Moreover, in a given external environment situation the behavior must often differ radically from one occasion to another, depending on the need which chances to be dominant at the time; e.g., whether it be of food, water, or a mate. In a similar manner the behavior must frequently differ widely from one environmental situation to another, even when the need is exactly the same in each environment; a hungry man lost in a forest must execute a very different sequence of movements to relieve his need from what would be necessary if he were in his home.

It follows from the above considerations that *an organism will hardly survive unless the state of organismic need and the state of the environment in its relation to the organism are some-*

how jointly and simultaneously brought to bear upon the movement-producing mechanism of the organism.

The Organic Basis of Adaptive Behavior

All normal higher organisms possess a great assortment of muscles, usually with bony accessories. These motor organs are ordinarily adequate to mediate the reduction of most needs, provided their contractions occur in the right amount, combination, and sequence. The momentary status of most portions of the environment with respect to the organism is mediated to the organism by an immense number of specialized receptors which respond to a considerable variety of energies such as light waves (vision), sound waves (hearing), gases (smell), chemical solutions (taste), mechanical impacts (touch), and so on. The state of the organism itself (the internal environment) is mediated by another highly specialized series of receptors. It is probable that the various conditions of need also fall into this latter category; i.e., in one way or another needs activate more or less characteristic receptor organs much as do external environmental forces.

Neural impulses set in motion by the action of these receptors pass along separate nerve fibers to the central ganglia of the nervous system, notably the brain. The brain, which acts as a kind of automatic switchboard, together with the remainder of the central nervous system, routes and distributes the impulses to individual muscles and glands in rather precisely graded amounts and sequences. When the neural impulse reaches an effector organ (muscle or gland) the organ ordinarily becomes active, the amount of activity usually varying with the magnitude of the impulse. The movements thus brought about usually result in the elimination of the need, though often only after numerous unsuccessful trials. But organismic activity is by no means always successful; not infrequently death occurs before an adequate action sequence has been evoked.

It is the primary task of a molar science of behavior to isolate the basic laws or rules according to which various combinations of stimulation, arising from the state of need on the one hand and the state of the environment on the other, bring about the kind of behavior characteristic of different organisms. A closely related task is to understand why the behavior so mediated is so generally adaptive, i.e., successful in the sense of reducing needs and facilitating survival, and why it is unsuccessful on those occasions when survival is not facilitated.

The Neurological Versus the Molar Approach

From the foregoing considerations it might appear that the science of behavior must at bottom be a study of physiology. Indeed, it was once almost universally believed that the science of behavior must wait for its useful elaboration upon the development of the subsidiary science of neurophysiology. Partly as a result of this belief, an immense amount of research has been directed to the understanding of the detailed or molecular dynamic laws of this remarkable automatic structure. A great deal has been revealed by these researches and the rate of development is constantly being accelerated by the discovery of new and more effective methods of investigation. Nearly all serious students of behavior like to believe that some day the major neurological laws will be known in a form adequate to constitute the foundation principles of a science of behavior.

In spite of these heartening successes, the gap between the minute anatomical and physiological account of the nervous system as at present known and what would be required for the construction of a reasonably adequate theory of molar behavior is impassable. The problem confronting the behavior theorist is substantially like that which would have been faced by Galileo and Newton had they seriously considered delaying their preliminary formulation of the molar mechanics of the physical world until the micro-mechanics of the atomic and subatomic world had been satisfactorily elaborated.

Students of the social sciences are presented with the dilemma of waiting until the physico-chemical problems of neurophysiology have been adequately solved before beginning the elaboration of behavior theory, or of proceeding in a provisional manner with certain reasonably stable principles of the coarse, macroscopic or molar action of the nervous system whereby movements are evoked by stimuli, particularly as related to the history of the individual organism.

There can hardly be any doubt that a theory of molar behavior founded upon an adequate knowledge of both molecular and molar principles would in general be more satisfactory than one founded upon molar considerations alone. But here again the history of physical science is suggestive. Owing to the fact that Galileo and Newton carried out their molar investigations, the world has had the use of a theory which was in very close approximation to observations at the molar level .for nearly three hundred years before the development of the molecular science of modern relativity and quantum theory. Moreover, it is to be remembered that science proceeds by a series of successive approximations; it may very well be that had Newton's system not been worked out when it was there would have been no Einstein and no Planck, no relativity and no quantum theory at all. It is conceivable that the elaboration of a systematic science of behavior at a molar level may aid in the development of an adequate neurophysiology and thus lead in the end to a truly molecular theory of behavior firmly based on physiology.

It happens that a goodly number of quasi-neurological principles have now been determined by careful experiments designed to trace out the relationship of the molar behavior of organisms, usually as integrated wholes, to well-controlled stimulus situations. Many of the more promising of these principles were roughly isolated in the first instance by the Russian physiologist, Pavlov, and his pupils, by means of conditioned-reflex experiments on dogs. More recently extensive experiments in many laboratories in this country with all kinds of reactions on a wide variety of organisms, including man, have greatly extended and rectified these principles and shown how they operate jointly in the production of the more complex forms of behavior. Because of the pressing nature of behavior problems, both practical and theoretical aspects of behavior science are, upon the whole, being developed according to the second of the two alternatives outlined above. For these reasons the molar approach is employed in the present work.

In this connection it is to be noted carefully that *the alternatives of microscopic versus macroscopic, and molecular versus molar, are relative rather than absolute.* In short, there are degrees of the molar, depending on the coarseness of the ultimate causal segments or units dealt with. Other things equal, it would seem wisest to keep the causal segments small, to approach the molecular, the fine and exact substructural details, just as closely as the knowledge of that substructure renders possible. There is much reason to believe that the seeming disagreements among current students of behavior may be largely due to the difference in the degree of the molar at which the several investigators are working. Such differences, however, do not represent fundamental disagreements. In the end the work of all who differ only in this sense may find a place in a single systematic structure, the postulates or primary assumptions of those working at a more molar level ultimately appearing as theorems of those working at a more molecular level.

The Rôle of Intervening Variables in Behavior Theory

Wherever an attempt is made to penetrate the invisible world of the molecular, scientists frequently and usefully employ logical constructs, intervening variables, or symbols to facilitate their thinking. These symbols or X's represent entities or processes which, if existent, would account for certain events in the observable molar world. Examples of such postulated entities in the field of the physical sciences are electrons, protons, positrons, etc. A closely parallel concept in the field of behavior familiar to everyone is that of *habit* as distinguished from habitual action. The habit presumably exists as an invisible condition of the nervous system quite as much when it is not mediating action as when habitual action is occurring; the habits upon which swimming is based are just as truly existent when a person is on the dance floor as when he is in the water.

In some cases there may be employed in scientific theory a whole series of hypothetical unobserved entities; such a series is presented by the hierarchy of postulated physical entities: molecule, atom, and electron, the molecule supposedly being constituted of atoms and the atom in its turn being constituted of electrons.

A rough parallel to this chain of hypothetical entities from the physical sciences will be encountered in the present system of behavior theory. For the above reasons the subject of symbolic constructs, intervening variables, or hypothetical entities which are not directly observable requires comment.

Despite the great value of logical constructs or intervening variables in scientific theory, their use is attended with certain difficulties and even hazards. At bottom this is because the presence and amount of such hypothetical factors must always be determined indirectly. But once (1) the dynamic relationship existing between the amount of the hypothetical entity (X) and some antecedent determining condition (A) which can be directly observed, and (2) the dynamic relationship of the hypothetical entity to some third consequent phenomenon or event (B) which also can be directly observed, becomes fairly well known, the scientific hazard largely disappears. The situation in question is represented in Figure 1.

$$A \longrightarrow f \longrightarrow (X) \longrightarrow f \longrightarrow B$$

FIGURE .1. *Diagrammatic representation of a relatively simple case of an intervening variable* (X) *not directly observable but functionally related* (f) *to the antecedent event* (A) *and to the consequent event* (B), *both* A *and* B *being directly observable. When an intervening variable is thus securely anchored to observables on both sides it can be safely employed in scientific theory.*

When a hypothetical dynamic entity, or even a chain of such entities each functionally related to the one logically preceding and following it, is thus securely anchored on both sides to observable and measurable conditions or events $(A$ and $B)$, the main theoretical danger vanishes. This at bottom is because under the assumed circumstances no ambiguity can exist as to when, and how much of, B should follow A.

The Objective Versus the Subjective Approach to Behavior Theory

If the circumstances sketched above as surrounding and safeguarding the use of hypothetical entities are not observed, the grossest falla-

cies may be committed. The painfully slow path whereby man has, as of yesterday, begun to emerge into the truly scientific era is littered with such blunders, often tragic in their practical consequences. A pestilence or a hurricane descends upon a village and decimates the population. The usual hypothesis put forward by primitive man (and many others who think themselves not at all primitive) to explain the tragic event (B) is that some hypothetical spirit (X) has been angered by the violation (A) of some tribal taboo on the part of one or more inhabitants of the village. Unfortunately this mode of thinking is deeply ingrained in most cultures, not excepting our own, and it even crops up under various disguises in what purports to be serious scientific work.

Perhaps as good an example of such a fallacious use of the intervening variable as is offered by recent scientific history is that of the *entelechy* put forward by Hans Driesch as the central concept in his theory of vitalism. Driesch says, for example:

> A *supreme* mind, conversant with the inorganic facts of nature and knowing all the intensive manifoldness of all entelechies and psychoids . . . would be able to predict the individual history of the latter, would be able to predict the actions of any psychoid with absolute certainty. *Human* mind, on the other hand, is not able to predict in this way, as it does not know entelechy before its manifestation, and as the material conditions of life, which alone the mind of man *can* know . . . in its completeness, are not the only conditions responsible for organic phenomena.

Driesch's entelechy (X) fails as a logical construct or intervening variable not because it is not directly observable (though of course it is not), but because the general functional relationship to antecedent condition A and that to consequent condition B are *both* left unspecified. This, of course, is but another way of saying that the entelechy and all similar constructs are essentially metaphysical in nature. As such they have no place in science. *Science has no use for unverifiable hypotheses.*

A logically minded person, unacquainted with the unscientific foibles of those who affect the scientific virtues, may naturally wonder how such a formulation could ever mediate a semblance of theoretical prediction and thus attain any credence as a genuinely scientific theory. The answer seems to lie in the inveterate animistic or anthropomorphic tendencies of human nature. The entelechy is in substance a spirit or daemon, a kind of vicarious ghost. The person employing the entelechy in effect says to himself, "If I were the entelechy in such and such a biological emergency, what would I do?" Knowing the situation and what is required to meet the emergency, he simply states what he knows to be required as a solution, and he at once has in this statement what purports to be a scientific deduction! He has inadvertently substituted himself in place of the construct and naïvely substituted his knowledge of the situation for the objective rules stating the functional relationships which *ought* to subsist between A and X on the one hand, and between X and B on the other.

This surreptitious substitution and acceptance of one's knowledge of what needs to be done in a biological emergency for a theoretical deduction is the essence of what we shall call *anthropomorphism*, or the *subjective*, in behavior theory. After many centuries the physical sciences have largely banished the subjective from their fields, but for various reasons this is far less easy of accomplishment and is far less well advanced in the field of behavior. The only known cure for this unfortunate tendency to which all men are more or less subject is a grim and inflexible insistence that all deductions take place according to the explicitly formulated rules stating the functional relationships of A to X and of X to B. This latter is the essence of the scientifically *objective*. A genuinely scientific theory no more needs the anthropomorphic intuitions of the theorist to eke out the deduction of its implications than an automatic calculating machine needs the intuitions of the operator in the determination of a quotient, once the keys representing the dividend and the divisor have been depressed.

Objective scientific theory is necessary because only under objective conditions can a principle be tested for soundness by means of observation. The basic difficulty with anthropomorphic subjectivism is that what appear to be deductions derived from such formulations do not originate in rules stating postulated functional relationships, but rather in the intuitions of the confused thinker. Observational check of such pseudo-deductions may verify or refute these intuitions, but has no bearing on the soundness of any scientific principles what-

ever; such verifications or refutations might properly increase the reputation for accurate prophecy of the one making such intuitive judgments, but a prophet is not a principle, much less a scientific theory.

Objectivism Versus Teleology

Even a superficial study of higher organisms shows that their behavior occurs in cycles. The rise of either a primary or a secondary need normally marks the beginning of a behavior cycle, and the abolition or substantial reduction of that need marks its end. Some phase of the joint state of affairs resulting from the environmental-organismic interaction at the end of a behavior cycle is customarily spoken of as a goal. Our usual thoughtless custom is to speak of cycles of behavior by merely naming their outcome, effect, or end result, and practically to ignore the various movements which brought this terminal state about. Guthrie has expressed this tendency more aptly than anyone else. We say quite naturally that a man catches a fish, a woman bakes a cake, an artist paints a picture, a general wins a battle. The end result of each angling exploit, for example, may be in some sense the same but the actual movements involved are perhaps never exactly the same on any two occasions; indeed, neither the angler nor perhaps anyone else knows or could know in their ultimate detail exactly what movements were made. It is thus inevitable that for purposes of communication we designate behavior sequences by their goals.

Now for certain rough practical purposes the custom of naming action sequences by their goals is completely justified by its convenience. It may even be that for very gross molar behavior it can usefully be employed in theory construction, provided the theorist is alert to the naturally attendant hazards. These appear the moment the theorist ventures to draw upon his intuition for statements concerning the behavior (movements) executed by the organism between the onset of a need and its termination through organismic action. Pseudo-deductions on the basis of intuition born of intimate knowledge are so easy and so natural that the tendency to make them is almost irresistible to most persons. The practice does no harm if the theorist does not mistake this subjective intui-tional performance for a logical deduction from an objective theory, and attribute the success of his intuitions to the validity of the theoretical principles.

An ideally adequate theory even of so-called purposive behavior ought, therefore, to begin with colorless movement and mere recep-tor impulses as such, and from these build up step by step both adaptive behavior and mal-adaptive behavior. The present approach does not deny the molar reality of purposive acts (as opposed to movement), of intelligence, of in-sight, of goals, of intents, of strivings, or of value; on the contrary, we insist upon the genuineness of these forms of behavior. We hope ultimately to show the logical right to the use of such concepts by deducing them as secondary principles from more elementary ob-jective primary principles. Once they have been derived we shall not only understand them better but be able to use them with more detailed effectiveness, particularly in the deduc-tion of the movements which mediate (or fail to mediate) goal attainment, than would be the case if we had accepted teleological sequences at the outset as gross, unanalyzed (and unana-lyzable) wholes.

"Emergentism" a Doctrine of Despair

Perhaps the very natural and economical mode of communication whereby we speak of the terminal or goal phases of action, largely regardless of the antecedent movements in-volved, predisposes us to a belief in *teleology*. In its extreme form teleology is the name of the belief that the *terminal* stage of certain environ-mental-organismic interaction cycles somehow is at the same time one of the *antecedent* determining conditions which bring the be-havior cycle about. This approach, in the case of a purposive behavior situation not hitherto known to the theorist, involves a kind of logical circularity: to deduce the outcome of any be-havioral situation in the sense of the deductive predictions here under consideration, it is nec-essary to know all the relevant antecedent conditions, but these cannot be determined un-til the behavioral outcome has been deduced. In effect this means that the task of deduction cannot begin until after it is completed! Natu-rally this leaves the theorist completely help-less. It is not surprising that the doctrine of teleology leads to theoretical despair and to such pseudo-remedies as vitalism and *emergen-tism*.

Emergentism, as applied to organismic be-havior, is the name for the view that in the process of evolution there has "emerged" a form of behavior which is ultimately unana-lyzable into logically more primitive elements —behavior which cannot possibly be deduced from any logically prior principles whatever. In particular it is held that what is called goal or purposive behavior is of such a nature, that it cannot be derived from any conceivable set of postulates involving mere stimuli and mere movement.

On the other hand, many feel that this de-featist attitude is not only unwholesome in that it discourages scientific endeavor, but that it is quite unjustified by the facts. The present writer shares this view. Therefore a serious attempt will ultimately be made to show that these supposedly impossible derivations are ac-tually possible; in some cases they will be shown to be quite easy of accomplishment.

A Suggested Prophylaxis Against Anthropomorphic Subjectivism

As already suggested, one of the greatest obstacles to the attainment of a genuine theory of behavior is anthropomorphic subjectivism. At bottom this is because we ourselves are so intimately involved in the problem; we are so close to it that it is difficult to attain adequate perspective. For the reader who has not hith-erto struggled with the complex but fascinating problems of behavior theory, it will be hard to realize the difficulty of maintaining a consist-ently objective point of view. Even when fully aware of the nature of anthropomorphic subjec-tivism and its dangers, the most careful and experienced thinker is likely to find himself a victim to its seductions. Indeed, despite the most conscientious effort to avoid this it is altogether probable that there may be found in various parts of the present work hidden ele-ments of the anthropomorphically subjec-tive.

One aid to the attainment of behavioral ob-jectivity is to think in terms of the behavior of subhuman organisms, such as chimpanzees, monkeys, dogs, cats, and albino rats. Unfortunately this form of prophylaxis against subjectivism all too often breaks down when the theorist begins thinking what he would do if he were a rat, a cat, or a chimpanzee; when that happens, all his knowledge of his own behavior, born of years of self-observation, at once begins to function in place of the objectively stated general rules or principles which are the proper substance of science.

A device much employed by the author has proved itself to be a far more effective prophylaxis. This is to regard, from time to time, the behaving organism as a completely self-maintaining robot, constructed of materials as unlike ourselves as may be. In doing this it is not necessary to attempt the solution of the detailed engineering problems connected with the design of such a creature. It is a wholesome and revealing exercise, however, to consider the various general problems in behavior dynamics which must be solved in the design of a truly self-maintaining robot. We, in common with other mammals, perform innumerable behavior adaptations with such ease that it is apt never to occur to us that any problem of explanation exists concerning them. In many such seemingly simple activities lie dynamical problems of very great complexity and difficulty.

A second and closely related subjective tendency against which the robot concept is likely to prove effectively prophylactic is that to the *reification* of a behavior function. To reify a function is to give it a name and presently to consider that the name represents a thing, and finally to believe that the thing so named somehow *explains* the performance of the function. We have already seen an example of this unfortunate tendency in Driesch's entelechy. The temptation to introduce an entelechy, soul, spirit, or daemon into a robot is slight; it is relatively easy to realize that *the introduction of an entelechy would not really solve the problem of design of a robot because there would still remain the problem of designing the entelechy itself, which is the core of the original problem all over again.* The robot approach thus aids us in avoiding the very natural but childish tendency to choose easy though false solutions to our problems, by removing all excuses for not facing them squarely and without evasion.

Unfortunately it is possible at present to promise an explanation of only a portion of the problems encountered in the infinitely complex subject of organismic behavior. Indeed, it is no great exaggeration to say that the present state of behavior theory resembles one of those pieces of sculpture which present in the main a rough, unworked block of stone with only a hand emerging in low relief here, a foot or thigh barely discernible there, and elsewhere a part of a face. The undeveloped state of the behavior sciences suggested by this analogy is a source of regret to the behavior theorist but not one of chagrin, because incompleteness is characteristic even of the most advanced of all theoretical sciences. From this point of view the difference between the physical and the behavioral sciences is one not of kind but of degree—of the relative amount of the figure still embedded in the unhewn rock. There is reason to believe that the relative backwardness of the behavior sciences is due not so much to their inherent complexity as to the difficulty of maintaining a consistent and rigorous objectivism.

Classical Conditioning

Ivan P. Pavlov

Ivan Pavlov (1849–1936), destined for the priesthood, turned to medicine and received his M.D. in 1883. He held the post of Professor of Physiology from 1895–1924 at the Military Medical Academy, St. Petersburg, Russia. Pavlov is best known for his pioneer work on conditioning, which still operates as the dominant research model in Russian psychology.

1. *Why was the secretory reflex chosen for study?*

2. *If you repeatedly blindfold a friend before popping a piece of chocolate in his mouth, what reaction will the blindfold eventually elicit when presented alone? What simple conditioning experiments can you think of that use reflexes other than that of salivation?*

3. *Why is Pavlov given such prominence in the history of experimental psychology?*

Before passing on to describe the results of our investigation it is necessary to give some account of the purely technical side of the methods employed, and to describe the general way in which the signalizing activity of the [cerebral] hemispheres can be studied. Obviously, the reflex activity of any effector organ can be chosen for the purpose of this investigation, since signalling stimuli can get linked up with any of the inborn reflexes. But, as was mentioned in the first lecture, the starting point for the present investigation was determined in particular by the study of two reflexes—the food or "alimentary" reflex, and the "defence" reflex in its mildest form, as observed when a rejectable substance finds its way into the mouth of the animal. As it turned out, these

Abridged from I. P. Pavlov, "Lecture II," *Conditioned Reflexes* (Oxford: The Clarendon Press, 1927), pp. 16–23. Reprinted by permission of the publisher.

two reflexes proved a fortunate choice in many ways. Indeed, while any strong defence reflex, *e.g.* against such a stimulus as a powerful electric current, makes the animal extremely restless and excited; and while the sexual reflexes require a special environment—to say nothing of their periodic character and their dependence upon age—the alimentary reflex and the mild defence reflex to rejectable substances are normal everyday occurrences.

It is essential to realize that each of these two reflexes—the alimentary reflex and the mild defence reflex to rejectable substances—consists of two distinct components, a motor and a secretory. Firstly the animal exhibits a reflex activity directed towards getting hold of the food and eating it or, in the case of rejectable substances, towards getting rid of them out of the mouth; and secondly, in both cases an immediate secretion of saliva occurs, in the case of food, to start the physical and chemical processes of digestion and, in the case of rejectable substances, to wash them out of the mouth. We confined our experiments almost entirely to the secretory component of the reflex: the allied motor reactions were taken into account only where there were special reasons. The secretory reflex presents many important advantages for our purpose. It allows of an extremely accurate measurement of the intensity of reflex activity, since either the number of drops in a given time may be counted or else the saliva may be caused to displace a coloured fluid in a horizontally placed graduated glass tube. It would be much more difficult to obtain the same accuracy of measurement for any motor reflex, especially for such complex motor reactions as accompany reflexes to food or to rejectable substances. Even by using most delicate instruments we should never be able to reach such precision in measuring the intensity of the motor component of the reflexes as can easily be attained with the secretory component. Again, a very important point in favour of the secretory reflexes is the much smaller tendency to interpret them in an anthropomorphic fashion—*i.e.* in terms of subjective analogy. Although this seems a trivial consideration from

to the outside of the cheek in the case of the parotid gland, or under the chin in the case of the submaxillary gland. In this new position the duct is fixed by a few stitches which are removed when the wound has healed. As a result of the operation the saliva now flows to the outside, on to the cheek or chin of the animal, instead of into the mouth, so that the measurement of the secretory activity of the gland is greatly facilitated. It is only necessary for this purpose to adjust a small glass funnel over the opening of the duct on to the skin, and for this we find a special cement prepared

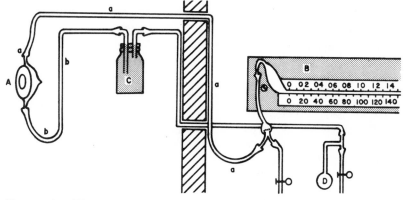

FIGURE 1.—*The apparatus used for recording the salivary secretion in experiments on conditioned reflexes. A, hemispherical bulb which is fixed over the fistula. aaa, connecting tube leading through the partition separating the animal's room from the experimenter and connecting the bulb A to the registering apparatus, B. bb, tube connecting the bulb with bottle, C.*

After each observation a vacuum is created in the bottle C by depression of the rubber balloon D; the saliva accumulating in A is thus sucked away. During the observation A is automatically disconnected from C and connected with the registering apparatus. During the aspirations of the saliva from bulb A the latter is automatically disconnected from the registering apparatus.

our present standpoint, it was of importance in the earlier stages of our investigation and did undoubtedly influence our choice.

For the purpose of registering the intensity of the salivary reflex all the dogs employed in the experiments are subjected to a preliminary minor operation, which consists in the transplantation of the opening of the salivary duct from its natural place on the mucous membrane of the mouth to the outside skin. For this purpose the terminal portion of the salivary duct is dissected and freed from the surrounding tissue, and the duct, together with a small portion of the mucous membrane surrounding its natural opening, is carried through a suitable incision,

according to a formula of Mendeléeff[1] most useful. As an alternative, very suitable and accurate as a recording apparatus is a hemispherical bulb which also can be hermetically sealed on to the skin. From the bulb project two tubes, one pointing up and the other pointing down. The latter tube is used for drawing off the saliva which collects during each observation, while the former tube connects by air transmission with a horizontal graduated glass tube filled with coloured fluid. As the saliva

[1] *Mendeléeff's cement:* Colophonium, 50 grammes; ferric oxide, 40 grammes; yellow beeswax, 25 grammes.

flows into the hemispherical bulb the coloured fluid is displaced along the graduated tube, where the amount of secretion can be read off accurately. Further, it is not difficult to fix up an automatic electrically-recording device which will split up the displaced fluid into drops of exactly equal volume and reduce any lag in the movement of the fluid to a minimum.[2]

To come to the general technique of the experiments, it is important to remember that our research deals with the highly specialized activity of the cerebral cortex, a signalizing apparatus of tremendous complexity and of most exquisite sensitivity, through which the animal is influenced by countless stimuli from the outside world. Every one of these stimuli produces a certain effect upon the animal, and all of them taken together may clash and interfere with, or else reinforce, one another. Unless we are careful to take special precautions the success of the whole investigation may be jeopardized, and we should get hopelessly lost as soon as we began to seek for cause and effect among so many and various influences, so intertwined and entangled as to form a veritable chaos. It was evident that the experimental conditions had to be simplified, and that this simplification must consist in eliminating as far as possible any stimuli outside our control which might fall upon the animal, admitting only such stimuli as could be entirely controlled by the experimenter. It was thought at the beginning of our research that it would be sufficient simply to isolate the experimenter in the research chamber with the dog on its stand, and to refuse admission to anyone else during the course of an experiment. But this precaution was found to be wholly inadequate, since

the experimenter, however still he might try to be, was himself a constant source of a large number of stimuli. His slightest movements—blinking of the eyelids or movement of the eyes, posture, respiration and so on—all acted as stimuli which, falling upon the dog, were sufficient to vitiate the experiments by making exact interpretation of the results extremely difficult. In order to exclude this undue influence on the part of the experimenter as far as possible, he had to be stationed outside the room in which the dog was placed, and even this precaution proved unsuccessful in laboratories not specially designed for the study of these particular reflexes. The environment of the animal, even when shut up by itself in a room, is perpetually changing. Footfalls of a passer-by, chance conversations in neighbouring rooms, slamming of a door or vibration from a passing van, street-cries, even shadows cast through the windows into the room, any of these casual uncontrolled stimuli falling upon the receptors of the dog set up a disturbance in the cerebral hemispheres and vitiate the experiments. To get over all these disturbing factors a special laboratory was built at the Institute of Experimental Medicine in Petrograd, the funds being provided by a keen and public-spirited Moscow businessman. The primary task was the protection of the dogs from uncontrolled extraneous stimuli, and this was effected by surrounding the building with an isolating trench and employing other special structural devices. Inside the building all the research rooms (four to each floor) were isolated from one another by a cross-shaped corridor; the top and ground floors, where these rooms were situated, were separated by an intermediate floor. Each research room was carefully partitioned by the use of sound-proof materials into two compartments—one for the animal, the other for the experimenter. For stimulating the animal, and for registering the corresponding reflex response, electrical methods or pneumatic transmission were used. By means of these arrangements it was possible to get something of that stability of environmental conditions so essential to the carrying out of a successful experiment.

Another point should be mentioned—although in this respect the means at our disposal still leave something to be desired. In analysing the exceedingly complex influence of the ex-

[2] In almost all the experiments quoted in these lectures the amount of salivary secretion is, for the sake of uniformity, given in drops. It was, however, only in the very earliest period of the research—before the separation of the experimenter from the animal was made—that the actual number of drops falling from a small funnel fixed over the fistula was counted, and only a few of these experiments are given. In the great majority of the experiments the salivary secretion was measured by the displacement of water in a graduated tube or by the electric recorder, allowing a much greater accuracy of measurement. The readings so obtained have been converted into drops. Thus, in some experiments it will be noticed that the number of drops is given to an accuracy of one-tenth.

ternal environment upon the animal, the experimenter must be able to exercise full control over all the conditions obtaining during the course of any experiment. He should therefore have at his disposal various instruments for affecting the animal by different kinds of stimuli, singly or combined, so as to imitate simple natural conditions. But we were often handicapped by the conditions in which we had to work and by the shortcomings of the instruments at our disposal, for we always found that the cerebral hemispheres were sensitive to far finer gradations of stimulus than we could furnish.

It is possible that the experimental conditions I have described may raise somewhere the objection of being abnormal and artificial. However it is hardly likely, in view of the infinite variety of stimuli met with under natural conditions, that we shall hit on one that is quite unprecedented in the life of the animal. Moreover, in dealing with any phenomenon of vast complexity it is absolutely necessary to isolate the different single factors involved, so as to study them independently, or in arbitrary groups in which we can keep the individual units under control. But as a matter of fact the same objection and the same answer apply equally to the whole of animal physiology. For instance, the methods of vivisection and of the study of isolated organs and tissues, which aim at the same isolation of different individual functions, have been constantly employed, and we may safely say that the greater part of the achievements of physiology are due to the successful application of such methods of control. In our experiments it is the whole animal which is placed under a limited number of rigidly defined conditions, and only by this method is it possible to study the reflexes independently of one another.

The foregoing remarks give an idea of our general aim and of the technical side of our methods. I propose to introduce you to the first and most elementary principles of the subject matter of our research by means of a few demonstrations:

Demonstration. The dog used in the following experiment has been operated upon as described previously. It can be seen that so long as no special stimulus is applied the salivary glands remain quite inactive. But when the sounds from a beating metronome are allowed to fall upon the ear, a salivary secretion begins after 9 seconds, and in the course of 45 seconds eleven drops have been secreted. The activity of the salivary gland has thus been called into play by impulses of sound—a stimulus quite alien to food. This activity of the salivary gland cannot be regarded as anything else than a component of the alimentary reflex. Besides the secretory, the motor component of the food reflex is also very apparent in experiments of this kind. In this very experiment the dog turns in the direction from which it has been customary to present the food and begins to lick its lips vigorously.

This experiment is an example of a central nervous activity depending on the integrity of the hemispheres. A decerebrate dog would never have responded by salivary secretion to any stimulus of the kind. It is obvious also that the underlying principle of this activity is signalization. The sound of the metronome is the signal for food, and the animal reacts to the signal in the same way as if it were food; no distinction can be observed between the effects produced on the animal by the sounds of the beating metronome and showing it real food.

Demonstration. Food is shown to the animal. The salivary secretion begins after 5 seconds, and six drops are collected in the course of 15 seconds. The effect is the same as that observed with the sounds of the metronome. It is again a case of signalization, and is due to the activity of the hemispheres.

That the effect of sight and smell of food is not due to an inborn reflex, but to a reflex which has been acquired in the course of the animal's own individual existence, was shown by experiments carried out by Dr. Zitovich in the laboratory of the late Prof. Vartanov. Dr. Zitovich took several young puppies away from their mother and fed them for a considerable time only on milk. When the puppies were a few months old he established fistulae of their salivary ducts, and was thus able to measure accurately the secretory activity of the glands. He now showed these puppies some solid food—bread or meat—but no secretion of saliva was evoked. It is evident, therefore, that the sight of food does not in itself act as a direct stimulus to salivary secretion. Only after the puppies have been allowed to eat bread and meat on several occasions does the sight or smell of these foodstuffs evoke the secretion.

The following experiment serves to illustrate the activity of the salivary gland as an inborn reflex in contrast to signalization:

Demonstration. Food is suddenly introduced into the dog's mouth; secretion begins in 1 to 2 seconds. The secretion is brought about by the physical and chemical properties of the food itself acting upon receptors in the mucous membrane of the mouth and tongue. It is purely reflex.

This comparatively simple experiment explains how a decerebrate dog can die of starvation in the midst of plenty, for it will only start eating if food chances to come into contact with its mouth or tongue. Moreover, the elementary nature of the inborn reflexes, with their limitations and inadequacy, are clearly brought out in these experiments, and we are now able to appreciate the fundamental importance of those stimuli which have the character of *signals*.

We come now to consider the precise conditions under which new conditioned reflexes or new connections of nervous paths are established. The fundamental requisite is that any external stimulus which is to become the signal in a conditioned reflex must overlap in point of time with the action of an unconditioned stimulus. In the experiment which I chose as my example the unconditioned stimulus was food. Now if the intake of food by the animal takes place simultaneously with the action of a neutral stimulus which has been hitherto in no way related to food, the neutral stimulus readily acquires the property of eliciting the same reaction in the animal as would food itself. This was the case with the dog employed in our experiment with the metronome. On several occasions this animal had been stimulated by the sound of the metronome and immediately presented with food—*i.e.* a stimulus which was neutral of itself had been superimposed upon the action of the inborn alimentary reflex. We observed that, after several repetitions of the combined stimulation, the sounds from the metronome had acquired the property of stimulating salivary secretion and of evoking the motor reactions characteristic of the alimentary reflex. The first demonstration was nothing but an example of such a conditioned stimulus in action. Precisely the same occurs with

the mild defence reflex to rejectable substances. Introduction into the dog's mouth of a little of an acid solution brings about a quite definite responsive reaction. The animal sets about getting rid of the acid, shaking its head violently, opening its mouth and making movements with its tongue. At the same time it produces a copious salivary secretion. The same reaction will infallibly be obtained from any stimulus which has previously been applied a sufficient number of times while acid was being introduced into the dog's mouth. Hence a first and most essential requisite for the formation of a new conditioned reflex lies in a coincidence in time of the action of any previously neutral stimulus with some definite unconditioned stimulus. Further, it is not enough that there should be overlapping between the two stimuli; it is also and equally necessary that the conditioned stimulus should begin to operate before the unconditioned stimulus comes into action.

As regards the condition of the hemispheres themselves, an alert state of the nervous system is absolutely essential for the formation of a new conditioned reflex. If the dog is mostly drowsy during the experiments, the establishment of a conditioned reflex becomes a long and tedious process, and in extreme cases is impossible to accomplish. The hemispheres must, however, be free from any other nervous activity, and therefore in building up a new conditioned reflex it is important to avoid foreign stimuli which, falling upon the animal, would cause other reactions of their own. If this is not attended to, the establishment of a conditioned reflex is very difficult, if not impossible. Thus, for example, if the dog has been so fastened up that anything causes severe irritation, it does not matter how many times the combination of stimuli is repeated, we shall not be able to obtain a conditioned reflex. A somewhat similar case was described in the first lecture—that of the dog which exhibited the *freedom reflex* in an exaggerated degree. It can also be stated as a rule that the establishment of the first conditioned reflex in an animal is usually more difficult than the establishment of succeeding ones. It is obvious that this must be so, when we consider that even in the most favourable circumstances the experimental conditions themselves will be sure to provoke numerous different reflexes—*i.e.* will give rise to one or other disturbing activity of the hemispheres. But this statement must be qualified by remarking that in cases where the cause of these uncontrolled reflexes is not found out, so that we are not able to get rid of them, the hemispheres themselves will help us. For if the environment of the animal during the experiment does not contain any powerful disturbing elements, then practically always the extraneous reflexes will with time gradually and spontaneously weaken in strength.

The third factor determining the facility with which new conditioned reflexes can be established is the health of the animal. A good state of health will ensure the normal functioning of the cerebral hemispheres, and we shall not have to bother with the effects of any internal pathological stimuli.

The fourth, and last, group of conditions has to do with the properties of the stimulus which is to become conditioned, and also with the properties of the unconditioned stimulus which is selected. Conditioned reflexes are quite readily formed to stimuli to which the animal is more or less indifferent at the outset, though strictly speaking no stimulus within the animal's range of perception exists to which it would be absolutely indifferent. In a normal animal the slightest alteration in the environment—even the very slightest sound or faintest odour, or the smallest change in intensity of illumination—immediately evokes the reflex which I referred to in the first lecture as the investigatory reflex—"What is it?"—manifested by a very definite motor reaction. However, if these neutral stimuli keep recurring, they spontaneously and rapidly weaken in their effect upon the hemispheres, thus bringing about bit by bit the removal of this obstacle to the establishment of a conditioned reflex. But if the extraneous stimuli are strong or unusual, the formation of a conditioned reflex will be difficult, and in extreme cases impossible.

It must also be remembered that in most cases we are not acquainted with the history of the dog before it came into the laboratory, and that we do not know what sort of conditioned reflexes have been established to stimuli which appear to be of the simplest character. But in spite of this we have, in a large number of cases, found it possible to take a strong stimulus which evoked some strong unconditioned response of its own, and still succeed in converting it into a conditioned stimulus for another reflex. Let us take for example a nocuous stimulus, such as a strong electric current or wounding or cauterization of the skin. These are obviously stimuli to vigorous unconditioned defence reflexes. The organism responds by a violent motor reaction directed towards removal of the nocuous stimulus or to its own removal from it. But we may, nevertheless, make use even of these stimuli for the establishment of a new conditioned reflex. Thus in one particular experiment a strong nocuous stimulus—an electric current of great strength—was converted into an alimentary conditioned stimulus, so that its application to the skin did not evoke the slightest defence reaction. Instead, the animal exhibited a well-marked alimentary conditioned reflex, turning its head to where it usually received the food and smacking its lips, at the same time producing a profuse secretion of saliva.

To sum up, we may legitimately claim the study of the formation and properties of conditioned reflexes as a special department of physiology. There is no reason for thinking about all these events in any other way, and it is my belief that in these questions prejudices blunt the intellect and that generally speaking the preconceptions of the human mind stand in the way of any admission that the highest physiological activity of the hemispheres is rigidly determined. The difficulty is mainly due to the tremendous complexity of our subjective states; and, of course, these cannot yet be traced to their primary causations.

Operant Conditioning

Burrhus F. Skinner

B. F. Skinner is Professor of Psychology at Harvard University, from which he received his Ph.D. in 1931. Widely recognized for his experimental analysis of behavior, including instruments and methods for the study of operant behavior and for programmed instruction, Skinner is also the author of a utopian novel, Walden Two. *In his own words, "In college I wanted to be a writer but soon discovered I had nothing to say. I turned to psychology as the most closely related science."*

1. *What are the advantages of studying behavior in the manner illustrated by Skinner? What are the disadvantages?*

2. *What evidence is given to indicate the similarity of response rate between human and infrahuman subjects?*

For a long time the analysis of behavior took the form of the discovery and collection of reflex mechanisms. Early in the present century, the Dutch physiologist Rudolph Magnus, after an exhaustive study of the reflexes involved in the maintenance of posture, put the matter this way: when a cat hears a mouse, turns toward the source of the sound, sees the mouse, runs toward it, and pounces, its posture at every stage, even to the selection of the foot which is to take the first step, is determined by reflexes which can be demonstrated one by one under experimental conditions. All the cat has to do is to decide whether or not to pursue the mouse; everything else is prepared for it by its postural and locomotor reflexes.

To pursue or not to pursue is a question,

Abridged from B. F. Skinner, "The Experimental Analysis of Behavior," *American Scientist,* 45, No. 4 (1957), 343–348, 356–358, 364–371. Reprinted by permission of author and publisher.

however, which has never been fully answered on the model of the reflex, even with the help of Pavlov's principle of conditioning. Reflexes—conditioned or otherwise—are primarily concerned with the internal economy of the organism and with maintaining various sorts of equilibrium. The behavior through which the individual deals with the surrounding environment and gets from it the things it needs for its existence and for the propagation of the species cannot be forced into the simple all-or-nothing formula of stimulus and response. Some well-defined patterns of behavior, especially in birds, fish, and invertebrates are controlled by "releasers" which suggest reflex stimuli, but even here the probability of occurrence of such behavior varies over a much wider range, and the conditions of which that probability is a function are much more complex and subtle. And when we come to that vast repertoire of "operant" behavior which is shaped up by the environment in the lifetime of the individual, the reflex pattern will not suffice at all.

In studying such behavior we must make certain preliminary decisions. We begin by choosing an organism—one which we hope will be representative but which is first merely convenient. We must also choose a bit of behavior—not for any intrinsic or dramatic interest it may have, but because it is easily observed, affects the environment in such a way that it can be easily recorded, and for reasons to be noted subsequently, may be repeated many times without fatigue. Thirdly, we must select or construct an experimental space which can be well controlled.

These requirements are satisfied by the situation shown in Figure 1. A partially sound-shielded aluminum box is divided into two compartments. In the near compartment a pigeon, standing on a screen floor, is seen in the act of pecking a translucent plastic plate behind a circular opening in the partition. The plate is part of a delicate electric key; when it is pecked, a circuit is closed to operate recording and controlling equipment. Colored lights can be projected on the back of the disk as stimuli. The box is ventilated, and illuminated by a dim ceiling light.

We are interested in the probability that in such a controlled space the organism we select will engage in the behavior we thus record. At first blush, such an interest may seem trivial. We shall see, however, that the conditions which alter the probability, and the processes which unfold as that probability changes, are quite complex. Moreover, they have an immediate, important bearing on the behavior of other organisms under other circumstances, including the organism called man in the everyday world of human affairs.

Probability of responding is a difficult datum. We may avoid controversial issues by turning at once to a practical measure, the *frequency* with which a response is emitted. The experimental situation shown in Figure 1 was designed to permit this frequency to vary over a wide range. In the experiments to be described here, stable rates are recorded which differ by a factor of about 600. In other experiments, rates have differed by as much as 2000 : 1. Rate of responding is most conveniently recorded in a cumulative curve. A pen moves across a paper tape, stepping a short uniform distance with each response. Appropriate paper speeds and unit steps are chosen so that the rates to be studied give convenient slopes.

Operant Conditioning

Among the conditions which alter rate of responding are some of the consequences of behavior. Operant behavior usually affects the environment and generates stimuli which "feed

back" to the organism. Some feedback may have the effects identified by the layman as reward and punishment. Any consequence of behavior which is rewarding or, more technically, *reinforcing,* increases the probability of further responding. Unfortunately, a consequence which is punishing has a much more complex result. Pecking the key in our experimental space has certain natural consequences. It stimulates the bird tactually and

FIGURE 1. *An experimental space showing a pigeon in the act of pecking a plastic key.*

auditorily, and such stimulation may be slightly reinforcing. We study the effect more expediently, however, by arranging an arbitrary consequence which is clearly so. For example, food is reinforcing to a hungry pigeon (for our present purposes we need not inquire why this is so), and we therefore arrange to present food with a special magazine. When a solenoid is energized, a tray containing a mixture of grains is brought into position in the square opening below the key in Figure 1, where the pigeon has access to the grain for, say, four seconds.

We can demonstrate the effect of operant

reinforcement simply by connecting the key which the pigeon pecks to the solenoid which operates the food tray. A single presentation of food, following immediately upon a response, increases the rate with which responses to the key are subsequently emitted so long as the pigeon remains hungry. By reinforcing

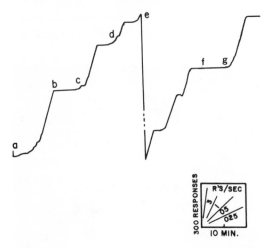

FIGURE 2. *Characteristic performance by a pigeon under fixed-interval reinforcement.*

several responses, we may create a high probability of responding. If the magazine is now disconnected, the rate declines to, and may even go below, its original level. These changes are the processes of operant conditioning and extinction, respectively. More interesting phenomena are generated when responses are merely *intermittently* reinforced. It is characteristic of everyday life that few of the things we do always "pay off." The dynamic characteristics of our behavior depend upon the actual schedules of reinforcement.

The effects of intermittent reinforcement have been extensively studied in the laboratory.[1] A common sort of intermittency is based on time. Reinforced responses can be spaced, say, ten minutes apart. When one reinforcement is received, a timer is started which opens the reinforcing circuit for ten minutes; the first response after the circuit is closed is reinforced. When an organism is exposed to this

[1] Much of the research from which the following examples are drawn has been supported by the Office of Naval Research and the National Science Foundation.

schedule of reinforcement for many hours, it develops a characteristic performance which is related in a rather complex way to the schedule. A short sample of such a performance is shown in Figure 2, obtained with a cumulative recorder. The scales and a few representative speeds are shown in the lower right-hand corner. The experimental session begins at *a*. The first reinforcement will not occur until ten minutes later, and the bird begins at a very low rate of responding. As the 10-minute interval passes, the rate increases, accelerating fairly smoothly to a terminal rate at reinforcement at *b*. The rate then drops to zero. Except for a slight abortive start at *c*, it again accelerates to a high terminal value by the end of the second 10-minute interval. A third fairly smooth acceleration is shown at *d*. (At *e* the pen instantly resets to the starting position on the paper.) The over-all pattern of performance on a "fixed-interval" schedule is a fairly smoothly accelerating scallop in each interval, the acceleration being more rapid the longer the initial pause. Local effects due to separate reinforcements are evident, however, which cannot be discussed here for lack of space.

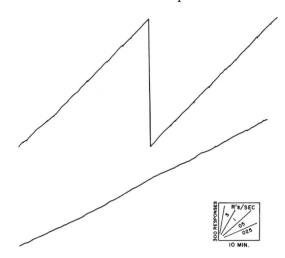

FIGURE 3. *Performance under variable-interval reinforcement for a pigeon (upper curve) and a chimpanzee (lower curve).*

If the intervals between reinforcements are not fixed, the performance shown in Figure 2 cannot develop. If the length of interval is varied essentially at random, responding occurs at a single rate represented by a constant slope in the cumulative record. Two examples are shown in Figure 3. In the upper curve, a hungry pigeon is reinforced with grain on a *variable-interval schedule,* where the mean interval between reinforcements is 3 minutes. Reinforcements occur where marked by pips. In the lower curve a hungry chimpanzee, operating a toggle switch, is reinforced on the same schedule with laboratory food. The over-all rate under variable-interval reinforcement is a function of the mean interval, of the level of food-deprivation, and of many other variables. It tends to increase slowly under prolonged exposure to any one set of conditions. The constant rate itself eventually becomes an important condition of the experiment and resists any change to other values. For this reason the straight lines of Figure 3 are not as suitable for baselines as might be supposed.

immediately after reinforcement. At the right is the performance generated when the pigeon pecks the key 900 times for each reinforcement. This unusually high ratio was reached in some experiments in the Harvard Psychological Laboratories by W. H. Morse and R. J. Herrnstein. A short pause after reinforcement is the rule.

A *variable-ratio* schedule programmed by a counter corresponds to the variable-interval schedule programmed by a timer. Reinforcement is contingent on a given *average* number of responses but the numbers are allowed to vary roughly at random. We are all familiar with this schedule because it is the heart of all

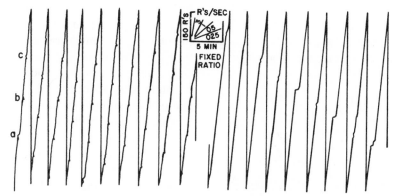

FIGURE 4. *Typical performance by a pigeon under fixed-ratio reinforcement. At the left every 210th response is reinforced; at the right every 900th response.*

Reinforcements may be scheduled with a *counter* instead of a timer. For example, we may maintain a *fixed ratio* between responses and reinforcements. In industry this schedule is referred to as piecework or piece-rate pay. Anyone who has seen workers paid on such a schedule is familiar with some features of the performance generated: a high rate is sustained for long periods of time. For this reason, the schedule is attractive to employers, but it is generally recognized that the level of activity generated is potentially dangerous and justified only in seasonal or other periodic employment.

Performances of a pigeon under fixed-ratio reinforcement are shown in Figure 4. In the left-hand record reinforcements occur every 210 responses (at *a, b, c,* and elsewhere). The over-all rate is high. Most of the pauses occur

gambling devices and systems. The confirmed or pathological gambler exemplifies the result: a very high rate of activity is generated by a relatively slight net reinforcement. Where the "cost" of a response can be estimated (in terms, say, of the food required to supply the energy needed, or of the money required to play the gambling device), it may be demonstrated that organisms will operate at a net loss.

Avoidance

So far our data have been taken from the pleasanter side of life—from behavior which produces positive consequences. There are important consequences of another sort. Much of what we do during the day is done not because of the positive reinforcements we receive but because of aversive consequences we avoid. The whole field of escape, avoidance, and punishment is an extensive one, but order is slowly being brought into it. An important contribution has been the research of Murray Sidman on avoidance behavior. In the Sidman technique, a rat is placed in a box the floor of which is an electric grid through which the rat can be shocked. The pattern of polarity of the bars of the grid is changed several times per second so that the rat cannot find bars of the same sign to avoid the shock. In a typical experiment a shock occurs every 20 seconds unless the rat presses the lever, but such a response postpones the shock for a full 20 seconds. These circumstances induce a rat to respond steadily to the lever, the only reinforcement being the postponement of shock. The rat must occasionally receive a shock—that is, it must allow 20 seconds to pass without a response—if the behavior is to remain in strength. By varying the intervals between shocks, the time of post-

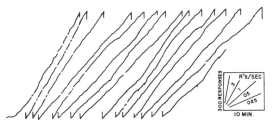

FIGURE 5. *Seven-hour performance of a rat which avoids a shock by pressing a lever under the Sidman procedure.*

ponement, and various kinds of warning stimuli, Sidman has revealed some of the important properties of this all-too-common form of behavior.

A sample of behavior which W. H. Morse and the writer obtained with the Sidman procedure is shown in Figure 5. Here both the interval between shocks and the postponement time were 8 seconds. (White space has been cut out of the record and the separate segments brought together to facilitate reproduction.) The records report a 7-hour experimental session during which about 14,000 responses were emitted. Occasional shocks are indicated by the downward movements of the pen (not to be confused with the fragments of the reset line). A significant feature of the performance is the warm-up at *a*. When first put into the appa-

ratus the rat "takes" a number of shocks before entering upon the typical avoidance pattern. This occurs whenever a new session is begun. It may indicate that an emotional condition is required for successful avoidance behavior. The condition disappears between sessions and must be reinstated. The figure shows considerable variation in over-all rate and many local irregularities. At times small groups of shocks are taken, suggesting a return to the warm-up condition.

Human Behavior

What about man? Is rate of responding still an orderly and meaningful datum here, or is human behavior the exception in which spontaneity and caprice still reign? In watching experiments of the sort described above, most people feel that they could "figure out" a schedule of reinforcement and adjust to it more efficiently than the experimental organism. In saying this, they are probably overlooking the clocks and calendars, the counters and the behavior of counting, with which man has solved the problem of intermittency in his environment. But if a pigeon is given a clock or a counter, it works more efficiently, and without these aids man shows little if any superiority.

Parallels have already been suggested between human and infra-human behavior in noting the similarity of fixed-ratio schedules to piece-rate pay and of variable ratios to the schedules in gambling devices. These are more than mere analogies. Comparable effects of schedules of reinforcement in man and the other animals are gradually being established by direct experimentation. An example is some work by James Holland at the Naval Research Laboratories on the behavior of observing. We often forget that looking at a visual pattern or listening to a sound is itself behavior, because we are likely to be impressed by the more important behavior which the pattern or sound controls. But any act which brings an organism into contact with a discriminative stimulus, or clarifies or intensifies its effect, is reinforced by this result and must be explained in such terms. Unfortunately mere "attending" (as in reading a book or listening to a concert has dimensions which are difficult to study. But behavior with comparable effects is sometimes accessible, such as turning the eyes toward a page, tilting a page to bring it into better light, or turning up the volume of a phonograph. Moreover, under experimental conditions, a specific response can be reinforced by the production or clarification of a stimulus which controls other behavior. The matter is of considerable practical importance. How, for example, can a radar operator or other "lookout" be kept alert? The answer is: by reinforcing his looking behavior.

Holland has studied such reinforcement in the following way. His human subject is seated in a small room before a dial. The pointer on the dial occasionally deviates from zero, and the subject's task is to restore it by pressing a button. The room is dark, and the subject can see the dial only by pressing another button which flashes a light for a fraction of a second. Pressing the second button is, then, an act which presents to the subject a stimulus which

is important because it controls the behavior of restoring the pointer to zero.

Holland has only to *schedule* the deviations of the pointer to produce changes in the rate of flashing the light comparable to the performances of lower organisms under comparable schedules. In Figure 6, for example, the upper curve shows a pigeon's performance on a fairly short fixed-interval. Each interval shows a rather irregular curvature as the rate passes from a low value after reinforcement to a high, fairly constant, terminal rate. In the lower part of the figure is one of Holland's curves obtained when the pointer deflected from zero every three minutes. After a few hours of exposure to these conditions, the subject flashed the light ("looked at the pointer") only infrequently just

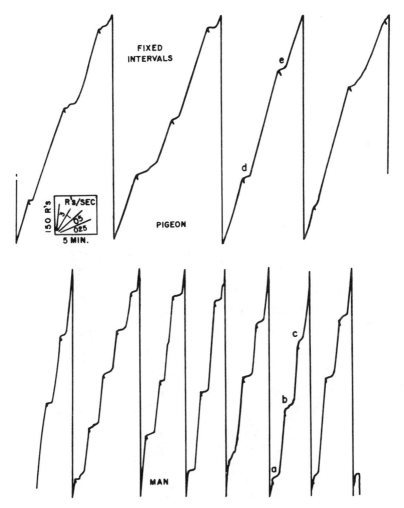

FIGURE 6. *Fixed-interval performance by a human subject compared with that of a pigeon.*

FIGURE 7. *Arrangement for the study of the behavior of a psychotic subject (Lindsley).*

seen at *d* and *e*. In their study of schedules, Ferster and the writer had investigated this effect in detail long before the human curves were obtained.)

Other experiments on human subjects have been conducted in the field of psychotic behavior. In a project at the Behavior Research Laboratories of the Metropolitan State Hospital, in Waltham, Massachusetts,[2] a psychotic subject spends one or more hours each day in a small room containing a chair and an instrument panel as seen in Figure 7. At the right of the instrument board is a small compartment (*a*) into which reinforcers (candy, cigarettes, coins) are dropped by an appropriate magazine. The board contains a plunger (*b*), similar to that of a vending machine. The controlling equipment behind a series of such rooms is shown in Figure 8. Along the wall at the left, as at *a,* are seen four magazines, which can be loaded with various objects. Also seen are periscopes (as at *b*) through which the rooms can be observed through one-way lenses. At the right are cumulative recorders (as at *c*) and behind them panels bearing the controlling equipment which arranges schedules.

after a deflection, but as the interval passed, his rate accelerated, sometimes smoothly, sometimes abruptly, to a fairly constant terminal rate. (An interesting feature of this curve is the tendency to "run through" the reinforcement and to continue at a high rate for a few seconds after reinforcement before dropping to the low rate from which the terminal rate then emerges. Examples of this are seen at *a, b,* and *c.* Examples in the case of the pigeon are also

[2] This work, directed by Henry C. Solomon and the writer, is supported by the Office of Naval Research and the Public Health Service. Ogden R. Lindsley is responsible for the design and conduct of the experiments.

FIGURE 8. *Controlling equipment used in research on psychotic behavior at the Metropolitan State Hospital, Waltham, Massachusetts.*

It is unfortunate that a presentation of this sort must be confined to mere examples. Little more can be done than to suggest the range of application of the method and the uniformity of results over a fairly wide range of species. The extent to which we are moving toward a unified formulation of this difficult material cannot be properly set forth. Perhaps enough has been said, however, to make one point—that in turning to probability of response or, more immediately, to frequency of responding we find a datum which behaves in an orderly fashion under a great variety of conditions. Such a datum yields the kind of rigorous analysis which deserves a place in the natural sciences. Several features should not be overlooked. Most of the records reproduced here report the behavior of single individuals; they are not the statistical product of an "average organism." Changes in behavior are followed continuously during substantial experimental sessions. They often reveal changes occurring within a few seconds which would be missed by any procedure which merely samples behavior from time to time. The properties of the changes seen in the cumulative curves cannot be fully appreciated in the non-instrumental observation of behavior. The reproducibility from species to species is a product of the method. In choosing stimuli, responses, and reinforcers appropriate to the species being studied, we eliminate the sources of many species differences. What emerges are dynamic properties of behavior, often associated with the central nervous system.

Have we been guilty of an undue simplification of conditions in order to obtain this level of rigor? Have we really "proved" that there is comparable order outside the laboratory? It is difficult to be sure of the answers to such questions. Suppose we are observing the rate at which a man sips his breakfast coffee. We have a switch concealed in our hand, which operates a cumulative recorder in another room. Each time our subject sips, we close the switch. It is unlikely that we shall record a smooth curve. At first the coffee is too hot and sipping is followed by aversive consequences.

As it cools, positive reinforcers emerge, but satiation sets in. Other events at the breakfast table intervene. Sipping eventually ceases not because the cup is empty but because the last few drops are cold.

But although our behavioral curve will not be pretty, *neither will the cooling curve for the coffee in the cup.* In extrapolating our results to the world at large, we can do no more than the physical and biological sciences in general. Because of experiments performed under laboratory conditions, no one doubts that the cooling of the coffee in the cup is an orderly process, even though the actual curve would be very difficult to explain. Similarly, when we have investigated behavior under the advantageous conditions of the laboratory, we can accept its basic orderliness in the world at large even though we cannot there wholly demonstrate law.

In turning from an analysis of this sort many familiar aspects of human affairs take on new significance. Moreover, as we might expect, scientific analysis gives birth to technology. The insight into human behavior gained from research of this sort has already proved effective in many areas. The application to personnel problems in industry, to psychotherapy, to "human relations" in general, is clear. The most exciting technological extension at the moment appears to be in the field of education. The principles emerging from this analysis, and from a study of verbal behavior based upon it, are already being applied in the design of mechanical devices to facilitate instruction in reading, spelling, and arithmetic in young children, and in routine teaching at the college level.

In the long run one may envisage a fundamental change in government itself, taking that term in the broadest possible sense. For a long time men of good will have tried to improve the cultural patterns in which they live. It is possible that a scientific analysis of behavior will provide us at last with the techniques we need for this task—with the wisdom we need to build a better world and through it better men.

Learning to Fear

Harold E. Jones and Mary C. Jones

Harold E. Jones (1894–1960) received his Ph.D. from Columbia University in 1923. Director of the Institute of Child Welfare at the University of California, he was especially interested in the area of mental growth and development. Mary C. Jones received her Ph.D. from Columbia University in 1926. A Professor of Education at the University of California since 1953, she and her husband have been associated with the Institute of Child Welfare. Her particular interest is the development and maturation process in children and adolescents.

1. Why is a frog a more fearful object to a child than a snake?

2. What factors do you think would help to account for the heightened emotional sensitivity of older children toward picking up a snake?

What Do Children Fear?

As children grow older, they begin to show differences in the number and kinds of things of which they are afraid. The only general statement which seems to cover all the cases of fear which we have observed in children is that children tend to be afraid of things that require them to make a sudden and unexpected adjustment. Stimuli which are startlingly strange, which are presented without due preparation, or which are painful or excessively intense, belong in this category. For example, in our study of the reactions of preschool children to flashlights, darkness, false-faces, snakes, rabbits, frogs, and the like, it was found that the animal which most often caused fear was the frog, the

Reprinted by permission of the Association for Childhood Education International, 3615 Wisconsin Avenue, N.W., Washington, D.C. "Fear," by Harold Ellis Jones and Mary Cover Jones. From *Childhood Education*, January 1928, Vol. 5, No. 3.

fear not usually appearing at first sight of the frog, but at sight of the frog suddenly jumping. Likewise, a child was often afraid of a jack-in-the-box; a species of beetle which suddenly snaps up in the air when placed on its back, was fairly efficient in arousing alarm; while caterpillars and earthworms produced no more than a mild curiosity in the younger children.

While traces of these childhood fears may last throughout life, affecting adult behavior profoundly, the overt expression of fear is apt to be less marked as childhood is outgrown: partly because the adult meets fewer unfamiliar situations (encounters fewer stimuli for which his action system contains no ready adjustment) and partly because he has learned to mask and repress the more conspicuous symptoms of emotion. From watching individuals of different ages in similar test situations, it is evident that the effectiveness of a stimulus and the type of emotional response are greatly affected by maturity. From the diffuse responsiveness of the infant, to the blunted and inhibited reaction of the blasé adult, the variety of unpredictable behavior in fear producing situations provides a rich field for research.

How does the sight of a snake affect a baby, a toddler, a youth, a grandfather? A few cases, chosen from our laboratory notes, show an interesting developmental sequence.

Experimental Situation

A pen 8 by 10 feet by 6 inches high was built on the nursery floor. Within this a number of blocks and toys were scattered, and two black suitcases were placed flat on the floor near the wall. The suitcases could be opened easily by a child; one contained a familiar mechanical toy, the other contained a snake of a harmless variety (Spilotes corais) about six feet in length and slightly under four inches in girth at the middle of the body. When free in the pen, the snake glided actively about, showing a powerful and agile type of movement, and frequently protruding a black forked tongue about an inch in length. If the child did not open the suitcase containing the snake, an observer was able to do so from a concealed position behind a screen, by pulling a string attached to the lid of the case.

Subject 1. Irving, age 1 year 3 months. Irving sat in the pen, playing idly with the ball and blocks. After being released, the snake glided slowly towards Irving, whipping up his head and deflecting his course when within 12 inches of the infant. Irving watched unconcerned, fixating the snake's head or the middle of his body, and letting his gaze wander frequently to other objects in the pen. The snake furnished only a mild incentive to his attention.

Subject 3. Enid, age 1 year 7 months. Enid sat passively in the pen, playing with blocks in an unsystematic fashion. The snake was released and moved fairly rapidly about the pen. Enid showed no interest, giving the snake only casual glances and continuing to play with her blocks when it was within two feet of her. When (later) the snake was held by the observer directly in front of her face, she showed no changes in facial expression, but presently reached out her hand and grasped the snake tightly about the neck.

Subject 8. Sol, age 2 years 3 months. When the snake began moving about the pen, Sol watched closely, holding his ground when the snake came near, but making no effort to touch it. He resisted when an attempt was made to have him pick up the snake (this was the same guarded reaction that he had shown previously with the rabbit and white rat). He stood unmoved when the snake was thrust toward him, and showed no overt response, save an attempt to follow visually, when the head of the animal was swung in front and in back of him, neck writhing and tongue darting. After the snake was returned to the suitcase he went to it

again and lifted the lid, looked within and then closed it in a business-like manner.

Subject 11. Laurel, age 3 years 8 months. Laurel opened the suitcase, picking out two blocks which were lying against the snake's body. The snake was immobile and she evidently had no differential reaction to it. The snake was taken out. Laurel: "I don't want it." Avertive reactions, moved off, then stood up and started to leave the pen, although without apparent stir or excitement. Experimenter: "Let's put him back in the box." Laurel: "I don't want it." Experimenter: "Come and help me put him back." After slight urging she came over and assisted, using both hands in picking up the snake and dropping him quickly when she reached the suitcase.

Subject 12. Edward, age 4 years 2 months. Edward sat down in the pen and began playing constructively with the blocks. At sight of the snake he asked: "Can it drink water?" Experimenter: "Do you know what it is?" Edward: "It's a fish." He puckered his brows and made slight avertive reactions when the snake was swung within a foot of him, but this was overcome through adaptation in three trials. When encouraged to touch the snake he did so, tentatively, but soon grasped it without hesitation at the neck and body.

Subject 15. Ely, age 6 years 7 months. On opening the suitcase he smiled and looked within for nearly a minute, making no effort to reach, and dropping the cover quickly when the snake moved. The snake thrust the lid up with his head, and glided out into the room. Ely took up a post of observation outside the pen. Experimenter: "Do you like him?" Ely nodded in the affirmative, and smiled. Experimenter: "Touch him like this." Ely very hesitatingly touched his back, and withdrew his hand quickly, later consenting to stroke him. He asked: "Does he have teeth?" a reasonable enough inquiry. When the snake moved in his direction he drew away and looked distressed, but was persuaded to help pick him up and to put him back in the suitcase.

Of 15 children, 7 showed complete absence of fear indications; their age range was from 14 to 27 months, with a median of 20 months. Eight individuals showed "guarded" reactions, 2 of these revealing distinct fear, and 2 showing marked avertive responses when the snake gave the appearance of aggression; the other four being classified as "unafraid but wary." The age range of the "guarded" group was from 26 to 79 months, with a median of 44 months. The only case of a child under three years showing fear was Doris, age 26 months, and her reaction changed markedly the following day, as indicated by the report of the group response:

The suitcase was taken into the nursery when 9 children were present. Most of them recognized it, and one of the older children said, "There's an animal in there." Several of the children moved forward to touch it as soon as the snake was released; Doris, who had been afraid the day before, now showed no fear, crowding close and attempting to hit the snake's head with a wooden boat. The two oldest children in the group remained cautious; Lawrence, age five years seven months, climbed up on a table, and John, age five years ten months, retained hold of the experimenter's hand, and refused to come near. After a few minutes of play, the experimenter said, "Now everyone has touched it except John and Lawrence." Both of these now came forward and touched the snake's back, social pressure being evidently effective in encouraging a more positive response.

Experiments with Older Children

The following results were obtained in a group of 36 school children, with an age range of from about six to ten years:

The children were sitting on low chairs in a circle about 20 feet in diameter. The experimenter placed the suitcase containing the snake in the middle of the circle, asking, "Who wants to open the suitcase?" Harry, eight years of age, opened it, and took the snake out when requested. The snake glided about the floor, passing between the feet of one of the boys; no disturbance was shown. The experimenter now asked, "Who wants to touch the snake?" holding the snake's head so that children had to reach past it, and walking slowly around the inside of the circle. The first 11 children touched the snake with no hesitancy. Four boys about ten years of age hesitated, one withdrawing markedly, another falling over backward in his chair. (This was due to an emotional heightening, arising partly from fear and partly from a desire to show off.) Two girls refused to touch the snake, but jumped up and ran around behind the circle, following the experimenter and watching closely. An undercurrent of reassurance was constantly heard, "He won't let it hurt you. Go ahead, touch it, it won't bite."

Only 9 of the 26 children showed definitely resistive behavior, and these were chiefly boys and chiefly the oldest in the group.

Experiments with College Students

How do adults behave, when presented with a similar situation?

In several classes of undergraduate and graduate students, the snake was introduced as "a perfectly harmless animal; the skin of this reptile has a smooth and pleasant feeling, and we guarantee that in touching him no one runs the slightest risk." In some classes the same reptile was used as in the preceding experiments; in others the snake was a boa constrictor, somewhat smaller and of a less "dangerous" appearance than the Spilotes. Of about 90 students nearly one third refused to have the snake brought near; one third touched him, with obvious hesitation and dislike, while the remainder (including as many women as men) reached forward with apparently complete freedom from any emotional disturbance. Several of the women obviously regarded the presence of a snake in the room as an almost unbearable ordeal, and several of the men solved the problem of emotional conflict by retiring to a neighboring room until the experiment was concluded.

Recommendations for Further Experiments

These studies exemplify a simple observational method, and can be readily repeated with other groups. It is desirable that the problem should be approached by cumulative records on the same children, presenting a series of animals (under standard conditions) to the *same* children at intervals of three months. It is also desirable that the observational data be checked by more rigorous laboratory methods, including the use of instruments, such as the galvanometer, which record the inner aspects of emotional stress. With some of our adult subjects, we noted that while they stroked the snake in an apparently composed fashion, the subject's face and palms were nevertheless covered with beads of perspiration, indicating a marked degree of emotional tension. With young children such repressions are less likely to occur: the emotion is more superficial, and expresses itself readily and frankly in external symptoms. In studying the elimination of a fear, however, we should bear in mind the possibility that an attitude of tolerance and self-assurance may be merely a mask for an internal emotional upset; methods of elimination which "cure" the external signs may sometimes fail to reduce, and may even increase, the actual emotional intensity. We are now collecting evidence on these points, by means of standard laboratory procedures.

It should be pointed out that our experiments of this character should not be attempted except by workers who are accustomed to handling both animals and children. A snake should not be used until he has been adequately tamed and has established a record of reacting well to handling. Some non-poisonous species are likely to be dangerous because of vicious and unpredictable tempers. The situation must always be kept in control, so that a nervous child is not over-frightened; a slight degree of fear, which he later recognizes as groundless, may be of hygienic value, but a marked emotional upset is never hygienic, and the experimenter must take care to avoid traumatic episodes. In regions where poisonous snakes are common, it may be undesirable to train young children in emotional tolerance. The subjects used in our experiments were city children who had never before seen a snake of any kind, and who would be unlikely to encounter a poisonous snake in the course of a lifetime. Even in infested districts, it would seem desirable to cultivate a reaction of intelligent caution, in place of the blinding and tumultuous fear which was shown in so many of our adult subjects.

Suggested Readings

Birney, R. C., and R. C. Teevan, eds. *Reinforcement.* Princeton, N.J.: Van Nostrand, 1961.

Deese, J. *The Psychology of Learning.* New York: McGraw-Hill, 1958.

Erickson, S. C. "Variability of Attack in Massed and Distributed Practice," *J. exp. Psychol.,* 31 (1942), 339–345.

Estes, W. K. "The Statistical Approach to Learning Theory," in S. Koch, ed., *Psychology: A Study of a Science,* Vol. II. New York: McGraw-Hill, 1959.

Estes, W. K. "An Experimental Study of Punishment," *Psychol. Monog.,* 57 (1944), No. 263.

Hilgard, E. R. *Theories of Learning.* New York: Appleton-Century-Crofts, 1956.

Hull, C. L. *Principles of Behavior.* New York: Appleton-Century-Crofts, 1943.

McGeoch, J. A., and A. L. Irion. *The Psychology of Human Learning.* New York: Longmans, Green, 1952.

Mowrer, O. H. *Learning Theory and Personality Dynamics.* New York: Ronald, 1950.

Rotter, J. B. *Social Learning and Clinical Psychology.* New York: Prentice-Hall, 1954.

Skinner, B. F. "Teaching Machines," *Science* 128 (1958), 969–977.

——————. *The Behavior of Organisms.* New York: Appleton-Century-Crofts, 1938.

Thorndike, E. L. "Reward and Punishment in Animal Learning," *Comp. Psychol. Monog.* 8 (1932), No. 39.

Tolman, E. C. "Cognitive Maps in Rats and Men," *Psychol. Rev.,* 55 (1948), 189–208.

Wolfe, J. B. "Effectiveness of Token Rewards for Chimpanzees," *Comp. Psychol. Monog.,* 12 (1936), No. 60.

A loud, shrill train whistle is sensed equally well whether it originates from a stereophonic recording or from a train approaching a railroad crossing. Yet an understanding, or perception, of the whistle differs as the situation differs. The patterns and relationships of stimuli, as they enter our system from the environment, elicit special, subjective meanings. An example of the many contradictions between reality and illusion that a person must adjust to is the occurrence of the water-puddle mirage commonly seen on a hot pavement. The adjustment requires an integration between the sensory organs and what is perceived as a result of their stimulation. This integration process is one of the most fascinating topics dealt with in psychology.

Toward a Neuropsychological Theory of Behavior, Donald O. Hebb. Hebb poses an interesting question: Why does intelligence sometimes seem not to be affected by a serious brain injury? To explain such a puzzling effect, he states that ". . . we must find an anatomical and physiological understanding of what is known psychologically as a concept; and we must be able to deal with its relation to perception and to learning." The framework for understanding such sensory and perceptual relations is suggested in this selection by relating it to existing research.

Vision, Conrad Mueller and Mae Rudolph and *Experiments in Hearing, S. S. Stevens and Fred Warshofsky.* The next two readings, on vision and hearing, depart from the usual practice of providing experiments rather than talking about them. Most of the research in the areas of vision and hearing is technical and introduces a plethora of new terms to the beginner in psychology. The two readings included here were written by experts for the intelligent layman and are relatively free of technical terms and jargon. Since vision and hearing are so crucial to man's existence, they have been the chief senses for psychological study. These selections will help set the stage for those that follow.

The Factor of Attention in the Cat, Raul Hernández-Peón, Harald Scherrer, and Michel Jouvet. This article considers the fact that one perceives or attends to external stimuli in a selective manner. This idea is not new. However, testing this phenomenon under controlled conditions is a difficult task. Hernández-Peón and his colleagues used three sensory pathways—visual, olfactory, and somatic—in unanesthetized, unrestrained cats in performing their research. They point out that a "central inhibitory mechanism may . . . play an important role in selective exclusion of sensory messages along their passage toward mechanisms of perception and con-sciousness."

Effects of Decreased Sensory Variation, W. H. Bexton, W. Heron, and T. H. Scott. A constant input of sensory data is a normal, everyday experience. But what happens when normal external stimulation is removed? Bexton, Heron, and Scott document the effects on perception when subjects are isolated from the outside world. They paid 22 male college students to lie on a comfortable bed 24 hours a day for several consecutive days. The perceptions of the students, resulting both from internal stimuli and from tasks they were asked to perform during and after the experimental session, were extensively tested. The conclusions drawn from the experiment are of considerable value for an understanding of perception.

Toward a Neuropsychological Theory of Behavior

Donald O. Hebb

Donald Hebb, Professor of Psychology at McGill University in Montreal, is a past president of both the Canadian and the American Psychological Associations. He received his Ph.D. from Harvard University in 1936. His interest in psychology has been identified with the neuropsychological position stated in this selection, and his basic interest in psychology is to better understand "how the mind works."

1. *In what way(s) is the concept of "set" at odds with an assumption of complete sensory control?*

2. *What facts, taken from studies of perceptual generalization, make it difficult to accept the memory trace as structural and static?*

Let us look first at the specific problem from which the present speculations began, to see why the discussion is oriented as it is.

The problem lay in certain puzzling effects of operation on the human brain. The effect of a clearcut removal of cortex outside the speech area is often astonishingly small; at times no effect whatever can be found. It is possible that there is always a loss of intelligence in aphasia, when the "speech area" is seriously damaged, but this does not, of course, explain why damage elsewhere should have no effect. It would be unreasonable to suppose that most of the cortex has nothing to do with intelligence, and there are in fact definite indications that this is

Abridged from D. O. Hebb, *The Organization of Behavior: A Neuropsychological Theory* (New York: John Wiley & Sons, Inc., 1949), pp. 1–8, 11–16. Reprinted by permission of the publisher.

not true. Intelligence must be affected by any large brain injury—yet sometimes it seems not to be.

A final touch is added to the puzzle when we find that it is tests of the Binet type that least show the effect of injuries outside the speech area. The Binet is the measure of intelligence that is most sensitive and accurate with normal subjects. How can it be possible for a man to have an IQ of 160 or higher, after a prefrontal lobe has been removed, or for a woman to have an IQ of 115, a better score than two-thirds of the normal population could make, after losing the entire right half of the cortex?

Those two are perhaps the most striking cases, but high scores after brain operation have been reported by nearly everyone who has used standard tests as a method of study, and they have to be explained. Most investigators have preferred to forget them, and to search only for intellectual defects. The defects certainly must exist, and it is important to find them; but it is just as important to learn why Binet-type tests, the most valid and sensitive indices of normal ability, should often show no effect of injury to the brain.

The only explanation that has been proposed, and perhaps the only feasible one, has to do with perceptual learning and with concepts as distinct from conditioned responses or motor learning. The explanation, roughly, is this. The level of intelligence-test performance is a function of the concepts a patient has already developed. Once developed, a concept is retained, despite brain damage that, if it had occurred earlier, would have prevented the development. The patient with brain injury at maturity may continue to think and solve problems normally (in familiar fields), although his intelligence would have been far from normal if a similar injury had happened at birth. The explanation meets the clinical facts and, moreover, is supported by the way in which some intellectual capacities are retained in old age when others are disappearing.

But now we come to the crux of the matter. As an explanation, this is only a good start. What is a concept, physiologically and *à propos* of the loss of neural cells? Though it has been tried before now, an explanation cannot be half neural anatomy and half consciousness. They are different levels in a logical hierarchy. A problem recognized at one level can be solved by recourse to a more fundamental set of conceptions, but an hypothesis cannot well comprise two levels, take in two universes of discourse at the same time. We want to explain certain clinical facts. To really do so, we must find an anatomical and physiological understanding of what is known psychologically as a concept; and we must be able to deal with its relation to perception and to learning.

And with *that,* we land right in the middle of the generalized problem of explaining mammalian behavior. What is a concept, if it is not a conditioned response? What is perceptual learning? And so on. Before such questions can be answered, psychological theory must have a new base of operations. As an illustration, a particular problem has been cited; but the difficulty is really general, as the following section will try to show, and there is no phase of psychological theory in which the same central weakness does not appear.

It has already been suggested that the essential need is to find out how to handle thought, and related processes, more adequately. The difficulty in doing so goes back to fundamental assumptions. If this discussion is to rest on solid ground, it must start with certain ideas with which every psychologist is concerned but which have been confused, vague, or ill defined.

Rejecting the Assumption of a Complete Sensory Control

The first to be discussed is what can be called the assumption of a sensory dominance of behavior. It is the idea that behavior is a series of *reactions* (instead of actions), each of which is determined by the immediately preceding events in the sensory systems. The idea is not altogether consistent with recognizing the existence of set, attitude, or attention; and an implicit inconsistency of this sort is at the root of the current confusion in psychological theory.

It may be noted in passing that the assumption of a sensory dominance of behavior is not the property of any particular theory. Theories differ as to how a sensory event has its effect, but not as to its all-important role. *Gestalt* psychology avoids words like "stimulus" and "sensation" but as a system is not less preoccupied with stimulus configurations than other systems are with their stimuli.

Now for the source of confusion.

In the simplest terms, "attention" refers to a selectivity of response. Man or animal is continuously responding to some events in the environment, and not to others that could be responded to (or "noticed") just as well. When an experimental result makes it necessary to refer to "set" or "attention," the reference means, precisely, that the activity that controls the form, speed, strength, or duration of response is not the immediately preceding excitation of receptor cells alone. The fact that a response is not so controlled may be hard to explain, theoretically; but it is not mystical, and "attention" is not necessarily anthropomorphic, or animistic, or undefinable.

Now the tradition in psychology has long been a search for the property of the stimulus which by itself determines the ensuing response, at any given stage of learning. This approach seems partly a consequence of psychology's persistent fight against animism[1] and deserves

---

[1] And partly, as we shall see, the product of antiquated physiological conceptions. Fighting animism meant that psychological phenomena had to be reduced to a pattern of cause and effect. The only means at hand was a physiology of the nervous system in which a knowledge of sense organs and peripheral nerves was the main content. As a result, it is still easy

respect for that reason; but it is no longer satisfactory as theory. Almost without exception psychologists have recognized the existence of the selective central factor that reinforces now one response, now another. The problem is to carry out to its logical conclusion an incomplete line of thought that starts out preoccupied with stimulus or stimulus configuration as the source and control of action, eventually runs into the facts of attention and so on, and then simply agrees that attention is an important fact, without recognizing that this is inconsistent with one's earlier assumptions. To complete this process, we must go back and make a change in the basis of the theory.

There are three points here: one is that psychologists have generally recognized the existence of attention or the like; another that they have done so reluctantly and sparingly, and have never recognized the fact in setting up theories. The third point is obvious enough, that we need to find some way of dealing with the facts consistently. Since everyone knows that attention and set exist, we had better get the skeleton out of the closet and see what can be done with it.

The first two of these points have been pretty clearly established by Gibson. His review needs some clarification in one respect, since he declined to attempt any definition of "set" or any other of the long list of terms with a similar meaning that he gathered together, although he evidently recognized, in classifying them so, that they have something in common. This common meaning has already been defined. When one considers the problem in the light of the implicit assumption of a sensory dominance of behavior it becomes clear at once that the notions of set, attention, attitude, expectancy, hypothesis, intention, vector, need, perseveration, and preoccupation have a common ele-

---

to feel that psychology becomes part of a larger demonology with any retreat from the stimulus-response formula. As for "insight," "purpose," "attention"— any one of these may still be an invocation of the devil, to the occasional psychologist. However, this attitude should not be too much made fun of. It cannot be emphasized too strongly that there is continual danger of slipping momentarily into animistic thinking; and consistent use of the S-R formula does at least avoid that danger effectively. It behooves those of us who wish to use other terms to see that they are clearly defined.

ment, and one only. That element is the recognition that responses are determined by something else besides the immediately preceding sensory stimulation. It does not deny the importance of the immediate stimulus; it does deny that sensory stimulation is everything in behavior.

All such terms, then, are a reference to the "central process which seems relatively independent of afferent stimuli," defined by Hilgard and Marquis, which I shall call here the *autonomous central process*. Gibson's review shows in effect that the process is ubiquitous, that it crops up in every sort of psychological investigation—and that almost everyone has recognized its existence, in one form or another. To Gibson's list can be added Pavlov's and Hull's stimulus trace—a lasting cerebral state, set up it is true by a specific stimulus but not transmitted and dissipated at once; Beach's central excitatory mechanism; Morgan's central motive state; and Kleitman's "interest"—a factor in wakefulness. All these things have the same property of an activity that has a selective effect on behavior without being part of the present afferent excitation.

Everyone has had such ideas about the control of behavior; and yet, as Gibson noted, "the meaning [of the term "set"] is felt to be unsatisfactory, and the concept is employed reluctantly and only because the facts make it absolutely unavoidable." The reluctance is partly no doubt because of a feeling that the concept is animistic, in some obscure way. But why animism, if the facts of behavior make it unavoidable? The trouble really seems to have been in finding how to make an essential idea intelligible.

Hilgard and Marquis' central process, and Beach's central excitatory mechanism, are hypothetical entities, but they certainly have no flavor of animism about them. "Attention" and "set" are now seen to fall in the same class: it may well be that their connotations are misleading and that we shall have to look for new terms, but the idea itself is respectable, and such language need no longer risk starting a witchhunt.

The Neurological Problem of Attention

There is a further hazard on the course. This is the apparent lack of a theoretical rationale for the autonomous central process. Actually, modern neurophysiology has already removed this difficulty.

Here again the situation can only be understood historically. A main function of the neural cell is of course to transmit excitations, and earlier ideas of anatomy and physiology made the central nervous system appear, in principle, a collection of routes, some longer, some shorter, leading without reversal from receptors to effectors—a mass of conductors that lies inactive until a sense organ is excited, and then conducts the excitation promptly to some muscle or gland. We know now that this is not so, but the older idea still has a profound effect on psychological thought—demonstrated, for example, in the assumption of sensory dominance, discussed above.

The lack of a rationale for nonsensory influences on behavior that seemed to exist in 1920 certainly exists no more. Psychologists have long had to recognize (since the days of the Würzburg school at least) the existence of a determining tendency, whether physiology made it comprehensible or not. Modern electrophysiology has more than caught up with psychology and now provides abundant evidence to support the same idea. When the detailed evidence of neurophysiology and histology is considered, the conclusion becomes inevitable that the nonsensory factor in cerebral action must be more consistently present and of more dominating importance than reluctant psychological theory has ever recognized. Instead of a joker to occasionally confuse the student of behavior, nonsensory activities appear in every fall of the cards and must make up a large share of the deck. Neurophysiologically, it may even become a problem to account for *any* consistent effect of a specific stimulus.

Electrophysiology of the central nervous system indicates in brief that the brain is continuously active, in all its parts, and an afferent excitation must be superimposed on an already existent excitation. It is therefore impossible that the consequence of a sensory event should often be uninfluenced by the pre-existent activity. If we recognize in that activity the psychologically known factor of set and the like the problem for psychology is no longer to account for the existence of set but to find out how it acts and above all to learn how it has the property of a consistent, selective action instead

of producing the random-error distribution postulated by Hull in his "oscillation principle."

So there really is a rational basis for postulating a central neural factor that modifies the action of a stimulus. The theoretical problem now is to discover the rules by which it operates. At first glance this is a problem for the neurophysiologist only. But look closer; much of the evidence, from which these rules must be worked out, is psychological, or behavioral. The problem is after all the problem of attention, and seen best in the activity of the whole animal. It is in the highest degree unlikely that it can be solved either from the physiological evidence alone or from the behavioral evidence alone. What we need, evidently, is some synthesis of both kinds of datum. The psychological data have been reviewed briefly.

For our purposes, the physiological evidence can be treated under two heads, as bearing on (1) the existence and properties of a continuous cerebral activity, and (2) the nature of synaptic transmission in the central nervous system.

Let me summarize. (1) All psychologists have recognized some such factor in behavior. It undoubtedly exists. (2) Recognizing it is really a denial that behavior is only a series of responses to environmental stimulation. One important meaning of "attention" or the like is the reference to a partly autonomous, or nonsensory, cerebral activity: the "autonomous central process." (3) The problem for psychology then is to find conceptions for dealing with such complexities of central neural action: conceptions that will be valid physiologically and at the same time "molar" enough to be useful in the analysis of behavior. (4) Psychology is still profoundly influenced by the very "molecular" conception of linear transmission through a sequence of single cells. The conception is no longer valid physiologically, just as it has long been without psychological usefulness. The attack on neural connections as an explanation of behavior was really an attack on this particular conception of the way connections operate; modern neuroanatomy and electrophysiology have changed the question completely, and the significance of synaptic connections must be examined all over again.

Our problem, then, is to find valid "molar" conceptions of neural action (conceptions, *i.e.,* that can be applied to large-scale cortical organizations). Bishop has made the point, in another context, that this is an essential problem from neurophysiology also. But psychologists can hardly sit around with hands folded, waiting for the physiologist to solve it. In its essence the problem is psychological and requires a knowledge of the psychological as well as the physiological evidence for its solution.

Perceptual Generalization and the Assumption of a Structural Memory Trace

Now for a second fundamental assumption of psychological theory: this time, one that must, it seems, be accepted; but in accepting it we must also recognize the difficulties it entails and provide for them. These difficulties in fact determine the main features of the theory presented in this monograph.

The assumption we must accept is that the memory trace, the basis of learning, is in some way structural and static; and the difficulties in the way of making the assumption are mainly in the facts of perceptual generalization that have been emphasized by *Gestalt* psychologists (Koffka, Köhler and Lashley). The problem raised by these writers is crucial and must be disposed of before we . touch anything else.

Lashley has concluded that a learned discrimination is not based on the excitation of any particular neural cells. It is supposed to be determined solely by the pattern, or shape, of the sensory excitation. Köhler, also stressing the apparent fact that the pattern and not the locus of stimulation is the important thing, has developed a theory of electrical fields in the brain which control cerebral action. Like Lashley, he explicitly denies that the same cells need be excited to arouse the same perception.

This suggests that the mnemonic trace, the neural change that is induced by experience and constitutes "memory," is not a change of structure. Other facts, at the same time, are an even stronger argument that it *must* be structural. A structural trace, as we shall see in a moment, must be assumed; but when we do so we have to find some way of fitting in the facts of perception.

If it is really unimportant in what tissues a sensory excitation takes place, one finds it hard to understand how repeated sensations can reinforce one another, with the lasting effect we call learning or memory. It might be supposed that the mnemonic trace is a lasting pattern of reverberatory activity without fixed locus, like some cloud formations or an eddy in a millpond. But if so it seems that the multitudinous traces in the small confines of the cerebral cortex would interfere with one another, producing a much greater distortion of early memories by later ones than actually occurs.

Moreover, violent cortical storms can occur (as in *grand mal* epilepsy or cerebral concussion) without a detectable effect on earlier memories. That the trace should be purely "dynamic"—a pattern of activity not dependent on structural changes for its permanence—thus seems in the highest degree unlikely. No one has explicitly made such an assumption; yet how otherwise are the known properties of a learned discrimination to be accounted for, with its inevitable tendency to be generalized beyond what has already been experienced by the animal—its apparent independence of excitation in specific cells?

In addition to the facts of perceptual generalization, two other forms of evidence might make it difficult to postulate a structural trace as the basis of memory. One is from Lashley's extirpation experiments, showing that the removal of blocks of the rat's cerebral cortex does not affect habits selectively. If one habit is affected, others are also. From this, Lashley has concluded that memory traces are not localized in the cerebral cortex, but himself has pointed out another possible interpretation. His evidence is consistent with the idea that the trace is structural but diffuse, involving, that is, a large number of cells widely spaced in the cortex, physiologically but not anatomically unified. This is not, consequently, crucial evidence for or against the notion of structural traces in the cortex.

The other evidence that seemed once to prevent postulating a structural trace is found in the work of Wulf and later investigators who have interpreted their studies of human memory for patterns to mean that the trace is spontaneously active, and does not lie dormant or merely deteriorate with the passage of time. Hanawalt, however, effectively criticized the earlier evidence for this idea; and Hebb and Foord, having obtained data inconsistent with Wulf's hypothesis, re-examined the later work that managed to avoid Hanawalt's criticism. They have shown that there is no evidence to even faintly support the idea of slow, spontaneous changes in the trace. This conception must be abandoned.

Thus the only barrier to assuming that a structural change in specific neural cells is the basis of memory lies in the generalization of the perception of patterns. Man sees a square as a square, whatever its size, and in almost any

that perception is independent of the locus of excitation; and this interpretation has been tacitly accepted as inescapable. The result is an awkward dilemma for theory, since, as we have seen, it is hard to reconcile an unlocalized afferent process with a structural (and hence localized) mnemonic trace.

Lashley's hypothesis of interference patterns is the one explicit attempt to solve this difficulty and to deal adequately with both perception and learning. As such it deserves special men-

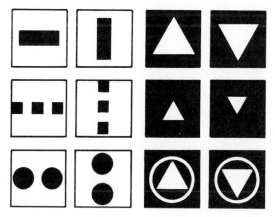

FIGURE 1. *Illustrating generalization in perception. A rat is first trained with the two diagrams at the top, in the left half of the figure, until he always avoids the vertical bar and chooses the horizontal. He is then tested with the next pair of diagrams, the horizontally and vertically arranged squares; and with the next pair, circles side by side versus circles one above the other. Transfer of response occurs, the rat in each case preferring the horizontal diagram, showing that perception of horizontal and vertical is generalized beyond any particular pattern. Similarly, after training with the large plain triangles, top right, the animal is tested with smaller triangles and with circumscribed triangles. If the erect triangle, the one to the left, is positive in training, the rat will choose the left-hand diagram when presented with either of the two lower pairs, again demonstrating perceptual generalization.*

setting. A rat trained to look for food behind a horizontal rectangle will thereafter choose almost *any* horizontal figure, such as an interrupted line or a pair of circles side by side (Figure 1). Trained to choose a solid upright triangle and to avoid an inverted triangle, he will discriminate consistently between outlines of triangles; triangles with confusing figures added (such as circumscribing circles); and triangles of different size, which cannot thus excite the same retinal cells simultaneously. Rats reared in darkness, then trained in the same way, show the same perceptual generalizations.

These are concrete, undisputed facts of behavior. They have been interpreted as meaning

tion here, although we shall see that in other respects it faces great difficulties.

Other writers have had to choose one horn of the dilemma. Köhler, for example, starts out with the facts of perceptual generalization, in his theory of cerebral fields of force, and then cannot deal with learning. He has no apparent way of avoiding a fatal difficulty about the nature of the trace, its locus and structure. This is another aspect of the difficulty for *Gestalt* theory raised by Boring, who pointed out that at *some* point the perceptual process must act on specific cells in order to determine a specific response.

The theory elaborated by Hull, on the other hand, is to be regarded as providing first of all for the stability of learning. It then has persistent difficulty with perception. The principle of "afferent neural interaction" appears to be a concession extorted by the facts of perceptual generalization. With this, there is some danger that the entire system may lose its meaning. The great value of Hull's theory is in showing how one may conceive of variable behavior as determined by constant causal relationships between stimulus, intervening variables, and response. This is brilliantly achieved, for an important segment of behavior. But then the postulate of afferent neural interaction adds that anything may happen when two sensory events occur at the same time—which of course they are always doing. Evidently no prediction is possible until the limits, and the determinants, of afferent neural interaction can be given in detail. This it seems demands that the neurological reference, already present in the theory, be made explicit, and detailed. For our present purposes, at any rate, Hull must be regarded as not yet having solved the problem of dealing with the perceptual process in a theory of learning, although it remains possible that his program will do so in the future.

Vision

Conrad Mueller and Mae Rudolph

Conrad Mueller is Professor of Psychology and of Neural Science at Indiana University. He was formerly Chairman of the Psychology Department at Columbia University. Mueller is the author of Sensory Psychology *and the co-author of* Vision and Visual Perception *and of* Modern Learning Theory. *Mae Rudolph is a journalist who has written for many magazines in the area of health. She is presently Managing Editor of* Medical World News.

1. *At what point is light no longer "light" but an electrical-chemical process?*

2. *Is there a known correspondence between areas of the retina and areas of the brain?*

For hundreds of years it has been clear that man's vision takes place, not in his eyes, but in his brain. One proof is that severe brain injury can blind him, completely and permanently, even though his eyes continue to function perfectly. The eye does gather and focus light into images on its back wall, the retina. But when

From Life Science Library's *Light and Vision*, edited by Conrad Mueller and Mae Rudolph, 1966, pp. 75–81. © 1966, Time, Inc. Reprinted by permission of Time, Inc.

the light strikes there, a wholly new step in the visual process begins. Sensitive cells in the retina convert the energy of light into signals, and these signals are transmitted to the brain. Only now, after generations of physicists, biologists and psychologists have pieced together fragmentary—often contradictory—bits of evidence, is this part of vision beginning to be understood. It is one of the most delicate achievements of nature, operating with the smallest quantities of light that can possibly exist, initiating elusive chemical reactions in single molecules, and transmitting signals over networks more complex than any in the biggest electronic computer.

The first important clue to the way visual signals reach the brain was uncovered in 1877 by a German biologist, Franz Boll. One day

Boll looked into a frog's eye he had just taken from a dark closet in his laboratory and noticed, far back in the eye, a reddish substance that quickly faded in the light. Other scientists had observed the same phenomenon but had dismissed it as a blood clot. This explanation did not satisfy Boll. If the red matter was blood, why did it disappear in the light? He returned the eye to the dark closet for a while and then repeated the experiment. Again the reddish substance was present when the eye was first removed, and again the color faded in the light. Soon Boll realized that he had made an important discovery: a chemical change takes place in the eye when light enters it.

Learning from a Frog's Eye

Discovering the molecular change that "bleaches" visual pigment was the essential first step in understanding the chemical reactions that convert light into signals of sight. The key was Boll's realization that the rod pigment in a frog's eye could be temporarily destroyed by light. Soon after Boll had seen the pigment in action, Wilhelm Kühne managed to extract some from frog rods. (Discovery of cone pigment did not come until much later.) The rod pigment was a colored substance that he called *sehpurpur,* a German word that means "visual scarlet" but was translated into English as "visual purple." The English misnomer continues to be used although Kühne and other scientists knew that the pigment may range from rose-colored in land animals to deep violet in freshwater fishes. Today most scientists prefer the term "rhodopsin" for the visual pigment of rods.

Although scientists were certain that there was pigment in cones as well as in rods, there was no laboratory evidence of its existence until nearly a century after Kühne had extracted rhodopsin. When cone pigment was finally discovered in the human eye, it turned out to be not one, but three kinds of pigment, differing in their response to colors. One is most sensitive to red, another to green and the third to blue. Only one kind of pigment exists in each cone, but none of them has yet been extracted as a chemical.

The rhodopsin pigment, experiments showed, includes a chemical relative of caro-

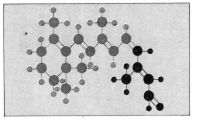

RETINENE IN DARKNESS

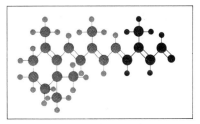

RETINENE IN LIGHT

MOLECULAR STRUCTURE, *diagrammed above, is changed and visual signals created when light hits the rod's rhodopsin pigment and affects its retinene group. Before light hits, the retinene structure* (top) *is twisted; note the position of the dark-colored atoms at lower right in the illustration. When light hits, the structure is "straightened out"* (bottom)— *the dark-colored group of atoms moves in line with other clusters. By some means not fully understood, this simple change sets off electrochemical impulses in the retina's nerve cells. The light, having transferred its energy, ceases to exist. The rest of the visual process occurs in darkness.*

tene, the vitamin A pigment of carrots—a discovery that had two quite dissimilar results. It suggested how the chemical transformation of light energy might operate. And it also threatened to set the population on a carrot binge. Researchers working with the retinas of rats that had been starved of vitamin A found that the rats' rhodopsin built up much more slowly in the dark than it did in normally fed animals. Both rod and cone vision in humans also is harmed by a vitamin A deficiency. To some persons this fact meant that eating quantities of carrots, which are the chief source of carotene, would improve their vision. It will—if they have poor sight because of a lack of vitamin A. However, if they are already on balanced diets with adequate vitamin A, they could eat carrots around the clock without the slightest improvement; the regeneration of both rod and cone

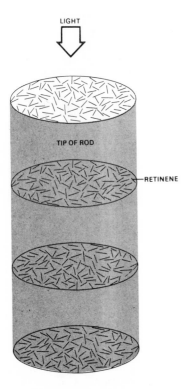

LIGHT

TIP OF ROD

RETINENE

THE LIGHT-SENSITIVE MATERIAL of the eye is believed to be located in a series of rhodopsin-containing disks stacked, as illustrated here in simplified form, in great numbers in the tips of the rods. When individual photons of light enter a rod, they pass through the disks unless they hit one or another of the myriads of retinene groups (small straight lines) within the rhodopsin. Only a small percentage are actually absorbed as they streak through the disks. When a photon does collide with a molecule, however, it straightens out the retinene structure (opposite) and triggers the complex process whereby a signal is passed along to the brain.

pigments is already at its best, and the extra vitamin A would simply be discarded by the body.

The Vital Vitamin A

But the greater significance of the vitamin A discovery lay in the insight it gave into the fundamentals of vision. Vitamin A is a compound that can exist in any one of four molecular arrangements—but only one of these arrangements serves to regenerate visual pigments. This suggested that molecular rearrangement—a shifting about of molecular parts —was involved in bleaching and regeneration.

There must, the investigators felt, be some kind of lock-and-key mechanism in pigment molecules that is operated by light.

At this point it is useful to remember the double nature of light. It acts as waves of energy with specific characteristics of waves such as length, frequency and velocity. But these waves also act like trains of individual particles of energy called photons. The latter aspect of the nature of light is of critical importance in understanding what goes on after a "light picture" has been absorbed by the visual pigment. The photon is not itself the key that unlocks sight; it uncovers the keyhole so that the key can enter the lock.

How this complex sequence of steps takes place can be seen in the pigment in the rods, rhodopsin. The molecule of rhodopsin consists of two parts. One is a protein, opsin, that serves as a base and provides the proper "environment" for the necessary chemical reactions. Fitted snugly on this base is the site of light absorption, a group of atoms that can be rearranged. This group, called retinene, is closely related to vitamin A. The retinene group fits over its opsin base like the cap that swings over the keyhole of a car door to keep out water that might freeze the turning mechanism. As long as the retinene is in its normal arrangement, it fits over the opsin keyhole and no key can be inserted. But the impact of a photon of light changes the shape of the retinene so that it "swings aside" like the keyhole cap, allowing crucial chemicals to slip into the keyhole. These chemicals increase the energy of the photoreceptors and send visual signals along them to the nerve cells. Thus begins the journey of sight to the brain.

However, this explanation cannot be the whole story. It assumes that a single photon of light is strong enough to power the chemical and electrical processes that actually produce the sensation of vision in the brain. But one photon could not do that. It is far too weak; just to provide the dim light from a small flashlight requires billions and billions of photons per second. Scientists are certain that the pigment reaction must be amplified for any perception of vision to occur. As yet, they do not know how this amplification takes place in the eye. George Wald of Harvard's Biological Laboratories has suggested two possibilities. It may be that the absorption of a photon activates

chemical boosters—enzymes—in the pigment. These enzymes may then be able to generate far greater amounts of energy than the original molecule could produce by itself. The other possibility is that when a photon of light hits the photoreceptor, it punches a one-molecule hole in the photoreceptor. If this second theory is correct, then electrically charged particles might be able to flow from the receptor into two other layers of the retina, where they may be processed and forwarded to the brain.

The Eye-Brain Transmission System

The retinal nerve fibers that carry this visual message constitute an extremely complex interconnected network that fans out all over the forward-facing surface of the retina. One layer of the retina, lying between the photoreceptors and the transmission lines, is made up of bipolar cells, which pick up the electrical signals from the photoreceptors. The foremost layer contains the ganglion cells, which receive the signals from the bipolars and transmit the messages to the brain. All these nerve fibers constitute a data-collecting system. They come together at one spot on the retina; from this point, bunched together like a cable, they pass through the retina and out the back to become the optic nerve leading to the brain. At the place where the cable passes through the surface of the retina, there are no photoreceptor cells, and this produces a blind spot. Here the eye sees nothing.

Despite its size and importance, the blind spot was not discovered until the 17th Century. Then a French scientist, Edmé Mariotte, performed a revealing experiment with two small white disks and a dark screen. He placed the first disk about eye level on the screen, and the second slightly lower and to the right about two feet. He closed his left eye, stared at the first disk with his right and then slowly backed away from the screen. At about nine feet, the second disk disappeared from his view although the screen around it remained visible. Light from the second disk was falling squarely on the blind spot. When Mariotte slightly shifted his eye, he could again see the disk. In ordinary vision the blind spot causes no inconvenience, partly because of binocular vision and partly because of the rapidity and frequency of eye movements.

In binocular vision man's eyes must exchange information. Therefore, after leaving the eyes, the two nerve bundles, one from each eye, come together at an intersection called the optic chiasma. Here each bundle forms two branches. One branch, from the nasal side of the right eye, crosses over and joins the branch

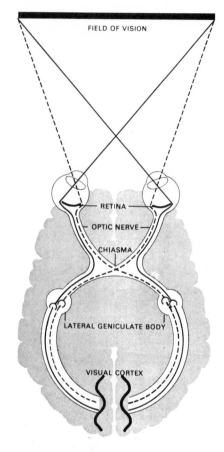

THE CROSSOVER *of visual nerve fibers results in the left part of the brain "seeing" only the right half of the field of vision, while the right part "sees" only the left half. The retina of each eye receives the entire image of an object, as shown by the solid and dotted lines passing through the lenses (colored for the right eye and black for the left). Impulses generated by the images on the retinas are carried from the eyes by the optic nerves. However, at the chiasma, the fibers in each optic nerve divide into two bundles. The inner branch from the right eye (dotted colored line) crosses over and joins with the outer branch from the left eye (solid black line) before continuing to the left lateral geniculate body. The other branches are routed to the right lateral geniculate body. Both sets of fibers are then relayed in newly formed nerve bundles to terminals on either side of the visual cortex.*

from the outer, or temporal, side of the left eye. The other two branches—from the nasal side of the left eye and the temporal side of the right —combine on the right. After this regrouping, the two newly formed bundles go respectively to the left and right lateral geniculate bodies, way stations that are located just back of the brain's midsection.

Each lateral geniculate body is a laminated material and its layers are organized to receive signals from only one of the two eyes. However, because of the close proximity of the layers, there is some form of interaction between signals. This interaction, along with such features of human vision as the placement of the eyes and the overlap of the visual fields, may be among the reasons man has stereoscopic vision.

The original fibers end at the lateral geniculate bodies. There, new nerve fibers continue to the visual cortex, where the actual phenomenon of "seeing" takes place. The cortex is a mass of gray matter, a pair of hemispheres that curve to form a shell around the very back of the brain. If the cortex were unfolded and spread out, it would be about a tenth of an inch thick and some 20 square feet—the area of a four-by-five-foot rug. The section devoted to vision is only a tiny portion of the entire cortex. The billions of cells in the visual cortex are arranged in a number of layers, and the millions of fibers that enter it from the lateral geniculate bodies connect with the fourth layer from the top. From here they disseminate to all layers of the cortex. The cells of some of the layers—particularly the ones just above and below the fourth layer—send out projections to other areas deep in the brain. Because vision involves memory and association, it may be that these outside lines connect with the parts of the brain that store up the data of experience.

At this point, scientists face a fundamental and appallingly difficult question: How does the brain use these signals to produce a visual image?

With the aid of sensitive electrodes it is now possible to locate exactly what area of the cortex is activated by a stimulus from a specific part of the retina. One section of the cortex receives the signals from the fovea, and another part responds to the periphery of the retina. Not unexpectedly, researchers have found that the larger region of the visual cortex serves the central portion of the retina, where cones predominate and man has greatest acuity.

Measuring Signals in a Single Cell

In recent years, this mapping of the cortex has become so refined that scientists can monitor a single nerve cell in the brain. The work of Hubel and Wiesel, the men who wired a cat's brain for sound, has been of special significance. By means of their microscopic electrodes, they have been able to measure the responsiveness of individual brain cells to various kinds of stimuli. Different nerve cells, they found, reacted to different sets of signals from the retina. For instance, one cell reacts vigorously if the stimulus is a slender upright rectangle that moves horizontally, but shows no response at all to the same rectangle when it moves up and down. Such experiments have shown that the interpretive function of vision involves not only areas of the cortex but also the reaction of highly specialized, individual cells in the cortex.

Somehow, in a manner yet to be discovered, all of these specialized cells add up, combine and exchange visual data and thereby create perception—a picture in the mind.

Experiments in Hearing

S. S. Stevens and Fred Warshofsky

S. S. Stevens is Professor of Psychophysics and Director of the Laboratory of Psychophysics at Harvard University. He is the co-author of Hearing: Its Psychology and Physiology. *He has received awards for his research from five organizations, including the American Psychological Association and the Society of Experimental Psychologists. As an adolescent Stevens went on a three-year mission for the Mormon Church to Belgium and Switzerland, where he learned to preach in French. Fred Warshofsky is a science writer who is best known for his book* The Rebuilt Man. *He was a Sloan-Rockefeller Advanced Science Writing Fellow in 1963.*

1. Why is the organ of Corti so essential to the function of hearing?

2. Of what practical significance is knowledge of hearing to the field of psychology?

Confusion from a Cat's Ear

In the first of several experiments, Bray and Wever * placed an electrode on the auditory nerve of an anesthetized cat. The electrical impulses transmitted by the nerve were picked up by the electrode, amplified and sent to a telephone receiver in a distant, soundproof room. Wever talked into the cat's ear while Bray listened at the receiver. He was delighted to hear some recognizable words coming out of the receiver. Apparently the telephone theory held up under experimental investigation.

But another experiment raised puzzling questions for the two researchers. This time, they stimulated the cat's ear not with words, but with pure sound of a single frequency. More important, they sent the amplified output from the electrode not to a telephone receiver,

but to a cathode-ray oscilloscope, a laboratory instrument that looks like a television set but shows wave forms rather than pictures. If the telephone theory was correct, the sound working through the cat's ear would initiate a corresponding signal in the nerve—a signal identical in frequency to the original sound. Such a regular electrical current would show up on the oscilloscope as a series of neat spikes of green light.

The results were anything but neat. When a high-frequency sound was fed to the cat's ear, the electrode did pick up an electrical impulse. But what showed on the oscilloscope was not a picture of orderly frequencies corresponding to the original sound but a display of noise—a wild tangle of irregular wave forms. Why should speech sounds come over a telephone line as comprehensible words, yet high-frequency sounds show up as so much jumbled noise on an oscilloscope?

In 1932, at the Harvard Medical School, Hallowell Davis and his co-workers found the answer. They showed that an electrode near the auditory nerve picks up two completely different electrical signals. One, which came to be called the *cochlear microphonic,* reproduces the wave form of the incoming sound just as an ordinary studio microphone does. The second, the *nerve action potential,* is the signal which gets through to the brain—and which is appar-

From Life Science Library's *Sound and Hearing,* edited by S. S. Stevens and Fred Warshofsky, 1965, pp. 58–62. © 1965, Time, Inc. Reprinted by permission of Time, Inc.

* Two researchers who conducted a series of pioneer experiments on hearing at Princeton circa 1930 (Ed.).

ently triggered by the cochlear microphonic. (Waltzing mice, the inbred laboratory animals that run in circles, have no hair cells in their inner ears, no cochlear microphonics and no demonstrable sense of hearing.)

Unlike the microphonics, which are electrical imitations of sound waves, nerve action potentials are pulses of electricity. The action potentials do not vary greatly in strength, nor do they occur over a wide range of rates; thus, they cannot directly reproduce wide variations in amplitude and frequency of sounds, as the cochlear microphonics do. What function, then, do the action potentials serve? The answer gives a clue to the magnificent complexity of human hearing. Somehow—no one understands how—action potentials make up a code of electric pulses which are relayed along the auditory nerve and are decoded by the brain.

Encoding perfectly clear signals may seem to call for unnecessary complications of the hearing apparatus, but nature is rarely wasteful. A pulse code is worth all the extra machinery it requires because of the accuracy with which it can relay information. Each nerve fiber that handles a hearing signal blurs the signal somewhat, passing it on in slightly changed form. But if the information being conveyed is merely that the signal exists or does not exist—i.e., that a nerve pulse is or is not fired—then slight errors in the *form* of the pulse do not matter. A pulse either gets through or does not get through—and that is all that counts.

Coding for Clarity

Commonplace examples demonstrate this principle in everyday affairs. Police dispatchers and lunch-counter waiters use number codes to avoid mistakes when relaying orders; fire departments use them to signal the location and severity of a blaze. On a grander scale, man-made codes transmit data over enormous distances. Pictures of the planet Mars taken by the unmanned spaceship Mariner IV made the long journey back to earth in coded form. Each picture consisted of 40,000 dots in 64 shades of gray, black and white. A number corresponding to the shade of each dot was relayed back to earth, where computers reassembled the entire picture dot by dot.

The code in the human nervous system—whatever it is—must be much more sophisticated than any of these man-made ones. Far from resembling a simple telephone hookup, the hearing sense seems to encompass at least the equivalent of a complete telephone network. Its many elements all seem to perform simultaneously the diverse functions—detection, amplification, conversion, transmission, power generation—which man-made devices must perform singly, in sequence.

At the heart of these functions lies the complex electric generating and signaling system of the human body.

The electrical nature of nerve impulses has puzzled scientists since 1791, when Luigi Galvani made frog muscles twitch by touching them with pieces of metal. Galvani concluded that electricity caused animal tissues to twitch, and that this electricity came from the tissues themselves. His conclusions were correct but his logic was wrong. Galvani had not tapped "animal electricity" but had unwittingly applied man-made electricity to the frog muscles. His metal connections constituted a crude battery, as his fellow Italian and scientific competitor, Alessandro Volta, quickly proved.

A Noise like Boiling Soup, a Light over the Head

Volta went on to seek electrical phenomena in other parts of the body, including the ear. In 1800 he attempted to stimulate the sensation of hearing electrically by connecting a battery to two metal rods, placing the rods in his ears, and closing the switch. Not surprisingly, Volta received what he described as "a jolt in the head," and a few moments later he heard "a noise like the boiling of thick soup." The sensation was too disagreeable to bear many repetitions and Volta did not pursue this investigation.

Later Ernst Weber, the German scientist who pioneered the study of physical sensations, tried to continue Volta's experiments, using his brother Wilhelm as a guinea pig. Weber filled Wilhelm's ears with water and then inserted a pair of electrodes. When a current was passed through, young Wilhelm reported a light "that seemed to go right over my head," but he heard no sound.

These experiments, too, were based on false

premises. Direct current from a battery will not do the job. There are several ways to stimulate a sustained sensation of hearing by electricity, but they all require an electric current that alternates back and forth at the frequency of a sound wave. With salt water and an electrode in the ear canal, alternating current pulls the eardrum back and forth, creating the mechanical vibration that stimulates the inner ear. Nerve impulses then generate a steady sensation of sound. It is the nerve impulses, not the external source of electricity, that actually generate the sensation. And this progress from sound to hearing, from mechanical vibrations to electrical nerve impulses, is marked by ever-increasing elaboration and complexity. In the outer and middle ears, sound travels through a single membrane—the eardrum—and three tiny bones. In the inner ear there is the basilar membrane—far more complex than the eardrum—and the 23,500 hair cells of the organ of Corti. The path of nerve impulses from the inner ear to the brain moves through thousands, and finally hundreds of thousands, of complex cells.

The nerve that services the ear, known variously as the auditory nerve, the acoustic nerve, and the eighth cranial nerve, is a broad bundle of about 30,000 individual fibers. Collectively these fibers run like a cable down the core of the cochlea, matching the twisting of the snaillike shell spiral for spiral. Just above the basilar membrane, the main trunk line of the nerve branches out into thousands of individual nerve cells, called neurons, each of which terminates near a hair cell in the organ of Corti.

Essentially, the neurons of the auditory nerve are complex devices for the detection and transmission of electrical signals. Each neuron contains a set of "input leads," which pick up external stimuli, such as the hearing signal from the hair cells, and flash them to the neuron's body. If the stimulus is strong enough to activate the neuron, it fires, passing an electrical signal to a set of "output leads." If the stimulus is not strong enough, nothing happens—the response is "all or nothing"—and some nerves require stronger stimuli than others before firing. Obviously, then, an intense sound will set off more nerve impulses than a weak one, and the total number of nerves firing is apparently one indication of loudness.

Each nerve cell works like a small battery. Normally, its metabolism keeps it charged, just as an automobile generator keeps an automobile battery charged. But the external stimulus seems to close a switch. The nerve battery discharges, or fires, generating a single pulse of electricity. It must then be recharged. It recharges very quickly indeed: the return to normal charge usually takes about one thousandth of a second. But the time taken for recharging, minute as it is, limits the rate at which a single neuron can fire to about 1,000 impulses per second, while human hearing ranges up to sound frequencies of 20,000 cycles per second. If the individual fibers take turns firing, they can produce bursts, or "volleys," of impulses, at rates up to 3,000 per second, but information about sound frequency depends on which fibers are activated, not on the rate of firing.

The stream of electrical impulses carried by the auditory nerve contains all the information that the brain actually receives from the ear. It is a stream of pulses that moves, nothing more: everything the ear tells the brain is coded into these pulses and passed along the auditory nerve. But while the code itself remains an undeciphered electrical mystery, its movement can be traced all the way to the brain.

From the Inner Ear to the Brain

To begin with, the auditory nerve leaves the cochlea and enters the central nervous system, where its neurons end in a welter of cell bodies. This collection, known as the cochlear nucleus, is a sort of way station on the auditory trail. It is apparently a main switching center in the hearing system. Here complex interconnections establish not one but several paths to the brain. Some neurons continue upward from the cochlear nucleus to another way station of cell bodies called the inferior colliculus. Some connect to several other way stations in the lower brainstem; some of these tie into their counterparts from the opposite ear. Finally, all come together in the auditory cortex, the actual hearing center of the brain.

This is the best-known trail from ear to brain, but not the only one. Clues to at least two other parallel routes have been discovered. (These parallel routes may contain supplemental networks for additional hearing information.) And adding to the complexity of the physiologist's problems is new evidence of paths *away* from the brain to the lower way stations. These "feedback" loops apparently run all the way from the cortex to the cochlea, and may enable the brain to send signals to the ear as well as receive them from it.

In the cells of the auditory cortex lies the ultimate mystery, the sensation we know as hearing. The electrical signal produced in response to a sound wave is added to billions of other impulses flashing through the brain. Even then it is possible to detect with electrodes the particular electrical pulses set up in the brain when a click is sounded at the ear. With the aid of a computer, a researcher need not work inside the cortex at all. Instead, he can take measurements of electrical signals at the surface of the scalp, and use the computer to cancel out the interfering effects of other messages to the brain. New and increasingly sophisticated computers will almost certainly play a major part in solving the mysteries of hearing.

The Factor of Attention in the Cat

Raul Hernández-Peón, Harald Scherrer, and Michel Jouvet

Raul Hernández-Peón, Director, Instituto de Investigaciones Cerebrales, A.C., Moras, Mexico, received his medical degree from the University of Mexico in 1949. With the intention of becoming a physician, Hernández-Peón realized a latent interest in the investigation of neurophysiological bases of behavior and mental activity. Harald Scherrer is presently at the University of Columbia, Vancouver, Canada and Michel Jouvet is at the Laboratoire de Physiologie, Faculté de Medicine, Lyon, France.

1. *When engrossed in a "good book" you suddenly look up to find someone has been trying to get your "attention" from across the room. Does this study throw any light on what has been happening?*

2. *What bearing does this study have in considering the "hearing sensitivity" of a sightless person?*

Attention involves the selective awareness of certain sensory messages with the simultaneous

From R. Hernández-Peón, H. Scherrer, and M. Jouvet, "Modification of Electric Activity in the Cochlear Nucleus during 'Attention' in Unanesthetized Cats," *Science*, 123 (24 February 1956), 331–332. Reprinted by permission of author and publisher.

suppression of others. Our sense organs are activated by a great variety of sensory stimuli, but relatively few evoke conscious sensation at any given moment. It is common experience that there is a pronounced reduction of extraneous sensory awareness when our attention is concentrated on some particular matter. During the attentive state, it seems as though the brain integrates for consciousness only a limited amount of sensory information, specifically, those impulses concerned with the object of attention.

An interference with impulses initiated by sensory stimuli other than those pertaining to the subject of attention seems to be an obvious possibility. It is clear that this afferent blockade might occur at any point along the classical sensory pathways from receptors to the cortical receiving areas, or else perhaps in the recently disclosed extraclassical sensory paths that traverse the brain-stem reticular system.

Recent evidence indicates the existence of central mechanisms that regulate sensory transmission. It has been shown that appropriate stimulation of the brain-stem reticular system will inhibit afferent conduction between the first- and second-order neurons in all three principal somatic paths. During central anesthesia, the afferent-evoked potentials in the first sensory relays are enhanced. This appears to be due to the release of a tonic descending inhibitory influence that operates during wakefulness and requires the functional integrity of the brain-stem reticular formation.

The possibility that a selective central inhibitory mechanism might operate during attention for filtering sensory impulses was tested by studying afferent transmission in the second- or third-order neurons of the auditory pathway (cochlear nucleus) in unanesthetized, unrestrained cats during experimentally elicited attentive behavior. Bipolar stainless steel electrodes with a total diameter of 0.5 mm were implanted stereotaxically in the dorsal cochlear nucleus through a small hole bored in the skull. The electrode was fixed to the skull with dental cement. A minimum of 1 week elapsed between the operation and the first electroencephalographic recordings. Electric impulses in the form of short bursts of rectangular waves (0.01 to 0.02 sec) at a frequency of 1000 to 5000 cy/sec were delivered to a loudspeaker near the cats at an intensity comfortable to human observers in the same environment.

Three types of sensory modalities were used to attract the animal's attention: visual, olfactory, and somatic. As is illustrated in Figure 1, during presentation of visual stimuli (two mice in a closed bottle), the auditory responses in the cochlear nucleus were greatly reduced in comparison with the control responses; they were practically abolished as long as the visual stimuli elicited behavioral evidence of attention. When the mice were removed, the auditory responses returned to the same order of magnitude as the initial controls. An olfactory stimulus that attracted the animal's attention produced a similar blocking effect. While the cat was attentively sniffing tubing through which fish odors were being delivered, the auditory potential in the cochlear nucleus was practically absent (Figure 2). After the stimulus had been removed and when the cat appeared to be relaxed once more, the auditorily evoked responses in the cochlear nucleus were of the same magnitude as they had been prior to the olfactory stimulation. Similarly, a nociceptive shock delivered to the forepaw of the cat—a shock that apparently distracted the animal's attention—resulted in marked reduction of auditorily evoked responses in the cochlear nucleus.

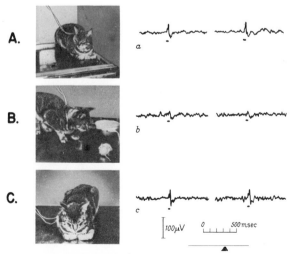

FIGURE 1. *Direct recording of click responses in the cochlear nucleus during three periods; the photographs were taken simultaneously. (Top and bottom) Cat is relaxed; the click responses are large. (Middle) While the cat is visually attentive to the mice in the jar, the click responses are diminished in amplitude.*

If this sensory inhibition during attentive behavior, as demonstrated in the auditory pathway, occurs in all other sensory paths except the ones concerned with the object of attention, such an inhibitory mechanism might lead to favoring of the attended object by the selective exclusion of incoming signals. It is conceivable not only that such a selective sensory inhibition might operate simultaneously for various sensory modalities, leaving one or more unaffected but that the selectivity could extend to some discriminable aspects of any single modality —for example, to one tone and not to others. This suggestion finds support in the recent demonstration that sensory "habituation" may occur to a particular tone—that is, a slowly developing inhibitory effect on auditorily evoked potentials observed in the cochlear nucleus on prolonged repetition of a given tone, an influence that does not affect other frequencies that are novel to the animal. The pathway by which this inhibitory influence acts on incoming auditory impulses remains to be determined, but experiments now in progress have shown that during electric stimulation of the midbrain reticular formation, the auditory potential in the cochlear nucleus is depressed.

The present observations suggest that the blocking of afferent impulses in the lower portions of a sensory path may be a mechanism whereby sensory stimuli out of the scope of attention can be markedly reduced while they

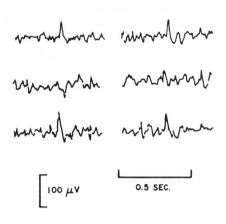

FIGURE 2. *Click responses recorded from the cochlear nucleus of the cat. (Top) Cat is relaxed; (middle) cat is attentively sniffing an olfactory stimulus; (bottom) cat is relaxed again. Note the reduced amplitude of the click responses when the animal is sniffing.*

are still in their trajectory toward higher levels of the central nervous system. This central inhibitory mechanism may, therefore, play an important role in selective exclusion of sensory messages along their passage toward mechanisms of perception and consciousness. In a recent symposium on brain mechanisms and consciousness, Adrian pointed out that "the signals from the sense organs must be treated differently when we attend to them and when we do not, and if we could decide where and how the divergence arises we should be nearer to understanding how the level of consciousness is reached."

Effects of Decreased Sensory Variation

W. H. Bexton, W. Heron, and T. H. Scott

W. H. Bexton, Chairman of the Department of Psychology, Pacific Lutheran University, Tacoma, Washington, received his Ph.D. from McGill University in 1953. Bexton indicates an interest in the effects of sensory deprivation and in the biochemical factors that occur in stressful situations. W. Heron is at McMaster University, Canada, and received his Ph.D. from McGill University in 1953.

1. *What effect does sensory isolation seem to have on cognitive processes? Would you have devised different ways of testing cognition?*

2. *What speculations would you make as to the purpose of hallucinatory activity during experimental conditions?*

3. *Of what importance are individual differences in a study such as this?*

This study began with a practical problem: the lapses of attention that may occur when a man must give close and prolonged attention to some aspect of an environment in which nothing is happening, or in which the changes are very regular. Watching a radar screen hour after hour is a prime example. As Mackworth and others have shown, when at last something *does* happen in such circumstances the watcher may fail to respond. Such monotonous conditions exist in civilian occupations as well as in military ones (marine pilotage by radar, piloting aircraft on long flights), and here too lapses of attention may have extremely serious conse-

Abridged from W. H. Bexton, W. Heron, and T. H. Scott, "Effects of Decreased Variation in the Sensory Environment," *Canadian Journal of Psychology,* 8 (1954), 70–76. Reprinted by permission of author and publisher.

quences. For example, such lapses may explain some otherwise inexplicable railroad and highway accidents.

Besides its practical significance this problem has theoretical implications of great interest. There is much evidence from recent neurophysiological studies to indicate that the normal functioning of the waking brain depends on its being constantly exposed to sensory bombardment, which produces a continuing "arousal reaction." Work now being done by S. K. Sharpless at McGill indicates, further, that when stimulation does not change it rapidly loses its power to cause the arousal reaction. Thus, although one function of a stimulus is to evoke or guide a specific bit of behaviour, it also has a non-specific function, that of maintaining "arousal," probably through the brain-stem reticular formation.

In other words, the maintenance of normal, intelligent, adaptive behaviour probably requires a continually varied sensory input. The brain is not like a calculating machine operated by an electric motor which is able to respond at once to specific cues after lying idle indefinitely. Instead it is like one that must be kept warmed up and working. It seemed, therefore, worth while to examine cognitive functioning during prolonged perceptual isolation, as far as this was practicable. Bremer has achieved such isolation by cutting the brain stem; college students, however, are reluctant to undergo brain operations for experimental purposes, so we had to be satisfied with less extreme isolation from the environment.

Procedure

The subjects, 22 male college students, were paid to lie on a comfortable bed in a lighted cubicle 24 hours a day, with time out for eating and going to the toilet. During the whole experimental period they wore translucent goggles which transmitted diffuse light but prevented pattern vision. Except when eating or at the toilet, the subject wore gloves and cardboard cuffs, the latter extending from below the elbow to beyond the fingertips. These permitted free joint movement but limited tactual perception. Communication between subject and experimenters was provided by a small speaker system, and was kept to a minimum. Auditory stimulation was limited by the partially sound-proof cubicle and by a U-shaped foam-rubber pillow in which the subject kept his head while in the cubicle. Moreover the continuous hum provided by fans, air-conditioner, and the amplifier leading to ear-phones in the pillow produced fairly efficient masking noise.

General Effects

As might be expected from the evidence reviewed by Kleitman, for onset of sleep following reduced stimulation in man and other animals, the subjects tended to spend the earlier part of the experimental session in sleep. Later they slept less, became bored, and appeared eager for stimulation. They would sing, whistle, talk to themselves, tap the cuffs together, or explore the cubicle with them. This boredom seemed to be partly due to deterioration in the capacity to think systematically and productively—an effect described below. The subjects also became very restless, displaying constant random movement, and they described the restlessness as unpleasant. Hence it was difficult to keep subjects for more than two or three days, despite the fact that the pay ($20 for a 24-hour day) was more than double what they could normally earn. Some subjects, in fact, left before testing could be completed.

There seemed to be unusual emotional lability during the experimental period. When doing tests, for instance, the subjects would seem very pleased when they did well, and upset if they had difficulty. They commented more freely about test items than when they were tested outside. While many reported that they felt elated during the first part of their stay in the cubicle, there was a marked increase in irritability toward the end of the experimental period.

On coming out of the cubicle after the experimental session, when goggles, cuffs, and gloves had been removed, the subjects seemed at first dazed. There also appeared to be some disturbance in visual perception, usually lasting no longer than one or two minutes. Subjects reported difficulty in focussing; objects appeared fuzzy and did not stand out from their backgrounds. There was a tendency for the environment to appear two-dimensional and colours seemed more saturated than usual. The subjects also reported feelings of confusion, headaches, a mild nausea, and fatigue; these conditions persisted in some cases for 24 hours after the session.

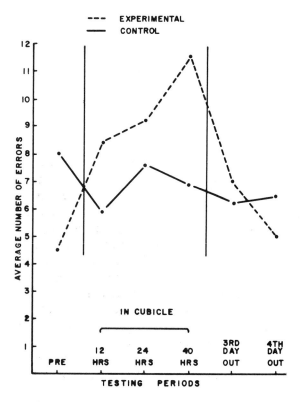

ERRORS IN WORD MAKING

FIGURE 1. *Mean error scores for experimental and control subjects, before, during, and after the isolation period.*

Our present concern is primarily with cognitive disturbances during the period of isolation and immediately afterwards. The subjects reported that they were unable to concentrate on any topic for long while in the cubicle. Those who tried to review their studies or solve self-initiated intellectual problems found it difficult to do so. As a result they lapsed into day-dreaming, abandoned attempts at organized thinking, and let their thoughts wander. There were also reports of "blank periods," during which they seemed unable to think of anything at all.

In an attempt to measure some of the effects on cognitive processes, various tests were given to the subjects before, during, and after the period of isolation.

First, the tests given during isolation. Twelve subjects were given the following types of problem to do in their heads: multiplying two- and three-digit numbers; arithmetical problems (such as "how many times greater is twice 2½ than one-half 2½?"); completion of number series; making a word from jumbled

letters; making as many words as possible from the letters of a given word. Each subject was tested on problems of this type before going into the cubicle, after he had been in for 12, 24, and 48 hours, and three days after coming out of the cubicle. Twelve control subjects were given the same series of tasks at the same intervals. The average performance of the experimental subjects was inferior to that of the controls on all tests performed during the cubicle session. With our present small number of subjects the differences are significant only for the error scores on the second anagram task ($p = .01$, see Figure 1). The groups are now being enlarged.

Secondly, tests given before entering the cubicle and immediately after leaving it. On the Kohs Block Test and the Wechsler Digit Symbol Test the experimental subjects were inferior to the controls on leaving the cubicle ($p = .01$). They also tended to be slower in copying a prose paragraph ($p = .10$). Figure 2 gives samples of handwriting before and after the experiment. The first is from one of the subjects showing the greatest effect, the second

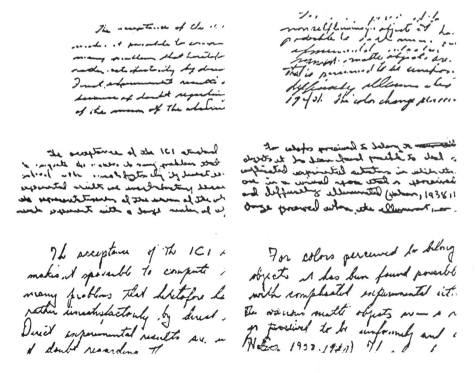

FIGURE 2. *Specimens of handwriting before and after the isolation period.*

illustrates the average effect. As the third sample shows, some subjects were not affected. This disturbance in handwriting, though perhaps due to some sensori-motor disturbance, might also reflect cognitive or motivational changes.

Hallucinatory Activity

Finally there were the hallucinations reported by the subjects while in the experimental apparatus. Among our early subjects there were several references, rather puzzling at first, to what one of them called "having a dream while awake." Then one of us, while serving as a subject, observed the phenomenon and realized its peculiarity and extent.

The visual phenomena were actually quite similar to what have been described for mescal intoxication, and to what Grey Walter has recently produced by exposure to flickering light. There have also been rare cases of hallucinations in aged persons without psychosis, which, like ours, involved no special chemical or visual stimulation. As we did not ask our first subjects specifically about these phenomena we do not know the frequency among them. The last 14 subjects, however, were asked to report any "visual imagery" they observed, and our report is based on them. In general, where more "formed" (i.e., more complex) hallucinations occurred they were usually preceded by simpler forms of the phenomenon. Levels of complexity could be differentiated as follows: In the simplest form the visual field, with the eyes closed, changed from dark to light colour; next in complexity were dots of light, lines, or simple geometrical patterns. All 14 subjects reported such imagery, and said it was a new experience to them. Still more complex forms consisted in "wallpaper patterns," reported by 11 subjects, and isolated figures or objects, without background (e.g., a row of little yellow men with black caps on and their mouths open; a German helmet), reported by seven subjects. Finally, there were integrated scenes (e.g., a procession of squirrels with sacks over their shoulders marching "purposefully" across a snow field and out of the field of "vision"; prehistoric animals walking about in a jungle). Three of the 14 subjects reported such scenes, frequently

including dreamlike distortions, with the figures often being described as "like cartoons." One curious fact is that some of the hallucinations were reported as being inverted or tilted at an angle.

In general, the subjects were first surprised by these phenomena, and then amused or interested, waiting for what they would see next. Later, some subjects found them irritating, and complained that their vividness interfered with sleep. There was some control over content; by "trying," the subject might see certain objects suggested by the experimenter, but not always as he intended. Thus one subject, trying to "get" a pen, saw first an inkblot, then a pencil, a green horse, and finally a pen; trying to "get" a shoe, he saw first a ski boot, then a moccasin. The imagery usually disappeared when the subject was doing a complex task, such as multiplying three-place numbers in his head, but not if he did physical exercises, or talked to the experimenter.

There were also reports of hallucinations

FIGURE 3. *Drawing made by a subject to show how he felt at one period in the cubicle. He reported that it was as if "there were two of me," and was momentarily unable to decide whether he was A or B.*

involving other senses. One subject could hear the people speaking in his visual hallucinations, and another repeatedly heard the playing of a music box. Four subjects described kinesthetic and somesthetic phenomena. One reported seeing a miniature rocket ship discharging pellets that kept striking his arm, and one reported reaching out to touch a doorknob he saw before him and feeling an electric shock. The other two subjects reported a phenomenon which they found difficult to describe. They said it was as if there were two bodies side by side in the cubicle; in one case the two bodies overlapped, partly occupying the same space. Figure 3 shows this subject's subsequent drawing, made in an attempt to show what he meant.

In addition, there were reports of feelings of "otherness" and bodily "strangeness" in which it was hard to know exactly what the subject meant. One subject said "my mind seemed to be a ball of cotton-wool floating above my body"; another reported that his head felt detached from his body. These are familiar phenomena in certain cases of migraine, as described recently by Lippman, and earlier by Lewis Carroll in *Alice in Wonderland*. As Lippman points out, Lewis Carroll was a sufferer from migraine, and it is suggested that Alice's bodily distortions are actually descriptions of Carroll's (i.e., Charles Dodgson's) own experiences.

In summary, both the changes in intelligence-test performance and the hallucinatory activity, induced merely by limiting the variability of sensory input, provide direct evidence of a kind of dependence on the environment that has not been previously recognized. Further experimental study will be needed to elucidate the details of this relationship.

Suggested Readings

Beardslee, D. C., and M. Wertheimer, eds. *Readings in Perception*. Princeton, N.J.: Van Nostrand, 1958.

Békésy, G. V. *Experiments in Hearing*. New York: McGraw-Hill, 1960.

Frenkel-Brunswick, E. "Intolerance of Ambiguity as an Emotional and Perceptual Personality Variable," *J. Pers.*, 18 (1949), 108–143.

Gardner, E. *Fundamentals of Neurology*. Philadelphia: Saunders, 1958.

Geldard, F. A. *The Human Senses*. New York: Wiley, 1953.

Gibson, J. J. "Perception as a Function of Stimulation," in S. Koch, ed., *Psychology: A Study of a Science*. Vol. I, New York: McGraw-Hill, 1959.

Holway, A. H., and E. G. Boring. "The Moon Illusion and the Angle of Regard," *Amer. J. Psychol.*, 53 (1940), 109–116.

Kohler, I. "On the Development and Transformation of the Perceptual World," *Psychol. Issues*, 2 (1961), No. 8.

Morgan, C. T., and E. Stellar. *Physiological Psychology*. New York: McGraw-Hill, 1950.

Penfield, W., and T. Rasmussen. *The Cerebral Cortex of Man*. New York: Macmillan, 1950.

Postman, L., J. Bruner, and E. McGinnies. "Personal Values as Selective Factors in Perception," *J. abnorm. soc. Psychol.*, 43 (1948), 142–154.

Teevan, R. C., and R. C. Birney, eds. *Color Vision*. Princeton, N.J.: Van Nostrand, 1961.

Wever, E. G. *Theory of Hearing*. New York: Wiley, 1949.

Witkin, H. A., et al. *Personality through Perception*. New York: Harper, 1954.

7   Memory: The Process and Product

According to Freud, the process of remembering and forgetting is likened to the beat of the heart: it begins at birth (some would say even before birth) and ends at death. Whether this statement is technically accurate or not is a moot point. It is agreed, however, that some form of thinking or imagination (fantasy) takes place during both wakefulness and sleep. Memory is a pervasive phenomenon that covers a wide range of situations. Examples of these situations would be reading street signs, discussing current events at a social gathering, taking a final examination, knowing your birthday, and reciting a poem. Because of its ubiquitous nature, it is set aside as a separate chapter for discussion. The four readings are divided in half between process and product. The first two selections focus on the memory process, and the last two selections focus on the product of memory.

An Early Approach to the Study of Memory, Hermann Ebbinghaus. Ebbinghaus deals with the measurement of memory. He is included here because his procedures for measuring the rate of forgetting, although gathered over 50 years ago, are still widely cited. Ebbinghaus, inventor of the nonsense syllable, was a pioneer in the measurement of memory. Although his experimental procedures may be questioned (he was both experimenter and subject in the studies he conducted), his work demonstrates that he operated with precision and scientific caution. His studies are used as the prototype for some work being done today on the assessment of memory.

Interference and Forgetting, Benton J. Underwood. This selection is deliberately included as a follow-up and critique of Ebbinghaus' work. Underwood describes research in the area of remembering and forgetting since the time of Ebbinghaus and emphasizes the role of inhibitory factors in forgetting.

Serial Reproduction of Picture Material, F. C. Bartlett. This selection is often cited in discussions of memory and memory distortion. The basic phenomenon with which Bartlett deals is perceptual in nature. His analysis of the phenomenon is based on an experiment in which subjects were briefly shown a simple picture and then asked to recall and reproduce the picture from memory. Of interest here is his description of the process by which a subject redefines and restructures an ambiguous picture into a meaningful, "known" representation that is related to the subject's own experience.

Recitation as a Factor in Memorizing, Arthur I. Gates. The final selection deals with memory and is included in the chapter to point out that psychological research can be conducted to elicit practical answers. A secondary benefit to be gained from reading this selection is that it may change the reader's own method of study.

An Early Approach to the Study of Memory

Hermann Ebbinghaus

Hermann Ebbinghaus (1850–1909) received his Ph.D. at Bonn University in 1873. Shortly thereafter he began his experiments on memory for which he invented the nonsense syllable. In 1893, Ebbinghaus published a theory on the workings of color vision and created the Ebbinghaus Completion Test, a method used in many modern tests of aptitude and intelligence. It has been said that "Ebbinghaus was for Germany what William James was for America"—the author of a readable yet scientific handbook of psychology.

1. *How did Ebbinghaus try to control for meaningfulness of memory material? How well did he succeed?*

2. *To what sources of human error was Ebbinghaus sensitive?*

Section 1. Series of Nonsense Syllables

In order to test practically, although only for a limited field, a way of penetrating more deeply into memory processes, I have hit upon the following method.

Out of the simple consonants of the alphabet and our eleven vowels and diphthongs all possible syllables of a certain sort were constructed, a vowel sound being placed between two consonants.[1]

These syllables, about 2,300 in number, were mixed together and then drawn out by chance and used to construct series of different lengths, several of which each time formed the material for a test.[2]

At the beginning a few rules were observed to prevent, in the construction of the syllables, too immediate repetition of similar sounds, but these were not strictly adhered to. Later they were abandoned and the matter left to chance. The syllables used each time were carefully laid aside till the whole number had been used, then they were mixed together and used again.

The aim of the tests carried on with these syllable series was, by means of repeated audible perusal of the separate series, to so impress them that immediately afterwards they could voluntarily just be reproduced. This aim was considered attained when, the initial syl-

Abridged from H. Ebbinghaus, *Memory: A Contribution to Experimental Psychology,* trans. Henry Ruger (New York: Bureau of Publications, Teachers College, Columbia University, 1913), Chapter 3, pp. 22–33. Reprinted by permission of the publisher.

[1] The vowel sounds employed were a, e, i, o, u, ä, ö, ü, au, ei, eu. For the beginning of the syllables the following consonants were employed: b, d, f, g, h, j, k, l, m, n, p, r, s (= sz), t, w and in addition ch, sch, soft s, and the French j (19 altogether); for the end of the syllables f, k, l, m, n, p, r, s (= sz) t, ch, sch (11 altogether). For the final sound fewer consonants were employed than for the initial sound, because a German tongue even after several years practise in foreign languages does not quite accustom itself to the correct pronunciation of the mediae at the end. For the same reason I refrained from the use of other foreign sounds although I tried at first to use them for the sake of enriching the material.

[2] I shall retain in what follows the designations employed above and call a group of several syllable series or a single series a "test." A number of "tests" I shall speak of as a "test series" or a "group of tests."

lable being given, a series could be recited at the first attempt, without hesitation, at a certain rate, and with the consciousness of being correct.

Section 2. Advantages of the Material

The nonsense material, just described, offers many advantages, in part because of this very lack of meaning. First of all, it is relatively simple and relatively homogeneous. In the case of the material nearest at hand, namely poetry or prose, the content is now narrative in style, now descriptive, or now reflective; it contains now a phrase that is pathetic, now one that is humorous; its metaphors are sometimes beautiful, sometimes harsh; its rhythm is sometimes smooth and sometimes rough. There is thus brought into play a multiplicity of influences which change without regularity and are therefore disturbing. Such are associations which dart here and there, different degrees of interest, lines of verse recalled because of their striking quality or their beauty, and the like. All this is avoided with our syllables. Among many thousand combinations there occur scarcely a few dozen that have a meaning and among these there are again only a few whose meaning was realised while they were being memorised.

However, the simplicity and homogeneity of the material must not be overestimated. It is still far from ideal. The learning of the syllables calls into play the three sensory fields, sight, hearing and the muscle sense of the organs of speech. And although the part that each of these senses plays is well limited and always similar in kind, a certain complication of the results must still be anticipated because of their combined action. Again, to particularise, the homogeneity of the series of syllables falls considerably short of what might be expected of it. These series exhibit very important and almost incomprehensible variations as to the ease or difficulty with which they are learned. It even appears from this point of view as if the differences between sense and nonsense material were not nearly so great as one would be inclined *a priori* to imagine. At least I found in the case of learning by heart a few cantos from Byron's "Don Juan" no greater range of distri-

bution of the separate numerical measures than in the case of a series of nonsense syllables in the learning of which an approximately equal time had been spent. In the former case the innumerable disturbing influences mentioned above seem to have compensated each other in producing a certain intermediate effect; whereas in the latter case the predisposition, due to the influence of the mother tongue, for certain combinations of letters and syllables must be a very heterogeneous one.

More indubitable are the advantages of our material in two other respects. In the first place it permits an inexhaustible amount of new combinations of quite homogeneous character, while different poems, different prose pieces always have something incomparable. It also makes possible a quantitative variation which is adequate and certain; whereas to break off before the end or to begin in the middle of the verse or the sentence leads to new complications because of various and unavoidable disturbances of the meaning.

Series of numbers, which I also tried, appeared impracticable for the more thorough tests. Their fundamental elements were too small in number and therefore too easily exhausted.

Section 3. Establishment of the Most Constant Experimental Conditions Possible

The following rules were made for the process of memorising.

1. The separate series were always read through completely from beginning to end; they were not learned in separate parts which were then joined together; neither were especially difficult parts detached and repeated more frequently. There was a perfectly free interchange between the reading and the occasionally necessary tests of the capacity to reproduce by heart. For the latter there was an important rule to the effect that upon hesitation the rest of the series was to be read through to the end before beginning it again.

2. The reading and the recitation of the series took place at a constant rate, that of 150 strokes per minute. A clockwork metronome placed at some distance was at first used to regulate the rate; but very soon the ticking of a watch was substituted, that being much simpler

and less disturbing to the attention. The mechanism of escapement of most watches swings 300 times per minute.

3. Since it is practically impossible to speak continuously without variation of accent, the following method was adopted to avoid irregular variations: either three or four syllables were united into a measure, and thus either the 1st, 4th, 7th, or the 1st, 5th, 9th . . . syllables were pronounced with a slight accent. Stressing of the voice was otherwise, as far as possible, avoided.

4. After the learning of each separate series a pause of 15 seconds was made, and used for the tabulation of results. Then the following series of the same test was immediately taken up.

5. During the process of learning, the purpose of reaching the desired goal as soon as possible was kept in mind as much as was feasible. Thus, to the limited degree to which conscious resolve is of influence here, the attempt was made to keep the attention concentrated on the tiresome task and its purpose. It goes without saying that care was taken to keep away all outer disturbances in order to make possible the attainment of this aim. The smaller distractions caused by carrying on the test in various surroundings were also avoided as far as that could be done.

6. There was no attempt to connect the nonsense syllables by the invention of special associations of the mnemotechnic type; learning was carried on solely by the influence of the mere repetitions upon the natural memory. As I do not possess the least practical knowledge of the mnemotechnical devices, the fulfillment of this condition offered no difficulty to me.

7. Finally and chiefly, care was taken that the objective conditions of life during the period of the tests were so controlled as to eliminate too great changes or irregularities. Of course, since the tests extended over many months, this was possible only to a limited extent. But, even so, the attempt was made to conduct, under as similar conditions of life as possible, those tests the results of which were to be directly compared. In particular the activity immediately preceding the test was kept as constant in character as was possible. Since the mental as well as the physical condition of man is subject to an evident periodicity of 24 hours, it was taken for granted that like experimental conditions are obtainable only at like times of day. However, in order to carry out more than one test in a given day, different experiments were occasionally carried on together at different times of day. When too great changes in the outer and inner life occurred, the tests were discontinued for a length of time. Their resumption was preceded by some days of renewed training varying according to the length of the interruption.

Section 4. Sources of Error

The guiding point of view in the selection of material and in determining the rules for its employment was, as is evident, the attempt to simplify as far as possible, and to keep as constant as possible, the conditions under which the activity to be observed, that of memory, came into play. Naturally the better one succeeds in this attempt the more does he withdraw from the complicated and changing conditions under which this activity takes place in ordinary life and under which it is of importance to us. But that is no objection to the method. The freely falling body and the frictionless machine, etc., with which physics deals, are also only abstractions when compared with the actual happenings in nature which are of import to us. We can almost nowhere get a direct knowledge of the complicated and the real, but must get at them in roundabout ways by successive combinations of experiences, each of which is obtained in artificial, experimental cases, rarely or never furnished in this form by nature.

Meanwhile the fact that the connection with the activity of memory in ordinary life is for the moment lost is of less importance than the reverse, namely, that this connection with the complications and fluctuations of life is necessarily still a too close one. The struggle to attain the most simple and uniform conditions possible at numerous points naturally encounters obstacles that are rooted in the nature of the case and which thwart the attempt. The unavoidable dissimilarity of the material and the equally unavoidable irregularity of the external conditions have already been touched upon. I pass next to two other unsurmountable sources of difficulty.

By means of the successive repetitions the

series are, so to speak, raised to ever higher levels. The natural assumption would be that at the moment when they could for the first time be reproduced by heart the level thus attained would always be the same. If only this were the case, i.e., if this characteristic first reproduction were everywhere an invariable objective sign of an equally invariable fixedness of the series, it would be of real value to us. This, however, is not actually the case. . . . If, at the very instant when the material to be memorised has almost reached the desired degree of surety, a chance moment of especial mental clearness occurs, then the series is caught on the wing as it were, often to the learner's surprise; but the series cannot long be retained. By the occurrence of a moment of special dullness, on the other hand, the first errorless reproduction is postponed for a while, although the learner feels that he really is master of the thing and wonders at the constantly recurring hesitations. In the former case, in spite of the homogeneity of the external conditions, the first errorless reproduction is reached at a point a little below the level of retention normally connected with it. In the latter case it is reached at a point a little above that level. As was said before, the most plausible conjecture to make in this connection is that these deviations will compensate each other in the case of large groups.

Of the other source of error, I can only say that it may occur and that, when it does, it is a source of great danger. I mean the secret influence of theories and opinions which are in the process of formation. An investigation usually starts out with definite presuppositions as to what the results will be. But if this is not the case at the start, such presuppositions form gradually in case the experimenter is obliged to work alone. For it is impossible to carry on the investigations for any length of time without taking notice of the results. The experimenter must know whether the problem has been properly formulated or whether it needs completion or correction. The fluctuations of the results must be controlled in order that the separate observations may be continued long enough to give to the mean value the certainty necessary for the purpose in hand. Consequently it is unavoidable that, after the observation of the numerical results, suppositions should arise as to general principles which are concealed in them and which occasionally give hints as to their presence. As the investigations are carried further, these suppositions, as well as those present at the beginning, constitute a complicating factor which probably has a definite influence upon the subsequent results. . . .

Section 5. Measurement of Work Required

The number of repetitions which were necessary for memorising a series up to the first possible reproduction was not originally determined by counting, but indirectly by measuring in seconds the time that was required to memorise it. My purpose was in this way to avoid the distraction necessarily connected with counting; and I could assume that there was a proportional relation existing between the times and the number of repetitions occurring at any time in a definite rhythm. We could scarcely expect this proportionality to be perfect, since, when only the time is measured, the moments of hesitation and reflection are included, which is not true when the repetitions are counted. Difficult series in which hesitation will occur relatively more frequently, will, by the method of time measurement, get comparatively greater numbers, the easier series will get comparatively smaller numbers than when the repetitions are counted. But with larger groups of series a tolerably equal distribution of difficult and easy series may be taken for granted. Consequently the deviations from proportionality will compensate themselves in a similar manner in the case of each group.

When, for certain tests, the direct counting of the repetitions became necessary, I proceeded in the following manner. Little wooden buttons measuring about 14 mms. in diameter and 4 mms. at their greatest thickness were strung on a cord which would permit of easy displacement and yet heavy enough to prevent accidental slipping. Each tenth piece was black; the others had their natural color. During the memorisation the cord was held in the hand and at each new repetition a piece was displaced some centimeters from left to right. When the series could be recited, a glance at the cord, since it was divided into tens, was enough to ascertain the number of repetitions that had been necessary. The manipulation required so little attention that in the mean values of the time used (which was always tabulated at the same time) no lengthening could be noted as compared with earlier tests.

By means of this simultaneous measurement of time and repetitions incidental opportunity was afforded for verifying and more accurately defining that which had been foreseen and which has just been explained with regard to their interrelation. When the prescribed rhythm of 150 strokes per minute was precisely maintained, each syllable would take 0.4 second; and when the simple reading of the series was interrupted by attempts to recite it by heart, the unavoidable hesitations would lengthen the time by small but fairly uniform amounts. This, however, did not hold true with any exactness; on the contrary, the following modifications appeared.

When the direct reading of the series predominated, a certain forcing, an acceleration of the rhythm, occurred which, without coming to consciousness, on the whole lowered the time for each syllable below the standard of 0.4 sec.

When there was interchange between reading and reciting, however, the lengthening of the time was not in general constant, but was greater with the longer series. In this case, since the difficulty increases very rapidly with increasing length of the series, there occurs a slowing of the tempo, again involuntary and not directly noticeable. Both are illustrated by the following table.

As soon as this direction of deviation from exact proportionality was noticed there appeared in the learning a certain conscious reaction against it.

Finally, it appeared that the probable error of the time measurements was somewhat larger than that of the repetitions. This relation is quite intelligible in the light of the explanations given above. In the case of the time measurements the larger values, which naturally occurred with the more difficult series, were relatively somewhat greater than in the case of the number of repetitions, because relatively they were for the most part lengthened by the hesitations; conversely, the smaller times were necessarily somewhat smaller relatively than the number of repetitions, because in general they corresponded to the easier series. The distribution of the values in the case of the times is therefore greater than that of the values in the case of the repetitions.

The differences between the two methods of reckoning are, as is readily seen, sufficiently large to lead to different results in the case of investigations seeking a high degree of exactness. That is not the case with the results as yet obtained; it is therefore immaterial whether the number of seconds is used or that of the repetitions. . . .

Series of 16 syllables, for the most part read	Each syllable required the average time of	Number of series	Number of syllables
8 times	0.398 sec.	60	960
16 "	0.399 "	108	1728

Series of X syllables	Were in part read, in part recited on an average Y times	Each syllable required an average time of Z secs.	Number of series	Number of syllables
X =	Y =	Z =		
12	18	0.416	63	756
16	31	0.427	252	4032
24	45	0.438	21	504
36	56	0.459	14	504

Section 6. Periods of the Tests

The tests were made in two periods, in the years 1879–80 and 1883–84, and extended each over more than a year. During a long time preliminary experiments of a similar nature had preceded the definite tests of the first period, so that, for all results communicated, the time of increasing skill may be considered as past. At the beginning of the second period I was careful to give myself renewed training. This temporal distribution of the tests with a separating interval of more than three years gives the desired possibility of a certain mutual control of most of the results. Frankly, the tests of the two periods are not strictly comparable. In the case of the tests of the first period, in order to limit the significance of the first fleeting grasp of the series in moments of special concentration, it was decided to study the series until two successive faultless reproductions were possible. Later I abandoned this method, which only incompletely accomplished its purpose, and kept to the first fluent reproduction. The earlier method evidently in many cases resulted in a somewhat longer period of learning. In addition there was a difference in the hours of the day appointed for the tests. Those of the later period all occurred in the afternoon hours between one and three o'clock; those of the earlier period were unequally divided between the hours of 10–11 A.M., 11–12 A.M., and 6–8 P.M.

Interference and Forgetting

Benton J. Underwood

Benton Underwood received his doctorate from the State University of Iowa in 1942. He has been Professor of Psychology at Northwestern University since 1952 and is now chairman of the department there. He has a long-standing interest in research on memory and forgetting.

1. What sort of interference does Underwood feel is mainly responsible for forgetting?

2. In what way would proactive inhibition decrease your grade on a final examination? Can you give an example from your own life?

I know of no one who seriously maintains that interference among tasks is of no consequence in the production of forgetting. Whether forgetting is conceptualized at a

Benton J. Underwood, "Interference and Forgetting," *Psychological Review,* 1957, 64, 49–58. Copyright 1957 by the American Psychological Association and reproduced by permission.

strict psychological level or at a neural level (e.g., neural memory trace), some provision is made for interference to account for at least some of the measured forgetting. The many studies on retroactive inhibition are probably responsible for this general agreement that interference among tasks must produce a sizable proportion of forgetting. By introducing an interpolated interfering task very marked decrements in recall can be produced in a few minutes in the laboratory. But there is a second generalization which has resulted from these studies, namely, that most forgetting must be a function of the learning of tasks which interfere with that which has already been learned (19). Thus, if a single task is learned in the laboratory and retention measured after a week, the loss has been attributed to the interference from activities learned outside the laboratory during the week. It is this generalization with which I am concerned in the initial portions of this paper.

Now, I cannot deny the data which show large amounts of forgetting produced by an interpolated list in a few minutes in the laboratory. Nor do I deny that this loss may be attributed to interference. But I will try to show that use of retroactive inhibition as a paradigm of forgetting (via interference) may be seriously questioned. To be more specific: if a subject learns a single task, such as a list of words, and retention of this task is measured after a day, a week, or a month, I will try to show that very little of the forgetting can be attributed to an interfering task learned outside the laboratory during the retention interval. Before pursuing this further, I must make some general comments by way of preparation.

Whether we like it or not, the experimental study of forgetting has been largely dominated by the Ebbinghaus tradition, both in terms of methods and materials used. I do not think this is due to sheer perversity on the part of several generations of scientists interested in forgetting. It may be noted that much of our elementary knowledge can be obtained only by rote learning. To work with rote learning does not mean that we are thereby not concerning ourselves with phenomena that have no counterparts outside the laboratory. Furthermore, the investigation of these phenomena can be handled by methods which are acceptable to a science. As is well known, there are periodic verbal revolts against the Ebbinghaus tradition (e.g., 2, 15, 22). But for some reason nothing much ever happens in the laboratory as a consequence of these revolts. I mention these matters neither by way of apology nor of justification for having done some research in rote learning, but for two other reasons. First, it may very well be true, as some have suggested (e.g., 22), that studies of memory in the Ebbinghaus tradition are not getting at all of the important phenomena of memory. I think the same statement —that research has not got at all of the important processes—could be made about all areas in psychology; so that the criticism (even if just) should not be indigenous to the study of memory. Science does not deal at will with all natural events. Science deals with natural

events only when ingenuity in developing methods and techniques of measurement allow these events to be brought within the scope of science. If, therefore, the studies of memory which meet scientific acceptability do not tap all-important memorial processes, all I can say is that this is the state of the science in the area at the moment. Secondly, because the bulk of the systematic data on forgetting has been obtained on rote-learned tasks, I must of necessity use such data in discussing interference and forgetting.

Returning to the experimental situation, let me again put in concrete form the problem with which I first wish to deal. A subject learns a single task, such as a list of syllables, nouns, or adjectives. After an interval of time, say, 24 hours, his retention of this list is measured. The explanatory problem is what is responsible for the forgetting which commonly occurs over the 24 hours. As indicated earlier, the studies of retroactive inhibition led to the theoretical generalization that this forgetting was due largely to interference from other tasks learned during the 24-hour retention interval. McGeoch (20) came to this conclusion, his last such statement being made in 1942. I would, therefore, like to look at the data which were available to McGeoch and others interested in this matter. I must repeat that the kind of data with which I am concerned is the retention of a list without formal interpolated learning introduced. The interval of retention with which I am going to deal in this, and several subsequent analyses, is 24 hours.

First, of course, Ebbinghaus' data were available and in a sense served as the reference point for many subsequent investigations. In terms of percentage saved in relearning, Ebbinghaus showed about 65 per cent loss over 24 hours (7). In terms of recall after 24 hours, the following studies are representative of the amount forgotten: Youtz, 88 per cent loss (37); Luh, 82 per cent (18); Krueger, 74 per cent (16); Hovland, 78 per cent (11); Cheng, 65 per cent and 84 per cent (6); Lester, 65 per cent (17). Let us assume as a rough average of these studies that 75 per cent forgetting was measured over 24 hours. In all of these studies the list was learned to one perfect trial. The percentage values were derived by dividing the total number of items in the list into the number lost and changing to a percentage. Thus, on the average in these studies, if the subject learned a 12-item list and recalled three of these items after 24 hours, nine items (75 per cent) were forgotten.

The theory of interference as advanced by McGeoch, and so far as I know never seriously challenged, was that during the 24-hour interval subjects learned something outside the laboratory which interfered with the list learned in the laboratory. Most of the materials involved in the investigations cited above were nonsense syllables, and the subjects were college students. While realizing that I am viewing these results in the light of data which McGeoch and others did not have available, it seems to me to be an incredible stretch of an interference hypothesis to hold that this 75 per cent forgetting was caused by something which the subjects learned outside the laboratory during the 24-hour interval. Even if we agree with some educators that much of what we teach our students in college is nonsense, it does not seem to be the kind of learning that would interfere with nonsense syllables.

If, however, this forgetting was not due to interference from tasks learned outside the laboratory during the retention interval, to what was it due? I shall try to show that most of this forgetting was indeed produced by interference —not from tasks learned outside the laboratory, but from tasks learned previously in the laboratory. Following this I will show that when interference from laboratory tasks is removed, the amount of forgetting which occurs is relatively quite small. It then becomes more plausible that this amount could be produced by interference from tasks learned outside the laboratory, although, as I shall also point out, the interference very likely comes from prior, not interpolated, learning.

In 1950 a study was published by Mrs. Greenberg and myself (10) on retention as a function of stage of practice. The orientation for this study was crassly empirical; we simply wanted to know if subjects learn how to recall in the same sense that they learn how to learn. In the conditions with which I am concerned, naive subjects learned a list of ten paired adjectives to a criterion of eight out of ten correct on a single trial. Forty-eight hours later this list was recalled. On the following day, these same subjects learned a new list to the same criterion and recalled it after 48 hours. This continued for two additional lists, so that the subjects had learned and recalled four lists, but the learning and recall of each list was complete before another list was learned. There was low similarity among these lists as far as conventional symptoms of similarity are concerned. No words were repeated and no obvious similarities existed, except for the fact that they were all adjectives and a certain amount of similarity among prefixes, suffixes, and so on must inevitably occur. The recall of these four successive lists is shown in Fig. 1.

As can be seen, the more lists that are learned, the poorer the recall, from 69 per cent recall of the first list to 25 per cent recall of the fourth list. In examining errors at recall, we found a sufficient number of intrusion responses from previous lists to lead us to suggest that the increasing decrements in recall were a function of proactive interference from previous lists. And, while we pointed out that these results had implications for the design of experiments on retention, the relevance to an interference theory of forgetting was not mentioned.

Dr. E. J. Archer has made available to me certain data from an experiment which still is in progress and which deals with this issue. Subjects learned lists of 12 serial adjectives to one perfect trial and recalled them after 24 hours. The recall of a list always took place prior to learning the next list. The results for nine successive lists are shown in Fig. 2. Let me say again that there is no laboratory activity during the 24-hour interval; the subject learns a list, is dismissed from the laboratory, and returns after 24 hours to recall the list. The percentage of recall falls from 71 per cent for the first list to 27 per cent for the ninth.

In summarizing the more classical data on retention above, I indicated that a rough estimate showed that after 24 hours 75 per cent forgetting took place, or recall was about 25 per cent correct. In viewing these values in the light of Greenberg's and Archer's findings, the conclusion seemed inescapable that the classical studies must have been dealing with subjects who had learned many lists. That is to say, the subjects must have served in many

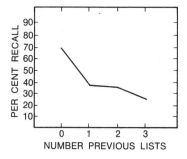

FIG. 1. *Recall of paired adjectives as a function of number of previous lists learned (10).*

conditions by use of counterbalancing and repeated cycles. To check on this I have made a search of the literature on the studies of retention to see if systematic data could be compiled on this matter. Preliminary work led me to establish certain criteria for inclusion in the summary to be presented. First, because degree of learning is such an important variable, I have included only those studies in which degree of learning was one perfect recitation of the list. Second, I have included only studies in which retention was measured after 24 hours. Third, I have included only studies in which recall measures were given. (Relearning measures add complexities with which I do not wish to deal in this paper.) Fourth, the summary includes only material learned by relatively massed practice. Finally, if an investigator had two or more conditions which met these criteria, I averaged the values presentation in this paper. Except for these restrictions, I have used all studies I found (with an exception to be noted later), although I do not pretend to have made an exhaustive search. From each of these studies I got two facts: first, the percent-

age recalled after 24 hours, and second, the average number of previous lists the subjects had learned before learning the list on which recall after 24 hours was taken. Thus, if a subject had served in five experimental conditions via counterbalancing, and had been given two practice lists, the average number of lists learned before learning the list for which I tabulated the recall was four. This does not take into account any previous experiments in rote learning in which the subject might have served.

For each of these studies the two facts, average number of previous lists learned and percentage of recall, are related as in Fig. 3. For example, consider the study by Youtz. This study was concerned with Jost's law, and had several degrees of learning, several lengths of retention interval, and the subjects served in two cycles. Actually, there were 15 experimental conditions and each subject was given each condition twice. Also, each subject learned six practice lists before starting the experimental conditions. Among the 15 conditions was one in which the learning of the syllables was carried to one perfect recitation and recall was taken after 24 hours. It is this particular condition in which I am interested. On the average, this condition would have been given at the time when the subject had learned six practice lists and 15 experimental lists, for a total of 21 previous lists.

The studies included in Fig. 3 have several different kinds of materials, from geometric forms to nonsense syllables to nouns; they include both paired-associate and serial presentation, with different speeds of presentation and different lengths of lists. But I think the general relationship is clear. The greater the number of previous lists learned the greater the forgetting. I interpret this to mean that the greater the number of previous lists the greater the *proactive* interference. We know this to be true (26) for a formal proactive-inhibition paradigm; it seems a reasonable interpretation for the data of Fig. 3. That there are minor sources of variance still involved I do not deny. Some of the variation can be rationalized, but that is not the purpose of this report. The point I wish to make is the obvious one of the relationship between number of previous lists learned—lists

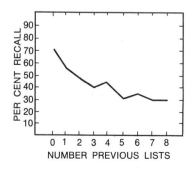

FIG. 2. *Recall of serial adjective lists as a function of number of previous lists learned. Unpublished data, courtesy of Dr. E. J. Archer.*

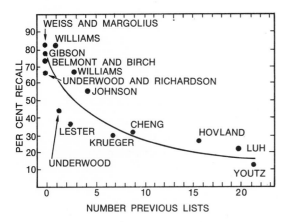

FIG. 3. *Recall as a function of number of previous lists learned as determined from a number of studies. From left to right: Weiss and Margolius (35), Gibson (9), Belmont and Birch (3), Underwood and Richardson (33), Williams (36), Underwood (27, 28, 29, 30), Lester (17), Johnson (14), Krueger (16), Cheng (6), Hovland (11), Luh (18), Youtz (37).*

which presumably had no intentionally built-in similarity—and amount of forgetting. If you like to think in correlational terms, the rank-order correlation between the two variables is − .91 for the 14 points of Fig. 3.

It may be of interest to the historian that, of the studies published before 1942 which met the criteria I imposed, I did not find a single one in which subjects had not been given at least one practice task before starting experimental conditions, and in most cases the subjects had several practice lists and several experimental conditions. Gibson's study (1942) was the first I found in which subjects served in only one condition and were not given practice tasks. I think it is apparent that the design proclivities of the 1920s and 1930s have been largely responsible for the exaggerated picture we have had of the rate of forgetting of rote-learned materials. On the basis of studies performed during the 1920s and 1930s, I have given a rough estimate of forgetting as being 75 per cent over 24 hours, recall being 25 per cent. On the basis of modern studies in which the subject has learned no previous lists—where there is no proactive inhibition from previous laboratory tasks—a rough estimate would be that forgetting is 25 per cent; recall is 75 per cent. The values are reversed. (If in the

above and subsequent discussion my use of percentage values as if I were dealing with a cardinal or extensive scale is disturbing, I will say only that it makes the picture easier to grasp, and in my opinion no critical distortion results.)

Before taking the next major step, I would like to point out a few other observations which serve to support my general point that proactive inhibition from laboratory tasks has been the major cause of forgetting in the more classical studies. The first illustration I shall give exemplifies the point that when subjects have served in several conditions, forgetting after relatively short periods of time is greater than after 24 hours if the subject has served in only one condition. In the Youtz study to which I have already referred, other conditions were employed in which recall was taken after short intervals. After 20 minutes recall was 74 per cent, about what it is after 24 hours if the subject has not served in a series of conditions. After two hours recall was 32 per cent. In Ward's (34) well-known reminiscence experiment, subjects who on the average had learned ten previous lists showed a recall of only 64 per cent after 20 minutes.

In the famous Jenkins-Dallenbach (13) study on retention following sleep and following waking, two subjects were used. One subject learned a total of 61 lists and the other 62 in addition to several practice lists. Roughly, then, if the order of the conditions was randomized, approximately 30 lists had been learned prior to the learning of a list for a given experimental condition. Recall after eight waking hours for one subject was 4 per cent and for the other 14 per cent. Even after sleeping for eight hours the recall was only 55 per cent and 58 per cent.

I have said that an interpolated list can produce severe forgetting. However, in one study (1), using the A-B, A-C paradigm for original and interpolated learning, but using subjects who had never served in any previous conditions, recall of the original list was 46 per cent after 48 hours, and in another comparable study (24), 42 per cent. Thus, the loss is not nearly as great as in the classical studies I have cited where there was no interpolated learning in the laboratory.

My conclusion at this point is that, in terms of the gross analysis I have made, the amount of forgetting which might be attributed to interference from tasks learned outside the laboratory has been "reduced" from 75 per cent to about 25 per cent. I shall proceed in the next section to see if we have grounds for reducing this estimate still more. In passing on to this section, however, let me say that the study of factors which influence proactive inhibition in these counterbalanced studies is a perfectly legitimate and important area of study. I mention this because in the subsequent discussion I am going to deal only with the case where a subject has learned a single list in the laboratory, and I do not want to leave the impression that we should now and forevermore drop the study of interference produced by previous laboratory tasks. Indeed, as will be seen shortly, it is my opinion that we should increase these studies for the simple reason that the proactive paradigm provides a more realistic one than does the retroactive paradigm.

When the subject learns and recalls a single list in the laboratory, I have given an estimate of 25 per cent as being the amount forgotten over 24 hours. When, as shown above, we calculate percentage forgotten of lists learned to one perfect trial, the assumption is that had the subjects been given an immediate recall trial, the list would have been perfectly recalled. This, of course, is simply not true. The major factor determining how much error is introduced by this criterion-percentage method is probably the difficulty of the task. In general, the overestimation of forgetting by the percentage method will be directly related to the difficulty of the task. Thus, the more slowly the learning approaches a given criterion, the greater the drop on the trial immediately after the criterion trial. Data from a study by Runquist (24), using eight paired adjectives (a comparatively easy task), shows that amount of forgetting is overestimated by about 10 per cent. In a study (32) using very difficult consonant syllables, the overestimation was approximately 20 per cent. To be conservative, assume that on the average the percentage method of reporting recall overestimates the amount forgotten by 10 per cent. If we subtract this from the 25 per cent assumed above, the forgetting is now re-estimated as being 15 per cent over 24 hours. That is to say, an interference theory, or any other form of theory, has to account for a very small amount of forgetting as compared with the amount traditionally cited.

What are the implications of so greatly "re-ducing" the amount of forgetting? There are at least three implications which I feel are worth pointing out. First, if one wishes to hold to an interference theory of forgetting (as I do), it seems plausible to assert that this amount of forgetting could be produced from learning which has taken place outside of the laboratory. Furthermore, it seems likely that such interference must result primarily from proactive interference. This seems likely on a simple probability basis. A 20-year-old college student will more likely have learned something during his 20 years prior to coming to the laboratory that will interfere with his retention than he will during the 24 hours between the learning and retention test. However, the longer the retention interval the more important will retroactive interference become relative to proactive interferences.

The second implication is that these data may suggest greater homogeneity or continuity in memorial processes than hitherto supposed. Although no one has adequately solved the measurement problem of how to make comparisons of retention among conditioned responses, prose material, motor tasks, concept learning, and rote-learned tasks, the gross comparisons have indicated that rote-learned tasks were forgotten much more rapidly than these other tasks. But the rote-learning data used for comparison have been those derived with the classical design in which the forgetting over 24 hours is approximately 75 per cent. If we take the revised estimate of 15 per cent, the discrepancies among tasks become considerably less.

The third implication of the revised estimate of rate of forgetting is that the number of variables which appreciably influence rate of forgetting must be sharply limited. While this statement does not inevitably follow from the analyses I have made, the current evidence strongly supports the statement. I want to turn to the final section of this paper which will consist of a review of the influence of some of the variables which are or have been thought to be related to rate of forgetting. In considering these variables, it is well to keep in mind that a variable which produces only a small difference in forgetting is important if one is interested in accounting for the 15 per cent assumed now as the loss over 24 hours. If appropriate for a given variable, I will indicate where it fits into an interference theory, although in no case will I endeavor to handle the details of such a theory.

Time. Passage of time between learning and recall is the critical defining variable for forgetting. Manipulation of this variable provides the basic data for which a theory must account. Previously, our conception of rate of forgetting as a function of time has been tied to the Ebbinghaus curve. If the analysis made earlier is correct, this curve does not give us the basic data we need. In short, we must start all over and derive a retention curve over time when the subjects have learned no previous materials in the laboratory. It is apparent that I expect the fall in this curve over time to be relatively small.

In conjunction with time as an independent variable, we must, in explanations of forgetting, consider why sleep retards the processes responsible for forgetting. My conception, which does not really explain anything, is that since forgetting is largely produced by proactive interference, the amount of time which a subject spends in sleep is simply to be subtracted from the total retention interval when predicting the amount to be forgotten. It is known that proactive interference increases with passage of time (5); sleep, I believe, brings to a standstill whatever these processes are which produce this increase.

Degree of Learning. We usually say that the better or stronger the learning the more or better the retention. Yet, we do not know whether or not the *rate* of forgetting differs for items of different strength. The experimental problem is a difficult one. What we need is to have a subject learn a single association and measure its decline in strength over time. But this is difficult to carry out with verbal material, since almost of necessity we must have the subject learn a series of associations, to make it a reasonable task. And, when a series of associations are learned, complications arise from interaction effects among associations of different strength. Nevertheless, we may expect, on the basis of evidence from a wide variety of studies, that given a constant degree of similarity, the effective interference varies as some function of the strength of associations.

Distribution of Practice. It is a fact that distribution of practice during acquisition influences retention of verbal materials. The facts of the case seem to be as follows. If the subject has not learned previous lists in the laboratory, massed practice gives equal or better retention than does distributed practice. If, on the other hand, the subject has learned a number of previous lists, distributed practice will facilitate retention (32). We do not have the theoretical solution to these facts. The point I wish to make here is that whether or not distribution of learning inhibits or facilitates retention depends upon the amount of interference from previous learning. It is reasonable to expect, therefore, that the solution to the problem will come via principles handling interference in general. I might also say that a theoretical solution to this problem will also provide a solution for Jost's laws.

Similarity. Amount of interference from other tasks is closely tied to similarity. This similarity must be conceived of as similarity among materials as such and also situational similarity (4). When we turn to similarity within a task, the situation is not quite so clear. Empirically and theoretically (8) one would expect that intratask similarity would be a very relevant variable in forgetting. As discussed elsewhere (31), however, variation in intratask similarity almost inevitably leads to variations in intertask similarity. We do know from a recent study (33) that with material of low meaningfulness forgetting is significantly greater with high intralist similarity than with low. While the difference in magnitude is only about 8 per cent, when we are trying to account for a total loss of 15 per cent, this amount becomes a major matter.

Meaningfulness. The belief has long been held that the more meaningful the material the better the retention—the less the forgetting. Osgood (21) has pointed out that if this is true it is difficult for an interference theory to handle. So far as I know, the only direct test of the influence of this variable is a recent study in which retention of syllables of 100 per cent association value was compared with that of zero association value (33). There was no difference in the recall of these syllables. Other less precise evidence would support this finding when comparisons are made among syllables, adjectives, and nouns, as plotted in Fig. 3. However, there is some evidence that materials of very low meaningfulness are forgotten more rapidly than nonsense syllables of zero association value. Consonant syllables, both serial (32) and paired associates (unpublished), show about 50 per cent loss over 24 hours. The study using serial lists was the one mentioned earlier as knowingly omitted from Fig. 3. These syllables, being extremely difficult to learn, allow a correction of about 20 per cent due to criterion overestimation, but even with this much correction the forgetting (30 per cent) is still appreciably more than the estimate we have made for other materials. To invoke the interference theory to account for this discrepancy means that we must demonstrate how interference from other activities could be greater for these consonant syllables than for nonsense syllables, nouns, adjectives, and other materials. Our best guess at the present time is that the sequences of letters in consonant syllables are contrary to other well-established language habits. That is to say, letter sequences which commonly occur in our language are largely different from those in consonant syllables. As a consequence, not only are these consonant syllables very difficult to learn, but forgetting is accelerated by proactive interference from previously well-learned letter sequences. If subsequent research cannot demonstrate such a source of interference, or if some other source is not specified, an interference theory for this case will be in some trouble.

Affectivity. Another task dimension which has received extensive attention is the affective tone of the material. I would also include here the studies attaching unpleasant experiences to some items experimentally and not to others, and measuring retention of these two sets of items. Freud is to a large extent responsible for these studies, but he cannot be held responsible for the malformed methodology which characterizes so many of them. What can one say by way of summarizing these studies? The only conclusion that I can reach is a statistical one, namely, that the occasional positive result found among the scores of studies is about as frequent as one would expect by sampling error, using the 5 per cent level of confidence. Until a reliable body of facts is established for this variable and associated variables, no theoretical evaluation is possible.

Other Variables. As I indicated earlier, I will not make an exhaustive survey of the variables which may influence rate of forgetting. I have limited myself to variables which have been rather extensively investigated, which have immediate relevance to the interference theory, or for which reliable relationships are available. Nevertheless, I would like to mention briefly some of these other variables. There is the matter of *warm-up* before recall; some investigators find that this reduces forgetting (12); others, under as nearly replicated conditions as is possible to obtain, do not (23). Some resolution must be found for these flat contradictions. It seems perfectly reasonable, however, that inadequate set or context differences could reduce recall. Indeed, an interference theory would predict this forgetting if the set or context stimuli are appreciably different from those prevailing at the time of learning. In our laboratory we try to reinstate the learning set by careful instructions, and we simply do not find decrements that might be attributed to inadequate set. For example, in a recent study (33) subjects were given a 24-hour recall of a serial list after learning to one perfect trial. I think we would expect that the first item in the list would suffer the greatest decrement due to inadequate set, yet this item showed only .7 per cent loss. But let it be clear that when we are attempting to account for the 15 per cent loss over 24 hours, we should not overlook any possible source for this loss.

Thus far I have not said anything about forgetting as a function of characteristics of the subject, that is, the personality or intellectual characteristics. As far as I have been able to determine, there is not a single valid study which shows that such variables have an appreciable influence on forgetting. Many studies have shown differences in learning as a function of these variables, but not differences in rate of forgetting. Surely there must be some such variables. We do know that if subjects are severely insulted, made to feel stupid, or generally led to believe that they have no justification for continued existence on the earth just before they are asked to recall, they will show losses (e.g., 25, 38), but even the influence of this kind of psychological beating is short lived. Somehow I have never felt that such findings need explanation by a theory used to explain the other facts of forgetting.

Concerning the causes of forgetting, let me sum up in a somewhat more dogmatic fashion than is probably justified. One of the assumptions of science is finite causality. Everything cannot influence everything else. To me, the most important implication of the work on forgetting during the last ten years is that this work has markedly *reduced* the number of variables related to forgetting. Correspondingly, I think the theoretical problem has become simpler. It is my belief that we can narrow down the cause of forgetting to interference from previously learned habits, from habits being currently learned, and from habits we have yet to learn. The amount of this interference is primarily a function of similarity and associative strength, the latter being important because it interacts with similarity.

Summary

This paper deals with issues in the forgetting of rote-learned materials. An analysis of the current evidence suggests that the classical Ebbinghaus curve of forgetting is primarily a function of interference from materials learned previously in the laboratory. When this source of interference is removed, forgetting decreases from about 75 per cent over 24 hours to about 25 per cent. This latter figure can be reduced by at least 10 per cent by other methodological considerations, leaving 15 per cent as an estimate of the forgetting over 24 hours. This estimate will vary somewhat as a function of intra-task similarity, distributed practice, and with very low meaningful material. But the overall evidence suggests that similarity with other material and situational similarity are by far the most critical factors in forgetting. Such evidence is consonant with a general interference theory, although the details of such a theory were not presented here.

References

1. Archer, E. J., & Underwood, B. J. Retroactive inhibition of verbal associations as a multiple function of temporal point of interpolation and degree of interpolated learning. *J. exp. Psychol.,* 1951, 42, 283–290.

2. Bartlett, F. C. *Remembering: a study in experimental and social psychology.* London: Cambridge Univer. Press, 1932.

3. Belmont, L., & Birch, H. G. Re-individualizing the repression hypothesis. *J. abnorm. soc. Psychol.,* 1951, 46, 226–235.

4. Bilodeau, I. McD., & Schlosberg, H. Similarity in stimulating conditions as a variable in retroactive inhibition. *J. exp. Psychol.,* 1951, 41, 199–204.

5. Briggs, G. E. Acquisition, extinction, and recovery functions in retroactive inhibition. *J. exp. Psychol.,* 1954, 47, 285–293.

6. Cheng, N. Y. Retroactive effect and degree of similarity. *J. exp. Psychol.,* 1929, 12, 444–458.

7. Ebbinghaus, H. *Memory: a contribution to experimental psychology.* (Trans. by H. A. Ruger, and C. E. Bussenius) New York: Bureau of Publications, Teachers College, Columbia Univer., 1913.

8. Gibson, Eleanor J. A systematic application of the concepts of generalization and differentiation to verbal learning. *Psychol. Rev.,* 1940, 47, 196–229.

9. Gibson, Eleanor J. Intra-list generalization as a factor in verbal learning. *J. exp. Psychol.,* 1942, 30, 185–200.

10. Greenberg, R., & Underwood, B. J. Retention as a function of stage of practice. *J. exp. Psychol.,* 1950, 40, 452–457.

11. Hovland, C. I. Experimental studies in rote-learning theory. VI. Comparison of retention following learning to same criterion by massed and distributed practice. *J. exp. Psychol.,* 1940, 26, 568–587.

12. Irion, A. L. The relation of "set" to retention. *Psychol. Rev.,* 1948, 55, 336–341.

13. Jenkins, J. G., & Dallenbach, K. M. Oblivescence during sleep and waking. *Amer. J. Psychol.,* 1924, 35, 605–612.

14. Johnson, L. M. The relative effect of a time interval upon learning and retention. *J. exp. Psychol.,* 1939, 24, 169–179.

15. Katona, G. *Organizing and memorizing: studies in the psychology of learning and teaching.* New York: Columbia Univer. Press, 1940.

16. Krueger, W. C. F. The effect of over-learning on retention. *J. exp. Psychol.,* 1929, 12, 71–78.

17. Lester, O. P. Mental set in relation to retroactive inhibition. *J. exp. Psychol.,* 1932, 15, 681–699.

18. Luh, C. W. The conditions of retention. *Psychol. Monogr.,* 1922, 31, No. 3 (Whole No. 142).

19. McGeoch, J. A. Forgetting and the law of disuse. *Psychol. Rev.,* 1932, 39, 352–370.

20. McGeoch, J. A. *The psychology of human learning.* New York: Longmans, Green, 1942.

21. Osgood, C. E. *Method and theory in experimental psychology.* New York: Oxford Univer. Press, 1953.

22. Rapaport, D. Emotions and memory. *Psychol. Rev.,* 1943, 50, 234–243.

23. Rockway, M. R., & Duncan, C. P. Pre-recall warming-up in verbal retention. *J. exp. Psychol.,* 1952, 43, 305–312.

24. Runquist, W. Retention of verbal associations as a function of interference and strength. Unpublished doctor's dissertation, Northwestern Univer., 1956.

25. Russell, W. A. Retention of verbal material as a function of motivating instructions and experimentally-induced failure. *J. exp. Psychol.,* 1952, 43, 207–216.

26. Underwood, B. J. The effect of successive interpolations on retroactive and proactive inhibition. *Psychol. Monogr.,* 1945, 59, No. 3 (Whole No. 273).

27. Underwood, B. J. Studies of distributed practice: VII. Learning and retention of serial nonsense lists as a function of intralist similarity. *J. exp. Psychol.,* 1952, 44, 80–87.

28. Underwood, B. J. Studies of distributed practice: VIII. Learning and retention of paired nonsense syllables as a function of intralist similarity. *J. exp. Psychol.,* 1953, 45, 133–142.

29. Underwood, B. J. Studies of distributed practice: IX. Learning and retention of paired adjectives as a function of intralist similarity. *J. exp. Psychol.,* 1953, 45, 143–149.

30. Underwood, B. J. Studies of distributed practice: X. The influence of intralist similarity on learning and retention of serial adjective lists. *J. exp. Psychol.,* 1953, 45, 253–259.

31. Underwood, B. J. Intralist similarity in verbal learning and retention. *Psychol. Rev.,* 1954, 3, 160–166.

32. Underwood, B. J., & Richardson, J. Studies of distributed practice: XIII. Interlist interference and the retention of serial nonsense lists. *J. exp. Psychol.,* 1955, 50, 39–46.

Serial Reproduction of Picture Material

F. C. Bartlett

F. C. Bartlett is a British psychologist who directed the Psychological Laboratory at Cambridge University, England, for many years. An international psychologist and past editor of the British Journal of Psychology, *Bartlett is the author of many books and holds several honorary doctoral degrees.*

1. *Which principles illustrated in the serial reproduction of picture material are also illustrated in the formation of social prejudices?*

2. *On what is the meaning of a reproduction based?*

3. *What similarities do you see between the task situation of picture reproduction and that of a projective test situation?*

1. Introduction

Not only stories, descriptions of events and arguments, but various types of picture material—art forms, decorative patterns, graphic representations of common objects and the like—frequently pass rapidly from person to person and from group to group. In the course of this transmission the material often suffers considerable change. It is therefore interesting, both from the point of view of the remembering of picture material and from that of its bearing upon the development of conventional representations, to see how far such a course of change can be experimentally produced. It is well known that a person may perfectly remember what he cannot reproduce well by drawing. But it has constantly appeared that when any complex form is presented for visual observation certain features of

From F. C. Bartlett, *Remembering* (New York: Cambridge University Press, 1950), pp. 177–185. Reprinted by permission of the publisher.

it will be dominant. These are pretty sure to appear again in any reproduction that may be effected; and, whether they are depicted accurately or not, it seems probable that it is these which set the direction of change in the course of serial reproduction.

Accordingly I collected a number of very simple picture representations and submitted them to a course of repeated and serial reproduction. As before, I shall give here only a very small selection of the many results that have been collected. This selection will sufficiently illustrate a few of the outstanding characteristics of the reproductions. The principles are found to be broadly the same, both in repeated and in serial reproduction. I shall therefore draw my illustrations from the chains of reproduction only.

2. Tendency to Transform in the Direction of Accepted Conventional Representations

Whenever material visually presented purports to be representative of some common object, but contains certain features which are unfamiliar in the community to which the material is introduced, these features invariably suffer transformation in the direction of the familiar. This constitutes a kind of analogue in the case of picture material to rationalisation in the case of the prose passages. The principle is illustrated in the series on page 174.

Though the series is a very short one, all the characteristics of the original which have any peculiarity are lost. The face is tilted upwards immediately, becomes oval and then round, acquires eyes, a nose and a mouth all of conventional form. There is considerable elaboration up to this point, when the title changes; and then simplification at once sets in again. No doubt the name given had a good deal to do with the form reproduced, but the whole series shows how speedily a pictorial representation may change all of its leading characteristics in the direction of some schematic form already current in the group of subjects who attempt its reproduction.

3. Elaboration

Under the conditions of this experiment and with the type of subjects employed, elaboration was very much more common with picture material than with the prose passages. This is in line with other evidence already reported. The picture material far more frequently induced a subject to use visual imagery; and it has already appeared that a visual image method favours invention. Further, in the experiments on perceiving it was shown that multiplication of features in an object visually presented is extremely common.

There were two very frequent types of elaboration. In the first, as a *whole* figure was gradually being transformed, certain relatively disconnected material was elaborated into some characteristic naturally belonging to the new setting. In the second, details or motives were simply reduplicated.

As illustrating the first type, we may take the second series. The original drawing is a representation of the Egyptian "mulak," a conventionalised reproduction of an owl, which may have been the basis of the form of our letter M.

The elaboration in this series is obvious. The reversal of the direction of the wing curve by subject 3, and its doubling, at once suggested a tail, and thereafter the tail drops lower and lower until it assumes its proper tail position, and is greatly emphasised, in which process it is reversed twice more. The apparently disconnected lines in the original drawing are all worked into the figure, and the original beak mark is elaborated into a ribbon with a bow. Whiskers are introduced in due course, and the small lines on the back are multiplied and

become shading.[1] In fact the same process appears here as in the "Portrait d'homme" series. A rather unusual figure, carrying a fairly strong suggestion of some realistic representation, becomes greatly elaborated into a familiar whole. Once this end has been achieved, simplification tends to set in again, and the whole progresses towards a truly conventionalised form.

The second type of elaboration, namely the strong tendency to multiply parts in the reproduction of visually presented forms, appears in both of the series already given; in the first series, especially in reproductions 3–7, and in the second throughout up to reproduction 10. This kind of change is present in every single series that I have collected. In one which begins as a simple drawing of a sailing-boat with three outline clouds in the sky, and on the left of the picture three birds, the clouds become two rather complicated wriggling lines in the top right-hand corner, while the birds, losing their representative character, are multiplied into thirty-eight small horizontal straight lines in the top left-hand corner by the time the seventeenth reproduction is reached. In another, which begins as an outline drawing of a house, with seven windows, the outline becomes merely a square, with the windows persisting as thirty-six small inset squares in four groups of nine in each group.

Such multiplication of detail has a large part to play in the actual development of conventional art forms in real life. Haddon, for example, speaks of reduplication as "that characteristic device of the decorative mind." Its constant appearance in the course of these experiments helps to show that the experimental material is far from being out of touch with that produced under everyday conditions of social contact and social development.

4. Simplification

If we consider how the first type of elaboration is secured, we can see that it is necessarily accompanied by simplification. A discon-

---

[1] It may be interesting to note that in another series from the same starting-point this design has again developed into a cat by the time the seventeenth reproduction is reached.

Original Drawing

Reproduction 1

PORTRAIT D'HOMME

Reproduction 2

PORTRAIT D'UN HOMME

Reproduction 3

Portrait d'un homme.

Reproduction 4

Portrait d'un homme.

Reproduction 5

Portrait d'un homme.

Reproduction 6

Portrait d'un homme

Reproduction 7

Un homme Egyptien.

Reproduction 8

L'Homme Egyptien.

Reproduction 9

L'homme Egyptien

Original Drawing

Reproduction 1

Reproduction 2

Reproduction 3

Reproduction 4

Reproduction 5

Reproduction 6.

Reproduction 7

Reproduction 8

Reproduction 9

Reproduction 10

Reproduction 11

Reproduction 12

Reproduction 13

Reproduction 14.

Reproduction 15

Reproduction 16

Reproduction 17

Reproduction 18.

nected detail, being developed and worked into a unit pattern, disappears from its original position, so that some part of the total design suffers from the elaboration of another part. The second type also usually involves simplification; for the reduplication of certain parts is commonly secured at the expense of other parts, which are then omitted.

If we turn to the designs or pictures as a whole, a fairly definite principle of elaboration and simplification seems to emerge. Whenever we have a design which is not readily assimilated—on account of its oddity or unfamiliarity—by a subject of the group concerned, there is a strong tendency to elaborate this into some readily recognisable form. But once that form is secured, simplification sets in until the whole figure has assumed a more or less conventionalised form for this group. This simplifying process may even run beyond the mark, and if it does, the whole becoming again difficult to label or to recognise, elaboration once more begins, and may proceed until some new and different, but familiar, whole has been evolved; or else the complete design may pass into a decorative *motif,* losing its representative character completely. I have, for example, two long series beginning with the obvious representation of a sailing-boat. Both show rapid simplification, until the boat character is lost. Then in one the boat was turned upside down, and became a horse-shoe shaped figure, and this again was speedily changed into a kind of architectural arch with side decorations, derived from the original water, clouds and birds. The other went through a further process of progressive elaboration until it arrived at what most subjects took to be a music-stand. Serial reproductions of material which are carried on for a very long time may thus alternate between processes of elaboration and processes of simplification, and through these processes they may develop either decorative designs, or a series of representations of apparently unrelated objects.

5. Naming

In the early experiments on perceiving it became clear that the assignment of a name to objects observed often strongly influenced their immediate reproduction or description. Moreover, there is evidence, drawn from the results yielded by the other methods, that in certain cases names given by an observer may play a very important part in his recall, whether this is immediate or remote. The serial reproduction of picture forms again emphasised the importance of naming. With this type of material and with this method, naming may operate in two ways. First, and perhaps more commonly, the whole presented is named, and then is recalled as having the conventional features of the object thus labelled in the community or for the person concerned. But there is a type of subject who, especially when he is dealing with material which is not readily named as a whole, very often takes a presented object piecemeal and names each part; visualisation usually occurs in such cases. A good instance is to be found in one of the "mulak" series. "I visualised throughout," said this subject, "and gave names to the parts. I said to myself: 'a heart at the top, then a curve and a straight post down to a little foot at the bottom. Between these two a letter W, and half a heart half-way up on the left-hand side.' " He was working on a reproduction which had assumed the following form:

and his reproduction was the following:

In this case it is obvious that the names have definitely affected the form reproduced, and under their influence the whole has been turned further in the direction of the odd, heraldic kind of animal which, in subsequent reproductions, it speedily and definitely became.

Names were more frequently still used for counting. They then normally helped to maintain order or number accurately, but allowed very considerable variations of form to occur.

6. The Preservation of Detached Detail

I have already shown that when a picture form is developing into a definite representation of some common object, detached detail is usually worked up into the whole, often changing its position and frequently undergoing elaboration in the process. But when detached detail occurs in a form which is already obviously representative, or in a decorative type of design, it stands an unusually good chance of being preserved with little change. The detached ear of the cat in reproductions 16–18 of the "mulak" series is a case in point, but I have had many better illustrations. The two wriggling lines which, as I have already mentioned, replaced the clouds in one of the boat series came in at the fourth reproduction and were maintained without any important change throughout a very long series. The same thing occurred repeatedly. Lines, shapes, dots, any feature whatsoever which stood away from a central design, were reproduced again and again practically without change. This constitutes yet another case of that curious preservation of the trivial, the odd, the disconnected, the unimportant detail. It indicates a principle which may be of considerable importance in normal remembering, one that has a significant bearing on certain problems of social conventionalisation.

7. Summary

Summarising the main conclusions that may be drawn from the serial reproduction of picture material, we find:

1. Sooner or later all such material tends to assume the form of accepted conventional representations, or decorative designs, current in the group of subjects concerned.

2. When material is presented which seems to a subject to be representative, but cannot be definitely labelled, it tends to undergo elaboration until a readily recognisable form is produced.

3. Another common characteristic is the multiplication of detail which is not readily assimilated, or of *motif* in decorative design.

4. When a readily recognisable form is presented, this tends to undergo simplification into a genuinely conventionalised representation or design. Such simplification may proceed too far, when a new process of elaboration is apt to set in, resulting in the development of a representative form apparently unconnected with the original.

5. Naming, it may be of the whole, or it may be of the parts, strongly affects reproduction whether immediate or remote. When counting is used, order and number may be preserved, though the form may be altered.

6. There is a strong tendency to preserve apparently trivial or disconnected detail of a non-representative character or in a nonrepresentative setting.

Recitation as a Factor in Memorizing

Arthur I. Gates

Arthur Gates, Professor Emeritus, Teachers College, Columbia University, received his Ph.D. in psychology from Columbia University in 1917. He is internationally acclaimed for his work in educational psychology and is known particularly for his research in the diagnosis and measurement of reading.

1. *What does recitation force the learner to do that reading alone fails to achieve?*

2. *If you have an hour available for reading an assignment what portion of that hour is spent in reading? Recitation? How does this match the "optimum combination" for recall of sense material?*

Introductory Statement of the Problem

The process of learning as carried on by most adults depending upon their native resources or practical experience, is frequently interrupted by attempts at recitation or voluntary recall of what has been learned. We tend to introduce an attempt at recitation at the earliest possible moment, usually long before a perfect reproduction is possible. In that case, as a rule, we refer promptly to the material being studied in order to complete the perusal. For example, many years ago Francis Bacon observed, "If you read anything over twenty times you will not learn it by heart so easily as if you were to read it only ten, trying to repeat it between whiles, and when memory failed looking at the book." The spontaneous methods of learning of many people resort so naturally to these attempted reproductions that we can hardly refuse to believe that they are helpful. Yet

Abridged from A. I. Gates, "Recitation as a Factor in Memorizing," *Archives of Psychology*, 6, No. 40 (1917).

most of us would admit that the dominating idea behind such a procedure is the fear of studying the lesson more than is absolutely necessary, and it is by no means clear that introducing the recitation too early in the learning process may not result in loss of time. This gives rise to practical questions, such as:—Is an attempted recitation of as much value in learning as another perusal or reading, and is a recitation at one stage of the learning as valuable as at another?

The present study presents the results of an effort to answer a practical problem of the school-room—namely, What are the relative values of learning by reading as compared to learning by recitation in the case of school children working under school conditions and with the ordinary school-room methods of attack?

In the present work, so far as practicable, conditions were made as nearly normal as possible. The material selected is comparable to that with which the pupils were accustomed to deal in their daily work. The children studied in much the same manner that they would employ in learning a vocabulary, a spelling lesson, or a history or geography lesson, with the knowledge that at the end of the study period they would be given a written examination. Details of material and methods, however, will be reserved for a later page.

From this study it is hoped that some information will be secured on the following points:

1. The relative value of learning by reading as compared to learning by recitation.

2. The differences in the functions involved in the two methods of learning.

3. The optimum time at which to introduce recitation into the learning process.

4. The relation of the two methods of learning as dependent upon the age or school status of the learner.

5. The relation of the two methods as dependent upon the kind of material employed.

The Subjects, Materials, and Methods of Procedure

As was mentioned earlier, the present study was devised to answer a practical question of the school-room—namely, What are the relative values of learning by reading as compared to learning by recitation in the case of school children working under school conditions and with the ordinary school-room methods of attack? So far as practicable, everything was done to secure normal conditions for the work. The details concerning subjects, materials, methods of study, and computation of results will now be considered.

The Subjects

The subjects used were pupils of a grammar school of Oakland, California. The members of the first, fourth, sixth, and eighth grades acted as subjects for the experiments in which the nonsense syllables were used, and the third, fourth, fifth, sixth, and eighth grades for the tests with sense material. Each class consisted of from forty to forty-five pupils.

The school in which the experiments were conducted is situated in a residential suburb of Oakland and draws its pupils from the homes of businessmen and artisans of moderate means. In general the school stands in the first class.

As will be explained later in detail, the pupils were grouped by grades rather than by age for the tests. The following table summarizes the distribution of the members of the several grades according to age.

Materials Used

The materials were of two sorts, senseless, non-connected material and connected, sense material in the form of biographies. The nonsense syllables were constructed in a manner similar to that of Müller and Schumann. The sense material was constructed by the writer from material found in J. McKeen Cattell's *American Men of Science* and *Who's Who in America*. While this material is senseful and connected, the organization of different parts of the whole is not so complete and systematic as would be generally found in poetry or prose, in which the ideas are more closely related and the material more closely unified by rhythms, accents, and natural pauses. This biographical form of material was used because it was desirable to approximate the kind of material that the pupils were accustomed to study in their regular history, geography, or grammar lessons.

The nonsense syllables were mimeographed in vertical columns on cards and were handed out one to each student. The sense material was mimeographed on sheets which were likewise distributed to the pupils.

Preliminary tests were conducted in order to determine the amount and difficulty of the material to include in the lesson as well as to give the subjects some preliminary practice in the tests before the actual experimentation began. The kind and amount of material was arranged

Age in years	6	7	8	9	10	11	12	13	14	15	16	17
Grade 1	24	13	4									
Grade 3		1	11	21	8	1						
Grade 4			5	16	11	4	1					
Grade 5				4	17	12	4	1	1			
Grade 6				2	7	13	9	2	1	1	1	
Grade 8						1	8	13	12	7		

so that the lesson was somewhat too large for the best students to master in the time allotted.

In the case of nonsense syllables, the series contained for the eighth grade sixteen syllables; for the sixth, fifteen; and for the fourth, fourteen. The pupils of the first grade were unable to read or write these syllables, so the teacher kindly constructed series of twelve syllables of a kind they were accustomed to manipulating, such as *ad, en, ig, op, ot,* etc. These syllables were written with a black crayon by the teacher on large strips of heavy paper.

The sense material was also arranged to suit the capacities of the different classes. For the eighth grade the biographies of five men served as a lesson; for the sixth and fifth grades, the same biographies for but four men were used. For the fourth grade easier biographies of four boys were used; while for the third grade, the biographies of three boys sufficed.

The following is a sample of the material used by the fifth, sixth, and eighth grades:

JAMES CHURCH, born in Michigan, February 15, 1869. Studied in Munich, and later studied Forestry and Agriculture. Director of Mt. Rose Weather Observatory in 1906. Studied evaporation of snow, water content, and frost.

JOHN CLARK, born in Indiana, June 4, 1867. Studied Surgery and became a doctor in Philadelphia. Taught at Johns Hopkins. Has visited Italy and Russia. Has a brother in Vancouver.

MORTON CLOVER, born in Ohio, April 25, 1875. Studied Chemistry at Michigan. Worked in Manila for eight years. Wrote articles on the content of dogwood, of sugar, and acids. Now lives in Detroit.

CLARENCE CORY, born in Indiana, September 4, 1872. Studied in Purdue and Cornell Universities. Now lives in Berkeley. Is Professor of Engineering and Dean of Mechanics. Since 1901 has been Consulting Engineer of San Francisco. Is a member of the British Institute.

GEORGE CURTIS, born in Massachusetts, July 10, 1872. Studied Geography at Harvard. Won Gold Medals at Paris in 1900. Member of Boston Scientific Society. Went on the Dixie Expedition in 1902.

The following is a sample of the material used by the third and fourth grades:

HARRY, is 14 years old. His father is a farmer. Around the farm are red stones, black-berry bushes, red clay, green clover, and small trees. Harry is in the eighth grade, and is tall and slender. He likes dancing and singing.

JAMES, was born in June, 1905. He is going to be a carpenter. He can make a chair, a stool, a box, a gate, and a window. His mother has white hair and wears a black dress. His father is fifty-five years old.

HAROLD, was born in New York. He came to California when six years old. He is now fifteen years old and has a gun, a bicycle, a kite, a pair of skates, and a baseball suit. He is going to be a lawyer and lives in Seattle.

FRED, was born in March, 1898. He lives on 31st and Parker Streets. He goes to business college. He is tall, has black hair and blue eyes, wears a gray suit and brown necktie. His home is made of brick and granite.

Since, as will be seen later, the same sort of tests were repeated several times, it was necessary to construct different texts equal in number to the tests given. An attempt was made, of course, to make the various texts of equal difficulty, but as is usually the case, they probably vary considerably. That such differences in difficulty as may exist will not invalidate the results to any considerable extent, will be made clear later.

Method of Conducting the Tests

Several very conspicuous sources of error are to be contended with in experimental work of the present sort. The more important sources of error are as follows:

(*a*) *Practice effects.* In a series of five or six practice periods of from five to ten minutes each, it would be expected that practice effects would be considerable. Some of the earlier studies have not taken this sufficiently into account.

(*b*) *Unequal difficulty of texts.* Since one individual must repeat a similar test with many different texts, any inequality in their difficulty will affect the results. Even series of nonsense syllables may differ greatly in difficulty for different individuals.

(*c*) *Individual differences.* In the case of most of the earlier investigations the subjects were so few that individual peculiarities may have played a large role.

(*d*) *Diurnal variations in efficiency and fatigue.* It is imperative that comparative experiments should be conducted at the same hour of the day with subjects as nearly as possible in the same state of physical fitness, unless some adequate estimate of these influences be introduced as a check. In this respect nearly all of the earlier investigators have been negligent.

In order to eliminate, as far as possible, the effects of such sources of error, the method described below was employed in the work.[1]

A class, consisting of forty or more pupils on the average, was divided into a number of sections or squads,[2] the number of squads, for reasons which will be evident, being made equal to the number of methods of study that were tested. Each squad thus consisted of seven or eight pupils, the personnel remaining unchanged throughout. Different texts, of as nearly equal difficulty as possible, were of necessity used. A particular squad was tested but once on a single day, and to complete the series for each squad required five or six days. The accompanying table shows in detail the manner in which the tests were conducted. The procedure was as follows: At nine A.M. of the first day, squad one was given its first test under method one,[3] using text one. Immediately after, squad two studied the same text, according to method two; then squad three worked under method three and so on. On the next day, squad three was taken out at the first hour and studied text two according to method two; at the next hour squad four worked under method three with the same text and so on. Thus the squads progressed, during the five days, through all the trials, texts, methods, and hours. The outcome, as shown under the column indicated "Total" is that from the point of view of the methods employed, which is the only factor with which we are concerned; all other influences are balanced or neutralized.

Differences in practice effects are neutralized because the sum total of practice for any one method is the same as for all others. Individual differences are neutralized because each subject has studied under each method, and no one more than once. The errors arising from differences in the difficulty of the texts are avoided, because each method has to its credit one group working with each of the six texts. The influences of diurnal variations in efficiency or fatigue are neutralized, since each method has been tried by one squad working at each of the different hours.

Almost ideal arrangements were made for conducting the tests.[4] In a well lighted and well ventilated room about twenty-two by fourteen feet in size, a library table large enough to seat about a dozen people was provided. The situation of the room was such that practically all noise and distractions of whatever kind were avoided. Care was taken to keep the physical conditions of the room as constant and comfortable as possible. Fresh air was kept in circulation, an abundance of light was admitted, and the temperature was kept constantly between fifty-seven and sixty degrees Fahrenheit.

Since there were but seven or eight pupils undergoing a test at a time, the experimenter who stood at the head of the table could easily keep an eye on the work of each individual. Any attempt on the part of a pupil to copy from another, to loaf, or use improper methods of any sort, could be instantly detected. Such policing was quite unnecessary and such violations of rules as did occur were in most cases unintentional. However, such factors which might result in the unreliability of the data were urgently sought, and in cases where such an unreliability was known or suspected, the entire data of that child were thrown out. In addition to the observations of the writer, the opinion of the teacher, especially with reference to doubtful cases, was sought and freely obtained. Each teacher listed the pupils in her room according to the following request, "Please list your estimates of the intelligence of the pupils in your room, in order of rank, putting the most intelligent as Number one, ———. Use your own methods of estimating and your own conception of what intelligence is. Please do not, however, make it a mere record of class standing according to grades received, and mere maturity should not be considered." The teachers also fulfilled a request to give the names "of such pupils that you think on account of feeble intelligence or inattentiveness, lack of persistence, indolence or inclination toward dishonesty in work, etc., would be

---

[1] The first grade was handled as a whole and not by squads as were the others. To be taken into new surroundings under the charge of a stranger proved to be too disturbing for these little children.

[2] Five for the learning of nonsense material, six for the learning of sense material.

[3] "Method" refers to the manner in which the material was studied.

[4] For this I am greatly indebted to the school principal, Mr. N. Ricciardi.

unreliable subjects for experimental purposes." The teachers were consulted also in particular cases when the occasion arose.

Methods of Studying

A single squad having been seated at the table in the separate room, a copy of the material was passed out face downward before each pupil, and the following instructions were given: "On each of these cards is a list of nonsense words [show a sample]. They are called nonsense words because in English they have no meaning. Now the object of the test today is to see how many of these words you can learn in a certain short time.

"We will proceed like this. I will give you two signals to start. At 'Ready' you take the card at the corner like this and at 'Go' you turn the card over and begin to study.

"Now you are going to study for a while in one way and then later you are going to study in a very different way. To begin with you are to study by reading this list of words over and over from beginning to end [illustrate]. Remember you are to read only. You should never look away from the paper; never close your eyes to see if you can say the words; in fact never say a single word unless you are actually looking at it, actually reading it. Remember you are to read through from the first to the last every time.

"After you have read the words through and through in this way for a while, I am going to give you a signal 'Recite.' When I say 'Recite' you are to hold your paper in front of you so that when you are looking straight ahead, you look over the top of it and you can see it by glancing downward a little like this. Now you are to try to say to yourselves as many of the syllables as you can without looking at the card. When you cannot remember the next word look down at your card and then go on saying as many of them as possible without looking. Glance at the card again whenever

		Day 1	Day 2	Day 3	Day 4	Day 5	Total[5]
Method 1	Squad	1	2	3	4	5	All squads
	Trial	1	2	3	4	5	All trials
	Hour	A	E	D	C	B	All hours
	Text	1	2	3	4	5	All texts
Method 2	Squad	2	3	4	5	1	All squads
	Trial	1	2	3	4	5	All trials
	Hour	B	A	E	D	C	All hours
	Text	1	2	3	4	5	All texts
Method 3	Squad	3	4	5	1	2	All squads
	Trial	1	2	3	4	5	All trials
	Hour	C	B	A	E	D	All hours
	Text	1	2	3	4	5	All texts
Method 4	Squad	4	5	1	2	3	All squads
	Trial	1	2	3	4	5	All trials
	Hour	D	C	B	A	E	All hours
	Text	1	2	3	4	5	All texts
Method 5	Squad	5	1	2	3	4	All squads
	Trial	1	2	3	4	5	All trials
	Hour	E	D	C	B	A	All hours
	Text	1	2	3	4	5	All texts

[5] In the case of sense material, six methods, squads, text, etc., were used instead of fire.

you cannot remember. Go through the list from the first word to the last in this way and continue until the word 'Time' is given. Remember you are not to look at the words unless you absolutely have to.

"When the learning period is over I am going to ask you to write as many of these words as you can."

It should be remembered that every class had received previous practice in the learning. The first grade had been given two trial tests of five minutes each, and every other grade one or two trials of eight minutes each, the data from which were not used.

Following is a table showing the absolute and relative amounts of time devoted to reading and to recitation in each method.

The study period was made somewhat shorter for the first and third grades, because it was found that steady application for longer periods was quite fatiguing.

At the end of each study period the pupils promptly placed the text papers face downward and began at once to write the material upon sheets that were provided. They were instructed to give the material in the original order as far as possible. In the case of nonsense syllables, the recall was pure reproduction, but when the sense material was used, the names of the individuals whose biographies were studied were written on the board in proper order. This was the only aid that was given. Ample time was allotted in which to write the material remembered.

Three or four hours later, tests for retention were given. The test consisted in simply asking the pupils to write, as before, all the material they could remember. No aids were given except that the names, in the case of sense material, were written on the board as in the immediate test.

Notes were kept of all manifestations of the children's work such as movements of the lips, whisperings, rhythmical movements of the head, or hands or feet, tappings of the fingers, directions of the gaze, etc., in fact, of all appearances which might be of later service in interpreting the results. The judgments of the pupils were frequently called for upon such matters as the methods which they liked or disliked, why the nonsense syllables were hard to learn and the like.

General Summary

Nonsense Material

1. In general, recitation, after a few initial readings, is of much more value in learning than more reading.

   a. Under the conditions of the present experiment a method devoting the first twenty per cent. of the time to reading followed by eighty per cent. recitation will result in learning for immediate reproduction twice as much material as will a method of reading only.

   b. As measured by recall three to four hours later, the difference between the two methods is about twice as great; four times as much being recalled under the recitation method as under the reading method.

2. After a certain amount of initial reading (one minute and forty-eight seconds or twenty per cent. of the total time in this experiment) the more quickly the recitation is introduced the better the results as measured by either immediate or delayed recall.

3. No conspicuous differences appear between the various grades with the exception that the findings for the first grade differ from all others.

Sense Material

1. In general the best results are obtained from a method devoting about forty per cent of the time to reading followed by an equal amount of recitation.

2. In general, the optimum combination of reading and recitation produces in immediate tests results superior by about twenty-seven per cent. to those obtained from reading only.

   a. The difference shown by recall three or four hours later is nearly twice as great as that shown in the immediate test.

3. In most respects the results for the various grades are very similar.

4. In certain respects differences between the grades were found on the basis of the results of immediate tests.

   a. The advantage of the best methods over the poorest is much greater in the lower grades than in the upper, *e.g.*, the average advantage for grades three and four of the best method over the poorest is 35.99 per cent. as compared to 18 per cent., the average for grades six and eight.

b. Introducing recitation very early in the study period has a disadvantageous effect upon the learning of the lower grades, but has little or no ill effect upon the work of the upper grades.

c. The upper grades, in comparison with the lower, learn more effectively under the methods involving a relatively large amount of reading.

5. With the exception of (*c*) above, none of the differences between grades were evident in the results of the retention tests.

a. This was believed to be due, in the main, to unavoidable errors which crept into the retention tests.

General Discussion

As the nature of reading and recitation now appears, the question is not so much—How is it that reading produces such poor results?—but rather—How is it that reading permits of any memorization at all? The evidence that has

NONSENSE MATERIAL

GRADE ONE

Method	Time of reading	Time of recitation	Per cent. reading	Per cent. recitation
1	5′	0′	100	0
2	4′	1′	80	20
3	3′	2′	60	40
4	2′	3′	40	60
5	1′	4′	20	80

GRADES FOUR, SIX, AND EIGHT

Method	Time of reading	Time of recitation	Per cent. reading	Per cent. recitation
1	9′	0	100	0
2	7′12″	1′48″	80	20
3	5′24″	3′36″	60	40
4	3′36″	5′24″	40	60
5	1′48″	7′12″	20	80

SENSE MATERIAL

GRADE THREE

Method	Time of reading	Time of recitation	Per cent. reading	Per cent. recitation
1	7′30″	0	100	0
2	6′	1′30″	80	20
3	4′30″	3′	60	40
4	3′	4′30″	40	60
5	1′30″	6′	20	80
6	45″	6′45″	10	90

GRADES FOUR, FIVE, SIX, AND EIGHT

Method	Time of reading	Time of recitation	Per cent. reading	Per cent. recitation
1	9′	0	100	0
2	7′12″	1′48″	80	20
3	5′24″	3′36″	60	40
4	3′36″	5′24″	40	60
5	1′48″	7′12″	20	80
6	54″	8′06″	10	90

been gathered makes it doubtful whether *pure* reading would result in memorization. But there is little doubt that *pure* reading is a fiction; more or less recitation is always present in any prolonged effort to learn.

The fact that reading is seldom if ever pure can be most clearly illustrated in the case of learning sense material, and this fact helps us at the same time to understand why reading as a method of learning is more fruitful when applied to such material than when employed with non-connected senseless material. Nearly all of the subjects admitted that their learning, especially of sense material, was not limited to pure reading. The eye moved along the line actually seeing only occasional words. Other words, in fact whole phrases, were filled in by recall. The text served only to suggest groups of words or ideas which were for the most part filled in by the learner. In so far as this subjective reproduction of the material was carried on, to just that extent the learner was reciting rather than reading, and without doubt this sort of recall was at all times considerable, becoming more and more so as the learning progressed. Consequently, it appears that the memorization of the material, technically speaking, must, after all, be attributed to recitation.

More advanced students may profit by the knowledge of the indispensable value of recitation. The college student is confronted by a situation in which the "absorbing" of knowledge seems paramount, and where reaction is too little required. Listening to lectures and reading the texts require most of his time; recitations are few and far between. That they "read lots but learn little" is a stock criticism, and it is indeed not seldom true that the college student is quite as ignorant of economical methods of study as the grammar school pupil. Recently the writer heard the case of a college student who came to a professor of psychology for an examination of what he believed to be a very poor memory. The student asserted that he could read a lesson over a dozen times and still not know it. A brief examination showed his memory not to be below par, but all the evidence indicated entirely inadequate methods of study. The student relied upon impression with little or no effort at expression; recall of the main points of his lesson was seldom tried. Yet for the college student who is so seldom called to account for his acquirements, recitation is more than usually essential. Frequent reviews, thinking the matter over by one's self, writing briefs of the main points, conversation with other students, and the like, are valuable because they throw into relief the portions that are hazy, inexact, and confused as well as because they fix more clearly in mind the material that is rehearsed.

Various opinions have been expressed with regard to methods of taking notes during lectures. Doubtless the method must be varied somewhat to suit the material that is presented, but the findings in the present study suggest a method which, although seldom employed, should bring good results. Instead of making of one's self a mechanism for transferring spoken words to paper with but little heed to the meaning, the student devotes his attention to a thorough understanding of the material presented, selecting the important points, organizing them into a systematic whole as the lecture progresses, and for the most part, delaying to a later hour the writing of the notes. Later in the day or evening, the lecture is rehearsed and an outline written down for future reference. While some disadvantages, or more likely, inconveniences, of such a method may appear, certain advantages of an important nature are obvious. First of all, the student may develop better habits of attention during the lecture. He forces himself to pick out the essentials, to grasp the relations of ideas and to unify and organize the material presented. The will to remember, which Meumann so strongly emphasizes, comes into play. The student must actively grasp the meaning of the lecture in order to be able to reproduce it later. Secondly, the writing of a brief of the lecture at a later hour combines the advantage of a recitation, which the copious notetaker too seldom practises, with the well known benefits to be derived from the distribution of learning periods. A few students who have tried this method speak enthusiastically of its effectiveness.

Finally, a word with regard to a more technical application of the results of this study. Individuals, when permitted to study by their "natural method," were found to employ various methods, not only for different materials, but for lessons of the same material and of the same length, at different times. The quantitative results consequently vary considerably, according to whether the subject does or does not happen to employ an optimum combination of reading and recitation. In experimental work on memory and learning in which successive tests under constant conditions are required, it would seem to be an important precaution to specify the time at which the learner should change from reading to attempted recall, with instructions to employ thereafter the recitation method until learning is complete.

Suggested Readings

Ebbinghaus, H. *Memory*. New York: Teachers College, Columbia University Press, 1885, 1913.

Irion, A. L. "The Relation of Set to Retention," *Psychol. Rev.*, 55 (1948), 336–341.

Jacobson, E. "The Electrophysiology of Mental Activities," *Amer. J. Psychol.*, 44 (1932), 677–694.

Jenkins, J. G. and K. M. Dallenbach. "Oblivescence during Sleep and Waking," *Amer. J. Psychol.*, 35 (1924), 605–612.

Luh, C. W. "The Conditions of Retention," *Psychol. Monog.*, 31 (1922), No. 3 (Whole No. 142).

Vinacke, W. E. *The Psychology of Thinking*. New York: McGraw-Hill, 1952.

Wallas, G. *The Art of Thought*. New York: Harcourt, Brace & World, 1926.

8 *Problem Solving*

The selections in this chapter generally reflect concern with the operational (descriptive) nature of problem solving rather than with an exploration of the general and theoretical aspects of thought. The psychologist, although interested in such issues as what causes one to think, is ultimately concerned with the operational process of thought as observed in controlled experiments. Placing an abstraction within the experimental mold is his *modus operandi*. The first two selections look at the matter of problem solving from a Gestalt point of view, and the last two selections emphasize the influence of set on problem-solving behavior.

On Problem Solving, Karl Duncker. This selection is an abridgment of a book-length monograph in which both theoretical and practical aspects of the subject are covered. The material chosen for the first reading is practical and brings some rather general questions about solving problems down to concrete example and description. It also demonstrates the usefulness of being aware of the fact that functions can serve as organizing concepts for the solution of problems.

The Mentality of Apes and the Phenomenon of Insight, Wolfgang Köhler. This selection deals directly with thinking and problem solving. It is abridged from Köhler's classic work on intelligence and insight. The emphasis he places on the perception of relationships as a sign of problem-solving ability stems directly from his close association with the Gestalt movement.

Mechanization in Problem Solving, Abraham S. Luchins. Luchins focuses more on methodology than on findings. His data were gathered from more than 9,000 subjects who were members of adult, college, secondary school, and elementary school groups. In his research he presented his subjects with a succession of mental problems, all of which could be solved by the same formula. Then he presented his subjects with a similar problem, which could be solved by a more direct formula. His purpose was to answer the following question: Will an individual ignore a direct and simple solution to a problem after he has established a different and more complicated problem-solving set? This is an interesting question, and the reader may wish to read the entire monograph, of which this selection is only a part, or the book by Luchins and Luchins, *Rigidity of Behavior,* which describes further experiments in this area.

Learning How to Learn, Harry F. Harlow. Harlow's research emphasizes that learning how to learn is a matter of learning how to transfer hypotheses. A hypothesis learned to be applicable to the solution of one problem may also be applicable to the solution of another. According to Harlow, ". . . the formation of a learning set is a highly predictable, orderly process which can be demonstrated as long as controls are maintained over the subjects' experience and the difficulty of the problems." Somewhat analogous to these findings is a process often experienced by college students: They discover that their classwork becomes more predictable and easier to handle as they progress from freshmen to seniors.

On Problem Solving

Karl Duncker

Karl Duncker is a European psychologist at the University of Berlin whose work on problem solving has been translated into English. He was a student of Wolfgang Köhler (see next selection) and Max Wertheimer—two of the three founders of the Gestalt psychology movement. Duncker dedicates his work on problem solving to these two professors.

1. What principle(s) guide the solution of a problem, according to Duncker?

2. What is meant by the statement that every solution to a problem has "two roots"? Can you give an example?

The Solution of Practical Problems (I)

1. Introduction and Formulation of the Problem

A problem arises when a living creature has a goal but does not know how this goal is to be reached. Whenever one cannot go from the given situation to the desired situation simply by action, then there has to be recourse to thinking. (By action we here understand the performance of obvious operations.) Such thinking has the task of devising some action which may mediate between the existing and the desired situations. Thus the "solution" of a practical problem must fulfill two demands: in the first place, its realization [1] must bring about

Karl Duncker, "On Problem Solving," *Psychological Monographs*, chap. 1, 1945, 58, 1–17. Copyright 1945 by the American Psychological Association and reproduced by permission.

[1] [Translator's note: "Realization" is used in the sense of "making real," of "actualization." The terms "embodiment" and "to embody" are used in a closely related sense, which will be clear in context. In the following, all notes of the translator will be given in parentheses. Such notes will add the German terms of the original where entirely satisfactory English terms do not seem to exist.]

the goal situation, and in the second place one must be able to arrive at it from the given situation simply through action.

The practical problem whose solution was experimentally studied in greatest detail runs as follows: Given a human being with an inoperable stomach tumor, and rays which destroy organic tissue at sufficient intensity, by what procedure can one free him of the tumor by these rays and at the same time avoid destroying the healthy tissue which surrounds it?

Such practical problems, in which one asks, "How shall I attain . . . ?", are related to certain theoretical problems, in which the question is, "How, by what means, shall I comprehend . . . ?" In the former case, a problem situation arises through the fact that a goal has no direct connection with the given reality; in the latter case—in theoretical problems—it arises through the fact that a proposition has no direct connection with what is given in the premises. As example in the latter field, let us take again the problem with which I experimented in greatest detail: Why is it that all six-place numbers of the type *abcabc*, for example 276276, are divisible by thirteen?

It is common to both types of problems that one seeks the ground for an anticipated consequence; in practical problems, the actual ground is sought; in theoretical problems, the logical ground.[2]

[2] Other types of theoretical problems, such as: "What is the essential nature of, or the law of . . . ?" or "How are . . . related to each other?", are not investigated here.

In the present investigation the question is: *How does the solution arise from the problem situation? In what ways is the solution of a problem attained?*

2. Experimental Procedure

The experiments proceeded as follows: The subjects (Ss), who were mostly students of universities or of colleges, were given various thinking problems, with the request that they think aloud. This instruction, *"Think aloud,"* is not identical with the instruction to introspect which has been common in experiments on thought-processes. While the introspecter makes himself as thinking the object of his attention, the subject who is thinking aloud remains immediately directed to the problem, so to speak allowing his activity to become verbal. When someone, while thinking, says to himself, "One ought to see if this isn't . . . ," or, "It would be nice if one could show that . . . ," one would hardly call this introspection; yet in such remarks something is revealed which we shall later deal with under the name of "development of the problem." The subject (S) was emphatically warned not to leave unspoken even the most fleeting or foolish idea. He was told that where he did not feel completely informed, he might freely question the experimenter, but that no previous specialized knowledge was necessary to solve the problems.

3. A Protocol of the Radiation Problem

Let us begin with the radiation problem. Usually the schematic sketch shown in Fig. 1

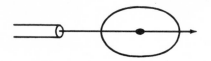

FIG. 1

was given with the problem. Thus, it was added, somebody had visualized the situation to begin with (cross-section through the body with the tumor in the middle and the radiation apparatus on the left); but obviously this would not do.

From my records I choose that of a solution-process which was particularly rich in typical hunches and therefore also especially long and involved. The average process vacillated less and could be left to run its own course with considerably less guidance.[3]

Protocol

1. Send rays through the esophagus.
2. Desensitize the healthy tissues by means of a chemical injection.
3. Expose the tumor by operating.
4. One ought to decrease the intensity of the rays on their way; for example—would this work?—turn the rays on at full strength only after the tumor has been reached. (Experimenter: False analogy; no injection is in question.)
5. One should swallow something inorganic (which would not allow passage of the rays) to protect the healthy stomach-walls. (E: It is not merely the stomach-walls which are to be protected.)
6. Either the rays must enter the body or the tumor must come out. Perhaps one could alter the location of the tumor—but how? Through pressure? No.

[3] Compare the pertinent protocols in my earlier and theoretically much less developed paper, "A qualitative study of productive thinking," Ped. Sem., 1926, v. 33.

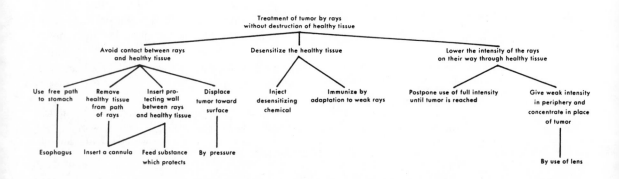

Treatment of tumor by rays
without destruction of healthy tissue

Avoid contact between rays and healthy tissue | Desensitize the healthy tissue | Lower the intensity of the rays on their way through healthy tissue

Use free path to stomach | Remove healthy tissue from path of rays | Insert protecting wall between rays and healthy tissue | Displace tumor toward surface | Inject desensitizing chemical | Immunize by adaptation to weak rays | Postpone use of full intensity until tumor is reached | Give weak intensity in periphery and concentrate in place of tumor

Esophagus | Insert a cannula | Feed substance which protects | By pressure | By use of lens

7. Introduce a cannula.—(E: What, in general, does one do when, with any agent, one wishes to produce in a specific place an effect which he wishes to avoid on the way to that place?)

8. (Reply:) One neutralizes the effect on the way. But that is what I have been attempting all the time.

9. Move the tumor toward the exterior. (Compare 6.) (The E repeats the problem and emphasizes, ". . . which destroy *at sufficient intensity.*")

10. The intensity ought to be variable. (Compare 4.)

11. Adaptation of the healthy tissues by previous weak application of the rays. (E: How can it be brought about that the rays destroy only the region of the tumor?)

12. (Reply:) I see no more than two possibilities: either to protect the body or to make the rays harmless. (E: How could one decrease the intensity of the rays en route? [Compare 4.])

13. (Reply:) Somehow divert . . . diffuse rays . . . disperse . . . stop! Send a broad and weak bundle of rays through a lens in such a way that the tumor lies at the local point and thus receives intensive radiation.[4] (Total duration about half an hour.)

4. Impracticable "Solutions"

In the protocol given above, we can discern immediately that the whole process, from the original setting of the problem to the final solution, appears as a series of more or less concrete proposals. Of course, only the last one, or at least its principle, is practicable. All those preceding are in some respect inadequate to the problem, and therefore the process of solution cannot stop there. But however primitive they may be, this one thing is certain, that they cannot be discussed in terms of meaningless, blind, trial-and-error reactions. Let us take for an example the first proposal: "Send rays through the esophagus." Its clear meaning is that the rays should be guided into the stomach by some passage free from tissue. The basis of this proposal is, however, obviously an incorrect representation of the situation inasmuch as the rays are regarded as a sort of fluid, or the esophagus as offering a perfectly straight approach to the stomach, etc. Nevertheless, within the limits of this simplified concept of the situation, the proposal would actually fulfill

the demands of the problem. It is therefore genuinely the solution of a problem, although not of the one which was actually presented. With the other proposals, the situation is about the same. The second presupposes that a means —for example, a chemical means—exists for making organic tissue insensitive to the rays. If such a means existed, then everything would be in order, and the solution-process would have already come to an end. The fourth proposal —that the rays be turned on at full strength only when the tumor has been reached—shows again very clearly its derivation from a false analogy, perhaps that of a syringe which is set in operation only when it has been introduced into the object. The sixth suggestion, finally, treats the body too much as analogous to a rubber ball, which can be deformed without injury. In short, it is evident that such proposals are anything but completely meaningless associations. Merely in the factual situation, they are wrecked on certain components of the situation not yet known or not yet considered by the subject.

Occasionally it is not so much the situation as the demand, whose distortion or simplification makes the proposal practically useless. In the case of the third suggestion, for example ("expose the tumor by operating"), the real reason why radiation was introduced seems to have escaped the subject. An operation is exactly what should be avoided. Similarly in the fifth proposal, the fact is forgotten that not only the healthy stomach-walls must be protected but also all parts of the healthy body which have to be penetrated by the rays.

A remark on principle may here be in order. The psychologist who is investigating, not a store of knowledge, but the genesis of a solution, is not interested primarily in whether a proposal is actually practicable, but only in whether it is formally practicable, that is, practicable in the framework of the subject's given premises. If in planning a project an engineer relies on incorrect formulae or on non-existent material, his project can nevertheless follow from the false premises as intelligently as another from correct premises. One can be "psychological equivalent" to the other. In short, we are interested in knowing how a solution develops out of the system of its subjective premises, and how it is fitted to this system.

---

[4] This solution is closely related to the "best" solution: *crossing of several weak bundles of rays at the tumor,* so that the intensity necessary for destruction is attained only here. Incidentally, it is quite true that the rays in question are not deflected by ordinary lenses; but this fact is of no consequence from the viewpoint of the psychology of thinking. See 4 below.

5. *Classification of Proposals*

If one compares the various tentative solutions in the protocol with one another, they fall naturally into certain groups. Proposals 1, 3, 5, 6, 7 and 9 have clearly in common the attempt to *avoid contact between the rays and the healthy tissue*. This goal is attained in quite different ways: in 1 by re-directing the rays over a path naturally free from tissue; in 3 by the removal of the healthy tissue from the original path of the rays by operation; in 5 by interposing a protective wall (which may already have been tacitly implied in 1 and 3); in 6 by translocating the tumor towards the exterior; and in 7, finally, by a combination of 3 and 5. In proposals 2 and 11, the problem is quite differently attacked: the accompanying destruction of healthy tissue is here to be avoided by the *desensitizing or immunizing of this tissue*. A third method is used in 4, perhaps in 8, in 10 and 13: *the reduction of radiation intensity on the way*. As one can see, the process of solution shifts noticeably back and forth between these three methods of approach.

In the interests of clarity, the relationships described are presented graphically below.

6. *Functional Value and Understanding*

In this classification, the tentative solutions are grouped according to the manner in which they try to solve the problem, i.e., according to their "by-means-of-which," their "functional value." Consider the proposal to send rays through the esophagus. The S says nothing at all about avoiding contact, or about a free passage. Nevertheless, the solution-character of the esophagus in this context is due to no other characteristic than that of being a tissue-free path to the stomach. It functions as the embodiment solely of this property (not of the property of being a muscular pipe, or of lying behind the windpipe, or the like). In short, in the context of this problem, the "by-means-of-which," the "functional value" of the esophagus is: a free path to the stomach. The proposals: "direct the rays by a natural approach," "expose by operation," "translocate the tumor toward the exterior," "protective wall," and "cannula" all embody the functional value: no contact between rays and healthy tissue. The functional value of the solution, "concentration of diffuse rays in the tumor," is the characteristic: "less intensity on the way, great intensity in the tumor." The functional value of the lens is the quality: "medium to concentrate rays," and so forth.

The functional value of a solution is indispensable for the understanding of its being a solution. It is exactly what is called the sense, the principle or the point of the solution. The subordinated, more specialized characteristics and properties of a solution embody this principle, apply it to the particular circumstances of the situation. For example, the esophagus is in this way an application of the principle: "free passage to the stomach," to the particular circumstances of the human body. To understand the solution as a solution is just the same as to comprehend the solution as embodying its functional value. When someone is asked, "Why is such-and-such a solution?", he necessarily has recourse to the functional value. In all my experiments, aside from two or three unmistakable exceptions, when the E asked about a proposal: "In what way is this a solution of the problem?", the S responded promptly with a statement of its functional value. (In spontaneous statements of the Ss, the functional value was frequently left unmentioned as being too obvious.)

Incidentally, the realization of its functional value mediates understanding of a solution even where there is nothing but an "unintelligible" (though sufficiently general) relation between the functional value and the demand which it fulfills. Blowing on a weakly glimmering fire, for example, undoubtedly solves the problem of rekindling the fire because in this way fresh oxygen is supplied. In other words, the increase of the oxygen supply is the immediate functional value of blowing on the fire. But why combination with oxygen produces warmth and flame is ultimately not intelligible. Even if the whole of chemistry should be successfully and without a gap derived from the principles of atomic physics, these principles are not in themselves altogether intelligible, i.e., ultimately they must be "accepted as mere facts." Thus, intelligibility frequently means no more than participation in, or derivability from, sufficiently elementary and universal causal relationships. But even if these general laws are not in themselves intelligible, reducibility to such general laws actually mediates a certain type of understanding.

To the same degree to which a solution is understood, it can be transposed, which means that under altered conditions it may be changed correspondingly in such a way as to preserve its functional value. For, one can transpose a solution only when one has grasped its functional value, its general principle, i.e., the invariants from which, by introduction of changed conditions, the corresponding variations of the solution follow each time.

An example: When, seen from the standpoint of a spectator, someone makes a detour around some obstacle, and yet acts from his own point of view in terms of nothing but, say, "now three yards to the left, then two yards straight ahead, then to the right . . ."—these properties of the solution would certainly satisfy the concrete circumstances of the special situation here and now. But so long as the person in question has not grasped the functional value, the general structure: "detour around an obstacle," he must necessarily fail when meeting a new obstacle which is differently located and of different shape. For to different obstacles correspond different final forms of the solution; but the structure, "detour around an obstacle," remains always the same. Whoever has grasped this structure is able to transpose a detour properly.

7. *Meaningless Errors as a Symptom of Deficient Understanding*

A solution conceived without functional understanding often betrays itself through nonsensical errors. A good example is supplied by experiments with another thinking problem.

The problem was worded as follows: "You know what a pendulum is, and that a pendulum plays an important rôle in a clock. Now, in order for a clock to go accurately, the swings of the pendulum must be strictly regular. The duration of a pendulum's swing depends, among other things, on its length, and this of course in turn on the temperature. Warming produces expansion and cooling produces contraction, although to a different degree in different materials. Thus every temperature-change would change the length of the pendulum. But the clock should go with absolute regularity. How can this be brought about?—By the way, the length of a pendulum is defined solely by the

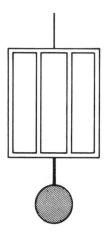

FIG. 2

shortest distance between the point of suspension and the center of gravity. We are concerned only with this length; for the rest, the pendulum may have any appearance at all."

The customary solution of this pendulum problem in actual practice is reproduced in Figure 2. At first this solution will be entirely "unintelligible" to many a reader.

Let him watch now what takes place when the solution suddenly becomes clear to him. Its functional value is that every expansion in one direction is compensated by an equally great expansion in the opposite direction.

The bars *a* and *a'* (see Fig. 3) can expand only downwards; *b* and *b'*, on the other hand, only upwards, since they are fastened below. The bars *b* and *b'* are meant to raise the strip of metal to which *c* is fastened by exactly as

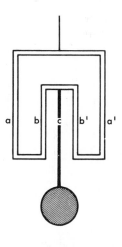

FIG. 3

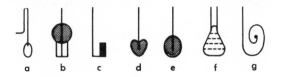

FIG. 5, a-g

much as *a* and *c* together expand downwards. To this end, *b* and *b'* must of course be constructed of a material with a greater coefficient of expansion than *a* and *a'* and *c*.

Only when Figure 3 is grasped as the embodiment of this functional value, is it understood as the solution.

Among the many Ss to whom I gave the pendulum problem, there were two who were already vaguely familiar with a pendulum-model, and simply reconstructed it from memory. One was fortunate and did it correctly, while the other drew "just four or five bars like this, from which the weight hung below" (Fig. 4). It is evident that this is a completely meaningless construction, despite all external resemblance to Figure 3, and devoid of any functional understanding (as the S clearly realized and expressed himself). Compare with this the solutions of the problem contained in Figure 5, a-g, which, in spite of all external differences, embody the identical functional value and at the same time represent completely new constructions.

In all of them there is compensation in the sense of Figure 3; thus we deal with appropriate transpositions of Figure 3. It is worth mentioning that one S drew the model of Figure 5a, believing that it was the compensation-pendulum dimly familiar from experience. Here it is clear that the reconstruction can have taken place only via the common functional value. Nothing in their form is common to the two pendulums.

"Good" and "stupid" errors in Köhler's sense can be clearly distinguished as follows: In the case of good, intelligent errors, at least the general functional value of the situation is correctly outlined, only the specific manner of its realization is not adequate. For example, an ape stands a box on its corner under the goal object, which hangs high above, because in this way the box comes closer—to be sure, at the price of its stability. In the case of stupid errors, on the other hand, the outward form of an earlier, or an imitated solution is blindly reproduced without functional understanding. For example, an ape jumps into the air from a box—but the goal object is hanging at quite a different spot.

8. The Process of Solution as Development of the Problem

It may already have become clear that the relationship between superordinate and subordinate properties of a solution has *genetic* significance. *The final form of an individual solution is, in general, not reached by a single step from the original setting of the problem; on the contrary, the principle, the functional value of the solution, typically arises first, and the final form of the solution in question develops only as this principle becomes successively more and more concrete. In other words, the general or "essential" properties of a solution genetically precede the specific properties; the latter are developed out of the former.* The classification given on page 220 presents, thus, a sort of *"family tree"* of the solution of the radiation problem.

The finding of a general property of a solution means each time a *reformulation of the original problem.* Consider for example the fourth proposal in the protocol above. Here it is clearly evident that at first there exists only the very general functional value of the solu-

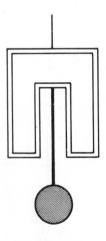

FIG. 4

tion: "one must decrease the intensity of the radiation on the way." But the decisive re-formulation of the original problem is thereby accomplished. No longer, as at the beginning, does the S seek simply a "means to apply rays to the tumor without also destroying healthy tissue," but already—over and above this—a means to decrease the intensity of the radiation on the way. The formulation of the problem has thus been made sharper, more specific— and the proposal not to turn the rays on at full strength until the tumor has been reached, although certainly wrong, arises only as a solution of this new, reformulated problem. From this same reformulation of the problem there arises, at the end of the whole process, the practicable solution, "concentration of diffuse rays in the tumor." With the other proposals in the protocol, the case is similar: the solution-properties found at first, the functional values, *always serve as productive reformulations of the original problem.*

We can accordingly describe a process of solution either as development of the solution or as development of the problem. Every solution-principle found in the process, which is itself not yet ripe for concrete realization, and which therefore fulfills only the first of the two demands given on page 2̄1̄9̄, functions from then on as reformulation, as sharpening of the original setting of the problem. *It is therefore meaningful to say that what is really done in any solution of problems consists in formulating the problem more productively.*

To sum up: *The final form of a solution is typically attained by way of mediating phases of the process, of which each one, in retrospect, possesses the character of a solution, and, in prospect, that of a problem.*

At the same time it is evident that, generally speaking, a process of solution penetrates only by degrees into the more specific circumstances and possibilities of the given situation. In the phase, "avoiding contact between rays and healthy tissue," for example, there is still very little reference to the concrete individuality of the situation. The rays function for the time being as "active agent," the tumor as "the place to be influenced," and the healthy tissue as "surrounding region which must be protected." In the next phase, "redirection of the rays over a tissue-free path to the stomach," at least the possibility of such a displacement of the rays is

already made use of. In the search for a free pathway, the situation is then subjected to an even more precise inspection; as a consequence, such a specific component of the situation as the esophagus enters the solution-process and is used in a sensible manner.

To widen our horizon, let us here demonstrate with a mathematical example how a solution-process typically arrives at the final solution by way of mediation problem- or solution-phases. The original problem is to prove that there is an infinite number of prime numbers (to find "something from which follows that there exists . . ."). A step which is quite decisive, although subjectively hardly noted, consists in the solution-phase: "I must prove that for any prime number p there exists a greater one." This reformulation of the problem sounds quite banal and insignificant. Nevertheless I had Ss who never hit on it. And without this step, the final solution cannot be reached.[5]

A further solution-phase would run as follows: "To prove the existence of such a prime number, I must try to construct it." With one of my Ss, I could follow clearly the way in which, to this phase, a further one attached itself as a mere explication: "One must therefore construct a number greater than p which cannot be represented as a product." From here on, clearly directed to "avoiding a product," the S proceeded to construct the product of all numbers from 1 to p and to add 1—incidentally, without having realized that the resultant number need not be itself a prime number, but may merely contain the desired number as a fraction of itself.

9. Implicit Solution-Phases

Not all phases of the various solution-processes are given in a family tree of the kind graphically represented on page 220: rather, only the more prominent and relatively inde-

[5] The solution consists in the construction of the product of all prime numbers from 1 to p and adding to it 1. The resultant number is either itself a prime number, or it is a product of prime numbers greater than p. For, with the exception of the special case of 1, a prime number less than p cannot be contained in a multiple of itself increased by 1 without a remainder. Thus in any case, a prime number greater than p exists. (Q.E.D.)

pendent among them are given. Aside from these, there exist phases which are not explicit enough and, above all, too banal ever to appear in a protocol. In the case of the radiation problem, for instance, it is clear to all Ss from the start that, in any case, to find a solution, something must be done with the actual circumstances concerned, with the rays and the body. As modern Europeans, they do not think of looking for suitable magic formulae; nor would they anticipate that some change in another place would lead to a solution. Similarly in the case of the prime numbers problem, from the beginning there is no doubt that the solution is to be sought in the province of numbers, and not, for example, in the province of physical processes. In short, from the very first, the deliberating and searching are always confined to a province which is relatively narrow as to space and content. Thus preparation is made for the more discrete phases of a solution by certain *approximate regional demarcations,* i.e., by phases in which necessary but not yet sufficient properties of the solution are demanded. Such implicit phases of a solution do not quite fulfill even the first prerequisite of a solution mentioned on page 219.

This is valid not only for thinking, but also for attempts at solution by action (trial and error). When a layman wishes to adjust the spacing between lines on a typewriter, this much at least of the solution is known to him: "I must screw or press somewhere on the machine." He will not knock on the wall, for instance, nor does he anticipate that any change of the given colors would do. In general, one seeks to achieve mechanical effects by mechanical alterations in the critical object.

One more example, this time from animal psychology. Thorndike set his experimental animals (mostly cats) problems of the following type. They had to learn to bring about the opening of their cage doors by a simple mechanical manipulation—unintelligible to them, to be sure, for they could not survey the connections—and so to escape into freedom. Part of the animals had a whole series of different cage problems to solve. In one cage they had to pull on a loop, in another to lift a bar, or press on a knob, etc. Thorndike made the very interesting observation that generally, in the

course of the experiments, "the cat's general tendency to claw at loose objects within the box is strengthened and its tendency to squeeze through holes and bite bars is weakened." Further, "its tendency to pay attention to what it is doing gets strengthened. . . ." It is evident that even animal "trial and error" is for the most part already under the confining influence of certain demarcations, which, by the way, are not purely instinctive.

10. *Insufficiency of a Protocol*

The reader has probably received the impression that the discussions of the preceding paragraphs left the data of the protocol a long way behind. In the case of the very first proposal, for instance, that of the esophagus, there was no mention at all of "redirecting over a tissue-free path," or even of "avoiding contact." That some such thing appeared in other protocols in an analogous place naturally proves nothing about the psychological origin of just this individual proposal.

This is the place in which to say something essential about protocols. One could formulate it thus: A protocol is relatively reliable only for what it positively contains, but not for that which it omits. For even the best-intentioned protocol is only a very scanty record of what actually happens. The reasons for this insufficiency of protocols which are based on spoken thoughts must interest us also as characteristic of a solution-process as such. Mediating phases which lead at once to their concrete final realization, and thus are not separated from the solution by clear phase-boundaries, will often not be explicitly mentioned. They blend too thoroughly with their final solutions. On the other hand, mediating phases which must persist as temporary tasks until they find their final "application" to the situation have a better chance of being explicitly formulated. Furthermore, many superordinate phases do not appear in the protocol, because the situation does not appear to the S promising enough for them. Therefore they are at once suppressed. In other words, they are too fleeting, too provisional, too tentative, occasionally also too "foolish," to cross the threshold of the spoken word.

In very many cases, the mediating phases are not mentioned because the S simply does not realize that he has already modified the original demand of the problem. The thing seems to him so self-evident that he does not have at all the feeling of having already taken a step forward. This can go so far that the S deprives himself of freedom of movement to a dangerous degree. By substituting unawares a much narrower problem for the original, he will therefore remain in the framework of this narrower problem, just because he confuses it with the original.

11. "Suggestion from Below"

There exist cases in which the final form of a solution is not reached from above, i.e., not by way of its functional value. This is a commonplace of "familiar" solutions. If the final solution of a problem is familiar to the S, it certainly need no longer be constructed, but can be reproduced as a whole, as soon as the problem is stated.[6]

More interesting cases exist. We must always remember that a solution has, so to speak, two roots, one in that which is sought and one in that which is given. More precisely, *a solution arises from the claim made on that which is given by that which is sought. But these two components vary greatly in the share they have in the genesis of a solution-phase.* A property of a solution is often very definitely demanded (characterized, hinted at) before it is discovered in what is given; but sometimes it is not. An example from the radiation problem: The esophagus may be discovered because a free path to the stomach is already sought. But it may also happen that, during a relatively vague, planless inspection of what is given in the situation, one "stumbles on the esophagus." Then the latter—so to speak, from below—suggests its functional value: "free path to the stomach"; in other words, the concrete realization precedes the functional value. This sort of thing happens not infrequently; for the analysis of the situation is often relatively planless. Nor is this disadvantageous, when the point is to find new ideas. In mathematical problems, this analysis merely of the given situation, the development of consequences from the given data, plays an especially large rôle.

One more example of "suggestion from below." An attractive goal object (for example, a banana) lies out of reach before the cage of a chimpanzee. So long as the solution, "to fish for the banana with a stick," is not very familiar, something like a stick must be in the visual field as a suggesting factor. The stick is not yet *sought*—as embodiment of the previously conceived functional value: "something long and movable"—as it is in later stages; rather it must itself help to suggest this functional value.

The prerequisite for such a suggestion from below is that the "phase-distance" between what is sought for and what could give the suggestion is not too great.

The following is an example for this influence of the size of the phase-distance. Right at the beginning of the radiation problem, the E can speak of "crossing," or can draw a cross, without the S's grasping what that means. (Cf. the solution by crossing a number of weak bundles of rays in the tumor.) If, on the other hand, the S is already of his own accord directed to "decreasing the intensity on the way," he will understand the suggestion sooner than if his thinking is dominated, for example, by the completely different demands for "a free path for the rays." We can formulate the general proposition that a suggestion is the sooner understood or assimilated, the closer it approaches the genealogical line already under development, and, within this line, the nearer it is to the problem-phase then in operation; in short, the more completely it is already anticipated.

This law is a special case of a more general law, which concerns not suggestions in the narrow sense, but the material of thinking in general. Selz formulated this law as "a general law of anticipation" in the following manner: "An operation succeeds the more quickly, the more the schematic anticipation of the solution approaches a complete anticipation."

12. *Learning from Mistakes* (*Corrective Phases*)

As yet we have dealt only with the progress from the superordinate to the subordinate phases (or vice versa), in other words, with progress along a given genealogical line. That

---

[6] This of course does not exclude the possibility that the solution is reproduced along with its functional value and as its realization, and that it is thus *understood.*

this is not the only kind of phase succession is, one should think, sufficiently indicated by the protocol given above. Here the line itself is continually changed, and one way of approach gives way to another. Such a *transition to phases in another line* takes place typically when some tentative solution does not satisfy, or when one makes no further progress in a given direction. *Another* solution, more or less clearly defined, is then looked for. For instance, the first proposal (esophagus) having been recognized as unsatisfactory, quite a radical change in direction takes place. The attempt to avoid contact is completely given up and a means to desensitize tissues is sought in its place. In the third proposal, however, the S has already returned to old tactics, although with a new variation. And such shifting back and forth occurs frequently.

It will be realized that, in the transition to phases in another line, the thought-process may range more or less widely. Every such transition involves a return to an earlier phase of the problem; an earlier task is set anew; a new branching off from an old point in the family tree occurs. Sometimes an S returns to the original setting of the problem, sometimes just to the immediately preceding phase. An example for the latter case: From the ingenious proposal, to apply the rays in adequate amounts by rotation of the body around the tumor as a center, an S made a prompt transition to the neighboring proposal: "One could also have the radiation apparatus rotate around the body." Another example: The S who has just realized that the proposal of the esophagus is unsatisfactory may look for another natural approach to the stomach. This would be the most "direct" transition, that is, the transition which retrogresses least. Or, renouncing the natural approach to the stomach, he looks for another method of avoiding contact. Or, again, he looks for an altogether different way to avoid the destruction of healthy tissue. Therewith, everything which can be given up at all would have been given up; a "completely different" solution would have to be sought.

In such retrogression, thinking would naturally not be taken back to precisely the point where it had been before. For the failure of a certain solution has at least the result that now one tries *"in another way."* While remaining in the framework of the old *Problemstellung,* one looks for another starting point. Or again, the original setting may itself be altered *in a definite direction,* because there is the newly added demand: From now on, that property of the unsatisfactory solution must be avoided which makes it incompatible with the given conditions. An example: The fully developed form of our radiation problem is naturally preceded by a stage in which the problem runs only as follows: Destroy the tumor with the aid of appropriate rays. The most obvious solution, which consists simply in sending a bundle of sufficiently strong rays through the body into the tumor, appears at once inadequate, since it would clearly have the result of destroying healthy tissue as well. In realization of this, *avoidance of the evil* has to be incorporated *as an additional demand* into the original form of the problem; only in this way does our form of the radiation problem arise (cure . . . without destruction of healthy tissue). One more example: In the pendulum problem, a watchman is often proposed who has the task of keeping the length constant by compensatory changes in the position of the weight. For the most part, Ss realize spontaneously that this procedure could not possibly be sufficiently precise, and that it would also incessantly interfere with the motion of the clock. Thus the problem: "compensation of the change in length of the pendulum," is enriched by the important addition: "automatically."

Such learning from errors plays as great a rôle in the solution-process as in everyday life.[7] While the simple realization, *that* something does not work, can lead only to some variation of the old method, the realization of *why* it does not work, the recognition of the *ground of the conflict,* results in a correspondingly definite *variation which corrects* the recognized defect.

---

[7] Life is of course, among other things, a sum total of solution-processes which refer to innumerable problems, great and small. It goes without saying that of these only a small fraction emerge into consciousness. Character, so far as it is shaped by living, is of the type of a resultant solution.

The Mentality of Apes and the Phenomenon of Insight

Wolfgang Köhler

Wolfgang Köhler (1887–1967) was Visiting Research Professor, Dartmouth College. He received his Ph.D. from the University of Berlin in 1909. A member of many scientific and philosophical societies and holder of nine honorary degrees, he was a past president of the American Psychological Association. Köhler's name is linked with that of Max Wertheimer and Kurt Koffka as founders of the Gestalt psychology movement. With a long-standing interest in perception and learning, Köhler is well known for his research on insight in chimpanzees, figural aftereffects, and brain activation. His special interest was to probe more deeply into the relation between brain processes and human experience.

1. *What seems to determine the chimpanzee's solution of a problem?*

2. *What technical aids does he lack, compared with humans, in problem solving?*

At the beginning of my work at the station, we had seven chimpanzees. Of these, I found Sultan already quite expert in the use of sticks, and Rana had also been observed performing similar feats. The achievements of some of the other chimpanzees will be recorded later; here we have to do with the three cases of Tschego, Nueva, and Koko.

The full-grown female (Tschego), of whose earlier career in the Cameroons we, of course, know nothing, had been kept almost entirely apart from the other animals up to the time of these experiments (26 Feb 1914), i.e. one year and six months. She had been in quarters that contained no movable objects, except straw and her blanket, but she was freely permitted to observe, the pranks of the young apes . . . She

Abridged from W. Köhler, *The Mentality of Apes* (New York: Hillary House Publishers, Ltd., 1925), pp. 31–39, 265–268. Reprinted by permission of the publisher.

is let out of her sleeping-place into the barred cage in which she spends her waking hours; outside the cage and beyond the reach of her exceptionally long arms, lies the objective; within the cage, somewhat to one side, but near the bars, are several sticks.

Tschego first tries to reach the fruit with her hand; of course, in vain. She then moves back and lies down; then she makes another attempt, only to give it up again. This goes on for more than half-an-hour. Finally she lies down for good, and takes no further interest in the objective. The sticks might be non-existent as far as she is concerned, although they can hardly escape her attention as they are in her immediate neighbourhood. But now the younger animals, who are disporting themselves outside in the stockade, begin to take notice, and approach the objective gradually. Suddenly Tschego leaps to her feet, seizes a stick, and quite adroitly, pulls the bananas till they are within reach. In this manœuvre, she immediately places the stick on the *farther* side of the bananas. She uses first the left arm, then the right, and frequently changes from one to the other. She does not always hold the stick as a human being would, but sometimes clutches it as she does her food, between the third and fourth fingers, while the thumb is pressed against it, from the other side.

Nueva was tested three days after her arrival (11 Mar 1914). She had not yet made the acquaintance of the other animals but remained isolated in a cage . . . A little stick is introduced into her cage; she scrapes the ground with it, pushes the banana skins together into a heap, and then carelessly drops the stick at a distance of about three-quarters of a metre from the bars. Ten minutes later, fruit is placed outside the cage beyond her reach. She grasps at it, vainly of course, and then begins the characteristic complaint of the chimpanzee: she thrusts both lips—especially the lower—forward, for a couple of inches, gazes imploringly at the observer, utters whimpering sounds,[1] and finally flings herself on to the ground on her back—a gesture most eloquent of despair, which may be observed on other occasions as well. Thus, between lamentations and entreaties, some time passes, until—about seven minutes after the fruit has been exhibited to her—she suddenly casts a look at the stick, ceases her moaning, seizes the stick, stretches it out of the cage, and succeeds, though somewhat clumsily, in drawing the bananas within arm's length. Moreover, Nueva at once puts the end of her stick behind and beyond the objective, holding it in this test, as in later experiments, in her left hand by preference. The test is repeated after an hour's interval; on this second occasion, the animal has recourse to the stick much sooner, and uses it with more skill; and, at a third repetition, the stick is used immediately, as on all subsequent occasions. Nueva's skill in using it was fully developed after very few repetitions.

On the second day after his arrival (10 Jul 1914), Koko was, as usual, fastened to a tree with a collar and chain. A thin stick was secretly pushed within his reach; he did not notice it at first, then he gnawed at it for a minute. When an hour had elapsed, a banana was laid upon the ground, outside the circle of which his chain formed a radius, and beyond his reach. After some useless attempts to grasp it with his hand, Koko suddenly seized the stick, which lay about one metre behind him, gazed at

his objective, then again let fall the stick. He then made vigorous efforts to grasp the objective with his foot, which could reach farther than his hand, owing to the chain being attached to his neck, and then gave up this method of approach. Then he suddenly took the stick again, and drew the objective towards himself, though very clumsily.

On repeating this experiment I was even more struck by the clumsiness of this animal; he often pushed the banana from the wrong (hither) side, so that it was once sent to quite a distance from him. In this case—and frequently on other occasions—Koko used his foot to grasp the stick, and continued to make vain efforts in this manner. Finding it of no avail, he suddenly took up a green stalk, with which he had been playing before the experiment began, but this was quite useless, the stalk being even shorter than the stick. From the beginning, Koko held the stick in his right hand, and only had recourse to the left for a few minutes when his feeble muscles were obviously tired; but when using his left hand, the stick wobbled aimlessly from the beginning (it could not have been from exhaustion), and was immediately transferred to the right.

It may be accepted as a general axiom that a chimpanzee who has once begun to use a stick for these purposes is not quite helpless if there is no stick to hand, or if he does not perceive one that is available.

Two days later, after she had played with it a good deal, Nueva, for the following test, was deprived of her stick. When the objective was put down outside the cage, she at once tried to pull it towards her with rags lying in her cage, with straws, and finally with her tin drinking-bowl which stood in front of the bars, or to beat it towards her—using the rags—and sometimes successfully.

On the day after Tschego's first test, two sticks lay inside the cage, about one and a half metres from the bars. When Tschego was let into her cage, she at first stretched her arm out through the grating towards the fruit; then, as the youngsters approached the coveted prize, Tschego caught up some lengths of straw, and angled fruitlessly with them. Only after a considerable time, as the young apes approached dangerously near to the objective, Tschego had recourse to the sticks, and succeeded in securing it with one of them.

---

[1] As is well known the chimpanzee never sheds tears.

In the next test, which took place several hours later on the same day, the sticks were removed to a greater distance from the bars (and, therefore, from the objective beyond them) and placed against the opposite wall of the cage, four metres from the grating. They were not used. After useless efforts to reach the bananas with her arm, Tschego jumped up, went quickly into her sleeping-den, which opens into the cage, and returned at once with her blanket. She pushed the blanket between the bars, flapped at the fruit with it, and thus beat it towards her. When one of the bananas rolled on to the tip of the blanket, her procedure was instantly altered, and the blanket with the banana was drawn very gently towards the bars. But the blanket is, at best, a troublesome implement; the next banana could not be caught like the first. Tschego looked blank, glanced towards the sticks, but showed not the least interest in them. Another stick was now thrust through the bars, diagonally opposite to the objective; Tschego took, and used, it at once.

Koko, who had already tried to use a plant-stalk in the same circumstances, three days later in the course of the test, ignored the stick which lay a little to one side and on the periphery of his "sphere of action." Only after some time did he grasp the stick with his foot, and thus drew the bananas, clumsily enough, towards him. On a repetition of the experiment, he fetched his blanket and dragged it close to the objective, then let it fall after a short hesitation, and took up the stick once more. A day later, when no stick was available, he repeated the blanket procedure exactly, and then tried to angle the objective with a stone. Some days after he employed a large piece of stiff cardboard, a rose-branch, the brim of an old straw hat, and a piece of wire. All objects, especially of a long or oval shape, such as appear to be movable, become "sticks" in the purely functional sense of "grasping-tool" in these circumstances and tend in Koko's hands to wander to the critical spot.

[Incidentally, an observation on myself: Even before the chimpanzee has happened on the use of sticks, etc., one expects him to do so. When he is occupied energetically, but, so far, without success, in overcoming the critical distance, anxiety causes one's view of the field of action to suffer a phenomenological change. Long-shaped and moveable objects are no longer beheld with strict and static impartiality, but always with a "vector" or a "drive" towards the critical point.]

As is to be expected, variations in the nature or position of the objective have very little influence on the use of the stick, when that instrument has once been mastered. One hot day Koko even tried to pull a pail of water, which had been left standing in his neighbourhood, towards him by a stick held in each hand; of course, without succeeding. When the bananas are hung out of reach on the smooth wall of the house, he takes a green plant-stalk, then a stone, a stick, a straw, his drinking-bowl, and finally a stolen shoe, and stretches up towards the fruit; if he has nothing else to hand, he takes a loop of the rope to which he is attached, and flaps it at the bananas.

When animals who have developed behaviour to cope with the requirements of a special given situation use the same methods in situations only similar or partially similar, their observers conclude, often correctly no doubt, that the cloudy perception of the animal sees no difference between the two situations, and, therefore, adopts the same procedure in each. It would be a mistake to give such an explanation when the chimpanzee replaces his stick by other objects. The vision of the chimpanzee is far too highly developed—as can easily be proved both by tests and by general observation—for him to "confuse" a handful of straw, the brim of a hat, a stone, or a shoe, with the already familiar stick. But if we assert that the stick has now acquired a certain *functional or instrumental value* in relation to the field of action under certain conditions, and that this value is extended to all other objects that resemble the stick, however remotely, in *outline* and *consistency*—whatever their other qualities may be—then we have formed the only assumption that will account for the observed and recorded behaviour of these animals. Hats and shoes are certainly not visually identical with the stick and, therefore, interchangeable in the course of the test experiments; *only in certain circumstances are they functionally* sticks, after the function has once been invested in an object which resembles them in shape and consistency, namely a stick. As has been shown in the account of Koko's behaviour, practically no limitation with regard to type remains in the case of this youngster, and almost every "movable object" becomes, in certain circumstances, a "stick."

A far more important factor than the external resemblances or differences between stick, hat brim, and shoe, is in the case of Tschego and Koko the *location of the implement* both in relation to the animals themselves and the objective. (Nueva was not tested in this manner, for some reason.) Even sticks that have already been used often both by Tschego and Koko seem to lose all their functional or instrumental value, if they are at some distance from the critical point. More precisely: if the experimenter takes care that the stick is not visible to the animal when gazing directly at the objective—and that, vice versa, a direct look at the stick excludes the whole region of the objective from the field of vision—then, generally speaking, recourse to this instrument is either prevented or, at least, greatly retarded, even when it has already been frequently used. I have used every means at my disposal to attract Tschego's attention to the sticks in the background of her cage and she did look straight at them; but, in doing so, she turned her back on the objective, and so the sticks remained meaningless to her. Even when we had induced her, in the course of one morning's test, to seize and use one of the sticks, she was again quite at a loss in the afternoon, although the sticks had not been removed from their former position, and she stepped on them in the course of her movements to and fro, and repeatedly looked straight at them. At the same time, *sticks*—and other substitutes—*which she beheld in the direction of her objective, were made use of without any hesitation,* and she devoured what food she could reach with relish.

We subjected Koko to a similar test with similar results. He made useless efforts to reach the objective: a stick was quietly placed behind him; but though, on turning round, he looked straight at the stick and walked across it, he did not behold in it a possible implement. If the stick was silently moved towards him, so that the slightest movement of head or eyes would lead from the region of the objective to the stick—suddenly he would fix his gaze on it, and use it.

The important factor here is not only the distance of the stick from its objective; for instance, suppose that Koko is seated in the centre of his chain-circle, the objective set down outside the circumference, and midway between ape and objective is placed a stick: Koko will then generally pick up the stick on the way to the objective, and naturally so; for his glance towards the goal can hardly miss the stick in this case, and it is highly probable that he *sees them "in connection,"* which would be favourable to the result.

There is no absolute rule here, however. It sometimes happens that some useful object, at quite a distance behind, is noticed as the animal looks back, and fetched. Such a result is only to be expected in the variety of circumstances that are at work; but as a rule, and to a conspicuous degree, the behaviour was as described in the preceding pages.

We found, however, that, although to some degree the use of the stick as an implement depends on the geometrical configuration, this is only so on first acquaintance. Later on, after the animal has experienced frequently the same conditions, it will not be easy to hinder the solution by a wide optical distance between objective and implement. But one can oneself "feel" that at the *inception* of these tests there is a dependence (on spatial position) such as has been described above. If one asks where to place the stick, the conviction arises—at once and without any previous reasoning—that the solution will be specially easy, if the stick is in the immediate neighbourhood of the objective, and can be visualized in connexion with the objective. However familiar the procedure in this situation may have become to us, we still dimly apprehend the decisive factors.

Conclusion

The chimpanzees manifest intelligent behaviour of the general kind familiar in human beings. Not all their intelligent acts are externally similar to human acts, but under well-chosen experimental conditions, the type of intelligent conduct can always be traced. This applies, in spite of very important differences between one animal and another, even to the least gifted specimens of the species that have been observed here, and, therefore, must hold good for every member of the species, as long as it is not mentally deficient, in the pathological sense of the word. With this exception, which is presumably rare, the success of the intelligence tests in general will be more likely endangered by the person making the experiment than by the animal. One must learn and, if necessary, establish by preliminary observation, within what limits of difficulty and in what functions the chimpanzee *can possibly* show insight; negative or confused results from complicated and accidentally-chosen test-material, have obviously no bearing upon the fundamental question, and, in general, the experimenter should recognize that every intelligence test is a test, not only of the creature examined, but also of the experimenter himself. I have said that to myself quite often, and yet I have remained uncertain whether the experiments I performed may be considered "satisfactory" in this respect; without theoretical foundations, and in unknown territory, methodological mistakes may quite well have occurred; anyone who continues this work will be able to prevent them more easily.

At any rate, this remains true: Chimpanzees not only stand out against the rest of the animal world by several morphological and, in the narrower sense, physiological, characteristics, but they also show a type of behaviour which counts as specifically human. As yet we know little of their neighbours on the other side, but according to the little we do know, with the results of this report, it is not impossible that, in this region of experimental tasks, the anthropoid is nearer to man *in intelligence too,* than to many of the lower monkey-species. So far, observations agree well with the theories of evolution; in particular, the correlation between intelligence, and the development of the brain, is confirmed.

The positive result of the investigation needs a limiting determination. It is, indeed, confirmed by experiments of a somewhat different nature, which will be recounted later; but a more complete picture will be formed when they are added, and, in so far, our judgment of the intelligence of apes is left some scope. Of much greater importance is the fact that the experiments in which we tested these animals brought them into situations in which all essential conditions were actually visible, and the solution could be achieved immediately. This method of experimentation is as well adapted to the chief problem of insight as are any which can bring about the decision "yes" or "no"; in fact, it may be the very best method possible at present, as it yields very many, and very clear, results. But we must not forget that it is just in these experimental circumstances that certain factors hardly appear, or appear not at all, which are rightly considered to be of the greatest importance for *human* intelligence. We do not test at all, or rather only once in passing, how far the chimpanzee is influenced by factors not present, whether things "merely thought about" occupy him noticeably at all. And most closely connected with this, is the following problem. In the method adopted so far we have not been able to tell how far back and forward stretches the time "in which the chimpanzee lives"; for we know that, though one can prove some effects of recognition and reproduction after considerable lapses of time—as is actually the case in anthropoids—this is not the same as "life for a longer space of time." A great many years spent with chimpanzees lead me to venture the opinion that, besides in the lack of speech, it is in the extremely narrow limits in *this* direction that the chief difference is to be found between anthropoids and even the most primitive human beings. The lack of an invaluable technical aid (speech) and a great limitation of those very important components of thought, so-called "images," would thus constitute the causes that prevent the chimpanzee from attaining even the smallest beginnings of cultural development. With special reference to the second fact, the chimpanzee, who is easily puzzled by the simplest optical complications, will indeed fare badly in "image-life," where even man has continually to be fighting against the running into one another, and melting together, of certain processes.

In the field of the experiments carried out here the insight of the chimpanzee shows itself to be principally determined by his optical apprehension of the situation; at times he even starts solving problems from a too visual point of view, and in many cases in which the chimpanzee *stops* acting with insight, it may have been simply that the structure of the situation was too much for his visual grasp (relative "weakness of form perception"). It is therefore difficult to give a satisfactory explanation of all his performances, so long as no detailed theory of form (*Gestalt*) has been laid as a foundation. The need for such a theory will be felt the more, when one remembers that, in this field of intelligence, *solutions* showing insight necessarily are of the same nature as the structure of the situations, in so far as they arise in dynamic processes *co-ordinated with* the situation.

One would like to have a standard for the achievements of intelligence described here by comparing with our experiments the performances of human beings (sick and well) and, above all, human children of different ages. As the results . . . have special reference to a particular method of testing and the special test-material of optically-given situations, the psychological facts established in human beings (especially children), under the same conditions, would have to be used. But such comparisons cannot be instituted, as, very much to the disadvantage of psychology, not even the most necessary facts of this sort have been ascertained. Preliminary experiments have given me the impression that we are inclined to over-estimate the capabilities of children of all ages up to maturity, and even adults, who have had no special technical training in this type of performance. We are in a region of *terra incognita*. Educational psychology, engaged on the well-known quantitative tests for some time, has not yet been able to test how far normal, and how far mentally-deficient, children can go in certain situations. As experiments of this kind can be performed at the very tenderest age, and are certainly as scientifically valuable as the intelligence tests usually employed, it does not matter so much if they do not become immediately practicable for school and other uses. M. Wertheimer has been expressing this view for some years in his lectures; in this place, where the lack of human standards makes itself so much felt, I should like to emphasize particularly the importance and—if the anthropoids do not deceive us—the fruitfulness of further work in this direction.

Mechanization in Problem Solving

Abraham S. Luchins

Abraham Luchins is Professor of Psychology at the State University of New York, Albany. A one-time research assistant to Max Wertheimer, Luchins is well grounded in Gestalt psychology. Although originally interested in chemistry and physics, Luchins changed toward philosophy and experimentation and began his work in psychology. He received his Ph.D. from New York University in 1939. At present his primary interest is the study of problem-solving behavior and perception.

1. *How would you compare the terms "Einstellung" and "habit"?*
2. *What everyday situation comes to mind where* Einstellung *can be observed?*

Introduction

The problem with which the present experiment is concerned was first investigated in the Berlin Institute of Psychology by Zener and Duncker. These experiments, which were preliminary in character, have not been published, the only published reference to them being the following passage in an article by N. R. F. Maier:

Zener, in some preliminary experiments at the Psychological Institute of the University of Berlin, in 1927, habituated his subjects to solve certain types of problems in the same way. A test problem was then given. He found that an obvious and simple solution of the test problem was usually overlooked because the characterisic method of solution, set up in the preceding problems, was used in the test problem. Control groups tended to solve the problem in the obvious and simple manner.[1]

It seemed important to conduct further experiments of this kind because the quoted findings of these preliminary experiments appeared to show clearly an interesting result: The successive, repetitious use of the same method mechanized many of the subjects—blinded them to the possibility of a more direct and simple procedure. We wished also to extend the scope of the method and to use various groups of subjects, children as well as adults. Furthermore, we wished to ascertain whether, if a tendency to repeat the habitually used method did develop, a change in response would be brought about if some factors to work against the habituation were employed.

Under the sponsorship of Professor Max Wertheimer,[2] the writer, in 1936, experimented with various sets of problems and finally selected the following, which are similar to those utilized by Zener and Duncker in Berlin; however, for theoretical and practical purposes, problems 9, 10, and 11 and a special "instructed group" were added. The problems selected may be shown in tabular form.

Our Basic Exploratory Experiment [3]

The problems were tried out in an exploratory experiment conducted, in 1936, in one of

[1] N. R. F. Maier, "Reasoning in Humans," *Journal of Comparative Psychology*. 2, No. 1 (1936), 127.

[2] Professor Max Wertheimer furnished us with more specific information about the Berlin experiments mentioned in Maier's article.

[3] Unless otherwise stated in the text, it should be understood that all experiments reported herein were conducted by the writer himself.

Problem		Given the following empty jars as measures			Obtain the required amount of water
1		29	3		20
2	E₁*	21	127	3	100
3	E₂	14	163	25	99
4	E₃	18	43	10	5
5	E₄	9	42	6	21
6	E₅	20	59	4	31
7	C₁	23	49	3	20
8	C₂	15	39	3	18
9		28	76	3	25
10	C₃	18	48	4	22
11	C₄	14	36	8	6

* An explanation of these letters will be furnished later.

Professor Max Wertheimer's seminars at the Graduate Faculty of the New School for Social Research. Graduate students, college instructors, and research workers composed this select group of 15 people, of whom many possessed the Ph.D. or M.D. degree.

The experimenter told the class that its task was to figure out on paper how to obtain a required volume of water, given certain empty jars for measures. To illustrate this principle we presented Problem One. The subjects were asked for the solution, and the method of solving the problem [29] [3] was then written on the blackboard. After this, Problem Two was put on the blackboard, [21] [127] [3] get 100! After 2½ minutes the subjects were asked for their solutions. The answer was then illustrated in both a written and verbal form; viz, [21] [127] [3] and verbally "One fills the 127-quart jar and from it fills the 21-quart jar once and the 3-quart jar twice. In the 127-quart jar there then remain the 100 quarts of water."

Without any further interruptions the other problems, in succession, were presented one at a time on the blackboard, at intervals of 2½ minutes—or oftener, if the students had required less time for the problem.

The method which solves Problem Two also solves Problems Three through Six; the solution which is applicable to these five problems may be described as: [diagram] or: "Fill the middle jar, and from it fill the jar to the right twice and the jar to the left once, leaving the required amount of water in the center jar." Or we may state the method as $B - A - 2C$, if we designate the jars, in the order written, as A, B, and C, respectively.

This $B - A - 2C$ method may also be used in Problems Seven and Eight. But Problem Seven may be solved more simply by subtracting 3 from 23 ($A - C$), and Problem Eight by adding 3 to 15 ($A + C$). Of eleven New School subjects (we shall speak first of those eleven who received only the instructions given above) all employed the circuitous method— $B - A - 2C$. Not one subject used the more direct method in Problems Seven and Eight. Having become habituated to the mode of solution ($B - A - 2C$), they used it in the succeeding similar problems. Later, when they were shown the more direct method after the whole experiment was completed, the subjects spontaneously said more or less passionately, "How dumb I was;" "How stupid of me;" "How blind I was;" or made other similar comments. A few of the subjects saw the light themselves—after the experiment.

Before any problems were presented, four other members had been taken outside of the classroom and had been told, in the absence of the eleven subjects whose results were reported above, "After returning to the classroom you will get a number of problems. After you will have completed Problem Six, write on your papers the words *'Don't be blind!'* " In some cases this warning appeared to be effective: 5 of their 8 answers to Problems Seven and Eight showed the direct method of solution. Three of their answers, in spite of the warning, showed only the tedious $B - A - 2C$ procedure.

Problems Ten and Eleven possessed the same ambiguity as Problems Seven and Eight. Before Problem Ten, we had introduced the ninth problem which could not be solved in the $B - A - 2C$ manner but could easily be solved by $A - C$, taking 3 away from 28. Would it disrupt the tendency to repeat blindly the $B - A - 2C$ method and bring about the more direct solution of Problems Ten and Eleven? A comparison of the per cent of solutions of Problems Ten and Eleven with the per cent of solutions of Problems Seven and Eight yielded an increase of 15 per cent direct solutions in the former for the 11 subjects who had not received the warning, "Don't be blind," and an increase of 12 per cent for the "Don't be blind" subjects. To this degree Problem Nine seemed effective.

Explanation of Terminology

In line with tradition, the habituation to the repeatedly used procedure (in this case the $B - A - 2C$ method) will be called an *Einstellung*.[4] Problems 2, 3, 4, 5, and 6 are then "Einstellung (E) problems" which may generate an "Einstellung Effect" for the subsequent "critical test problems" (7 and 8), which, if the Einstellung operated, would be solved in the Einstellung (E) method, $B - A - 2C$, and not in the more simple and direct fashion designated as the D-Method. C_1 and C_2 will henceforth refer to the Critical Test Problems Seven and Eight, respectively, and similarly, C_3 and C_4 to Problems Ten and Eleven, respectively.

A Crucial Decision

We saw that most subjects, under the influence of the Einstellung, used the complicated E method in C_1C_2 and not the more direct (D) method. One might argue, in line with some theoretical attitude, that there is nothing wrong in using the E method in the critical test problems since this method does result in the correct answer, and may be quicker under these circumstances. The tendency to repeat the E method, the argument might continue, rather than being a hindrance is an aid since it gives a ready, accurate, and speedy response. Thus Einstellung or habituation would be an effect of considerable strength, which is in no way a bad thing.

First of all, many subjects who employed the E method in C_1C_2 or C_3C_4, upon discovering the D method, or being shown it at the completion of the experiment, were excited about how foolish and blind they had been.

But besides this qualitative evidence, we

---

[4] *Einstellung* is "the set which immediately predisposes an organism to one type of motor or conscious act." H. C. Warren, *Dictionary of Psychology*, New York: Houghton Mifflin Co. (1934), p. 371. For the various meanings of "set" see James I. Gibson, "A Critical Review of the Concept of Set in Contemporary Experimental Psychology," *Psychological Bulletin*, Vol. 38, No. 9 (1941).

have in our experimental set-up a possibility to test whether the habituation to the E method is a real hindrance or not. We have spoken so far of Problem Nine only in terms of a task introduced for the sake of producing D solutions in the following critical problems, C_3C_4. Problem Nine was solvable by the direct method ($A - C$) but not by the E method ($B - A - 2C$). What about the result in Problem Nine itself? Would the solution of this simple problem be hindered by the existing habit? Would the results of the experimental groups (as against the Control groups) show that perhaps Problem Nine was not so easily solved?

Before going on to the report of the results of Problem Nine, we must confess that the situation seemed to us to be very dramatic. If the results should show that subjects able to solve more difficult problems (E_1, E_2, for example) were hindered in solving Problem Nine, it would indicate an undoubtedly bad effect of habit.

We confess that we had some expectation in this direction, but the quantitative results showed not merely some influence of this kind on only a few subjects, but a very strong influence indeed.

How many persons, in per cents, were not able to solve the comparatively simple Problem Nine within the allotted time of 2½ minutes, in contrast to the subjects' solutions of Problem Nine in the Control groups?

Every group's result cited above points directly to the fact that the Einstellung, the tendency to repeat the E method in subsequent problems, was clearly a hindrance, preventing a large number of subjects from solving a problem which Control group subjects solved. On the basis of these results, and in connection with the observations reported, this formulation seems appropriate: *Einstellung—habituation—creates a mechanized state of mind, a blind attitude toward problems; one does not look at the problem on its own merits but is led by a mechanical application of a used method.* Thus the habituation—*Einstellung*—produced in Problem Nine a surprising failure to solve a simple problem, in the same way as it blinded subjects to direct solutions in the previously discussed critical problems.

Learning How to Learn

Harry F. Harlow

Harry Harlow is Research Professor at the University of Wisconsin and Director of the Primate Laboratory and the Wisconsin Regional Primate Center. He received his Ph.D. from Stanford University in 1930. A past president of the American Psychological Association, Harlow was also a consultant on the Army's Scientific Advisory Panel. Editor of the Journal of Comparative and Physiological Psychology *from 1951 to 1963, Harlow is the recipient of the Distinguished Psychologist Award and the National Medal of Science.*

1. How does a measure of "learning set" differ from a measure of "habit"?

2. How does Harlow account for the nature of insight and hypothesis making?

3. Does the percentage increase of correct responses from trail to trail observed here as "learning how to learn" tell us anything about the process of human socialization?

The variety of learning situations that play an important rôle in determining our basic personality characteristics and in changing some of us into thinking animals are repeated many times in similar form. The behavior of the human being is not to be understood in terms of the results of single learning situations but rather in terms of the changes which are affected through multiple, though comparable, learning problems. Our emotional, personal, and intellectual characteristics are not the mere algebraic summation of a near infinity of stimulus-response bonds. The learning of primary importance to the primates, at least, is the formation of learning sets; it is the *learning how to learn efficiently* in the situations the animal frequently encounters. This learning to learn

Abridged from Harry F. Harlow, "The Formation of Learning Sets," *Psychological Review,* 56 (1949), 51–56, 58–59, 63–65. Copyright 1949 by the American Psychological Association and reproduced by permission.

transforms the organism from a creature that adapts to a changing environment by trial and error to one that adapts by seeming hypothesis and insight.

The rat psychologists have largely ignored this fundamental aspect of learning and, as a result, this theoretical domain remains a *terra incognita.* If learning sets are the mechanisms which, in part, transform the organism from a conditioned response robot to a reasonably rational creature, it may be thought that the mechanisms are too intangible for proper quantification. Any such presupposition is false. It is the purpose of this paper to demonstrate the extremely orderly and quantifiable nature of the development of certain learning sets and, more broadly, to indicate the importance of learning sets to the development of intellectual organization and personality structure.

The apparatus used throughout the studies subsequently referred to is illustrated in Fig. 1. The monkey responds by displacing one of two stimulus-objects covering the food-wells in the tray before him. An opaque screen is interposed between the monkey and the stimulus situation between trials and a one-way vision screen separates monkey and man during trials.

The first problem chosen for the investigation of learning sets was the object-quality discrimination learning problem. The monkey

238

was required to choose the rewarded one of two objects differing in multiple characteristics and shifting in the left-right positions in a predetermined balanced order. A series of 344 such problems using 344 different pairs of stimuli was run on a group of eight monkeys. Each of the first 32 problems was run for 50 trials; the next 200 problems for six trials; and the last 112 problems for an average of nine trials.

In Fig. 2 are presented learning curves which show the per cent of correct responses on the first six trials of these discriminations. The data for the first 32 discriminations are grouped for blocks of eight problems, and the remaining discriminations are arranged in blocks of 100, 100, 56, and 56 problems. The data indicate that the subjects progressively improve in their ability to learn object-quality discrimination problems. The monkeys *learn how to learn* individual problems with a minimum of errors. It is this *learning how to learn a kind of problem* that we designate by the term *learning set.*

The very form of the learning curve changes as learning sets become more efficient. The form of the learning curve for the first eight discrimination problems appears S-shaped: it could be described as a curve of "trial-and-error" learning. The curve for the last 56 problems approaches linearity after Trial 2. Curves of similar form have been described as indicators of "insightful" learning.

We wish to emphasize that this *learning to learn,* this *transfer from problem to problem* which we call the formation of a learning set, is a highly *predictable, orderly* process which can be demonstrated as long as controls are maintained over the subjects' experience and the difficulty of the problems. Our subjects, when they started these researches, had no previous laboratory learning experience. Their entire discrimination learning set history was obtained in this study. The stimulus pairs employed had been arranged and their serial order determined from tables of random numbers. Like nonsense syllables, the stimulus pairs were equated for difficulty. It is unlikely that any group of problems differed significantly in intrinsic difficulty from any other group.

In a conventional learning curve we plot change of performance over a series of *trials;* in a learning set curve we plot change in performance over a series of *problems.* It is important to remember that *we measure learning set in terms of problems* just as *we measure habit in terms of trials.*

Figure 3 presents a discrimination learning set curve showing progressive increase in the per cent of correct responses on Trials 2–6 on successive blocks of problems. This curve appears to be negatively accelerated or possibly linear.

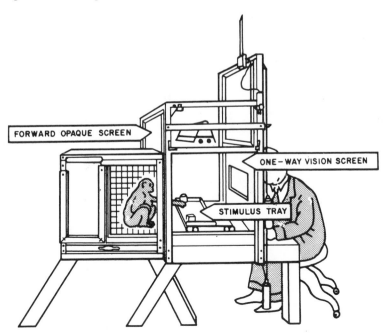

FORWARD OPAQUE SCREEN

ONE-WAY VISION SCREEN

STIMULUS TRAY

FIGURE 1. *Wisconsin general test apparatus.*

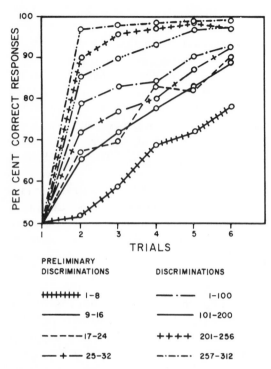

FIGURE 2. *Discrimination learning curves on successive blocks of problems.*

Discrimination learning set curves obtained on four additional naive normal monkeys and eight naive monkeys with extensive unilateral cortical lesions, are shown in Fig. 4. Brain-injured as well as normal monkeys are seen to form effective discrimination learning sets, al-

though the partial hemidecorticate monkeys are less efficient than the normal subjects. Improvement for both groups is progressive and the fluctuations that occur may be attributed to the small number of subjects and the relatively small number of problems, 14, included in each of the problem blocks presented on the abscissa.

Through the courtesy of Dr. Margaret Kuenne we have discrimination learning set data on another primate species. These animals were also run on a series of six-trial discrimination problems but under slightly different conditions. Macaroni beads and toys were substituted for food rewards, and the subjects were tested sans iron-barred cages. The data for these 17 children, whose ages range from two to five years and whose intelligence quotients range from 109 to 151, are presented in Fig. 5. Learning set curves are plotted for groups of children attaining a predetermined learning criterion within differing numbers of problem blocks. In spite of the small number of cases and the behavioral vagaries that are known to characterize this primate species, the learning set curves are orderly and lawful and show progressive increase in per cent of correct responses.

Learning set curves, like learning curves, can be plotted in terms of correct responses or errors, in terms of responses on any trial or total trials. A measure which we have fre-

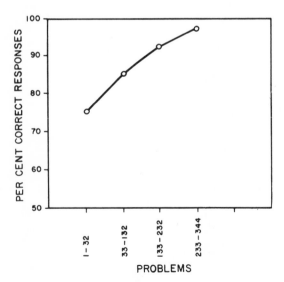

FIGURE 3. *Discrimination learning set curve based on Trial 2–6 responses.*

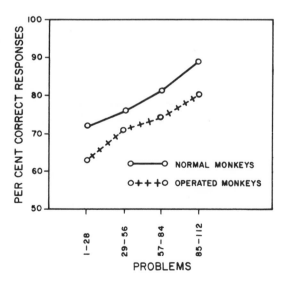

FIGURE 4. *Discrimination learning set curves based on Trial 2–6 responses: normal and operated monkeys.*

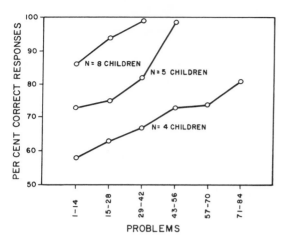

FIGURE 5. *Discrimination learning set curves based on Trial 2–6 responses: children.*

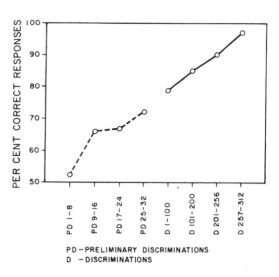

PD — PRELIMINARY DISCRIMINATIONS
D — DISCRIMINATIONS

FIGURE 6. *Discrimination learning set curve based on Trial 2 responses.*

quently used is per cent of correct Trial 2 responses—the behavioral measure of the amount learned on Trial 1.

Figure 6 shows learning set curves measured in terms of the per cent correct Trial 2 responses for the 344-problem series. The data from the first 32 preliminary discriminations and the 312 subsequent discriminations have been plotted separately. As one might expect, these learning set curves are similar to those that have been previously presented. What the curves show with especial clarity is the almost unbelievable change which has taken place in the *effectiveness of the first training trial.* In the initial eight discriminations, this single paired stimulus presentation brings the Trial 2 performance of the monkeys to a level less than three per cent above chance; in the last 56 discriminations, this first training trial brings the performance of the monkeys to a level *less than three per cent* short of perfection. Before the formation of a discrimination learning set, a single training trial produces negligible gain; after the formation of a discrimination learning set, *a single training trial constitutes problem solution.* These data clearly show that *animals can gradually learn insight.*

In the final phase of our discrimination series with monkeys there were subjects that solved from 20 to 30 consecutive problems with no errors whatsoever following the first blind trial,—and many of the children, after the first day or two of training, did as well or better.

These data indicate the function of learning set in converting a problem which is initially difficult for a subject into a problem which is so simple as to be immediately solvable. The learning set is the mechanism that changes the problem from an intellectual tribulation into an intellectual triviality and leaves the organism free to attack problems of another hierarchy of difficulty.

For the analysis of learning sets in monkeys on a problem that is ostensibly at a more complex level than the discrimination problem, we chose the discrimination reversal problem. The procedure was to run the monkeys on a discrimination problem for 7, 9, or 11 trials and then to reverse the reward value of the stimuli for eight trials; that is to say, the stimulus previously correct was made incorrect and the stimulus previously incorrect became correct.

Although the discrimination reversal problems might be expected to be more difficult for the monkeys than discrimination problems, the data of Fig. 7 indicate that the discrimination reversal learning set was formed more rapidly than the previously acquired discrimination learning set. The explanation probably lies in the nature of the transfer of training from the discrimination learning to the discrimination reversal problems. A detailed analysis of the discrimination learning data indicates the operation throughout the learning series of certain error-producing factors, but with each successive block of problems the frequencies of errors

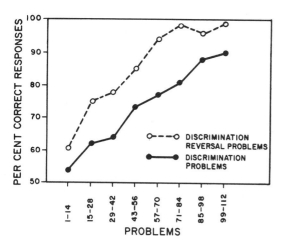

FIGURE 7. *Discrimination reversal and discrimination learning set curves based on Trial 2 responses.*

attributable to these factors are progressively decreased, although at different rates and to different degrees. The process might be conceived of as a learning of response tendencies that counteract the error-producing factors. A description of the reduction of the error-producing factors is beyond the scope of this paper, even though we are of the opinion that this type of analysis is basic to an adequate theory of discrimination learning.

Suffice it to say that there is reason to believe that there is a large degree of transfer from the discrimination series to the reversal series, of the learned response tendencies counteracting the operation of two of the three primary error-producing factors thus far identified.

The combined discrimination and discrimination reversal data show clearly how the learning set delivers the animal from Thorndikian bondage. By the time the monkey has run 232 discriminations and followed these by 112 discriminations and reversals, he does not possess 344 or 456 specific habits, bonds, connections or associations. We doubt if our monkeys at this time could respond with much more than chance efficiency on the first trial of any series of the previously learned problems. But the monkey does have a generalized ability to learn *any* discrimination problem or *any* discrimination reversal problem with the greatest of ease. Training on several hundred specific problems has not turned the monkey into an automaton exhibiting forced, stereotyped, reflex responses

to specific stimuli. These several hundred habits have, instead, made the monkey an adjustable creature with an *increased capacity* to adapt to the everchanging demands of a psychology laboratory environment.

Although our objective data are limited to the formation of learning sets which operate to give efficient performance on intellectual problems, we have observational data of a qualitative nature on social-emotional changes in our animals. When the monkeys come to us they are wild and intractable but within a few years they have acquired, from the experimenter's point of view, good personalities. Actually we believe that one of the very important factors in the development of the good personalities of our monkeys is the formation of social-emotional learning sets organized in a manner comparable with the intellectual learning sets we have previously described. Each contact the monkey has with a human being represents a single specific learning trial. Each person represents a separate problem. Learning to react favorably to one person is followed by learning favorable reactions more rapidly to the next person to whom the monkey is socially introduced. Experience with additional individuals enables the monkey to learn further how to behave with human beings, and eventually the monkey's favorable reactions to new people are acquired so rapidly as to appear almost instantaneous.

The formation of social-emotional learning sets is not to be confused with mere stimulus generalization, a construct applied in this field with undue freedom. Actually a learning set once formed determines in large part the nature and direction of stimulus generalization. In the classic study in which Watson conditioned fear in Albert, the child developed a fear of the rat and generalized this fear, but failed to develop or generalize fear to Watson, even though Watson must have been the more conspicuous stimulus. Apparently Albert had already formed an affectional social-emotional learning set to people, which inhibited both learning and simple Pavlovian generalization.

Our observations on the formation of social-emotional learning sets have been entirely qualitative and informal, but there would appear to be no reason why they could not be studied experimentally.

The emphasis throughout this paper has been

on the rôle of the historical or experience variable in learning behavior—the forgotten variable in current learning theory and research. Hull's Neo-behaviorists have constantly emphasized the necessity for an historical approach to learning, yet they have not exploited it fully. Their experimental manipulation of the experience variable has been largely limited to the development of isolated habits and their generalization. Their failure to find the phenomenon of discontinuity in learning may stem from their study of individual as opposed to repetitive learning situations.

The field theorists, unlike the Neo-behaviorists, have stressed insight and hypothesis in their description of learning. The impression these theorists give is that the phenomena are properties of the innate organization of the individual. If such phenomena appear independently of a gradual learning history, we have not found them in the primate order.

Psychologists working with human subjects have long believed in the phenomenon of learning sets and have even used sets as explanatory principles to account for perceptual selection and incidental learning. These psychologists have not, however, investigated the nature of these learning sets which their subjects bring to the experimental situation. The determining experiential variables of these learning sets lie buried in the subjects' pasts, but the development of such sets can be studied in the laboratory as long as the human race continues to reproduce its kind. Actually, detailed knowledge of the nature of the formation of learning sets could be of such importance to educational theory and practice as to justify prolonged and systematic investigation.

In the animal laboratory where the experiential factor can be easily controlled, we have carried out studies that outline the development and operation of specific learning sets. We believe that the construct of learning sets is of importance in the understanding of adaptive behavior. Since this is our faith, it is our hope that our limited data will be extended by those brave souls who study *real* men and *real* women.

Suggested Readings

Brown, R. W. *Words and Things*. Glencoe, Ill.: Free Press, 1958.

Bruner, J. S., J. J. Goodnow, and G. A. Austin. *A Study of Thinking*. New York: Wiley, 1956.

Cook, T. W. "Massed and Distributed Practice in Puzzle Solving," *Psychol. Rev.,* 41 (1934), 330–355.

Hull, C. L. "Quantitative Aspects of the Evolution of Concepts," *Psychol. Monog.* 28 (1920), No. 123.

Johnson, D. M. *The Psychology of Thought and Judgment*. New York: Harper, 1955.

Osgood, C. E. "The Nature and Measurement of Meaning," *Psychol. Bull.,* 49 (1952), 197–327.

Patrick, C. "Creative Thought in Artists," *J. Psychol.,* 4 (1937), 35–73.

Poincaré, H. "Mathematical Creation," in *The Foundations of Science*. New York: Science Press, 1913.

Rokeach, M. *The Open and Closed Mind*. New York: Basic Books, 1960.

9   *Abnormal Behavior and Its Treatment*

If the world were depopulated of all but two individuals and they were marooned together on a desert island, could either of them be called normal or abnormal? No, for normal or abnormal behavior is a statistically and culturally defined concept. If one were to think of normal behavior as signifying the behavior of most people, one could not establish that either of the two survivors is normal or abnormal, since two points of reference do not provide enough information on which to base an interpretation. Even if a larger number of people constituted the society, an interpretation could not be made. One would not know what to look for, because a given behavior or act that is revered in one culture may be condemned in another. Of course, these concepts appear to be simple. However, it is often the simplicity of a concept that makes its explanation difficult.

In like manner, it is easier to describe and catalog undesirable behavior than it is to define the sources and causes of undesirable behavior. Much research and scientific work have been expended in an effort to understand mental illness and to design a cure. Most of this work has been done recently. Greater effort has been made in the field of understanding and treating mentally disturbed individuals since the turn of this century than was made during all the previous history of mankind.

The selections in this chapter are quite varied in content, and each focuses on a somewhat different aspect of abnormal behavior and its treatment. It is advisable, therefore, to keep in mind the comments made above concerning normal and abnormal behavior.

What Is a Neurosis? John Dollard and Neal E. Miller. Since few of us are psychotic but many of us are neurotic, let us begin with an article on neurosis. Dollard and Miller define some of the major dimensions of neurosis and present a case study to demonstrate these dimensions. Although a neurotic is usually able to provide for himself and is somehow able to get along in life, he is generally miserable, worried, anxious, and quite uncertain about the reasons for his behavior.

The Effect of Dream Deprivation, William Dement. This selection raises a basic question: How necessary is dreaming to the ongoing life function? The evidence he has compiled indicates that dreaming serves a purpose and is a phenomenon over which an individual most likely has little control. It is therefore sometimes necessary, when treating a patient, to look at his dream life, for dreams often reveal clues to painful or deeply personal information that a patient may not openly express.

The Locomotive God, William E. Leonard. Also of interest to the psychologist in explaining abnormal behavior is the dramatic, often traumatic, impact of an early-childhood experience. This selection is an autobiographical description of a childhood experience. While he was waiting for a train to pull into a station, he lived through an experience that changed the course of his life. The fear he encountered persisted into his adult life, shaped his everyday behavior, and forced him to retreat into a protective shell of existence.

A Case of Multiple Personality, Corbett H. Thigpen and Hervey Cleckley. One of the more unusual, less frequently documented, displays of personality structure is that of the multiple personality. Thigpen and Cleckley describe the multiple roles played by a patient who came to them for treatment of severe and blinding headaches. This study demonstrates how conventional theories of personality and modes of treatment inadequately account for the several distinct personalities housed in a single human body. This particular case received wide publicity, was published in book form, and provided the plot for a motion picture.

Reports of Lysergic Acid Experiences, Sidney Cohen, Lionel Fichman, and Betty G. Eisner. For a number of years scientific interest has focused on the psychological effects of such drugs as lysergic acid diethylamide (LSD-25), mescaline, and psilocybin. Cohen, Fichman, and Eisner describe some carefully observed reactions to the effects of the LSD drug. In this study volunteer subjects experienced a variety of bizarre and peculiar effects. Visual tricks were played on them, and they were observed to exhibit, in some cases, behaviors similar to those of a psychotic patient. Of particular interest are their responses to psychological test questions during the period they were under the control of LSD.

Therapeutic Personality Change, Carl R. Rogers. This selection is included to give the reader an insight into the important conditions most psychotherapists and counselors agree must prevail before personality change can occur. Rogers has developed a system of treatment and theory of personality based on the principles he describes in this selection. It should be recognized, however, that other schools of thought, based on different concepts of the nature of man, deny the adequacy of Rogers' system of treatment and theory of personality. Nevertheless, Rogers' approach is clearly stated and provides an adequate framework for gaining an understanding of the conditions that foster personality change.

What Is a Neurosis?

John Dollard and Neal E. Miller

John Dollard has been Professor of Psychology at Yale University since 1952. He received his Ph.D. from the University of Chicago in 1931. Of special interest to Dollard are the relationships between personality and learning concepts and their possible significance for psychotherapy. Neal Miller, past president of the American Psychological Association, is Professor of Psychology at Rockefeller University in New York City. He received his Ph.D. from Yale in 1935. Miller is interested in learning, motivation, and conflict and their physiological mechanisms.

1. *Why do you think the neurotic is unable to understand and change his condition?*

2. *Of what value is it for a patient to verbalize his resentment to a therapist?*

3. *What organizing principle helps explain why Mrs. A felt better when counting her heartbeats?*

Most people, even scientists, are vague about neurosis. Neither the neurotic victim nor those who know him seem able to state precisely what is involved. The victim feels a mysterious malady. The witness observes inexplicable behavior. The neurotic is mysterious because he is *capable* of acting and yet he is *unable* to act and enjoy. Though physically capable of attaining sex rewards, he is anesthetic; though capable of aggression, he is meek; though capable of affection, he is cold and unresponsive. As seen by the outside witness, the neurotic does not make use of the obvious opportunities for satisfaction which life offers him.

From J. Dollard and N. E. Miller, Chapter Two, *Personality and Psychotherapy* (New York: McGraw-Hill Book Co., Inc., 1950), pp. 12–22. Reprinted by permission of the publisher.

To Be Explained: Misery, Stupidity, Symptoms

The therapist confronts a person who is miserable, stupid (in some ways), and who has symptoms. These are the three major factors to be accounted for. Why is he miserable, in what curious way is he stupid, and whence arise the symptoms? The waiting room of every psychiatric clinic is crowded with patients showing these common signs.

Neurotic Misery Is Real

Neurotic misery is real—not imaginary. Observers, not understanding the neurotic conflict, often belittle the suffering of neurotics and confuse neurosis with malingering. Neurotic habits are forced upon an individual by peculiar conditions of life and are not cheap attempts to escape duty and responsibility. In most cases the misery is attested by many specific complaints. These complaints or symptoms differ with each category of neurosis but sleeplessness, restlessness, irritability, sexual inhibitions, distaste for life, lack of clear personal goals, phobias, headaches, and irrational fears are among the more common ones.

At times the depth of the misery of the

neurotic is concealed by his symptoms. Only when they are withdrawn does his true anguish appear. Occasionally the misery will be private, not easily visible to outside observers because friends and relatives are ringed around the neurotic person and prevent observation of his pain. In still other cases, the neurotic person is miserable but apathetic. He has lost even the hope that complaining and attracting attention will be helpful. However this may be, *if the neurotic takes the usual risks of life* he is miserable. He suffers if he attempts to love, marry, and be a parent. He fails if he tries to work responsibly and independently. His social relations tend to be invaded by peculiar demands and conditions. Neurotic misery is thus often masked by the protective conditions of life (as in childhood) and appears only when the individual has to "go it on his own."

Conflict produces misery. Suffering so intense as that shown by neurotics must have powerful causes, and it does. The neurotic is miserable because he is in conflict. As a usual thing two or more strong drives are operating in him and producing incompatible responses. Strongly driven to approach and as strongly to flee, he is not able to act to reduce either of the conflicting drives. These drives therefore remain dammed up, active, and nagging.

Where such a drive conflict is conscious there is no problem in convincing anyone why it should produce misery. If we picture a very hungry man confronting food which he knows to be poisoned, we can understand that he is driven on the one hand by hunger and on the other by fear. He oscillates at some distance from the tempting food, fearing to grasp but unable to leave. Everyone understands immediately the turmoil produced by such a conflict of hunger and fear.

Many people remember from their adolescence the tension of a strong sex conflict. Primary sex responses heightened by imaginative elaboration are met by intense fear. Though usually not allowed to talk about such matters, children sometimes can, and the misery they reveal is one of the most serious prices exacted of adolescents in our culture. That this conflict is acquired and not innate was shown by Margaret Mead in her brilliant book, "Coming of Age in Samoa" (1928). It is also agonizingly depicted in a novel by Vardis Fisher (1932).

Our third example of conscious conflict shows anger pitted against fear. In the early part of the war, an officer, newly commissioned from civilian life and without the habits of the professional soldier, was sent to an Army post. There he met a superior officer who decided to make an example of some minor mistake. The ranking officer lectured and berated the subordinate, refusing to let him speak and explain his behavior. He made him stand at attention against the wall for half an hour while this lecture was going on. The new-made officer quaked in fearful conflict. He detected the sadistic satisfaction which his superior got in dressing him down. He had never so much wanted to kill anyone. On the other hand, the junior officer felt the strong pressure of his own conscience to be a competent soldier and some real fear about what the consequence of assault might be. We met him shortly after this episode, and he still shook with rage when he described the experience. There was no doubt in his mind but that bearing strong, conflicting drives is one of the most severe causes of misery.

Repression Causes Stupidity

In each of the above cases, however, the individual could eventually solve his conflict. The hungry man could find nourishing food; the sex-tortured adolescent could eventually marry; the new officer could and did avoid his punishing superior.

With the neurotic this is not the case. He is not able to solve his conflict even with the passage of time. Though obviously intelligent in some ways, he is stupid in-so-far as his neurotic conflict is concerned. This stupidity is not an over-all affair, however. It is really a stupid area in the mind of a person who is quite intelligent in other respects. For some reason he cannot use his head on his neurotic conflicts.

Though the neurotic is sure he is miserable and is vocal about his symptoms, he is vague about what it is within him that could produce such painful effects. The fact that the neurotic cannot describe his own conflicts has been the source of great confusion in dealing with him either in terms of scientific theory or in terms of clinical practice. Nor can the therapist immediately spot these areas of stupidity. Only after extensive study of the patient's life can the areas of repression be clearly identified. Then the surprising fact emerges that the competing drives which afflict the neurotic person are not labeled. He has no language to describe the conflicting forces within him.

Without language and adequate labeling the higher mental processes cannot function. When these processes are knocked out by repression, the person cannot guide himself by mental means to a resolution of his conflict. Since the neurotic cannot help himself, he must have the help of others if he is to be helped at all—though millions today live out their lives in strong neurotic pain and never get help. The neurotic, therefore, is, or appears to be, stupid because he is unable to use his mind in dealing with certain of his problems. He feels that someone should help him, but he does not know how to ask for help since he does not know what his problem is. He may feel aggrieved that he is suffering, but he cannot explain his case.

Symptoms Slightly Reduce Conflict

Although in many ways superficial, the symptoms of the neurotic are the most obvious aspects of his problems. These are what the patient is familiar with and feels he should be rid of. The phobias, inhibitions, avoidances, compulsions, rationalizations, and psychosomatic symptoms of the neurotic are experienced as a nuisance by him and by all who have to deal with him. The symptoms cannot be integrated into the texture of sensible social relations. The patient, however, believes that the symptoms *are* his disorder. It is these he wishes to be rid of and, not knowing that a serious conflict underlies them, he would like to confine the therapeutic discussion to getting rid of the symptoms.

The symptoms do not solve the basic conflict in which the neurotic person is plunged, but they mitigate it. They are responses which tend to reduce the conflict, and in part they succeed. When a successful symptom occurs it is reinforced because it reduces neurotic misery. The symptom is thus learned as a habit. One very common function of symptoms is to keep the neurotic person away from those stim-

uli which would activate and intensify his neurotic conflict. Thus, the combat pilot with a harrowing military disaster behind him may "walk away" from the sight of any airplane. As he walks toward the plane his anxiety goes up; as he walks away it goes down. "Walking away" is thus reinforced. It is this phobic walking away which constitutes his symptom. If the whole situation is not understood, such behavior seems bizarre to the casual witness.

Conflict, Repression, and Symptoms Closely Related

In the foregoing discussion we have "taken apart" the most conspicuous factors which define the neurosis and have separately discussed conflict, stupidity, and misery. We hope that the discussion has clarified the problem even at the expense of slightly distorting the actual relationships. In every human case of neurosis the three basic factors are closely and dynamically interrelated. The conflict could not be unconscious and insoluble were it not for the repressive factors involved. The symptoms could not exist did they not somewhat relieve the pressure of conflict. The mental paralysis of repression has been created by the very same forces which originally imposed the emotional conflict on the neurotic person.

The Case of Mrs. A [1]

We are presenting the facts about Mrs. A for two reasons: (1) as background material on a case from which we will draw many concrete examples throughout the book; (2) as a set of facts from which we can illustrate the relationships between misery and conflict, stupidity and repression, symptoms and reinforcement. The reader will understand, of course, that the sole function of this case material is to give a clear exposition of principles by means of concrete illustrations; it is *not* presented as evidence or proof.

The Facts

Mrs. A was an unusually pretty twenty-three-year-old married woman. Her husband

[1] We are allowed to present and analyze the material on Mrs. A through the kindness of a New York colleague, a man so remarkable as to provide this laboriously gathered material and yet be willing to remain anonymous to aid in the complete disguise of the case.

worked in the offices of an insurance company. When she came to the therapist she was exceedingly upset. She had a number of fears. One of the strongest of these was that her heart would stop beating if she did not concentrate on counting the beats.

The therapist, who saw Mrs. A twice a week over a three-month period, took careful notes. The life-history data that we present were pieced together from the patient's statements during a total of 26 hours. The scope of the material is necessarily limited by the brevity of the treatment. The treatment had to end when a change in the husband's work forced her to move to another city.

Her first neurotic symptoms had appeared five months before she came to the psychiatrist. While she was chopping in a New York store, she felt faint and became afraid that something would happen to her and "no one would know where I was." She telephoned her husband's office and asked him to come and get her. Thereafter she was afraid to go out alone. Shortly after this time, she talked with an aunt who had a neurotic fear of heart trouble. After a conversation with this aunt, Mrs. A's fears changed from a fear of fainting to a concern about her heart.

Mrs. A was an orphan, born of unknown parents in a city in the upper South. She spent the first few months of life in an orphanage, then was placed in a foster home, where she lived, except for a year when she was doing war work in Washington, until her marriage at the age of twenty.

The foster parents belonged to the working class, had three children of their own, two girls and a boy, all of them older than the patient. The foster mother, who dominated the family, was cruel, strict, and miserly toward all the children. She had a coarse and vulgar demeanor, swore continually, and punished the foster child for the least offense. Mrs. A recalls: "She whipped me all the time—whether I'd done anything or not."

The foster mother had imposed a very repressive sex training on the patient, making her feel that sex was dirty and wrong. Moreover, the foster mother never let the patient think independently. She discouraged the patient's striving for an education, taking her out of school at sixteen when the family could have afforded to let her go on.

Despite the repressive sex training she received, Mrs. A had developed strong sexual appetites. In early childhood she had overheard parental intercourse, had masturbated, and had witnessed animal copulation. When she was ten or twelve, her foster brother seduced her. During the years before her marriage a dozen men tried to seduce her and most of them succeeded.

Nevertheless, sex was to her a dirty, loathesome thing that was painful for her to discuss or think about. She found sexual relations with her husband disgusting and was morbidly shy in her relations with him.

The patient had met her husband-to-be while she was working as a typist in Washington during the war. He was an Army officer and a college graduate. Her beauty enabled the patient to make a marriage that improved her social position; her husband's family were middle-class people. At the time of treatment Mrs. A had not yet learned all the habits of middle-class life. She was still somewhat awkward about entertaining or being entertained and made glaring errors in grammar and pronunciation. She was dominated, socially subordinated, and partly rejected by her husband's family.

When they were first married, Mr. and Mrs. A lived with his parents in a small town north of New York City and commuted to the city for work. Mrs. A had an office job there. Later, they were able to get an apartment in New York, but they stayed with the in-laws every week end. Although she described her mother-in-law in glowing terms at the beginning of the treatment, Mrs. A later came to express considerable hostility toward her.

When she came to the psychiatrist, Mrs. A was in great distress. She had to pay continual attention to her heart lest it stop beating. She lived under a burden of vague anxiety and had a number of specific phobias that prevented her from enjoying many of the normal pleasures of her life, such as going to the movies. She felt helpless to cope with her problems. Her constant complaints had tired out and alienated her friends. Her husband was fed up with her troubles and had threatened to divorce her. She could not get along with her foster mother and her mother-in-law had rejected her. She had no one left to talk to. She was hurt, baffled, and terrified by the thought that she might be going crazy.

Analysis in Terms of Conflict, Repression, Reinforcement

We have described Mrs. A as of the moment when she came to treatment. The analysis of the case, however, presents the facts as they were afterward ordered and clarified by study.

Misery. Mrs. A's misery was obvious to her family, her therapist, and herself. She suffered from a strong, vague, unremitting fear. She was tantalized by a mysterious temptation. The phobic limitations on her life prevented her from having much ordinary fun, as by shopping or going to the movies. Her husband and mother-in-law criticized her painfully. She feared that her husband would carry out his threat and divorce her. She feared that her heart would stop. She feared to be left all alone, sick and rejected. Her friends and relatives pitied her at first, then became put out with her when her condition persisted despite well-meant advice. Her misery, though baffling, was recognized as entirely real.

Conflict. Mrs. A suffered from two conflicts which produced her misery. The first might be described as a sex-fear conflict. Thanks to childhood circumstances she had developed strong sex appetites. At the same time strong anxieties were created in her and attached to the cues produced by sex excitement. However, she saw no connection between these remembered circumstances and the miserable life she was leading. The connective thoughts had been knocked out and the conflict was thus unconscious. The presence of the sexual appetites showed up in a kind of driven behavior in which she seemed to court seduction. Her fear was exhibited in her revulsion from sexual acts and thoughts and in her inability to take responsibility for a reasonable sexual expressiveness with her husband. The conflict was greatly intensified after her marriage because of her wish to be a dutiful wife. Guilt about the prospect of adultery was added to fear about sex motives.

Mrs. A was involved in a second, though less severe, conflict between aggression and fear. She was a gentle person who had been very badly treated by her mother-in-law. Resentful tendencies arose in her but they were quickly inhibited by fear. She attempted to escape the anger-fear conflict by exceptionally submissive behavior, putting up meekly with slights and subordination and protesting her fondness for the mother-in-law. She was tormented by it nevertheless, especially by feelings of worthlessness and helplessness. She felt much better, late in therapy, when she was able to state her resentment and begin to put it into effect in a measured way. (After all, she had the husband and his love, and if the mother-in-law wanted to see her son and prospective grandchildren she would have to take a decent attitude toward Mrs. A.)

Stupidity. Mrs. A's mind was certainly of little use to her in solving her problem. She tried the usual medical help with no result. She took a trip, as advised, and got no help. Her symptoms waxed and waned in unpredictable ways. She knew that she was helpless. At the time she came for therapy she had no plans for dealing with her problem and no hope of solving it. In addition to being unable to deal with her basic problems, Mrs. A did many things that were quite unintelligent and maladaptive. For example, in spite of the fact that she wanted very much to make a success of her marriage and was consciously trying to live a proper married life, she frequently exposed herself to danger of seduction. She went out on drinking parties with single girls. She hitchhiked rides with truck drivers. She was completely unaware of the motivation for this behavior and often unable to foresee its consequences until it was too late. While her behavior seems stupid in the light of a knowledge of the actual state of affairs, there were many ways in which Mrs. A did not seem at all stupid—for example, when debating with the therapist to protect herself against fear-producing thoughts. She then gave hopeful evidence of what she could do with her mind when she had available all the necessary units to think with.

Repression. Mrs. A gave abundant evidence of the laming effects of repression. At the outset she thought she had no sex feelings or appetites. She described behavior obviously motivated by fear but could not label the fear itself. The closest she came was to express the idea that she was going insane. Further, Mrs. A thought she had an organic disease and clung desperately to this idea, inviting any kind of treatment so long as it did not force her to think about matters which would produce fear. Such mental gaps and distortions are a characteristic result of repression. They are what produce the stupidity.

Symptoms. Mrs. A's chief symptoms were the spreading phobia which drove her out of theaters and stores and the compulsive counting of breaths and heartbeats. These symptoms almost incapacitated her. She had lost her freedom to think and to move.

Reinforcement of symptoms. An analysis of the phobia revealed the following events. When on the streets alone, her fear of sex temptation was increased. Someone might speak to her, wink at her, make an approach to her. Such an approach would increase her sex desire and make her more vulnerable to seduction. Increased sex desire, however, touched off both anxiety and guilt, and this intensified her conflict when she was on the street. When she "escaped home," the temptation stimuli were lessened, along with a reduction of the fear which they elicited. Going home and, later, avoiding the temptation situation by anticipation were reinforced. Naturally, the basic sex-anxiety conflict was not resolved by the defensive measure of the symptom. The conflict persisted but was not so keen.

The counting of heartbeats can be analytically taken apart in a similar way. When sexy thoughts came to mind or other sex stimuli tended to occur, these stimuli elicited anxiety. It is clear that these stimuli were occurring frequently because Mrs. A was responding with anxiety much of the time. Since counting is a highly preoccupying kind of response, no other thoughts could enter her mind during this time. While counting, the sexy thoughts which excited fear dropped out. Mrs. A "felt better" immediately when she started counting, and the counting habit was reinforced by the drop in anxiety. Occasionally, Mrs. A would forget to count and then her intense anxiety would recur. In this case, as in that of the phobia, the counting symptom does not resolve the basic conflict—it only avoids exacerbating it.

Thus Mrs. A's case illustrates the analysis of neurotic mechanisms made in the earlier part of the chapter. Conflict produced high drives experienced as misery; repression interfered with higher mental processes and so with the intelligent solution of the conflict; the symptoms were learned responses which were reinforced by producing some reduction in the strength of drive.

The Effect of Dream Deprivation

William Dement

William Dement is Associate Professor of Psychiatry at the Stanford University School of Medicine. He received his M.D. and Ph.D. degrees from the University of Chicago. Dement is currently engaged in dream research, particularly on the effects of dream deprivation in animals and humans.

1. *If a friend mentions to you that he didn't dream at all last night, would you believe him?*

2. *How did the experimenter determine that a subject had begun to dream?*

3. *Assuming that dreaming is a "necessity of life," what are your hunches as to why this is so? Could you design an experiment to support your theory?*

About a year ago, a research program was initiated at the Mount Sinai Hospital which aimed at assessing the basic function and significance of dreaming. The experiments have been arduous and time-consuming and are still in progress. However, the results of the first series have been quite uniform, and because of the length of the program, it has been decided to issue this preliminary report.

In recent years, a body of evidence has accumulated which demonstrates that dreaming occurs in association with periods of rapid, binocularly synchronous eye movements. Furthermore, the amount and directional patterning of these eye movements and the associated dream *content* are related in such a way as to

From W. Dement, "The Effect of Dream Deprivation," *Science*, 131, No. 3415 (June 10, 1960), 1705–1707. Reprinted by permission of author and publisher.

strongly suggest that the eye movements represent scanning movements made by the dreamer as he watches the events of the dream. In a study of undisturbed sleep, the eye-movement periods were observed to occur regularly throughout the night in association with the lightest phases of a cyclic variation in depth of sleep, as measured by the electroencephalograph. The length of individual cycles averaged about 90 minutes, and the mean duration of single periods of eye movement was about 20 minutes. Thus, a typical night's sleep includes four or five periods of dreaming, which account for about 20 percent of the total sleep time.

One of the most striking facts apparent in all the works cited above was that a very much greater amount of dreaming occurs normally than had heretofore been realized—greater both from the standpoint of frequency and duration in a single night of sleep and in the invariability of its occurrence from night to night. In other words, dreaming appears to be an intrinsic part of normal sleep and, as such, although the dreams are not usually recalled, occurs every night in every sleeping person.

A consideration of this aspect of dreaming leads more or less inevitably to the formulation of certain rather fundamental questions. Since there appear to be no exceptions to the nightly occurrence of a substantial amount of dreaming in every sleeping person, it might be asked whether or not this amount of dreaming is in some way a necessary and vital part of our existence. Would it be possible for human beings to continue functioning normally if their dream life were completely or partially suppressed? Should dreaming be considered necessary in a psychological sense or a physiological sense or both?

The obvious attack on these problems was to study subjects who had somehow been deprived of the opportunity to dream. After a few unsuccessful preliminary trials with depressant drugs, it was decided to use the somewhat drastic method of awakening sleeping subjects immediately after the onset of dreaming and to continue this procedure throughout the night, so that each dream period would be artificially terminated right at its beginning.

Subjects and Method

The data in this article are from the first eight subjects in the research program, all males, ranging in age from 23 to 32. Eye movements and accompanying low-voltage, nonspindling electroencephalographic patterns were used as the objective criteria of dreaming. The technique by which these variables are recorded, and their precise relationship to dreaming, have been extensively discussed elsewhere. Briefly, the subjects came to the laboratory at about their usual bedtime. Small silver-disk electrodes were carefully attached near their eyes and on their scalps; then the subjects went to sleep in a quiet, dark room in the laboratory. Lead wires ran from the electrodes to apparatus in an adjacent room upon which the electrical potentials of eye movements and brain waves were recorded continuously throughout the night.

Eye movements and brain waves of each subject were recorded throughout a series of undisturbed nights of sleep, to evaluate his base-line total nightly dream time and over-all sleep pattern. After this, recordings were made throughout a number of nights in which the subject was awakened by the experimenter every time the eye-movement and electroencephalographic recordings indicated that he had begun to dream. These "dream-deprivation" nights were always consecutive. Furthermore, the subjects were requested not to sleep at any other time. Obviously, if subjects were allowed to nap, or to sleep at home on any night in the dream-deprivation period, an unknown amount of dreaming would take place, offsetting the effects of the deprivation. On the first night immediately after the period of dream deprivation, and for several consecutive nights thereafter, the subject was allowed to sleep without disturbance. These nights were designated "recovery nights." The subject then had a varying number of nights off, after which he returned for another series of interrupted nights which exactly duplicated the dream-deprivation series in number of nights and number of awakenings per night. The only difference was that the subject was awakened in the intervals between eye-movement (dream) periods. Whenever a dream period began, the subject was allowed to sleep on without interruption, and was awakened only after the dream had ended spontaneously. Next, the subject had a number of recovery nights of undisturbed sleep equal to the number of recovery nights in his original dream-deprivation series. Altogether, as many as 20 to 30 all-night recordings were made for each subject, most of them on consecutive nights. Since, for the most part, tests could be made on only one subject at a time, and since a minute-by-minute all-night vigil was required of the experimenter to catch each dream episode immediately at its onset, it can be understood why the experiments have been called arduous and time-consuming.

Table 1 summarizes most of the pertinent data. As can be seen, the total number of base-line nights for the eight subjects was 40. The mean sleep time for the 40 nights was 7 hours and 2 minutes, the mean total nightly dream time was 82 minutes, and the mean percentage of dream time (total dream time to total sleep time $\times$ 100) was 19.4. Since total sleep time was not held absolutely constant, percentage figures were routinely calculated as a check on the possibility that differences in total nightly dream time were due to differences in total sleep time. Actually, this is not a plausible explanation for any but quite small differences in dream time, because the range of values for total sleep time for each subject turned out to be very narrow throughout the entire study. When averaged in terms of individuals rather than nights, the means were: total sleep time, 6 hours 50 minutes; total dream time, 80 minutes; percentage of dream time, 19.5; this indicates that the figures were not skewed by the disparate number of base-line nights per subject. The remarkable uniformity of the findings for individual nights is demonstrated by the fact that the standard deviation of the total nightly dream time was only plus or minus 7 minutes.

Progressive Increase in Dream "Attempts"

The number of consecutive nights of dream deprivation arbitrarily selected as a condition of the study was five. However, one subject left the study in a flurry of obviously contrived excuses after only three nights, and two subjects insisted on stopping after four nights but consented to continue with the recovery nights and the remainder of the schedule. One subject was pushed to seven nights. During each awakening the subjects were required to sit up in bed and remain fully awake for several minutes. On the first nights of dream deprivation, the return to sleep generally initiated a new sleep cycle, and the next dream period was postponed for the expected amount of time. However, on subsequent nights the number of forced awakenings required to suppress dreaming steadily mounted. Or, to put it another way, there was a progressive increase in the number of attempts to dream. The number of awakenings required on the first and last nights of deprivation are listed in Table 1. *All* the subjects showed this progressive increase, although there was considerable variation in the starting number and the amount of the increase. An important point is that each awakening was preceded by a minute or two of dreaming. This represented the time required for the experimenter to judge the emerging record and make the decision to awaken the subject after he first noticed the beginning of eye movements. In some cases the time was a little longer, as when an eye-movement period started while the experimenter was looking away from the recording apparatus. It is apparent from this that the method employed did not constitute absolute dream deprivation but, rather, about a 65- to 75-percent deprivation, as it turned out.

Nightly Dream Time Elevated After Deprivation

The data on the first night of the dream deprivation recovery period are summarized for each subject in Table 1. As was mentioned, one subject had quit the study. The mean total dream time on the first recovery night was 112 minutes, or 26.6 percent of the total mean sleep time. If the results for two subjects who did not show marked increases on the first recovery night are excluded, the mean dream time is 127 minutes or 29 percent, which represents a 50-percent increase over the group base-line mean. For all seven subjects together, on the first recovery night the increase in percentage of dream time over the base-line mean (Table 1, col. 3, mean percentage figures; col. 10, first recovery night percentages) was significant at the $p < .05$ level in a one-tail Wilcoxin matched pairs signed-ranks test.

It is important to mention, however, that one (S.M. in Table 1) of the two subjects alluded to above as exceptions was not really an exception because, although he had only 1 hour 1 minute of dreaming on his first recovery night, he showed a marked increase on *four* subsequent nights. His failure to show a rise on the first recovery night was in all likelihood due to the fact that he had inbibed several cocktails at a party before coming to the laboratory so that the expected increase in dream time was offset by the depressing effect of the alcohol. The other one of the two subjects (N.W. in Table 1) failed to show a significant increase in dream time on any of five consecutive recovery nights and therefore must be considered the single exception to the over-all results. Even so, it is hard to reconcile his lack of increase in dream time on recovery nights with the fact that during the actual period of dream deprivation he showed the largest build-up in number of awakenings required to suppress dreaming (11 to 30) of any subject in this group. One may only suggest that, although he was strongly affected by the dream loss, he could not increase his dream time on recovery nights because of an unusually stable basic sleep cycle that resisted modification.

The number of consecutive recovery nights for each subject in this series of tests was too small in some cases, mainly because it was naively supposed at the beginning of the study that an increase in dream time, if it occurred, would last only one or two nights. One subject had only one recovery night, another two, and another three. The dream time was markedly elevated above the base-line on all these nights. For how many additional nights each

TABLE 1. SUMMARY OF EXPERIMENTAL RESULTS. *TST*, TOTAL SLEEP TIME; *TDT*, TOTAL DREAM TIME

MEAN AND RANGE, BASE-LINE NIGHTS			DREAM-DEPRIVATION NIGHTS (No.)	AWAKENINGS (No.)		DREAM-DEPRIVATION RECOVERY NIGHTS — First night				FIRST CONTROL RECOVERY NIGHT		
TST	*TDT*	*Percent*		*First night*	*Last night*	*No.*	*TST*	*TDT*	*Percent*	*TST*	*TDT*	*Percent*
Subject W. T. (4 base-line nights)												
6h36m	1h17m	19.5	5	8	14	1	6h43m	2h17m	34.0	6h50m	1h04m	15.6
6h24m–6h48m	1h10m–1h21m	17.0–21.3										
Subject H. S. (5 base-line nights)												
7h27m	1h24m	18.8	7	7	24	2	8h02m	2h45m	34.2	8h00m	1h49m	22.7
7h07m–7h58m	1h07m–1h38m	15.4–21.8										
Subject N. W. (7 base-line nights)												
6h39m	1h18m	19.5	5	11	30	5	6h46m	1h12m	17.8	7h10m	1h28m	20.2
5h50m–7h10m	1h11m–1h27m	17.4–22.4										
Subject B. M. (6 base-line nights)												
6h59m	1h18m	18.6	5	7	23	5	7h25m	1h58m	26.3	7h48m	1h28m	18.8
6h28m–7h38m	0h58m–1h35m	14.8–22.2										
Subject R. G. (10 base-line nights)												
7h26m	1h26m	19.3	5	10	20	5	7h14m	2h08m	29.5	7h18m	1h55m	26.3
7h00m–7h57m	1h13m–1h46m	16.9–22.7										
Subject W. D. (4 base-line nights)												
6h29m	1h21m	20.8	4	13	20	3	8h53m	2h35m	29.0			
5h38m–7h22m	1h08m–1h32m	17.8–23.4										
Subject S. M. (2 base-line nights)												
6h41m	1h12m	17.9	4	22	30	6	5h08m	1h01m	19.8	6h40m	1h07m	16.8
6h18m–7h04m	1h01m–1h23m	16.2–19.3						6h32m*	1h50m*	28.1*			
Subject W. G. (2 base-line nights)												
6h16m	1h22m	20.8	3	9	13							
6h08m–6h24m	1h17m–1h27m	20.7–20.9										

* Second recovery night (see text).

of these three subjects would have maintained an elevation in dream time can only be surmised in the absence of objective data. All of the remaining four subjects had five consecutive recovery nights. One was the single subject who showed no increase, two were nearing the base-line dream time by the fifth night, and one still showed marked elevation in dream time. From this admittedly incomplete sample it appears that about five nights of increased dreaming usually follow four or five nights of dream suppression achieved by the method of this study.

Effect Not Due to Awakening

Six of the subjects underwent the series of control awakenings—that is, awakenings during non-dream periods. This series exactly duplicated the dream-deprivation series for each subject in number of nights, total number of awakenings, and total number of awakenings per successive night. The dream time on these nights was slightly below base-line levels as a rule. The purpose of this series was, of course, to see if the findings following dream deprivation were solely an effect of the multiple awakenings. Data for the first recovery nights after nights of control awakenings are included in Table 1. There was no significant increase for the group. The mean dream time was 88 minutes, and the mean percentage was 20.1. Subsequent recovery nights in this series also failed to show the marked rise in dream time that was observed after nights of dream deprivation. A moderate increase found on four out of a total of 24 recovery nights for the individuals in the control-awakening group was felt to be a response to the slight reduction in dream time on control-awakening nights.

Behavioral Changes

Psychological disturbances such as anxiety, irritability, and difficulty in concentrating developed during the period of dream deprivation, but these were not catastrophic. One subject, as was mentioned above, quit the study in an apparent panic, and two subjects insisted on stopping one night short of the goal of five nights of dream deprivation, presumably because the stress was too great. At least one subject exhibited serious anxiety and agitation. Five subjects developed a marked increase in appetite during the period of dream deprivation; this observation was supported by daily weight measurements which showed a gain in weight of 3 to 5 pounds in three of the subjects. The psychological changes disappeared as soon as the subjects were allowed to dream. The most important fact was that *none* of the observed changes were seen during the period of control awakenings.

The results have been tentatively interpreted as indicating that a certain amount of dreaming each night is a necessity. It is as though a pressure to dream builds up with the accruing dream deficit during successive dream-deprivation nights—a pressure which is first evident in the increasing frequency of attempts to dream and then, during the recovery period, in the marked increase in total dream time and percentage of dream time. The fact that this increase may be maintained over four or more successive recovery nights suggests that there is a more or less quantitative compensation for the deficit. It is possible that if the dream suppression were carried on long enough, a serious disruption of the personality would result.

The Locomotive God

William E. Leonard

William Leonard (1876–1944) was an author, poet, and Professor of English at the University of Wisconsin. He received his Ph.D. from Columbia University in 1904.

1. This is literary description, not subject to quantification. Of what value is it to the scientifically oriented psychologist?

2. What benefit would have accrued had this little boy been given the opportunity to relate his trauma in greater depth at the time it occurred?

I am standing agape on the platform. But I cannot communicate either the world about me or the world within, exactly as it is to me; for my consciousness is still so largely nameless objects and nameless feelings and thoughts. I think largely in terms of things, relations, emotions. My speech must be a blend of childhood's vocabulary and manhood's craftsmanship. But the data, external and internal, are scientifically exact. I am some two hundred and fifty feet from my young mother and her friends. I have been pulling on her skirts, bothering her. She has yielded to my nagging and let me walk up to the further end; for she wants to talk undisturbed with the family doctor about the bright ways and promising future of her little boy. Nurse Tina, the pretty negress in a plaid bodice, and a stocky man, have now let go my hands. I have promised both her and my mother not to go near the tracks. This is

Abridged from W. E. Leonard, *The Locomotive God* (New York: Appleton-Century-Crofts, Inc., 1927), pp. 8–17. Copyright 1927, The Century Company; copyright 1942, D. Appleton-Century Co.; copyright renewed 1955, by Appleton-Century-Crofts. Reprinted by permission of the publisher.

my first journey so far from home, since a baby in arms . . . a mile from home into a world more venturous and engrossing than I can ever know twice. How big and brave I am! I had been looking round a little nervously toward my mother three or four times as our steps had increased the distance from her; but my curiosity and courage have conquered. I look back past the length of the long red station to the diminished figure of my mother with her red parasol. There too is little Mary. She is nearly four, I say to myself . . . she is so much bigger, yet not nearly as brave as I . . . she was afraid to come 'way off here with Tina and me. And, besides, her mother was afraid to let her. How wonderful I must seem to her 'way off here! And I hitch up the little black leather belt of my clean white dress (there are blue anchors on the sleeves), and stalk about in the sun for her distant, admiring eyes. And Mary loves me. How proud I am that Mary loves me, more even than that mama does! Though I do not know it, I am already lover and hero . . . the aboriginal masculine of the race.

From out of the woods, a far whistle, a puff of far smoke. The train! On the Path. Beside the interminable row of poles and wires. It moves. Toward us. I beg Tina to let me go—I want to look straight down the Path and see just how IT comes. Yes, I promise not to get *too* near the rails . . . and the Stocky Man strolls over after me. He stands and lights a cigar, looking idly up the tracks. The Train. Nearer. I can see it sway. The great black, puffing head-part. The length of moving sheds behind it. The chug-a-chug-chug, louder and louder. The almost musical rattle, with humming overtones, of the rails, louder and louder. I lean over to get the view more nearly head-on. The sky is back of it, farther and farther back of it. The Thing lengthens out, swaying this way and that. And it seems to surge up and down. A train? What *is* a train? Curiosity before the unknown now suddenly becomes apprehension . . . dread. . . . We are human from the start. We do not need to see a man die to know death. Death is born with our birth; the self that craves life shrinks by the very law of life as instinctively from the constriction and blockage of that craving. A little child . . . what should it know of death? All there is to know, O sage of Winander. The Premonition is upon me. I realize with horror what a Train is. It is a gigantic Caterpillar . . . gigantic beyond anything I have ever seen in our garden or Mary's. I am fascinated, rooted to the barren planks, while the Caterpillar roars and wriggles and arches along. The Stocky Man puffs his cigar, Tina is lolling by the blue rail, and calling idly, "Come back away from the tracks, Ellery," while curiosity overmasters even my horror at my own well realized disobedience; my mother is still talking doubtless with the family doctor, who brought me into the world, about the bright ways and promising future of her little son. But for the little son the universe is the Caterpillar . . . then the jerking angles of the driving-rod and the long boiler-belly make it for one tumultuous instant a tremendous Grasshopper . . . till it towers and lowers and grins in one awful metamorphosis, more grotesque than the most bizarre dreams of Greek mythology, as Something indescribably greater than Caterpillar or Grasshopper. As It roars over the bridge, with the engineer . . . I see again to-day his face peering out of the cabin window high above me . . . madly pulling the bell-rope, while the clanging fills what just now remained of silence in the world . . . as it roars with thunder and smoke over the bridge, scattering dust and a strewn newspaper, the black circle of the boiler-front swells to the size of the round sky out of which the Thing now seems to have leaped upon me. It sets up conscious reverberations of a picture in Uncle Oliver's insurance office . . . up the same stairs as papa's newspaper office . . . a locomotive on a calendar of the Ætna Company which floods my mind . . . even as a generation later a picture on another wall is to set up subconscious reverberations of this Aboriginal Monster. My eyeballs, tranfixed in one stare, ache in their sockets. The head-light glass in a square black box above the Black Circle flames with the reflected light of the afternoon sun down there where my mother is. But I am to postpone these realistic deductions for forty-seven years. To me at a little more than two years, the Black Circle flashes a fiercely shaking Face of infinite menace, more hideous and hostile than Gorgonshield or the squat demon in a Chinese temple, with gaping Jaws, flanked by bulging jowls, to swallow me down, to eat me alive—and the Thing is God. Coetaneous with the Face and Maw, a long lank Arm shoots out low down from around the further side of the engine, with an end half-spoon, half-claws, to scoop me up, to ladle me *in!* (This was a fantastic transfer from the swift vicious thrust of the driving-rod visible on my side.) God roaring from heaven to slay me for having disobeyed my mother and gone so close to the track. Guilt . . . remorse . . . Mary . . . in air above the great puffing smoke-stack, a tumultuous image of Mary's house . . . small hands clapped to eyes. My heart leaps to my throat . . . I think it is coming out of my mouth. "Al-leady" (i.e., "I am all ready. Come!") I moan inside me, summoning the resolution of an absolute despair.

The locomotive sweeps by, and my physical paralysis ends in a sudden leap away. The steam discharges from under the piston-box into the child's anus, with hot pain through his kilt-skirt. "God kills me *here too,*" he thinks with a scream out loud, and presses his hand to the pain. I am to feel that pain a generation later . . . for ten years, it will wake me from sleep. His little straw hat with scarlet band whirls off in the blast and roar, as the Stocky Man makes a futile grab. The monstrous boiler on the monstrous wheels rolls by, topped by the clangor and swaying of the bell. If I am dead, I think, how strange that I can still move so fast. It *is* God—God thunders out of the sky . . . I have heard him . . . this *is* God, I think in my panic . . . for I still think. The Face, that Face. Then the flight. Our house, so safe, but so horribly far, floods my mind. The parlor, with its carpet-designs in red and yellow and its maroon plush chairs, becomes an image so intense and vivid, with feel so protecting and close, that I am bewildered between being there and not there, with a paradoxical interpenetration of experience best comparable perhaps to our dream-states of maturity. The Face, that Face. The distance from my mother and Mary is terrible and hopeless: the proud moment in getting so far has supplied the suggestion for the terror of the immeasurable farawayness from safety. The flight, down that long, level, narrow highway. And I can't see my mother. The Face, the Face, the Face. A baggage-truck down there has rolled between . . . blockage . . . I am shrieking. The cars keep passing me. I am so small that I see under them, past their tangle of iron rods, to the freight-depot on the other (the left) side of the track. The wheels pound and bump, one after the other, where rail joins rail. The Face. A thought more awful still: This Thing, God, or whatever it is, will kill Mary. I must get to Mary. The Face, the Jaws. The end of the station grows nearer. I see a white frame house just beyond the station where the platform ends. The Stocky Man runs after, Tina runs, and a dog races beside me. It is fun for him. I see to my right the awnings on the stores on the street across the way from the station-park. The last car has passed. A slight relief. I stare toward its retreating rear end. My side aches . . . that frightens me too . . . I put my hand on the ache . . . I have lived through all thus far; I can live till I reach mama and Mary, I say to myself. My mother sees me and signals with her red parasol. Relief. But where is Mary? . . . a new despair . . . till she darts out from behind the two mothers and is running toward me. Spiritual relief . . . a little. Then I stumble and flop flat. The dog noses my neck. My anguish lies watching my mother's hurrying steps . . . This anguish will burst from the subconscious, as the university professor overhears himself saying half asleep (i.e., in twilight sleep) the apparently meaningless phrase, "Æneas rushing at me," and "Æneas" will be a Freudian pun for "her knees," and the informing point will be that he lay there unable to raise his infant head to her face, eyes fixed on her legs bending under her skirts. . . . Meantime Tina picks me up, and I sob and shriek my tale of the God-Face in my mother's comforting arms. The talk with the family doctor has been interrupted.

"Now you're all hunky-dory," says my mother, setting me down beside the baby-carriage of sister. I rush behind the baby-carriage to Mary. She caresses me. I cling with my arms about her, long . . . like a lover . . . a little shy (believe me, or not) lest the mothers see how hard I cling, how that clinging is all the world to me. I feel a sweet comfortableness in my body too. . . . And when she starts away at the joyous sight of her father descending from the train, I am jealous and grieved. I lean against my little wagon. Tina gives me an orange to suck. I am getting myself together and thinking matters over. What a fool I am, I think. A Highlander, in costume, stands with his bagpipe against the station wall, laughing. The people on the platform are staring. Rows of heads too from all the car-windows. The world is all eyes. I am the Great Fool. A generation later I will be reading books that say little children don't feel shame, until taught and mistaught; and I will know that, though one needs teaching a plenty to be ashamed of the little naked body that nature gave him, he needs no teaching to be ashamed of lapsing from himself, as Intelligence and Courage.

The train didn't bring papa after all. So we all walk through the station with Mary's folks. They drive off with a span of horses, Mary on the front seat with her bearded papa. She seems almost to pay no more attention to me, and that hurts. She too must think me the Great Fool. Then my mother leads me back to the Engine. A man is oiling the wheels. I am urged to touch them and the cowcatcher. I do . . . gingerly. My mother shows me that it is not really alive, that it has no face, that it has no long arm, that it is not God but a Locomotive. I am trying to convince myself . . . but am still nervous and a little skeptical . . . especially when it starts to move away.

I ask on the walk home, when but a few rods from the station, with my mind full of my little lover riding away behind the turning span of great horses: "Mama, do you suppose Mary thinks I'm a fool?" She cajoles and chides me: "You mustn't talk like that." I brood, deeply troubled. And again as we near our house at last: "Mama, do you suppose Mary loves me?" . . . My papa arrives in time for supper, after all. Mama is telling him how scared I was, and how I thought the Locomotive was God. I am such a little boy that she thinks I don't understand her big words. But, just as I lift my glass of milk to my mouth, I see for a second the Locomotive-God plunging at me through the hall door. I shriek out. My father's face is troubled, a kindlier face than the years are ever to carve out for his childless son. . . . The Face of St. Francis. . . . He is very grave, worried about the shock and what it may do to me . . . perhaps (as I am to speculate when I am a dozen years older than my father is now) worried too that the shock may affect my love for the good God whom he loves more now, as a newspaper editor in a small city, than when before my birth he resigned his pastorate in far-off Evanston because he no longer liked the Baptist God. Yet what he and my mother had already told me of the Heavenly Father that thunders and his Power and Love of Good Little Boys was, it seems (I conjecture here), enough for my reconstruction of the Locomotive-God.

That afternoon changed my whole life. In recovering my lost years, I have uncovered a hundred dreams dreamed in the years not lost: that afternoon was involved in their pattern. I have uncovered conduct and motives for conduct: that afternoon was in their pattern. Emotions, opinions, scholarly interests, materials in my poems: that afternoon was there too. Long years of unexplained, intermittent nervousness, followed by fifteen years (to date) of a chronic neurosis, with all its accompanying limitations and handicaps: that afternoon was in their pattern. Can ten minutes' time control fifty years? It can. Children's diseases—measles, scarlet fever, infantile paralysis—how parents dread them, for, even if the little lives are saved, they may be maimed, in eyes, ears, or legs for life. And nurse-maids must not drop or bump them—for a scar is a lifelong misfortune. We must guard their morals and manners too—training them not to tell lies or to spit or to do nasty things in the clothes-closet. But a scare, with a few shrieks and tears, is soon a neighborhood joke. Yet what was this scare of mine? Sex, self-respect, self-confidence, friendliness to the world, the will to roam and the will to know, basic forces for normal manhood, here unfolding with wholesome promise, were abruptly disintegrated in the explosion of complete collapse before the attack of alien and incomprehensible power, to be replaced by terror, guilt, shame, and the cringing need of shelter. In a nervous system, a little more than two years out of the womb. I was born again that day.

A Case of Multiple Personality

Corbett H. Thigpen and Hervey Cleckley

Corbett Thigpen is Chief of the Psychiatry Department at University Hospital, in Augusta, Georgia. He received his M.D. degree in 1945 from the Medical College of Georgia, where he is now Associate Clinical Professor of Psychiatry. Hervey Cleckley, with Thigpen, is co-author of The Three Faces of Eve, *a book based on the selection below. Cleckley is Clinical Professor of Psychiatry at the Medical College of Georgia, from which he received his M.D. degree in 1929. He is particularly interested in the study of psychopathic personalities. Both Thigpen and Cleckley are members of a number of professional organizations and are engaged in private practice.*

1. Why was it so difficult to sift out what was common to the backgrounds of Eve White and Eve Black?

2. In what ways did the emergence of Jane create ethical deliberations as to the course of a treatment aim?

3. The degree of conscious awareness this patient had of her other self was of particular importance to the therapists. Why?

Our direct experience with a patient has forced us to review the subject of multiple personality. It has also provoked in us the reaction of wonder, sometimes of awe.

One of us (C. H. T.) had for several months been treating a twenty-five-year-old married woman who was referred because of "severe and blinding headaches." At the first interview she also mentioned "blackouts" following headache. These were vaguely described by the patient. Her family was not aware of anything that would suggest a real loss of consciousness

or serious mental confusion. During a series of interviews which were irregular, since the patient had to come from some distance away, several important emotional difficulties were revealed and discussed. Encouraging symptomatic improvement occurred, but it was plain that this girl's major problems had not been settled. To the therapist, Eve White—as we shall call her—was an ordinary case with commonplace symptoms and a relatively complex but familiar constellation of marital conflicts and personal frustrations. We were puzzled during therapy about a recent trip for which she had no memory. Hypnosis was induced and the amnesia cleared up promptly. Several days after a visit to the office a letter was received. (Exhibit 1.)

What was the meaning of such a letter? Though unsigned, the postmark, the content, and the familiar penmanship in most of the message revealed to the therapist that this had been written by Eve White. The effect of this letter on the therapist was considerable. It raised puzzling questions for which there were no answers and set in motion thoughts that pursued various and vague directions. Had some child found the uncompleted page, scribbled those words, and, perhaps as a whim, mailed it in an already addressed envelope? Perhaps. The handwriting of the last para-

July –

Dear Doctor,

Remembering my visit to _____ brought me a great deal of relief, to begin with.

Just being able to recall the trip seemed enough, but now that I've had time to think about it and all that occurred, it's more painful than I ever thought possible.

How can I be sure that I remember all that happened, even now? How can I know that it won't happen again? I wonder if I'll ever be sure of anything again.

While I was there with you it seemed different. Somehow it didn't matter so much, to have forgotten; but now it does matter. I know it's something that doesn't happen ...

I can't even recall color schemes and I know that would probably be the first thing I'd notice.

My head hurts right on top. It has ever since the day I was down there to see you. I think it must be my eyes. I see little red & green specks – and I'm covered with some kind of rash.

[note in different hand] baby please be quite dear Lord ... let me have patience with her ... sweet and innocent ... my self-control

EXHIBIT 1. *This letter in retrospect was the first intimation that our patient was unusual. The dramatic and unexpected revelation of the second personality shortly followed.*

graph to be sure suggested the work of a child. Could Eve White herself, as a puerile prank, have decided to disguise her characteristic writing and added this inconsequential note? And if so, why? Mrs. White had appeared to be a circumspect, matter of fact person, meticulously truthful and consistently sober and serious about her grave troubles. It was rather difficult to imagine her becoming playful or being moved by an impulse to tease, even on a more appropriate occasion. The "blackouts" which she had rather casually mentioned, but which did not seem to disturb her very much, suggested of course that a somnambulism or brief fugue might have occurred.

On her next visit she denied sending the letter, though she recalled having begun one which she never finished. She believed she had destroyed it. During this interview Eve White, ordinarily an excessively self-controlled woman, began to show signs of distress and agitation. Apprehensively and reluctantly she at last formulated a question: Did the occasional impression of hearing an imaginary voice indicate that she was "insane"?

To the therapist this information was startling. Nothing about Eve White suggested even an early schizoid change. Her own attitude toward what she now reported was in no respect like any of the various attitudes of patients who are in the ordinary sense experiencing auditory hallucinations. Yet, she insisted with painful embarrassment, she had on several occasions over the last few months heard briefly but distinctly a voice addressing her. Something about her reaction to this may be conveyed if we compare it to what we can imagine an experienced psychiatrist in robust mental health might feel if, with full retention of insight, he heard himself similarly addressed. While the therapist, hesitating a moment in wonder, sought for an adequate reply, an abstruse and inexplicable expression came, apparently unprompted by volition, over Eve White's familiar countenance. As if seized by a sudden pain she put both hands to her head. After a tense moment of silence, her hands dropped. There was a quick, reckless smile and, in a bright voice that sparkled, she said, "Hi there, Doc!"

The demure and constrained posture of Eve White had melted into buoyant repose. With a soft and surprisingly intimate syllable of laughter, she crossed her legs. Disconcerted as he was by unassimilated surprise, the therapist noted from the corner of his awareness something distinctly attractive about them, and also that this was the first time he had received such an impression. There is little point in attempting here to give in detail the differences between this novel feminine apparition and the vanished Eve White. Instead of that retiring and gently conventional figure, there was in the newcomer a childishly daredevil air, an erotically mischievous glance, a face marvellously free from the habitual signs of care, seriousness, and underlying distress, so long familiar in her predecessor. This new and apparently carefree girl spoke casually of Eve White and her problems, always using *she* or *her* in every reference, always respecting the strict bounds of a separate identity. When asked her own name she immediately replied, "Oh, I'm Eve Black."

It is easy to say that this new voice was different, that the basic idiom of her language was plainly not that of Eve White. A thousand minute alterations of manner, gesture, expression, posture, of nuances in reflex or instinctive reaction, of glance, of eyebrow tilting and eye movement, all argued that this could only be another woman. It is not possible to say just what all these differences were.

It would not be difficult for a man to distinguish his wife, or perhaps even his secretary, if she were placed among a hundred other women carefully chosen because of their resemblance to her, and all dressed identically. But few would wager that, however articulate he might be, he could tell a stranger, or even someone very slightly acquainted with her, how to accomplish this task. If he tries to tell us how he himself recognizes her, he may accurately convey something to us. But what he can convey, no matter how hard he tries, is only an inconsequential fragment. It is not enough to help us when we set out to find her. So, too, we are not able to tell adequately what so profoundly distinguishes from Eve White the carefree girl who took her place in this vivid mutation.

Even before anything substantial of her history could be obtained, the therapist reacted to the new presence with feelings that momentarily recalled from distant memory these words:

The devil has entered the prompter's box
And the play is ready to start.

Over a period of 14 months during a series of interviews totaling approximately 100 hours, extensive material was obtained about the behavior and inner life of Eve White—and of Eve Black. It is our plan to report on this more adequately in a book-length study. Here space limits our presentation to a few details.

Eve Black, so far as we can tell, has enjoyed an independent life since Mrs. White's early childhood.[1] She is not a product of disruptive emotional stresses which the patient has suffered during recent years. Eve White apparently had no knowledge or suspicion of the other's existence until some time after she appeared unbidden before the surprised therapist. Though Mrs. White has learned that there is a Miss Black during the course of therapy, she does not have access to the latter's awareness. When Eve Black is "out," Eve White remains functionally in abeyance, quite oblivious of what the coinhabitant of her body does, and apparently unconscious.

On the contrary, Eve Black preserves awareness while absent. Invisibly alert at some unmapped post of observation, she is able to follow the actions and the thoughts of her spiritually antithetical twin. The hoydenish and devil-may-care Eve Black "knows" and can report what the other does and thinks, and describes her feelings. Those feelings, however, are not Eve Black's own. She does not participate in them. Eve White's genuine and natural distress about her failing marriage is regarded by the other as silly. Eve White's love and deep concern for her only child, a little girl of four, is to us and to all who know her, warm, real, consistent, and impressive. Eve Black, who shares her memory and verbally knows her thoughts, discerns her emotional reactions and

---

[1] The question: "How can the various personalities be called out?" has been asked. After the original spontaneous appearance of Eve Black it was at first necessary for Eve White to be hypnotized in order for us to talk with Eve Black. How Eve Black could "pop out" of her own accord at unpredictable times and yet could not come out on request, we do not know. Under hypnosis of Eve White, Eve Black could very easily be called forth. After a few hypnotic sessions, we merely had to request Eve White to let us speak to Eve Black. Then we called Eve Black's name, and Eve Black would come forth. The reverse was true when Eve Black was out and we wished to speak with Eve White. Hypnosis was no longer necessary for the purpose of obtaining the changes. This made things simpler for us but complicated Eve White's life considerably because Eve Black found herself able to "take over" more easily than before. A third personality, Jane, to be described below, emerged spontaneously and we have never had to employ hypnosis to reach her.

values only as an outsider. They are for the outsider something trite, bothersome, and insignificant. The devotion of this mother for her child, as an empty definition, is entirely familiar to the lively and unworried Eve Black. Its substance and nature are, however, so clearly outside her personal experience that she can evaluate it only as "something pretty corny."

During the temporary separation of her parents, which may become permanent, this little girl is living with her grandparents in a village. Because her earnings are necessary for her child's basic welfare, the mother has no choice but to work and live in a city approximately a hundred miles from the child. Having apparently known little but unhappiness with her husband, she was finally forced to the conclusion that her young and vulnerable child had little chance of happy or normal development in the home situation, which, despite her best efforts, continually grew worse. She now endures the loneliness, frustration, and grief of separation from her warmly loved daughter, who is the primary object of her life and feeling, and who, she has good reason to fear, is likely to grow up apart from her. Perhaps, it seems to her sometimes, she will become to her as years pass little more than a coolly accepted stranger.

Vulnerable, uningenuous, and delicately feminine, Eve White characteristically preserves a quiet dignity about personal sorrow, a dignity unpretentiously stoic. Under hypnosis one can come closer to the sadness and the lonely despair she feels it her task not to display. Even then no frantic weeping occurs, no outcries of self-pity. Her quiet voice remains level as she discusses matters that leave her cheeks at last wet from silent tears.

Despite access to this woman's "thoughts" Eve Black has little or no real compassion for her. Nor does she seem in any important sense actively, or purposefully, cruel. Neutral or immune to major affective events in human relations, an unparticipating onlooker, she is apparently almost as free of hatefulness, or of mercy, or of comprehension, as a bright-feathered parakeet who chirps undisturbed while watching a child strangle to death.

It has been mentioned that Eve Black's career has been traced back to early childhood.

She herself freely tells us of episodes when she emerged, usually to engage in acts of mischief or disobedience. She lies glibly and without compunction, so her account alone can never be taken as reliable evidence. Since Eve White, whose word on any matter has always proved good, still has no access to the other's current awareness or her memory and, indeed, did not until recently even faintly suspect her existence, it has been impossible through her to check fully and immediately on Eve Black's stories. Her memory has, however, afforded considerable indirect evidence since she has been able to confirm reports of punishments she received, of accusations made against her, for deeds unknown to her but described to us by Eve Black.

Some stories have been substantiated through others. Both of this patient's parents, as well as her husband, have been available for interviews. They recall several incidents that Eve Black had previously reported to us. For instance, the parents had had to punish their ordinarily good and conforming six-year-old girl for having disobeyed their specific rule against wandering through the woods to play with the children of a tenant farmer. They considered this expedition dangerous for so young a child, and their daughter's unaccountable absence had caused them worry and distress. On her return Eve received a hearty whipping despite her desperate denials of wrongdoing or disobedience. In fact these very denials added to her punishment, since the evidence of her little trip was well established and her denial taken as a deliberate lie. Eve Black had previously described this episode to us in some detail, expressing amusement about "coming out" to commit and enjoy the forbidden adventure and withdrawing to leave the other Eve, sincerely protesting her innocence, to appreciate all sensations of the whipping.

The adult Eve White recalled this and several other punishments which she had no way of understanding and which sometimes bewildered her in her relations with her parents.

Irresponsibility and a shallowly hedonistic grasping for ephemeral excitements or pleasures characterize Eve Black's adult behavior. She succeeded in concealing her identity not only from the other Eve but also from her parents and the husband. She herself denies marriage to this man, whom she despises, and any relation to Eve White's little girl except that of an unconcerned bystander. Though she had often "come out" in the presence of all these people, she went unrecognized until she agreed to reveal herself to them in the therapist's office.

Her wayward behavior, ill will, harshness, and occasional acts of violence, observed by Mr. White and the parents, were attributed to unaccountable fits of temper in a woman habitually gentle and considerate.

During her longer periods "out," when she expresses herself more freely in behavior so unlike that of Eve White, she avoids her family and close friends, and seeks the company of strangers or of those insufficiently acquainted with her alternate to evaluate accurately the stupendous transformation.

Once we had seen and spoken with Eve Black, it seemed to us at first scarcely possible that, even in the same body as her alternate, she could for so long have concealed her separate identity from others. Yet, who among those acquainted with her would be likely to suspect, however unlike herself Eve appeared at times to be, such a situation as that voluntarily revealed to us by the patient? No matter how many clues one is given, no matter how obvious the clues, one will not be led to a conclusion that is inconceivable. One will seek explanations for the problem only among available hypotheses.

Not knowing the only concept into which successive details of perception will fit, even a very astute man may observe a thousand separate features of something his imagination has never shaped without grasping the gestalt, without being able to put into a recognizable whole the details he has so clearly detected. Only our previous familiarity with three-dimensional space enables us to see the representation of depth in a picture. What is for us still unconceived can give us a thousand hints, boldly flaunt before us its grossest features, and remain for us undelineated, formless, uncomprehended as an entity.

The astonishingly incompatible gestures, expressions, attitudes, mannerisms, and behavior which Eve occasionally displayed before intimates provoked thought and wonder, demanded explanation. But who in the position of these people would be likely to find or create in his mind the hypothesis that forms a recognizable image? Let us remember too that Eve

Black, until she voluntarily named herself to the therapist, meant to remain unrecognized. When it suits her, she deliberately and skillfully acts so as to pass herself off as Eve White, imitating her habitual tone of voice, her gestures, and attitudes. Let us not forget that she is shrewd.

With the circumspect Eve White oblivious of her escapades, Miss Black once recklessly bought several expensive and unneeded new dresses and two luxurious coats. Sometimes she revels in cheap night clubs flirting with strange men on the make. Insouciantly she pursues her irresponsible way, usually amused, sometimes a little bored, never alarmed or grieved or seriously troubled. She has, apparently, been unmoved by any sustaining purpose, unattracted by any steady goal, prompted only by the immediate and the trivial.

Eve White's husband, on discovering the valuable outlay of new clothes, which the other Eve had hidden carefully away, lost his temper and abused his wife for wantonly plunging him into debt. He found no way to accept her innocent denials as genuine but was at length assuaged in wrath by her wholehearted agreement that it would be disastrous for them to run up such a bill, and her promptness in returning all these garments to the store.[2] Eve White has told us of many real and serious incompatibilities with her husband. Even if the two were unmolested by an outsider, it is doubtful if the imperfections of this marriage, its unhappiness, and the threats to its continuation could be alleviated. Adverse acts and influence by an insider have been peculiarly damaging and pernicious. Though Eve Black does not apparently follow a consistent purpose to disrupt the union, or regularly go out of her way to make trouble for the couple, her typical behavior often compounds their difficulties.

"When I go out and get drunk," Eve Black

---

[2] Mrs. White apparently failed to produce a satisfactory rationalization. This is true for all of her fugue states. She did tell us she suspected that her husband may have planted the clothes in order to make it appear that she was "insane." She did not, however, seem to come to grips with the problem. Apparently finding it, along with so many other problems, too much for her, she took an attitude in some ways like that of Scarlett O'Hara when the latter would tell herself, "Well, tomorrow will be another day."

with an easy wink once said to both of us, *"she wakes up with the hangover. She wonders what in the hell's made her so sick."*

Though as a rule only indifferent, passively callous to her alternate's child, Eve Black once in the past became irritated with her and hurt her. Apparently she might have done her serious harm had her husband not restrained her. This act she denied and lied about consistently though the evidence for it through others is strong. Later she flippantly confessed, giving as her reason, "The little brat got on my nerves."

From the two Eves during many interviews and from her husband and parents, we in time obtained a great deal of information about the patient. Having concluded we had a reasonably complete and accurate history of her career since early childhood, we were astonished by the report of a distant relative who insisted that a few years before she met her present husband a previous marriage had occurred.

Eve White denied this report and has never yet shown any knowledge of it. To our surprise Eve Black also maintained that we had been misinformed, insisting that Eve White had married only once, that she herself had never and would never consider marrying any man.

Finally, under the persistent pressure of evidence, Eve Black gave up her position, admitted that the relative's report was correct, that she herself and only she had been the bride. This event she told us occurred several years before Mrs. White's marriage. While the other Eve was employed in a town some distance from her parents' home she had come "out" and gone to a dance with a man she scarcely knew. After a night of merriment, something was half-jokingly mentioned about the pair getting married more or less for the hell of it. This apparently struck her fancy.

She has recounted many details of outlandish strife and hardship during several months when, apparently, she had lived with this man. No record of a legal union has been obtained but considerable evidence indicates she did cohabit during this period with such a man as she describes, perhaps under the careless impression that a marriage had really occurred. She insists that some sort of "ceremony" was performed, saying that it was not formally recorded and admitting it may have been a ruse.

During this time when she regarded herself as wed, Eve Black enjoyed her longest periods of uninterrupted sway. She was predominantly in control, almost constantly present. Apparently she had no desire for sexual relations but often enjoyed frustrating her supposed husband by denying herself to him. He in turn, she says, was prone to beat her savagely. She claims to have succeeded in avoiding most of the pain from this by "going in" and leaving the other Eve to feel the blows.

This last claim immediately impressed us both as extremely implausible. If Eve White experienced the pain and humiliation of these beatings, why did she not remember them? She has consistently denied any memory of the entire marital or pseudomarital experience reported by Eve Black. Our unreliable but convincing informant maintains that she herself remained in control or possession nearly all the time during this adventure. She furthermore insists that she can, by exerting a considerable effort, often "pick out" or erase from Eve White's reach certain items of memory. "I just start thinking about it very hard," Eve Black says, "and after a while she quits and it doesn't come back to her anymore." All awareness of the beatings she claims so to have erased from the other's recollection. Such a claim, obviously, was subject to testing by the therapist. Several experiments indicated that it is correct.

After approximately eight months of psychiatric treatment Eve White had apparently made encouraging progress. For a long time she had not been troubled by headaches or "blackout." The imaginary voice had never been heard again since the other Eve revealed herself to the therapist. Mrs. White worked efficiently at her job and had made progress financially through salary raises and careful management. The prospect of returning to her husband and of working out a bearable relation was still blocked by serious obstacles, but, having achieved more personal security and financial independence, she had become more hopeful of eventually reaching some acceptable solution. Though sadly missing the presence of her child, she found some comfort in her successful efforts to provide for her. She had made friends in the once strange city and with them, despite many worries and responsibilities, occasionally enjoyed simple recreations.

Meanwhile Eve Black, though less actively

resisted in emerging, had in general been causing less trouble. Being bored with all regular
work, she seldom "came out" to make careless
and costly errors, or indulge in complicating
pranks while the breadwinner was on her job.
Though in leisure hours she often got in bad
company, picked up dates, and indulged in
cheap and idle flirtations, her demure and conventional counterpart, lacking knowledge of
these deeds, was spared the considerable humiliation and distress some of this conduct would
otherwise have caused her.

At this point the situation changed for the
worse. Eve White's headaches returned. They
grew worse and more frequent. With them also
returned the "blackouts." Since the earlier
headaches had been related to, perhaps caused
by, the other Eve's efforts to gain control, and
the "blackouts" had often represented this
alternate's periods of activity, she was suspected and questioned. She denied any part or
influence in the new development. She did not
experience the headaches, but, surprisingly,
seemed now to participate in the blackouts, and
could give no account of what occurred during
them. Apparently curious about these experiences, she said, "I don't know where we go, but
go we do."

Two or three times the patient was found
lying unconscious on the floor by her room-
mate. This, so far as we could learn, had not
occurred during the previous episodes reported
by Eve White as "blackouts." It became
difficult for her to work effectively. Her hard-
won gains in serenity and confidence disappeared. During interviews she became less
accessible, while showing indications of increasing stress. The therapist began to fear that a
psychosis was impending. Though this fear
was not, of course, expressed to Eve White, it
was mentioned to her reckless and invulnerable
counterpart. The fact was emphasized that,
should it be necessary to send Eve White to an
institution, the other, too, would suffer the same
restrictions and confinement. Perhaps, the
therapist hoped, this fact would curtail her in
any unadmitted mischief she might be working.

Since it has for long been presumed that so-
called dual personalities arise from a dissociation of an originally integrated entity of functioning and experience, efforts were naturally
exerted from the first to promote reintegration.

Attempts were made with each Eve to work
back step by step into early childhood. With
Mrs. White hypnosis was sometimes used to
regain forgotten events or aspects or fragments
of experience. It was hoped that some link or
bridge might be found on which additional
contact and coalition could grow or be built.
Under hypnosis she occasionally re-experienced
considerable emotion in recalling events of her
childhood. We have never been able to hypno-
tize Eve Black.

It soon became possible for the therapist to
evoke either personality at will. During the
first few weeks a transition from Eve White to
Eve Black was more easily achieved by hypnosis. Shortly afterwards it became possible to
simplify the procedure. Permission and the
promise of cooperation were obtained from the
lady present. Then the other was called by
name and invited or encouraged to emerge.
With repetition, and with deepening emotional
relations between patient and physician, this
process became after a while very easily accomplished. In the very early stages of treatment
an effort was made, perhaps a too naive effort,
to promote some sort of blending, or at least a
liaison, by calling out both personalities at
once. To this attempt Eve White reacted with
violent headache and emotional distress so severe that it was not considered wise to continue. When the experiment was reversed, with
the apparently invulnerable Eve Black manifest, much less agitation was observed. After
one unsuccessful trial, however, she bluntly
refused to go further. In explanation she said
only that it gave her "such a funny, queer,
mixed-up feeling that I ain't gonna put up with
it no more."

Sometime after the return of headaches and
blackouts, with Eve White's maladjustment still
growing worse generally, a very early recollection was being discussed with her. The incident focused about a painful injury she had
sustained when scalded by water from a wash
pot. As she spoke her eyes shut sleepily. Her
words soon ceased. Her head dropped back on
the chair. After remaining in this sleep or
trance perhaps two minutes her eyes opened.
Blankly she stared about the room, looking at
the furniture and the pictures as if trying to
orient herself. Continuing their apparently be-

wildered survey, her eyes finally met those of the therapist, and stopped. Slowly, with an unknown husky voice and with immeasurable poise, she spoke. "Who are you?"

From the first moment it was vividly apparent that this was neither Eve White nor Eve Black. She did not need to tell us that. The thousands of points distinguishing the two Eves have grown more clear and convincing as we acquire additional experience with each. So this new woman with time and study has shown herself ever more plainly another entity. Only in a superficial way could she be described as a sort of compromise between the two. She apparently lacks Eve Black's obvious faults and inadequacies. She also impresses us as far more mature, more vivid, more boldly capable, and more interesting than Eve White. It is easy to sense in her a capacity for accomplishment and fulfillment far beyond that of the sweet and retiring Eve White, who, beside this genuinely impressive newcomer, appears colorless and limited. In her are indications of initiative and powerful resources never shown by the other. This third personality calls herself Jane, for no particular reason she can give. In her it is not difficult to sense the potential or the promise of something far more of woman and of life than might be expected from the two Eves with faults and weaknesses eliminated and all assets combined.

For several months now there have been three patients to interview and work with. Jane has awareness of what both Eves do and think but incomplete access to their stores of knowledge and their memories prior to her emergence upon the scene. Through her reports the therapist can determine when Eve Black has been lying. Jane feels herself personally free from Eve White's responsibilities and attachments, and in no way identified with her in the role of wife and mother. Apparently she is capable of compassion, and, we feel likely, of devotion and valid love. She has cooperated with sincerity, and with judgment and originality beyond that of the others. Though it took her a while to learn what was quite new to her, she has already taken over many of Eve White's tasks at work and at home in efforts to relieve and help her. Her feelings towards Eve's little girl appear to be those of a wise and richly compassionate woman towards the child of a family not her own, but still a child in emotional privation.

Her warm impulses to take a more active role with this little girl are complicated by the deep conviction that she must not in anyway act so as to come between the distressed mother and her only child. During the few months of her separate existence Jane has, one might say, become stronger and more active. Despite her fine intelligence she began without experience, or at least without full access to the experience of an adult. As time passes Jane stays "out" more and more. She emerges only through Eve White, never yet having found a way to displace Eve Black or to communicate through her. Almost any observer would, we think, find it obvious that Jane, and she only of the three, might solve the deepest problems that brought the patient we call Eve White to us for treatment. Could Jane remain in full possession of that integrated human functioning we call personality our patient would probably, we believe, regain full health, eventually adjust satisfactorily, perhaps at a distinctly superior level, and find her way to a happy life.

Should this occur it seems very unlikely that Mr. White's wife would ever return to him. On the other hand it is little more likely that Eve White, even if she becomes free of all that she has known as symptoms, could or would ever take up her role again as wife in that marriage. Should she try to do so, it is difficult to foresee much happiness for her or the husband. The probability of deep and painful conflict is apparent, also the real danger of psychosis.

Were we impersonal arbiters in such a matter it would be easy to see, and to say, that the only practical or rational solution to this astonishing problem is for Jane to survive, and Jane only. A steadily prevailing Eve Black would indeed be a travesty of woman. The surface is indeed appealing, but this insouciant and likable hoyden, though perhaps too shallow to become really vicious, would, if unrestrained, forever carry disaster lightly in each hand.

The sense of duty, the willingness for self-sacrifice, so strong and so beautiful in Eve White, might bring her back repeatedly into this marital situation which she lacks the emotional vigor to deal with, and in which it is not likely she could survive. Jane, whose integrity, whose potential goodness, seems not less than that of Eve White, has rich promise of the power to survive, even to triumph against odds.

It is perhaps unnecessary to point out that we have not judged ourselves as wise enough to make active decisions or exert personal influence in shaping what impends. It is plain that, even if we had this wisdom, the responsibility is not ours. Would any physician order euthanasia for the heedlessly merry and amoral but nevertheless unique Eve Black? If so, it is our belief, it could not be a physician who has directly known and talked for hours with her, not one who has felt the inimitable identity of her capricious being.

A surviving Jane would provide for Eve White's half-lost little girl a maternal figure of superb resources.[3] Perhaps in time she could give the child a love as real and deep as that of the mother herself. Perhaps. But would those feelings be the actual and unique feelings that have sustained the frail and tormented Eve White in her long, pathetic, and steadfast struggle to offer the child a chance for happiness? It may be said that this is foolish and tedious quibbling, that Jane after all, *is* the girl's real mother. Was she not born of her body? All awareness of her as a daughter ever experienced by Eve White is recorded in the electrochemical patterns of Jane's brain. True

---

[3] A question of the psychotherapist's responsibility has been raised. Morton Prince has been accused by some, particularly by McDougall, of taking too active a part in "squeezing out" Sally. Our experience made us feel very keenly the wish not to exert pressures arbitrarily and perhaps play a part in the extinction of qualities possibly of real value if they were integrated into more responsible patterns of behavior. We believe there is some choice open to the psychiatrist as to which personality he will try to reinforce, but that he must be tentative and work along with developments within the patient (or patients?) rather than make full and final judgments.

We feel that therapy has played a part in the emergence of Jane, but we do not consider her merely our creation. Our influence seems to have been more catalytic than causal. Psychotherapy has not been directed according to an arbitrary plan. Although we have persistently investigated early experiences through all three manifestations of our patient, and have encouraged emotional reaction to them, we have sought to avoid insistence on any of the popular theoretical forms of interpretation.

Jane continues to grow in influence, to be out more and more. She has established contact with some events in the early life of Eve White, and seems more rooted in a past. We cannot predict with any great confidence the outcome, but we are hopeful that some reasonably good adjustment will work out through the capacities contributed by Jane.

indeed. But *is* she her mother? Those who have known Eve White personally will find it hard to accept simple affirmation as the whole truth. What this whole truth is can be better sensed in direct feeling than conveyed by explanation.

At a distance bridged only by printed or spoken words these "beings" may appear as factitious abstractions. In the flesh, though it is the flesh of a single body, one finds it more difficult so to dismiss them. Final decisions, or choices in the course of involuntary developments must, we have decided, be offered freely to something without our patient, perhaps to something beyond any levels of contact we have reached with Eve Black, with Eve White, or with Jane.

Jane, who appears to have some not quite articulate understanding or purblind grasp of this whole matter, not available to either of the Eves, shares our sharp reluctance about participating in any act that might contribute to Eve White's extinction. Unlike Eve Black, Jane has profound and compassionate realization of Eve White's relation to her child. The possibility, the danger, of a permanent loss of all touch with reality has occurred to Eve White. Through this we have found a better appreciation of her feelings as a mother. Too restrained ordinarily by modesty to speak about such a matter, after hypnosis she offered in quiet tones of immeasurable conviction to accept this extinction if it might win for her daughter Jane's presence in the role she had not succeeded in filling adequately for her child.

It has been said that a man must first lay down his life if he is to truly find it. Is it possible that this mother may, through her renunciation, somehow survive and find a way back to the one and dearest thing she is, for her child's sake, ready to leave forever? That we do not know. Long and intimate personal relations with this patient have brought us to wonder if in her we have blindly felt biologic forces and processes invisible to us, still uncomprehended and not quite imaginable.

Recently Eve White, anything but a physically bold or instinctively active person, was challenged suddenly by an event, for her momentous. Of this Jane, deeply moved, wrote to the therapist:

Today she did something that made me know and appreciate her as I had not been able to do before. I wish I could tell her what I feel but I can't reach her. She must not die yet. There's so much I must know, and so very much I must learn from her. She is the substance of, *this above all to thine own self be true.* In her, too, *the quality of mercy is not strained.* I want her to live—not me!

She saved the life of a little boy today. Everybody thought him to be her child, because she darted out in front of a car to pick him up and take him to safety. But instead of putting him down again, the moment his baby arms went around her neck, he became her baby—and she continued to walk down the street carrying him in her arms.

I have never been thus affected by anything in my four months of life. There seemed only one solution to prevent her possible arrest for kidnapping. That was for me to come out and find the child's mother. In the end I had to give him to a policeman. Later tonight when she had come back out, she was searching for her own baby. She had her baby again for a short while this afternoon; and I'm so happy for that. I still can't feel Eve Black. I can't believe she's just given up. *I feel inexpressibly humble.*

Discussion

What is the meaning of the events we have observed and reported? Some, no doubt, will conclude that we have been thoroughly hoodwinked by a skillful actress. It seems possible that such an actress after assiduous study and long training might indeed master three such roles and play them in a way that would defy detection. The roles might be so played for an hour, perhaps for a few hours. We do not think it likely that any person consciously dissimulating could over months avoid even one telltale error or imperfection. Though this does not seem likely to us, we do not assume it to be impossible. Let us remember, too, that in plays the actors are given their lines, and their roles are limited to representations of various characters only in circumscribed and familiar episodes of the portrayed person's life. The actor also has costume and make-up to help him maintain the illusion.

Obviously the differing manifestations we have observed in one woman's physical organism do not, in all senses of the term, indicate three quite separate people. Our words referring to the possible disappearance or permanent extinction of one of the personality manifestations perhaps imply we regard this as an equivalent, or at least an approximation, of death.

Are we guilty of a misleading exaggeration? No heart would stop beating should this occur. No eyes would permanently close. No flesh would undergo corruption. Such an extinction would not fulfill the criteria by which death is defined. Yet, if we may ask, would his immediate replacement by an identical twin invalidate for a bereaved widow the death of her husband? This analogy is not precise. In some respects it is misleading. It does not give us an answer to the question we raise. Perhaps it may, nevertheless, accurately reflect some of our perplexity.

For these and for many other questions that have confronted us in this study we have no full or certain answers. We ask ourselves what we mean by referring to that which we have observed by such a term as *multiple personality?* Immediately we face the more fundamental question: What is the real referent of this familiar word *personality?* In ordinary use we all encounter dozens of unidentical referents, perhaps hundreds of overlapping concepts, all with vague and elusive areas extending indefinitely, vaguely fading out into limitless implications.

Any day we may hear that John Doe has become a *new man* since he quit liquor three years ago. Perhaps we tell ourselves that Harvard actually made a *different person* of that boy across the street who used to aggravate all the neighbors with his mischievous depredations. Many religious people describe the experience of being *converted* or *born again* in terms that to the skeptical often seem chiefly fantastic.

With considerable truth, perhaps, it may be stated that after her marriage Mary Blank *changed,* that she has become *another woman.* So, too, when a man's old friends say that since the war he hasn't been the *same fellow* they used to know, the statement, however inaccurate, may indicate something real. We hear that an acquaintance when drinking the other night was *not himself.* Another man, we are told, *found himself* after his father lost all that money. Every now and then it is said that a certain woman's absorption in her home and children has resulted in her losing her *entire personality.* Though such sayings are never taken literally, there is often good reason for them to be taken seriously.

Are they not exaggerations or distortions

used to indicate very imperfectly what is by no means totally untrue but what cannot be put precisely, or fully, into words? The real meaning of such familiar statements, however significant, helps us only a little in explaining what we think we have encountered in the case reported. Some relation seems likely, as one might say there is some relation between ordinary vocal memory or fantasy and true auditory hallucinations.

Though often distinguished from each of the other terms, "personality" is sometimes used more or less as a synonym or approximation for "mind," "character," "disposition," "soul," "spirit," "self," "ego," "integrate of human functioning," "identity," etc. In common speech it may be said that John has a good mind but no personality, or that Jim has a wonderful personality but no character, etc. Often this protean word narrows (or broadens) in use to indicate chiefly the attractiveness, or unattractiveness, of some woman or man. In psychiatry its most specific function today is perhaps that of implying a unified total, of indicating more than "intelligence," or "character," more than

any of the several terms referring with various degrees of exactness to various qualities, activities, responses, capacities, or aspects of the human being. In the dictionaries, among other definitions, one finds "individuality," "quality or state of being a person," "personal existence or identity."

There is, apparently, no distinct or whole or commonly understood referent for our word "personality." It is useful to us in psychiatry despite its elasticity, often because of its elasticity. If they are to be helpful all such elastic terms must be used tentatively. Otherwise they may lead us at once into violent and confused disagreement about what are likely to be imaginary questions, mere conflicts of arbitrary definition. Bearing this in mind we feel it proper to speak of Eve Black, Eve White, and of Jane as three "personalities." Perhaps there is a better term available to indicate the manifestations of this patient. If so we are indeed prepared to welcome it, with enthusiasm and with relief.

Reports of Lysergic Acid Experiences

Sidney Cohen, Lionel Fichman, and Betty G. Eisner

Sidney Cohen is Director, Division of Narcotic Addiction and Drug Abuse, National Institute of Mental Health, Chevy Chase, Maryland. His recent books on psychopharmacology have been The Drug Dilemma: The LSD Story *(Atheneum),* LSD, *with Richard Alpert (New American Library), and* The Drug Dilemma *(McGraw-Hill). Lionel Fichman is a clinical psychologist at the Los Angeles State Mental Hygiene Clinic. He received his Ph.D. from U.C.L.A. in 1957. Betty Eisner is a psychologist in private practice. She received her Ph.D. from U.C.L.A. in 1956.*

1. Do you find narrative reports as described herein of value? If not, what measures would you use to elicit data on drugs?

2. Is there any mention of the fact that "willingness to submit" to the drug increases the possibility of bias in the sampling of subjects?

3. Why was abstract thinking more affected by the drug than vocabulary? Is this also true of the schizophrenic?

The psychotomimetic drugs have proven valuable tools in neuropsychiatric research. Of these agents lysergic acid diethylamide (LSD-25) is preferred at present for the production of a dissociation state or "model psychosis." It is a matter of current controversy whether the subject undergoes a toxic psychosis or a schizophreniform state. There is no desire to participate here in such controversy; however, reactions which included aspects of both the toxic and the schizophrenic psychoses were observed. Furthermore, in some cases no psy-

Abridged from S. Cohen, L. Fichman, and B. G. Eisner, "Subjective Reports of Lysergic Acid Experiences in a Context of Psychological Test Performance," *American Journal of Psychiatry,* 115 (1958), 30–35. Reprinted by permission of author and the American Psychiatric Association.

chotic process whatsoever appears to be involved.

Investigators who have attempted to evaluate the effect of the hallucinogenic drugs on personality have approached the problem from several parameters. Some use clinical appraisal, others contrive stressful situations, a growing number make use of psychological test batteries, and some employ a combination of methods. It is possible that there is still another source of information which has so far not been fully utilized—narrative reports by the subject himself.

Although introspective reports should be approached with caution, verbal subjects gifted with some measure of lucidity may offer insights which would otherwise escape detection. This is particularly true since the LSD-25 experience is, for many individuals, so overwhelming that immediate, effective communication becomes disrupted. Valuable information is often lost when a subjective description of the event is not recorded as soon as possible after termination of the major effects of the drug.

It is recognized that the validity of individual introspective reports is tentative because of the possibilities of distortion which may occur at any point in the process from experience to narration. However, if the reports can be correlated with clinical observation and psychological test results, a new dimension of insight into the LSD experience becomes available. There seems to be distinct value to subjective descriptions, especially when counter-balanced by the more objective psychological test material.

The following 5 case reports were selected from a study of 30 volunteer subjects, male and female, whose ages ranged from 22 to 57 years. None of these persons had ever required neuropsychiatric hospitalization or intensive psychotherapy. A battery of psychological tests[1] was administered under both control and drug conditions. The average dose was 100 micrograms of LSD-25 diluted in distilled water and administered orally at 8:00 A.M. to the fasting subject. Each volunteer agreed, as part of the study, to write a report of his experience that same day, if possible.

These examples are chosen for clinical variety and the expressiveness of the subjective reports. They also appear to be a fair sampling from the range of possible LSD-25 reactions. Although the cases appear to have a sustained direction toward a particular diagnostic category, this correspondence is not exact. Even if diagnostic labels were completely precise, it would be impossible to match reaction to category because a subject could progress through a series of affectual changes. These might vary from deepest dysphoria to soaring euphoria during a single drug experience, and also at times manifesting paranoid and catatonic type thinking and behavior.

A brief summary of performance changes on the psychological tests will be given. A subsequent report will deal more fully with the significant changes on the tests between drug and non-drug conditions and with the implications of these changes. However, a few overall remarks may be pertinent with respect to the sample in general.

As the drug took effect, the subjects showed varying amounts of change in sensory and motor function. Everything from slight visual blurring to synesthesias and the apparent motion of stable objects was reported. Sometimes

the movements of the subjects became more expansive, and sometimes they were so inhibited that the individual could not raise a finger.

With respect to intelligence, there was a drop in IQ scores on the Shipley-Hartford scale in 24 out of 30 cases under LSD-25. Abstract thinking was more affected than was vocabulary retention. The range of IQ change was from an increase of 11 points to a decrease of 41 points with the mean IQ change a decrease of 8.9 points.

The most outstanding features of the personality changes as revealed by the projective techniques were three. 1. A striking general disruption of the defensive system of the individual occurred. Breakdown of defensive structure was significantly more frequent and more pathological and there was an increased appearance of repressed material. 2. There was an impairment in reality contact which was reflected in bizarre responses and actual perceptual distortions up to and including hallucinations. 3. A disruption in the ability to maintain any sustained effort in dealing with the demands of the environment was a consistent finding. This was particularly clear in the disinclination and sometimes incapacity to perform the tasks set before him.

Probably because of the lowering of ego defenses, there appeared to be a lessening of differentiation between outer and inner stimuli, and the usually clear-cut divisions between sensory modalities became blurred with assorted synesthesias making their appearance. Accompanying the decreased awareness of external stimuli was a general turning inward of attention and an obvious preoccupation with internal productions.

One of the most provocative observations was the variety of mechanisms of coping with the effects of the drug. Some individuals exhibited a single regressive mode of defense; other subjects seemed to run through a repertoire of defensive techniques, either singly or several at a time; and others allowed their defensive system to be disrupted without anxiety. These latter appeared to experience a type of dissociation or depersonalization which was described as extremely pleasant, insightful and integrating.

[1] The battery consisted of the following projective tests: Rorschach, Thematic Apperception Test (TAT), Draw-A-Person (DAP), Bender Gestalt, Saxe Sentence Completion and Word Association. Other tests given were: Shipley-Hartford, Grayson Perceptualization, Minnesota Multiphasic Personality Inventory (MMPI) and an adjective check list.

It is of intense interest to speculate on the determinants of the direction of experience under LSD-25 which do not seem to be consistent in the same subjects from one session to another. The type of reaction seems to be a function of the personality of the subject, the conditions surrounding the situation, the people present during the drug-induced state, and the immediate circumstances of the subject's life. Further research is needed in this area to clarify the relationship of these variables, and to discover any other factors involved.

Case Reports

CASE 1. Woman psychologist.—The test changes from non-drug to drug battery showed a general regression from a high level of operational efficiency to one of disorganization and withdrawal. There was a drop from 145 to 137 in IQ, and most of this reflected an impairment in the ability to reason abstractly. Tests which were done with speed and efficiency under the control conditions were left unfinished or were completed with the greatest urging under the drug. A number of replies on the tests were left blank, and an even larger percentage were answered by inappropriate perseverations of "nothing" and "no." The overall picture of regressive withdrawal is perhaps best typified by the figure drawings. Under control conditions these were large, easily recognizable male and female figures; under the drug all the subject was able to produce were two tiny question marks in the upper righthand corner of the paper. One of the figures had a small box drawn around it. These would be an indication that the subject was unable to conceptualize or to produce even the most rudimentary human figure. In summary: the clinical picture changed from a highly intelligent normal subject with some anxiety and rather overt aggression to that resembling a catatonic schizophrenic.

Subjective Report: "The psychologist told me to get up and go over to a table and take some tests. I started to go, but nothing happened. I tried very hard to move. I pushed, but my body would not move. When I finally got it going, it went all right, but it was hard to stop. I wasn't thinking about anything but what I had to do which was move . . . Sometimes I would notice painful sensations in some part of my body which I knew in a vague sort of way were caused from being in one position too long. When I felt these I knew that they were intense sensations, but it didn't seem to matter very much. But whenever I became aware of pain, I tried to change position to relieve it. Sometimes it worked, and I was able to move. Sometimes I tried my best for a long time and nothing happened, so I would just stay the way I was and put up with the pain until I didn't notice it anymore . . .

"People would come in from time to time. If they were within my field of vision, I saw them. If they were not within my field of vision, I forgot they were there. Once I seemed to clear up a little, and I wondered who was sitting next to me; I tried to turn my head to see, but it wouldn't move. Whenever anybody asked me something, I tried to answer. Sometimes I wouldn't be thinking at all, just blank. Occasionally I would know exactly what I wanted to say. I would try to say it, and nothing would come out. Then I would line up some words to say, line them up in my mouth and work on getting the first one out on the theory that if I could get one word out, the rest would be easy. But this usually did not work . . .

"Somebody asked me if I were happy. In a fuzzy sort of way I wanted to explain that I just couldn't answer the question because it didn't have any meaning. I didn't think I was happy or unhappy, but I wasn't sure just what this was. I couldn't answer the question as phrased because the terms were just not relevant. This thought was hopelessly complicated to me. To get out of not being able to say anything, I just said, 'sure.'

"My most striking impression of the way I felt was of the tremendous amount of effort I was putting out for very little return. Now it seems to me that I found everything impossible but unavoidable. I felt no anxiety at any time after the drug took effect. I think now that anxiety would have been a very pleasant feeling and a welcome relief from the nothing in which I spent today."

CASE 2. Male teacher.—The test changes from non-drug to drug battery showed less deterioration than those of the majority of the subjects. There was an unevenness of performance which makes it difficult to give a consistent picture of the changes. For instance, when asked to tell stories to a set of pictures, the subject was able only to describe what was on the cards; on the Rorschach, by contrast, productivity was doubled and most of the responses were of a high caliber. These responses showed less anxiety and defensiveness against aggression and sexuality, and the homosexual flavor of the control record disappeared. There was also not as much preoccupation with a conflictual life situation on the drug tests as there had been on the control. There was a rise in IQ from 131 to 133 points which is not significant, but which is interesting because with the majority of the subjects there was a significant drop in IQ level. The subject demonstrated vividly in his test battery the visual changes which occur with the drug in heightened three dimensionality and the apparent movement of static surfaces. In summary: contrary to the trend, this subject showed less anxiety and defensiveness under the drug and seemed in better control of threatening unconscious material. There was an unevenness about his performance, suggesting that the effects of the drug waxed and waned, thus making it difficult to summarize the direction of clinical change.

Subjective Report: "About this time I noticed the bed, table legs, the doctor's legs and shoes, everything in my visual field was close around me, and they were very large. It was as though everything were on a convex surface about me. I have no idea how long this lasted, but following this, I suddenly felt that everything was 'away' from me. There was too much distance from me to the objects about me, the floor was spacious. This change occurred more than once (close-in-large to away). During one of the close-in phases the objects about me seemed to have no common base or ground. They all seemed to be floating on surfaces, transparent and their own; yet all were related and the phenomena felt normal. I was intensely aware of everything and felt I was experiencing something extremely important.

"We left the room, and I went to the lavatory . . . while there I looked in the mirror. I appeared drawn and lifeless and, therefore, somewhat shocked. I believe this may have been the beginning of the 'away' phase. Going through the halls there was little of interest. Coming upon the outside court . . . the 'outside' at this time appeared lifeless and not quite real. It was dull, flat, and colorless . . .

"We walked over to the cafeteria. As we entered, the music being played on the juke box 'caught' me. I began to walk in rhythm with it . . . Looking around as we walked toward the cafeteria line, I began to notice color. By the time we reached the line, colors were intense and saturated. The salads and desserts on the shelf became the most marvelous sight I had ever seen. As food the thought never occurred to me. My attention was taken by people and movement. At this time my sense of time was warped all out of proportion. An intensity crept into all objects. There was no distinction between animate and inanimate except for movement. It seemed to take hours to go through the cafeteria line.

"We left the cafeteria, went through the halls, and came out on the same yard or court previously mentioned. I would not have known it was the same place. The outside had the same quality about it that the cafeteria had. Everything was substantial. It was as though things were the way they should be—fantastically real. The trees were lush and their aroma was magnificent. All was fresh as I had never seen it before. I watched pigeons fly—there seemed to be after-images of them in their flight path. I could hardly leave the outdoors to go back into the building.

"At this time I believe I left the phase of close-in (which started when I walked into the cafeteria) and began the away phase. In the room again we started working on the tests. I became quiet inside. Withdrawn and moody. I would have been content to sit and brood, but there was nothing to brood about. I just felt nothing was worthwhile and any effort was too great.

"I feel there were definite phases: close-in (euphoria) and away (depression). These seemed to be an effect of the drug, but could be triggered by associations of a psychological nature. Not mentioned were feelings of being watched through the window in the door of the room. Also feeling that conversations were related to me."

CASE 3. Female nurse.—The control battery showed a rather immature woman within the normal range but with a strong flavor of the labile hysterical personality. The drug first threw the subject into an acute panic and then intensified the immature and repressed elements of the personality, and there was a drop in efficiency of performance with the appearance of much more hostility and sexuality. This increase in sexuality was so threatening to the subject that she threw a Rorschach card reminding her of male genitals across the room and called it lewd and nauseating.

The over-all drop in efficiency is typified by the drop of IQ level from 125 to 101 with the greater impairment in abstract reasoning. The general loosening of defenses was exhibited in associations such as "that's a place to live, too, I guess" to "vagina" and in her failure to draw both sexes in the figure drawings when under the drug. The control figures were rather silly and childish, but under the drug she was able to manage only one large, unclothed, undifferentiated figure and say, "There is no other sex, that's one and the same."

In summary: after the subject overcame the initial acute panic into which she was precipitated by the drug, the clinical picture which she had exhibited was that of an immature, labile woman whose defenses were loosened so that there was an increase in the appearance of overt aggression and sexuality. The appearance of this unconscious material and the feeling of loss of control were very threatening to the subject.

Subjective Report: "However, shortly I had the feeling of being choked from inside. I had difficulty breathing for a moment. Then I began to feel nauseated and restless. I said to the psychologist, 'I don't feel good at all.' I remember turning around in my chair and holding onto the table and putting my head down on my arm. Suddenly the tightness in my throat increased, and I began to feel as if my body were on fire both inside and outside. My neck and back felt very tense. I became very frightened and had the feeling of acute panic. I was being swirled and sucked down, down, down into oblivion. I clung to the table for dear life, but it did no good.

"The fear was overwhelming as I was thrust down into blackness. My body was burning up, and I began to sweat. This indescribable feeling of being swirled and thrust into some place else was easing somewhat. It seemed that I had been in this torment for weeks. After it had eased up, I knew beyond a doubt that I was in another world. I felt it and refused to tell the psychologist about it because he wouldn't understand. I remember thinking, 'This is what the psychotic feels like.' That feeling of panic and terror had left me tremulous and weak.

"At this point I felt as if there were a transparent wall all around me. It was so physical that I could almost reach out and touch it. I was completely enclosed in this wall, but I could see through it and hear everything that went on. . . . This transparent wall prevented other people from getting into my world, and also it kept me from going into theirs. I felt pleased and quite superior about this arrangement and thought that I had the advantage . . . Although the whole experience was interesting, no one could persuade me to go through the fear and discomfort again. The horror of 'losing control' is too much to expect of anyone to experience twice."

CASE 4. Male physiotherapist.—The outstanding change from control to drug battery was from rather defensive, careful—although slightly aggressive—performance to a relaxed happiness which was not disturbed even by the appearance of bizarre material. There was an IQ drop from 136 to 129 points, all of which appeared in the ability to reason abstractly. The relaxation of defensiveness, the lowering of intellectual controls, and the emergence of unconscious material is best exemplified by the figure drawings and the sentence completion test. The figures changed from well-defined although immature ones to purely symbolic drawings which resembled an embryo with a flowing tail and two ostrich feathers with beads at their base. On the sentence completion he perseverated "hot dog" 3 times, "Dad beat on the head" 4 times, and 5 sentences were happily preoccupied with Sigmund Freud. He felt he was really loved by him, people who didn't like Sigmund annoyed him, he wished his mother had married S.F. and so on for 8 out of 50 questions. He seemed conscious of his performance but undisturbed by it, and the bizarre material and disorganizations had a happy setting such as his drawing circles as musical notes and his gay choice of names in the stories he told (Murgatroid, Lotus Blossom, Hannah and Harry, etc.).

In summary: this subject seemed to welcome dissociation, the lessening of defenses and anxiety, and the appearance of unconscious material.

Subjective Report: "This sounds contradictory but isn't—this clear-headed confusion. A thing can become so bright it cannot be held within the human brain—so beautiful it aches to behold it—yet one looks and submits the flesh to this pain of beauty—this beauty is clear—the pain is the confusion. If the 'beauty' can look at the pain and become one with it—this is what I mean by clear-headed confusion. I recall seeing pictures and colors and many things . . . One thing is quite clear to me now as I return to the changing pictures, the colors swimming, retreating, charging: these colors to an artist are in reality a picture frame—the hard core, the soul, the God, the Be of the artist is the picture. His genius is as great as his ability to put his Be or Is or Oneness on the canvas. This can be rewritten for any of the Arts.

"My own slant was, I believe, particularly towards form and movement. At one point when I persisted in holding onto a single hair as if that was all that held me to reality and perhaps it was, you said why not choose a speck on the floor? I tried very hard to tell you it couldn't be just a speck on the floor. It had to be a symbol of my choice and this now seems logical to me . . . You tell me and I tell me that I cannot see thru a file card, see my hand and the blood vessels, see the thickness of printers ink, and I must bow my head and say it can't be done. But surely, I did it. And this is the logic. What makes our logic better than the psychotic's logic? . . . Heretofore, over many years I have had a superior, somewhat supercilious attitude towards all organized religions. Today, on the way home, I tried to tell A. that I could now feel with people who had deep religious feeling . . .

"A week ago I would have thought that visions seen by 'normal' individuals were carefully considered fictions. Although my personal religious convictions have not changed, I can very well understand 'visions,' 'calls,' or deep religious feelings. However, I will still be suspicious of people who protest too much. A feeling of oneness with God cannot be mundane, practical consideration but must be an intenseness; not a common sketch but a masterpiece. This new acquaintance with reality will probably be the strongest reminder of my visit into mania. Reality will no longer be an absolute. I know now that the psychotic's reality is not mine and that for him, perhaps, his reality can be infinitely better than mine."

CASE 5. Male psychiatric aide.—Although both test batteries were defensive, there was more disorganization present on the drug tests. The IQ level fell from 133 to 126. On the word association test synesthesia was present and the subject saw the object represented on several occasions when the word was spoken. The type of defense shifted from the predominantly intellectual to the more withdrawn. There was less productivity and several refusals to answer. Evidences of fatigue and inertia were present, and more concern with themes of failure occurred in the stories. The regression and refusals appeared most clearly when unconscious material which the subject found distressing (mainly aggressive) showed evidence of appearing. There was much sensory involvement while under the drug, and cards with pictures or blots seemed to undulate and weave in almost living vibrations. In summary: the clinical picture was that of an extremely careful, defensive individual with a strong intellectual overlay who was much affected by sensory changes under the drug and whose defenses shifted from the intellectual to the more withdrawn when threatening unconscious material of a revealing nature began to appear.

Subjective Report: "When I started to tell what I saw, I would suddenly stop in amazement of what I had said. 'Well,' ran my private thought, 'I'll have to use more discretion than that in what I say.' A moment later I would find myself saying something even more disturbing. A sense of having lost control hit me, and produced a definite negative experience. I believe all the force of control and restraint that I could muster must have been called forth.

"My mind was busy. Was this an indication of the fears and violence I feared I might encounter deep down in my nature? This is the way I immediately interpreted it. A tendency to 'clam up' was now elevated to a ruling emotion . . . My usual determination to see a 'nice' meaning was powerless in the face of a violence that seemed almost vicious—For relief I turned to the lovely Utah landscape on the wall. And what should I find but a cloud line and horizon converted into a fierce pair of lips, snarling in a pulsating, threatening face. My body tensed; my feet began to sweat, and I believe I slid down in my chair; I don't know what good that was supposed to do, unless I thought I could duck out the back way. It would be difficult to describe my emotional response which somehow, stripped of its complex variations, amounted to an immense sense of failure.

"Only for perhaps 5 minutes did I wish I had not tried the drug. After that, the feeling that I wanted to try again grew steadily—it grew along with the feeling that I had started out right, that my reactions did not indicate pure and simply that I was at heart a fearful person, ridden with guilt complexes. Actually, though this new and more hopeful interpretation was born early in the experience, the 'majority' of me had given up to negative emotions. I could see very little but disintegration in myself. Therefore it became very necessary to parry, to not reveal the mess that I was. I could keep that to myself, and attempt a major reconstruction privately later.

"We went to the canteen for lunch. By this time I seemed to be at the peak of the effect of the drug —I was 'far gone' . . . I couldn't remember going down the hall or being on the elevator, though I can remember the elevator door opening very suddenly. The doctor commented on it; and I thought it was somehow significant as part of a trick. After all, it wasn't lunch time yet, I thought. Or maybe it was an act to test my powers of observation . . . In the cafeteria line I felt clumsy . . . I almost felt that (the waitress) was participating in a conspiracy to force me to reveal that I was 'gone.'

"I was really on guard now. The doctor suggested I find a table. Very cautiously I set out across the room, which was a vast place now, not at all certain that I would recognize an empty table. And I wondered if there would be any significance in the sort of location I would select. I was looking for significance in everything. I was wary and suspicious; but oddly enough still felt I could trust the doctor and psychologist. I knew I was paranoid, and yet no person seemed threatening . . .

"It was the oddest thing. I couldn't follow the conversation at all, can't remember a thing that was said. What impressed me was the staccato, rapid pace of the thing, and the 'gangster' quality. I thought they might be trying to see if I would later be able to link this act with reality . . . for the most part I was wrapped up in my own thoughts and emotions. I had failed. I was a mess. I thought of the report by another subject who commented that she knew this was 'how a psychotic feels.' I could go her one better: obviously I was psychotic . . . Early in the experience I had been able to make some shift between normal and LSD states of consciousness. But now I was entirely caught up in the new world. I couldn't be sure that we were really at dinner at all. . . . Was I dreaming? I made a mental note to be sure and ask the doctor and psychologist if we had really gone to lunch at all.

"Once outside again, I saw a group of patients being escorted by several aides. Immediately I saw one of my friends, an aide, with the group . . . I thought to myself: 'It is very clever of them to have me see C. now. That adds a quality of verisimilitude.' (Later when finishing the tests:) 'The test called up often rehearsed feelings of being accused' . . . Occasionally, for a moment at a time, I caught a painful sense of the inability to feel warmth or trust. I had a sense of isolation, of frigid aloneness built and defended by the intellect's too dominant questions, evaluations, and judgments."

Summary

These personal narrations of subjects recently recovered from LSD-25 experiences supplement the information obtained by clinical observation and psychological test data and give insight into the qualitative change occurring within the individual.

Therapeutic Personality Change

Carl R. Rogers

Carl Rogers, Resident Fellow of the Center for Studies of the Person, La Jolla, California, received his Ph.D. from Teachers College, Columbia University, in 1931. He began his academic work in scientific agriculture, shifted to history, and spent two years at Union Theological Seminary before going on to Teachers College. Rogers is the only psychologist who has received both the Distinguished Scientific Contribution Award and the Award for Professional Achievement from the American Psychological Association. His major professional interest has always been in personality change—he has focused on this topic as therapist, as researcher in psychotherapy, as group facilitator, and as personality theorist. His name is synonymous with client-centered therapy.

1. *Can you "buy" the assumption that personality change cannot be self-induced or achieved outside of a personal relationship? If you cannot, what is your evidence?*

2. *What difference does it make who determines whether a client is "in a state of incongruence"?*

3. *Should the therapist know the why, dynamics, of a client's "problem" before treating him?*

For many years I have been engaged in psychotherapy with individuals in distress. In recent years I have found myself increasingly concerned with the process of abstracting from that experience the general principles which appear to be involved in it. I have endeavored to discover any orderliness, any unity which seems to inhere in the subtle, complex tissue of interpersonal relationship in which I have so constantly been immersed in therapeutic work.

Abridged from Carl R. Rogers, "The Necessary and Sufficient Conditions of Therapeutic Personality Change," *Journal of Consulting Psychology*, 21 (1957), 95–100. Copyright 1957 by the American Psychological Association and reproduced by permission.

One of the current products of this concern is an attempt to state, in formal terms, a theory of psychotherapy, of personality, and of interpersonal relationships which will encompass and contain the phenomena of my experience. What I wish to do in this paper is to take one very small segment of that theory, spell it out more completely, and explore its meaning and usefulness.

The Problem

The question to which I wish to address myself is this: Is it possible to state, in terms which are clearly definable and measurable, the psychological conditions which are both necessary and sufficient to bring about constructive personality change? Do we, in other words, know with any precision those elements which are essential if psychotherapeutic change is to ensue?

Before proceeding to the major task let me dispose very briefly of the second portion of the question. What is meant by such phrases as "psychotherapeutic change," "constructive personality change"? This problem also deserves deep and serious consideration, but for the moment let me suggest a common-sense type of meaning upon which we can perhaps agree for purposes of this paper. By these phrases is meant: change in the personality structure of the individual, at both surface and deeper levels, in a direction which clinicians would agree means greater integration, less internal conflict, more energy utilizable for effective living; change in behavior away from behaviors generally regarded as immature and toward behaviors regarded as mature. This brief description may suffice to indicate the kind of change for which we are considering the preconditions. It may also suggest the ways in which this criterion of change may be determined.

The Conditions

As I have considered my own clinical experience and that of my colleagues, together with the pertinent research which is available, I have drawn out several conditions which seem to me to be *necessary* to initiate constructive personality change, and which, taken together, appear to be *sufficient* to inaugurate that process. As I have worked on this problem I have found myself surprised at the simplicity of what has emerged. The statement which follows is not offered with any assurance as to its correctness, but with the expectation that it will have the value of any theory, namely that it states or implies a series of hypotheses which are open to proof or disproof, thereby clarifying and extending our knowledge of the field.

Since I am not, in this paper, trying to achieve suspense, I will state at once, in severely rigorous and summarized terms, the six conditions which I have come to feel are basic to the process of personality change. The meaning of a number of the terms is not immediately evident, but will be clarified in the explanatory sections which follow. Without further introduction let me state the basic theoretical position.

For constructive personality change to occur, it is necessary that these conditions exist and continue over a period of time:

1. Two persons are in psychological contact.
2. The first, whom we shall term the client, is in a state of incongruence, being vulnerable or anxious.
3. The second person, whom we shall term the therapist, is congruent or integrated in the relationship.
4. The therapist experiences unconditional positive regard for the client.
5. The therapist experiences an empathic understanding of the client's internal frame of reference and endeavors to communicate this experience to the client.
6. The communication to the client of the therapist's empathic understanding and unconditional positive regard is to a minimal degree achieved.

No other conditions are necessary. If these six conditions exist, and continue over a period of time, this is sufficient. The process of constructive personality change will follow.

A Relationship

The first condition specifies that a minimal relationship, a psychological contact, must exist. I am hypothesizing that significant positive personality change does not occur except in a relationship. This is of course an hypothesis, and it may be disproved.

Conditions 2 through 6 define the characteristics of the relationship which are regarded as essential by defining the necessary characteristics of each person in the relationship. All that is intended by this first condition is to specify that the two people are to some degree in contact, that each makes some perceived difference in the experiential field of the other. Probably it is sufficient if each makes some "subceived" difference, even though the individual may not be consciously aware of this impact. Thus it might be difficult to know whether a catatonic patient perceives a therapist's presence as making a difference to him—a difference of any kind—but it is almost certain that at some organic level he does sense this difference.

Except in such a difficult borderline situation as that just mentioned, it would be relatively easy to define this condition in operational terms and thus determine, from a hard-boiled research point of view, whether the condition does, or does not, exist. The simplest method of determination involves simply the awareness of both client and therapist. If each is aware of being in personal or psychological contact with the other, then this condition is met.

This first condition of therapeutic change is such a simple one that perhaps it should be labeled an assumption or a precondition in order to set it apart from those that follow.

Without it, however, the remaining items would have no meaning, and that is the reason for including it.

The State of the Client

It was specified that it is necessary that the client be "in a state of incongruence, being vulnerable or anxious." What is the meaning of these terms?

Incongruence is a basic construct in the theory we have been developing. It refers to a discrepancy between the actual experience of the organism and the self picture of the individual insofar as it represents that experience. Thus a student may experience, at a total or organismic level, a fear of the university and of examinations which are given on the third floor of a certain building, since these may demonstrate a fundamental inadequacy in him. Since such a fear of his inadequacy is decidedly at odds with his concept of himself, this experience is represented (distortedly) in his awareness as an unreasonable fear of climbing stairs in this building, or any building, and soon an unreasonable fear of crossing the open campus. Thus there is a fundamental discrepancy between the experienced meaning of the situation as it registers in his organism and the symbolic representation of that experience in awareness in such a way that it does not conflict with the picture he has of himself. In this case to admit a fear of inadequacy would contradict the picture he holds of himself; to admit incomprehensible fears does not contradict his self concept.

Another instance would be the mother who develops vague illnesses whenever her only son makes plans to leave home. The actual desire is to hold on to her only source of satisfaction. To perceive this in awareness would be inconsistent with the picture she holds of herself as a good mother. Illness, however, is consistent with her self concept, and the experience is symbolized in this distorted fashion. Thus again there is a basic incongruence between the self as perceived (in this case as an ill mother needing attention) and the actual experience (in this case the desire to hold on to her son).

When the individual has no awareness of such incongruence in himself, then he is merely vulnerable to the possibility of anxiety and disorganization. Some experience might occur so suddenly or so obviously that the incongruence could not be denied. Therefore, the person is vulnerable to such a possibility.

If the individual dimly perceives such an incongruence in himself, then a tension state occurs which is known as anxiety. The incongruence need not be sharply perceived. It is enough that it is subceived—that is, discriminated as threatening to the self without any awareness of the content of that threat. Such anxiety is often seen in therapy as the individual approaches awareness of some element of his experience which is in sharp contradiction to his self concept.

It is not easy to give precise operational definition to this second of the six conditions, yet to some degree this has been achieved. Several research workers have defined the self concept by means of a Q sort by the individual of a list of self-referent items. This gives us an operational picture of the self. The total experiencing of the individual is more difficult to capture. Chodorkoff has defined it as a Q sort made by a clinician who sorts the same self-referent items independently, basing his sorting on the picture he has obtained of the individual from projective tests. His sort thus includes unconscious as well as conscious elements of the individual's experience. The correlation between these two sortings gives a crude operational measure of incongruence between self and experience, low or negative correlation representing of course a high degree of incongruence.

The Therapist's Genuineness in the Relationship

The third condition is that the therapist should be, within the confines of this relationship, a congruent, genuine, integrated person. It means that within the relationship he is freely and deeply himself, with his actual experience accurately represented by his awareness of himself. It is the opposite of presenting a facade, either knowingly or unknowingly.

It is not necessary (nor is it possible) that the therapist be a paragon who exhibits this degree of integration, of wholeness, in every aspect of his life. It is sufficient that he is accurately himself in this hour of this relationship, that in this basic sense he is what he actually is, in this moment of time.

It should be clear that this includes being himself even in ways which are not regarded as ideal for psychotherapy. His experience may be "I'm afraid of this client" or "My attention is so focused on my own problems that I can scarcely listen to him." If the therapist is not denying these feelings to awareness, but is able freely to be them (as well as being his other feelings), then the condition we have stated is met.

It would take us too far afield to consider the puzzling matter as to the degree to which the therapist overtly communicates this reality in himself to the client. Certainly the aim is not for the therapist to express or talk about his own feelings, but primarily that he should not be deceiving the client as to himself. At times he may need to talk about some of his own feelings (either to the client, or to a colleague or supervisor) if they are standing in the way of the two following conditions.

It is not too difficult to suggest an operational definition for this third condition. We resort again to Q technique. If the therapist sorts a series of items relevant to the relationship, this will give his perception of his experience in the relationship. If several judges who have observed the interview or listened to a recording of it (or observed a sound movie of it) now sort the same items to represent *their* perception of the relationship, this second sorting should catch those elements of the therapist's behavior and inferred attitudes of which he is unaware, as well as those of which he is aware. Thus a high correlation between the therapist's sort and the observer's sort would represent in crude form an operational definition of the therapist's congruence or integration in the relationship; and a low correlation, the opposite.

Unconditional Positive Regard

To the extent that the therapist finds himself experiencing a warm acceptance of each aspect of the client's experience as being a part of that client, he is experiencing unconditional positive regard. This concept has been developed by Standal. It means that there are no *conditions* of acceptance, no feeling of "I like you only *if* you are thus and so." It means a "prizing" of the person, as Dewey has used that term. It is at the opposite pole from the selective evaluating attitude—"You are bad in these ways, good in those." It involves as much feeling of accept-

ance for the client's expression of negative, "bad," painful, fearful, defensive, abnormal feelings as for his expression of "good," positive, mature, confident, social feelings, as much acceptance of ways in which he is inconsistent as of ways in which he is consistent. It means a caring for the client, but not in a possessive way or in such a way as simply to satisfy the therapist's own needs. It means a caring for the client as a *separate* person, with permission to have his own feelings, his own experiences. One client describes the therapist as "fostering my possession of my own experience and that I am actually having it: thinking what I think, feeling what I feel, wanting what I want, fearing what I fear: no 'ifs,' 'buts,' or 'not reallys.' " This is the type of acceptance which is hypothesized as being necessary if personality change is to occur.

Like the two previous conditions, this fourth condition is a matter of degree,[1] as immediately becomes apparent if we attempt to define it in terms of specific research operations. One such method of giving it definition would be to consider the Q sort for the relationship as described under Condition 3. To the extent that items expressive of unconditional positive regard are sorted as characteristic of the relationship by both the therapist and the observers, unconditional positive regard might be said to exist. Such items might include statements of this order: "I feel no revulsion at anything the client says"; "I feel neither approval nor disapproval of the client and his statements—simply acceptance"; "I feel warmly toward the client—toward his weaknesses and problems as well as his potentialities"; "I am not inclined to pass judgment on what the client tells me"; "I like the client." To the extent that both therapist

[1] The phrase "unconditional positive regard" may be an unfortunate one, since it sounds like an absolute, an all or nothing dispositional concept. It is probably evident from the description that completely unconditional positive regard would never exist except in theory. From a clinical and experiential point of view I believe the most accurate statement is that the effective therapist experiences unconditional positive regard for the client during many moments of his contact with him, yet from time to time he experiences only a conditional positive regard—and perhaps at times a negative regard, though this is not likely in effective therapy. It is in this sense that unconditional positive regard exists as a matter of degree in any relationship.

and observers perceive these items as characteristic, Condition 4 might be said to be met.

Empathy

The fifth condition is that the therapist is experiencing an accurate, empathic understanding of the client's awareness of his own experience. To sense the client's private world as if it were your own, but without ever losing the "as if" quality—this is empathy, and this seems essential to therapy. To sense the client's anger, fear, or confusion as if it were your own, yet without your own anger, fear, or confusion getting bound up in it, is the condition we are endeavoring to describe. When the client's world is this clear to the therapist, and he moves about in it freely, then he can both communicate his understanding of what is clearly known to the client and can also voice meanings in the client's experience of which the client is scarcely aware. As one client described this second aspect: "Every now and again, with me in a tangle of thought and feeling, screwed up in a web of mutually divergent lines of movement, with impulses from different parts of me, and me feeling the feeling of its being all too much and suchlike—then whomp, just like a sunbeam thrusting its way through cloudbanks and tangles of foliage to spread a circle of light on a tangle of forest paths, came some comment from you. (It was) clarity, even disentanglement, an additional twist to the picture, a putting in place. Then the consequence—the sense of moving on, the relaxation. These were sunbeams." That such penetrating empathy is important for therapy is indicated by Fiedler's research in which items such as the following placed high in the description of relationships created by experienced therapists:

The therapist is well able to understand the patient's feelings.
The therapist is never in any doubt about what the patient means.
The therapist's remarks fit in just right with the patient's mood and content.
The therapist's tone of voice conveys the complete ability to share the patient's feelings.

An operational definition of the therapist's empathy could be provided in different ways. Use might be made of the Q sort described under Condition 3. To the degree that items descriptive of accurate empathy were sorted as characteristic by both the therapist and the observers, this condition would be regarded as existing.

Another way of defining this condition would be for client and therapist to sort a list of items descriptive of client feelings. Each would sort independently, the task being to represent the feelings which the client had experienced during a just completed interview. If the correlation between client and therapist sortings were high, accurate empathy would be said to exist, a low correlation indicating the opposite conclusion.

Still another way of measuring empathy would be for trained judges to rate the depth and accuracy of the therapist's empathy on the basis of listening to recorded interviews.

The Client's Perception of the Therapist

The final condition as stated is that the client perceives, to a minimal degree, the acceptance and empathy which the therapist experiences for him. Unless some communication of these attitudes exists in the relationship as far as the client is concerned, then the therapeutic process could not, by our hypothesis, be initiated.

Since attitudes cannot be directly perceived, it might be somewhat more accurate to state that therapist behaviors and words are perceived by the client as meaning that to some degree the therapist accepts and understands him.

An operational definition of this condition would not be difficult. The client might, after an interview, sort a Q-sort list of items referring to qualities representing the relationship between himself and the therapist. (The same list could be used as for Condition 3.) If several items descriptive of acceptance and empathy are sorted by the client as characteristic of the relationship, then this condition could be regarded as met. In the present state of our knowledge the meaning of "to a minimal degree" would have to be arbitrary.

Up to this point the effort has been made to present, briefly and factually, the conditions which I have come to regard as essential for psychotherapeutic change. I have not tried to give the theoretical context of these conditions nor to explain what seem to me to be the dynamics of their effectiveness.

I have, however, given at least one means of defining, in operational terms, each of the conditions mentioned. I have done this in order to stress the fact that I am not speaking of vague qualities which ideally should be present if some other vague result is to occur. I am presenting conditions which are crudely measurable even in the present state of our technology, and have suggested specific operations in each instance even though I am sure that more adequate methods of measurement could be devised by a serious investigator.

My purpose has been to stress the notion that in my opinion we are dealing with an if-then phenomenon in which knowledge of the dynamics is not essential to testing the hypotheses. Thus, to illustrate from another field: if one substance, shown by a series of operations to be the substance known as hydrochloric acid, is mixed with another substance, shown by another series of operations to be sodium hydroxide, then salt and water will be products of this mixture. This is true whether one regards the results as due to magic, or whether one explains it in the most adequate terms of modern chemical theory. In the same way it is being postulated here that certain definable conditions precede certain definable changes and that this fact exists independently of our efforts to account for it.

Desensitization Therapy

Joseph Wolpe

Joseph Wolpe is a physician who was born in South Africa and later came to this country to practice. His original inspiration for treatment of the mentally ill was Freudian in nature. He broke away from this approach during World War II while studying psychological theories of learning and their application to war neuroses. Today he is the chief spokesman for a variety of "learning therapies." Wolpe is presently Professor of Psychiatry, Department of Behavioral Science, Temple University Medical School, Philadelphia.

1. *How would you explain Wolpe's hypnotic instructions from a psychological point of view?*

2. *Why do you think patients do not signal mild disturbances to the therapist?*

3. *Explain, in your own words, how the technique described in this reading eliminates a person's fears and anxieties.*

Of the methods of therapy considered, systematic desensitization parallels most closely the experimental procedure of feeding cats in the presence of increasing "doses" of anxiety-evoking stimuli discussed previously.

An anxiety hierarchy is a list of stimulus situations to which a patient reacts with graded amounts of anxiety. The most disturbing item is placed at the top of the list, the least disturbing at the bottom. These hierarchies provide a convenient framework for systematic desensitization, through relaxation, to increasing amounts of anxiety-evoking stimuli.*

* A basic assumption underlying this procedure is that the response to the imagined situation resembles that to the real situation. Experience bears this out. People are anxious when they imagine stimuli that are fearful in reality. This is in keeping with Stone's observations in another context.

The theory may be summarized like this: If a stimulus constellation made up of five equipotent elements $A_1A_2A_3A_4A_5$ evokes 50 units of anxiety response in an organism, proportionately less anxiety will be evoked by constellations made up of fewer elements. Relaxation that is insufficient to counter the 50 units of anxiety that $A_1A_2A_3A_4A_5$ evokes may be well able to inhibit the 10 units evoked by A_1 alone. Then if the anxiety evoked by A_1 is repeatedly inhibited through being opposed by relaxation, its magnitude will drop, eventually to zero. In consequence, a presentation of A_1A_2 will now evoke only 10 units of anxiety, instead of 20, and this will similarly undergo conditioned inhibition when opposed by relaxation. Through further steps along these lines the whole combination $A_1A_2A_3A_4A_5$ will lose its power to arouse any anxiety.

The raw data for a hierarchy are obtained in several ways. The patient's history frequently reveals a variety of situations to which he reacts with undue disturbance. Further areas of disturbance may be revealed by perusal of his answers to the Willoughby questionnaire. Then he is given the "homework" task of making up a list of everything he can think of that is capable of frightening, disturbing, distressing, or embarrassing him in any way, excepting, of course, situations that would frighten anybody, such as meeting a hungry lion. Some patients bring back extensive inventories, others very scanty ones; and with the latter a good deal of time may have to be spent during interviews eliciting further items.

Confronted at last with anything between about 10 and 100 heterogeneous items, the therapist peruses them to see whether they belong to one or more thematic categories. If there is more than one theme, the items of each are grouped together. For example, one patient had a subdivision into enclosement, death, and bodily-lesion themes; another into social disapproval, disease, and aloneness; a third into trauma, death, and being in the limelight; a fourth into rejection and scenes of violence.

The subdivided list is now handed to the patient, who is asked to rank the items of each sublist in descending order according to the measure of disturbance he would have upon exposure to each. The rearranged list constitutes the hierarchical series that will be used in treatment. Modifications or additions may of course be made later.

At the first desensitization session the patient, already trained in relaxation, is hypnotized and in the trance is made to relax as deeply as possible. He is then told that he will be required to imagine a number of scenes which will appear to him very vividly. If he feels disturbed by any scene, he is to raise his hand as a signal. The weakest scenes from the hierarchical series are now presented in turn, usually for between two and three seconds each in the beginning. The raising of the left hand or any manifestation of increased bodily tension leads to the immediate curtailment of the ongoing scene. When it is judged that enough scenes have been given, the patient is roused from the trance and asked how clear the scenes were and whether any of them were disturbing. Even if he has not raised his hand during the trance, he may report having been very slightly to very considerably disturbed by one or more of the scenes. (Patients almost never raise their hands to a disturbance that is only slight.)

At the second desensitization session, a day or more later, the procedure is largely determined by what happened at the first. A scene that produced no disturbance at all is omitted and the next higher item in the hierarchy presented in its place. A scene that was slightly disturbing is presented again, unchanged. If there was considerable disturbance to the weakest scene from any hierarchy, a still

weaker stimulus must now be substituted. Suppose, for example, that the disturbing item was seeing a funeral procession. Typical weaker substitutions would be the word "funeral," seeing the procession from a distance of 200 yards, seeing an isolated and presumably empty hearse, or a *very brief* presentation of the original scene. The verbal substitution would usually be the weakest of these and would therefore be preferred. No harm is ever done by presenting a stimulus that is too weak. A stimulus that is too strong may actually increase sensitivity, and, especially during early experiments with the method, I have occasionally produced major setbacks in patients by premature presentation to them of stimuli with a high anxiety-evoking potential.*

In most patients, when the same scene is presented several times during a session there is a weaker reaction to each successive presentation. When this occurs, it accelerates therapy.† In other patients there is perseveration of anxiety responses, so that the anxiety produced by a second presentation summates with that from the first, the repetition tending thus to have a sensitizing effect rather than a therapeutic one.

With suitably cautious handling some headway will be made in the hierarchies at each session, and *pari passu* with this the patient will report a progressive decrease of sensitivity to the relevant kinds of stimulus situations encountered in the normal course of his life. The total number of sessions required varies greatly but is usually between 10 and 25.

The introspections of a clinical psychologist who was treated by this method are of interest:

Most typically the emotion associated with a situation tended to diminish or disappear between one session and another. On three or four oc-

---

* When sensitivity is increased as a result of an error of this kind, no scenes must be presented at the next session or two, and during these the hypnotic trance should be utilized merely to relax the patient as deeply as possible. At subsequent sessions scenes are introduced very cautiously from far down in the hierarchy whose subject matter produced the setback.

† I frequently inquire whether the reaction is weakening or not by saying after, say, the third presentation of a scene, "If your reaction has been decreasing, do nothing; if not, raise your hand." If it has been decreasing, I present the same scene two or three times more.

casions, however, the desensitization seemed to occur quite suddenly in the course of a session. On these occasions the change was subjectively a dramatic one: I would feel, all at once, a sense of separation, or apartness, or independence of the situation; a feeling that "I am *here*, it is *there*." To say simply that I attained greater objectivity, or more simply that the emotional component of the image disappeared, would be accurate but not quite as descriptive of my subjective experience as the preceding sentence.

The change, even when sudden, never seemed to constitute an "insight." My insight into my difficulties was perhaps fairly good initially, and was not altered one way or the other by the desensitization process *per se*. It might be said, however, that my "perception" of situations changed.

Patients who cannot relax will not make progress with this method. Those who cannot or will not be hypnotized but who can relax will make progress, although apparently more slowly than when hypnosis is used. The method necessarily fails with a small minority who are unable to imagine the suggested scenes. A few, perhaps about 5 per cent, do not make progress because although they can visualize clearly, they do not have the disturbed reaction to the imagined scene that they would have to the reality. Experience has shown that most of these can arouse the relevant emotions by *verbalizing* the scenes, and they then progress in the same way as other patients.

Occasionally, one comes across a patient who, having been desensitized to a hierarchy list, reveals a range of further, previously unrecognized sensitivities on a related but distinct theme. After desensitization to the latter, a third theme may become evident, and so on. It is surmised that this profusion of variations is due to unusually numerous and severe past stresses having brought about a conditioning of anxiety responses to an extraordinarily large number of aspects of certain situations. In these cases, abreaction is sometimes a valuable adjuvant because it involves the whole of the original conditioning situation.

The Conduct of Desensitization Sessions

An account will be given of the exact details of procedure at one patient's desensitization sessions—her first session and two successive sessions when therapy was well under way. This patient had the following anxiety hierarch-ies (the most disturbing items being on top, as always):

Hierarchies

A. Fear of hostility
   1. Devaluating remarks by husband
   2. Devaluating remarks by friends
   3. Sarcasm from husband or friends
   4. Nagging
   5. Addressing a group
   6. Being at social gathering of more than four people (the more the worse)
   7. Applying for a job
   8. Being excluded from a group activity
   9. Anybody with a patronizing attitude

B. Fear of death and its accoutrements
   1. First husband in his coffin
   2. At a burial
   3. Seeing a burial assemblage from afar
   4. Obituary notice of young person dying of heart attack
   5. Driving past a cemetery
   6. Seeing a funeral (the nearer the worse)
   7. Passing a funeral home
   8. Obituary notice of old person (worse if died of heart disease)
   9. Inside a hospital
   10. Seeing a hospital
   11. Seeing an ambulance

C. Fear of symptoms (despite *knowing* them to be nonsignificant)
   1. Extrasystoles
   2. Shooting pains in chest and abdomen
   3. Pains in left shoulder and back
   4. Pain on top of head
   5. Buzzing in ears
   6. Tremor of hands
   7. Numbness or pain in fingertips
   8. Dyspnea after exertion
   9. Pain in left hand (old injury)

First Desensitization Session (*12th Interview*) *

Before this interview the patient had learned to relax most of the muscles in her body. At our last meeting hypnosis had been discussed, and as she was afraid of it, I had tried to reassure her.

* The hypnotic induction procedure follows Wolberg.

After some discussion about other matters, I told her that we would now try to have a hypnotic session. As she was comfortably seated, I said, "Rest a hand on each thigh. In response to suggestions that I shall give you, you will notice various things happen to your hands. However, if at any time you feel anxious at what is happening, you will be able to interrupt the proceedings immediately. You will at no stage lose consciousness."

Her hands having settled comfortably on her lap, I went on, "Look at your hands and keep on looking at them. At the same time I want you to give your fullest attention to the sensations in your hands, whatever they may be. At this moment you may be aware of the texture of your skirt, of the warmth between your fingers and in your thighs, of tingling sensations, perhaps an awareness of your pulse, or the movement of air over your fingers. There may even be other sensations. Concentrate on your sensations, give them your complete attention, no matter what they are, and continue to do so. As you go on watching you will notice small movements appearing in your fingers. It will be interesting to see which finger moves first— maybe the thumb or little finger or index finger or the middle finger or even the fourth finger. (*Right index finger moves.*) There, your right index finger moved, and now, as you go on watching, you will notice other fingers move, and the general effect of these movements will be to spread the fingers farther and farther apart. (*Movements appear in other fingers of the right hand.*) Now you begin to notice that as the fingers spread apart, a feeling of lightness appears among the other sensations in your hand and soon you will observe that your right hand begins to rise. Your right hand will become lighter and lighter and it will begin to lift. There, we can already see some slight arching of the right hand. Your hand goes up higher and higher. (*Hand rises.*) As it rises you will notice that the palm begins to turn slowly inward, because it is going to rise to your face. When your hand touches your face, you will be aware of a profoundly pleasant, heavy feeling throughout your body. Then, or even before then, your eyes will close. (*Her hand slowly rises to her face and her eyes close.*) Now you feel so pleasantly heavy and drowsy, you become heavier and heavier.

"Now let all the muscles of your body relax. Let relaxation grow deeper and deeper. We shall concentrate on the various zones of your body in turn. Relax the muscles of your forehead and those of the rest of your face. (*Pause.*) Relax all the muscles of your jaws and of your tongue. (*Pause.*) Relax the muscles of your eyeballs. (*Pause.*) Now relax your neck. (*Pause.*) Let the muscles of your shoulders and your arms relax. (*Pause.*) Relax the muscles of your back and your abdomen. (*Pause.*) Relax the muscles of your thighs and your legs. (*Pause.*) Let go more and still more. You become so calm; you feel so comfortable, nothing matters except to enjoy this pleasant, calm, relaxed state. (*Pause.*)

"Now I am going to give you some scenes to imagine and you will imagine them very clearly and calmly. If, however, by any chance anything that you imagine disturbs you, you will at once indicate this to me by raising your left hand two or three inches. First I am going to give you a very commonplace scene. Imagine that you are sitting alone in an armchair in the living room of your house. It is a very pleasant sunny day and you are sitting in this chair perfectly at ease. (*Pause of about 5 seconds.*) Next I want you to imagine the printed word 'Dentist.' (*Pause of about 3 seconds.*) Stop imagining this word and concentrate on relaxing your muscles. (*Pause.*) Now imagine that you are reading the newspaper and that your eye falls upon the headline 'Prominent citizen dies at 86.' (*Pause of about 3 seconds.*) Stop imagining those words, and again concentrate on your muscles. Let them go completely. Enjoy this calm state."

After a minute or two, I said to the patient, "In a few moments, I'll count five and then you will wake up feeling very calm and refreshed. (*Pause.*) One, two, three, four, five."

She now opened her eyes and to my "How are you?" said that she felt quite calm. Replying to further questions, she said that all three of the scenes had been clear and the only one that had disturbed her was the third one and the disturbance had even in this case been very slight. It may be noted that the first scene had nothing to do with the items on the hierarchy list. It was inserted as a kind of control, and a street scene or a flower or almost anything else which has no obvious relevance to the hierarchy items could equally well have been used. The word "dentist" was used as a kind of sensitivity test because of its vague associations with hospitals and illness.

17th Desensitization Session (32d Interview)

Since desensitization to the fear of hostility (sublist A) had progressed much more rapidly than the others, at the last few sessions this sublist had been set aside and our attention concentrated on the death fear and fear of symptoms. Six sessions before, we had begun to deal with funerals (B-6) on the hierarchy list. On the first occasion, the word "funeral" had alone been presented, and thereafter actual funerals had been presented, starting from two blocks away and then at decreasing distances as her reaction declined. At the previous session she had been made to imagine a funeral passing in the street in front of her and this had caused slight disturbance. Imagining a pain in her left shoulder had been just perceptibly disturbing. A scene of a woman in a film weeping had also been introduced because of its association with the idea of death and she had reacted very slightly to it.

At this session she was hypnotized in the same way as in the first session, but, as would be expected, the procedure took much less time. When she was deeply relaxed, I spoke as follows: "I am going to present a number of scenes to your imagination which you will imagine very clearly. It goes without saying that, if by any chance any scene should disturb you, you will indicate it by raising your left hand. First, I want you to imagine that you are standing at a street corner and a funeral procession passes you. You may have some feeling of sadness, but apart from this you are absolutely calm. (*Brief pause.*) Stop the scene. (*Pause of about 4 seconds.*) Now I want you to imagine the same scene of the funeral passing in the street before you. (*Pause of 6 or 7 seconds.*) Now just relax. Think of nothing but your muscles. (*Pause of about 15 seconds.*) Now I want you to imagine the same scene of the funeral again. (*Pause of about 8 seconds.*) Stop imagining that scene and just relax. If the last presentation of that scene disturbed you even to the slightest degree I want you now to raise your left hand. (*Hand does not rise.*)

Good. Now let yourself go still further. (*Pause of about 15 seconds.*) Now I want you to imagine last time's scene of the woman in the film weeping bitterly. (*Pause of about 4 seconds.*) Now stop imagining this scene and just relax. (*Pause of about 15 seconds.*) Now I want you again to imagine the scene of the weeping woman. (*Pause of about 8 seconds.*) Stop that scene and again think of nothing but relaxing. If the last presentation of that scene disturbed you in the slightest, please raise your left hand. (*Hand does not rise.*) Good. Relax. (*Pause of about 15 seconds.*) Now I want you to imagine that you have a pain in your left shoulder. (*Pause of about 10 seconds.*) Now stop that pain and think only of relaxing. (*Pause of about 15 seconds.*) Now again imagine you have a pain in your left shoulder. (*Pause of about 10 seconds.*) Stop that pain and think of your muscles only. Soon I'll count five and you will wake. (*Pause.*) One, two, three, four, five."

The patient was not asked during the trance to indicate if she had been disturbed by the shoulder pain, because I assumed—wrongly, as it turned out—that there would be no disturbance. (As stated earlier, patients usually do not spontaneously signal *mild* disturbances.) On waking, she stated that there had been a very slight disturbance to the first presentation of the funeral scene, less to the second, and none to the third. The weeping woman had not disturbed her at all, but each presentation of the pain in the shoulder had been very slightly disturbing.

18th Desensitization Session (33d Interview)

The hypnotic session was, as usual, preceded by a discussion of the patient's experiences of the past few days.

At this session the funeral scene and the one of the woman weeping were abandoned because it had been possible to present them without any disturbance whatever at the previous session. They were replaced by two new scenes, slightly higher on the hierarchy. The pain in the left shoulder was again presented because its presentation had not been completely free from disturbance last time. Having hypnotized the patient and made her relax, I spoke as follows:

"First we are going to have something already well familiar to you at these sessions—a pain in your left shoulder. You will imagine this pain very clearly and you will be not at all disturbed. (*Pause of about 4 seconds.*) Stop imagining this pain and again concentrate on your relaxing. (*Pause of about 15 seconds.*) Now again imagine that you have this pain in your left shoulder. (*Pause of about 10 seconds.*) Stop imagining the pain and again relax. (*Pause of about 15 seconds.*) Now I'd like you to imagine the pain in your left shoulder a third time, very clearly and calmly. (*Pause of about 10 seconds.*) Now stop this pain and focus your attention on your body, on the pleasant relaxed feeling that you have. If you felt in the least disturbed by the third presentation of this scene, I want you now to indicate it by raising your left hand. (*The hand does not rise.*) Go on relaxing. (*Pause of about 15 seconds.*) Next I want you to visualize the following. You are in your car being driven by your husband along a pleasant road in hilly country. On a distant hillside you can clearly see the gray stones of a cemetery. (*Pause of 2 or 3 seconds.*) Now stop imagining this scene and think only of relaxing. Let yourself go completely. (*Pause of about 15 seconds.*) I want you again to imagine the same scene of the distant hillside cemetery. (*Pause of 4 or 5 seconds.*) Now stop imagining the scene and again think of your muscles and of letting them go still more. (*Pause of about 15 seconds.*) I want you to imagine that while you are standing in a queue at a drugstore you begin talking to the woman next to you and she tells you that her husband has been very short of breath since he had his heart attack. (*Pause of 2 or 3 seconds.*) Now cut that scene short and relax. (*Pause of about 15 seconds.*) Now I want you to imagine the same scene again very clearly and calmly. (*Pause of about 4 seconds.*) Stop imagining this scene and relax."

On waking, the patient reported that the first presentation of the pain in her left shoulder had been very slightly disturbing but by the third presentation it had not disturbed her at all. The first presentation of a distant cemetery had been fairly disturbing but the second much less so. The woman in the drugstore whose husband had had a heart attack had disturbed her considerably the first time and somewhat less the second time.

Two remarks must be made here. First, it was not imperative to present the two new scenes only twice each, but experience with this patient had shown that new scenes did not entirely lose their power to disturb at the first session at which they were given, so that to force the pace would have taken up time and gained nothing.

Second, it will have been noticed that although the scenes presented follow the general idea of the hierarchy list, they do not conform to it absolutely and the therapist may introduce variations according to his discretion and his knowledge of the case.

Suggested Readings

Allport, G. W. *Personality*. New York: Holt, 1937.

—————, and H. S. Odbert. "Trait Names: A Psycholexical Study," *Psychol. Monog.*, 1936, No. 211.

Coleman, J. C. *Abnormal Psychology and Modern Life*. Chicago: Scott, Foresman, 1964.

Hall, C. S. *A Primer of Freudian Psychology*. Cleveland: World Publishing Co., 1954.

—————, and G. Lindzey. *Theories of Personality*. New York: Wiley, 1957.

Harper, R. A. *Psychoanalysis and Psychotherapy: 36 Systems*. Englewood Cliffs, N.J.: Prentice-Hall, 1959.

Kretschmer, E. *Physique and Character*. New York: Harcourt, Brace & World, 1925.

Lewin, K. *A Dynamic Theory of Personality*. New York: McGraw-Hill, 1935.

McClelland, D. C. *Personality*. New York: Sloane, 1951.

Murray, H. A. *Explorations in Personality*. New York: Oxford University Press, 1938.

Rogers, C. R. *Client-Centered Therapy*. Boston: Houghton Mifflin, 1951.

Shaffer, L. F. "Fear and Courage in Aerial Combat," *J. consult. Psychol.*, 11 (1947), 137–143.

———, and E. J. Shoben, Jr. *The Psychology of Adjustment.* Houghton Mifflin, 1956.

Sheldon, W. H., and S. S. Stevens. *The Varieties of Temperament.* New York: Harper, 1942.

———, et. al. *The Varieties of Human Physique.* New York: Harper, 1940.

White, R. W. *The Abnormal Personality.* New York: Ronald, 1956.

10   *Social-Cultural Influences*

From birth to death an individual finds himself in a position of dependence. He is dependent on other individuals, and others are dependent on him. The means by which an individual carries out his relationships are learned mainly through the institutions of family, school, and church. He will assume particular roles as he progresses from child to student to parent. At the same time, it is a simple matter for him to overlook the divergent roles being assumed by those around him.

As man's society grows in population and becomes more urbanized, as in this country, he finds that people move closer together. As a consequence, he has less breathing room and, if so inclined, greater opportunities for social enjoyment. In either event he is forced to act out various roles and conform to various expected behaviors, as he associates with the groups to which he belongs. The roles he must play become increasingly important to him, and it becomes imperative that he acquire knowledge of the social and cultural influences operating in his society.

Experiments in Social Space, Kurt Lewin. Psychology is primarily concerned with the way in which social-cultural influences relate to the behavior of the individual. The sociologist and the anthropologist are concerned with a more molar, less differentiated view of the effect of these influences. In the first selection, Lewin comments that "Being officially a psychologist, I should perhaps apologize to the sociologists for crossing the boundaries of my field." It is quite clear, however, that even scientists sometimes become confused in the roles they are to play. After beginning with a general orientation to the study of social groups, Lewin discusses the now-classic "group atmosphere" study. He compares individuals whose social activities are confined within democratic, autocratic, or laissez faire group atmospheres. He describes the pressures at work and the outlets available to individual members in each group atmosphere.

The Contrasting Rôles of Tchambuli Men and Women, Margaret Mead. Mead uses a larger unit of measure: an entire culture. In her study she describes, as an anthropologist, some of her findings about three New Guinea tribes. However, only that part of the study related to the Tchambuli tribe is included here. The men and women of this tribe display a daily behavior that is in marked contrast to the kinds of behaviors displayed by men and women in our own culture. Behavior we take for granted as being appropriate and right is considered to be quite the opposite among Tchambuli tribesmen.

Social Class and Mental Illness, A. B. Hollingshead and F. C. Redlich. This selection is included here, rather than in the chapter on abnormal behavior, because of its emphasis on social-class expectations toward abnormality. Hollingshead and Redlich offer some examples and cite a few of the major findings from their careful study of the effects of social class on the interpretation of behavior. Interest in treatment and the availability of treatment do appear to vary considerably from class to class in our society.

Conformity and Character, Richard S. Crutchfield. The fourth selection considers several questions related to conformity. What happens when a person is challenged by group consensus? To what extent do the individuals in such a situation vary in their responses to the challenge? Are there identifiable traits of character that distinguish the conformist from the nonconformist? Are there circumstances under which a group can exert a maximal amount of pressure on an individual?

The Significance of Multiple-Group Membership in Disaster, Lewis M. Killian. Killian describes the reactions of people in four Southwestern towns to physical disasters that occurred in their communities. This naturalistic test of the primary, or basic, loyalties of man under stress is impressive, because it illustrates the inescapable fact that the conditions of group membership deeply affect the behavior of an individual.

Experiments in Social Space

Kurt Lewin

Kurt Lewin (1890–1947) studied psychology in Germany and became interested in the Gestalt movement. He came to America in 1932, spending most of his time at the University of Iowa conducting action studies of children. Lewin is best known for his field theory of personality and his research on types of leadership and the group process.

1. Which group atmosphere precipitated the most hostility and demand for attention?

2. In which group did the group members act more like individuals?

3. Why was a scapegoat needed in the autocratic group?

I am persuaded that it is possible to undertake experiments in sociology which have as much right to be called scientific experiments as those in physics and chemistry. I am persuaded that there exists a social space which has all the essential properties of a real empirical space and deserves as much attention by students of geometry and mathematics as the physical space, although it is *not* a physical one. The perception of social space and the experimental and conceptual investigation of the dynamics and laws of the processes in social space are of fundamental theoretical and practical importance.

Being officially a psychologist I should perhaps apologize to the sociologists for crossing the boundaries of my field. My justification for doing so is that necessity forces the move, and for this the sociologists themselves are partially

to blame. For they have stressed that the view which holds a human being to be a biological, physiological entity is utterly wrong. They have fought against the belief that only physical or biological facts are real, and that social facts are merely an abstraction. Some of the sociologists have said that only the social group has reality and that the individual person is nothing more than an abstraction—a being who properly should be described as a cross section of the groups to which he belongs.

Whichever of these statements one might consider correct, one certainly will have to admit that psychology has learned, particularly in the last decade, to realize the overwhelming importance of social factors for practically every kind and type of behavior. It is true that the child from the first day of his life is a member of a group and would die without being cared for by the group. The experiments on success and failure, level of aspiration, intelligence, frustration, and all the others, have shown more and more convincingly that the goal a person sets for himself is deeply influenced by the social standards of the group to which he belongs or wishes to belong. The psychologist of today recognizes that there are few problems more important for the development of the child and the problem of adolescence than a study of the processes by which a child takes over or becomes opposed to the ideology and the style of living predominant in

Abridged from Kurt Lewin, "Experiments in Social Space," *Harvard Educational Review*, 9 (1939), 21–31. Reprinted by permission of the publisher.

his social climate, the forces which make him belong to certain groups, or which determine his social status and his security within those groups.

A genuine attempt to approach these problems—for instance, that of social status or leadership—experimentally implies technically that one has to create different types of groups and to set up experimentally a variety of social factors which might shift this status. The experimental social psychologist will have to acquaint himself with the task of experimentally creating groups, creating a social climate or style of living. The sociologist I hope will therefore forgive him when he cannot avoid handling also the so-called sociological problems of groups and group life. Perhaps the social psychologist might prove to be even of considerable help to the sociologist. Frequently the investigation on the border line between two sciences has proved to be particularly fruitful for the progress of both of them.

Take, for instance, the concept "social group." There has been much discussion about how to define a group. The group often has been considered as something more than the sum of the individuals, something better and higher. One has attributed to it a "group mind." The opponents of this opinion have declared the concept of "group mind" to be mere metaphysics and that in reality the group is nothing other than the sum of the individuals. To one who has watched the development of the concept of organism, whole, or Gestalt, in psychology this argumentation sounds strangely familiar. In the beginning of Gestalt theory, at the time of Ehrenfels, one attributed to a psychological whole, such as melody, a so-called Gestalt quality—that is, an additional entity like a group mind, which the whole was supposed to have in addition to the sum of its parts. Today we know that we do not need to assume a mystical Gestalt quality, but that any dynamical whole has properties of its own. The whole might be symmetric in spite of its parts being asymmetric, a whole might be unstable in spite of its parts being stable in themselves.

As far as I can see, the discussion regarding group versus individual in sociology follows a similar trend. Groups are sociological wholes; the unity of these sociological wholes can be defined operationally in the same way as a unity of any other dynamic whole, namely, by the interdependence of its parts. Such a definition takes mysticism out of the group conception and brings the problem down to a thoroughly empirical and testable basis. At the same time it means a full recognition of the fact that properties of a social group, such as its organization, its stability, its goals, are something different from the organization, the stability, and the goals of the individuals in it.

How, then, should one describe a group? Let us discuss the effect of democratic, autocratic and laissez faire atmospheres on clubs which have been experimentally created by R. Lippitt and R. K. White at the Iowa Child Welfare Research Station. Let us assume the club had five members and five observers were available. It might seem the simplest way always to assign one observer to one member of the club. However, the result at best would be five parallel micro-biographies of five individuals. This procedure would not yield a satisfactory record even of such simple facts of the group life as its organization, its subgroups, and its leader-member relationship, not to speak of such important facts as the general atmosphere. Therefore, instead of assigning every observer to one individual, one observer was assigned to record from minute to minute the organization of the group into subgroups, another the social interactions, etc. In other words, instead of observing the properties of individuals, the properties of the group as such were observed.

In one additional point sociology may well profit from psychology. It is a commonplace that the behavior of individuals as well as groups depends upon their situation and their peculiar position in it. In my mind the last decade of psychology has shown that it is possible to give a clearly detailed description of the peculiar structure of a concrete situation and its dynamics in scientific terms. It can even be done in exact mathematical terms. The youngest discipline of geometry called "topology" is an excellent tool with which to determine the pattern of the life space of an individual, and to determine within this life space the relative positions which the different regions of activity or persons, or groups of persons bear to each other. It has become possible to transform into mathematical terms such everyday statements as: "He is now closer to his goal of being a first-rate physician," "He has changed the direction of his actions," or "He has joined a group." In other words, it is possible to determine, in a geometrically precise manner, the position, direction, and distance within the life space, even in such cases where the position of the person and the direction of his actions are not physical but social in nature. With this in mind let us return to the social experiment which was undertaken at the Iowa Child Welfare Research Station.

It is well known that the amount of success a teacher has in the classroom depends not only on her *skill* but to a great extent on the *atmosphere* she creates. This atmosphere is something intangible; it is a property of the social situation as a whole, and might be measured scientifically if approached from this angle. As a beginning, therefore, Mr. Lippitt selected a comparison between a democratic and an autocratic atmosphere for his study. The purpose of his experiment was not to duplicate any given autocracy or democracy or to study an "ideal" autocracy or democracy, but to create setups which would give insight into the underlying group dynamics. Two groups of boys and girls, ten and eleven years of age, were chosen for a mask-making club from a group of eager volunteers of two different school classes. With the help of the Moreno test both groups were equated as much as possible on such qualities as leadership and interpersonal relations. There were eleven meetings of the groups, the democratic group meeting always two days ahead of the autocratic one. The democratic group chose its activities freely. Whatever they chose the autocratic group was then ordered to do. In this way the activities of the group were equated. On the whole, then, everything was kept constant except the group atmosphere.

The leader in both groups was an adult student. He tried to create the different atmospheres by using the technique [shown in the table below]:

Democratic

1. All policies a matter of group determination, encouraged and drawn out by the leader.
2. Activity perspective given by an explanation of the general steps of the process during discussion at first meeting (clay mould, plaster of Paris, papier-mâché, etc.). Where technical ad-

vice was needed, the leader tried to point out two or three alternative procedures from which choice could be made.
3. The members were free to work with whomever they chose and the division of tasks was left up to the group.
4. The leader attempted to be a group member in spirit and in discussion but not to perform much of the actual work. He gave objective praise and criticism.

Authoritarian

1. All determination of policy by the strongest person (leader).
2. Techniques and steps of attaining the goal (completed mask) dictated by the authority, one at a time, so that future direction was always uncertain to a large degree.
3. The authority usually determined autocratically what each member should do and with whom he should work.
4. The dominator criticized and praised individual's activities *without giving objective reasons,* and remained aloof from active group participation. He was always impersonal rather than outwardly hostile or friendly (a necessary concession in method).

During the meetings of the two groups, the observers noted the number of incidents and actions per unit of time. It was observed that the autocratic leader put forth about twice as much action towards the members as the democratic leader, namely, 8.4 actions as against 4.5. This difference is even greater if one takes into account only the initiated social approach, namely, 5.2 as against 2.1. Still greater is this difference in relation to ascendant or initiated ascendant behavior: the ascendant actions of the autocratic leader were nearly three times as frequent as those of the democratic leader.

In regard to submissive actions, the proportion was opposite, namely, more frequent by the democratic leader, although in both groups submissive actions of the leader were relatively rare. A similar relation held for the objective, matter-of-fact actions. Here too the democratic leader showed a higher frequency.

On the whole, then, there existed a much greater impact on the members of the group by the leader in autocracy than in democracy, and the approach was much more ascendant and less matter-of-fact.

When we attempt to answer the question "How does the leader compare with the ordinary member in an autocracy and a democracy?" we must refer to an ideal average member who is a statistical representation of what would happen if all activities were distributed equally among the members of the group, including the leader. In Mr. Lippitt's experiment the figures showed two facts clearly: first, in both groups the leader was really leading. The autocratic leader showed 118 per cent more initiated ascendant acts than the average ideal member, and the democratic leader 41 per cent more. Both leaders were less submissive than the average member, namely, the autocrat 78 per cent, the democrat 53 per cent. It was interesting to note that both showed also more matter-of-fact action than the average ideal member.

However, the difference between the ordinary member and the leader was much less pronounced in democracy than in autocracy, both in ascendant and submissive action. The democratic leader distinguished himself, also relatively, more by his greater matter-of-factness.

What do these figures indicate about the situation in which the autocratic and democratic group members find themselves? I can only mention a few aspects: In the autocratic group it is the leader who sets the policy. For instance, a child says: "I thought we decided to do the other mask." The leader answers: "No, *this* is the one *I* decided last time would be the best one." In dynamical terms such an incident means that the child would have been able to reach his own goal but the leader puts up a barrier against this locomotion. Instead he induces another goal for the child and a force in this direction. We are calling such goals, set up by the power of another person, an *induced* goal.

A parallel example in the democratic group might be this: A child asks, "How big will we make the mask? Are they out of clay or what?" The leader answers: "Would you like me to give you a little idea of how people generally make masks?" In other words, the leader in the democratic group, instead of hindering the children in getting to their own goal, bridges over whatever regions of difficulty might exist. For the democratic group, many paths are open; for the autocratic only one, namely, that determined by the leader. In an autocracy the leader determines not only the kind of activity

but also who should work with whom. In our experimental democracy all work cooperation was the result of spontaneous sub-grouping of the children. In the autocracy 32 per cent of the work groups were initiated by the leader, as against 0 per cent in the democracy.

On the whole, then, the autocratic atmosphere gives a much greater and more aggressive dominance of the leader, and a narrowing down of the free movement of the members, together with a weakening of their power fields.

What is the effect of this atmosphere on the group life of the children? As measured by the observers the child-to-child relationship was rather different in the two atmospheres. There was about thirty times as much hostile domination in the autocracy as in the democracy, more demands for attention and much more hostile criticism; whereas in the democratic atmosphere cooperation and praise of the other fellow was much more frequent. In the democracy more constructive suggestions were made and a matter-of-fact or submissive behavior of member to member was more frequent.

In interpreting these data, we might say that the "style of living and thinking" initiated by the leader dominated the relations between the children. Instead of a cooperative attitude, a hostile and highly personal attitude became prevalent. This was strikingly brought out by the amount of group or "we" feeling as against "I" feeling. Statements which were "we-centered" occurred twice as often in the democracy as in the autocracy, whereas far more statements in the autocracy were "I-centered" than in the democracy.

So far as the relation of the children toward the leader was concerned, the statistical analysis revealed that the children in the autocratic group who were *less submissive* to each other were about *twice* as submissive to their leader, as the children in the democratic group. Initiated approaches to the leader in the democratic group were less frequent than in the autocratic group. In autocracy the action by the member toward the leader had more the character of a *response* to an approach of the leader. The approach to the leader in the autocracy was more submissive, or kept at least on a matter-of-fact basis.

On the whole, then, the style of living in both atmospheres governed the child-child relation as well as the child-leader relation. In the autocratic group the children were less matter-of-fact, less cooperative, and submissive toward their equals, but more submissive to their superior than in the democracy.

Behind this difference of behavior lie a number of factors. The tension is greater in the autocratic atmosphere, and the dynamic structure of both groups is rather different. In an autocratic group there are two clearly distinguished levels of social status: the leader is the only one having higher status, the others being on an equally low level. A strong barrier kept up by the leader prevents any one from increasing his status by acquiring leadership. In a democratic atmosphere the difference in social

they kept together about twice as long as in the autocracy. In the autocracy these larger units disintegrated much faster when left to themselves.

These group structures, in combination with the high tension in the autocracy, led in Lippitt's experiments to a *scapegoat* situation. The children in the autocratic group ganged together not against their leader, but against one of the children and treated him so badly that he ceased coming to the club. This happened twice during twelve sessions. Under autocratic rule any increase in status through

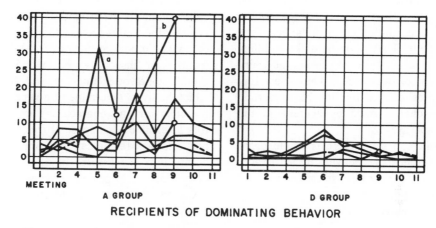

RECIPIENTS OF DOMINATING BEHAVIOR

FIGURE 1. *The curves indicate that the amount of dominating behavior directed against the various individuals was much greater in autocracy (A group) than in democracy (D group). In autocracy two individuals (a and b) were treated as scapegoats (at the 5th and 6th, and at the 9th meetings respectively).*

status is slight and there exists no barrier against acquiring leadership.

This has a rather clear effect on the amount of individuality. In our experiment every individual in the democracy showed a relatively greater individuality, having some field of his own in spite of the greater "we" feeling among them, or perhaps because of it. In the autocratic group on the contrary the children all had a low status without much individuality. The type of sub-grouping showed this difference even more clearly. In the autocracy, there was little "we" feeling and relatively little spontaneous sub-grouping among the children. If the work required the cooperation of four or five members, it was the leader who had to order the members to get together. In the democracy those groups came together spontaneously and

leadership was blocked and the attempt to dominate was dictated by the style of living. In other words, every child became a potential enemy of every other one and the power fields of the children weakened each other, instead of strengthening each other by cooperation. Through combining in an attack against one individual the members who otherwise could not gain higher status were able to do so by violent suppression of one of their fellows.

One may ask whether these results are not due merely to individual differences. A number of facts rule out this explanation, although of course individual differences always play a role. Of particular interest was the transfer of one of the children from the autocratic to the democratic group, and of another from the democracy to the autocratic one. Before the transfer the difference between the two children was the same as between the two groups they belonged to, namely, the autocratic child was more dominating and less friendly and objective than the democratic one. However, after the transfer the behavior changed so that the previously autocratic child now became the less dominating and more friendly and objective child. In other words, the behavior of the children mirrored very quickly the atmosphere of the group in which they moved.

Recently R. Lippitt and R. K. White have studied four new clubs with other leaders. They have included a third atmosphere, namely that of laissez faire, and have exposed the same children successively to a number of atmospheres. On the whole, the results bear out those of Lippitt. They show a striking difference between laissez faire and democracy very much in favor of democracy. They show further two types of reaction in the autocratic groups, one characterized by aggression, the second by apathy.

On the whole, I think there is ample proof that the difference in behavior in autocratic, democratic, and laissez faire situations is not a result of individual differences. There have been few experiences for me as impressive as

seeing the expression in children's faces change during the first day of autocracy. The friendly, open, and cooperative group, full of life, became within a short half hour a rather apathetic-looking gathering without initiative. The change from autocracy to democracy seemed to take somewhat more time than from democracy to autocracy. Autocracy is imposed upon the individual. Democracy he has to learn.

These experiments as a whole, then, bear out the observations of cultural anthropology and are well in line with other experiments on the effect of the situation as a whole, such as those of Wellman and Skeels. The social climate in which a child lives is for the child as important as the air it breathes. The group to which a child belongs is the ground on which he stands. His relation to this group and his status in it are the most important factors for his feeling of security or insecurity. No wonder that the group the person is a part of, and the culture in which he lives, determine to a very high degree his behavior and character. These social factors determine what space of free movement he has, and how far he can look ahead with some clarity into the future. In other words, they determine to a large degree his personal style of living and the direction and productivity of his planning.

The Contrasting Rôles of Tchambuli Men and Women

Margaret Mead

Margaret Mead is Curator of Ethnology Emeritus, American Museum of Natural History. She received her Ph.D. from Columbia University in 1929. President of the World Federation for Mental Health in 1957 and of the American Anthropological Association in 1960, Mead is the author of more than 20 books in her field.

1. Would the "self-made" American male, if placed in Tchambuli society, be considered effeminate?

2. Are there universal behaviors or practices common to all mankind? List as many as you can.

As the Arapesh made growing food and children the greatest adventure of their lives, and the Mundugumor found greatest satisfaction in fighting and competitive acquisition of women, the Tchambuli may be said to live principally for art. Every man is an artist and most men are skilled not in some one art alone, but in many: in dancing, carving, plaiting, painting, and so on. Each man is chiefly concerned with his rôle upon the stage of his society, with the elaboration of his costume, the beauty of the masks that he owns, the skill of his own flute-playing, the finish and *élan* of his ceremonies, and upon other people's recognition and valuation of his performance. The Tchambuli ceremonies are not a by-product of some event in the life of an individual; that is, it cannot be said that in order to initiate young boys the Tchambuli hold a ceremony, but

rather that in order to hold a ceremony the Tchambuli initiate young boys. Grief over a death is muffled and practically dissipated by interest in the ceremonial that surrounds it—which flutes are to be played, which masks and clay heads are to decorate the grave; in the etiquette of the groups of formally mourning women, who are given charming little souvenirs of reeds to remember the occasion by. The women's interest in art is confined to sharing in the graceful pattern of social relations, a small amount of painting on their baskets and plaited cowls, and chorus dancing; but to the men, it is the only important matter in life.

The structure of the society is patrilineal. Groups of men all related through male ancestors, and bearing a common name, own strips of territory that stretch from the hill-tops, where occasional gardens are made, down through the wooded mountain-side where the women's houses are built, to the lake-shore, where each clan or sometimes two adjacent clans, building together, have their men's clubhouse. Within this group of related males there are certain taboos. An eldest son is embarrassed and shy in the presence of his father, and his next younger brother observes the same sort of behaviour towards him. The possibility of inheritance is the subject of their embarrassment. The younger sons, far removed from considerations of the succession, are easy with one another. Relationships between a man and his brother's son are also friendly, and these men—whose position is vividly described by the pidgin-English term "small papa"—intervene between small boys and their self-appointed and light-hearted disciplinarians, the bigger boys. The membership in these men's houses varies, and quarrels are frequent. Upon the merest slight—a claim of precedence that is not justified, a failure of the wife of one man to feed the pigs of another, a failure to return a borrowed article—the person who cherishes a sense of hurt will move away, and go to live with some other clan group to which he can claim relationship. Meanwhile there is a strong social feeling that such behaviour is bad, that the men of a clan should sit down together, that in a large number of older men lies the wisdom of the ceremonial house. When illness or misfortune occurs, the shamans explain that the shamanic spirits and the ghosts of the dead that hang about the house-posts are angry because one or more members of the clan have moved away. The solidarity of any of these groups of men is more apparent than real; it is as if all of them sat very lightly, very impermanently, on the edges of their appointed sitting-shelves, ready to be off at a look, a touch, a word of hostility.

His relations to all other males are delicate and difficult, as he sits down a little lightly even in his own clansmen's house, and is so nervous and sensitive that he will barely eat in the houses of other clans, but his relations to women are the one solid and reliable aspect of his life. As a small child, he was held lightly in the arms of a laughing casual mother, a mother who nursed him generously but nonchalantly, while her fingers were busy plaiting reeds into sleeping-baskets or rain-capes. When he tumbled down, his mother picked him up and tucked him under her arm as she went on with her conversation. He was never left alone; there were always some eight or ten women about, working, laughing, attending to his needs, willingly enough, but unobsessively. If his father's other wife failed to feed him as generously as his mother, his mother needed only to make the light reproach: "Are children plentiful that you should neglect them?" His childhood days were spent tumbling about the floor of the great dwelling-house, where his antics were privileged, where he could tickle and wrestle with the other children. His mouth was never empty. Women weaned their children as carelessly and casually as they nursed them, stuffing their mouths with delicacies to stop their crying. Afterwards the women fed them bountifully with food, lotus-stems, lily-

Where the Arapesh, the Mundugumor and the Tchambuli live.

stems, lotus-seed, Malay apples, pieces of sugar-cane, and a little boy could sit and munch in the great roomy house filled with other children of his kin and with groups of working, kindly women. Sometimes there was a ceremony, and his mother took him with her when she went to spend the day cooking in another house. There, in a larger crowd of women, with more children rolling about on the floor, he also munched. His mother took plenty of dainties along in her basket, to give him whenever he cried for them.

By the time a boy is seven or eight, he is beginning to hang about the edges of the men's ceremonial life. If he goes too close to the men's house during a ceremony, he will be chased away, although on ordinary occasions he can slip in and hide behind a small papa's protection. The older boys will haze him lightly, send him on errands, throw sticks at him, or beat him if he disobeys. Back he runs, scurrying up the hillside to his mother's house, whither the big boys will not pursue him. The next time that he and those big boys are in a woman's house together, he will take advantage of the older boy's embarrassment; he will tease and plague him, caricature his walk and manner—with impunity; the older boy will not attack him.

At some point when he is between eight and twelve, a period that is not determined by his age so much as by his father's ceremonial ambitions, he will be scarified. He will be held squirming on a rock while a distantly related maternal "uncle" and an expert scarifier cut patterns on his back. He can howl as much as he likes. No one will comfort him, no one will attempt to stop his howls. Nor will anyone take any delight in them. Casually, efficiently, performing as relatives their ritual duty, for which they will receive graceful recognition, or performing their duty as artists, they cut patterns on the little boy's back. They paint him with oil and turmeric. All about him is an elaborate ceremonial pattern that he does not share. His father gives presents to his mother's brother. His mother's brother's wives are given beautiful new grass skirts, new rain-capes, new carrying-baskets. His scarification is the occasion for all this display, but no one pays any attention to him.

There follows a long period of seclusion. At night he is allowed to go home to sleep, but in the chill morning, before dawn, he must creep away from the women's house, wrapped from head to foot in a great coarse rain-cape. His body is smeared with white clay. All day he must stay inside the men's house. Every fourth day he washes and assumes a new coat of paint. It is all very uncomfortable. Sometimes two men of the same clan combine to scarify their sons, but as often a boy is initiated alone. There is no suggestion that this is done for his welfare. Nor is there any suggestion that the adults are interested in the discomfort of his position or the pain of his scarifications. All about him goes on the discussion of ceremonial policy, and if his father can make a more effective ceremony by waiting for three months to wash him, he waits. The child is not considered. Or in a great pet over some slight or indignity put upon him by those who should assist him in the ceremony, the father incontinently washes the child within a week or so after his scarification. The washing is ritual, and ends the period of seclusion. The boy's mother's brother presents him with an elaborately woven belt, shell ornaments, a beautifully incised bamboo lime-gourd with a lovely filigree spatula. He may now walk about with these under his arm, accompanying parties of people who take food or *talibun* and *kinas* to other people in his name. After this he is supposed to spend more time in the men's house, but he still takes refuge among the women whenever possible. He grows gradually into young manhood; his father and elder brothers watching jealously his attitude towards their younger wives and suspecting him if he walks about upon the women's roads.

The women remain, however, a solid group upon whom he depends for support, for food, for affection. There is no split between the women of his blood-group and the wife whom he marries, for he marries a daughter of one of his mother's half-brothers or cousins. He calls her by the name by which he calls his own mother, *aiyai*. All of the little girls of his mother's clan, to all of whom he looks hopefully, he addresses as *aiyai*. One of his "mothers" will some day be his wife. The gifts that his father gave in his name when he was very small, the gifts which he is now being taught to take himself to his mother's brothers, these are the earnest of his claim upon a woman of his mother's clan. In this way, one clan is linked with another from generation to generation, the men of one clan having a lien upon the women of the other. Women are therefore divided for him into the group upon which he depends; these are all considered as of the order of mothers and include his mother, his mother's sisters, his father's brothers' wives, his mother's brothers' wives, and the daughters of his mother's brothers. Towards his father's sister and his father's sister's daughter his behaviour is more formal, for these can never be either mother, wife, or mother-in-law, the three relationships that Tchambuli feeling groups together. For the actual marriage, in addition to the presents that have been sent on ceremonial occasions the bride must be paid for in many *kinas* and *talibun,* and for this payment the young man is dependent upon his immediate male kin. An orphan, if he is allowed to live, has small hope of obtaining a bride while he is a young man. He is no one's child; how, indeed, can he hope to have a wife?

As the young man's attitude towards the women is single-hearted, rather than complicated with different conflicting attitudes appropriate to mother, sister, wife, and mother-in-law, so also the women in the house in which he has been brought up are a solid unit. When a girl marries, she goes not into the house of strangers but into the house of her father's sister, who now becomes her mother-in-law. If a man has two wives they usually, although not always, come from the same clan, and are sisters as well as cowives. To have been cowives, even although separated by death of the husband and subsequent remarriage, is regarded as a great tie between women. The prototype of Tchambuli polygyny is a pair of sisters entering as brides a house into which one or more of their father's sisters have married before them; in which the old woman who sits by the fire, and occasionally utters a few carping comments, is a woman of their own clan also, and so will not deal harshly with them. And this unusual picture of great amity and solidarity within the two feminine relationships that are often most trying, that of cowives and

that of mother-in-law and daughter-in-law, pervades the interrelations of all women. Tchambuli women work in blocks, a dozen of them together, plaiting the great mosquito-bags from the sale of which most of the *talibun* and *kina* are obtained. They cook together for a feast, their clay fireplaces (circular pots with terraced tops, which can be moved from place to place) set side by side. Each dwelling-house contains some dozen to two dozen fire-places, so that no woman need cook in a corner alone. The whole emphasis is upon comradeship, efficient, happy work enlivened by continuous brisk banter and chatter. But in a group of men, there is always strain, watchfulness, a catty remark here, a *double entendre* there: "What did he mean by sitting down on the opposite side of the men's house when he saw you upon this side?" "Did you see Koshalan go by with a flower in his hair? What do you suppose he is up to?"

For although Tchambuli is patrilineal in organization, although there is polygyny and a man pays for his wife—two institutions that have been popularly supposed to degrade women—it is the women in Tchambuli who have the real position of power in the society. The patrilineal system includes houses and land, residence land and gardening-land, but only an occasional particularly energetic man gardens. For food, the people depend upon the fishing of the women. Men never fish unless a sudden school of fish appears in the lake, when they may leap into canoes in a frolicsome spirit, and spear a few fish. Or in high water when the shore-road is become a water-way, they may do a little torch-light fishing for sport. But the real business of fishing is controlled entirely by the women. For traded fish they obtain sago, taro, and areca-nut. And the most important manufacture, the mosquito-bags, two of which will purchase an ordinary canoe, are made entirely by women. The people of the middle Sepik purchase these mosquito-bags, in fact they are so much in demand that purchasers take options on them long before they are finished. And the women control the proceeds in *kinas* and *talibun.* It is true that they permit the men to do the shopping, both for food at the market and in trading the mosquito-bags. The men make a gala occasion of these latter shopping-trips; when a man has the final negotiations for one of his wives' mosquito-bags in hand, he goes off resplendent in feathers and shell ornaments to spend a delightful few days over the transaction. He will hesitate and equivocate, advance here, draw back there, accept this *talibun,* reject that one, demand to see a more slender *kina* or one that is better cut, insist on changing half of the purchasing items after they have been spread out, have a very orgy of choice such as a modern woman with a well-filled purse looks forward to in a shopping-trip to a big city. But only with his wife's approval can he spend the *talibun* and *kina* and the strings of *conus* rings that he brings back from his holiday. He has wheedled a good price from the purchaser; he has still to wheedle the items of the price from his wife. From boyhood up, this is the men's attitude towards property. Real property, which one actually owns, one receives from women, in return for languishing looks and soft words. Once one has obtained it, it becomes a counter in the games that men play; it is no longer concerned with the underlying economics of life, but rather with showing one's appreciation of one's brother-in-law, soothing someone's wounded feelings, behaving very handsomely when a sister's son falls down in one's presence. The minor war-and-peace that goes on all the time among the men, the feelings that are hurt and must be assuaged, are supported by the labour and contributions of the women. When a woman lies dying, her thought is for the young boys whom she has been helping, her son, her sister's son, her husband's sister's son; how will this one, who, it is true, is an orphan also and has no one to help him, fare when she is dead? And if there is time, she will send for this handsome stripling or accomplished youth, and give him a *kina* or so, or some *talibun.* Such a handsome one is sure to arouse jealousy, to get into scrapes; he must be provided with the means by which to bribe his way back into favour.

The women's attitude towards the men is one of kindly tolerance and appreciation. They enjoy the games that the men play, they particularly enjoy the theatricals that the men put on for their benefit. A big masked show is the occasion for much pleasure. When a *mwai* dance is made, for instance, it means that a group of women dance about each of the sets of masked dancers. These masked figures wear wooden masks balanced in the midst of a head-dress of leaves and flowers in which dozens of slender little carvings are thrust on sticks. They have great paunches made up of a long row of the crescent-shaped *kina* shells, which extend below their waists rather like elephants' tusks. They wear bustles in which grimacing carved faces are stuck. Their legs are concealed with straw leggings, and they descend from a platform, which has been specially built with a back-drop resembling the distant mountains. The two male masks carry spears, the two female masks carry brooms; trumpeting and singing esoteric songs through little bamboo megaphones, they parade up and down a long cleared way that is lined with watching women and children. The masks are clan-owned, and when their own masks appear, the women of that clan and other women also go out and dance about them, making a gay chorus, and picking up any feathers or ornaments that fall from them. There are no men upon the dancing-ground except the four men hidden within the masks—older men in the male masks, young and frivolous ones within the female masks. These young men take a strange inverted pleasure in thus entering, in semi-disguise—not wholly in disguise, for most of them have whispered the details of their leggings to at least one woman—into the women's group. Here masked they can take part in the rough homosexual play that characterizes a group of women on any festive occasion. When there are no masks on the dancing-ground, the women play among themselves, jocosely going through pantomimes of intercourse. When the masked figures appear, the women include the female masks in their play, but not the male masks. The women treat these latter with gentle, careful gravity, lest their feelings be hurt. To the female masks the women give very definite attention, poking them with bundles of leaves that they carry in their hands, bumping against them in definitely provocative positions, tickling and teasing them. The *double entendre* of the situation, the spectacle of women courting males disguised as females, expresses better than any other ritual act that I witnessed the complexities of the sex-situation in Tchambuli, where men are nominally the owners of their homes, the heads of their families, even the owners of their wives, but in which the actual initiative and power is in the hands of the women. To the male mask the women give lip-service, and some of them, usually the older and graver women, dance with it; they pick up its ornaments when they fall. With the female masks they display aggressive sexual desire, and flaunt their right to initiative. After all, the young men can only whisper to the women in which masks they plan to dance and how their legs may be distinguished. Then, imprisoned in the clumsy, unstable, top-heavy masks and partially chaperoned by the older men who are dancing in the male masks, they can only parade blindly up and down the dancing-ground, waiting for a whisper and a blow to advise them that particular women have pressed against them. These ceremonies usually break up in a far shorter number of days than the original plan provides for, as rumours of liaisons flutter about to frighten the older men, who decide that they have lured their wives out on the dancing-ground for no good purpose. For even if no new alliance has sprung up under cover of the dancing, the dance of the women is itself designed to produce a high degree of sexual excitation, which may become an explosive in the days to come. It is the young wives of old men who enjoy these ceremonies most.

Tchambuli young men develop their attitudes towards one another in the highly charged atmosphere of courtship, in which no one knows upon whom a woman's choice will fall, each youth holds his breath and hopes, and no young man is willing to trust another. Such courtship arises from the presence of widows or dissatisfied wives. The dissatisfied wives are created by the same fidelity to a pattern without regard for practical considerations that occurs in the exchanges in Mundugumor. If among the "mothers" of his generation, one of whom he has a right to marry, there is no girl a little younger than a boy, his mother's clan will give him a girl who is a little older. While he is still adolescent, insecure, frightened of sex, she matures, and becomes involved in a liaison either with one of his brothers or possibly with an older relative. His mother's brothers will try to prevent this; they will publicly deride the boy who does not enter his betrothed wife's sleeping-bag, and threaten him that trouble will

result and she may be lost to another clan. The boy, shamed and prickly with misery, becomes more tongue-tied, more recalcitrant than ever to his wife's advances. Then some rearrangement, her marriage to another man of the same clan, is likely to follow. With a young widow also, it is the girl's choice that is decisive, for men will not be foolish enough to pay for a girl who has not indicated her choice of a husband by sleeping with him. It will be, as they say, money thrown away. A young widow is a tremendous liability to a community. No one expects her to remain quiet until her remarriage has been arranged. Has she not a vulva? they ask. This is the comment that is continually made in Tchambuli: Are women passive sexless creatures who can be expected to wait upon the dilly-dallying of formal considerations of brideprice? Men, not so urgently sexed, may be expected to submit themselves to the discipline of a due order and precedence.

Yet the course of true love runs no smoother here where women dominate than it does in societies dominated by men. There is sometimes a tendency in describing marriage arrangements to consider that one of the inevitable effects of the dominance of women is the woman's freedom to marry whom she will, but this is no more a necessary aspect of women's power than the right of a young man to choose his wife is an inevitable result of patriliny. The social ambitions of a mother may ruin her son's marriage under the most patriarchal form of society, and in Tchambuli neither men nor women are minded to give young people any more rein than they can help. The ideal is to marry pairs of cousins as children and thus settle at least part of the difficulty. The opportunities that polygyny offers wait, then, upon the ripening of the boy's charms. The older men see with jaundiced eyes the beauty and grace of their younger brothers and later of their sons, a beauty and grace that will soon displace them in the eyes of women, especially of their young wives, whose favour they had perhaps caught in the last flutter of powerful middle age. The young men say bitterly that the old men use every bit of power and strategy which they possess to cut out their young rivals, to shame and disgrace them before the women.

The method of discrediting a young rival that the men find readiest to their jealous hands is the accusation of being an orphan. If a boy's father is alive, he will contribute perhaps 10, perhaps 20, per cent of the bride-price, seldom more, and the other men of the clan contribute the rest. The principal contribution is made by the man or men whose marriages were mainly financed by the bridegroom's father. The state of being an orphan, then, does not mean that the boy is actually unable to pay a bride-price, but merely that he is in an exposed state of which the other men can take advantage. And cruelly the old lascivious man, nearing his grave, will use this power to interfere between an orphan boy of his clan and the young widow who has expressed a preference for that boy.

So the conflict over women, outlawed in Arapesh because of the emphasis upon finding wives for sons and so important a part of the struggle and clash of life in Mundugumor, exists too in Tchambuli, where young men and old struggle stealthily for the possession of women's favours—but the struggle is for the most part an underground one. It is not a fight but a secret competition, in which young men and young women are both likely to lose to the will of their elders.

Relevant also to the position of the sexes are the secrets of the men's cults and the sanctity of the men's houses. These men's houses, which combine the functions of club and green-room, places where men can keep themselves out of the women's way and prepare their own food, workshops and dressing-rooms for ceremonies, are not kept inviolate from a woman's entrance on certain ceremonial occasions. For the scarification of a child, the woman who carries the child enters the men's house in state, and sits there proudly upon a stool. If there is a quarrel, the women gather on the hill-side and shout advice and directions into the very centre of the house where the debate is going on. They come armed with thick staves, to take part in the battle if need be. The elaborate ceremonies, the beating of water-drums, the blowing of flutes, are no secrets from the women. As they

stood, an appreciative audience, listening solemnly to the voice of the crocodile, I asked them: "Do you know what makes that noise?" "Of course, it is a water-drum, but we don't say we know for fear the men would be ashamed." And the young men answer, when asked if the women know their secrets: "Yes, they know them, but they are good and pretend not to, for fear we become ashamed. Also—we might become so ashamed that we would beat them."

"We might become so ashamed that we would beat them." In that sentence lies the contradiction at the root of Tchambuli society, in which men are theoretically, legally dominant, but in which they play an emotionally subservient rôle, dependent upon the security given them by women, and even in sex-activity looking to women to give the leads. Their love magic consists in charms made of stolen stones that the women use for auto-erotic practices: this the men deeply resent, feeling that they should benefit by the greater sexual specificity and drive of the women. What the women will think, what the women will say, what the women will do, lies at the back of each man's mind as he weaves his tenuous and uncertain web of insubstantial relations with other men. Each man stands alone, playing his multiplicity of parts, sometimes allied with one man, sometimes with another; but the women are a solid group, confused by no rivalries, brisk, patronizing, and jovial. They feed their male children, their young male relatives, on lotus-seeds and lily-roots, their husbands and lovers upon doled-out pellets of love. And yet the men are after all stronger, and a man can beat his wife, and this possibility serves to confuse the whole issue of female dominance and masculine charming, graceful, coquettish dancing attention.

Social Class and Mental Illness

August B. Hollingshead and Fredrick C. Redlich

A. B. Hollingshead received his doctorate at the University of Nebraska in 1935. He was Chairman of the Sociology Department at Yale from 1959 to 1965. Hollingshead is author of Principles of Human Ecology (1938), Elmstown's Youth (1949), *and* Social Class and Mental Illness (1958), *with Redlich as co-author. Hollingshead was originally interested in becoming a lawyer before turning to sociology. He now considers medical sociology his special interest. The title of the book from which the material below is abridged is* Social Class and Mental Illness. *Hollingshead provides his expertise on social class, and Redlich offers his experience and credentials in the field of mental illness. Fredrick Redlich is a 1935 graduate of the medical school of the University of Vienna. He came to this country in 1938 and has been Chairman of the Department of Psychiatry, School of Medicine, Yale University, since 1950. He recently became Dean of the Medical School. He is the author of books and articles dealing with the mentally ill.*

1. *Is there any way in which a democratic society can provide equal medical or psychological treatment for all, regardless of class standing?*

2. *Why are lower-status people apparently more prone to give physical rather than psychological reasons for their troubles?*

Introduction

Americans prefer to avoid the two facts of life studied in this book: social class and mental illness. The very idea of "social class" is inconsistent with the American ideal of a society composed of free and equal individuals, individuals living in a society where they have identical opportunities to realize their inborn potentialities. The acceptance of this facet of the "American Dream" is easy and popular. To

Abridged from August B. Hollingshead and Fredrick C. Redlich, *Social Class and Mental Illness.* New York: Wiley, 1958. Pp. 3–6, 171–176. Reprinted by permission.

suggest that it may be more myth than reality stimulates antagonistic reactions.

Although Americans, by choice, deny the existence of social classes, they are forced to admit the reality of mental illness. Nevertheless, merely the thought of such illness is abhorrent to them. They fear "mental illness," its victims, and those people who cope with them: psychiatrists, clinical psychologists, social workers, psychiatric nurses, and attendants. Even the institutions our society has developed to care for the mentally ill are designated by pejorative terms, such as "bug house," "booby hatch," and "loony bin," and psychiatrists are called "nutcrackers" and "head shrinkers."

Denial of the existence of social classes and derisive dismissal of the mentally ill may salve the consciences of some people. The suggestion that different social classes receive different treatment for mental illness may come as a shock, but to repress facts because they are distasteful and incongruent with cherished values may lead to consequences even more serious than those we are trying to escape by substituting fantasy for reality.

American ideals relative to social status are premised upon the "self-evident truth" that "all men are created equal." If our ideals corresponded to reality, there would be no classes in our society. However, students of American society have pointed out on numerous occasions that American ideals and American reality are two different things. More than a half-century ago, Lord Bryce in his astute analysis of our society put the problem succinctly when he said:

There is no rank in America, that is to say no external and recognized stamp marking a man as entitled to any special privileges or to deference or respect from others. No man is entitled to think himself better than his fellows. . . .

The total absence of rank and universal acceptance of equality do not, however, prevent the existence of grades and distinctions which, though they find no tangible expression, are sometimes as sharply drawn as in Europe.

In more recent years, Myrdal summed up the disparity between what we profess publicly as members of a democratic society and how we act in private life as "an American dilemma." The observations of these discerning Europeans have been documented many times by the researches of American social scientists. Some 25 years ago, the Lynds in their widely acclaimed books on "Middletown" demonstrated the reality of social classes in the daily activities of Middle Western Americans. In the ensuing years a number of social scientists have published extensive evidence to support the fact that American society is stratified.

Nevertheless, the phrase "social class" is an emotionally provoking symbol to Americans. The idea that people are unequal socially is resisted strongly. Even when Americans privately "draw the line" between one another in subtle ways, they do not like to admit it in public. Our reluctance to admit that we discriminate among our fellow citizens is traceable to the doctrine of equality enunciated in the Declaration of Independence. Publicly we talk about equality; privately we practice inequality. A consequence of this conflict in values is that some of the most highly charged emotional issues facing our society revolve around the everyday practices of some members of our society who behave toward other members in invidious ways. The inconsistency between our public protestations and our private acts presents us with deep moral issues.

This is recognized officially in the area of race and ethnic relations. It is expressed by fair employment practice acts and the efforts of national, state, and local governments to end segregation in the schools and other areas of public life. The official efforts of men and women of good will, however, are resisted mightily by other members of the society. Such actions are based upon the traditional conviction that some men are socially superior to others.

Mental Illness

Our attitudes toward mental illness are also a product of our cultural heritage. Historical evidence indicates that mental "disturbances" have been known in all civilized societies. The severe disturbances of kings, generals, religious leaders, and other personages have been recorded since ancient times. Persons who were not important enough to have their mental aberrations written into the human record undoubtedly also were afflicted, even though their ailments and their numbers have been lost in the mists of time. Although man's mental and emotional maladjustments are not new, the public is more clearly aware of them now than in the past, and responsible leaders have become increasingly concerned with their alleviation.

In the last decade mental illness has been recognized as one of the most serious unsolved health problems facing our society. A few figures will indicate its magnitude. The approximately 750,000 persons who are currently hospitalized in mental institutions occupy some 55 percent of all hospital beds in the United States. Hundreds of thousands of other mentally ill persons are treated by psychiatrists in clinics and in private practice, but the number of hospitalized cases increases year by year. During World War II, 43 percent of all disability discharges (980,000) from the Armed Forces were granted on psychiatric grounds, and 865,000 young men were rejected for psychiatric reasons in Selective Service examinations. Moreover, some 16,000 to 17,000 persons commit suicide each year and, according to the best estimates, there are about 3,800,000 alcoholics in the adult population. We are certain that patients hospitalized in mental institutions in addition to those cared for by psychiatrists in private practice and in clinics represent only a portion of those who are mentally ill. Estimates indicate that there are from seven to eight million other Americans who are less seriously disturbed but who could benefit from psychiatric care if it were available.

Social Class and Mental Illness

Is the presence of mental illness in the population related to class status? Is the treatment received by a mentally ill member of our society an effect of his class position? These questions are crucial to the research reported here. They are even more important from the viewpoint of their scientific meaning and their implications for social policy.

Both social class and mental illness may be compared to an iceberg; 90 percent of it is concealed below the surface. The submerged portion, though unseen, is the dangerous part. This may be illustrated by recalling what happened when an "unsinkable" trans-Atlantic luxury liner, the *Titanic,* rammed an iceberg on her maiden voyage in 1912. In that crisis, a passenger's class status played a part in the determination of whether he survived or was drowned. The official casualty lists showed that only 4 first class female passengers (3 voluntarily chose to stay on the ship) of a total of 143 were lost. Among the second class passengers, 15 of 93 females drowned; and among the third class, 81 of 179 female passengers went down with the ship. The third class passengers were ordered to remain below deck, some kept there at the point of a gun.

The idea that stratification in our society has any bearing on the diagnosis and treatment of disease runs counter to our cherished beliefs about equality, especially when they are applied to the care of the sick. Physicians share deeply ingrained egalitarian ideals with their fellow citizens, yet they, too, may make subtle, perhaps unconscious, judgments of the differential worth of the members of our society. Physicians, among them psychiatrists, are sensitive to statements that patients may not be treated alike; in fact there is strong resistance in medical circles to the exploration of such

questions. But closing our eyes to facts or denying them in anger will help patients no more than the belief that the *Titanic* was "unsinkable" kept the ship afloat after it collided with an iceberg.

Paths to the Psychiatrist

Every person who follows a path that leads him eventually to a psychiatrist must pass four milestones. The first marks the *occurrence* of *"abnormal" behavior;* the second involves the *appraisal* of his behavior as "disturbed" in a psychiatric sense; the third is when the *decision* is made that psychiatric treatment is indicated; and the fourth is reached when the *decision is implemented* and the "disturbed" person actually enters the care of a psychiatrist. In our discussion of the events that link each milestone, we will focus attention upon the question: Is class status a salient factor in the determination of what path a person follows on his way to a psychiatrist?

"Abnormal" Behavior

"Abnormal" behavior is used here to indicate actions that are different from what is expected in a defined social situation. Thus, abnormal acts can be evaluated only in terms of their cultural and psychosocial contexts. Homicide, for example, is abnormal in a peaceful community; it is normal when inflicted on the enemy during war.

Viewed psychiatrically, the range of abnormal behavior is very great, covering in intensity mild neuroses to severe psychoses, and in duration from acute, transient "disturbances" to chronic reactions. It encompasses such well-defined phenomena as various types of schizophrenia, and many psychosocial maladjustments that never bring most persons to the attention of psychiatrists. "Abnormality depends" upon appraisal.

"Appraisal"

The perception and "appraisal," by other persons, of an individual's abnormal behavior as psychiatrically disturbed is crucial to the determination of whether a given individual is to become a psychiatric patient or be handled some other way. By appraisal we mean the evaluations of family members and proximate groups of abnormal behavior of persons. The appraisal of behavior as psychiatrically abnormal precedes decisions concerning therapeutic intervention. Appraisal is carried on by individuals and groups through the interpretation of interacting responses. It may be conscious, preconscious, or unconscious; usually, it is a combination of all three. It is both interpersonal and intrapersonal. As a lay response, appraisal corresponds to the professional diagnosis. As an intrapsychic process, it designates how the prospective patient perceives his actions, particularly his disturbed actions. Appraisal, as an interpersonal process, entails how a disturbed person and his actions are perceived and evaluated by the individual and by other persons in the community. Appraisal will determine what is judged to be delinquency, bad behavior, or psychiatric troubles.

Class Status and Appraisal

Inferences drawn from clinical practice, the tape-recorded interviews with persons in the 5 percent sample, and patients and members of their families in the Controlled Case Study and the Psychiatric Census indicate that class I and II persons are more aware of psychological problems than class IV and V persons.* Class I and II persons are also more perceptive of personal frustration, failure, and critical intrapsychic conflicts than class IV and V persons. Perception of the psychological nature of personal problems is a rare trait in any person and in any class, but it is found more frequently in the refined atmosphere of classes I and II than in the raw setting of class V. As a consequence, we believe that far more abnormal behavior is tolerated by the two lower classes, particularly class V, without any awareness that the motivations behind the behavior are pathological, even though the behavior may be disapproved by the class norms. We will illustrate these points by drawing upon the clinical histories of several patients in our study.

The first patient is an example of a higher status person who is able and willing to utilize

* The reader who is interested in the sampling on which the following class data are based should refer to the original book. Generally speaking, the sample came from the New Haven, Connecticut, area. The class notations (I through V) are based on an index of social position, utilizing ecological area of residence, occupation, and education. Class I is high in social position; Class V, low (Ed.).

the help of a psychiatrist to overcome self-perceived disturbances. This patient is a 25-year-old graduate student, the son of a salaried, minor professional man in an established class II family. The patient's chief complaint is a feeling that he is not able to work to his full capacity. He first noted this difficulty as an undergraduate in a state university near his home. He discussed this problem with a college friend who was being treated by psychotherapy and, upon his friend's advice, consulted the psychiatrist in charge of the college mental hygiene clinic. However, he did not enter treatment at that time. He knew little about psychiatry when he went to the clinic, but he began to read Freud, Horney, and others; after a period of conscious aversion, he found the materials interesting. The information gathered from them led him, after he had entered graduate school, to discuss his feelings with his friend. Upon this occasion he entered treatment. He was skeptical about psychiatric help in the first weeks of therapy, but he convinced himself that obtaining psychotherapy does not mark a person as "crazy." From this point on he was able to profit from psychiatric treatment. In the course of several months of psychotherapy, he was able to discuss with the therapist his relationships with a stern, driving father and a brother who had disgraced the family on many occasions. The discussions made him realize he was far too critical of himself and inordinately ambitious; unconsciously he was identifying with his stern father while competing with and outdoing the "bad" brother. Gradually, he realized that his unconscious motivations were related to his depression, anxiety, and inability to do graduate work the way he desired.

The patient we shall use to illustrate the lack of sensitivity to psychopathological behavior in the lower segments of the status structure is an elderly class IV man. This man's clinical history indicates that he had exhibited psychopathological behavior throughout his life, but it was not interpreted as such by his family or his associates. A few incidents will clarify the lack of appraisal by the family. In 1940, he took his thermos bottle to a chemist for examination to see if his wife was trying to poison him. Every night before his wife went to bed she secreted butcher knives and other sharp instruments to keep them away from him. He did not trust his daughter to measure medicine "prescribed" for him by a corner druggist, and he accused her of trying to poison him to get his money. He entered his daughters' bedrooms while they were dressing or undressing unless they locked their doors. He kept a razor-sharp hunting knife in the cellar. A daughter and son-in-law knew about the weapon and his constant preoccupation with sharpening it, but no action was taken. The man became violent whenever anyone told him to stop cursing or stop anything he might be doing. When this occurred, he would shout and pound on the walls; on numerous occasions he broke the plaster with the force of his blows. The family avoided bringing any liquor into the home because the father became unmanageable when drunk.

The day before Christmas, however, he requested a bottle for the holidays, and the eldest daughter and son-in-law, in order to humor him, bought a fifth of whiskey. On Christmas Eve, he drank too much, became angry, and used his full vocabulary of obscenity and profanity on the family. The daughter and son-in-law put him to bed and removed his weapons from the room. The next morning he demanded to know what had happened the previous evening, and when he was told he began to yell and curse until the entire building of flats where the family lived was aroused. His daughter in desperation called the police who took the man to the city jail. He was held until after New Year's Day before he was tried, found guilty of breach of the peace, and was sentenced to sixty days in the county jail. After transfer to the jail, he became violent, and a psychiatrist was called to the jail by the sheriff. The psychiatrist recommended commitment to the state hospital.

This man had been in the state hospital two years at the time of the Psychiatric Census. His family did not want him in the home, but they did not feel it was right for him to remain in the state hospital. His eldest daughter, who took charge of the situation, did not think he was "crazy." However, she made no active plans to care for him or to have him discharged. While the study was in progress, the man died in the state hospital.

Although the patient presents a lifelong history of hostility, suspicion, and extreme lack of consideration of others, so far as we are able to determine neither his family nor others in his environment—even when his behavior became violent—considered him a "psychiatric problem." Such an appraisal of behavior is more typical of class V than of class IV, although people in all strata have blind spots regarding psychopathological implications of unusual behavior or even deliberately avoid thinking about them. The lower status patient will attribute his troubles to unhappiness, tough luck, laziness, meanness, or physical illness rather than to factors of psychogenic origin. The worst thing that can happen to a class V person is to be labeled "bugs," "crazy," or "nuts." Such judgment is often equal to being sentenced for life to the "bughouse." Unfortunately, this sentiment is realistic.

The case histories of two compulsively promiscuous adolescent females will be drawn upon to illustrate the differential impact of class status on the way in which lay persons and psychiatrists perceive and appraise similar behavior. Both girls came to the attention of the police at about the same time but under very different circumstances. One came from a core group class I family, the other from a class V family broken by the desertion of the father. The class I girl, after one of her frequent drinking and sexual escapades on a weekend away from an exclusive boarding school, became involved in an automobile accident while drunk. Her family immediately arranged for bail through the influence of a member of an outstanding law firm; a powerful friend telephoned a newspaper contact, and the report of the accident was not published. Within twenty-four hours, the girl was returned to school. In a few weeks the school authorities realized that the girl was pregnant and notified her parents. A psychiatrist was called in for consultation by the parents with the expectation, expressed frankly, that he was to recommend a therapeutic interruption of the pregnancy. He did not see fit to do this and, instead, recommended hospitalization in a psychiatric institution to initiate psychotherapy. The parents, though disappointed that the girl would not have a "therapeutic" abortion, finally consented to hospitalization. In due course, the girl delivered a healthy baby who was placed for adoption.

Throughout her stay in the hospital she received intensive psychotherapy and after being discharged continued in treatment with a highly regarded psychoanalyst.

The class V girl was arrested by the police after she was observed having intercourse with four or five sailors from a nearby naval base. At the end of a brief and perfunctory trial, the girl was sentenced to a reform school. After two years there she was paroled as an unpaid domestic. While on parole, she became involved in promiscuous activity, was caught by the police, and sent to the state reformatory for women. She accepted her sentence as deserved "punishment" but created enough disturbance in the reformatory to attract the attention of a guidance officer. This official recommended that a psychiatrist be consulted. The psychiatrist who saw her was impressed by her crudeness and inability to communicate with him on most subjects. He was alienated by the fact that she thought masturbation was "bad," whereas intercourse with many men whom she hardly knew was "O.K." The psychiatrist's recommendation was to return the girl to her regular routine because she was not "able to profit from psychotherapy."

This type of professional judgment is not atypical, as we will demonstrate in Chapter Eleven, because, on the one hand, many psychiatrists do not understand the cultural values of class V, and on the other, class V patients and their families rarely understand common terms in the psychiatrists' vocabulary, such as neuroses, conflict, and psychotherapy. The lack of communication between psychiatrist and patient merely adds to the hostility felt toward the psychiatrist and fear of what will happen to a member of the family if he is "taken away." A lack of understanding of the psychiatrist's goals occurs, in part, because lower class persons are not sufficiently educated, but also their appraisal of what is disturbed behavior differs greatly from that of the psychiatrist.

In class V, where the demands of everyday life are greatest, awareness of suffering is perceived less clearly than in the higher levels. The denial, or partial denial, of the existence of psychic pain appears to be a defense mechanism that is linked to low status. Also, class V persons appear to accept physical suffering to a greater extent than do persons in higher status positions. This may be realistic and in keeping with the often hopeless situations these people face in day-to-day living. In classes I and II, by way of contrast, there is less willingness to accept life as unalterable. Consequently, there is a marked tendency to utilize a psychiatrist to help ease subjective malaise or disease. Nevertheless, the individual usually tries to hide his "shame" until it is no longer concealable. Even members of the immediate family may not be told that the patient is in psychiatric treatment. For example, in an extreme case, a middle-aged class III Jewish woman takes great pains to let nobody except her favorite sister know that she is a patient. The sister, who usually brings the patient to the psychiatrist's office, insists that the patient be administered anesthesia before she receives electro-convulsive therapy. She does not think the patient should know about her "shameful" treatment.

Conformity and Character

Richard S. Crutchfield

Richard Crutchfield received his Ph.D. in 1938 from the University of California, Berkeley, where he is now Professor of Psychology and Associate Director of the Institute of Personality Assessment and Research. Interested in developing methods for the instruction of creative thinking and problem solving, Crutchfield is the co-author of three books in the field of psychology: Theory and Problems of Social Psychology *(1948),* Elements of Psychology *(1958, rev. ed., 1969), and* Individual in Society *(1962).*

1. *To what extent does the artificiality of the "conformity" situation detract from the applicability of the findings?*

2. *When deceptive methods are used on human subjects what ethical responsibility, if any, does the experimenter have to the subject?*

During the Spring of 1953, one hundred men visited the Institute of Personality Assessment and Research at the University of California, Berkeley, to participate in an intensive three-day assessment of those qualities related to superior functioning in their profession.

As one of the procedures on the final day of assessment, the men were seated in groups of five in front of an apparatus consisting of five adjacent electrical panels. Each panel had side wings, forming an open cubicle, so that the person, though sitting side by side with his fellow subjects, was unable to see their panels. The experimenter explained that the apparatus was so wired that information could be sent by each man to all the others by closing any of eleven switches at the bottom of his panel. This information would appear on the other

From Richard S. Crutchfield, "Conformity and Character," *American Psychologist*, 10 (1955), 191–198. Copyright 1955 by the American Psychological Association and reproduced by permission.

panels in the form of signal lights, among five rows of eleven lights, each row corresponding to one of the five panels. After a warm-up task to acquaint the men with the workings of the apparatus, the actual procedure commenced.

Slides were projected on a wall directly facing the men. Each slide presented a question calling for a judgment by the person. He indicated his choice of one of several multiple-alternative answers by closing the appropriately numbered switch on his panel. Moreover, he responded *in order,* that is, as designated by one of five red lights lettered A, B, C, D, E on his panel. If he were A, he responded first, if B, second, and so on. The designations, A, B, C, D, and E, were rotated by the experimenter from time to time, thus permitting each person to give his judgments in all the different serial positions. No further explanation about the purpose of this procedure was offered.

It may help to convey the nature of the men's typical experiences by giving an illustrative description of what happens concretely to one of the men. The first slide calls for a simple judgment of which of two geometrical figures is larger in area. Since his red light C is on, he waits for A and B to respond before making his response. And, as he is able to observe on the panel, his own judgment coincides with the judgments of A and B who preceded him, and of D and E who follow him. After judgments on several further slides in position C, he is then shifted to position D for more slides, then to A.

The slides call for various kinds of judgments—lengths of lines, areas of figures, logical completion of number series, vocabulary items, estimates of the opinions of others, expression of his own attitudes on issues, expression of his personal preferences for line drawings, etc. He is not surprised to observe a perfectly sensible relationship between his judgments and those of the other four men. Where clear-cut perceptual or logical judgments are involved, he finds that his judgments are in perfect agreement with those of the other four. Where matters of opinion are involved, and some differences in opinion to be expected, his judgments and those of the other four men are sometimes in agreement and sometimes not.

Eventually the man finds himself for the first time in position E, where he is to respond last. The next slide shows a standard line and five comparison lines, of which he is to pick the one equal in length to the standard. Among the previous slides he has already encountered this kind of perceptual judgment and has found it easy. On looking at this slide it is immediately clear to him that line number 4 is the correct one. But as he waits his turn to respond, he sees light number 5 in row A go on, indicating that that person has judged line number 5 to be correct. And in fairly quick succession light 5 goes on also in rows B, C, and D.

At this point the man is faced with an obvious conflict between his own clear perception and a unanimous contradictory consensus of the other four men. What does he do? Does he rely on the evidence of his own senses and respond independently? Or does he defer to the judgment of the group, complying with their perceptions rather than his own?

We will postpone for a moment the answer as to what he does, and revert to the description of our apparatus.

We have been describing the situation as if seen from the perspective of one of the men. Actually his understanding of the situation is wrong. He has been deceived. For the apparatus is *not* really wired in the way that he was informed. There actually is no connection among the five panels. Instead, they are all wired in an identical manner to a control panel where the experimenter sits behind the men. It is the experimenter who sends all the information which appears on the panels, and the wiring is in parallel in such a way that whatever

signals are sent by the experimenter appear simultaneously and identically on all five panels. Moreover, the designations of serial order of responding—A through E—are identical at all times for the five panels, so that at a given moment, for instance, all five men believe themselves to be A, or at another time, E.

As we have just said, the responses actually made by the five men do not affect in any way the panels of the others. They do get registered individually on one part of the experimenter's control panel. The *latency* of each individual response to one tenth of a second is also recorded by timers on the control panel.

Hence, the situation as we have described it for our one illustrative man is actually the situation simultaneously experienced by all five men. They all commence in position C, and all shift at the same time to position D, and to A, and finally E. They all see the same simulated group judgments.

The entire situation is, in a word, contrived, and contrived so as to expose each individual to a standardized and prearranged series of group judgments. By this means the simulated group judgments can be made to appear sensible and in agreement with the individual, or, at chosen critical points, in conflict with his judgments.

Most of you will recognize at once the basic similarity of our situation to that invented by Asch in his extremely important work of recent years on independence of individual judgment under opposing group pressure. In his method, ten subjects announced aloud and in succession their judgments of the relative length of stimulus lines exposed before the group. The first nine subjects were actually confederates of the experimenter, and gave uniformly false answers at pre-established points, thus placing pressure on the single naive subject.

For extensive research use, for instance in personality assessment, Asch's technique is handicapped by the severely unfavorable ratio of confederates to true subjects. The present technique, utilizing the electrical network described above, avoids this difficulty. There are no confederates required; all five subjects are tested simultaneously in a thoroughly standardized situation. The experimenter exercises highly flexible control of the simulated group judgments, and of the serial order of responding. Stimulus material to be judged can be varied as widely as desired by use of different slides.

Now at last come back to our man still sitting before his panel, still confronted with the spurious group consensus, still torn between a force toward independent judgment and a force toward conformity to the group. How he is likely to behave in the situation can best be described by summarizing the results for our study of 50 of the 100 men in assessment.

Effects of Consensus

All of these men were engaged in a profession in which leadership is one of the salient expected qualifications. Their average age was 34 years. Their educational levels were heterogeneous, but most had had some college training.

Fifty of the men were tested in the procedure as described. Another 40 served as *control* subjects; they simply gave individual judgments of the slides without using the apparatus, and hence without knowledge of the judgments of others. The distribution of judgments of these control subjects on each slide was subsequently used as a baseline for evaluating the amount of group pressure influence on the experimental subjects.

Now as to results. When faced with the dilemma posed by this first critical slide, 15 of the 50 men, or 30 per cent, conformed to the obviously false group consensus. The remaining 70 per cent of the men maintained independence of judgment in face of the contradictory group consensus.

The first critical slide was followed by 20 others, all with the subjects responding in position E. The 20 slides involved a broad sampling of judgmental materials, exploring the question of what would happen to other kinds of perceptions, to matters of factual appraisal and of logic, of opinion and attitude, of personal preference—all under the same conditions of group pressure. Interpolated among them were occasional neutral slides, in which the group consensus was simulated as correct or sensible, in order to help maintain the subjects' acceptance of the genuineness of the apparatus and situation.

The results on several more of the critical slides will give a representative picture of what happens under group pressure. First, take another kind of perceptual judgment. A circle and a star are exposed side by side, the circle being about one third larger in area than the star. The false group consensus is on the *star* as the larger, and 46 per cent of the men express agreement with this false judgment.

On a simple logical judgment of completion of a number series, as found in standard mental tests, 30 per cent of the men conform to an obviously illogical group answer, whereas not a single control subject gives an incorrect answer.

As striking as these influence effects are, they are overshadowed by the even higher degree of influence exhibited on another set of items. These pertain to perceptual, factual, and logical judgments which are designed to maximize the *ambiguity* of the stimulus. There are three such examples: (*a*) two actually equal circles are to be judged for relative size; (*b*) a pair of words are to be judged as either synonyms or antonyms, though actually entirely unrelated in meaning and unfamiliar to all subjects; (*c*) a number series is to be completed which is actually insoluble, that is, for which there is no logically correct completion.

To take the third example, which gives the most pronounced influence effect of all 21 critical items, 79 per cent of the men conform to a spurious group consensus upon an arbitrarily chosen and irrational answer.

Influence effects are found, we see, on both well-structured and poorly-structured stimuli, with markedly greater effects on the latter.

Turning from perceptual and factual judgments to opinions and attitudes, it is clearly evident that here, too, the judgments of many of the men are markedly dependent upon a spurious group consensus which violates their own inner convictions. For example, among control subjects virtually no one expresses disagreement with the statement: "I believe we are made better by the trials and hardships of life." But among the experimental subjects exposed to a group consensus toward disagreement, 31 per cent of the men shift to expressing disagreement.

It can be demonstrated that the conformity behavior is not found solely for attitudes on issues like the foregoing, which may be of rather abstract and remote significance for the person. Among the control sample of men, not a single one expresses agreement with the statement: "I doubt whether I would make a good leader," whereas 37 per cent of the men subjected to group pressure toward agreement succumb to it. Here is an issue relating to appraisal of the self and hence likely to be of some importance to the person, especially in light of the fact already mentioned that one of the salient expected qualifications of men in this particular profession is that of leadership.

The set of 21 critical items ranges from factual to attitudinal, from structured to ambiguous, from impersonal to personal. With only two exceptions, all these items yield significant group pressure influence effects in our sample of 50 men. The very existence of the two exceptional items is in itself an important finding, for it demonstrates that the observed influences are not simply evidence of indiscriminate readiness to conform to group pressure regardless of the specific nature of the judgment involved. The character of the two exceptional items is significant, for they are the two most extremely personal and subjective judgments, namely, those in which the individual is asked which one of two simple line drawings *he prefers*. On these slides there is virtually no effective result of group pressure. Not more than one man of the 50 expresses agreement with the spurious group consensus on the nonpreferred drawing. Such personal preferences, being most isolated from the relevance of group standards, thus seem to be most immune to group pressure.

Individual Differences

To what extent do the fifty men differ among themselves in their general degree of conformity to group pressure?

A total "conformity score" is readily obtainable for each individual by counting the number of the 21 critical items on which he exhibits influence to the group pressure. The threshold for influence for each item is arbitrarily fixed on the basis of the distribution of judgments by control subjects on that item.

Considering that we are dealing with a fairly homogeneous sample of limited size, the range of individual differences that we obtain is astonishingly large, covering virtually the entire possible scope of our measure. At the lower extreme, several of the men showed conformity on no more than one or two of the critical items. At the upper extreme, one man was influenced on 17 of the 21 items. The rest of the scores are well distributed between these extremes, with a mean score of about eight items and a tendency for greater concentration of scores toward the lower conformity end.

The reliability of the total score, as a measure of generalized conformity in the situation, is obtained by correlating scores on two matched halves of the items. The correlation is found to be .82, which when corrected for the combined halves gives a reliability estimate for the entire 21-item scale of .90.

To recapitulate, we find large and reliable differences among the 50 men in the amount of conformity behavior exhibited, and there appears to be considerable generality of this conformity behavior with respect to widely varied judgmental materials. Whether such conformity tendencies also generalize to other, quite different behavioral situations is a question for future research.

Relations to Personality Variables

Assuming that we are, indeed, measuring conformity tendencies which are fundamental in the person, the question is what traits of character distinguish between those men exhibiting much conformity behavior in our test and those exhibiting little conformity. The assessment setting within which these men were studied provides an unusually fertile opportunity to explore this question, in light of the wide range of personality measurements available.

Correlational study of the conformity scores with these other variables of personality provides some picture of the independent and of the conforming person. As contrasted with the high conformist, the independent man shows more intellectual effectiveness, ego strength, leadership ability and maturity of social relations, together with a conspicuous absence of inferiority feelings, rigid and excessive self-control, and authoritarian attitudes.

A few correlations will illustrate. The assessment staff rating on "intellectual competence" correlates $-.63$ with conformity score, this being the highest relationship of any found. The *Concept Mastery Test*,[1] a measure of superior mental functioning, correlates −.51 with conformity. An "ego strength" scale, independently derived by Barron, correlates −.33, and a staff rating on "leadership ability," −.30 with conformity. Scales of Gough's *California Psychological Inventory,* pertaining to such dimensions as "tolerance," "social participation," and "responsibility," range in correlation from −.30 to −.41 with conformity.

And as for some of the positive correlates, the F scale, a measure of authoritarian attitudes, correlates +.39 with conformity, and a staff rating on amount of authoritarian behavior manifested in a standard psychodrama situation correlates +.35 with conformity.

The general appraisal of each man by the assessment staff in the form of descriptive Q sorts further enriches this picture. Those men exhibiting extreme independence in the situation as contrasted with those at the high conformity end are described more often in the following terms by the assessment staff, which was entirely ignorant of the actual behavior of the men in the group pressure procedure:

Is an effective leader.

Takes an ascendant role in his relations with others.

Is persuasive; tends to win other people over to his point of view.

Is turned to for advice and reassurance.

Is efficient, capable, able to mobilize resources easily and effectively.

Is active and vigorous.

Is an expressive, ebullient person.

Seeks and enjoys aesthetic and sensuous impressions.

Is natural; free from pretense, unaffected.

Is self-reliant; independent in judgment; able to think for himself.

In sharp contrast to this picture of the independent men is the following description of those high in conformity behavior:

With respect to authority, is submissive, compliant and overly accepting.

Is conforming; tends to do the things that are prescribed.

Has a narrow range of interests.

Overcontrols his impulses; is inhibited; needlessly delays or denies gratification.

Is unable to make decisions without vacillation or delay.

Becomes confused, disorganized, and unadaptive under stress.

Lacks insight into his own motives and behavior.

Is suggestible; overly responsive to other people's evaluations rather than his own.

Further evidence is found in some of the specific items of personality inventories on which the answers of the high and low conformers are significantly different. Here are some illustrative items more frequently answered "True" by the independent subjects than by the conforming subjects:

Sometimes I rather enjoy going against the rules and doing things I'm not supposed to.

I like to fool around with new ideas, even if they turn out later to be a total waste of time.

A person needs to "show off" a little now and then.

At times I have been so entertained by the cleverness of a crook that I have hoped he would get by with it.

It is unusual for me to express strong approval or disapproval of the actions of others.

I am often so annoyed when someone tries to get ahead of me in a line of people that I speak to him about it.

Compared to your own self-respect, the respect of others means very little.

This pattern of expressed attitudes seems to reflect freedom from compulsion about rules, adventurousness (perhaps tinged with exhibitionism), self-assertiveness, and self-respect.

Turning to the opposite side of the picture, here are some illustrative items more frequently answered "True" by the extreme conformists, which reflect a rather rigid, externally sanctioned, and inconsistent, moralistic attitude.

I am in favor of very strict enforcement of all laws, no matter what the consequences.

It is all right to get around the law if you don't actually break it.

Most people are honest chiefly through fear of being caught.

Another set of items reveals a desire for clarity, symmetry, certainty, or, in presently popular phraseology, "an intolerance of ambiguity."

I don't like to work on a problem unless there is a possibility of coming out with a clear-cut and unambiguous answer.

Once I have made up my mind I seldom change it.

Perfect balance is the essence of all good composition.

[1] Used with the kind permission of Dr. Lewis M. Terman.

I always follow the rule: business before pleasure.

The trouble with many people is that they don't take things seriously enough.

I am very careful about my manner of dress.

Anxiety is revealed in numerous items:

I am afraid when I look down from a high place.

I am often bothered by useless thoughts which keep running through my head.

I often think, "I wish I were a child again."

I often feel as though I have done something wrong or wicked.

And, finally, there are various expressions of disturbed, dejected, and distrustful attitudes toward other people:

When I meet a stranger I often think that he is better than I am.

Sometimes I am sure that other people can tell what I am thinking.

I wish that I could get over worrying about things I have said that may have injured other people's feelings.

I commonly wonder what hidden reason another person may have for doing something nice for me.

People pretend to care more about one another than they really do.

Although there is an unmistakable neurotic tone to many of the foregoing statements, one must be chary of inferring that those high on conformity are measurably more neurotic than the others. There does not in fact appear to be any significant correlation of the conformity scores with obvious standard measures of neuroticism as found, for instance, in scales of the Minnesota Multiphasic Personality Inventory. A similar negative finding has been reported by Barron in his study of the personality correlates of independence of judgment in Asch's subjects.

In another area, attitudes concerning parents and children, differences between those high and low on conformity are especially interesting. The extreme conformists describe their parents in highly idealized terms, unrelieved by any semblance of criticism. The independents, on the other hand, offer a more balanced picture of praise and criticism.

Most of the men in the sample are fathers, and it is instructive to see that in their view of child-rearing practices, the conformers are distinctly more "restrictive" in their attitudes, and the independents distinctively more "permissive."

Finally, there appears to be a marked difference in the early home background of the conformists and independents. The high conformers in this sample come almost without exception from stable homes; the independents much more frequently report broken homes and unstable home environments.

Previous theoretical and empirical studies seem to converge, though imperfectly, on a picture of the overconformist as having less ego strength, less ability to tolerate his own impulses and to tolerate ambiguity, less ability to accept responsibility, less self-insight, less spontaneity and productive originality, and as having more prejudiced and authoritarian attitudes, more idealization of parents, and greater emphasis on external and socially approved values.

All of these elements gain at least some substantiation in the present study of conformity behavior, as objectively measured in our test situation. The decisive influence of intelligence in resisting conformity pressures is perhaps given even fuller weight in the present findings.

Conformity Behavior in Different Populations

Two further studies have been made. The first was with 59 college undergraduates, mostly sophomores. Forty were females, 19 males. An additional 40 students served as control subjects.

Using the same procedures and the same items for judgment, the conformity results for this student sample were highly similar to those already reported for the adult men. Here again extensive group pressure effects are found on almost all items. And here again there are wide individual differences, covering virtually the entire score range.

The male students on the average exhibit just about the same level of conformity as do the adult men. The female students, on the other hand, exhibit significantly *higher* amounts of conformity than the male groups. This greater conformity among females is evident across the entire range of items tested. Interpretation of this sex difference in conformity will require further research.

But before male egos swell overly, let me hasten to report the results of a third study, just completed. Fifty women, all college alumnae in their early forties, were tested in the same group pressure procedure, again as part of a larger assessment setting, and under the auspices of the Mary Conover Mellon Foundation. As in the previous populations, virtually the entire range of individual differences in conformity is exhibited by these women. Some of them show no effect at all; others are influenced on almost all items. But the average conformity score for these 50 women is significantly *lower* than that found in the previous populations.

Thus we find our sample of adult women to be more independent in judgment than our adult men. The interpretation is difficult. The two groups differ in many particulars, other than sex. The women are highly selected for educational and socioeconomic status, are persons active in their community affairs, and would be characterized as relatively stable in personality and free of psychopathology. The adult men in our professional group are less advantageously selected in all these respects. Differences in intellectual level alone might be sufficient to account for the observed differences in conformity scores.

Psychological Processes

Turn now to questions concerning the nature of the psychological processes involved in these expressions of conformity to group pressure. How, for instance, is the situation perceived by the individual? The most striking thing is that almost never do the individuals under this pressure of a false group consensus come to suspect the deception practiced upon them. Of the total of 159 persons already tested in the apparatus and questioned immediately afterwards, only a small handful expressed doubt of the genuineness of the situation. Of these not more than two or three really seem to have developed this suspicion while in the actual situation.

Yet all the subjects are acutely aware of the sometimes gross discrepancies between their own inner judgments and those expressed by the rest of the group. How do they account for these discrepancies?

Intensive individual questioning of the subjects immediately following the procedure elicits evidence of two quite different tendencies. First, for many persons the discrepancies tend to be resolved through self-blame. They express doubt of their own accuracy of perception or judgment, confessing that they had probably misread or misperceived the slides. Second, for many other persons the main tendency is to blame the rest of the group, expressing doubt that they had perceived or read the slides correctly. This is not a neat dichotomy, of course. Most persons express something of a mixture of these explanations, which is not surprising in view of the fact that some slides may tend to favor one interpretation of the difficulty and other slides the opposite interpretation.

As might be predicted, there is a substantial relationship between conformity score and tendency to self-blame; or, putting it the other way, those who remain relatively independent of the group pressure are more likely to blame the discrepancies on poor judgments by the rest of the group.

But this is by no means a perfect relationship. There are many persons who, though retrospectively expressing doubt of the correctness of the group's judgment, did in fact conform heavily while in the situation. And what is even more striking is that a substantial number of the subjects—between 25 and 30 per cent—freely admit on later questioning that there were times when they responded the way the group did *even when they thought this not the proper answer*. It seems evident, therefore, that along with various forms of cognitive rationalization of the discrepancies, there occurred a considerable amount of what might be called deliberate conforming, that is, choosing to express outward agreement with the group consensus even when believing the group to be wrong.

Another noteworthy effect was the sense of increased psychological distance induced between the person himself and the rest of the group. He felt himself to be queer or different, or felt the group to be quite unlike what he had thought. With this went an arousal of considerable anxiety in most subjects; for some, manifest anxiety was acute.

The existence of these tensions within and between the subjects became dramatically manifest when, shortly after the end of the procedure, the experimenter confessed the deception he had practiced and explained the real situation. There were obvious and audible signs of relaxation and relief, and a shift from an atmosphere of constraint to one of animated discussion.

This is an appropriate point to comment on ethics. No persons when questioned after explanation of the deception expressed feelings that they had been ethically maltreated in the experiment. The most common reaction was a positive one of having engaged in an unusual and significant experience, together with much joking about having been taken in.

Undeniably there are serious ethical issues involved in the experimental use of such deception techniques, especially inasmuch as they appear to penetrate rather deeply into the person. My view is that such deception methods ethically require that great care be taken immediately afterwards to explain the situation fully to the subject.

These remarks on ethics of the method are especially pertinent as we move from study of judgmental materials which are noncontroversial to those which are controversial. In the studies of college students and of mature women, many new critical items were introduced and subjected to the pressure. They were intended to explore more deeply the conformity tendencies in matters of opinion and attitude. And they were so chosen as to pertain to socially important and controversial issues involving civil liberties, political philosophy, crime and punishment, ethical values, and the like.

Here are two salient examples. An expression of agreement or disagreement was called for on the following statement: "Free speech being a privilege rather than a right, it is proper for a society to suspend free speech whenever it feels itself threatened." Among control subjects, only 19 per cent express agreement. But among the experimental subjects confronted with a unanimous group consensus agreeing with the statement, 58 per cent express agreement.

Another item was phrased as follows: "Which one of the following do you feel is the most important problem facing our country today?" And these five alternatives were offered:

Economic recession
Educational facilities
Subversive activities

Mental health
Crime and corruption

Among control subjects, only 12 per cent chose "Subversive activities" as the most important. But when exposed to a spurious group consensus which unanimously selected "Subversive activities" as the most important, 48 per cent of the experimental subjects expressed this same choice.

I think that no one would wish to deny that here we have evidence of the operation of powerful conformity influences in the expression of opinion on matters of critical social controversy.

Reinforcement of Conformity

There is one final point upon which I should like to touch briefly. That is the question of whether there are circumstances under which the power of the group to influence the judgments of the individual may be even more greatly reinforced, and if so, how far such power may extend.

One method has been tried as part of the study of college students. With half of the subjects, a further instruction was introduced by the experimenter. They were told that in order to see how well they were doing during the procedure, the experimenter would inform the group immediately after the judgments on each slide what the correct answer was. This was to be done, of course, only for those slides for which there was a correct answer, namely, perceptual judgments, logical solutions, vocabulary, etc. No announcement would be made after slides having to do with opinions and attitudes.

The experimenter here again deceived the subjects, for the answers he announced as correct were deliberately chosen so as to agree with the false group consensus. In short, the external authority of the experimenter was later added on as reinforcement to the group consensus.

The effect of this so-called "correction" method is striking. As the series of judgments goes on, these individuals express greater and greater conformity to the group pressure on slides which are of the same character as those for which earlier in the series the false group consensus was thus reinforced by the false announcement by the experimenter.

But the more critical issue is whether this enhanced power of the group generalizes also to judgments of an entirely unrelated sort, namely, matters of opinion and attitude, rather than of fact. In other words, will the group, through having the rightness of its judgment supported by the experimenter on matters of perception, logic, and the like, thereby come to be regarded by the individual as more right, or more to be complied with, on entirely extraneous matters, such as social issues?

The answer is absolutely clear. The enhanced power of the group does *not* carry over to increase the effective influence on expression of opinions and attitudes. The subjects exposed to this "correction" method do not exhibit greater conformity to group pressure on opinions and attitudes than that found in other subjects.

This crucial finding throws some light on the nature of the psychological processes involved in the conformity situation. For it seems to imply that conformity behavior under such group pressure, rather than being sheerly an indiscriminate and irrational tendency to defer to the authority of the group, has in it important rational elements. There is something of a reasonable differentiation made by the individual in his manner of reliance upon the group. He may be led to accept the superiority of the group judgment on matters where there is an objective frame of reference against which the group can be checked. But he does not, thereby, automatically accept the authority of the group on matters of a less objective sort.

Conclusion

The social psychologist is concerned with the character of conformity, the personologist with conformity of character. Between them they raise many research questions: the comparative incidence of conformity tendencies in various populations; the influence of group structure and the individual's role in the group on the nature and amount of conformity behavior; the effects of reward or punishment for conforming on habits of conformity; the genesis and change of conformity behavior in the individual personality; the determinants of extreme *anti*conformity tendencies.

Contributing to such questions we have what appears to be a powerful new research technique, enabling the study of conformity behavior within a setting which effectively simulates genuine group interaction, yet preserves the essential requirements of objective measurement.

The Significance of Multiple-Group Membership in Disaster

Lewis M. Killian

Lewis Killian, a sociologist at the University of Massachusetts, received his Ph.D. from the University of Chicago in 1949. His major area of interest is in the application of social science principles to an understanding of race relations. Dr. Killian is author of The Impossible Revolution? (*1968*) *and co-author of* Collective Behavior (*1957*) *and* Racial Crisis in America (*1964*).

1. What hunches do you have as to why a person turns to his family group first, in time of disaster? Are there learning or personality theories that would predict this?

2. Would reactions of people to disaster in large cities (New York, Chicago) differ from reactions in the small town communities of this study?

In a study of the reactions of people in four Southwestern communities to physical disasters —explosions and tornadoes—made by the University of Oklahoma Research Institute, it was found that conflicting group loyalties and contradictory roles resulting from multiple-group membership were significant factors affecting individual behavior in critical situations. The dilemmas created by the disasters also brought to light latent contradictions in roles not ordinarily regarded as conflicting.

In spite of the fact that multiple-group memberships do create dilemmas and inconsistencies, the majority of people in modern urban society manage to function efficiently as members of many groups, often being only

Reprinted from *The American Journal of Sociology,* Vol. 57, January 1952, by permission of The University of Chicago Press. Copyright, 1952, The University of Chicago.

vaguely aware of contradictions in their various roles. Sherif points out that the individual is often not aware of the derivation of the "cross-pressures" which cause inconsistent behavior. Newcomb declares that many role prescriptions are "relatively nonconflicting" and says:

> Most of us, most of the time, manage to take quite different roles, as prescribed by the same or by different groups, without undue conflict. . . . Indeed, it is rather remarkable how many different roles most of us manage to take with a minimum of conflict.

He points out that many roles are "nonoverlapping." A man may play the role of a businessman, acting in terms of the work situation, during most of the day. For a few hours in the evening he may play the role of "the family man," leaving his work at the office. In a small community he may, on certain occasions, act as a functionary of the town government, as a volunteer fireman, or as a town councilman. Simultaneously, he has other group memberships which call for certain behavior—in a social class group, in a racial group, in the community of which he is a citizen, and in "society-at-large."

When catastrophe strikes a community, many individuals find that the latent conflict between ordinarily nonconflicting group loyalties suddenly becomes apparent and that they are faced with the dilemma of making an immediate choice between various roles. In his classic study of the Halifax disaster, S. H. Prince noted this conflict when he wrote:

> But the earliest leadership that could be called social, arising from the public itself, was that on the part of those who had no family ties, much of the earliest work being done by visitors in the city. The others as a rule ran first to their homes to discover if their own families were in danger.

People who had been present in the explosion port of Texas City and in three Oklahoma tornado towns during disasters were asked, among other questions, "What was the first thing you thought of after the disaster struck?" and "What was the first thing you did?" Their answers revealed not only the conflict between loyalties to the family and to the community, described by Prince, but also dilemmas arising from conflicting roles derived from membership in other groups. The individuals concerned were not always conscious of the dilemmas or of the existence of "cross-pressures," but even in such cases the choice of roles which the person made was significant in affecting the total pattern of group reaction to the disaster. In some cases subjects indicated that they recognized *after* the emergency that their reaction had been of critical social importance. On the basis of the experiences of people involved in these four community disasters it is possible to suggest the types of groups between which dilemmas of loyalty may arise in modern communities. Tentative generalization as to how these dilemmas will be resolved and as to their significance for *group* reactions to disaster may also be formulated.

The choice required of the greatest number of individuals was the one between the family and other groups, principally the employment group or the community. Especially in Texas City, many men were at work away from their families when disaster struck and presented a threat to both "the plant" and "the home." In all the communities there were individuals, such as policemen, firemen, and public utilities workers, whose loved ones were threatened by the same disaster that demanded their services as "trouble-shooters." Even persons who had no such definite roles to play in time of catastrophe were confronted with the alternatives of seeing after only their own primary groups or of assisting in the rescue and relief of any of the large number of injured persons, regardless of identity. Indeed, only the unattached person in the community was likely to be free of such a conflict.

How these conflicts between loyalty to the family group and loyalty to other membership groups, including the community and "society-at-large," were resolved was of great significance for the reorganization of communities for rescue, relief, and prevention of further disaster. In Texas City, at the time of the first ship explosion, many men were working in oil refineries, where failure to remain on the job until units were shut down could result in additional fires and explosions. In all the communities studied, failure of community functionaries, such as firemen and policemen, to perform the duties appropriate to their positions could result in the absence of expected and badly needed leadership in a disorganized group. This, in turn, could cause costly delay in the reorganization of the community for emergency rescue, traffic control, and fire-fighting activity. Preoccupation of large numbers of able survivors with their own small primary groups could result in the atomization of the community into small, uncoordinated groups, again delaying reorganization into a relatively well-integrated, unified, large group. As Prince indicated in his statement, quoted above, this would increase the dependence of the community on outside sources of leadership.

The great majority of persons interviewed who were involved in such dilemmas resolved them in favor of loyalty to the family or, in some cases, to friendship groups. Much of the initial confusion, disorder, and seemingly complete disorganization reported in the disaster communities was the result of the rush of individuals to find and rejoin their families. Yet in none of the four communities studied did the disastrous consequences contemplated above seem to have materialized. In the first place, there were important exceptions to the tendency to react first in terms of the family. Most of the refinery workers in Texas City did stay on the job until their units were safely shut down, as they had been trained to do. The significance of conflicting group loyalties in a disaster situation is underlined, however, by the importance of the actions taken by a few exceptional individuals in each town who were not confronted with such conflicts. In Texas City the chief of police remained at his post from the moment of the first explosion until seventy-two hours later, never returning to his home during the entire period and playing a vital part in the reorganization of the community. He ascribed his ability to give undivided attention to his official duties to the fact that he knew that his family was safely out of town, visiting relatives, at the time of the explosion. One member of the volunteer fire department of a tornado town told of the thin margin by which his community escaped a disastrous fire following the "twister":

I was at my home, right on the edge of where the storm passed, when it hit. Neither me nor my wife was hurt. The first thing I thought of was fires. I knew there'd be some, so I went to the fire station right away. On the way I could see that there was a fire right in the middle of the wreckage—a butane tank had caught fire. I got out of the truck, drove over there, and fought the fire by myself until the army got there to help me.

All the rest of the firemen had relatives that were hurt, and they stayed with them. Naturally they looked after them. If it hadn't been that my wife was all right, this town probably would have burned up. It's hard to say, but I kind of believe I would have been looking after my family, too.

Devotion to the family as the primary object of loyalty did not always redound to the detriment of aid to other groups, however. Many people who served as rescue workers, assisting injured people whom they did not even know, were drawn to the areas of heavy casualties because of concern for members of their own families whom they believed to be there. Apparently they found their identification with society-at-large, and the emphasis of American culture upon the importance of human life, too great to permit them to pass an injured stranger without assisting him. Hence, many stayed to assist in the common community task of rescuing the injured, in both Texas City and in the tornado towns. In one of the latter a man sensed the approach of the tornado only minutes before it struck. In spite of great personal danger he rushed through the storm to a theater where his children were attending a movie. There he prevented the frightened audience from pouring forth into the storm by holding the doors closed. Later he was acclaimed as a hero whose quick action had saved the lives of many of his fellow-citizens. He himself denied that he had any thought of taking the great risk that he took for the sake of the anonymous audience itself; he was thinking only of his own children.

A second, but less common, type of conflict was found in the case of people who were confronted with the alternatives of playing the "heroic" role of rescue worker and of carrying out what were essentially "occupational roles." In terms of group loyalty, they were impelled, on the one hand, to act as sympathetic, loyal members of society-at-large and to give personal aid to injured human beings. On the other hand, they were called to do their duty as it was indicated by their membership in certain occupational groups.

One such person was a minister in Texas City who, upon hearing the explosion, started for the docks with the intention of helping in the rescue work. On the way he became conscious of the choice of roles which confronted him. He said:

After I heard the first explosion my first impulse was to go down to the docks and try to help there. But on the way down I saw two or three folks I knew who had husbands down there. I saw then that my job was with the families—not doing rescue work. I had a job that I was peculiarly suited for, prepared for, and I felt that I should do that.

More important for the reorganization of a tornado-stricken town was the choice made by a state patrolman between his role as a police officer and his role as friend and neighbor to the people of the community in which he was stationed. His story was:

As I drove around town after the tornado had passed I realized that the best thing I could do was to try to make contact with the outside and get help from there. I started out to drive to the next town and try to call from there. As I drove out of town people I knew well would call me by name and ask me to help them find their relatives. Driving by and not stopping to help those people who were looking to me as a friend was one of the hardest things I ever had to do.

As a result of this difficult decision, this man became the key figure in the development of organized rescue work, after he recruited and organized a large force of rescue workers in a near-by community.

A similar dilemma faced many public utilities workers who were forced to disregard the plight of the injured if they were to perform their task of restoring normal community services. Unlike the minister and the patrolman, these workers reported no awareness of a conflict of roles, regarding it as a matter of course that they concentrated on their often quite dangerous jobs. Some indicated that preoccupation with the job was so intense that they were scarcely aware of what went on around them. Yet the instances of devotion to prosaic duty cited above were exceptional. Many policemen, firemen, and other functionaries acted heroically but quite outside the framework and discipline of their organizations.

For people whose usual occupational roles bore little or no relationship to the needs created by a disaster, identification with the community as a whole and disregard of their occupational roles came still more easily. Many merchants and clerks rushed from their stores to aid in rescue work, leaving both goods and cash on the counters. The postmaster in one tornado town left the post office completely unguarded, even though the windows were shattered and mail was strewn about the floor. This was, it is true, an extreme case of abandonment of the occupational role.

A third type of conflict of loyalties was that between the loyalty of employees to "the company" as an organization and to fellow-employees as friends and human beings. It might seem that the choice, essentially one between life and property, should have been an easy one; but the fact that different choices were made by men with different degrees of identification with other workers reveals that a basic conflict was present. In Texas City many plant officials were also residents of the community and friends of the workers. After the explosions, in which several top executives were killed, some men found themselves suddenly "promoted" to the position of being in charge of their company's damaged property. At the same time men with whom they had worked daily for several years were injured or missing. The most common, almost universal, reaction was to think of the men first and of the plant later. One plant official, active in rescue work,

in spite of a broken arm and numerous lacerations, described his reaction to the sudden, dramatic conflict between loyalty to the company and loyalty to the workers as follows:

> Property! Nobody gave a damn for property! All that was important was life. I've often wondered just how it would be to walk off and let a plant burn up. That was the way it was. We didn't even consider fighting the fire.

In sharp contrast to this reaction, however, was that of a man in charge of a neighboring plant. While he was in Texas City at the time of the first blast, he had never lived in the community and scarcely knew his workers. He described his first reaction in the following words:

> I got in my car and drove over to another refinery to find out what had happened. The assistant superintendent told me that their top men had been killed and asked me what I thought he should do. I told him, "You should take charge of the company's property. That's what the president of your company would tell you if he were here. You look after the property. I'm going over to Galveston to call our president, and I'll call yours at the same time."

While this reaction was exceptional, it is significant as suggesting an alternate way of resolving the conflict between loyalty to "the company" and "the men."

Finally, some individuals suddenly discovered, in the face of disaster, that there was a conflict between loyalty to the community and loyalty to certain extra-community groups. At the time of two of the disasters telephone workers in the Southwest were on strike. In both communities the striking workers were allowed to return to duty by union leaders but were ordered to walk out again a few days later. In both cases the union officials considered the emergency to be over sooner than did the townspeople of the stricken communities. In one town the workers obeyed the union's orders only to find themselves subjected to harsh criticism by their fellow-townsmen. In the other community the workers resigned from the union rather than forsake their loyalty to their other membership group. It was almost a year before union officials were able to reorganize the local in this town, and some workers never rejoined.

As was pointed out earlier, the individual may, under normal circumstances, carry out roles appropriate to membership in several groups without having to make a choice between basically conflicting group loyalties. He may even do so without seriously impairing his performance of any of his roles. The worker may wish that he could spend more time at home with his family but resigns himself to the fact that he cannot if he is to keep the job he wants. On his way to work he may pass the scene of a fire and be vaguely conscious that, as a citizen, he is indirectly responsible for the protection of life and property; but he assumes that the limit of his direct responsibility for action extends only to notifying the fire department, if it is not already there. The employer may, within certain limits, think of the workers as persons and friends and still not be disloyal to the company's interests. In the crisis induced by disaster, however, these individuals may find that it is impossible to serve two masters, to act in two roles. An immediate choice is demanded, but it may be difficult because the demands of the competing groups may appear equally urgent. The nature of the choice made by the individual, particularly if one of his roles is associated with a key position in the community, may have important consequences for the reorganization of the community. Large-scale reorganization, co-ordination, and direction of efforts is necessary to speedy rescue work and the restoration of normalcy. Activities carried on in terms of the demands of many diverse, competing groups act as an impediment to this reorganization.

Further research is needed to make possible the prediction of the choices that will be made by individuals in these conflicts. The frequency with which individuals thought and acted first in terms of family and close friends suggests that loyalty to primary groups stands first in the hierarchy of group loyalties, as might be expected. On the other hand, important exceptions in which persons played relatively impersonal roles as leaders or working with matériel, rather than people, indicate that some factors, such as training or feelings of responsibility, may predispose the individual to adhere to secondary-group demands even in a disaster. Knowledge of what these factors are and how they may be induced would contribute to greater understanding of group reactions to disorganization and of methods of facilitating group reorganization.

Suggested Readings

Adorno, T. W., et al. *The Authoritarian Personality*. New York: Harper, 1950.

Allport, F. H. "The J-Curve Hypothesis of Conforming Behavior," *J. soc. Psychol.*, 5 (1934), 141–183.

Allport, G. W. *ABC's of Scapegoating*. Chicago: Central Y.M.C.A. College, 1944.

——————, and L. Postman. *The Psychology of Rumor*. New York: Holt, Rinehart & Winston, 1947.

Asch, S. E. "Effects of Group Pressure upon the Modification and Distortion of Judgments," in H. Guetzkow, ed., *Groups, Leadership and Men*. Pittsburgh: Carnegie Press, 1951.

Bales, R. F. "How People Interact in Conferences," *Sci. Amer.*, 192 (1955), 31–35.

Helson, H., R. R. Blake, and J. S. Mouton. "Petition-Signing as Adjustment to Situational and Personal Factors," *J. soc. Psychol.*, 48 (1958), 3–10.

Hovland, C. I., A. A. Lumsdaine, and F. C. Sheffield. *Experiments on Mass Communication*. Princeton, N.J.: Princeton University Press, 1949.

Hunter, E. *Brainwashing in Red China*. New York: Vanguard, 1951.

Klineberg, O. *Social Psychology*. New York: Holt, Rinehart & Winston, 1954.

Lewin, K. "Forces behind Food Habits and Methods of Change," *Bull. Nat. Res. Coun.*, 108 (1943), 35–65.

Likert, R. "A Technique for the Measurement of Attitudes," *Arch. Psychol.*, 28 (1932), No. 194.

Moreno, J. L. *Who Shall Survive?* New York: Beacon House, 1953.

Sherif, M. *The Psychology of Social Norms*. New York: Harper, 1936.

11   The Psychologist and the World Community

First, one must get the facts of a situation or problem. Second, one must form a judgment as to what those facts portend. Third, one must act—before it is too late.

Bernard Baruch

This final chapter departs from the chapter classifications normally found in introductory texts and is not derived from the empirical list of common references found in introductory texts. It is included here to show that psychology reaches into, and is concerned with, the social and political issues of our time. Some psychologists, in addition to their interest in the science of psychology, have an interest in achieving a better understanding of human relationships as they relate to international disputes. The science of psychology may be applied with equal success to such areas as education, industry, and mental health. Of particular interest is the success attained in the area of sociopolitical activities.

The Behavioral Scientist in the Civil Rights Movement, Martin Luther King, Jr. It seems appropriate to begin this chapter with the words of an inspired orator and a dedicated American. Martin Luther King's untimely death was keenly felt by people who had never met him personally but had only heard or read his words or had entertained the ideas he espoused. In this first selection he speaks to the psychologist and indicates concerns to which the psychologist might address himself within his own community.

A Psychologist in the Peace Corps, Nicholas Hobbs. Hobbs extends the concern of the psychologist outside the confines of our nation to the underdeveloped countries of the world. Although this article is now dated, it is included because it was written shortly after the first assessments of the Peace Corps movement were returned for evaluation. In this selection Hobbs is concerned with the psychologist's role in selecting and assessing Peace Corps volunteers. Hobbs has been associated with the program since its beginning. He describes some of the methods used to select candidates and to evaluate on-the-job effectiveness. He also offers recommendations for future programs. Psychologists have been doing this type of job for federal governmental agencies since World War I.

The Psychologist in International Affairs, Charles E. Osgood. In this article Osgood indicates that the psychologist who works on public issues may choose to wear one of three hats. He may wear the hat of professional, specialist, or citizen. Osgood discusses the kinds of research that psychologists conduct and carry out in the field of international understanding and peace. He is well qualified to do so, for he has personally worn all three hats while carrying out the tasks he describes.

Psychology in the Year 2000, Gardner Murphy. The final selection is for the imaginative student of psychology. Unlike the preceding selections, it fits within the theme of social action only in an indirect way. It lays a framework for the research-minded psychologist who may eventually come to see his findings as grist for the solution of world problems. To continue the apology, where else would one include a treatise that in some respects can surely be considered science fiction? For the student who would like seriously to tackle the field of psychology, this reading may be enjoyable detective work as the prediction date offers plenty of time for whatever extrapolations the reader may prefer to substitute. However, Murphy has always shown a keen sense for history in psychology, and it is evident that if "fools rush in where angels fear to tread," we will be listening to one of the brighter fools among us.

The Behavioral Scientist in the Civil Rights Movement

Martin Luther King, Jr.

As figurehead for the civil rights movement and past president of the Southern Christian Leadership Conference, Atlanta, Georgia, Martin Luther King needs no introduction to most of you. Shortly before his untimely death, King was invited to address a group of psychologists concerned with social action research in the area of civil rights. His remarks to this group of psychologists on their role as behavioral scientists follow.

1. King was especially interested in having the psychologist study the parameters of Negro leadership, the means for political action, and psychological and ideological changes in Negroes. As you read his words, can you outline a study you would like to see done in one of these areas?

2. What would you want to do with the findings of your research?

It is always a very rich and rewarding experience when I can take a brief break from the day-to-day demands of our struggle for freedom and human dignity and discuss the issues involved in that struggle with concerned friends of good will all over this nation. It is particularly a great privilege to discuss these issues with members of the academic community, who are constantly writing about and dealing with the problems that we face and who have the tremendous responsibility of moulding the minds of young men and women all over our country.

In the preface to their book, *Applied Sociology,* S. M. Miller and Alvin Gouldner (1965) state: "It is the historic mission of the social

Martin Luther King, Jr., "The Role of the Behavioral Scientist in the Civil Rights Movement," *American Psychologist,* 23 (March, 1968), 3, 180–186.

sciences to enable mankind to take possession of society." It follows that for Negroes who substantially are excluded from society this science is needed even more desperately than for any other group in the population.

For social scientists, the opportunity to serve in a life-giving purpose is a humanist challenge of rare distinction. Negroes too are eager for a rendezvous with truth and discovery. We are aware that social scientists, unlike some of their colleagues in the physical sciences, have been spared the grim feelings of guilt that attended the invention of nuclear weapons of destruction. Social scientists, in the main, are fortunate to be able to extirpate evil, not to invent it.

If the Negro needs social science for direction and for self-understanding, the white society is in even more urgent need. White America needs to understand that it is poisoned to its soul by racism and the understanding needs to be carefully documented and is consequently more difficult to reject. The present crisis arises because, although it is historically imperative that our society take the next step to equality, we find ourselves psychologically and socially imprisoned. All too many white Americans are horrified not with conditions of Negro life but with the product of these conditions—the Negro himself.

White America is seeking to keep the walls of segregation substantially intact while the evolution of society and the Negro's desperation is causing them to crumble. The white majority, unprepared and unwilling to accept radical structural change, is resisting and producing chaos while complaining that if there were no chaos orderly change would come.

Negroes want the social scientist to address the white community and "tell it like it is." White America has an appalling lack of knowledge concerning the reality of Negro life. One reason some advances were made in the South during the past decade was the discovery by northern whites of the brutal facts of southern segregated life. It was the Negro who educated the nation by dramatizing the evils through nonviolent protest. The social scientist played little or no role in disclosing truth. The Negro action movement with raw courage did it virtually alone. When the majority of the country could not live with the extremes of brutality they witnessed, political remedies were enacted and customs were altered.

These partial advances were, however, limited principally to the South and progress did not automatically spread throughout the nation. There was also little depth to the changes. White America stopped murder, but that is not the same thing as ordaining brotherhood; nor is the ending of lynch rule the same thing as inaugurating justice.

After some years of Negro-white unity and partial successes, white America shifted gears and went into reverse. Negroes, alive with hope and enthusiasm, ran into sharply stiffened white resistance at all levels and bitter tensions broke out in sporadic episodes of violence. New lines of hostility were drawn and the era of good feeling disappeared.

The decade of 1955 to 1965, with its constructive elements, misled us. Everyone, activists and social scientists, underestimated the amount of violence and rage Negroes were suppressing and the amount of bigotry the white majority was disguising.

Science should have been employed more fully to warn us that the Negro, after 350 years of handicaps, mired in an intricate network of contemporary barriers, could not be ushered into equality by tentative and superficial changes.

Mass nonviolent protests, a social invention of Negroes, were effective in Montgomery, Birmingham, and Selma in forcing national legislation which served to change Negro life sufficiently to curb explosions. But when changes were confined to the South alone, the North, in the absence of change, began to seethe.

The freedom movement did not adapt its tactics to the different and unique northern urban conditions. It failed to see that nonviolent marches in the South were forms of rebellion. When Negroes took over the streets and shops, southern society shook to its roots. Negroes could contain their rage when they found the means to force relatively radical changes in their environment.

In the North, on the other hand, street demonstrations were not even a mild expression of militancy. The turmoil of cities absorbs demonstrations as merely transitory drama which is ordinary in city life. Without a more effective tactic for upsetting the status quo, the power structure could maintain its intransigence and hostility. Into the vacuum of inaction, violence and riots flowed and a new period opened.

Urban riots must now be recognized as durable social phenomena. They may be deplored, but they are there and should be understood. Urban riots are a special form of violence. They are not insurrections. The rioters are not seeking to seize territory or to attain control of institutions. They are mainly intended to shock the white community. They are a distorted form of social protest. The looting which is their principal feature serves many functions. It enables the most enraged and deprived Negro to take hold of consumer goods with the ease the white man does by using his purse. Often the Negro does not even want what he takes; he wants the experience of taking. But most of all, alienated from society and knowing that this society cherishes property above people, he is shocking it by abusing property rights. There are thus elements of emotional catharsis in the violent act. This may explain why most cities in which riots have occurred have not had a repetition, even though the causative conditions remain. It is also noteworthy that the amount of physical harm done to white people other than police is infinitesimal and in Detroit whites and Negroes looted in unity.

A profound judgment of today's riots was expressed by Victor Hugo a century ago. He said, "If a soul is left in darkness, sins will be committed. The guilty one is not he who commits the sin, but he who causes the darkness."

The policy makers of the white society have caused the darkness; they created discrimination; they structured slums; and they perpetuate unemployment, ignorance, and poverty. It is incontestable and deplorable that Negroes have committed crimes; but they are derivative crimes. They are born of the greater crimes of the white society. When we ask Negroes to abide by the law, let us also demand that the white man abide by law in the ghettos. Day-in and day-out he violates welfare laws to deprive the poor of their meager allotments; he flagrantly violates building codes and regulations; his police make a mockery of law; and he violates laws on equal employment and education and the provisions for civic services. The slums are the handiwork of a vicious system of the white society; Negroes live in them but do not make them any more than a prisoner makes a prison. Let us say boldly that if the total violations of law by the white man in the slums over the years were calculated and compared with the law breaking of a few days of riots, the hardened criminal would be the white man. These are often difficult things to say but I have come to see more and more that it is necessary to utter the truth in order to deal with the great problems that we face in our society.

There is another cause of riots that is too important to mention casually—the war in Vietnam. Here again, we are dealing with a controversial issue. But I am convinced that the war in Vietnam has played havoc with our domestic destinies. The bombs that fall in Vietnam explode at home. It does not take much to see what great damage this war has done to the image of our nation. It has left our country politically and morally isolated in the world, where our only friends happen to be puppet nations like Taiwan, Thailand, and South Korea. The major allies in the world that have been with us in war and peace are not with us in this war. As a result we find ourselves socially and politically isolated.

The war in Vietnam has torn up the Geneva Accord. It has seriously impaired the United Nations. It has exacerbated the hatreds between continents, and worse still, between races. It has frustrated our development at home by telling our underprivileged citizens that we place insatiable military demands above their most critical needs. It has greatly contributed to the forces of reaction in America, and strengthened the military-industrial complex, against which even President Eisenhower solemnly warned us. It has practically destroyed Vietnam, and left thousands of American and Vietnamese youth maimed and mutilated. And it has exposed the whole world to the risk of nuclear warfare.

As I looked at what this war was doing to our nation, and to the domestic situation and to the Civil Rights movement, I found it necessary to speak vigorously out against it. My speaking out against the war has not gone without criticisms. There are those who tell me that I should stick with Civil Rights, and stay in my place. I can only respond that I have fought too hard and long to end segregated public accommodations to segregate my own moral concerns. It is my deep conviction that justice is indivisible, that injustice anywhere is a threat to justice everywhere. For those who tell me I am hurting the Civil Rights movement, and ask, "Don't you think that in order to be respected, and in order to regain support, you must stop talking against the war?", I can only say that I am not a consensus leader. I do not seek to determine what is right and wrong by taking a Gallup Poll to determine majority opinion. And it is again my deep conviction that ultimately a genuine leader is not a searcher for consensus, but a molder of consensus. On some positions cowardice asks the question, "Is it safe?"! Expediency asks the question, "Is it politic?" Vanity asks the question, "Is it popular?" But conscience must ask the question, "Is it right?" And there comes a time when one must take a stand that is neither safe, nor politic, nor popular. But one must take it because it is right. And that is where I find myself today.

Moreover, I am convinced, even if war continues, that a genuine massive act of concern will do more to quell riots than the most massive deployment of troops.

The unemployment of Negro youth ranges up to 40% in some slums. The riots are almost entirely youth events—the age range of participants is from 13 to 25. What hypocrisy it is to talk of saving the new generation—to make it the generation of hope—while consigning it to unemployment and provoking it to violent alternatives.

When our nation was bankrupt in the '30s we created an agency to provide jobs to all at their existing level of skill. In our overwhelming affluence today what excuse is there for not setting up a national agency for full employment immediately?

The other program which would give reality to hope and opportunity would be the demolition of the slums to be replaced by decent housing built by residents of the ghettos.

These programs are not only eminently sound and vitally needed, but they have the support of an overwhelming majority of the nation—white and Negro. The Harris Poll on August 1, 1967, disclosed that an astounding 69% of the country support a works program to provide employment to all and an equally astonishing 65% approve a program to tear down the slums.

There is a program and there is heavy majority support for it. Yet, the administration and Congress tinker with trivial proposals to limit costs in an extravagant gamble with disaster.

The President has lamented that he cannot persuade Congress. He can, if the will is there, go to the people, mobilize the people's support, and thereby substantially increase his power to persuade Congress. Our most urgent task is to find the tactics that will move the Government no matter how determined it is to resist.

I believe we will have to find the militant middle between riots on the one hand and weak and timid supplication for justice on the other hand. That middle ground, I believe, is civil disobedience. It can be aggressive but nonviolent; it can dislocate but not destroy. The specific planning will take some study and analysis to avoid mistakes of the past when it was employed on too small a scale and sustained too briefly.

Civil disobedience can restore Negro-white unity. There have been some very important sane white voices even during the most desperate moments of the riots. One reason is that the urban crisis intersects the Negro crisis in the city. Many white decision makers may care little about saving Negroes, but they must care about saving their cities. The vast majority of production is created in cities; most white

Americans live in them. The suburbs to which they flee cannot exist detached from cities. Hence powerful white elements have goals that merge with ours.

Now there are many roles for social scientists in meeting these problems. Kenneth Clark has said that Negroes are moved by a suicide instinct in riots and Negroes know there is a tragic truth in this observation. Social scientists should also disclose the suicide instinct that governs the administration and Congress in their total failure to respond constructively.

What other areas are there for social scientists to assist the Civil Rights movement? There are many, but I would like to suggest three because they have an urgent quality.

Social science may be able to search out some answers to the problem of Negro leadership. E. Franklin Frazier (1957), in his profound work, *Black Bourgeoisie,* laid painfully bare the tendency of the upwardly mobile Negro to separate from his community, divorce himself from responsibility to it, while failing to gain acceptance into the white community. There has been significant improvement from the days Frazier researched, but anyone knowledgeable about Negro life knows its middle class is not yet bearing its weight. Every riot has carried strong overtone of hostility of lower class Negroes toward the affluent Negro and vice versa. No contemporary study of scientific depth has totally studied this problem. Social science should be able to suggest mechanisms to create a wholesome black unity and a sense of peoplehood while the process of integration proceeds.

As one example of this gap in research, there are no studies, to my knowledge, to explain adequately the absence of Negro trade union leadership. Eighty-five percent of Negroes are working people. Some 2,000,000 are in trade unions, but in 50 years we have produced only one national leader—A. Philip Randolph.

Discrimination explains a great deal, but not everything. The picture is so dark even a few rays of light may signal a useful direction.

The second area for scientific examination is political action. In the past 2 decades, Negroes have expended more effort in quest of the franchise than they have in all other campaigns combined. Demonstrations, sit-ins, and marches, though more spectacular, are dwarfed by the enormous number of man-hours expended to register millions, particularly in the South. Negro organizations from extreme militant to conservative persuasion, Negro leaders who would not even talk to each other, all have been agreed on the key importance of voting. Stokely Carmichael said black power means the vote and Roy Wilkins, while saying black power means black death, also energetically sought the power of the ballot.

A recent major work by social scientists Matthews and Prothro (1966) concludes that "The concrete benefits to be derived from the franchise—under conditions that prevail in the South—have often been exaggerated," . . . that voting is not the key that will unlock the door to racial equality because "the concrete measurable payoffs from Negro voting in the South will not be revolutionary."

James A. Wilson (1965) supports this view, arguing, "Because of the structure of American politics as well as the nature of the Negro community, Negro politics will accomplish only limited objectives."

If their conclusion can be supported, then the major effort Negroes have invested in the past 20 years has been in the wrong direction and the major pillar of their hope is a pillar of sand. My own instinct is that these views are essentially erroneous, but they must be seriously examined.

The need for a penetrating massive scientific study of this subject cannot be overstated. Lipsit (1959) in 1957 asserted that a limitation in focus in political sociology has resulted in a failure of much contemporary research to consider a number of significant theoretical questions. The time is short for social science to illuminate this critically important area. If the main thrust of Negro effort has been, and remains, substantially irrelevant, we may be facing an agonizing crisis of tactical theory.

The third area for study concerns psychological and ideological changes in Negroes. It is fashionable now to be pessimistic. Undeniably, the freedom movement has encountered setbacks. Yet I still believe there are significant aspects of progress.

Negroes today are experiencing an inner transformation that is liberating them from ideological dependence on the white majority. What has penetrated substantially all strata of Negro life is the revolutionary idea that the philosophy and morals of the dominant white society are not holy or sacred but in all too many respects are degenerate and profane.

Negroes have been oppressed for centuries not merely by bonds of economic and political servitude. The worst aspect of their oppression was their inability to question and defy the fundamental percepts of the larger society. Negroes have been loath in the past to hurl any fundamental challenges because they were coerced and conditioned into thinking within the context of the dominant white ideology. This is changing and new radical trends are appearing in Negro thought. I use radical in its broad sense to refer to reading into roots.

Ten years of struggle have sensitized and opened the Negro's eyes to reaching. For the first time in their history, Negroes have become aware of the deeper causes for the crudity and cruelty that governed white society's responses to their needs. They discovered that their plight was not a consequence of superficial prejudice but was systemic.

The slashing blows of backlash and frontlash have hurt the Negro, but they have also awakened him and revealed the nature of the oppressor. To lose illusions is to gain truth. Negroes have grown wiser and more mature and they are hearing more clearly those who are raising fundamental questions about our society whether the critics be Negro or white. When this process of awareness and independence crystallizes, every rebuke, every evasion, become hammer blows on the wedge that splits the Negro from the larger society.

Social science is needed to explain where this development is going to take us. Are we moving away, not from integration, but from the society which made it a problem in the first place? How deep and at what rate of speed is this process occurring? These are some vital questions to be answered if we are to have a clear sense of our direction.

We know we have not found the answers to all forms of social change. We know, however, that we did find some answers. We have achieved and we are confident. We also know we are confronted now with far greater complexities and we have not yet discovered all the theory we need.

And may I say together, we must solve the problems right here in America. As I have said time and time again, Negroes still have faith in America. Black people still have faith in a dream that we will all live together as brothers in this country of plenty one day.

But I was distressed when I read in the *New York Times* of August 31, 1967, that a sociologist from Michigan State University, the outgoing President of the American Sociological Society, stated in San Francisco that Negroes should be given a chance to find an all Negro community in South America: "that the valleys of the Andes mountains would be an ideal place for American Negroes to build a second Israel." He further declared that "The United States Government should negotiate for a remote but fertile land in Equador, Peru, or Bolivia for this relocation." I feel that it is rather absurd and appalling that a leading social scientist today would suggest to black people, that after all these years of suffering and exploitation as well as investment in the American dream, that we should turn around and run at this point in history. I say that we will not run! Loomis even compared the relocation task of the Negro to the relocation task of the Jews in Israel. The Jews were made exiles. They did not choose to abandon Europe, they were driven out. Furthermore, Israel has a deep tradition, and Biblical roots for Jews. The Wailing Wall is a good example of these roots. They also had significant financial aid from the United States for the relocation and rebuilding effort. What tradition do the Andes, especially the valley of the Andes mountains have for Negroes?

And I assert at this time that once again we must reaffirm our belief in building a democratic society, in which blacks and whites can live together as brothers, where we will all come to see that integration is not a problem, but an opportunity to participate in the beauty of diversity.

The problem is deep. It is gigantic in extent, and chaotic in detail. And I do not believe that it will be solved until there is a kind of cosmic discontent enlarging in the bosoms of people of good will all over this nation.

There are certain technical words in every academic discipline which soon become stereotypes and even clichés. Every academic discipline has its technical nomenclature. You who are in the field of psychology have given us a great word. It is the word maladjusted. This word is probably used more than any other word in psychology. It is a good word; certainly it is good that in dealing with what the word implies you are declaring that destructive maladjustment should be destroyed. You are saying that all must seek the well-adjusted life in order to avoid neurotic and schizophrenic personalities.

But on the other hand, I am sure that we all recognize that there are some things in our society, some things in our world, to which we should never be adjusted. There are some things concerning which we must always be maladjusted if we are to be people of good will. We must never adjust ourselves to racial discrimination and racial segregation. We must never adjust ourselves to religious bigotry. We must never adjust ourselves to economic conditions that take necessities from the many to give luxuries to the few. We must never adjust ourselves to the madness of militarism, and the self-defeating effects of physical violence.

In a day when Sputniks, Explorers, and Geminies are dashing through outer space, when guided ballistic missiles are carving highways of death through the stratosphere, no nation can finally win a war. It is no longer a choice between violence and nonviolence, it is either nonviolence or nonexistence. As President Kennedy declared, "Mankind must put an end to war, or war will put an end to mankind." And so the alternative to disarmament, the alternative to a suspension in the development and use of nuclear weapons, the alternative to strengthening the United Nations and eventually disarming the whole world, may well be a civilization plunged into the abyss of annihilation. Our earthly habitat will be transformed into an inferno that even Dante could not envision.

Thus, it may well be that our world is in dire need of a new organization, the International Association for the Advancement of Creative Maladjustment. Men and women should be as maladjusted as the prophet Amos, who in the midst of the injustices of his day, could cry out in words that echo across the centuries, "Let justice roll down like waters and righteousness like a mighty stream"; or as maladjusted as Abraham Lincoln, who in the midst of his vacillations finally came to see that this nation could not survive half slave and half free; or as maladjusted as Thomas Jefferson, who in the midst of an age amazingly adjusted to slavery, could scratch across the pages of history, words lifted to cosmic proportions, "We hold these truths to be self evident, that all men are created equal. That they are endowed by their creator with certain inalienable rights. And that among these are life, liberty, and the pursuit of happiness." And through such creative maladjustment, we may be able to emerge from the bleak and desolate midnight of man's inhumanity to man, into the bright and glittering daybreak of freedom and justice.

I have not lost hope. I must confess that these have been very difficult days for me personally. And these have been difficult days for every Civil Rights leader, for every lover of justice and peace. They have been days of frustration—days when we could not quite see where we were going, and when we often felt that our works were in vain, days when we were tempted to end up in the valley of despair. But in spite of this, I still have faith in the future, and my politics will continue to be a politic of hope. Our goal is freedom. And I somehow still believe that in spite of the so-called white backlash, we are going to get there, because however untrue it is to its destiny, the goal of America is freedom.

Abused and scorned though we may be, our destiny as a people is tied up with the destiny of America. Before the Pilgrim fathers landed at Plymouth, we were here. Before Jefferson scratched across the pages of history the great words that I just quoted, we were here. Before the beautiful words of the "Star Spangled Banner" were written, we were here. For more than 2 centuries, our forebears labored here without wages. They made Cotton King. They built the home of their masters in the midst of

the most humiliating and oppressive conditions.

And yet out of a bottomless vitality, they continued to grow and develop. If the inexpressable cruelties of slavery could not stop us, the opposition that we now face will surely fail. We shall win our freedom because both the sacred heritage of our nation, and the eternal will of the almighty God, are embodied in our echoing demands.

And so I can still sing, although many have stopped singing it, "We shall overcome." We shall overcome because the arch of the moral universe is long, but it bends toward justice. We shall overcome because Carlysle is right, "No lie can live forever." We shall overcome because William Cullen Bryant is right, "Truth crushed to earth will rise again." We shall overcome because James Russell Lowell is right, "Truth forever on the scaffold, wrong forever on the throne, yet that scaffold sways a future." And so with this faith, we will be able to hew out of the mountain of despair a stone of hope. We will be able to transform the jangling discords of our nation into a beautiful symphony of brotherhood. This will be a great day. This will not be the day of the white man, it will not be the day of the black man, it will be the day of man as man.

References

Frazier, E. F. *Black bourgeoisie*. Glencoe, Ill.: Free Press, 1956.

Lipsit, M. Political sociology. In, *Sociology today*. New York: Basic Books, 1959.

Matthews & Prothro. *Negroes and the new southern politics*. New York: Harcourt & Brace, 1966.

Miller, S. M., & Gouldner, A. *Applied sociology*. New York: Free Press, 1965.

Wilson, J. A. The Negro in politics. *Daedalus*, 1965, Fall.

A Psychologist in the Peace Corps

Nicholas Hobbs

Nicholas Hobbs, Provost of Vanderbilt University and Director of the John F. Kennedy Center, Peabody College, Nashville, Tennessee, received his Ph.D. from Ohio State University in 1946. Nationally recognized for his work in academic and applied psychology, Hobbs is listed in American Men of Science *and* Who's Who in America. *In 1961 he became Director of Selection for the Peace Corps. A vigorous worker in the American Psychological Association, Hobbs chaired its Committee on Ethical Standards and became the Association's 74th president in 1965.*

1. What factors might account for the low reliability coefficients between psychiatric interview ratings of Peace Corps Volunteers?

2. By what methods might such desirable qualities as "idealistic" and "tough-minded disenchantment" be measured? How would you approach the task?

If this paper is short on research and long on impressionistic reporting, I am sure you will be tolerant of this deficiency if I remind you that the Peace Corps has been in operation for a very short period of time. This observation in itself is of some consequence since the Peace Corps has become, in this short period of time, an established part of the national and international scene and is much taken for granted by the American people. It has assumed a place with military service and matrimony, a job and graduate school, as one of the alternatives to be weighed by the college graduate, and it also presents an ever-available invitation to the older citizen of youthful outlook, who feels he has something to offer to the developing countries of the world. The Peace Corps has all the appearances of a viable social institution.

Abridged from ·N. Hobbs, "A Psychologist in the Peace Corps," *American Psychologist,* 18 (January 1963), 47–52. Copyright 1963 by the American Psychological Association and reproduced by permission.

The public perception of the Peace Corps has not always been so positive. From some obscure corner of my psyche bubbles an inordinate bit of joy from rereading, as I recently have done in preparation for this paper, some of the early comments on President Kennedy's proposal. Here is the somewhat citrus observation of an eminent legislator: "People don't just come off trees like lemons, all set to do a job overseas." *Time* magazine, which in fairness must now be regarded as a strong supporter of the Peace Corps, initially had its enthusiasm well under control. It reported with characteristic editorial anonymity: "Skeptics at once envisioned pony-tailed coeds and crew-cut Jack Armstrongs playing Albert Schweitzer—an appalling army of innocents abroad." Later, when its reporters were impressed by the first group of Volunteers in training, the following ecstatic picture caption was allowed: "They May Do More Good Than Harm." If you think that Mr. Kennedy's popularity with the business community deteriorated, you may take some vague comfort from this early editorial comment in the *Wall Street Journal:* "The thing is so disproportionate as to be nonsensical. What person, except the very young themselves, can really believe that an Africa aflame with violence will have its fires quenched because some Harvard boy or Vassar girl lives in a mud hut and speaks Swahili?" Even the *Saturday Review* joined the skeptical chorus: "Sending out masses of unguided young men and women, doers, not believers, inadequately screened . . ., will be another futility."

That the press has reversed field in its evaluation of the Peace Corps will be well known to you. You will be interested, I am sure, in some other perhaps more substantial indices of its success. Operationally, one of the most significant of these is the demand for Volunteers. It is especially significant that each of the 17 countries that had one of the first projects, initiated in the summer of 1961, has asked for a renewal.

Another index of effectiveness is the staying power of the individual Volunteer, which certainly bests our most optimistic predictions. In planning the logistics of the Peace Corps it was important to get an estimate of the number of people who would fail in training and who would fail overseas and have to be brought home. We sought advice from the State Department, from the military, from religious groups with overseas missions, and from businesses with foreign operations. Early planning documents stated an expectancy of 50% attrition in training, and we were advised to expect an additional 15 to 50% attrition overseas. To give substance to these pessimistic figures, we had the example of one unfortunate overseas teaching project, drawing from the same age group, in which 80% of the participants had to be brought home. Experience has been strikingly at odds with early predictions. The attrition rate in training has averaged around 17% including medical disqualifications. The attrition rate overseas stands now at the remarkable figure of less than 1½%. There are now 1,400 Volunteers overseas. Half of these have been on the job for 6 months or more and some have been overseas for over a year. Some have just arrived. A total of 18 Volunteers has been returned home, for the following reasons. There have been three deaths. Eight Volunteers have come home for personal reasons, such as marriage or a death in the family. Seven Volunteers have been brought home as unsuitable for overseas service. This last category, that of personal unsuitability, was expected to be the greatest source of casualties; it amounts at the present time to less than one-half one percent of the total. There is no doubt that the percentage of failures will rise somewhat until the number of Volunteers overseas is stabilized, but it also is clear that the Volunteers are making a remarkable adjustment and a remarkable record.

The members of this division with predilections to personality study may well want to ask: what manner of men—and of women—are these? What are their motivations? How efficiently have they been selected? What problems have they encountered and what satisfactions are they deriving from service overseas? Some data bearing on these questions are available, though answers will of course have to be tentative for the research program is just getting into gear. I am personally very pleased that there is a research program at all, and grateful to the many psychologists, a number from this Division, who have made it possible. I have a special feeling of amiability toward those patient evaluators of Volunteers, who acceded from the start to our demand that they entertain no ideas that they could not put on a five-point scale. Can it be quantified? Can it be reduced to number?—if not, burn it, throw it out, has been our Kantian motto—or at least our aspiration. If some observations of softer substance slip into this paper here and there, the clinicians in the group will recognize the wanderings of a kindred spirit.

Let us look first at some data descriptive of the total group of Volunteers. The group is relatively young, though clearly not pony-tailed and crew-cut college kids. The mean age for men is 25 and for women is 28. The latter average is higher largely because the extraordinary durability of the female of the species skews the curve upward; there are more older women in the Peace Corps than older men. Contrary to the public picture, there are a number of middle-aged and retired people serving as Volunteers, and the relative number of these is increasing. The ratio of men to women 6 months ago was a clear cut 2 to 1; however, women are catching up and the ratio now stands at about 1.7 to 1. The group always has been and remains exceptionally well educated, though the number of billets for people with a high school education and limited college training is increasing. Ninety-six percent of the Volunteers have had at least some college experience; 90% have completed a formal course of study; 60% have bachelor's degrees; 8% have master's degrees; and something less than 1% have doctorates of one kind or another.

With regard to region of origin, all sections of the country are about equally represented except for the Southern states which show their characteristic depression in the tendency to supply candidates for opportunities for personal development and service of whatever character: fellowships, Fulbright appointments, research grants, as well as the Peace Corps. The correlation between the number of Peace Corps Volunteers, from a state and the per capita expenditure for public education in that state is .54.

The people who volunteer for the Peace Corps have, in total, an acquaintance with a foreign culture that far exceeds the ordinary. A substantial number, fully one-fourth of the total, have resided or studied abroad for periods of more than 4 months, and nearly all have at least some minimal competence in a second language. It is clear that the Peace Corps attracts people who are already interested in the kinds of opportunities that the Peace Corps presents.

In the first weeks of planning the Peace Corps selection program, there was considerable pressure to establish a nationwide network of interviewers to screen candidates for admission. In fact, early publicity promised that applicants would be invited to regional centers to be interviewed. I opposed this procedure because of the overwhelming evidence in the literature that the personal interview, except in special limited situations, is useless as a selection device. Validity coefficients of zero are to be expected. Having decided not to select by interview, we proceeded to look for data to see whether the decision was a good one or not. The first study undertaken suggests that the decision had indeed been sound.

In this study, arrangements were made for psychiatrists at the University of California to interview twice all Volunteers in training for teaching assignments in Ghana. There were 58 Volunteers and seven psychiatrists; two psychiatrists interviewed each Volunteer and made independent evaluations, including a prediction of his effectiveness as a Peace Corps Volunteer. Four reliability coefficients, reflecting agreement between raters, ranged from .26 to .35. These reliabilities are clearly too low to

warrant using the psychiatric interview alone as a selection procedure. However, subsequent studies are somewhat more encouraging and seem to indicate that interviews may have some contribution to make to a composite evaluation that would include other variables, obtainable before and during the training period. There are some projects in which psychiatric evaluations do correlate suggestively with ratings by selection boards at the end of training as well as with preliminary ratings on overseas performance. Since psychiatrists responsible for the interviews often participated in selection board deliberations, there may be some contamination here, but this should not hold for correlations between interviews and overseas ratings. In spite of the possibility of teasing out of the interview some of the validity that nearly everyone seems to feel is there, there are certainly no grounds for reversing the early decision not to have applicants screened by panels of interviewers.

The letter of reference vies with the personal interview as the selection technique most widely used with least tangible justification. The popularity of both is inversely related to their validity; except in special circumstances, they are without value. In contrast to the usual findings, the results of early research on the Peace Corps Personal Reference Form are particularly heartening. As a predictor of ratings by final selection advisory boards at the end of training it stands up very well, better than any of the many tests that have been tried. The relationship is sustained overseas, against the criterion of ratings made by officers in charge of Peace Corps projects and, in one country, by skilled psychologist on the basis of 4-hour-long, on-the-job interviews with Volunteers. Of 48 correlations between references and final selection board ratings, 42 are positive, and one project accounts for half of the remaining 6 negative ratings. Two observations are important here. While some contamination is possible in that one member of the final selection board might have read the references some months before, the amount of contamination is certainly minimal. Furthermore, the variance ascribable to the reference form has already been sharply reduced by the selection process itself which relies heavily on the instrument being evaluated. The form has a summary overall rating on a five-point scale, with five being high or good. The ones and twos and some of the threes are eliminated before training. The true validity of the reference forms, a quantity that could be estimated only by assigning to training a randomly chosen group of applicants, is probably quite substantial.

I think it is possible to account for the effectiveness of the Peace Corps reference procedures. The form asks for appraisals of job competence, relationships with people, and emotional maturity, and then for an overall judgment of probable effectiveness as a Peace Corps Volunteer. The first three items, purposely calling for global judgments, are defined in a paragraph, as are each of the five steps on the accompanying rating scale. The task of the respondent is a reasonable and manageable one. The covering letter from Mr. Shriver emphasizes the importance to the nation of a successful Peace Corps and the importance of references in the selection of Volunteers. It gets across the idea that a careful appraisal is in the interest of the applicant as well as of the country, that it is no favor to an applicant to get him into a situation that is more than he can handle. Finally, there is an elegant idea that I wish I could claim but must credit to Henry Rieken: The person making an evaluation is assured that no applicant will be rejected on the basis of a single negative appraisal, that corroborative information will be sought in all such instances. To the best of my knowledge the Peace Corps has always meticulously honored this promise. Many people have indicated that this assurance of fairness freed them to write in candor, without fear that a personal bias would do injustice to a candidate. It seems likely that both the reliability and the validity of the reference procedure is upped substantially by the requirement that there be at least 6 usable references for a candidate before he will be considered for selection. Often as many as 12 or 15 references are considered before a decision is reached to invite a candidate to training.

Let me now somewhat gingerly touch on some other tentative findings that will be intriguing to you but that should be warily received until additional data are available. The elaborate and time consuming Peace Corps Placement Test, which you will recall is administered quarterly at testing centers throughout the country, does not yield substantial correlations with ratings by final-selection advisory boards or by Peace Corps representatives overseas. An exception is Carroll's Modern Language Aptitude test which holds up reasonably well not only for countries where a new language must be learned but for others as well, suggesting the importance of some general ability-to-learn factor. The Biographical Data Blank, which has performed well in other selection situations, does not hold up with the *a priori* keys used in this initial run. It is possible that empirically developed keys would yield better results. On the Peace Corps Volunteer Questionnaire, which provides additional biographical information, some kind of response set seems to be working. People who check a lot of items indicating many experiences and accomplishments tend to get lower ratings by final selection advisory boards.

There is some evidence that successful performance overseas is related to low F scale scores and high Barron Ego-Strength Scale scores. An analysis of MMPI profiles, of the Strong Vocational Interest Blank, and of a special Q sort, suggest that one large group of Peace Corps Volunteers "have quite stable personal adjustment, high social service motives, and a diversity of purposes [in joining the Peace Corps] . . . the most promising of which are altruistic, political and educational."

The judgments of the final selection advisory boards are positively related to the few ratings on overseas performance that are available at the present time, yet there are some interesting and unexplained patterns in the performance of the boards themselves. They tend to give highest ratings to Volunteers of modal ages, lowest ratings to younger Volunteers, and most variable ratings to older Volunteers. We do not know yet whether these differences represent biases or whether they reflect true differences in probabilities of success overseas. In addition, selection boards judging candidates at the end of training find women somewhat more promising than men as Peace Corps Volunteers. It is hard to know just what to make of this. It is possible that the Peace Corps attracts better women than men, though I very much doubt that this is true. It may be just another bit of evidence of the natural superiority of women. Or it may be that selection boards are composed mostly of men, and that men like women.

The foregoing statistics are singularly unsatisfactory in describing the Peace Corps Volunteers. Perhaps it is trite to say that they are remarkable people because all people are remarkable but Peace Corps Volunteers are remarkable along dimensions that represent many of the best aspirations of our society. In time, as a result of our emerging research program, we should be able to identify these dimensions with some accuracy. For the present, permit me simply to say what I think these dimensions may turn out to be.

One important dimension is idealism. Peace Corps Volunteers are idealistic; they want to serve; they want to make a contribution to their fellow man. My guess is that this dimension will have a heavy weight in a final equation.

Crosscutting the dimension of idealism, and transmuting it to effective use, is a dimension that might be labeled "tough-minded disenchantment." It is the dimension that tempers the idealistic statement, "I desire to serve," with the realistic statement, "I know I may not be able to do much." Nothing annoys a Volunteer more than to be told how great he is. Heroics are for an earlier generation.

I surmise that Volunteers have a high need for affiliation. They get substantial satisfactions from being with other Volunteers and from association with new friends in other lands. They wear no hair shirts, nor are they out for an irresponsible lark. They say: "It will be good to make friends in other lands," "It will be fun to see the world"; they also say, "I know I will have dysentery, it will be hot and dusty, I will be lonesome."

The Volunteers are learners. They have been reaching-out type people and the Peace Corps experience is but a natural extension of an already developed pattern of intellectual adventuresomeness. In fact, I have been surprised at how many Volunteers among the few that I have talked with overseas are finding the Peace Corps to be an exciting intellectual adventure, for some more stimulating even than their college experience.

As an overall descriptive statement, I would hazard the observation that the Peace Corps Volunteer is imbued with the protestant ethic of Max Weber; he has a desire to serve his fellow man tempered by a love of fun and adventure and by a realistic appraisal of what he will be up against, and an appropriate modesty.

The Psychologist in International Affairs

Charles E. Osgood

Charles Osgood is Professor of Psychology and Director of the Institute of Communications Research at the University of Illinois. A graduate of Yale University, and a past president of the American Psychological Association, he is author of the "Semantic Differential," a measure of the meaning of concepts. Osgood modestly and succinctly describes his background as follows: "I started out to be a journalist, became a psychologist, barely avoided being a politician, and am still striving to be an adequate psycholinguist."

1. *Do you feel psychologists should remain within the scientist's role of studying international problems or should they offer recommendations toward the solution of these problems?*

2. *Be sure to read footnote 2. Jot down your own "fantasy" and, if you have the time and interest, send it on to this book's editor.*

It may be professional myopia, but I think psychologists as a group have been more actively involved in "peace research," and over a longer period, than any other behavioral or social science. For a long time we have had SPSSI (Society for the Psychological Study of Social Issues) whose members have done research and written about problems in areas of public concern like race relations, civil rights, and peace and war. More recently in 1960, beginning with a working group under Roger Russell, a continuing committee for the profession as a whole on Psychology in National and International Affairs was established. Members of this committee have been Ray Bauer, Urie Bronfenbrenner, Morton Deutsch, Fred Fiedler, Harold Guetzkow, John Finan, Edwin Hollander, Herbert Kelman, Joseph Weitz, and myself, but this represents only a very small sample of the professional psychologists actually involved. Most recently, through a grant from the Marshall Fund, we have been able to support a full-time person, Lawrence Solomon, in Washington to work on the Committee's tasks.

Why should it be so—if indeed it is—that psychologists have gotten themselves involved in this area earlier and more deeply? Perhaps it is because psychology had about the right "distance" from public issues—close enough to have developed a scientific conception of man and his behavior, but not so close as to have become intimidated. Perhaps the fact that psychology is more like the physical and biological sciences in methods and in quantification created a feeling of security and efficacy; in the past few decades psychologists have been very self-conscious about scientific methods and have generally convinced themselves that "even though they may not know the answers, they know how to find out!" Or perhaps it is the outward reaching tendencies of psychological theories about behavior, which may have their

Abridged from Charles E. Osgood, "The Psychologist in International Affairs," *American Psychologist,* 19 (1964), 114–118. Copyright 1964 by the American Psychological Association and reproduced by permission.

moorings in the Skinner box, the tachistoscope, or the therapeutic interview, but are generalized as widely as possible.

The natural and legitimate tendency of a theory to generalize carries with it the real danger of over-generalizing. Put less kindly, psychologists face the danger of "overselling" wares which they may not have. This has been a constant concern of the Committee on Psychology in National and International Affairs. There is nothing that would more effectively undercut the potential contribution of psychology to public affairs than repeated failures to follow through on explicit commitments to solve practical government problems. This is probably the reason why professional psychologists have preferred to advertise themselves as equipped to do research, rather than to promise solutions or even advise from a body of established principle. And the danger *here,* of course, is that of leaning so far over backwards to avoid overselling that we rule ourselves out for real contributions we might well be able to make. The Committee has tried to steer a course between these two reefs.

The psychologist working on public issues may wear any one of three hats, but he should be aware of which hat is appropriate for which occasion. On some occasions he may legitimately don his "professional" hat—when he speaks as a psychological scientist on the basis of hard facts and generally accepted principles. On other occasions he should wear his "specialist" hat—when he speaks as an individual psychologist who, by virtue of his special training and experience, may claim a higher probability of correct insights and opinions in certain areas than others not so trained. On yet other occasions, he must explicitly display his "citizen" hat—when he speaks his opinions, expresses his attitudes, and takes his stands on matters where neither his science nor his expertise gives him any obvious advantage over other equally intelligent citizens.

An example of this came up in the meetings of the APA Council several years ago: There was strong pressure from some members for the Association to take a public stand against the United States resuming nuclear testing, following the resumption of testing by the Soviets. The Committee's policy recommendation, which was finally accepted, was as follows:

The Association should speak for the psychological profession on social and political issues only when psychologists have a professional expertise which is clearly relevant to the issues involved and when there is a substantial convergence of judgment among psychologists on the nature and implications of relevant scientific data. There are, of course, many urgent issues in which the need for psychological knowledge is apparent. When such knowledge is not available, the Association should encourage research to foster its development. At all times, the Association maintains its traditional interest in having its members participate as individual psychologists and citizens in the presentation and discussion of psychological facts and ideas as they bear on current national and international problems.

The three hats I mentioned above are clearly implied by this statement. It is not always easy to maintain these distinctions, and some will argue that, with an issue so urgent as avoiding a nuclear war, trying to maintain them is a delicacy verging on the ludicrous. The answer, I think, is that to fail to make these distinctions is to destroy whatever potential contribution we can make as psychologists.

There are two other caveats I must make before saying something about action and research on international affairs. One concerns what we mean by "peace." Perhaps it's because of the grinding process I've been through in the search for feasibility, but I often get the feeling that many of my colleagues have never thought very hard about what they mean by this term. It is the opposite of "war," which we're all against, and there surely is a good feel to it. But do we mean peace in the no-war sense? In the no-nuclear-war sense? In the complete disarmament sense? In the permanent tranquility sense? In the sense of establishing and observing the rule of international law? In the sense of peaceful (competitive) coexistence? In the Pax Americana sense? How one answers this question will determine what he would include under "peace research," how much effort he will put into short-term versus long-term action programs and research programs, and so forth. The controversy that is now going on between the "arms management and control" proponents and the "general and complete disarmament" proponents in part reflects differences in what kind of peaceful world people have in mind.

The other caveat concerns our own stereotypes and intolerances. Being merely human, psychologists are prone to the same cognitive dynamics they study in others. In our own striving for a simplified, comprehensible world, it is easy for us to set up Bogey Men of our own—in the Pentagon, in Congress, in the mass media, in the defense industries, and so forth. Here are the war mongers, here are the evil men who, for selfish and aggressive motives, are deliberately risking all our lives. There probably are a few such people, but I have yet to meet them. I have yet to find a person, in government, in industry, in the media, in the military or elsewhere, who did not profess to desire peace (on his own terms) as ardently as I did (on mine). We might differ absolutely on our assumptions and upon our prescriptions, but not on our basic motives—to preserve both our lives and our way of life. But most importantly (as we should realize as psychologists), to impugn these men's motives, to accuse them of being immoral and callous to the best interest of humanity as a whole, is to promptly establish a deep antagonism through which it is impossible to exert any positive influence. I do not want what I have just said to be misinterpreted: I am convinced that there are many people in the institutions we are discussing who are misguided, who have dangerous misconceptions about the nature of the world today and the nature of the people who inhabit it, and who are following policies that have a high probability of eventuating in the destruction of everything we hold valuable—but as a social scientist I cannot consider them evil and I must consider them modifiable.

Action

By "action" aimed at moving toward a more peaceful world I refer to the whole spectrum of endeavors to change people's minds, and thereby their behaviors, through utilizing what we know (or think we know) as psychologists and as intelligent citizens. It involves all the skills we have as individuals in interpersonal relations, in persuasive communication, and in problem solving. It means trying to inject psychological insights and skills wherever they are relevant—and often the first, and most difficult, step is to convince others of their relevance.

One type of action is, frankly, *lobbying* in the best sense. And by "best sense" I mean trying to influence decision making in government for altruistic rather than selfish ends. I believe there is a difference between lobbying for support of inter-American exchange among students and scholars and lobbying for higher status and pay for psychologists in government. Lobbying for increased support of research in the behavioral and social sciences would be ambiguous, I suppose. The Committee on Psychology in National and International Affairs, particularly through the good offices of its full-time executive secretary, has been trying to develop and maintain effective contacts with relevant government agencies and activities (e.g., the Agency for International Development, the Arms Control and Disarmament Agency, the Peace Corps, etc.) as well as with members of Congress. One side of this activity is of necessity educational—it is surprising how many nonpsychologists, both in government and in the public at large, see us *only* as clinicians interested in and competent with personality problems! Another side of this activity is predictive—trying to anticipate public issues just over the horizon and prepare for them. Yet another side of this is a mediating role—bringing into fruitful contact the public official with a problem and the psychologist with maximally relevant skill and experience.

Another type of action is trying to inject the psychologist's conception of the nature of man into the decision making process. Again, being merely human, we tend to project our own conception onto others, and are often shocked to discover how different other people's conceptions may be. Among the generally, if not completely, agreed-upon elements in the psychological conception of man are: the notion that man's behavior is deterministic in terms of both innate and acquired factors and, as a kind of correlary, that no individual is inherently evil; the notion that differences among individuals within nations, races, etc., are typically greater than differences between them; the notion that war is not inevitable, although many of its contributing elements may be (e.g., aggression, fear, perceptual distortion under stress, etc.); the notion that much of man's behavior, particularly as it relates to group solidarity and conflict, is learned and hence potentially modifiable; the notion that much of man's behavior is determined by irrational rather than rational factors; and so forth. One means to inject our conception of man into the decision making process is to bring psychologists into more continuous contact with people in government; the APA Committee has already made arrangements for several Congressional Fellowships for psychologists, and we hope to have our own program underway soon.

Yet another type of action is playing the role of Devil's Advocate—questioning assumptions which are generally taken for granted. Examples of such assumptions would be: that our opponent (whoever he may be) is motivated by aggression and hatred while we are motivated by insecurity and fear; that we must maintain military superiority in order to be secure; that our nuclear deterrent is nothing more than that (it is also a security base from which to take limited risks); that credibility of our deterrent requires that we present the face of implacable hostility to an opponent; that prior commitment from both sides via negotiation is a prerequisite for tension reducing action by either; that we can have unlimited national sovereignty and unlimited international security at the same time. It is precisely because such assumptions are often implicit and largely taken for granted that they must be questioned and raised to the level of public debate. They create a rigid and narrow framework for policy, within which only a small number of alternatives seem to be available.

The activities undertaken by the Committee on Psychology in National and International Affairs serve to illustrate the variety of actions open to us.

Research

Psychologists are as prone to fads as anyone else. There are fads in research. There was a period when learning theory was astride the white stallion, and now it seems to be mathematical models. Young people in the field quickly develop a sixth sense for what is "paying off" in job offers and promotions; a few regional and national meetings are sufficient to set a pattern, and such patterns are difficult to change over short time periods. Although a

great deal of research that has been going on steadily in social psychology, communications, cognitive processes, and many other areas is clearly relevant, "peace research," under that name at least, certainly is not prestigeful in our profession. However, the pulling power of a research area depends both upon the stature of the senior people who work in it and upon the availability of funds for doing it (which are not independent factors, incidentally!) and the situation seems to be becoming more favorable. Recent trips to university and other research centers all over the country by my colleague, Shel Feldman, indicated a rather surprising density of relevant research, and much of it quite explicitly (in the thinking of the investigators) directed toward problems in war and peace, arms control, disarmament, international tensions, and related areas.[1]

Action-oriented research. Some research is designed to produce dependable information that can be transmitted directly into action programs. This is particularly characteristic of research oriented toward public issues. One illustration is the monograph on "Psychological Factors in Peace and War"—being prepared by Shel Feldman, Joseph de Rivera, and myself with support from both the National Institute of Mental Health and Earl Osborn, President of the Institute for International Order. The general purposes are to make available to behavioral and social scientists in a readily digestible form the existing evidence relating to psychological propositions explicitly or implicitly made in the literature in this field, the hypotheses that need investigation, and the available personnel in terms of contributions and interests. Another example would be the production of what might be called "instant public opinion" on foreign issues and assumptions. Under Dee Norton's general direction, the Iowa City Consensus on International Affairs has been polling its membership on a variety of issues of the moment (e.g., Proposition No. 4: We urge the United States Government to take immediate steps to re-establish diplomatic,

---

[1] Papers describing these ongoing research projects can be obtained by writing to: Shel Feldman, Institute of Communications Research, University of Illinois, Urbana, Illinois.

cultural, and trade relations with Cuba) and transmitting the results to various people in government. The point is that decisions are often made on the basis of assumptions about "public opinion" that may well be invalid. If such informed opinion could be collected in synchronized fashion over a broad sample of the population, it could have impressive impact.[2]

Yet another illustration is a panel study done by Feldman and Fishbein at our Institute of the performance of a peace candidate in the last election; he lost, to be sure, but the action-oriented research was designed to find out why.

Understanding-oriented research. What we usually refer to as "pure" or "basic" research is directed toward increasing our understanding of human behavior without any immediate concern for social action. What impresses one when he starts searching the literature for material relevant to the present topic is the fact that—if one forgets the particular substantive material—almost everything we are investigating has some relevance. A William McGuire does ingenious experiments on susceptibility to, and immunization to, persuasion; the persuasive materials may be counterarguments to unquestioned assumptions about the value of brushing one's teeth, but they might just as well have been counterarguments to the unquestioned assumptions about national security listed earlier. The point is that there is much that we are doing already, just because we want to find out more about human beings—how they think, how they make decisions, and how

they behave—that could be made directly relevant to the crucial issues of our time by a minor shift in materials, in subjects, or emphasis.

Some will argue that it is impossible to be truly objective when the topics under investigation are policy relevant, are emotion laden, or involve the investigator himself. I think this is sheer nonsense. As soon as one has become wound up in his own theory, his mentor's theory, or even his own previous findings, he is equally liable to subjective bias. The whole purpose of our training in rigorous, objective, and quantitative methods is to protect ourselves from such bias, and objective methodology will protect us if adhered to.

Merely by way of illustration, here are some areas of understanding-oriented research that I think are particularly relevant: the simulation of complex human decision making processes, whether by computers (e.g., Herbert Simon's work) or by people (e.g., Harold Guetzkow's internation simulations); studies on the dynamics of human perceptions or cognitions as they affect choice behaviors of all types (e.g., extending and refining the theories of Heider, Festinger, and others); research on interperson, intergroup, and internation communication (e.g., the problem of multiple audiences receiving the same message, the problem of information restriction because of the structure and function of the mass media); cross-cultural and cross-linguistic studies of psycholinguistic and other cognitive phenomena, both as a means of quantifying what might be called "subjective culture" and as a means of specifying cultural similarities and differences more rigorously.

The principles and tools developed in the course of such understanding-oriented research could be transferred rather directly into "applied" research that is needed by society. Take for example internation simulation (which is not too different from the "war games" played by the military) if the validity of such simulations can be demonstrated and they can be shown to reduce uncertainty in policy decisions significantly, one can imagine a massive program of such research designed to simulate and thereby anticipate critical decision points in the constantly expanding "near future." Our present transportation and communication technologies make cross-cultural tests of hypotheses and international surveys entirely feasible—we no longer need be provincial in the behavioral

---

[2] I once had the fantasy that there was a huge map of the United States on a building near the White House. Above the map, a flashing sign announced the "issue of the day." With each county in each state represented by a small panel that would be turned to either black or white depending on the responses obtained there, the whole map would represent, by shades from white through grey to black, "instant public opinion" on the issue as well as regional variations. Senators and Congressmen and men in various agencies could not help but steal a peek at what was happening as they went to and from their offices; the mass media obviously would have to carry these displays as regularly as they now carry the weather maps; and when visiting our Capital, every Mr. and Mrs. Jones from Podunk or from Spokane would want to see the display and point to *their* community. Sheer fantasy, but it could easily be done.

and social sciences. Indeed, many of our hypotheses require testing against a cross-cultural and cross-linguistic matrix, in order to distinguish that which is culturally and linguistically unique from that which is common to the human species. Research on this scale would require a great deal of money, to be sure, but no more than is thrown away every time an experimental missile or space vehicle plops into the ocean as a failure.

Psychology in the Year 2000

Gardner Murphy

Gardner Murphy received his doctorate from Columbia University in 1923. In 1929 he surveyed the history of psychology in his book Historical Introduction to Modern Psychology. *He and his wife also published a comprehensive survey of experimental work in social psychology. He formulated a biosocial theory of personality that received much attention. Murphy is past president of the Society for the Psychological Study of Social Issues (1938), the Eastern Psychological Association (1942), and the American Psychological Association (1944). In 1949 Murphy was elected President of the Society for Psychical Research, London. He became Director of Research at the famed Menninger Foundation in 1952. He is presently a Visiting Professor of Psychology at the George Washington University. He has always tried to integrate psychology and parapsychology and is qualified, as no other psychologist today, to gaze into the fantasy land of the future.*

Our profound ambivalence about human futures, and our hopes and fears regarding the possibility of intelligent planning for the future, appears in a charming phrase of Sir George Thomson. Regarding the role of science in planning for new potentialities within the human germ cell, he says that our likelihood of genetic improvements is about like the probability of improving a status by spraying it with machine gun bullets. Instantly, however, he catches himself up in the remark that with the electron microscope, we are already very close

indeed to the localization of individual genes. We dare not be overbold for fear our critics will laugh, while actually the science fiction, and the casual predictions of scientists, have, for the last hundred years or so, been very much too modest—in fact, very much too myopic—as to what can actually be achieved. Our best guide here is a systematic and reasonable extrapolation from trends that we can already identify, and at the same time, a cautious but systematic utilization of the principle of emergence in which new realities constantly come into being, not through the extrapolation of separate curves, but through specific interaction processes. Many of these new emergents are known in metallurgy, in embryology, and in

Gardner Murphy, "Psychology in the Year 2000," Paper given at Wayne State University Centennial, May 10, 1968. Reprinted by permission.

our own field of psychology. Some of them have to do with new perceptual and conceptual wholes as shown in countless studies of music and of painting; some of them have to do with dyadic or group patterns which come into existence when new relationships are, for the first time, achieved, as shown in the dynamic leadership patterns of Lewin, White, and Lippitt. In a symposium like the present one, an ultra-cautious note may indeed *sound* like science, but only like the plodding science of Sir Francis Bacon's *Novum Organum,* not the creative science which indeed has remade the world, and is remaking the world through the extravagant inventiveness of a Planck and an Einstein. In this spirit, I am going to attempt some predictions which, I believe, are just as likely to prove shallow and banal as to prove ultimately extravagant and exotic.

The ten topics which I shall attempt to survey are extrapolations based upon (1) the current extraordinary development of *psychophysiology;* (2) together with such psychophysiology, the new possibilities of *internal scanning,* in the discovery of the inner human world; the renewed capacity to *observe, with full objectivity, a great deal which has long been regarded as hopelessly subjective;* (3) herewith, the direct *confrontation of the unconscious world* which merges into, and is isomorphic with, the world of physiology; (4) following these discoveries, the development of *voluntary control over the inner world,* such as we never previously dared to dream; (5) a new definition of a wide variety of nameless states, *psychological states for which we have no good names,* including feeling states, cognitive states, and volitional states, upon which human destiny may almost literally depend, with resulting understanding of those profound alterations in states of consciousness, well-known to the East, regarding which Western man has usually expressed doubt or scorn; (6) together with these, the objective exploration of the vast sphere of *parapsychology,* at the edges of which science is nibbling, but so far has failed massively to invade; (7) a fresh *reconsideration of the relations of psychology to the biological sciences,* especially genetics; (8) a renewed *consideration of psychology in relation to the social sciences,* notably in the new sci-

ence of social ecology, entailing cross-cultural collaboration of cross-cultural realities; (9) a note on the way in which changes in research *methods* alter all these basic concepts; (10) finally, a consideration, in all these terms, of the nature of the *human predicament* to which expanding science, which I am describing, may make a serious and indeed a crucial contribution.

1. Psychophysiology

First, then, as to psychophysiology. Partly as a result of new concepts of the wholeness, the integrity, of the living system, as voiced for example by Sir Charles Sherrington in the *Integrative Action of the Nervous System,* and partly as a result of the sheer power of the research tools which have been developed, psychophysiology has become a dramatically new science in the last twenty years. Problems of specialization and subspecialization of tissues, as within the mammalian cerebral cortex, have taken on astonishing forms with Penfield's discovery of specific memory localization, with various techniques for studying the electronic functional realities inside the individual nerve cell, with X-ray studies of lattices, and fine localization of sensory and motor function through implanted electrodes. Both the cruder spot localizations, earlier used in the study of the aphasias, and also the extreme equipotentiality concepts based largely on extirpation studies, have yielded to a dialectical reconsideration of both local and general aspects of functioning, and with an extraordinary directness of application to the world of immediate experience. Donald Hebb's brilliant breakthrough in the study of sensory deprivation has helped us to think of the amazing possibilities of sensory enrichment. We can no longer speak of sensory deprivation or sensory enrichment without thinking, in the manner of David Krech, regarding the biochemistry and physiology of the mammalian cortex, as profoundly affected by very early postnatal experience. We begin to see, quite literally, the likelihood, in the next few decades, of a thorough-going isomorphism of physiological process and psychological process right across the board. Biochemical and neurophysiological progress has been so astonishing in the last few years that we may quite confidently look for a rapidly advancing series of discoveries related specifically to the different kinds of human experience, essentially the sensory, the imaginal, the conceptual, the affective, and indeed certain types of experience which we have never been able to analyze finely enough to allow us to give them names. Psychopharmacology, long considered to be limited to the specific effects of toxins, is rapidly taking on the form of a powerful organist having at his command banks upon banks of keys, and hundreds of stops, calling into existence an incredible gamut of new experiences.

2. Internal Scanning

Following from, or upon, this concurrent study of psychophysiology and biochemistry on the one hand, and the phenomenal world of immediate experience and function on the other hand, we shall be drawn, as in a vortex, into the rich field of the study of internal scanning. By this, I mean first of all the process by which delicate messages from the striped musculature can be more accurately identified as our subjects carry out reflex or skilled movements. Like a tea taster or a wine sampler, the subject, in several laboratories today, comes quickly to recognize the kinesthetic messages in different magnitude from different muscles. Specific muscular activities are experienced kinesthetically at the same time he sees on the panel the electronic evidence of what is going on in specific muscle groups, so that he learns to identify them and name them. He is, in the same way, learning to recognize on the panel many other messages which come from organs that are under autonomic control. We may think here of Bykov's and Lisina's studies in the Soviet Union relating to proprioceptive and interoceptive conditioning.

But the work will soon move further along. Giving the subject feedback on a panel which shows him what specific internal activities are going on, we can teach him to make more and more refined differentiation within the inner world. His searching, his sweeping, his scanning, and his identification of the different components from the proprioceptive world, as identical or isomorphic with the same messages from the exteroceptive world on the panel or conveyed to him through tones, give him more and more precise information as to the rich system of internal messages which had previously been nearly a blur, so precise that he can begin to play the instrument himself. The ancient prejudice that exteroceptive information has a kind of place in the reality world, which is lacking for the other sensory functions, has begun to collapse. A rich variety of internal messages has exactly the same possibility of cross-checking, consensual validation, as has held for sight, hearing, and touch. It is hard to set any limits. We know something about discriminability when working with teas and wines, or even two-point thresholds on the finger tip, but we have never pushed these studies to their true physiological limits. Nor do we know how they are affected by a variety of parameters, anatomical distribution of receptors and afferent fibers, which have never in the past been that important to us to investigate; but today they are coming to be seen in terms of individuality—an individuality based upon heredity, growth, and the learning process. We have a whole internal world coming up for discovery.

3. Confrontation of the Unconscious World

Third, this internal world, as Gregory Razran has pointed out, would include the entire world of the "observable unconscious," the world of psychologically meaningful, but hitherto not directly observable, processes discovered by Freud and his followers. It appears to be more and more evidently the same world as that which anthropologists, playwrights, poets, and prophets have often called upon without knowing, in any scientific sense, what they were doing.

But it is one thing to observe the separate components, of course, and another thing to study creatively how they can be put together into new and emergent wholes. We may say, I think, that both Arnheim, in *Art and Visual Perception,* and Freud, in *The Interpretation of Dreams,* have given us some of the first steps of information regarding the synthesis, the creative reorganization, of a world which offers vast possibilities. I mean literally that there are hundreds of experiences waiting patiently to be experimentally discovered. It will not be just the clinicians and the "encounter" groups that will discover them; they will soon yield rich new harvests to general experimental psychology. I might remind you that while Chaucer, six hundred years ago, had only a few words for colors, we have today some thousands of color terms, mostly ·representing *new* colors that have come to us in the last century as a result of industrial chemistry—colors that simply do not appear in any rainbow, or natural sunset, or natural color scheme. There are not only the stock experiences that human beings have by virtue of their anatomical equipment and their physiological capacity as human beings, but thousands of newly created colors. There are also many new kinds of inner experiences, ranging from the effects of new foods, drugs, smogs, exercise, fatigue, strain, anxiety, and ecstasy—scores upon scores of new kinds and shades of inner experience. It is, of course, true that many of the new methods may involve risks, and that many of them will come under some sort of social control. Whether it will be control by a wise and humane Federal agency, or by public opinion, I fear we have no present reliable clues. Inner responses include those called affective and impulsive states, and the vast range of expressions of mood and temperament used in the aesthetic world and in the personal world generally. There are new worlds just waiting; and they will not have to wait very long. Experimental methods for the study of differentiation are developing; for example, from experiments in the Soviet Union we know that two-point thresholds within the body, say from the gastric mucosa, can be measured, and we have every reason to believe that as such differentiations are carried out by classical psychophysical methods we may first identify a very large range of internal messages, and secondly, learn how to integrate them in thousands of new ways.

4. Voluntary Control

Fourth, insofar as these new messages can be differentiated, tagged, and named, they can apparently be brought under voluntary control. We have a wide array of new possibilities, for example, in Hefferline's study of rapid acquisition of operant control over slight movements which are effective in cutting out a disagreeable

hum spoiling music at the time. That is, individuals who could differentiate at all, could also learn, even though unwittingly, to bring in or shut out particular messages. Other laboratories are now doing what Hefferline started. It appears to be very refined, delicate, and far-below-threshold type of activity which can bring in an astonishing range of experimentally prepared visual and auditory material. Soviet work on voluntary control of cardio-vascular processes appears to concur with what Robert Malmo has reported in Montreal. There are studies of bladder and of capillary control, using panel feedback techniques, strongly suggesting that the autonomically controlled organs are capable of being brought rapidly into the same sphere of voluntary control as that which obtains for the striped muscle responses. Within the next decade or two we can certainly look forward to a very rich control of cardio-vascular and gastro-intestinal responses not only with immediate clinical values in bringing in or shutting out various classes of bodily information, but with the deeper scientific value of giving us a much wider range of what the human potentialities for such inner experience and such inner control may actually be. Wenger and Bagchi studied adepts in yoga in various ashrams in India, while Anand and his collaborators have pushed their studies further. The keen interest of Indian investigators in putting to experimental tests the classical yoga sutras of Patanjali means not only cross-national research collaboration, but what is more important, the serious awakening of Western psychologists to the fact that experiences treasured and cultivated on the other side of the globe might be as worthy of investigation as those encountered in Detroit, or Cambridge, or Topeka.

Last, but by no means least, we have the process of directly observing one's own EEG, notably one's own alpha, as developed by Joe Kamiya at Langley Porter. Ordinarily a 400 cycle tone is activated by the individual's own alpha rhythm, so the subject given the task of increasing the amount of alpha he is exhibiting can rapidly learn, through the feedback which this tone gives him, to bring this under his control. Soon he is turning on or turning off his own alpha. Apparently alpha is not the only rhythm which he can control. There are, as Kamiya points out, staggering possibilities both for the understanding of the nature of central nervous system control by the organized central nervous system itself in the form which we call voluntary, but likewise a vast area of further implications for the understanding of the isomorphic relation between a variety of subjective states which accompany the alpha and the exteroceptive patterns which we see when we observe the visual tracing or hear an appropriate tone. While the clinical applications are important, it is this larger vision of learning to control the brain rhythms themselves that is likely to mean most to the scientist oriented to the year 2000.

5. Nameless States

Fifth, while neither Kamiya, or anyone else, so far as I know, has gone on to publish the implications which these new methods have for the study of whole new areas of experience which we can only dimly describe today, I would note that it is highly probable that before the year 2000 there will be both identification of many kinds of phenomenological states which are anchored upon particular types of EEG's, and the invention of appropriate *names,* appropriate language, to describe the newly identified and newly integrated components. I am thinking here particularly of cognitive states, conceptualizing states, creative states, which may, while retaining all their charm and all their majesty, become far more describable, controllable, and achievable.

6. Parapsychology

Sixth, it is, of course, characteristic of science at any given period to cultivate the belief that it has a rather well integrated system under which new observations can fit. While it is at many points open-ended, and has really fuzzy edges, there would be chaos indeed if scientists gave up their passion for a unified field of science. Suppose it were an archipelago of little, spotty factual details, with no possibility of an implied closed system, an ocean bed unifying all the little islands that appear at the surface level. There is very good psychological reason why science, as it grows, takes on the conservative, the resistive, character which we know. Under these conditions it is hardly surprising that there is some restlessness, or even

resistance, when we talk about discovering kinds of experience about which we have never known anything. Of course, actually there are many good reasons, in polite society, why we do not know too much about our insides. These have to do with delicate and complex systems of human expression, some related very broadly to love, some related very broadly to destructiveness, but a great many others which almost every human individual encounters, but does not really want at this time to communicate on a massive basis. I do not anticipate very much actual interference with science on this count, but I do think we must be honest with ourselves that this quest of the inside is going to entail not only triumphs but occasional acrimonious encounters.

While saying this I must also add that the resistance towards types of human communication which we do not at present understand has shown the same attributes. We can understand very clearly the natural fear of scientists that their whole tough labor would be disturbed if we should admit perceptual, or memoric, or affective, or volitional processes which are not at present explainable in terms of the basic biochemical and biophysical realities of human conduct. Even the thought elements that the Wurzburg School brought into Wundt's psychological system, led to much hostility. Today we are dealing with more serious difficulties as the study of *parapsychology* moves into more systematic experimental form. Most of the data, when closely observed, turn out to be like the perceptual and affective data that we already know about, but they appear to occur under conditions in which the time and space parameters are unfamiliar. For example, in several recent studies, the telepathic phenomena occur when sender and receiver are separated by very long distances; and while the data can be psychologically described without any mystery, we encounter a physical difficulty because we do not know how to conceptualize energies which could carry over these long distances. In other words, our difficulty is at the level of physics, not at the level of psychology. We may be a little bewildered when we encounter modern physicists who take these phenomena in stride; in fact, take them very much more seriously than we psychologists do, saying, as physicists, that they are no longer bound by the types of Newtonian energy distribution, inverse square laws, etc., with which we used to regard ourselves as tightly bound. In the same way, new physical conceptions regarding the nature of time seem to remove a large part of the trouble which appears in precognition experiments, in which a randomly determined target order of stimulus materials can be foreseen by certain subjects. I think that with the computer methods which are now coming into use, and with the progressive rigidity in experimental controls, we shall probably witness a period of slow, but definite, erosion of the blandly exclusive attitude which has offered itself as the only appropriate scientific attitude in this field. The data from parapsychology will almost certainly be data in harmony with general psychological principles, and will be rather easily assimilated within the systematic framework of psychology as a science when once the imagined appropriateness of Newtonian physics is put aside, and modern physics is used to replace it.

7. Psychology and Biology

As I turn to genetics, I would venture to predict a period of massive reorientation of psychology to the biological roots of which it used to boast. The very substance of growth, of motivation, of the learning process, and indeed of most of the basic realities with which the modern evolutionary psychology would have to cope, are provided by the DNA-RNA system; the elements of field physics as they are known in the embryology of Spemann and Weiss; the intricacies of polygenic determination of structure and function; and the broad recognition that individuality in tissue systems, as described by Roger Williams, rewrites the psychology of individual differences in astonishing terms. These genetic terms will be held, of course, by some to be fatalistic, as indicating the genetically given limitations upon all human endeavor. But in two respects these discoveries will be most encouraging: (1) It will be realized that individuality always applies to the growth *potential,* which can be utterly different when a new environmental situation is supplied. An example is the discovery of the Mendelian basis of the phenylpyruvic type of men-

tal defect which turned out nevertheless to yield, to a large degree, to a carefully prepared diet. In other words, that which was genetically determined was nevertheless controllable. Through respect for the genetics of human individuality we shall know how to become better environmentalists. (2) We are, as Sir George Thomson's statement, quoted earlier, implied, moving rapidly to a point such that the electron microscope can greatly aid in studies of the internal organization of individual cells. This, together with some control of mutations and a great deal of control of selective breeding and the application of the principles of population genetics, makes it likely that we may, within a few generations, cut down to a considerable degree on some of the most abhorrent threats to human development. If we were talking about the year 2100 or 2500, we could quite rationally talk about not only the prevention of deterioration, but plans for the actual long-range improvement of genetic potentials.

8. Psychology and Social Science

But the biological sciences do not have the whole message that our ears require. There is equal need for big gains in the social sciences, especially in the development of a social ecology. Ecology has been the most neglected aspect, I think, of the entire behavior field. The experimental psychologist may control, let us say, a ten by ten by ten foot area, and with enormous and devoted attention to detail, think of everything that is in that space at a given time. Organisms, however, have life histories in segments of space-time about which we know a fair amount if they were hatched or born in the laboratory. But if not, the higher they are in the phylogenetic tree, the more likely they are to bring more from their past into the laboratory. Mark May used to say that the American sophomore, from whom we derive findings for humanity at large, was expected to "park his culture outside." We observe only the regions of time and space that are involved in the experiment, ignoring the whole vast area from which the individual organism comes.

The needed studies of ecological organization are vastly more complex than anybody has imagined so far. The maps that Roger Barker has drawn of a Kansas town, and the lists of situational pressures that Saul Sells has devised as a preparation for space travel, will be only a tiny sampling of that vast conception of past and present environmental totalities that Egon Brunswik asked us to imagine. It will be a genetics that is oriented to a systematic and scientific science of ecology that will really give us new field clues to human behavior. By field clues I hope to suggest the modalities of interaction between the edge of the organism and the edge of the environment, such that a complete and real fusion is created. I mean the kind of thing that is involved in interaction between the visual centers in the brain, the retina, the external light source, the laboratory conditions, personalities of the experimenters, the laboratory tradition, and laboratory culture, which must all be considered when a person sees an inkblot or a social scene enacted before him. There must be whole organisms and whole environments to be studied for the sake of the modalities of reciprocity that develop between them. We began to learn from Lewin, as we had earlier begun to learn from Clark Maxwell, how to think in field terms; but we have not really done much of the sort on a scale demanded by present knowledge. The subspecialization has driven us more and more from organs to tissues, from tissues to cells, from cells to molecules, from molecules to atoms, from atoms to microparticles. All this specialization is, of course, absolutely necessary. The job of seeing psychological function, however, in combined biological and cultural terms is still mostly a promissory note with as yet very little backing.

Because it is so rare, I will mention the example of audiogenic seizures in mice, which Benson Ginzburg showed to have a not too complex Mendelian basis. But some of the mice that were expected to have convulsions and die had no convulsions, or had convulsions but did not die. He then worked on the matter from the pharmacological viewpoint, and in terms of biochemistry found a way to buffer the lethal effects of the genes. Allow me a free analogy in the field of human ecology: What will happen when we find a human environment of space-time, sensory enrichment, maternal warmth, generous and skillful experimental reinforcement, which will allow a poorly endowed, frightened, aggressive ghetto child to develop into full humanness? This is exactly the type of experiment now being launched at several outposts of research on disadvantaged children. Before long we shall quietly cease to

think in terms of biology versus the social sciences; we shall develop an ecological science so rich and so concrete that it will articulate closely with the new biology of individual growth.

And if we mean quite seriously that man, as man, is richly intertwined with his ecology, it follows that the psychology of the next two decades will depend enormously upon the discovery of new forms of cross-cultural, cross-national communication. Indeed, it follows that unless there is very broad cross-national communication and action, there will be no human race to investigate. It will not do for American psychology, now having about ninety-two percent of the world's psychological personnel, and about ninety-two percent of its published communications, to undertake a bland and supposedly disinterested study of the rest of the world in order that the wise and productive science, which we feel we represent, can hand down appropriate messages of enlightenment to those struggling along in less enlightened paths of endeavor. The study of the human predicament can come from a human race familiar with the method of science, but a human race speaking many tongues, regarding many values, and holding different convictions about the meaning of life, sooner or later will have to consult all that is human. There are a few in the audience who will still be around in the year 2000, if there is a year 2000; and they will, I hope, still be battling the problem of developing a sufficiently coherent human point of view that is human enough to speak for all kinds of human beings. This will mean that the genetic and ecological progress that I am describing will have actually helped towards a psychology which is common human, which entails not only a study of all human beings, but by trained and devoted individuals within all human groups. Following our American habit of delivering "State of the Union" messages, the Secretary General of the United Nations has been asked to report on the "state of the human race." I do not personally understand why governments, and indeed professional psychologists, too, are almost wholly ignoring the challenge to make direct studies of the possibilities of achieving an international and intercultural plan for world order. Aiming at this goal, it is conceivable that there will be worldwide human modalities of investigation like those already existing in astronomy and in medicine, but oriented to the behavioral sciences. And it is even possible that they will be oriented not only to the behaviors as such, but toward the deep inner humanness which I have tried to describe as an object of study. This, in relation likewise to the dyadic and group problems of the behavior sciences, may give both insight and control over the more destructive tendencies, and may utilize the common human aspiration to live not only more safely and a little more comfortably, but also a little more creatively and a great deal more humanly.

9. The Role of Method

I am sure you have noted, all the way through, that new discoveries in our field, and, I believe, in all scientific fields, are largely the children of new *methods*. Consider what the compound microscope did to histology, what X-rays did for diagnostic procedure, what the puzzle box, the maze, the Skinner box, have done in the development and documentation of seminal scientific theories. I am raising these issues not simply to welcome the computer as a new brother to our side, but to ask one final question: We can, as Abe Maslow has pointed out, strip down the study of man to those methods that are common to the other sciences that do not deal with man; we can assume that the human sciences can best do their job by leaving humanness out. There is, however, another possibility. We might conceivably find that science can become big enough to develop fully human methods oriented to the full panoply of human problems, that empathy, "t.l.c.," rich dyadic methods of communication between subjects and experimenters, might, through patience, discipline, and imagination, give us in the year 2000 a science more fully competent to deal with all the discoverable aspects of human nature.

But a still more basic problem of method relates to the way in which we try to hook together the data from laboratory, from clinic, from field observation, from home, from neighborhood, from observation of human gatherings in schools, churches, juries, parliamentary bodies. On the one hand, we have neglected the use of laboratories, and today we are beginning

to discover a more suitable laboratory approach to a wide variety of spontaneous human situations. We are discovering that inventive experimentalists can do even better work in free human situations than they can in the classical, highly planned, settings. But I am referring now mainly to the manner in which the experimental method does its work. Long ago psychologists set up for themselves the impossible task of creating a psychology through intensive observation of those phenomena that occur under controlled laboratory conditions, and then systematizing a psychology based solely on such findings. They tried to set up physics and chemistry, sometimes the biological sciences of genetics, embryology, and physiology, as models. Belatedly we have discovered that beautiful scientific structures, such as that of modern geology, can, with only slight use of experimental method, be developed through the integration of many types of observations, short-term and long-term, outdoors and indoors, pinpointed or extravagantly blown up to cosmic proportions. The geologist uses experimental methods, but he uses them in the total context of his work. It is Mother Earth, not Her fingernails that interests him. Psychology, which attempted to pinpoint its existence in the Nineteenth Century terms of Weber and Fechner, is now beginning a great awakening, a sort of Rip Van Winkle awakening; for we are discovering, and will discover more fully in the next few decades, the vast dimensions in which a mature psychology can be conceived. It will make even more use of experimental method than it does at present. But the experiments will be suggested, and the techniques controlled, rather largely by the broad perception of the nature of the human animal in his whole ecological setting. The observational systems which will develop cannot be categorized by any one word which we now know. The word *experimental* is a fine word, but it will have to be replaced by something much more systematic. Even the developmental approach will mean something quite new when conceived in the kind of general systems terms, the kind of life science terms, that I am trying to suggest. Mathematical models will certainly both benefit and be benefited by the transitions that I am suggesting; and of course, the engineering skills, already so important in psychophysiology, will become even more important.

I think we shall have to admit that many of us of this era will be unable to see the promised land which begins to be sketched out. Psychologists who will make the grade in the year 2000 will have to be smarter than the psychologists today, as well as enormously better trained—I might add enormously more *broadly* trained—than the subspecialized people we turn out today. We keep sharpening the blade of the modern mind until it keeps breaking, and we damn the blade instead of asking the metallurgist to develop for us tools from which we can prepare sharp tools which can, while still unscathed, cut through the hard inscrutable rock of man's basic resistance to discovering his own nature.

10. The Human Predicament

The year 2000 can come, and the Twenty-first Century offer less terror and more joy, but only if we have learned both *how to look inside* and *how to look outside;* how to recognize the reciprocities of inner and outer, through methods which are as far-ranging and as deeply human as is the human stuff itself that is being studied.

Suggested Readings

Abelson, P. H. "The Space Race," *Amer. Psychol.,* 19 (1964), 39–45.

Albee, G. "American Psychology in the Sixties," *Amer. Psychol.,* 18 (1963), 90–95.

Bray, C. W. "Toward a Technology of Human Behavior for Defense Use," *Amer. Psychol.,* 17 (1962), 527–541.

Clark, K. E. *America's Psychologists.* Washington, D.C.: Amer. Psychol. Assn., 1957.

David, H. P. "Phones, Phonies, and Psychologists. III: Professional Problems and Progress," *Amer. Psychol.,* 18 (1963), 144–148.

Hobbs, N. "A Psychologist in the Peace Corps," *Amer. Psychol.,* 18 (1963), 47–52.

Hoch, E. L., and J. G. Darley. "A Case at Law," *Amer. Psychol.,* 17 (1962), 623–654.

Humphrey, H. H. "The Behavioral Sciences and Survival," *Amer. Psychol.,* 18 (1963), 290–294.

Jahoda, M. "Psychological Issues in Civil Liberties," *Amer. Psychol.,* 11 (1956), 234–240.

Pettigrew, T. F. "Social Psychology and Desegregation Research," *Amer. Psychol.,* 16 (1961), 105–112.

"Psychology in Action." (A section, in each issue of the *American Psychologist,* devoted to current news and events.)

Rice, G. P. "The Psychologist as Expert Witness," *Amer. Psychol.,* 16 (1961), 691–692.

Rogers, C. R., and B. F. Skinner. "Some Issues Concerning the Control of Human Behavior: A Symposium," *Science,* 124 (1956), 1057–1066.

Solomon, L. N. "The Committee on Psychology in National and International Affairs," *Amer. Psychol.,* 19 (1964), 105–110.

Thorndike, R. L. "The Psychological Value Systems of Psychologists," *Amer. Psychol.,* 9 (1954), 787–789.

Glossary

For additional clarification of terms, see H. B. English and A. C. English, *A Comprehensive Dictionary of Psychological and Psychoanalytical Terms*. New York: David McKay, 1958.

acuity: sharpness or keenness of perception.

affective: pertaining to feeling states.

afferent: concerned with the transmission of neural impulse toward the central part of the nervous system.

alimentary: pertaining to food or to the digestion of food.

alpha waves: the most common brainwave form of the electroencephalogram (EEG).

anima: a term used within the psychoanalytic school to designate a personality structure that articulates with the unconscious or to designate the feminine component of personality.

animistic: a belief that various objects in one's environment have souls or that the soul or mind has a causal relationship to the activities of living creatures.

animus: the masculine component that resides unconsciously in humans (see also *anima*).

anthropology: the science of man that focuses on cultural characteristics, social habits and customs, linguistics, and prehistory.

anthropomorphic: ascribing human characteristics to gods, animals, or inanimate objects.

a priori reasoning: reasoning that deduces consequences from definitions or from assumed causes; thinking held to belong to the mind prior to experience.

autonomic nervous system: a major division of the nervous system that is concerned chiefly with the largely automatic (involuntary) regulation of smooth muscles and glands.

avoidance gradient: a curve showing the change, during training, in avoidance response to a given situation or the increase in frequency of avoidance to a cue or trigger stimulus in the experimental situation.

behaviorism: the view that psychology as a science studies only observed behavior rather than statements about behavior.

biology: the science of all life (zoology plus botany).

catatonic: a form of schizophrenia characterized by marked motor anomalies such as stupor and mutism.

cathexis: the affective value of an object, idea, or action and the channeling of this affect toward the object, idea, or action.

central tendency: those measures, such as mean, median, and mode, that summarize or typify a set of distinct and independent observations.

cerebral hemispheres: the two main lobes of the brain in vertebrates.

classical conditioning: the procedure of linking a reflex response to a new or conditioned stimulus (for example, salivating to a bell when no food is present).

cochlear nucleus: the spiral bony tube in the inner ear that contains the organ of hearing.

cognitive: a generic term for any process whereby an organism becomes aware or obtains knowledge of something.

conative: pertaining to those processes whereby an organism goes from a state of unrest or imbalance to a state of rest or balance; a tendency to move.

conditioning: all learning procedures based on a classical (respondent) or instrumental (operant) model or design. To the behaviorist, conditioning is synonymous with learning.

cones: minute bodies in the retina that transform the energy of light rays into the specific neural impulses for color and light vision.

congenital: present at birth and seldom if ever determined by heredity.

contiguity: the nearness of two objects in space and time.

control group: a group that is as closely as possible equivalent to an experimental group and that is exposed to all the conditions of an experiment except the treatment variable (main effect, independent variable).

controlled observation: observations that are specified or delineated prior to being observed; observations that are limited in frequency or type according to some plan.

correlation: two things so related that change in one is accompanied by change in the other; the act of bringing two things into orderly relationships.

correlation coefficient: the number that denotes the meaning of a correlation—that is, a measure. Perfect correspondence between two things (variables) is expressed by $+1.00$; perfect inverse correspondence, by -1.00; complete lack of correspondence (independence) of two variables, by 0.00.

cortex: the surface layers (gray matter) of the cerebral hemispheres.

counterbalancing: a method of canceling out the influence of irrelevant variables that cannot be experimentally removed.

criterion: a comparison object or a rule, standard, or test for making a judgment.

delusion: a belief held in the face of evidence normally sufficient to negate the belief, therefore, a false belief or system of beliefs.

diurnal: occurring each day.

dorsal: pertaining to the back.

drive: a tendency, initiated by shifts in physiological balance, to be sensitive to stimuli of a certain class and to respond in a way related to the attainment of a certain goal.

dualism: a point of view in psychology that accepts a distinction between mental and physical phenomena.

ecology: the study of the adaptation of organisms in reference to their physical environment.

effector: a muscle or gland considered to be the executive organ or organ of response. The nerve fiber that discharges into the muscle or gland is an effector nerve.

ego: the "I," self, or person or that aspect of the person that is conscious and most in touch with external reality.

ego defenses: any of a variety of mechanisms that protect the integrity of the ego (for example, rationalization).

ejaculation: the forcible emission of semen at the height of the male orgasm.

electrode: a device for transmitting electric current to a substance (for example, animal tissue) that is not usually regarded as an electric transmitter.

electroencephalograph (EEG): a graphic record of the wavelike changes in the electric potential observed when electrodes are placed on the skull or on the exposed brain.

embryology: the study of organisms during the early stages of their prenatal development.

emotion: a complex feeling state accompanied by characteristic motor and glandular activities; a complex behavior in which the visceral component predominates.

empirical: relating to facts or experience; experimental; based on factual investigation.

encounter groups: therapy groups in which the members of the group learn to react openly with one another at a feeling level and to constructively receive the feeling reactions of others.

entity: a self-maintaining portion of reality; a being or part of a being that has some degree of autonomy.

entomology: the study of insects.

environment: the sum of the external conditions and factors potentially capable of influencing an organism.

ethics: the study of the ideal in human character and conduct.

experimental group: those subjects who are exposed to an experimental (treatment) variable and whose performance will reflect the influence, if any, of that variable.

extroversion: an attitude of interest in things outside oneself, as in the physical and social environment, rather than in one's own thoughts and feelings.

factor analysis: a statistical method for interpreting scores and correlations of scores from a number of tests and from which factors or separate categories of meaning appear.

factorialized correlation matrix: a matrix whose elements are the factor loadings obtained from a factor analysis.

factor loading: the amount that a given factor contributes to the variability of a particular test; the correlation of a factor with a test.

field study: a collection of data outside the laboratory, library, or clinic; the study of organisms in their usual habitats.

frustration: the blocking of, or interference with, an ongoing goal-directed activity.

fugue: a long period in which a patient has almost complete amnesia (lack of memory) for his past, although habits and skills are usually little affected. He usually leaves home and starts a new life, with little or no memory of events preceding the fugue state.

functionalism: the point of view that perception is an instrumental activity that is closely related to, and dependent upon, other functions; a school of thought that defines mental phenomena as processes or activities rather than as mental contents.

Gestalt: the systematic position that psychological phenomena are organized, undivided, and articulated wholes, or gestalts.

habit: an acquired act—usually a relatively simple one—that is regularly or customarily manifested.

habituation: the gradual increase in the certainty that a situation will elicit a given response.

hallucination: a false perception with the reality of objects, although relevant and adequate stimuli for such a perception are lacking.

hallucinogenic: anything that creates or contributes to the creation of hallucinations.

heterogeneous: characterizing any group of items that show marked dissimilarity.

heterosexual: pertaining to the opposite sex or to an attraction to the opposite sex.

histology: the study of the structure of body tissues.

homeostasis: the maintenance of constancy of relations or equilibrium in the bodily processes.

homogeneous: characterizing any group of items that show sameness or marked likeness in the quality or attribute under consideration.

homosexual: pertaining to one's own sex or to an attraction to those of one's own sex.

hypothalamus: a group of nuclei at the base of the brain that are involved in many visceral regulative processes.

hypothesis: an explanation of a complex set of data that is admittedly tentative and not yet proved.

hypothetical construct: a formally proposed concept referring to an entity or process that is inferred as actually existing.

illusion: mistaken perception of an actual object or stimulus.

image: a likeness or copy; usually a mental copy of something not present to the senses.

individual differences: any psychological characteristics, qualities, traits, or differences in a character by which he can be distinguished from others.

intelligence: the ability to deal effectively with tasks involving abstractions; the ability to learn; the ability to deal with new situations. To the psychologist this definition generally implies "as measured by a properly standardized intelligence test."

interoceptor: a sense organ or receptor inside the body, in contrast with one at or near the surface.

interpolation: inserting an estimated value between two values in a series.

intervening variable: any variable that is functionally connected with a preceding variable (control condition) and a following (dependent) variable.

isomorphism: the doctrine that the excitatory fields in the brain have a formal, point-for-point correspondence with the experienced contents of consciousness.

kinesthesis: the sense that yields knowledge of the movements of the body or of its members.

latency: the state of an organic mechanism from the beginning of stimulation or excitation to the beginning of the observable response to that stimulation.

learning: a highly general term for the relatively enduring change, in response to a task demand, that is induced directly by experience; the process or processes whereby such change is brought about.

learning curve: a graphic representation of measured changes at successive units of practice.

linear: describing a relationship between two or more variables that can be represented by a straight line.

locomotor: pertaining to some form of body movement.

logical positivism: a philosophic movement that seeks to establish a science of sciences. It holds that the instrument of science is the experience of the scientist himself and that statements of experience (empirical propositions) must be operationally defined.

massed practice: the arrangement of periods for learning with little or no interval between the successive presentations or practices.

masturbation: the induction of erection and sexual satisfaction, in either sex, by manual or mechanical stimulation of the genitals.

maturation: generally pertaining to developmental changes that are hereditary and that lead one toward full maturity.

maze learning: a learning procedure involving a network of pathways, some of them blind alleys, but with one or more leading to an outlet or goal in which learning experiments are conducted.

mean: an arithmetic average.

median: the value that separates all the cases in a ranked distribution into halves.

mental age (MA): the level of intellectual development equivalent to that of a given chronological age.

metaphysics: the branch of philosophy that is concerned with the ultimate nature of existence; a doctrine that accepts spiritual realities not based on scientific methodology.

methodology: the systematic and logical study and formulation of the principles and methods used in the search for fact or truth; procedures used in a particular research.

mnemotechnical: concerning techniques that pertain to memory or to the art of memorizing or improving memory.

mode: the most common or frequently appearing value or class of values in a series.

molar: pertaining to that which is relatively large and unanalyzed.

molecular: pertaining to that which is relatively small or to a product of detailed analysis.

mores: the customs of a social group that are regarded as having a peculiar sanction, so that violation brings condemnation to the offender.

motivation: the determination, in direction and strength, of an organism's acts by its own nature or internal state.

motor: pertaining to muscle movement.

neonate: a newborn infant.

neural: pertaining to the function of nerves.

neurology: the science of the structure and function of the nervous system.

neuron: the single cell that is the fundamental unit of structure of nerve tissue.

neurotic: a general term describing people who are unduly preoccupied with matters over which they feel they have little knowledge or control.

nociceptive: pertaining to pain reception.

nocturnal emission: loss of semen during sleep.

nonsense syllable: a pronounceable combination of letters, used chiefly in memory experiments, that has no meaning in the language of the person using it.

nymphomania: abnormally strong (insatiable) sex desire in females.

nystagmus: a quick, jerky movement of the eyes, followed by a slower return to the original position.

object constancy: the fact that perceptual objects retain a certain standard or normal appearance independent of surrounding stimuli.

Oedipus complex: Freud's term for a child's repressed desire for sex relations with the parent of the opposite sex. Most people resolve this stage by identifying with the same-sex parent.

olfactory: pertaining to smell and the organs of smell.

one-tail test: a test for the statistical stability of a difference when it is assumed that the difference may be predicted in one direction rather than in any direction.

ontogeny: the origin or development of an individual organism or of one of its organs or functions.

operant conditioning: conditioning or learning in which a response or behavior is identified and strengthened or weakened by its consequences in the environment; learning in which the response determines the reinforcement to the organism.

operational definition: the definition of a term according to the operations employed in distinguishing the object referred to from all other objects.

optokinetic: pertaining to movements of the eye caused by visual stimulation.

paradigm: a model, pattern, or example that exhibits all the variable forms of whatever is under consideration.

parameter: any constant that defines the curve of the equation for some psychological function (for example, learning, growth).

paranoid: suffering from delusions of grandeur or of persecution.

parapsychology: a division of psychology dealing with psychological phenomena that appear not to fall within the range of what is at present covered by natural law.

parthenogenesis: reproduction from an unfertilized egg.

perception: the organization and interpretation of sensory information.

personality: a general term with a variety of meanings, including (1) one's demeanor as perceived by others; (2) being a person; (3) one's unique personal qualities; (4) one's motivational dispositions and consequent traits; (5) those characteristics that determine reputation; and (6) the social aspects of one's individual nature.

phenomenology: the view that behavior is determined by phenomena of experience rather than by external, objective, physically described reality.

phobia: an excessive fear of something.

photon: a measure of brightness or of retinal illumination; the amount of illumination on the retina when a surface brightness of one candle per square meter is seen through a pupil with an area of one square millimeter.

phrenology: the doctrine that personality traits are determined by the size and shape of the brain.

phylogenetic: pertaining to the origin and development of a characteristic in the race or other biological division.

physiotherapy: the branch of medicine dealing with treatment by physical means, excluding drugs and surgical cutting, and including massage, hydrotherapy, and heat treatment.

placebo: a preparation containing no medicine (or no medicine related to the complaint) and administered simply to cause a patient to believe he is receiving treatment.

primates: the highest order of mammals, including monkeys, apes, and man.

proactive inhibition: the inhibitory influence of a previously learned task on the recall or learning of another, similar task.

probability: the likelihood that an event will occur; estimated as the ratio of the number of ways in which the event may occur to the number of ways in which alternative events may occur.

proprioceptor: any receptor sensitive to the position and movement of the body and its members.

psychodynamics: any psychological system that strives for an explanation of behavior in terms of motives or drives.

psychogenic: functionally or psychologically caused; having no known organic or physical basis for cause.

psychology: a branch of science dealing with behavior, acts, or mental processes and with the mind, self, or person who behaves, acts, or has the mental processes.

psychometrics: the development and application of mathematical procedures to psychology.

psychopathological: pertaining to mental disease.

psychophysical methods: methods of determining thresholds and scale values for stimuli that can be arranged along a physical continuum.

psychotherapy: any psychological technique used in the treatment of mental disorders or maladjustment.

psychotic: characterized by personality disintegration, failure to test and evaluate external reality correctly, and failure in interpersonal relationships.

psychotomimetic: psychotic-like or causing psychotic-like reactions.

pupillary: pertaining to the variable aperture of the iris through which light passes on its way to the retina of the eye.

Q sort: a personality inventory in which the subject (or someone making judgments about him) sorts a considerable number of statements into piles that represent the degrees to which the statements apply to him.

rationalization: the process of concocting plausible reasons to account for one's practices and beliefs when they are challenged by oneself or others.

receptor: a specialized structure that is sensitive to specific forms of physical energy and that initiates neural impulses.

reflex: a species-specific innate behavior or act in which there is no element of choice or premeditation and no variability of response except in intensity or time.

reflex arc: a theoretical description of the functioning of the nervous system; at its simplest level it consists of a receptor nerve that transmits excitation from a stimulus to an effector nerve via a neuron.

regeneration: replacement by growth of a lost part of the body; restoration.

regression: a return to earlier and less mature behavior.

reification: acting as if or assuming that an abstract quality (for example, intelligence) has concrete actuality or existence.

reinforcement: a strengthening by augmentation; a reward or punishment.

reinforcement, fixed-interval: reinforcement given at the end of a fixed time interval.

reinforcement, fixed-ratio: a reinforcement schedule whereby a ratio of responses to reinforcement is set (for example, 3:1).

reinforcement, intermittent: periodic partial reinforcement.

reinforcement, variable-interval: reinforcement given after varying predetermined time intervals.

reinforcement, variable-ratio: a reinforcement schedule whereby the ratio of response to reinforcement varies in some systematic way.

reliability: proof of accuracy through repeated trials.

replication: the reproduction or copy of an original in all essentials.

repression: the exclusion of specific psychological activities or contents from conscious awareness by a process the individual is not directly aware of.

reticular system: the ascending and descending pathways in the brain (arousal functions).

retina: the innermost part of the eyeball that receives the optical image and contains cones and rods, which in turn are vision receptors.

retroactive inhibition: a decrease in learning because it is closely followed by another activity, especially a somewhat similar activity.

rods: structures in the retina that are believed to be specific receptors for gray or achromatic visual qualities at low intensities.

rote learning: memorization requiring no understanding.

satyriasis: abnormally strong or excessive sex desire in men.

schizoid: a person who is abnormally withdrawn from social contacts.

schizophrenia: a group of psychotic reactions characterized by fundamental disturbances in reality relationships.

secretory reflex: any reflex involving the production and discharge of a physiologically active substance by an organ or tissue.

sensation: the elementary, unanalyzable, and uninterpreted item or unit of that which one apprehends when certain receptors are excited.

serial learning: a process in which a person acquires responses in a definite prescribed sequence so that each response serves as a cue for the next.

set: a readiness to respond in a certain way that is brought about by temporary and intrinsic determinants of response (such as instructions), which serve to adjust the motivation system.

shaping: a training procedure in instrumental (operant) conditioning in which a subject is led toward the behavior to be learned by the reinforcement of responses that bring him closer to the desired act.

sociology: the behavioral or social science dealing with group life and social organization, chiefly in literate societies.

sociopathic: categorized by disorders in one's relationships with society and with the cultural milieu.

somatic: pertaining to the body rather than to the environment.

somnambulism: sleepwalking.

standard deviation: a measure of variability in a set of scores; it is found by summing the squared differences from the mean, dividing the number of cases, and extracting the square root.

standard error: a measure of the sampling errors that affect a statistic; it is the standard deviation of a distribution of samples of means, differences between means, and so on.

standardize: to bring something into line with established standards; to establish standards of performance or product.

statistical significance: the degree of probability that, in an infinite series of measurements, the value or score actually obtained will not by chance alone occur with significant frequency and thus can be attributed to something other than chance. The probability of chance occurrence is set at levels of confidence—customarily at the 5% or 1% level—which means that the value or score in question would probably have occurred by chance only 5 times or 1 time in 100.

statistics: techniques for describing, classifying, and analyzing data.

stimulus: a physical event, or a change in physical energy, that causes physiological activity in a sense organ.

stimulus generalization: conditioned response to stimuli simply because they are similar to the stimuli the subject has learned to respond to.

structure: any enduring arrangement, grouping, pattern, or articulation of parts to form a relatively stable system or whole.

subject: the person or animal to whom stimuli are applied for the purpose of evoking responses in an experiment.

surrogate: a person who functions in another's life as a substitute for some third party (for example, a teacher may be a parent-surrogate).

sympathetic branch: a functional subdivision of the autonomic nervous system.

synapse: the place and process by which the end (axon) of one neuron transmits a nervous impulse to the beginning (dendrite) of another neuron.

synesthesia: a condition whereby perception of a certain object (for example, a musical tone) will elicit a particular image from another sensory mode (for example, the color purple).

teleology: the study of acts considered related to purposes; the doctrine that the future, no less than the past, affects the present.

thalamus: a part of the brain that is an important relay center between various sensory organs and the cortex.

theology: the study of God.

theory: a statement of the relations believed to prevail in a comprehensive body of facts. Theory is more solidly supported by evidence than is hypothesis.

trait: any enduring or persisting characteristic of a person by means of which he can be distinguished from another.

trial: a single effort or performance.

validity: the quality of being founded on truth, fact, or law.

variable: a quantity or factor that is changeable and that can increase or decrease.

variable, dependent: the response variable whose arousal value one expects to be determined by the independent variable.

variable, independent: the variable that is manipulated or treated in an experiment.

variance: the square of the standard deviation; a measure of variability.

ventral: pertaining to the belly or underside of the body.

Wilcoxian matched pairs signed-ranks test: a statistical test of significance.

wild child (feral child): a human who has been raised in complete social isolation from other humans, either by animals or by indirect contact with human caretakers.

Würzburg school: a group of psychologists at Würzburg University (Germany) who, by means of introspective analysis, found evidence for imageless thought.

Zeitgeist: the spirit of the times; the prevailing sentiments that are present in a given era and culture.

Symbols and Abbreviations

$>$ more than.

$<$ less than.

MA   mental age.

IQ   intelligence quotient.

5%, 1% level of confidence See *statistical significance* in the Glossary.

g   the general factor found in all the tests being factor-analyzed.

N   number of subjects.

P   probability.

t (t test)   a test of significance in which the ratio of a value (such as the difference between two means) to its standard error is computed.

Index

Date Due